The Book of
Poverty and Wealth

S W E D E N

F I N L A N D

KÓLA PEN.

BALTIC SEA

ÅLAND IS.

NYSTAD
ÅBO

HANGÖ

HELSINGFORS

DAGÖ IS.

ÖSEL IS.
ARENSBURG

HAMBURG

PERNAU

REVAL

ESTONIA

LIVONIA

RIGA

Dvina
Västern

DORPAT

NÁRVAGA

INGRIA

SESTRÓ
RETSK

ST. PETERSBURG

NÖTEBORG

SÉBEZH

STÁRAIA RÚSA

GRODNO

PÓLOTSK

NÉVEL

VÉLIZH

GOLÓVCHINO

LESNÁIA

SMOLENSK

VÉTKA

STARODÚB

BRIANSK

CHERNIGOV

NÓVGOROD
SÉVERSKII

KIEV

PUTÍVL

BÉLGOROD

PEREVÓLOCHNA

POLTÁVA

IZIÚM

ZMIÉV

DONÉTSK

TAGANRÓG

CHERKÁSSK

CRIMEA

ROSTÓV

AZÓV

Straits
of Kerch

BLACK SEA

CAUCASUS MTS.

TÉREK River

DÉRBENT

BAKÚ

KARELIA

Lake
Ládoga

VÝBORG

KEXHOLM

PETROZAVÓDSK

OLÓNETS

Lake Onéga

POVENÉTS

SOLOVÉTSKI IS.

SORÓKA

White Sea

ARCHANGEL
KHOLMOGÓRY

P O M O R E

Onega
River

Northern River

IÁRENSK

VELÍKII ÚSTIUG

SOLVYCHEGÓDSK

Výchegda R.

Súkhona R.

VÓLOGDA

TÓTMA

SOLIKÁMSK

U R A L   M O U N T A I N S

PSKOV

Lake
Ilmen

NÓVGOROD

USTRÉKA

BOROVICHI

ÚSTIUZHNA

VÝSHNII
VOLOCHÓK

TVER'

KÁSHIN
IAROSLÁVL

KOSTROMÁ

ÚNZHA

ZVENÍGOROD

VIÁZMA

MOSCOW

PEREIASLÁVL
ZALÉSSKII

SÚZDAL

Kliáz'ma River

NÍZHNII
NOVGOROD

SÉRPUKHOV

OKÁ R.

KOLÓMNA
RIAZAN'

MÚROM

KAZAN

Kama R.

TÚLA

KÁSHIRA

ALÉKSIN

MTSENSK

Mókcha River

Súra River

SARÁNSK

SIMBÍRSK

NÍZNII
LOMOV

ÍNSAR

NADÉENO
USOLE

SÉRGIEVSK

Sok R.

UFÁ

Belaia River

BÉLAIA

Buzulúk River

SÝZRAN'

SAMÁRA

Samára River

SÝZRAN'

VORÓNEZH

TAMBÓV

PÉNZA

Uzá R.

Khopét River

SARÁTOV

Medvéditsa

DOÑ River

BÍtiug River

OSKÓL River

Donéts River

Seversky

Dnepr

DNEPR

Kalmius R.

Seim River

Sosna R.

PÁNSHIN
GORODÓK

TSARÍTSYN

Lake Elton

Volga River

Iaik River

ASTRAKHAN

CASPIAN

SEA

RUSSIAN EMPIRE 1725

OTTOMAN EMPIRE

BATTLEFIELD

0   km   500

Translators' Note

This translation of Iván Pososhkóv's *Kniga o skúdosti i bogátstve* is based on the MS published by the late B.B. Kafengauz in 1951. It is not a very good text: often one of the other readings in the (incomplete) *apparatus criticus* or the text of the *editio princeps* of 1842 is clearly to be preferred. The translator-editor has, in such simple cases, chosen the best text without specific comment, and also in frequent other cases corrected small but obvious errors, e.g. plural instead of singular verb or vice versa. There remain some two dozen passages which do not make satisfactory sense according to any version available to the translators. The proposed emendations are listed on p. 431–2.

The translation is intended above all to be clear and readable, removing all ambiguities as to what Pososhkóv is trying to say. This has led to considerable reordering of the syntax, which is both lax and convoluted after the manner of his time, and extensive repunctuation. In other respects the translators have tried to retain the flavour of Pososhkóv's language (one can scarcely call it style) by hinting at the elements of biblical Church Slavonic and obsolescent officialese in it and avoiding too modern a vocabulary. Apart from a small number of recently borrowed western European words, most of which were necessarily used by any Russian writing about Tsar Peter's rule (and naturally remain in the translation), Pososhkóv's vocabulary, indeed his whole literary manner, belongs to pre-Petrine Russia.

The transliteration of personal and place-names follows to a large extent the usage of the Library of Congress with notation of stress. Readers unfamiliar with Russian should ignore apostrophes (as in Terént'ev) and pronounce *ë* as *yo* (e.g. Mogilëv). Anglicized place-names have not been stressed. Printed Russian documents are dated in the Old Style.

Acknowledgements

We wish to record our warm thanks to the British Academy, the Master and Fellows of Christ's College, Cambridge and the Twenty-Seven Foundation for their generosity in making grants which have made possible the publication of this volume. Our gratitude is also due to all those friends and colleagues who, over the years, have helped us with advice and information, in particular Professor J.H. Elliott, Professor J.L.H. Keep and Dr Jonathan Shepard. Furthur we thank the Literary and Linguistic Computing Centre, University of Cambridge, for preparing a computerized concordance of *The Book of Poverty and Wealth* and Dame Elizabeth Hill for introducing us to that work many years ago.

Christ's College, Cambridge   L.R.L.
Selwyn College, Cambridge   A.P.V.

Contents

Stanford University Press
Stanford, California
© 1987 L. R. Lewitter and Alexis Vlasto
Originating publisher: The
Athlone Press, London
First published in the U.S.A. by
Stanford University Press, 1986
Printed in Great Britain
ISBN 0-8047-1361-8
LC 86-61841

IVÁN POSOSHKÓV

The Book of
Poverty and Wealth

Edited and translated by
A.P. VLASTO and L.R. LEWITTER

Introduction and Commentaries by
L.R. LEWITTER

Stanford University Press
Stanford, California
1987

Abbreviations

AAE	=	*Akty, sobrannye . . . Arkheograficheskoiu ekspeditsieiu Imperatorskoi Akademii Nauk*, 4 vols, SPg, 1836
AE	=	*Arkheograficheskii Ezhegodnik*
AI	=	*Akty Istoricheskie, sobrannye i izdannye Arkheograficheskoiu komissieiu*, 5 vols, SPg, 1841–2
BL	=	British Library
CASS	=	*Canadian-American Slavic Studies*
ChOIDR	=	*Chteniia v Imperatorskom Obshchestve Istorii i Drevnostei Rossiiskikh pri Moskovskom Universitete*
CMRS	=	*Cahiers du monde russe et soviétique*
DAI	=	*Dopolneniia k Aktam istoricheskim*, sobrannye i izdannye Arkheograficheskoiu komissieiu, 12 vols, SPg, 1846–72
DDPV	=	*Dopolnenie k Deianiiam . . .*, edited by I.I. Golikov, 18 vols, M, 1790–7
DP	=	*Doklady i prigovory, sostoiashchiesia v Pravitel'stvuiushchem senate v tsarstvovanie Petra Velikogo*, edited successively by N.V. Kalachev and N.F. Dubrovin, 6 vols, SPg, 1880–1901
DPV	=	*Deianiia Petra Velikogo, mudrogo preobrazovatelia Rossii . . .*, edited by I.I. Golikov, 12 vols, M, 1788–9
ES	=	*Entsiklopedicheskii slovar'*, edited by I.E. Andreevskii and others, SPg (Brockhaus-Efron), 1890–1907
IA	=	*Istoricheskii Arkhiv (sbornik* 1936–54, journal 1954–62)
IANSSSR	=	*Izvestiia Akademii Nauk SSSR*
IORIaS	=	*Izvestiia Otdeleniia Russkogo Iazyka i Slovesnosti Akademii Nauk*
ISSSR	=	*Istoriia SSSR*
IZ	=	*Istoricheskie Zapiski*
JfGO	=	*Jahrbücher für Geschichte Osteuropas*
L	=	Leningrad

M	=	Moscow

M = Moscow

ODD = *Opisanie dokumentov i del, khraniashchikhsia v arkhive sviateishego Pravitel'stvuiushchego sinoda*, SPg, 1868–1914

Opisanie MAMIu = *Opisanie dokumentov i bumag, khraniashchikhsia v Moskovskom arkhive Ministerstva iustitsii*, M, 1869–1916

PB = *Pis'ma i bumagi imperatora Petra Velikogo*, edited successively by A.F. Bychkov, A.I. Andreev and others, SPg, 1887–1918, L, 1946–

PRO = Public Record Office

PRP = *Pamiatniki russkogo prava*, 8 vols, M, 1952–61 (vols VI and VIII edited by K.A. Sofronenko, vol. VII by L.V. Cherepnin).

PSZ = *Polnoe sobranie zakonov Rossiiskoi Imperii*. Sobranie pervoe s 1649 g. po 12 dekabria 1825, SPg, 1830

RANION = Rossiiskaia assosiatsiia nauchno-issledovatel'skikh institutov obshchestvennykh nauk

RBS = *Russkii Biograficheskii Slovar'*

Sb.ORIaS = *Sbornik statei, chitannykh v Otdelenii russkogo iazyka i slovesnosti Imperatorskoi Akademii Nauk*

Sb.RIO = *Sbornik Imperatorskogo Russkogo Istoricheskogo Obshchestva*

SEER = *Slavonic and East European Review*

SGGD = *Sobranie gosudarstvennykh gramot i dogovorov, khraniashchikhsia v Gosudarstvennoi kollegii inostrannykh del*, 5 pts, M, 1813–94

SIE = *Sovetskaia Istoricheskaia Entsiklopediia*, edited by E.M. Zhukov, M, 1961–76

SPg = St Petersburg

SR = *Slavic Review*

VI = *Voprosy Istorii*

ZA = *Zakonodatel'nye akty Petra I*, compiled by N.A. Voskresenskii, edited by B.I. Syromiatnikov, vol. I, M, 1945

ZfOG = *Zeitschrift für Osteuropäische Geschichte*

ZhMNP = *Zhurnal Ministerstva Narodnogo Prosveshcheniia*

ZIAN = *Zapiski Imperatorskoi Akademii Nauk*

ZIFF = *Zapiski Istoriko-Filologicheskogo Fakul'teta S. Peterburgskogo Universiteta*, SPg

Introduction

The Historical Background

J'aurais bien mieux fait d'éviter tous ces détails de combats donnés chez les Sarmates, et d'entrer plus profondément dans le détail de ce qu'a fait le Czar pour le bien de l'humanité. Je fais plus de cas d'une lieue en carré défrichée que d'une plaine jonchée de morts. (Voltaire to the Crown Prince Frederick, 1737)

I

Iván Pososhkóv and his
Book of Poverty and Wealth

Russia under Peter the Great as seen by foreign eyewitnesses. Pososhkóv, the native eyewitness. His life and writings. The Book of Poverty and Wealth, *its connection with Križanić's* Politika, *cameralism and mercantilism. Pososhkóv as political polemicist.*

The student of the reign of Peter the Great is well provided with contemporary accounts of Russia set down by observant and well-informed foreigners in full awareness of the magnitude of the events which it was their good fortune to witness. Even the professional diplomats among them did not record their impressions solely for the benefit of their chiefs but did so for their private purposes, perhaps with a view to going into print at the right moment. For already the curiosity of the reading public was being aroused by the 'improvements which the tsar had made among his people, whereby he had become formidable to his neighbours and gained universal applause'.[1] And yet, valuable documents though they are, their scope is limited, being as a rule confined to the same subjects presented in different combinations and proportions: religion, the system of government, the armed forces, the revenue, the coinage, trade and public security. The material thus arranged makes up a useful but strictly conventional 'Companion to Russia' for the statesman or the private observer of the European scene.

The earliest of these works are two accounts of Russia in the year 1710, one by the Emperor Joseph I's agent (later resident) Otto Pleyer, the other by the British envoy (later ambassador) Charles Whitworth. Both works were published posthumously, Whitworth's in 1758, Pleyer's in 1872. The second is a fairly short memorandum written in the heavy officialese of the period and, unlike Pleyer's dispatches (some of which had been published earlier), of minor interest. Whitworth, on the other hand, was the first of a long line of distinguished Russian experts at the Foreign Office; his account surpasses Pleyer's in conciseness, lucidity and accuracy. A critical survey of the country's territory, frontiers, climate, population, social structure, administrative organization, coinage, trade, natural wealth and armed forces, it includes an appraisal of

Russia's leading political personalities, beginning with the tsar himself. Whitworth's *Account* does indeed, as its editor has put it, show 'what lasting benefits ambassadors and foreign ministers might confer on mankind beyond the temporary utility of negotiating and sending intelligence'.[2]

The same may justly be said of the Danish envoy Just Juel, whose diary, published in Danish in 1893 and in translation in 1899, covers the critical years between the tsar's victory over the Swedes at Poltáva (1709) and his ill-fated expedition to the Pruth (1711). Juel, who was a naval officer by profession, had as keen an eye to the social as to the political scene and kept his diary as meticulously as if it had been a log book. Another Scandinavian, J. P. von Strahlenberg, a Swedish officer, was taken prisoner at Poltáva and repatriated in 1722; in the intervening period, having accepted an offer to enter the tsar's service, he spent many years in Siberia where he worked as a cartographer and made three maps of the country. These were apparently destroyed but Strahlenberg's treatise entitled *Das nord und östliche Theil von Europa und Asia* was published in Stockholm in 1730; it is the work of an amateur geographer, ethnographer, philologist, antiquary and historian, and a mine of recondite information about Russia and Siberia. Strahlenberg deliberately abstained from treating of any of 'the actions and undertakings of the Monarch which are already made public'[3] but the analysis of the conflicting opinions expressed about the tsar by his contemporaries was revealing enough to elicit a detailed commentary from the historian and government servant V. N. Tatíshchev (1686–1750), the author of an unfinished history of Russia.[4]

The bulky volume entitled *Das veränderte Russland* is the work of yet another diplomat, F. C. Weber, and consists of three parts published successively in 1721, 1738 and 1740. Of these the first, which covers Weber's stay in Russia as Hanoverian envoy between 1714 and 1719, is the most valuable but the whole work suffers from the defect, avowed by the author himself, of having been begun as a diary and only later filled out with new material and furnished with a commentary. The author's aim, however, was constant throughout: to demonstrate the principal means by which Tsar Peter effected improvements in the religion, laws, customs and habits, armed forces, navigation, trade and arts and sciences of Russia, thus laying the foundations of its newly acquired might. Weber's treatment of his subject, apart from being unsystematic, was also deliberately uncritical; in Weber's own words the reader would look in vain for any faults or failings in this description of Peter the Great's deeds.[5]

It was possibly Weber's prolixity that caused the future Frederick the Great, in a letter to Voltaire, to object to the supposed 'privilège du diffus' which yet another German writer on the subject might be tempted to abuse. But the writer in question, J. G. Vockerodt, who had just returned to Berlin from St Petersburg after serving for eighteen years as secretary to the Prussian legation, showed no such leanings. The crown prince regarded him as a man of sense and intelligence, truthful and well versed in Russian affairs and therefore the person best suited to answer in detail the twelve questions concerning Russia which Voltaire, who was already contemplating a work on Peter the Great, had requested Frederick to put to 'un serviteur éclairé'. Voltaire was seeking information about the state of civilization in Muscovy, the changes effected in the Church, the system of government, military organization, trade, public works, projects and buildings undertaken, exploration and colonization carried out, advances made in learning and the establishment of educational institutions, changes in customs and manners, the rise or decline in the number of inhabitants, the composition of the population and the state of the revenue. In November 1737 Frederick was able to send Voltaire Vockerodt's memoir on Russia under Peter the Great, written in complete ignorance of the use for which it was intended. Later unjustly dismissed by Voltaire as no longer relevant and published only in 1872, Vockerodt's work remains to this day an historical source of the greatest value.[6]

Their usefulness notwithstanding, all the accounts of Petrine Russia discussed so far suffer from the same deficiency: their authors' deliberate detachment – diplomatic or scholarly – from the realities of everyday life. To these political commentators the condition of the populace, being of no professional interest, could be no more than an object of occasional curiosity, or, at best, of fleeting sympathy. The one exception to this rule is the author of *The State of Russia under the Present Tsar* (published in 1716), John Perry, a civil engineer whose status in Russia as a foreign specialist was so insecure that in the end he had to be spirited out of the country in Charles Whitworth's retinue. Perry's experiences were as close to those of a Russian as any foreigner could have undergone: he had incurred the tsar's disfavour, been subjected to arbitrary and unjust treatment by his boyars, and suffered the consequences of the depreciation of the coinage. The high position which in virtue of his skill as a designer of canals and harbour installations he occupied in the enchanted circle of the tsar's technical experts was of a kind to which many a Russian might well have aspired. During his stay Perry had acquired something of a stake in the condition of Russia; he 'wanted to have been married in the country to a woman for whom he had long had a great esteem'[7] and might have settled there if he had received the remuneration to which he considered himself entitled.

This high degree of personal involvement in local affairs would explain Perry's evident interest in Russia's economic problems and his wish to contribute to their solution. In his opinion, the means of enriching the tsar and his people were to be found in the development of trade and manufactories under a less oppressive and more equitable system of government. He takes an optimistic view of Russia's economic potential: 'Was but industry cultivated and encouraged as it is in England and other free countries, the product of it might be much further improved, Trade be extended, the People made happy, and the

Czar of Muscovy . . . might in a short time become equal in power and strength
to any Monarch on Earth.' Perry sees not only 'injudicious administration' but
the general oppression of the people as major obstacles to social improvement.[8]
In this respect he comes close to the most authoritative witness of all, Iván
Pososhkóv, the author of *The Book of Poverty and Wealth*.[9] Although Pososhkóv
never set foot outside Russia and, being an autodidact, was less well educated
than his country's Western observers, his knowledge of local conditions was
more intimate than theirs and covered a longer period. The scope of his enquiry
may be narrower than that of Weber's survey but his perception, sharpened by
the experience of a lifetime spent in the handling of practical affairs, is more
acute.

The life of Iván Tíkhonovich Pososhkóv has been the subject of much careful
study and research by a succession of Russian scholars and most recently by the
late B. B. Kafengauz whose monograph contains all the essential facts which it
has been possible to discover about this pioneer of early capitalism. Having
made his fortune as a fiscal agent of the state – a publican in both senses of the
word – by collecting toll and distilling and selling spirits at a handsome profit to
himself, he finally rose to a higher and more productive level of economic
activity by setting up a manufactory.

Pososhkóv, the descendant of several generations of artisans and craftsmen –
silversmiths – but nominally a peasant, was born in 1652 near Moscow on an
estate which formed part of the tsar's demesne. In 1671 he was living in
Moscow as a townsman (*posádskii chelovék*) enrolled in the *Baráshskaia slobodá*,
one of the surburban settlements obliged to perform work for the tsar's household.[10] In the late 1680s, together with a brother, he owned a distillery in the
uézd of Aléksin, in the region of Túla (where at that time Russia's iron industry
was concentrated). Between 1690 and 1692 he was engaged in various commercial activities in Moscow. It was about this time that Pososhkóv, obviously
hitherto an Old Believer, allowed himself to be persuaded to make the sign of
the cross with two fingers instead of three. Pososhkóv deliberately plays down
the political implications and deeper religious meaning of this act when referring to it in an autobiographical aside in his *Zérkalo ochevídnoe* (*The Manifest
Mirror*), a disquisition directed against the schismatics and in its extended
version also against the Lutherans.[11] His sister apparently abandoned Old
Belief only temporarily.

In the years 1694 to 1696 Pososhkóv designed and constructed a coining
press commissioned by the *stárets* Avraámii of the Andréevskii monastery as a
gift for Tsar Peter. It is not clear when Pososhkóv joined the Mint or when he
reached the rank of master minter (*ustávnyi dénezhnyi máster*), his official
designation on the roll of the Arsenal (*Oruzhéinaia paláta*) in 1704. The
circumstances are obscured by the fact that in Moscow at the beginning of the
eighteenth century coins were minted in several different workshops (*dénezhnye*

dvorý) under the general direction of General-Admiral and General Field-Marshal F. A. Golovín (1650–1706) in his capacity as director of the Arsenal from 1697 and from 1700 also of the *Zolotáia paláta* and the *Serébrianaia paláta*, the gold and the silver workshops in the Kremlin which were amalgamated with the Arsenal in 1700.[12] It would appear that Pososhkóv, having begun by executing occasional commissions between 1696 and 1697, worked regularly for the Mint from 1697 and joined its establishment not later than 1700. It is likely that he was employed by the workshop which in 1699 began to mint the copper coins referred to by Pososhkóv in Chapter 9. In 1700 and 1701, however, he seems also to have worked on his own account as a distiller or as a silversmith.

In January 1697 he was questioned in the *Preobrazhénskii prikáz* – the department which *inter alia* investigated matters affecting the security of the state – in connection with the enquiry into the authorship and allegedly subversive contents of a memorandum submitted to Peter I by Avraámii[13] but no action was taken against Pososhkóv. Some time between January and March of that year he was received by the tsar and allowed to demonstrate his ballistic invention – a barrier of muskets mounted on *chevaux de frise*; in 1699–1700 he wrote his first memorandum on coinage. In the early years of the new century Pososhkóv tried his hand at prospecting and discovered some natural dyes, petroleum and sulphur. In 1700 he wrote the *Donoshénie o rátnom povedénii* ('A Memorandum on the Conduct of Military Affairs'), an enquiry into the causes of the setbacks recently suffered by the Russian army in the initial phase of the war with Sweden. This memorandum he presented in 1701 to his chief, Golovín.

Before 1704 Pososhkóv wrote a draft memorandum known as *Donoshénie o ispravlénii vsekh neispráv* ('On the Making Good of all Shortcomings') which foreshadows many of the views later expressed in his major works. In 1703 or 1704 he wrote the first letter to the acting head of the hierarchy, metropolitan Stefán (Iavórskii), on matters relating to the clergy; the second followed in 1708 and the third in 1710. In 1704 Pososhkóv petitioned the tsar for a licence to manufacture playing cards for an annual royalty of 2,000 roubles. The licence was granted and with it, from the Arsenal, a subsidy of 200 roubles and some tools, but Pososhkóv and his partners could not raise the rest of the required working capital and the venture was abandoned. Between about 1704 and 1708, having presumably left the Mint, Pososhkóv worked as a master distiller at the *Bol'shói krúzhechnyi dvor* (the Crown distillery and emporium of spirits in Moscow; the Crown had the monopoly of distilling which from 1716 it enforced vigorously by taking over unlicensed private stills). In 1708 Pososhkóv appears to have been dismissed from his post on a charge of misdemeanour. He petitioned to be transferred in the same capacity to St Petersburg or to the province of Ingria; the request was refused. In the summer of 1708, at the time of the revolt of the Bashkirs, the commandant of Kazan requested that, pending the arrival of a fully qualified engineer, Pososhkóv be put in charge of repairing the fortifications, but it is not known whether he was ever seconded to Kazan.

In 1708 Pososhkóv wrote his second memorandum on coinage and the *Zérkalo ochevídnoe* (*The Manifest Mirror*). Whatever charges had been levelled against him must have been dropped, for in 1709 or early in 1710 he was appointed official master distiller at Nóvgorod where he was also concerned with the stamping of official paper (*gérbovaia bumága*) introduced as a new source of revenue in 1699[14] and, oddly, with the construction of fountains or waterworks. His hydraulic activities precede those of the two foreigners engaged in 1721 to construct fountains in St Petersburg and at Peterhof.[15] In 1712 he was instrumental in setting up the Crown pharmacy in Nóvgorod and in the same year began to write the *Zaveshchánie otécheskoe* (*The Paternal Testament*) – a book of fatherly advice, moral and practical, wider in its scope than the *Domostrói* (*The Book of Household Management*) whose last chapter it brings to mind.[16] As before, Pososhkóv took care to be in the good graces of the higher clergy – a habit which in the end contributed to his undoing. In Nóvgorod he met the metropolitan Job (?–1716) more than once and it seems likely that through him Pososhkóv made the acquaintance of Ioanníkii Likhúda (Licudi, 1633–1717) who with his brother Sofrónii (1652–1730) had been moved to Nóvgorod by the ecclesiastical authorities in 1706. Sofrónii left for Moscow in 1707 but Ioanníkii remained in Nóvgorod till 1716.[17] It is possible that from him Pososhkóv learnt something of Western political institutions and ideas. One wonders whether there existed in Nóvgorod in the entourage of Job a discussion group or circle similar to, but more progressive in outlook than, the one centred on the *stárets* Avraámii in Moscow at the end of the previous century.

In 1714 Pososhkóv, through the good offices of Feodósii (Ianóvskii), archimandrite of the St Alexander-Névskii monastery, leased from one of its dependent houses a building in Nóvgorod obviously intended for industrial or commercial use. From Nóvgorod Pososhkóv seems to have made several expeditions to St Petersburg on business, bringing with him foodstuffs and a variety of goods for sale. On two occasions he carried letters of introduction from the metropolitan of Nóvgorod, Job – in 1712 to the recently appointed vice-governor of Petersburg, Ia. N. Rímskii-Kórsakov, in 1713 to Ia. F. Dolgorúkii (1639–1720), the head of his family and the senior senator. Pososhkóv's earnings from various sources other than his official appointment (his salary, though nominally adequate, was not paid regularly) enabled him to leave the tsar's service in 1715 or 1716 and between 1716 and 1717 to buy two adjacent messuages (*dvorý*) in St Petersburg for 400 roubles and in 1720 and 1721 two more in Nóvgorod for 100 roubles.

In 1718 he wrote his third memorandum (no longer extant) on coinage which may never have reached the tsar. In 1719 Pososhkóv completed the *Zaveshchánie* (*Testament*). Between 1719 and 1725 he bought a total of fourteen parcels of land in the region of Káshin (about half-way between Tver' and Iaroslávl') and in the *pogóst* (settlement) of Ustréka, to the east of Borovichí, on the river Uvér' (a northern confluent of the Msta). The second locality was within comparatively easy reach of Nóvgorod; the distance between the two was about 190 km as the crow flies. On a piece of land belonging to the church at Ustréka, Pososhkóv established a distillery for which the thirty male peasants on the two small estates bought by him in the vicinity provided the labour. The management of the land and of the distillery was in the hands of Pososhkóv's wife's nephew, Aleksandr Mikháilov. It seems likely that the distillery supplied the three licensed liquor shops which Pososhkóv ran in Nóvgorod. The setting up of the fourteen stills cost Pososhkóv over 1,000 roubles, for the land nearby he paid 539 roubles and for the hamlet near Káshin 750 roubles. In all cases the sellers were men of service (*sluzhílye liúdi*) of one sort or another or the widows of such men. Thus Pososhkóv, himself an 'agriculturalist', became the owner of 258 *desiatíny*[18] of land (some 700 acres or 283 hectares) and the master of fifty male peasants. Strange as it may seem, this kind of relationship was not uncommon in Pososhkóv's lifetime as the ownership by non-*dvoriáne* of land inhabited by peasants was not expressly prohibited until 1730.[19] Between 1721 and 1724 Pososhkóv also farmed the collection of tolls (*tamózhennyi sbor*) at Ustréka.

In February 1724 he completed *The Book of Poverty and Wealth* (*Kníga o skúdosti i bogátstve*) which, in his own words, he had begun three years earlier. However, internal evidence suggests that the triennium may have been preceded by a period of preliminary work at least equally long.

Throughout his life Pososhkóv borrowed and occasionally lent money; he sued and was sued for debt. At his death he owed 2,350 roubles, including 1,100 to various individuals, among them eight *posádskie liúdi* (townsmen) in Nóvgorod, and 1,076 roubles to the exchequer in arrears of rent for farming the tolls. Pososhkóv did not buy land for purely agricultural purposes but rather in order to equip himself for further entrepreneurial activity. In the summer of 1725, after the death of Peter I, Pososhkóv applied to the *Manufaktúr-kollégiia* (College or Board of Manufactories) for permission to establish in Nóvgorod a workshop (*zavód*) for the manufacture of calamanco and linen. His land was to supply the labour (and presumably also some of the raw materials) but Pososhkóv looked to the state to provide him with the necessary technical personnel and some of the equipment: he asked for two master craftsmen, one weaver and two looms (out of the proposed five or six) to be assigned to him from the Crown manufactories. Pososhkóv's request was apparently granted in part or in full, the workshop was established and eventually passed into the hands of Pososhkóv's son Nikolái. In August 1725 Pososhkóv was arrested, probably in consequence of the heterodox views expressed in *The Book of Poverty and Wealth* and perhaps also in connection with the proceedings against the archbishop (since 1720) of Nóvgorod, Feodósii (Ianóvskii), among whose books and papers a copy of *The Book of Poverty and Wealth* was found.[20] Pososhkóv died in prison on 1 February 1726 OS.

The likeness of Pososhkóv – miscellaneous writer, projector, entrepreneur, self-made capitalist – that could be reconstructed from these data would be one of a garrulous busybody, a well-meaning but persistent giver of gratuitous advice, a mechanically minded Ivan-of-all-trades, an astute man of business and also something of an amateur theologian who liked to move in ecclesiastical circles. It is not often that a person of so eminently practical a temperament is given to theorizing and is determined and literate enough to set his views down on paper. Posterity has every reason to praise these qualities since in the writings of Pososhkóv is to be found a picture of Petrine Russia which is unique in being contemporary, many-sided and the work of a man who in the social sense of the word, and in that sense alone, may be described as ordinary.

It is easy enough to trace Pososhkóv's ascent in the social scale; it is much harder to fit his one socio-economic work into the history of ideas in and outside Russia. It was suggested a long time ago that Pososhkóv may have been influenced by Juraj Križanić's unpublished discourses on government, commonly known as *Politika* (written between 1663 and 1666), which *The Book of Poverty and Wealth* in some respects resembles. Admittedly some of the subject-matter – trade and handicrafts, agriculture, legal institutions, warfare – is similar and the analogy between Križanić's short section on craftsmanship and some of Pososhkóv's utterances on the artisans is indeed striking. Nevertheless, there is not enough evidence to prove that Pososhkóv borrowed this or that idea or piece of information from Križanić. The *Politika* is primarily a treatise on government whose purpose is to discover the best ways of protecting the body politic from harm and enhancing the power, prosperity, well-being and glory of the state. It introduces at great length a programme of reform which includes the creation of privileged estates subordinated to the Crown, the abolition of commercial monopolies and the control of foreign trade by the monarch. It upholds the principle of absolute monarchy but finds much to criticize in the Muscovite political tradition. Its general intention, which is presumably to introduce the Russians to the elements of political thought, has very little to do with the essentially fiscal purpose of Pososhkóv's treatise. The feature which the two works share most conspicuously is a thoroughgoing hatred of foreigners as economic intruders and competitors. The only difference here is that of degree: compared to Križanić's, Pososhkóv's is a mild case of xenophobia.

In any case the question of Križanić's possible influence on Pososhkóv – still open – is only of secondary importance. When Križanić insists that a poor kingdom means a poor king and Pososhkóv declares that the peasants' wealth is the wealth of the tsar,[21] it does not necessarily follow that Pososhkóv had read Križanić, nor does it greatly matter whether he had done so or not. What is significant is that an idea which had long been in circulation in western Europe had finally found its way into Russia. Križanić may well have culled it from the densely packed pages of his main authority on economics, the *Consilia pro aerario* (Advice concerning all treasuries, civil, ecclesiastical and military, public and private, or laws, arts and remedies whereby the chests of rulers and the purposes of subjects ... may be filled, multiplied, enriched and maintained, etc.), by one of the 'early' cameralist writers, Faust ab Aschaffenburg. Because of its practical purpose and of the juristic propensity of its author, the *Consilia*, together with other productions of the cameralist school, would have been of greater interest to Pososhkóv than the *Politika*.

The Austro-German cameralists, 'middle', 'early' and 'late', have been described as 'administrative technologists' and their work as 'a theory of managing natural resources and human capacities so that they would be most lucrative for the prince in whose interest the management was conducted'.[22] Their most noteworthy representatives in Pososhkóv's lifetime were J. J. Becher (1635–82), W. von Schröder, FRS (1640–88) and P. W. von Hörnigk (1640–1714). All three were directly or indirectly associated with the Emperor Leopold I. It was the self-imposed task of the cameralists to offer to rulers detailed advice on the most effective ways of securing a regular revenue, required for the fulfilment of their political aims, without bringing ruin on their subjects. In the words of Schröder, they believed that it was profitable for the state that the ruler should have the reins of power in his hand and money in his chest. If this phraseology savours of a narrowly monetarist conception of wealth and power it is because the cameralists for the most part subscribed to the principles of the mercantile system. In its wider and modern interpretation mercantilism – when it is not dismissed as devoid of adequate meaning – is seen as a set of policies calculated to supply the state, by means of favourable balance of trade, with the ready money needed by its subjects for internal and external trade, investment and accumulation. From these aims spring the ideals of self-sufficiency, manu-facturing enterprise, commercial predominance and national solidarity.

Within the meaning of these shorthand definitions, Križanić, although obviously influenced by both mercantilism and cameralism, belongs to neither school. *A fortiori* the same has to be said of Pososhkóv, a backwoodsman isolated from the intellectual life of western and central Europe. And yet, informed as it is by a desire for the improvement in the fortunes of the state in the supposedly common interest of ruler and subject, Pososhkóv's work re-flects, as if in a curved mirror, some of the concerns and ideals of the cameralists. Many of the topics discussed in *The Book of Poverty and Wealth* – taxation, penury, population, internal and external trade, craftsmanship, manu-facturing, coinage, the land survey, law and order – are the subject-matter of cameralist literature. The full title of Pososhkóv's treatise recalls the descriptive headings of the works of some of the cameralists. Who can tell whether this affinity is due to the direct but obscure influence of some individual, to hearsay, to reading, to intellectual osmosis or perhaps to a natural similarity in the response to the challenge offered at different times and in different parts of Europe by a crisis originating in a dangerous deficiency in a country's resources?

These questions have to remain unanswered but it may be noted that in Sweden, which was losing ground to Russia, Schröder's *Fürstliche Schatz- und Rent-Kammer*, without finding an imitator, was read in 1711–12 and some of the advice contained in it was acted on in 1713.[23] Nor were the cameralists quite unknown in Russia. A Russian translation of the same book by Schröder is listed among the manuscripts owned by Prince D. M. Golítsyn (1665–1737). Whether it was read by its owner or anyone else we do not know. It is tempting to think that it may have been known to Pososhkóv who mentions his acquaintance with Golítsyn at the beginning of Chapter 3 but the temptation must be resisted if only because the date of the translation is unknown. Another cameralistic item in Golítsyn's collection was Johann Joachim Becher's *Politische Discurs von den eigentlichen Ursachen dess Auff- und Abnehmen der Städt Länder und Republicken. In Spezie, wie ein Land Volckreich und Nahrhafft zu machen und eine rechte Societatem civilem zu bringen*, first published in Frankfurt in 1668, also in Russian translation. A third was Christian Georg Bessel's *Schmiede des politischen Glücks, darinnen viele nützliche Lehren enthalten* (Frankfurt and Hamburg, 1673), possibly in the original.

Pososhkóv's cameralism, such as it was, was what Albion Small has called 'cameralism of the book' in contradistinction to 'cameralism of the bureau',[24] which, it may be assumed, was that of the foreign bureaucrats who were active in Peter I's new central administration from about 1717. Despite the gap between the two varieties of cameralism it will be noticed that quite a few of Pososhkóv's proposals come so close to some of the reforms decreed by Peter as to give the impression that the author of *The Book of Poverty and Wealth* was knocking on doors that were being opened by the professional practitioners of cameral science. In the writings of the theorists of the middle period they could find the principles upon which to base their advice with regard to money, trade and industry.[25] The economic programme adopted by Tsar Peter on the advice of his (for the most part) foreign counsellors in the closing years of his reign, though patently more coherent, more systematic, more rational, was not unlike that drawn up about the same time by Pososhkóv, save for the lack of any ethical foundation.

In submitting to the tsar unsolicited proposals for reform Pososhkóv was not alone. A few men, more highly placed than he, sent in memoranda on subjects connected with public finance, trade and industrial development. Others, closer in their social origins to Pososhkóv but for the most part advancing towards high office and described as 'Moscow progressives', presented their views on topics more closely connected with the life of the community: runaway peasants, theft and brigandage, the proper dispensation of justice. None of these memoranda rival the scope or depth of Pososhkóv's investigation.[26]

On the face of it the subject-matter of *The Book of Poverty and Wealth* is public finance. The declared purpose of its author, who is at once a Christian moralist and a political economist, is to find ways of setting in motion an antiquated and stagnant economy, among them the improvement of public morality and economic behaviour. But behind the economist and the moralist lurks the political polemicist who occasionally makes himself heard. As Pososhkóv examines the fabric of Russian society he utters *obiter dicta* which, when pieced together, amount to a withering criticism of the existent posture of public affairs. The blame for the failure of the well-intentioned efforts of the tsar and his small team of henchmen to improve government and society falls on the obstructive actions and attitudes of the privileged hereditary governing caste. Corrupt, self-seeking and often remiss, it has a vested interest in dishonesty and inefficiency. By reason of its status and its numerical strength it is immune from punishment. For once the remedy lies not in legislation and regulation, for which Pososhkóv has as great a weakness as any armchair reformer, but in political action: the tsar should recruit his servants from among the lower and uncorrupted strata of the population whose members, unendowed with wealth and influence, will be more amenable than the traditional élite.[27] The proposal goes far beyond the opportunity for advancement offered to outsiders by the Table of Ranks of 1722, and could easily have been denounced as impertinent and seditious by those in authority who had no patience with Pososhkóv.

Had *The Book of Poverty and Wealth* not been preserved, posterity would have found itself unable to contemplate 'the enterprises carried out under Peter' from a point of view which the imaginative Vockerodt considered to be as rewarding as the historical. 'Consider', he suggested, 'an ordinary Russian townsman or peasant – social categories untouched by Peter's efforts to civilize his subjects – and see how far their intelligence and mental powers extend. You will soon notice that in general, in all matters in which he is not hampered by prejudice proper to his land or his religion, the Russian has a really sound natural intelligence and good judgment coupled with an uncommon ability to grasp the essence of things, great readiness to find effective means by which to achieve his ends and to use opportunities to his advantage as they arise. Most of them have considerable natural eloquence and an ability to plead their case well.'[28] Pososhkóv's literary personality fits this description perfectly. Narrow-minded, in many respects ignorant, prejudiced, repetitive, long-winded, sententious, at times incoherent he may be, but his last and best work, the only one of its kind, is a historical document of far greater value than the contemporary accounts mentioned earlier. Without *The Book of Poverty and Wealth* we would lack an oblique but consistent and detailed assessment by a Russian of the effect – positive, negative or neutral – of the domestic policies of Peter I on the life of the common people of his realm. Only here can we catch a glimpse of ordinary people going about their business, buying, selling or producing goods, attending church or failing to do so, litigating, lying in gaol or begging and, further afield, beyond the confines of legality, taking to violent crime, deserting from the army or abandoning their dwellings to flee from the tax-collector. It is for this reason that since Pogódin first published Pososhkóv's great work in 1842 few if any social or economic historians of the reign of Peter have been able to ignore Pososhkóv's treatise or deny themselves the opportunity of quoting from it. Outside the USSR, however, even those historians who have a good reading knowledge of present-day Russian might be discouraged by the often archaic vocabulary, the abstruse terminology and the loose syntax of the text. Besides, the absence of a translation of *The Book of Poverty and Wealth* into a western European language has deprived the student of Russian history who does not read Russian of the possibility, offered by Pososhkóv, of taking a look at Petrine Russian through a borrowed pair of Russian eyes.

But to provide a bare translation is not enough. For one thing many of the facts contained and opinions expressed in the original need to be verified or explained. Hence the Commentaries. For another, although *The Book of Poverty and Wealth* is a self-contained treatise it gains depth from being seen against its extensive and kaleidoscopic historical background, consisting of two epochs which are seldom examined in apposition.

Neither Pososhkóv's mentality nor the intent of his treatise can be fully understood without a preliminary examination of the social and political environment in which he grew to maturity. Pososhkóv was born in 1652 – the year in which Níkon became Patriarch; he had reached manhood by the end of the reign of Alekséi Mikháilovich when the future Peter the Great was barely two-and-a-half years of age. The intervening period coincides with the aftermath of the promulgation of the *Code* (*Ulozhénie*) of 1649, the annexation of the Ukraine, the Church schism, the promulgation of the New Trade Regulations (*Nóvyi torgóvyi ustáv*) and with the conflicts leading up to the peasant uprising of 1670–1. Pososhkóv's formative years, about which little is known, coincide with the reign of Fëdor Alekséevich (1676–82) and the regency of Sófia Alekséevna (1682–9). By the beginning of the joint reign (until 1689) of Peter I and Iván Alekséevich, Pososhkóv was on the threshold of middle age; his view of the world had been formed and his scale of values fixed.

Russian Society at the End of the Seventeenth Century

The service state. The Church. The disruptive effect of Old Belief. Social change after 1649. Territorial expansion. The Cossacks. Peasant unrest and migration. The emergence of the dvoriáne. *Wars. The Ukraine. The population of Russia and the distribution of land in 1678. Industrial enterprise. Foreign trade. Taxation. Landed estates. The* prikázy *or departments of state. The regional administration. Centralization. The regency of Sófia Alekséevna (1682–9).*

In the midst of this spectacle of continuous change, now orderly, now violent, one feature stands out as constant and decisive: the nature and function of the state. The political system which Peter I was to inherit from his predecessors has much in common with Max Weber's *Leiturgiestaat*, that universal regime of services and exactions under which the activities of most individuals are subjected to physical restrictions, economic constraints and bureaucratic controls for the benefit of the state. The members of various sections of society are kept in their hereditary stations in perpetuity: the peasants are bound to the land, the craftsmen to their trades, the office-holders to their posts. The most profitable sectors of the economy are monopolized by the state, the taxes are excessive and for their collection in full men of property are held personally responsible. The system as a whole is administered by a body of officials whose practices curtail personal freedom and economic enterprise.

Križanić, in writing about Muscovy as he knew it in the 1660s, blames the harshness of the system of government for making men indifferent to life itself and, all the more so, insensible to honour and morals. 'The place', he observes, 'is full of taverns, monopolies and prohibitions, concessionaires, tax collectors, customs officials and secret informers so that everywhere men are under constraint; they can do nothing of their free will and are unable to benefit from what they have acquired by their sweat and labour. Instead they have to work and trade in secrecy and in silence, in fear and trembling, and have to hide before the innumerable officials – plunderers and wrongdoers or, to call them by their proper name, executioners. And as the tax collectors and tormentors of the peasantry do not receive adequate pay, they cannot act equitably because necessity drives them to seek their own advantage and accept gifts from the wrongdoers.'[29]

Russian society at the close of the seventeenth century resembled the unattractive model of the *Leiturgiestaat* not only in its essence but also in many points of detail: witness such profitable commodities as the principal articles of overseas trade regrated by the tsar's treasury and farmed out or monopolized; the sale, and at times the production too, of alcoholic liquor likewise reserved; various categories of the urban population obliged to act as commissaries for the tsar's treasury and as farmers of the liquor monopoly; the collectors of revenue held personally responsible for the delivery of the entire proceeds due from a particular collection; the landholders expected to supervise the payment of taxes by the peasants on their land. The creation by the state, towards the end of the reign of Peter the Great, of craft corporations to suit its own economic ends was to complete the analogy. Another feature of the service state – the ownership of the state by the monarch – was particularly marked in Muscovy. The tsar considered himself to be and by common consent was the ground landlord, as it were, of all immovable property – landed estates, commercial premises, urban messuages. The landholders – men of service (*sluzhílye liúdi*), the urban population (*posádskie liúdi*), peasants – owed him rent in the form of military service, tax and ancillary service in various combinations and degrees.[30]

The outright ownership of land without any obligation on the part of the owner to serve the sovereign was considered incompatible with the interests of the service state. For this reason the law of the land restricted and controlled the alienation of landed property, be it by inheritance, exchange, lease or assignment. The absence – apart from the Church – of independent corporations and the existence of a direct connection between the central authorities and the various sections of society under their control appears to have been peculiar to Muscovy. The Church, without forming part of the service state, was accommodated within it. But even here there is a hint of a service nexus. The portions of land assigned in the seventeenth century by the state to parish churches were for the most part detached from estates held or owned by men of service. This simple reallocation suggests that the state regarded the parish clergy as its spiritual servants. The Patriarch was wholly subservient to the tsar and could not take a single step without his approval and consent. The one Patriarch – Níkon – to challenge the nature of this relationship was driven from the field.[31]

As might be expected, the service state had scant regard for the basic needs and higher aspirations of individuals. At the bottom of the social scale the attachment of the peasantry to the land contributed to a condition of constant unrest; higher up, in the urban communities, to a sense of injury. The average trader or artisan had little chance of growing rich – or less poor – without receiving preferential treatment from the tsar. Any advancement beyond the bounds of a man's inherited station or any substantial economic gain occurred only by way of exception. The internal economic activities of so static a society could not – without overburdening the population – keep pace with the financial demands of an ambitious dynasty committed to a course of territorial expansion to the detriment of an enfeebled Polish Republic. Unlike the service states of late antiquity, Muscovy under the patrimonial rule of Alekséi Mikháilovich and his successors was an empire not in decline but in the making, not a graveyard but a potential breeding-ground of a state-sponsored capitalism. Favourable external economic factors assisted the expansionist policy of the Muscovite service state; the demand in the maritime countries of western Europe for Russian primary products helped the tsar's treasury to meet the cost of territorial conquest.[32]

The legal framework of the Muscovite service state is to be found in the *Ulozhénie* or *Code* associated with the name of Tsar Alekséi Mikháilovich. At the beginning of June 1648 Moscow was for ten days convulsed by tumult. Rioting, looting and armed assault reinforced demands and petitions for the redress of grievances and the convocation of an Assembly of the Land (*Zémskii sobór*). In July the tsar convoked the *sobór* for 1 September with a view to resolving the underlying social conflicts and bringing about a long-term settlement. In January 1649 the *Code* was approved and printed for distribution to the departments of state (*prikázy*) and seats of authority in the provinces.

Henceforth in the state of Muscovy justice in all matters was to be dispensed even-handedly and the *Code* was to remain fixed and inviolate. The last and weightiest juridical monument of the Muscovite period, it also constitutes, as Shchápov suggests, the first attempt to regulate by statute the activities of the whole community in so far as such activities affected the interests of the state. From now on the tsar's government, instead of allowing the inhabitants of various localities to seek exemptions and dispensations in accordance with their particular needs, positively required his subjects to comply with the law. The *Code* marked a further advance in the process of centralization in so far as a territory as vast as that of Muscovy could be subjected to such a process. As well as being a code of civil law whose provisions extend into the spheres of property and inheritance, and a code of criminal law, it also embodies in statutory form the obligations and restrictions imposed by the service state on all subjects and the privileges granted to some. By ordering the return of all runaways without a period of grace it attached the peasants to the land of their respective landlords. In a similarly indirect manner it defined the duties and character of the various social groups. The peasants were to till the land and remain on it; the traders and artisans were to join the urban communities (*posády*), pay tax, perform official duties at the bidding of the tsar and produce or sell goods; the men of service (*sluzhílye* or *rátnye liúdi*) were to be called to the colours in times of war and were entitled to hold or own landed estates.

The twenty-five chapters of the *Code* legislate, in a rather haphazard order, for a variety of aspects of both ecclesiastical and civil life; many of its provisions continued to affect social relations in the first quarter of the next century and are therefore relevant to a number of matters discussed in *The Book of Poverty and Wealth*. Thus Chapters 10 and 15 deal with judicial procedure, 11 and 12 with the dispensation of justice to peasants and with their liabilities and movements, 16 and 17 with landed estates; 18 is devoted to fees for the sealing of documents, 19 to the reorganization of the inhabitants of the urban areas (*posádskie liúdi*), 21 to robbery and theft, 22 to capital punishment.[33]

The social barriers erected and the restrictions on physical mobility imposed by the *Code* in order to protect the various groups, as well as individuals, from mutual encroachment and depredation did not usher in a period of social stability. Muscovy was to remain in a chronic state of flux and tension, constantly subject to civil strife, expanding her territory in war but, not surprisingly, failing to develop her economic resources beyond the minimum required for the security of the state. During the summer of 1648 the commotion in Moscow was followed by similar outbreaks in other parts of the country, including Siberia. The summer of 1650 saw more unrest in Pskov and Nóvgorod followed by a wave of violence in the surrounding countryside in the winter of 1650–1. In 1662 in Moscow the introduction of copper coinage, added to other causes of discontent such as high taxation, the scarcity and rising prices of grain, as well as reverses suffered in the war with Poland, led in July to an outbreak of rioting and organized mob violence which had to be suppressed by the military garrison. The period between the beginning of 1670 and November 1671 saw the peasant uprising led by the Cossack Stepán Rázin.[34]

In response to representations made before the Assembly by the deputies of the urban population the provisions made by Chapter 19 of the *Code* had set in motion a reorganization of the *posády*. The object of this operation was, for the benefit of the tsar's treasury and the taxpayer alike, to put an end to the unfair advantage enjoyed at the expense of the rest of the community by the inhabitants of the 'blank' (*bélye*), that is to say 'exempt', settlements (*slóbody*), established within or close to the *posády* by the Patriarch, bishops, monasteries, boyars and other landlords. The inhabitants of these 'liberties' – traders, artisans and the like, including migrants from the countryside – in virtue of the immunity of these areas paid no taxes, rendered no services to the sovereign and did not share in the civic tasks of the *posád*. Under the Russian system of joint responsibility for the total obligations to be discharged by a community, urban or rural, the departure from it of any one member increased proportionately the collective liability of the rest.

The wholesale exemption conferred by the tsar on any particular area within a *posád* had an adverse effect on the remaining members of the community: as well as bearing a heavier burden of tax they had to compete with those who paid none. The *slóbody* were duly sequestrated, joined to the *posády* and subjected to all the ordinary obligations incumbent on the inhabitants 'in accordance with their possessions and earnings'.[35] Peasants living in the exempted settlements and originating from estates belonging to their founders were to return there forthwith. Conversely, traders who had moved to villages must return to their *posády*; likewise men who had acquired exemption from all obligations to the tsar and duties to the community by pledging their persons to a protector or hiring themselves out to an employer, must be reintegrated in the *posád*. The *Code* attached the urban population as firmly to its communities as it bound the peasants to the land: all *posádskie* must henceforth reside in the *posády* of which they were members. As a result of this measure the number of holdings occupied by *posádskie liúdi* rose from 31,567 in 1648 to 41,662 in 1652 and again from that figure to 49,788 by the late 1670s. It has been estimated that by the end of the century there were 52,500 such holdings in Russia and Siberia.[36]

One of the principal achievements of the *Code* of 1649 was to set out in detail the terms on which landed estates – *pomést'ia* and *vótchiny* – were to be held by secular occupiers. Their rights – in many respects more extensive than before – and duties are the subject of Chapters 16 and 17. The contents of these chapters make it clear that contrary to a widely held but fallacious belief,[37] the *pomést'ia* and the *vótchiny* did not differ from one another in their essence, as is the case with feudal and allodial estates, but rather constituted two species of the same genus: land granted by the tsar in recompense for service but remaining under his ultimate control. The difference between the two lay in the degree of proprietorial rights enjoyed by the holder. The *vótchinnik* came closer to absolute ownership since in his lifetime he was free to part with his land at will – though not in favour of monasteries or members of the clergy. The endowment with a *pomést'e*, on the other hand, placed a servant of the tsar under an obligation to perform various military or civil duties. The restrictions governing the conveyance of land by exchange, gift, sale or bequest between members of specified groups of men of service, established in different regions and responsible to different authorities, applied as much to *vótchiny* as to *pomést'ia*. The *pomést'e* must not be bequeathed or assigned or otherwise alienated and at first, from about the middle of the sixteenth century, was allowed on the death of the holder to pass only to his son or sons.

From the early seventeenth century successive *ukázy* extended the proprietorial rights of holders of *vótchiny* and *pomést'ia* alike. Thus in 1611 the principle was established that not only the sons but also the widow and daughters of the deceased *poméshchik* were entitled to an interest in the estate held by him in his lifetime. The *Code* of 1649 confirmed and in some respects widened these concessions. The *vótchinniki* were allowed to acquire more land by buying *vótchiny* from their kinsmen and by extending the area of ploughland within the boundary of a *vótchina* and – but only by leave of the tsar – by buying *pomést'ia* and converting them into *vótchiny*. The *Code* also confirmed the rights of holders of *vótchiny* which had been sold to them from the uninhabited lands in the gift of the sovereign and allowed men of service in certain districts to buy as *vótchiny* uninhabited *pomést'ia* for which no tenants could be found. The holders of *pomést'ia*, too, benefited from the *Code*. Thus a *poméshchik* was allowed to retain his estate beyond his period of useful service or to let it on lease for the rest of his life to a kinsman, provided that men or money were contributed from the *pomést'e* in place of the holder's military service. If the *poméshchik* died without leaving a male heir, his widow and daughters were now formally allowed to receive portions of the estate for their maintenance (with the right to assign them to another holder) or as a jointure or dowry.

Under the *Code* a *pomést'e* vacated by the death of a bachelor was assigned by the authorities to any of his kinsmen who might be landless or inadequately endowed with land. The exchange of *pomést'ia*, by leave of the tsar, had long been allowed between men of service belonging to the same category, on condition that the two estates were of the same size and that both were inhabited or uninhabited. The *Code* allowed the exchange of *pomést'ia* which were not wholly equal in size, as well as the exchange of secular for ecclesiastical or monastic estates. Even more valuable from the point of view of the landholder was the permission granted by the *Ulozhénie* to exchange *pomést'ia* for *vótchiny* and vice versa, by leave of the tsar and in conformity with a special procedure, provided that in consequence no peasants were transferred from a *pomést'e* to a *vótchina*. While continuing to restrict the size of *pomést'ia* appropriate to each category of men of service and the amount of arable land within the limits of each *pomést'e* and *vótchina*, the *Ulozhénie* yet again allowed the holders of *pomést'ia* as well as of *vótchiny* to seek official approval for the increase in the area of arable land within the boundaries of their estates effected by the ploughing up of meadows and the clearing of forests. In certain cases such areas might now be permanently added to the *vótchina* or *pomést'e* to make up for the poor or mediocre quality of the ploughland in proportion to the original area of such land on the estate. Finally, the *Ulozhénie* allowed the hereditary men of service of the most junior rank (*boiárskie déti*) resident in the borderlands on the middle and lower Oká to apply for grants of *pomést'ia* from unassigned land (*díkie poliá*) in that region. The size of such grants was related to the amount of land already held by the petitioners.

In sum, the service state was going to considerable lengths within a restrictive and hierarchical system of land tenure to reward and encourage its landed men of arms and to give them greater security of tenure as well as to accommodate their dependents and descendants. In consequence of this policy the *pomést'e* came increasingly to resemble the *výsluzhennaia vótchina* – the hereditary estate earned in the tsar's service. This occurred all the more naturally as *vótchiny*, whether granted or bought, were most frequently areas of land carved out of the *pomést'ia*.[38]

The proprietorial rights of holders of *vótchiny* and *pomést'ia* under the *Code*, apart from creating something of a market in real estate, enhanced the mobility of landholders in general and assisted the south-eastward advance of the frontier.[39] Yet even the richest agricultural land was unproductive unless it was populated by peasants obliged to render service or pay rent to the landholder. It must have seemed, therefore, that the greatest single boon conferred by the *Code*, in keeping with the rationale of the service state, on landlords (including the Crown), was the binding of the peasants to the land.

The *Zémskii sobór* of 1648–9 took away from the Church in privileges and material advantages almost as much as it gave to the men of service 'by descent'[40] although it did not go as far as granting their request that the monastic estates be confiscated and distributed among them. The *Ulozhénie* did, however, withdraw from their ecclesiastical founders and landlords and assign to the sovereign the urban settlements and quarters (*slóbody* and *posády*) whose inhabitants had been exempt from paying tax and rendering service to the state. The *Code* also prohibited the monasteries and the clergy from acquiring any more *vótchiny* of any kind by purchase, bequest or mortgage. Soon after the publication of the *Code*, presumably in order not to put the ecclesiastical law at a disadvantage by comparison with the civil, it was decided to produce a printed edition of a canonical collection of ecclesiastical laws – *Kórmchaia kníga* – analogous to the Byzantine *Nomokanon*, but its publication was held up until 1653 by the new Patriarch, Níkon, elected in 1652.[41]

The Church in general, and the Patriarch in particular, although subject to interference on the part of the secular authorities, had long enjoyed a high degree of immunity with a generous measure of judicial autonomy. In consequence the Patriarch, the bishops and the superiors of certain monasteries with their lands and administrative organization were, in civil actions, answerable only before the high officials of the *Prikáz Bol'shógo dvortsá* (the office of the sovereign's palace) acting on behalf of the tsar in consultation with representatives of the clergy, whereas below that level justice was dispensed, with much overlapping of authority and without any clear definition of territorial limits, by the Patriarch, the bishops, the monasteries and the civil authorities or by mixed tribunals. The laity at large had good reason to complain of the difficulty of obtaining justice in a contest at law with a cleric or a dependant of the Church under so cumbersome a system and one so given to bias.

These faults were but partially corrected by the decision made by the tsar in council in 1641 to delegate the judicial authority over the hierarchy with its lay dependants (as exercised by the *Prikáz Bol'shógo dvortsá*) to various other appropriate *prikázy*. The state had long exercised control over the Church by the agency of the boyars (in this instance high officials), appointed by the tsar and answerable to him, in the Patriarch's judicial and administrative departments, as well as in the diocesan administration. It was left to the *sobór* (assembly) of 1648–9 to complete this process by placing the clergy (but not the Patriarch or his demesne) as well as the monasteries with their subordinates and the inhabitants of their lands, in all matters outside the sphere of ecclesiastical discipline, under the jurisdiction of the secular authorities – the *voevódy* (prefects) in the provinces and the *prikázy* in Moscow. The higher judicial authority over the clergy was vested in the *Monastýrskii prikáz*, formerly a branch of the *Prikáz Bol'shógo dvortsá*, partly staffed by ecclesiastics who were soon to be replaced by laymen. The only ecclesiastic to retain his jurisdiction in all matters over his direct subordinates and the inhabitants of his demesne was the Patriarch.

This exception was not enough to win the approval of the new Patriarch, Níkon, who saw in the establishment of the *Monastýrskii prikáz*, where even disputes between ecclesiastics were adjudicated upon by laymen, an attempt to diminish the authority of the priesthood at the very time when he himself was preparing to secure for his office a standing and power equal to those of the tsar in the secular sphere and to renew the spiritual strength of the Church by carrying out a revision of the liturgy and of the ritual. Finding his purpose crossed at the very outset, Níkon denounced the *Code* as an accursed book and its contents as diabolical and drawn up at the prompting of Antichrist. At his instance the Church assemblies of 1654, 1655 and 1656 sanctioned the reform of the liturgical books, rites and ceremonies in accordance with contemporary Greek usage; that of 1656 excommunicated the adherents of the ancient ritual, henceforth to be known as Old Ritualists or Old Believers.

Thus a new cause of tension, a schism, arose in a country hitherto united in its religious life but already troubled by repeated disturbances in Moscow and in other towns and by growing discontent in the countryside. In the trial of strength with Tsar Alekséi, Níkon overplayed his hand. In 1658 he abandoned his throne in protest against the tsar's displeasure at the usurpation by the Patriarch of the style of Great Sovereign Lord (reserved for the tsar) and was formally deposed by the council of 1666 but his strictures against the *Monastýrskii prikáz* were not held against him, indeed they caused the assembly of 1667 to review the entire question of secular jurisdiction over the clergy. The decision arrived at and duly confirmed by the tsar reversed that of the assembly of 1648–9: the Church had won the day.

Although in 1669 the tsar, in consultation with the Patriarch of Moscow, two Eastern Patriarchs and the 'hallowed assembly' of representatives of the clergy, ruled that a priest who had committed a criminal offence would be deprived of orders and handed over to the secular authorities, the principle of exemption from secular jurisdiction in all other proceedings against the clergy remained in force. Priests and monks were no longer to be brought before secular tribunals. The *Monastýrskii prikáz* was not abolished immediately but survived for a further ten years during which period it concerned itself with the taxation of ecclesiastical lands and the provision of administrative links between monasteries and dioceses. The Church assembly of 1675 removed secular officials from the ecclesiastical administration. The 'hallowed assembly' (*osviashchёnnyi sobór*)[42] of high ecclesiastics which had joined the *zémskii sobór* of 1648–9 continued to take part in the deliberations of the boyar *dúma* and occasionally, when a new policy was inaugurated or a general crisis occurred (as befell in 1682 and 1689), the Patriarch moved to the front of the political stage.[43]

By reason of its ritualistic traditionalism Old Belief quickly became a cause with which many of the deprived and discontented could and did easily identify themselves, and one which seemed worthy of martyrdom. The persecution of its adherents by the authorities after the council of 1667 added a new stream to the flood of runaways pouring into the area of the lower Don; many of these and other Old Believers were soon to take part in the peasant rebellion of 1670–1. Its leader, Stepán Rázin, claimed the patronage of the deposed Patriarch who was said to be accompanying Rázin's flotilla in a barge covered with black velvet, a living symbol not of Old Belief but of a challenge to the powers that be. By contrast, the resistance offered by the monks of the Solovétskii monastery between 1668 and 1676 to the spiritual authority of the official Church, soon supported by a military expedition, suggested that the schismatics were a danger to both Church and tsar. This zeal for the 'old faith' also fed the discontent of the *strel'tsý*.[44] About half of those who rebelled in 1682 against the predominance of the Narýshkin faction, as well as their leader, Prince I. A. Khovánskii, were Old Believers. Further disturbances were caused by the Old Believers in the area of the river Medvéditsa (a tributary of the Don) in 1688–89.[45]

If the tsar and his government saw in the *Code* a definitive act of social justice,[46] a permanent readjustment of the concessions enjoyed by, and obligations incumbent upon, the various constituent groups of Muscovite society, any assumption as to the finality of the new dispensation was soon to be disproved: changing circumstances militated against the perpetuation of the renovated system in its entirety. The accommodation with the Church has already been noted; no major change was called for in the treatment of the *posád* or the peasantry but the organization and endowment of the men of service were ill suited to rewarding individuals for their part in a succession of wars – with Poland from 1654 to 1656, with Sweden from 1656 and 1658 and again with Poland from 1658 to 1667.

The men of service 'by descent' fell into three main groups – *dúmnye* (members of the boyar *dúma*), *moskóvskie* (based on Moscow) and *gorodovýe* (based on the outlying garrisons) – and eleven categories, each governed by strict rules as to how much land their members were allowed to hold as *pomést'ia*, on what terms and in which areas. Grants of land in the form of transfers from *pomést'ia* to *vótchiny* were generally made by the tsar for the benefit of a particular body of men rather than to individuals. But in rewarding his intimate counsellors with *vótchiny* from the Crown demesne the tsar was able to display exceptional generosity and often did so on an extravagant scale. Especially lavish treatment, usually accompanied by promotion to the rank of boyar, was extended to those who were related to the tsar by marriage: the Stréshnevs through Evdokíia Lukiánovna, the second wife of Mikhaíl Fëdorovich, the Miloslávskiis through Maríia Ilínichna, the first wife of Alekséi Mikháilovich and the Narýshkins through Natáliia Kiríllovna his second wife (and mother of Peter I). In their treatment of those who were not thus privileged, the authorities tried to observe the principle that men of service must not receive *pomést'ia* or acquire *vótchiny* outside the district in which they were registered for service but this policy was thwarted by the dynamic of the Muscovite state and its growing population: six-and-a-half million in the mid-sixteenth century, seven million at the end of that century, ten-and-a-half million in 1678 (after the annexation of the Ukraine). Territorial expansion and internal colonization demanded more rapid social advancement and greater freedom of physical movement – with their concomitant economic benefits – than could officially be sanctioned.

The conquest and settlement of the steppe lying to the south and the southeast of the centre – the *Zamoskóvnyi krái* – had proceeded at a rapid pace and was protected from the Crimean and Nogái Tatars and from other nomadic tribes by a defensive line – the *Zaséchnaia chertá*, consisting of natural defences – rivers, lakes, marshes, ravines – linked by abatis and, in treeless areas, by palisades, ramparts and trenches. In the 1630s this military frontier ran some 80 km to the south of the lower Oká and its central point was Túla. The central point of the new Bélgorod line, set up between 1636 and 1640, lay some 400 km to the south of Túla. The Iziúm line begun in 1679 eventually acquired the shape of an irregular V marked by the rivers Kolomák, Mzha, Sévernyi Donéts and Oskól, its apex touching the confluence of the Donéts and the Kazënnyi Toréts some 200 km to the south of Iziúm. This area known as the *Slobodskáia Ukraïna* was colonized largely by migrants from both the left and the right bank Ukraine, Cossacks and peasants. The Cossacks, formed into territorial regiments, guarded this outer line of defence against the incursions of the Crimean Tatars. The so-called 'Sýzran'' line, a branch of the Simbírsk line (which ran from that place to Tambóv and was completed in 1648), was built in two stages: between 1676 and 1680 along the lower Móksha as far as Pénza, and after 1681 from that point along the lower Surá and Sýzran' and beyond to Nadéeno Usól'e.[47]

An important part in the defence of the Muscovite frontier was played by the Cossacks of whom (the Ukraine apart) there were two kinds. The so-called garrison (*gorodovýe*) Cossacks were enlisted men of service – remunerated, endowed for life with parcels of land and exempt from taxation; they manned fortresses and frontier posts whence they sent out patrols and made forays into the steppe. The other kind were the communities of 'free' Cossacks, semi-independent military societies which elected their own officers.

In the first half of the seventeenth century the Don and Iaík Cossacks were still but loosely allied to the tsar and given to some waywardness in their relations with his government but nevertheless formed an effective outer line of defence against the Tatars and other nomadic tribes. The original Don Cossacks were Tatars but from the 1560s the various bands of marauders, hunters and fishermen on the Don were made up of runaways from central Russia and perhaps also of Russian galley slaves escaped from Turkish captivity. The Don Cossacks did not achieve unity until about the end of the first quarter of the seventeenth century; from then on they were reinforced by a steady influx of Russian migrants – men of service, *posádskie liúdi*, free peasants – who formed the nucleus of the upper stratum of 'husbandmen' (*domovítye kazáki*) – alongside a stream of runaways and outcasts who drifted into and out of the ragged rank and file (*golyt'bá*). The 'husbandmen' were established in the area to the west of the lower Don, their less reputable brethren infested the region to the east of the upper Don. After 1644 the headquarters of the Don Cossacks were located at Cherkássk, about 100 km to the north-east of Azóv which they had succeeded in seizing from the Turks in 1637 and holding till 1642. In 1671 it was the Cossacks of Cherkássk who delivered the rebel chief Stepán Rázin into the hands of the authorities; later in that year the Don Cossacks in a body swore allegiance to the tsar. The Iaík (Ural) Cossacks were established on the right bank of the bend of the river of that name, roughly from a point close to the source of the river Samára. The free Cossack community on the river Térek in the Caucasus was an offshoot of the Don Cossacks but, being very much smaller, was of no great military importance.[48]

By the 1670s the south-eastern borderlands had been made secure and allowed for a change of policy in the colonization of those areas. In 1637 boyars and all men of service registered in Moscow were prohibited from petitioning for *pomést'ia* and from acquiring *vótchiny* in the area to the west of the Don between the old and the new military frontier, presumably on the grounds that the intrusion into that area of men of service from the upper echelons would interfere with the effective defence of the frontier by their inferiors. The 1650s and 1660s saw some relaxation of this restriction which was lifted in 1672. By now men of service from Moscow and the central provinces were settling in those outlying areas on *pomést'ia* granted by the tsar, *vótchiny* bought from his treasury or obtained from private owners by purchase or exchange or simply seized by force from their weaker juniors, the enlisted men of service (*sluzhílye po pribóru*). The successive measures adopted between 1672 and 1701 to prevent such displacement only testify to the frequency and success of these irregular proceedings. If the land was uninhabited the newcomer would settle it with his own peasants or with runaways.

The abolition by the *Code* of 1649 of the statutory period of grace, ten years for runaways and fifteen for peasants carried off against their will, did not achieve the desired result of tying the peasants to the land occupied by their masters. As taxation by the state and exploitation by the landlord increased, so the flood of migration to the south and south-east swelled, helping to populate the borderlands but depleting the central regions to the detriment of both land-holders and treasury. Some of the aggrieved and discontented peasants tried by stealth to enter a *posád* while the more adventurous ones sought in the south-eastern borderlands landlords who were more considerate and less easily moved by demands for extradition. Many fugitives were even more strongly attracted to the regions where no landlords were to be found and where the tsar's edict did not run – the middle and lower Volga, the region of the middle Don and its tributaries including the Sévernyi Donéts, under the sway of the Don Cossacks, and the territories of the Iaík Cossacks. In areas under their control the authorities, determined to check this outflow of valuable manpower, retrieved the fugitives with ruthless brutality, provoking a correspondingly fierce resistance on the part of a growing mass of aggrieved and revengeful peasants. This reaction culminated in the uprising of 1670–1 led by the Cossack Stepán Rázin. At different times it ranged over nearly half the country's territory, from Unzhá 200 km due north of Nízhnii Nóvgorod in the north to Astrakhan in the south and from Zmiëv on the Sévernyi Donéts in the south-west to Kazan in the north-east. The uprising was put down by the government with the utmost severity, regardless of the cost in human lives and material damage.[49]

As under the impact of migration and colonization territorial bounds were broken and legal restrictions disregarded, so it became more difficult to maintain the distinction between the *vótchina* and the *pomést'e*. Similarly the term *dvorianín* originally used only in apposition to designate certain categories of *sluzhílye liúdi* came to be applied to the whole hierarchy of men of service except, at the top, the boyars and, at the bottom, the enlisted categories whose members in the border areas held land of the tsar collectively, became liable to personal taxation in the period 1674–81 and were eventually absorbed into the peasantry.

Official policy, presumably under pressure brought to bear by the *sluzhílye liúdi*, tended towards the transformation of the bulk of groups covered by this term, including the most junior and marginal category, the *déti boiárskie*, into an exclusive caste barred at the entry and at the exit. The *Ulozhénie* had forbidden the *déti boiárskie* to change their status for that of a slave (*kholóp*), as they had been apt to do in order to evade service; from 1678 peasants and *posádskie* were no longer to be admitted to the higher status of *déti boiárskie* after completing a period of service by enlistment. Exclusiveness and immobility were setting in after the state of flux which had prevailed earlier in the century. In the 1660s it had not been uncommon for the sons of *posádskie liúdi*, of priests and of boyars' retainers to win promotion from the ranks of the army or of petty officialdom, and to be rewarded with the grant of a *pomést'e* or of a *vótchina*, thus giving rise to a new line of *dvoriáne*. In the mid-seventeenth century prominent merchants – *gósti* or members of the *gostínaia sótnia* – who had carried out commissions for the tsar were able to acquire the hereditary status of *dvorianín* and membership of the *dúma* on being appointed as *diakí* or principals in a department of state (*prikáz*).

Having shown its willingness to protect the men of service from the intrusion of thrusting outsiders, the state was the better able to reward merit and efficiency within the barriers of privilege. Only a few more years were to elapse before the order of precedence within the caste of established men of service – *méstnichestvo* – based on birth and seniority was to be abandoned.[50]

Although the *Code* of 1649 devotes a whole chapter (Chapter 7) to the service of all men of arms in the state of Muscovy, it makes no reference to the institution of *méstnichestvo*. This was an elaborate set of rules which determined precedence and seniority in all the branches of the tsar's service – in the army, in the administration and at court. As a practice it went back to the days of the grand-principality of Moscow, as an institution it was officially recognized from the end of the fifteenth century and consistently applied from the reign of Vasílii III Ivánovich (1505–33). Based on lineage in so far as it took account of the positions held in the past not only by the competitors concerned but also by their ancestors, *méstnichestvo* could not prevent the ruler from choosing the man best suited to a particular appointment; it also protected the vested interests of certain powerful boyar families and their followers.

By the mid-sixteenth century the counter-action taken by the state to check *méstnichestvo* had resulted only in making the tsar and the boyar *dúma* the arbiters in disputes over precedence and in introducing the practice of service for a limited period, especially for the duration of a military campaign, without the observation of precedence. In all other respects *méstnichestvo* was at variance with the natural tendency of the service state to set up a hierarchy suited to its needs and subject to its complete control, as well as with the policy of investing the tsar's servants with land and rewarding them with honour and office on grounds of utility and merit rather than of birth. Such treatment rather than the observance of *méstnichestvo* also answered the ambitions of the new men who were making their way up from the middle ranks of the *sluzhílye liúdi* registered in Moscow and in the provincial garrison towns. It did not, presumably, suit their less successful rivals whose anxiety to maintain the positions secured to them by tradition would account for the persistence of *méstnichestvo*. It was defended by men of rank – whose descendants in consequence of the abolition of precedence would be prevented from stepping into positions of power and influence – and attacked by their inferiors in the hierarchy. One such man is reported to have remarked, presumably with satisfaction, that 'nowadays all of us, big and small alike, owe our livelihood to the tsar's favour',[51] a significant testimony to the growing degree of mutual dependence between the tsar and the rank and file of the men of service 'by descent'.

Méstnichestvo was formally abolished in January 1682 on purely technical grounds: when the battalion replaced the regiment as the basic unit throughout the army it was found that there were not enough men of service of the appropriate age and standing to supply the full quota of officers. But the change in the organization itself was introduced because in the recent Turkish campaign *méstnichestvo* had proved an impediment to military efficiency. Its elimination from the army was used as an opportunity for the abolition of the outdated system of precedence as a whole. Pedigree, however, remained a means of determining the place of a *dvorianín* in the official hierarchy with the result that the scions of old princely and boyar families did not lose the traditional advantages derived from high birth and inherited wealth. Peter I is said in retrospect to have condemned *méstnichestvo* as a 'harsh and harmful custom which had acquired the force of law'[52] but even he, for all his readiness to reward individual endeavour, refrained from relating every service rank, civil and military, to merit without regard to birth. Yet the abolition of precedence could not by itself bring about full military efficiency. Since native technical expertise was lacking, only foreign experts could help and teach the tsar's subjects to organize and train the new regiments, set up on the Western model, to produce some of the necesary arms and ammunition and to build ships. A foreign colonel is known to have been in charge of the regular recruitment of such specialists in Amsterdam as early as 1675.[53]

As well as reaping the benefits of colonization, the men of service also bore the brunt of the many wars waged by Russia in this period. Between May 1654 and October 1656 and again between September 1658 and the summer of 1667 Russia was at war with Poland. The cause of the conflict was the Ukraine: in 1654 the Ukrainian Cossacks under their hetman Bogdán Khmel'nítskii, who had raised a rebellion against Poland in 1648, swore allegiance to the tsar. The invasion of Poland by Sweden in 1655 caused Russia to fight Sweden in the intervening period – May 1656–May 1658 – as a precaution against becoming the object of further Swedish expansion. The Russo-Swedish peace treaty concluded at Kardis in June 1661 left Sweden in possession of Ingria and the western shore of Lake Ládoga held by her since 1617 under the treaty of Stolbóvo. By the terms of the armistice with Poland signed early in 1667 at Andrusovo, Russia gained Bélaia, Smolensk, Chernígov, Starodúb with the surrounding regions, the left bank Ukraine and Kiev – nominally for two years but in fact for good; in 1678 the city was formally exchanged for Sébezh, Nével' and Vélizh in White Russia. The Zaporózh'e, the area to the south of the Dnieper rapids inhabited by the Ukrainian Cossacks, was declared a Russo-Polish condominium.

Thus the supremacy in the basin of the Dnieper as far south as the lands of the Crimean Tatars passed from Poland to Muscovy, a change fraught with many immediate as well as long-term consequences. The acquisition of Kiev with its academy and printing press was to have a stimulating effect on the religious life and intellectual development of Muscovy; the occupation of the left bank of the Dnieper brought her face to face with Turkey. In 1672 the Turks occupied the Polish province of Podolia and assumed authority over the right bank Ukraine through the person of its hetman, Pëtr Doroshénko. In 1676 the Russians compelled him to declare his loyalty to the tsar, and in the following year the Turks invaded the right bank Ukraine. The Russo-Turkish War of 1677–81 was a struggle for dominance over the Ukraine. In 1686, again at Andrusovo, Russia and Poland concluded a treaty of permanent peace and of alliance against the Turks and Tatars; the unsuccessful Crimean campaigns fought by Russia in 1687 and 1689 were undertaken in accordance with its terms. The alliance made Russia an active supporter of the Holy League consisting of the Emperor, Venice and Poland. In the event of the victory of the League over Turkey, Russia's contribution to the joint military effort might be rewarded with access to the Black Sea. For the time being her only seaport and sole point of contact, however remote, with the commercial nations of the west was Archangel at the mouth of the northern Dviná.[54]

The population of Russia in 1678 has been put at 10.5 million. Out of that total the peasants are estimated to have accounted for 9.6 million, the townspeople for 0.5 million and the landholders, clergy, officials and the army treated as one category, for 0.4 million. The following data indicate the relative economic strength of the Crown, of the main social groups and their component categories in 1678. Out of 833,603 holdings (*dvorý*) subject to tax (*tiáglo*) only a small proportion, 92,000 (11.3 per cent), were in the hands of *posádskie liúdi* and peasants holding land direct of the sovereign (*chernosóshnye krest'iáne*); of the rest 83,000 holdings (9.8 per cent) were on the Crown demesne, 118,000 (14.2 per cent) on ecclesiastical lands of various denominations ('patriarchal', 'episcopal', 'monastic'), 88,000 (10.5 per cent) on lands owned or held by boyars, but the majority of the total, 432,000 holdings (54 per cent), were in the hands of other men of service. In considering these figures originally adduced by Kliuchévskii[55] to show the growing economic strength of the men of service and of the ruling class in relation to the taxpaying strata of the population it is also useful to bear in mind the number of boyars in relation to the amount of land held by them. Assuming that all the holdings attributed to the ninety-seven boyars were in their hands (and none in the hands of their adult sons) this works out at about 907 holdings per head, but this high average figure does not reflect the enormous wealth of those to whom the tsar chose to show his particular favour. Thus Fëdor Alekséevich gave away 6,274 holdings out of which 2,186 went to Prince V. V. Golítsyn (1643–1714) who had not yet reached the peak of his career.[56]

Numerically small but economically important, industrial entrepreneurs were attracted to Muscovy by the opportunity of rapid enrichment but their expectations were not always fulfilled. Of the three foreign pioneers of the iron industry and indeed of all manufacturing in Russia – Andreas Vinius of Amsterdam, Peter Marselis (a Danish subject of Dutch descent) and Thielmann Akkema of Harlingen in Friesland – who in 1634 obtained a joint concession for the mining, founding and working of iron, the first was squeezed out by his partners in 1644 and the second at his death (in 1675) left debts to the value of 11,000 roubles. Only Marselis died (in 1672) a rich man but after many vicissitudes, having been in and out of favour with the tsar on whose pleasure, like all men in his position, he had depended for charters, leases, subsidies, exemptions, contracts and privileges.

At one time Marselis was on good terms with A. L. Ordýn-Nashchókin, the tsar's principal counsellor and the author of the New Trade Regulations which may have originated in a memorandum submitted by Marselis. By 1662 Marselis and Akkema operated ten ironworks – four situated to the north-west of Túla on the river Túlitsa (a confluent of the Úpa), another four to the north-west of Sérpukhov in the *uézd* of Kashíra (as it then was) on the river Skniga and one on the Protvá (both confluents of the Oká), and another on the Ugódka, close to their conjunction. Eight of these works in that year are known to have employed a total of forty-five craftsmen and three charcoal-burners, all foreigners, as well as native workers from the Crown demesne assigned to the manufactories by the tsar. Marselis and Akkema were the official and principal domestic suppliers of iron to the government and of munitions to the army. In the years 1668–73 the Túla works alone supplied about 656 tonnes of iron bars and pig iron, 154,169 hand grenades, 25,313 shell grenades and 42,718 cannon-balls. By 1675 the output of iron and munitions in Muscovy appears to have been large enough to satisfy home needs and to leave a surplus for export. In that year Peter Marselis the younger sent from Archangel to an unknown destination overseas 116 cannon, 33,742 cannon-balls, 2,934 grenades, 2,356 musket barrels and 157 tonnes of bar iron. The one item of military equipment not to be produced in Russia in that period in sufficient quantities was the complete firelock. Marselis's and Akkema's works also served more peaceful purposes by manufacturing iron doors, roofing sheets and salt-pans; with the co-operation of the local blacksmiths they produced sickles as well as halberds and entrenching tools. On the premature death in 1690 of Christian Marselis, a son of the younger Peter, the seven works extant in the regions of Túla and Kashíra were assigned to Lev Kiríllovich Narýshkin, an uncle of Tsar Peter, and soon afterwards entered on a period of decline.

Under Marselis and Akkema the works had also supplied the anchors for the first Russian warship, the *Orël* ('Eagle'), commissioned by Tsar Alekséi in 1667, together with some auxiliary craft, for trade with Persia in the Caspian. Early in 1668 in a shipyard at the junction of the Oká with the Volga, fifteen Dutch ship's carpenters and a Russian labour force set to work under the direction of a Dutch entrepreneur; the *Orël* was launched in May and the smaller craft were built during the summer; the flotilla, soon to be joined by another ship, arrived at Astrakhan a year later only to be destroyed by Rázin and his men in 1670.

Alongside the Marselis-Akkema complex other metallurgical works were to be found in Russia, including those originally established about 1650 by the boyar B. I. Morózov in the area of Zvenígorod, where guns were cast from Swedish iron, and the copper, iron and steel works set up in 1678 on the north-western shore of Lake Ládoga by the entrepreneur Heinrich Butenant (who first entered the scene as a guardian of Christian Marselis, a minor). These works (seventeen in all), the arsenal and the cannon foundry in Moscow and three powder-mills, provided Muscovy with a solid industrial base for her army and her defence lines. The remainder of the manufactories established in the same period can be counted on the fingers of one hand: a cloth factory, a silk-mill, a paper-mill, a glass works and a linen factory. The first three of these were no longer active at the end of the regency of Sof'ia Alekséevna.[57]

In the eyes of the merchants of western Europe, the Muscovy of Alekséi Mikháilovich and of his direct successors was a source of such native primary products as hemp, potash, weidash, tar, tallow, hides, furs (occasionally also of grain), and a channel of trade between East and West. The principal articles to be conveyed by this route south-eastwards were copper ore, metal and manu-factured goods (such as pins, needles and mirrors), while raw silk, cotton fabrics, morocco leather, spices, drugs and essential oils were carried in the opposite direction. From northern and western Europe the Russians bought for their own use and consumption metals (mainly from Sweden), arms (from Holland), gunpowder, wines, spices, cloth, spangled fabrics, dyestuffs, paper and sundry other goods. In the mid-seventeenth century 75 per cent of Russian overseas trade passed through Archangel whose southern antipode was Astrakhan, the principal centre for trade with the Balkans and Constantinople being Putívl' on the river Séim in the Ukraine.

In the centre and in the north the most active foreign traders were the Dutch who, Dr Samuel Collins complained, 'like locusts swarm in Moscow and eat bread out of Englishmen's mouths; they are more in number, and richer, and spare no gifts to attain their ends'[58] – namely, to buy raw materials and half-finished goods cheaply in this semi-colonial mart, transport them in their own ships to Amsterdam and sell them there at a high profit. Inland the foreign merchants tended to employ native agents as buyers on their behalf, thus bypassing the Russian middleman and, much to his dissatisfaction, depriving him of a chance of making a profit. The Russian merchants also complained that the tolls exacted from them by the authorities were too numerous, too heavy and lacking in uniformity. The Tolls and Customs Regulations of 1653 (*Tamózhennyi ustáv*) sought to make the system of collection simpler and fairer by introducing a rate of 5 per cent on the purchase and on the sale of goods alike. Foreigners were required to pay duty in addition to these charges but the Russian merchants, traders and *posádskie liúdi* in general still considered themselves to be at a disadvantage and persisted in their complaints.

In 1667 the New Trade Regulations (*Nóvyi torgóvyi ustáv*) were introduced in order to effect a general and permanent improvement in the terms on which Muscovy conducted her foreign trade 'for the sake of the revenue from customs and tolls as well as for the material benefit of the population at large'.[59] The New Regulations favoured the native merchant in that they deterred his foreign competitor from trading inland – provided he did not choose to pose as a Russian. At Archangel and in the frontier towns the foreigner paid, in ducats or rix-dollars, 4 or 5 per cent duty on the sale of his goods (depending on whether they were sold by weight or by the piece); but for carrying his merchandise inland – if he was fortunate enough to obtain the tsar's express permission to trade thus – he paid a transit charge of 10 per cent, again in foreign currency, and a further duty or toll of 6 per cent in Russian money on any goods sold inland. Wine attracted a special and heavy duty at the rate of between 20 and 50 rix-dollars per barrel. Foreigners were debarred from engaging in retail trade and from trade with one another except at Archangel and subject to the payment of duty at 5 per cent. Russian merchants on the other hand continued to pay the standard toll of 5 per cent on all transactions; furthermore, when they bartered native goods with foreign merchants or used the proceeds of the sale of such goods for the purchase of foreign goods, they paid no duty on these transactions (having already paid the standard toll on the purchase of the native goods). The duty on Russian goods exported by foreign merchants was, like the import duty, charged at the rate of 4 or 5 per cent. The only concession which the New Regulations appeared to make to the foreigner was the exemption from duty of goods bought by him for export and paid for in ducats or rix-dollars. This particular regulation could have worked to the detriment of the Russian merchant who was obliged to exchange the proceeds of the transaction with the tsar's treasury at the official fixed rate of one rouble for one ducat and 50 kopecks for one rix-dollar, whereas the commercial rate fluctuated between 114 and 125 kopecks for the ducat and 52 and 57 kopecks for the dollar. It may be assumed, however, that the Russian recipient of the currency will have adjusted his selling price to the official rate of exchange, with the probable result that the foreigner lost on the purchase as much as he saved on the duty, if not more.

This provision underlines the twofold purpose of the New Trade Regulations: to benefit the Russian merchants and traders by deterring foreigners from trading inland and to provide the tsar's treasury with specie on favourable terms as the rix-dollars were recoined and issued as roubles at a profit of 28 per cent. The collection of tolls and customs was an obligation towards the tsar's treasury incumbent on the urban communities (*posády*) and discharged by their representatives who were elected to serve for one year. The treasury derived a further profit from exports by pre-empting on the tsar's behalf such goods as grain, hemp, potash, weidash, Siberian rhubarb and raw silk and selling them direct to foreign merchants. On one occasion, in 1662, hemp, potash, weidash, tallow, hides and sable pelts were declared the tsar's monopoly, an example later to be followed by Peter I. The New Trade Regulations may well have increased the profits of Russian merchants and traders, although evidence on this point is lacking. It did not, however, produce a spectacular and permanent increase in the customs duties and tolls levied at Archangel. In the first half of the seventeenth century the revenue from this source fluctuated between 24,000 and 40,000; in the second half between 60,000 and 80,000 roubles. The peak figure of just over 82,000 roubles for 1675–6 and for 1687–9 quoted as evidence of improvement, had already been exceeded – if we accept Kilburger's statistics – in 1658, 1660 and 1661.[60] However that may be, in 1679–80 indirect taxation – tolls, customs duties and the alcohol excise – accounted for 53 per cent of the total public revenue of 1,220,367 roubles. Sixty-two per cent of this sum was spent on the army, just over 19 per cent on the central administration, including the tsar's palace.[61]

In the reign of Alekséi Mikháilovich the authorities collected from the urban and rural population a large number of direct taxes. The most substantial of these was the *strelétskaia pódat'*, raised in money or in kind – rye and oats – for the maintenance of the *strel'tsý* (musketeers). Later to be contemptuously described by Peter I as 'janissaries',[62] the *strel'tsý* had by the middle of the seventeenth century become something of a hereditary military caste without official status. Endowed with plots of land, they also engaged in trade and handicrafts in their spare time. Their growing numerical strength – from about 37,500 in 1651 to well over 20,000 in Moscow and 27,000 in provincial garrisons some two decades later – and political importance were due to their new role as a security force. Eventually only between 5 and 30 per cent of this force took part in the military operations carried out by an army which in 1680 is said to have been capable of mustering about 91,000 levied troops – two thirds foot soldiers and one third horse – and 16,000 mounted men of service. These figures could explain the otherwise puzzling ability of the Muscovite state – until 1682 – to suppress any movement of internal revolt and to wage war on its neighbours irrespective of any adverse effect that military set-backs might have on the home front.

The wars and unrest of the 1650s had obliged the tsar's government to increase the number of garrisons consisting of *strel'tsý* and to make provision for their subsistence; in the 1670s, as relations between Russia and Turkey deteriorated, measures had to be taken at further expense to prevent the Tatars from making incursions into Russia from their territories on the Black Sea in support of their Turkish allies. In 1672, as a means of raising the necessary funds, the incidence and nature of the *strelétskaia pódat'* were adjusted to the paying capacity of the population. The rate at which the tax for the *strel'tsý* was levied in northern Russia, where it was discharged in cash, was somewhat reduced; in the rest of the country it was commuted from kind to cash at a corresponding rate in the towns and raised in rural areas where payment in kind continued. Henceforth, as a rule, inhabitants of the sovereign's land in northern Russia paid the *strelétskaia pódat'* in cash, as did the urban population in the whole country, whereas the rural population – the peasants on private and ecclesiastical estates – paid in kind.

In 1681 the government took a further step towards the simplification and unification of the tax system which was to be finally achieved under Peter the Great. The various petty imposts which made up about 21 per cent of the total revenue from direct taxation (apart from special charges on incomes and on the use of premises) as against 79 per cent derived from the *strelétskaia pódat'* were amalgamated in a single tax under that name. The required annual receipt from this source was set at the actual cost of maintaining the *strel'tsý* in 1679 – 107,227 roubles, a reduction of the previous estimate by about one third. The census completed in the same year for the first time registered the number of households instead of areas of agricultural land with their inhabitants. On this basis the required total was imposed on the various localities placed in one of ten categories and related to a sliding scale which rose from 80 kopecks to 2 roubles per household (*dvor*). The rest of the operation the central authorities delegated, as before, to the urban and rural communities (*posád, mir*), holding the elective officers of each responsible for the collection of the full amount of the tax. The total liability, now calculated on the basis of the number of households, was divided by each community among its members in proportion to their possessions and earnings. Whatever the merits of this system may have been initially, it was towards the end of the seventeenth century a further and unwelcome addition to the large number of services performed for the tsar's government by his subjects free of charge and against their will. On private and ecclesiastical estates the landholder was responsible for the orderly collection of the *strelétskaia pódat'*. The tax itself survived under a modernized name until the early years of the next century.[63]

On the land held by the men of service 'by descent' the reign of Fëdor Alekséevich saw an even closer convergence of the *pomést'e* and the *vótchina*. The regulations concerning the succession to *vótchina* were tightened: from 1679 a *vótchina* other than one acquired by purchase could not be bequeathed but passed by descent to the kinsmen of the holder. By contrast, in 1676 the rule governing the exchange of *vótchiny* and *pomést'ia* had been relaxed by being interpreted in a sense which brought the transaction close to a sale. It was officially stated that no limit would be placed on the difference in the size of the estates exchanged, with the implication that even a substantial difference could be made up in cash. It is hard to reconcile the existence of this loophole with the continued restriction on the formal alienation of *pomést'ia*. A *pomést'e* could be let on lease by a superannuated holder and by the widow and daughters of a deceased one but could not be assigned for money by a serving holder who was allowed to part with only one half of his *pomést'e* provided he did so free of charge.[64]

It is characteristic of the Muscovite system of government that between 1672 and 1683 the *strelétskaia pódat'* should have been collected by the *strelétskii prikáz*, for Muscovy had neither a ministry of finance nor a ministry of war, nor indeed any other department of state in the modern sense of the term. The building in the Kremlin erected specially for the *prikázy* about 1680 looks like the headquarters of a highly centralized bureaucracy but housed under one roof the staffs of only seven out of eighty *prikázy*. Each *prikáz* (department or office of state) was headed by a *sud'iá* (a magistrate), usually a member of the *dúma* (see below), and manned by a small team of *d'iakí* assisted by a corresponding number of clerks – *pod'iáchie*. The total strength of a *prikáz* could be as large as 400 or as small as three.

This high degree of concentration of bureaucratic manpower was not matched by a corresponding degree of co-ordination. A *prikáz* was essentially a commission – permanent or temporary – appointed by the tsar to exercise authority on his behalf in discharging tasks as varied as the dispensation of justice to certain categories of the population, the collection of particular taxes and dues, the supervision of public works, the organization of various corps of the army, the control over the tenure of landed estates together with adjudication on disputes arising therefrom, and the retrieval of runaway peasants. Not only the four main judicial (*súdnye*) *prikázy*, but most other *prikázy* too, exercised judicial as well as executive – including fiscal – authority over those sections of the population to which its functions appertained. Even the *prikáz* in charge of foreign affairs, the *Posól'skii*, exercised jurisdiction over foreign merchants in Russia and was responsible for the administration of certain recently annexed territories such as the Ukraine and the region of Smolensk.

Towards the end of the seventeenth century, the drawbacks of the system of *prikázy* – heterogeneous, straggling and unwieldy – were making themselves acutely felt but were only temporarily overcome by grouping – that is, by the subordination of several departments to one chief – or by experiments in amalgamation. The attempt made in 1680 to create a single revenue department by attaching to the *Prikáz Bol'shói kazný* (of the Grand Treasury[65]) two other main fiscal *prikázy* proved impracticable and was abandoned after three years as was the attempt to attach three predominantly territorial *prikázy* to the *Posól'skii prikáz*. The combination of centralism with the lack of distinction between the process of law and administrative procedure made for interminable and notorious delays in the dispensation of justice and these in turn opened the door to bribery and corruption.[66]

A similar lack of unity and coherence can be seen in the regional administration of the tsar's dominions. In the patchwork and crisscross pattern of civil and military territorial divisions resulting from many decades of disorderly development one basic unit is clearly discernible – the *uézd* (district), administered from a *górod* (fortified town) by a *voevóda* (prefect). Not all *voevódy*, however, nor all *gorodá* in the 250 or so *uézdy*, were of equal standing. Thus in Siberia Toból'sk was the administrative capital from which the work of the other centres – Tomsk, Eniséisk and Iakútsk – was directed. A similar organization was in force in other frontier regions and some other outlying towns – Archangel, Nóvgorod, Pskov, Smolensk, Bélgorod, Astrakhan, Kazan – where the *voevóda* as a rule headed a department not unlike a *prikáz* and exercised extensive military, judicial and executive authority including, in Siberia, the right to assign duties and *pomést'ia* to the men of service. Like the head of a *prikáz* the *voevóda* held, as it were, a personal commission from the tsar and although the duties and powers of a *voevóda* were never formally defined in general terms, each one received from the tsar detailed instructions (*nakáz*) in writing. The *voevóda* together with his associates – *d'iakí* or *pod'iáchie* (senior and junior clerks) – was responsible for the maintenance of public order and external security, the effective collection and proper disbursement of revenue and the performance of state service in the town or towns and territory assigned to him.

The powers of the *voevóda* were at once too wide – the further away from Moscow the more open to abuse – and too restricted, since he must not depart from his instructions or take any initiative without the sanction of higher authority in the capital. At the same time, only the fear of punishment consequent upon a formal complaint from a group of inhabitants or an investigation by a special inspector would restrain him from abusing his position at the expense of the local inhabitants. In the second half of the seventeenth century the appointment to the post of *voevóda* was still regarded by its holder as an official invitation to feather his nest. By way of a precaution against excess the *voevóda*'s term of office did not usually exceed two or three years. The system as a whole undoubtedly suffered from the worst effects of both centralism and devolution, but in the absence of an army of trained officials to carry out the commands of the tsar, of his boyars and of the *prikázy*, the *voevódy* kept a tight grip on his subjects through the length and breadth of Muscovy, from Smolensk to Iakútsk and from Archangel to Astrakhan.[67]

Such freedom of action as the Moscow *prikázy* themselves enjoyed under the *Code* of 1649 was confined to straightforward matters only; any issues regarded as controversial must be reported upon to the Sovereign Lord and Grand Duke of All the Russias and his boyars, *okól'nichie* (dignitaries close to the tsar's person) and councillors (*dúmnye liúdi*) who were to sit together in conclave and transact all the sovereign's business in accordance with his instructions. The members of this body – commonly referred to as the *boiárskaia dúma*, sixty-seven in number in 1688 and ninety-seven in 1678–9 – many of whom stood at the head of the various *prikázy*, were bound by oath not to transact any business without the knowledge of the sovereign; an unlikely occurrence since the *dúma* sat under the chairmanship of the tsar and only in his absence under that of the boyar senior by descent to all the others. The Patriarch and the chief ecclesiastical dignitaries – 'the hallowed assembly' – were not *ex officio* members of the *dúma* but often took part in its deliberations.

The limited degree of the authority delegated to it by the tsar may be gauged from the three variants in the formula used to record or announce official acts: 'the tsar has ordained and the boyars have pronounced' or 'after a hearing in the presence of the boyars the tsar has pronounced' or, quite simply, 'the tsar has ordained'. The wording of the extended formulae indicates whether the matter had for the most part been discussed in joint sessions of the tsar and the *dúma* or whether the decision was made by the tsar after a joint hearing with the boyars. All three variants reflect accurately the absolute character of the Muscovite monarchy – an autocracy based on the power of officialdom, the army and the Church and tempered in its harshness only by inefficiency and venality.

In the second half of the seventeenth century as prolonged periods of absence of the tsar and the court, especially in wartime, and the growing volume of business tended to hamper the work of the *dúma* as a single body, it was found more convenient, and perhaps also considered more expedient, to concentrate the work of the *dúma* in special committees to which urgent and controversial issues might be referred by the *prikázy*. Two of these committees acquired a semi-permanent character: the *blízhniaia* (inner) *dúma* and the *rasprávnaia paláta* (executive chamber). The first functioned in the reign of Alekséi Mikháilovich only and consisted of the tsar's intimate councillors (some of whom, apparently, were not members of the *dúma* proper); the second, having originated under Tsar Alekséi, was at its most active between 1681 and 1694 in a judicial capacity. Long before that time the *Zémskii sobór* (Assembly of the Land) had lost the authority which it had exercised in 1613 when it elected the first tsar of the house of Románov, Mikhaíl Fëdorovich, or in 1648–9 when it had promoted and approved the *Ulozhénie*. The last assembly of similar status and consequence was that of 1653 which approved the decision of the government to accept the offer of the Zaporozhian hetman, Bogdán Khmel'nítskii, to recognize the suzerainty of the tsar in place of the king of Poland over the Cossacks together with their cities and lands in the Polish Ukraine. At the assemblies held after that date the provincial men of service 'by descent' and the upper strata of the *posádskie liúdi* in towns other than Moscow were under-represented or, like their social inferiors, not represented at all. The later *sobóry* were not so much assemblies as meetings between the central authorities and selected representatives of the more in-fluential social groups – the clergy, the men of service, the merchants. These gatherings were called at irregular intervals to discuss specific problems, mostly of an economic nature such as trade or the coinage or to add weight to decisions already taken in principle, as in 1682 the abolition of *méstnichestvo* and in 1683-4 the conclusion of a definitive peace treaty with Poland. The assembly which in April 1682 approved the accession of the juvenile Peter I – soon to be replaced by Sófia Alekséevna as regent (on behalf of Peter and his half-brother Iván) – consisted largely of men of service and was a *Zémskii sobór* only in name. Political representation – which had never been strong – was a thing of the past.[68]

In contrast with the reigns of Alekséi Mikháilovich (1645–76) and Fëdor Alekséevich (1676–82) the regency of the tsarevna Sófia Alekséevna (1682–9) was a period not of social but rather of political instability caused by the absence of a law of succession and by a dynastic feud between the maternal families of the claimants to the throne, Iván Alekséevich born, like Sófia, of Maríia Il'ínichna Miloslávskaia, the first wife of Alekséi Mikháilovich, and Peter, his son by his second wife, Natáliia Kiríllovna Narýshkina.

The revolt in 1682 of the chronically discontented Moscow *strel'tsý*, in its essence a mutiny of the garrison troops of the capital, was turned by the new commanding officer, Prince I. A. Khovánskii, Sófia Alekséevna and her kinsmen in the Miloslávskii camp against their various political rivals. In the massacre of 15 May nearly seventy boyars, officials and military commanders of mixed allegiance, including some pillars of the previous reign and three prominent members of the Naryshkin family, perished at the hands of the *strel'tsý*. Soon afterwards the joint rule of the tsars Iván and Peter was proclaimed, with Sófia Alekséevna as regent. The decisive factor, however, which helped Sófia to bring the turbulent *strel'tsý* under control was a show of force by the provincial men of service who, at Sófia's call, had begun to advance on Moscow. The failure of the two military expeditions to the Crimea led by Sófia's favourite, Prince V. V. Golítsyn, in 1687 and 1689 weakened her position and strengthened that of her opponents. The Naryshkins exposed a plot by the latest commander of the *strel'tsý*, F. L. Shaklovítyi, to make Sófia's rule permanent by having her crowned, accused him of preparing the assassination of the leaders of the Naryshkin party and later, by their conduct, suggested that Tsar Peter himself was on the list of intended victims. In September 1689 Sófia, deserted by the *strel'tsý*, the majority of whom went over to the Naryshkins, entered a convent. Her rule, despite its dramatic beginning and end, described by a contemporary as 'orderly',[69] was followed by the 'disorderly' and unofficial rule of the tsaritsa Natáliia Kiríllovna who died in 1694. The sickly and incapable Iván Alekséevich died in 1696.[70]

The assets and liabilities of the political inheritance to which Peter I succeeded in the 1690s were fairly evenly balanced but many of the forces behind them were in a state of direct opposition to one another. The service state was a pliable instrument of government policy. The loyalty of the men of service was beyond question, the appetite of some of their number for virgin soil in the steppe promoted the process of Muscovy's territorial expansion but the price paid for their co-operation was the recalcitrance and pent-up anger of a peasantry reduced to servitude. The Patriarch had been subordinated to the tsar but the discord brought about by the schism had permanently weakened the authority of both Church and state. The *Code* of 1649, in prescribing norms and procedures, had strengthened the hand of the government but did not establish the rule of law. The administration was inefficient and corrupt, the levies of men of service were antiquated and unwieldy. The country as a whole was rich in human and material resources but underdeveloped and lacking in skilled labour, professional expertise and commercial initiative. With Sweden in possession of the Baltic seaboard, Muscovy's trade with the maritime countries of western Europe was handled from Archangel by alien middlemen. In foreign relations Muscovy was newly aligned with Poland against the Turk but its cultural affinities were yet uncertain. The reign of Peter was to witness and indeed to effect the resolution of many of these contradictions to the advantage of the service state rather than for the benefit of its subjects for whom Pososhkóv speaks in *The Book of Poverty and Wealth*.

III

Peter I and the Modernization
of the Service State

Religious and intellectual life. The contrast with Western Europe. 1700: a turning-point. The Turkish war. The Rátusha *established (1698). The outbreak of the Great Northern War (1700). The Church without a Patriarch. The weakness of the Russian army. The beginnings of St Petersburg (1703), the capture of Narva and Dorpat (1704). The mobilization of labour; conscription. Changes in the administrative and fiscal organization (1708–15). The northern war. The creation of the Senate (1711). War with Turkey (1710–13). Further gains on the Baltic.* Polizey *and* Cultur. *The character of the rule of Peter I. Continued colonization in the south-east. The northern war (1714–18). The death of Charles XII and of the tsarevich Alekséi Petróvich. Peter I embarks on a programme of systematic and comprehensive reform. Judicial reform. The* Artíkul Vóinskii *(Articles of War, 1715). The failure of the rule of law. 'Quis custodiet . . .?' The Petrine* Polizeystaat *and the modern police state. The last years of the Great Northern War and the peace of Nystad (1721). The regulation of the succession (1722). A new official hierarchy: the Table of Ranks (1722). The* dvoriánstvo. *The* iúnkers. *The* Vótchinnaia kollégiia *and the tacit allodification of* pomést'ia. *The* gerol'dméister *(chief herald) as taskmaster of the* dvoriáne. *Education. The Ecclesiastical Regulation (1721) fits the clergy into the framework of the service state. The Holy Synod. Peter I hostile towards monasticism. The revival of the Department of Monasteries (1701). Tsar Peter as Head and Governor of the Church. The office of* óber-prokurór *of the Holy Synod established (1722). The plight of the Old Believers.*

For the moment the domain of the youthful Grand Sovereign Tsar and Grand Duke was in a state of flux. The general condition of the country remained archaic. In economic terms Russia was still a primary-producing country, in political terms a service state with a ragged military frontier and a rapidly diminishing popular representation. At the same time the extension of the tsar's dominions to the banks of the Dnieper and beyond had enriched and renewed Muscovy's religious and intellectual life. Even before the occupation of Kiev by Russian troops in 1665, Níkon's immediate predecessor, Patriarch (1642–52) Joseph, had come to recognize that the accuracy of liturgical texts could not be ensured without recourse to scholarship, whereupon Tsar Alekséi had invited some Kievan monks to come to Moscow and apply their knowledge of Greek and Latin to that end. After 1655 Kiev – that outpost of Western Catholic baroque culture reconciled with the tenets of Orthodoxy by the scholars of the college founded by Peter Mohíla – had fallen under the sway of the tsar. In subsequent years dozens of Ukrainian monks transferred to various parts of Muscovy by the ecclesiastical authorities brought with them a knowledge of the liberal arts, of Latin, occasionally also of Greek and some knowledge of Roman Catholic dogmatic theology. In Moscow in the 1650s and 1660s some Kievan monks – among them Simeon (Pëtróvskii-Sitnianóvich) of Pólotsk – ran two more or less formal teaching establishments, each under the auspices of a monastery.

These activities were revived in the 1680s by which time, however, under the influence of Patriarch Ioakím (elected in 1674) the Greek orientation had come temporarily to replace the Latin as the educational trend favoured by the authorities. In a school established under Ioakím's patronage about 1680 only Greek and Slavonic were taught. On this foundation the Helleno-Greek Academy, later to be known as 'Slavonic, Greek and Latin', officially opened in January 1686, was based. The Patriarch himself had spent two years as a monk in a monastery near Kiev but had learnt to read and write only after being appointed Father Superior of a monastery in 1657. It is all the more surprising – and reassuring – to learn that in the sixteenth and seventeenth centuries the secular clergy and merchants were, as a rule, literate, as were over 50 per cent of all landholders, large and small, about 20 per cent of the *posádskie liúdi* and 15 per cent of the peasantry. From the modest scholastic achievements of the clergy in Moscow the tsar's government derived little practical benefit beyond a few translators supplied to the *Posól'skii prikáz* (the department of foreign relations). Simeon of Pólotsk, the versatile and erudite court pedagogue, writer of sermons and versifier who took it upon himself to exhort the Muscovites to defy the infidel Turk, was an exception. As a poet he found neither patron nor public. The national culture was for the most part enshrined in the religious life of the people and symbolized by the icon and the monastery. The majority of the institutions – schools, universities, private printing presses, libraries, learned societies – whose pupils, members or users contribute to the make-up of a secular and urban culture, were as yet alien to Russia. At the same time the tendency towards secularization, discernible in the work of the narrative writers, icon painters and church builders in the latter part of the century, did denote a changing outlook and a susceptibility to extraneous influence. It was in this atmosphere of change that the young tsar was growing up.[71]

During his visit to Holland and England in 1697 and 1698 Tsar Peter could not but have been struck by the contrast between the bustling prosperity of those countries and the debilitating stagnation of his own. On his return from western Europe he was faced with the task of disciplining the *strel'tsý* after their third and last rebellion in March–June 1698. Between August and October of that year and again in January and February 1699, Moscow and Preobrazhénskoe (the seat of the *Preobrazhénskii prikáz*)[72] were the scenes of torture and mass executions. Nearly 800 *strel'tsý* were executed during the first period and (if the information is correct) 342 in the second; the tsar himself took an active part in the questioning of the accused. Western observers were deeply shocked by this display of savagery but the tsar continued to treat the differences between his country and those of western Europe as ones of degree rather than of kind, and therefore capable of being eliminated by mechanical adjustment.

Once order had been restored the tsar was able to attend to the attenuation of the more glaring contrasts between Russia and the West by decreeing the abolition of some external peculiarities of Russian life and the introduction of new ways. As the official record or *Journal* of the activities of Peter the Great has it, in 1699 the translation and printing of many books began – books on engineering, artillery, mechanics and other useful arts, also of historical books and calendars. In the same year 'the School of Navigation was established alongside schools where other subjects were taught . . . His Majesty gave permission to all his subjects to travel to foreign European countries for study which until then had been forbidden . . . His Majesty also began to put his signature to communications addressed by him to other Christian monarchs. This had not often been done before by Russian monarchs who used only their seal . . His Majesty also saw fit to abandon the old Russian attire and ordered all his subjects to dress after the fashion of other Christian lands, also to shave off their beards. At the end of the year [7208 OS] New Year's Day was fixed for 1 January 1700 [instead of 1 September 7209] – the beginning of the new year was celebrated by a Holy Liturgy at the Uspénskii cathedral in Moscow followed by a display of fireworks and a three-gun salute.'[73]

In virtue of its membership of the Holy League Russia was a European power but without direct access to western Europe by land or sea. From the earliest years of his reign Tsar Peter concentrated his efforts on resolving this paradox by the acquisition of a seaport closer to western Europe than Archangel. In 1695 he revived the flagging activities of the League by leading an expedition against Azóv. In the following year, with the help of artillerymen and military engineers who had been seconded from the Imperial army at the tsar's request, the Russians succeeded in capturing the fortress from the Turks. Eventually, under the terms of the peace treaty concluded with Turkey in 1700 Russia kept Azóv and the surrounding area but Russian ships were prohibited from sailing beyond the straits of Kerch into the Black Sea.

Tsar Peter's determination to conquer and hold Azóv contrasts sharply with the diffidence of his predecessors in an analogous situation. In 1641 the

Assembly of the Land (*Zémskii sobór*), upon being informed that to hold Azóv (which the Don Cossacks had captured in 1637 on their own initiative) would require an outlay of 221,000 roubles apart from the cost of building the necessary fortifications, decided to abstain from action. In 1696 after a period of rapid territorial expansion Russia was better able to bear the cost and no difficulties were allowed to stand in the way of the tsar's ambitious schemes. A harbour was to be built at Taganróg, so 20,000 men of service of inferior rank were to be sent there from the southern border to provide the labour. Azóv had to be populated, so it was decided to bring over 3,000 families from the *ponizóvye gorodá* – the fortified places on the Volga roughly between Nízhnii Nóvgorod and Kazan – as well as 3,000 *strel'tsý* and soldiers from the Moscow garrison.

A fleet was wanted but before the establishment of the Admiralty *prikáz* in 1700 the requisite technical and administrative services were lacking. The difficulty was overcome by adding the cost and physical task of shipbuilding to the taxes and services due from the population at large. The holders of large estates – the boyars, the Patriarch, the bishops, the monasteries – were made responsible for the construction and equipment of one ship for every 8,000 peasant households on ecclesiastical, and for every 10,000 on secular, lands. These proportions were applied in the creation of thirty-eight 'companies' of landholders, each of which represented the total number of households deemed to be capable of producing one ship. Some of the 'companies', rather than rely on their own devices, farmed out the work to foreign entrepreneurs. Men of service whose lands were inhabited by under one hundred households were simply taxed at the rate of half a rouble for each one. The *posádskie liúdi* together with the peasants on the sovereign's land in the northern regions (*Pomór'e, pomórskie gorodá*) were ordered to build twelve ships, the *gósti* – the foremost merchants of Moscow engaged in the lucrative foreign trade – two ships as a punishment for having sought exemption from contributing to the cost of the fleet. In order to enable them to shoulder this burden they were, for the year 1697, exempted from paying the extraordinary 10 per cent tax on income from commercial transactions. The *gósti* were also made responsible for collecting the ship-money from the *posády* and from the peasants in the north, as well as for organizing and supervising the work in the shipyards at Vorónezh. In 1698 they were the first collective to obtain permission from the tsar to supply money instead of ships. The tax gathered from the smaller landholders was used by the treasury to meet the cost of its own shipbuilding programme.[74]

To repulse an attack on Azóv mounted by the Crimean and Nogái Tatars in 1697, 35,000 men were requisitioned. These *dátochnye liúdi* (supplied men) were to be levied from estates held by the clergy, the monasteries and the higher secular dignitaries. The *poméshchiki* and *vótchinniki* registered in Moscow were ordered to present themselves in person with an armed retinue and, in addition, to supply one horseman for every hundred, and one foot soldier for every fifty peasant households on their estates. Those *poméshchiki* and *vótchinniki* who as holders of civil offices were not required to bear arms were to supply one infantryman for every thirty households while those who were not serving in any capacity were to supply one horseman for every hundred households and one foot soldier for every fifty. Any enlisted men of service who were not called up were required to contribute one rouble a head in cash; each peasant household paid 25 kopecks.

In 1699 as a precaution against a resumption of the war with Turkey another levy was ordered. The clergy and the higher dignitaries were again ordered to supply men at the same rate as before or, where the requisite number of men was wanting, to pay 11 roubles in place of each one. The higher secular dignitaries who had recently held a command or had been seconded abroad were to supply one infantryman for every fifty households on their land, as were landholders registered in Moscow and due for service; on taking up service they were to supply one infantryman and one horseman for every 150 peasant households while those who had fewer than fifty households on their land were instead to pay cash at the prescribed rate; those who were not being called up for service but were employed in a civil capacity – retired men of service, widows, spinsters and minors – were to supply soldiers at the rate of one for every thirty households or pay 11 roubles in place of each one. In the same year the *posády* too supplied their quota of men for the army, volunteers were enrolled (not for the first time, as this had already been done in 1632) and the adolescent sons of *dvoriánie* were registered for future service.

The gist of these minutiae indicates that the principles governing the performance and financing of military service established in the second half of the sixteenth century were still in force: from those who held land of the tsar without paying for it with service, money was to be collected to pay for men; the peasants and *posádskie liúdi* supplied men as well as paying the direct taxes which covered most of the military expenditure of the state. The same principles and methods, applied with greater vigour and intensity, enabled Peter I in a critical period – in the thick of a war, after the virtual disbandment of the Moscow *strel'tsý* – to make the fullest use of his country's human and monetary resources. The recruiting campaign, nominally completed by the end of 1701, produced a total of 33,234 men, 32,130 of whom were drafted into the army and 1,104 into the navy.[75]

The orderly way in which the merchants, traders and artisans of Russia discharged their joint responsibility for the naval armament begun in 1697 may have put the tsar in mind of the desirability of bringing them together permanently in a single body. Such acquaintance as he had with the corporate organization of the administrative and business activities of the prosperous town-dwellers of England and Holland may have strengthened this wish but the immediate motive for bringing into existence on 1 September 1698 the *Burmísterskaia paláta* (chamber of burgomasters), soon to be renamed *Rátusha* (from the German *Rathaus* = town hall), was prompted by fiscal considerations. The service state charged the merchants and the *posádskie liúdi* with the collection of the bulk of the indirect taxes – the tolls and the liquor excise which produced about 45 per cent of the entire revenue – and it seemed prudent for this reason alone to protect them from the abuses and extortions perpetrated by the tsar's officials. It made sense to assume that the yield from the taxes gathered by those unpaid and unhonoured collectors would improve in proportion to the betterment of their lot. The simplest way of achieving this result was to allow them to manage their own affairs. The *ukáz* of 30 January 1699 accordingly exempted from the ministrations of the officials in the *prikázy* in Moscow and of the *voevódy* and their underlings – the *prikáznye liúdi* – in the provinces, all the sections of the population under the direct control of the Crown: these comprised the *posádskie liúdi* proper as well as any members of other categories of the population engaged in trade or handicrafts and residing in urban areas, and also the peasants, tradesmen and artisans living on the sovereign's land and on the Crown demesne. All these communities were granted a considerable measure of autonomy but the label of 'self-government' attached to this institution by some of its historians[76] obscures its true and less benevolent purpose – the collection in full, under pain of a fine, of all direct and indirect taxes.

In the provinces, in urban as well as in rural areas, the elected officers – *burmístry* – managed not only the financial but also the judicial affairs of the various communities – hearing private pleas, taking official proceedings, adjudicating in commercial disputes. In Moscow the corresponding functions were discharged by a board of *burmístry* elected by various sections of the *posád*. The *Rátusha* also took over from the various *prikázy* the overall responsibility for the affairs of the urban population in the country as a whole, including the receipt of the revenue collected by the *burmístry* throughout the land. The official status of the *Rátusha* came close to that of an office of state: the *burmístry* in Moscow were authorized to send instructions to various *prikázy* and to their counterparts in the provinces and, on specified days, to report to the tsar on matters concerning their department. Little is known, however, about the day-to-day working of the system because the records of the *Rátusha* have apparently gone astray.[77]

The expeditions against Azóv undertaken by Tsar Peter with the intention of ultimately establishing himself on the Black Sea were not unconnected with his future conquests on the Baltic and on the Caspian. In Riga, Narva and later St Petersburg he saw not merely the antipodes of Azóv and Astrakhan but the terminal points of the last stage of a new trade route leading from the Far East through Persia to western Europe. With these considerations in mind, in

August 1700 the tsar joined the operation which together with King Christian IV of Denmark and Augustus II of Poland (also Elector of Saxony) he had planned for a concerted and rapid seizure of some of Sweden's overseas possessions. The Danish occupation of Holstein had already been frustrated by the intervention of an Anglo-Dutch fleet and now the invasion of Livonia by the Saxons and of Ingria by the Russians was unexpectedly and successfully resisted by the Swedes. In October the Saxons were forced to withdraw from Riga, and in November the Russians were heavily defeated at Narva by the youthful Charles XII. The intended *Blitzkrieg* had turned out to be a mere flash in the pan but in the course of time it developed into the Great Northern War which kept Russia and Sweden locked in combat until 1721. With their calculations thus upset, Peter I and his collaborators were obliged from the end of 1700 to concentrate all their efforts on the conduct of the war. The tsar's principal concern was to raise all the money, manpower and equipment required for the creation of a large modern army (and soon also of a Baltic navy) capable of fending off and in the end defeating a powerful enemy. To achieve these aims the tsar continued to use the existing machinery of the service state which he found to be in urgent need of modernization.[78]

In October 1700 the Patriarch Adrian died but the tsar decided against the appointment of a successor. The motives for this decision were at once political and economic. It had been suggested to the tsar by some of his advisers that a period of delay was desirable in order to enable him, as autocrat, to impose his authority on the Church and to consider a new regime for the ecclesiastical lands. The Patriarch's responsibilities were therefore for the time being divided. To Stefán (Iavórskii), metropolitan of Riazán' since April of that year, the tsar assigned, in December 1700, the ecclesiastical duties of the primate, and to the *Monastýrskii prikáz*, revived for the purpose in January 1701, his judicial and administrative responsibilities. The original scope of that *prikáz* was accordingly extended and under the direction of a layman, the boyar I. A. Músin-Pushkin, it became to all intents and purposes a ministry of church affairs. The collection of tax from ecclesiastical estates for the tsar's treasury was one of its many duties and its principal contribution to the war effort. Thus began the integration of the Church with the service state, a process to be completed in 1721.[79]

The traditional organization of the state had produced the necessary quantity of money, men and guns but had failed to muster an army capable of standing up to the most formidable fighting force in northern Europe. At Narva the Russians lost between 8,000 and 10,000 men and the whole of their artillery. In the memorandum on the conduct of military affairs which he submitted in 1701 to the boyar F. A. Golovín, Pososhkóv pours scorn on the unreformed Russian army and especially on the cavalrymen mounted on bony mares, seedy, ill-clad, carrying blunt sabres but incapable of wielding any arm whatever, who scattered before the enemy at Narva. Pososhkóv declares to have seen more than one *dvorianín* who did not know how to load a musket, let alone fire it. When these warriors happen to kill two or three Tatars, he wrote, they are filled with astonishment and congratulate themselves on their success, ignoring their own losses even though they may be as high as 100 men. He had heard some trustworthy and by no means poor *dvoriáne* say that their main concern was not to kill an enemy but to return home and pray to God that they might serve the Great Sovereign Lord without drawing their swords. This was no wild exaggeration: it is known from other sources that only two out of every ten *dvoriáne* registered in Moscow presented themselves for service. Tsar Peter's official *Journal* explained the weakness of the Russian army: only one infantry regiment was made up of seasoned soldiers, the two guards regiments had only been in action twice (at Azóv) but had never confronted a regular army in the field; as for the rest, with the exception of some of the colonels, the officers were as raw as the men.[80]

Charles XII's involvement in Poland allowed Peter I enough respite to put Russia on a war footing and even for a while to regain the strategic initiative in the northern theatre. More taxes were imposed and more men levied, the army was reorganized, retrained and re-equipped, once again with the help of officers from the West. These efforts were rewarded in October 1702 with the capture of the fortress of Nöteborg at the source of the Nevá; the Russians took Narva in July 1704 (thus completing their conquest of Ingria) and Dorpat in Estonia in August of that year. In May 1703 they had taken the fortress of Nyenskans at the confluence of the Nevá and the Ókhta; on 29 June on a small island in the mouth of the Nevá, chosen as the site of a new fortress, the foundation stone of a church was laid; both buildings were named after SS Peter and Paul whose feast day it was.

The decision to gain and maintain a foothold on the Baltic at this perilous junction shows Tsar Peter at his most determined. From the autumn of 1704, at a time when Charles XII's back was only temporarily turned and Peter could not assume that he was safe from a Swedish counter-stroke by land or sea, he looked upon the place known as *Sankt Piterbúrkh* as the future capital of Russia. By the autumn of 1705 the Admiralty dockyards protected by a fortress roughly opposite that of SS Peter-and-Paul had been completed, and in April 1706 the first ship to be built there was launched.

The labour for this and similar undertakings was secured by adapting to novel circumstances the traditional prestations incumbent on the taxpaying categories of the population: the supply of hands and material for the construction and upkeep of fortifications (*gorodovóe i ostrózhnoe délo*) and of men for pioneering duties in the army (*posóshnaia slúzhba*). The men supplied for these purposes, formerly known as *posóshnye liúdi*, were now referred to simply as *rabótnye* – workmen – and their services were required for longer spells over a longer period but in its essence the system of compulsory labour remained unchanged. The labour in the docks was conscripted from specified localities for an indefinite period, as in 1705 when 500 carpenters were called up or again in 1707 when over 3,000 workmen were drafted for the dressing of timber. At times of acute labour shortage carpenters were hired for limited periods and received 4 roubles a month whereas the conscripts received on the average 90 kopecks a month and a food ration consisting as a rule of bread and salt; only the most highly skilled were rewarded in addition with payments of between 8 and 12 roubles a year.

From 1704 40,000 workmen requisitioned each year at the rate of one from between fourteen and sixteen households were assigned to building duties in St Petersburg during the period between April and October, at first in three rotas but from 1706 in two, with the possibility of extension for three or more months. In practice the number of workmen thus mobilized did not exceed 20,000 each year but the burden weighed heavily enough on the men themselves and on their communities where households which did not send a workman paid a special contribution towards the maintenance of those sent by the others. The scheme nevertheless remained in force until 1718. In 1710, faithful to the colonizing tradition of the service state, the tsar ordered the compulsory transfer to St Petersburg of 4,720 families of *posádskie liúdi*. Men were also conscripted for public works at Vorónezh, Azóv and at Taganróg where, in 1707, 26,226 men are said to have been employed in building the harbour.[81]

In the army by 1705 the initial phase of the somewhat haphazard raising of levies gave place to wholesale and periodic conscription at the rate of one man from a fixed number – twenty or fifty or eighty – peasant households (*dvorý*), without any relation to the status or the official duties of their landlords. These men, drafted for the whole of their fighting lives into a modern regular standing army in the making, now became officially known as recruits (*rékruty*). Special levies were still, however, raised from among particular categories of the population such as *posádskie liúdi*, scribes in government service, and peasants or retainers on monastic estates. A separate levy of 1,000 men for the navy was first raised in 1703. The twenty-one main and thirty-two subsidiary levies raised between 1699 and 1725 produced 248,187 men for the army alone; in 1725 the field army effectives numbered about 130,000 men.

In the administration the policy which was aimed at the concentration of the collection of revenue in the *Rátusha* was superseded in the second half of 1706 by a contrary and centrifugal tendency which led to the creation in the provinces of large administrative units – *gubérnii* (governments) – and the appointment of *gubernátory* (governors), though office and territory were not as yet necessarily concomitant. The pressure of events strengthened this trend. As the Swedes advanced towards central Russia and in 1707–8 the peasant and

Cossack revolt associated with the name of its principal leader, Bulávin, raged on the Don, the Khopër and the Sévernyi Donéts, it became necessary for reasons of strategy and internal security to tighten the grip of the authorities on the provinces. In December 1708 the tsar decreed that 'for the common good' eight *gubérnii* were to be formed. Their chiefs were commanded to concern themselves with the collection of revenue and 'all matters in the *gubérnii*', each of which was to contribute its quota towards the cost of maintaining specified regiments of the cavalry, the infantry and the garrison troops. The *gubérniia* of Moscow was also to meet the cost of the general staff and of the guards. In the interests of efficiency and accountability the revenue thus allocated was to pass direct from its source to its destination by the hands of commissaries representing in each *gubérniia* the regiments corresponding to it.

The immediate superiors of these commissaries were the *gubérnskie komissáry*, controlled in turn by a hierarchy of *krigs-komissáry* (military commissaries). As a result of these changes, by 1712 the collection of revenue together with the rest of the administrative system had been temporarily placed under a quasi-military régime. The *voevódy* (prefects) were replaced by governors, and in those provinces which were on a war footing, by military governors. Unlike their predecessors who were commissioned personally by the tsar, the governors were expected to act in accordance with uniform instructions issued on the tsar's behalf. The province and the *uézd*, the territorial units comprised by the *gubérniia*, were administered respectively by an *ober-komendánt* and a *komendánt*. The governor was assisted by several *land-ríkhtery* (sheriffs) who, as well as dispensing justice, performed a variety of administrative duties; he was to be advised, and to some extent controlled, by a council of *landráty* (district magistrates), eight, ten or twelve in number, according to the size of the *gubérniia*. These councillors, originally appointed by the Senate, were from 1714 to be elected by the local *dvoriáne*. In 1715 under yet another and, as it turned out, provisional reorganization, the areas in which no garrisons were stationed and which were subdivided into *dóli* ('lots') of approximately 5,536 peasant households each were put in the charge of *landráty* who in this capacity acted as full-time officials.

The depredations committed by this succession of outlandishly named civil and military officers were no less severe than the harm done up and down the country in the last years of the previous period by the 'advancers of [the tsar's] profit' (*príbyl'shchiki*) who according to John Perry vexed the common people so much that they had but little heart or desire for any industry. The first *príbyl'shchiki* were appointed early in 1705 with instructions 'to increase the revenue without overburdening the people' – a conundrum never to be resolved in Tsar Peter's day. In Moscow the rich and powerful members of the various communities (*slóbody*) did not scruple to shift the burden of tax and service on to the shoulders of their poorer and defenceless brethren. With the creation of the *gubérnii* between 1708 and 1710 the role of the *Rátusha* as a central agency for the collection of tax came to an end and in consequence its local branches – the *posády* in the provinces – found themselves at the mercy of the nearest *voevóda* or governor.[82]

The changes effected in the regional administrative system between 1708 and 1715 are more properly described as hand-to-mouth contrivances than as systematic reform. It will be seen that not more than one of these innovations, the *gubérnii*, stood the test of time and only in a modified form. But however inefficient and wasteful these makeshifts were, they did succeed in their principal purpose of enabling the army to conduct an orderly defensive campaign and ultimately to defeat the enemy. The Russo-Swedish war did not enter into its critical phase until January 1708 when Charles XII occupied Grodno with the intention of marching on Moscow. Early in July 1708 he narrowly defeated the Russians at Golóvchino but General A. L. Lewenhaupt's failure to arrive in time from the north with supplies of food and ammunition caused the king to change his plan. Instead of marching to Moscow via Smolensk he turned south towards Nóvgorod-Séverskii where supplies could be obtained and whence Moscow might still be reached. However, after the defeat and the losses in men and material inflicted by the Russians on Lewenhaupt at Lesnáia, Charles XII had no choice but to seek winter quarters and succour in the Ukraine from Iván Mazepa, hetman of the left bank Cossacks since 1687. Having made secret overtures to the Swedes in the summer, Mazepa openly deserted the tsar in October and encouraged them to enter the Ukraine.

In April 1709 Charles XII laid siege to the fortress of Poltáva garrisoned by 4,000 Russians. At the end of June, although himself incapacitated by a wound in the foot, he accepted the challenge of the tsar who had moved into the area with the intention of fighting a decisive battle. The Russian army consisting of 158 battalions of infantry, 17 regiments of cavalry and 72 field guns, a total of 42,000 men, faced a Swedish force of 24,000 men and four field guns. In the battle which began in the small hours and ended by 11 a.m. on 27 June the Swedes were driven from the field leaving behind 9,234 dead and 2,864 wounded. The remnant of the Swedish army retreated southwards only to suffer a final defeat and the humiliation of surrender at Perevólochna. Charles XII and Mazepa at the head of a small party of Swedes and Cossacks succeeded in crossing the Dnieper into the Zaporózh'e and eventually reaching Turkish territory. The destruction of the Swedish army at Poltáva was ultimately seen to have tilted the balance of power in eastern Europe in favour of Russia but it did not end the war and Charles XII's presence in Turkey before long led to the renewal of hostilities between Peter I and the sultan.[83]

Turkey declared war on Russia in November 1710. In February 1711, before setting out for Poland to lead his ill-fated expedition to the river Pruth, the tsar decreed that there should be a 'Governing Senate to act in Our absence'. The creation of the Senate completed a process begun at the end of the seventeenth century when the boyar *dúma* was outliving its usefulness as a consultative and legislative assembly of the chief dignitaries at court and in the central administration. Tsar Peter had begun to attend meetings of the *dúma* (or strictly speaking of the council commonly referred to as 'the boyars') regularly in 1688. Of the two extended formulae mentioned earlier as being used in the promulgation of official acts only one – 'the tsar has ordained and the boyars have pronounced' – remained in use until the beginning of the next century. From about 1696, however, this formula was at variance with the practice newly adopted by the tsar: in keeping with the personal nature of his rule he would issue an *ukáz* in his own name or announce his decisions in response to questions put to him in writing by his officials. The resolution of a council held in October 1696 to deal with the apportionment of the cost of building a fleet begins with the significantly impersonal expression: 'Resolved . . .'. In January 1699 two important *ukázy* were validated not, as had hitherto been the practice, by several *d'iakí*, but by one clerk (*dúmnyi d'iak*), a prelude, it has been suggested, to the tsar's signing his ordinances himself.

By the turn of the century the *dúma* had ceased to be a consultative and legislative assembly and had become an executive committee; only its judicial functions remained unchanged. The *dúma* had been diminishing in size as well as in importance because new boyars were not appointed to replace those who had died. During the period 1698–1701 the number of members of the *dúma*, after having been allowed to decline from 182 to 112, dropped to 86. Tsar Peter made a habit of employing the boyars not only as *voevódy* but also as his personal representatives or diplomatic agents with the result that many members of the *dúma* were absent from Moscow on duty: 24 in 1699 and 22 in 1700. Nor did all the members of the *dúma* who were at hand receive summonses to meetings. In 1699 and 1700 on three occasions, out of a total of 78 members, 63, 69 and 51 respectively were called upon to attend, and on one occasion in 1701, 47 out of 61. The matters about which decisions were taken at the meetings were few and of minor importance. It is not clear in what circumstances this senescent body was replaced by the council of ministers (or heads of *prikázy* – *konsíliia minístrov*) which is known to have been active by March 1704. The council met under the chairmanship of the tsar as and when necessary and was attended by designated 'ministers' concerned with the business of the day.

The creation of the Senate – on the face of it a hastily contrived measure – nevertheless marks a stage in the transition from personal to bureaucratic rule in the Russian service state. For although, perhaps in order to remind his entourage of the absolute and permanent nature of his authority, the tsar took care at intervals to stress the original purpose of the Senate which was to govern in the tsar's absence, it soon acquired a permanent existence and became at first the nucleus and eventually an essential component of the new bureaucracy.

The Senate consisted of nine members and a secretary. From its inception it was the highest judicial and administrative body in the land; its functions ranged from the publication of the tsar's ordinances to the interpretation of the existing laws and enactments; it was the Senate which in the last decade of Peter I's reign was to deliberate on the reorganization of the central and regional administration and scrutinize the draft of the Table of Ranks and of the *Ecclesiastical Regulation*. In establishing the Senate the tsar somewhat casually completed the new administrative structure based on the *gubérniia* by superimposing on it a co-ordinating central authority. The commissaries for each *gubérniia* were expected, when required, to wait upon the senators, to supply them with information and to receive their instructions. In 1711 the tsar ruled that the decisions of the Senate were to be unanimous although, when it came to an irreconcilable difference of opinion, a senator who dissented from his colleagues was allowed to register his objection in writing. The final decision rested with the tsar.[84]

The war declared by Turkey in November 1710 began early in 1711 with two unsuccessful attacks carried out by her allies, the Crimean Tatars. At the end of June, on the banks of the river Pruth in Moldavia, the Turks encircled and attacked with superior forces the main body of the Russian army. The Russians repulsed the enemy but having suffered heavy casualties and run short of supplies, sued for peace. By the treaty signed on 12 July 1711 and finally confirmed in 1713, Turkey recovered Azóv with the surrounding area on the bay of Taganróg, and the Russians agreed to destroy all the fortifications erected by them since 1700 on the Turkish frontier between the Don and the Dnieper. The southern fleet, deprived of its harbour became useless; the razing of the two fortresses, Novobogoróditskii and Kámennyi Zatón, on the left bank of the Dnieper just to the north and to the south of the rapids and close to the lands of the Crimean Tatars, exposed the settlements on the fortified lines in southern and south-eastern Russia to repeated depredations – almost every year between 1713 and 1725 – by Tatar and Turkish raiding parties.

This setback was more than outweighed by successes in the Baltic theatre. Between June and September 1710 the Russians had gained complete control of Karelia, Livonia and Estonia by capturing Viborg, Riga and Reval. Viborg served as a base for the Finnish campaign waged by land and sea from August 1712. In July 1713 the Russians took Helsingfors, the last anchorage of the Swedish fleet in the Gulf of Finland. After winning the battle of Nappo in February 1714 they occupied nearly the whole of southern Finland. In the war at sea the battle of Hangö Head marked a turning-point. In August 1714 the Russian galley fleet under General-Admiral F. M. Apráksin overwhelmed the Swedish flotilla under Schoutbynacht Nils Ehrenskiöld. Tsar Peter led the first of the three Russian attacks. After anchoring at Åbo the Russian galley fleet occupied the Åland islands, unhindered by the Swedes. St Petersburg was now secure from attack, and with the senators in permanent residence from 1713, ranked as a capital city. The initiative in the war in the eastern Baltic is said at this point to have passed to the Russians. Nevertheless, two years later Swedish ships were again cruising off Åland and hindering Apráksin from making a descent on the Swedish mainland. Meanwhile Charles XII having left Turkey and crossed the continent at lightning speed joined his countrymen in the fortress of Stralsund and took charge of its defence in November 1714. He left for Sweden towards the end of December 1715 on the eve of the surrender of the fortress to the tsar's Prussian, Danish and Saxon allies. Victory over Sweden seemed to be within the grasp of the northern league but as it turned out, the northern crisis was yet to come.[85]

It is tempting to look upon the year 1714 – the year of the battle of Hangö and of Charles XII's return to western Europe after spending five years in Turkey – as critical in the development of the service state under Peter I, and December of that year as one of symbolic significance. In that month Heinrich Fick, a native of Hamburg, was setting out for Russia. This man (of whom more will be said later) was to play a bigger part than any other – Brius or Osterman, for example – apart from the tsar himself, in the final reconstitution of Russia's civil and financial administration. But Fick did not arrive in St Petersburg until about a year later, and when the antecedents of the new policy are examined it soon becomes apparent that he did not initiate it.

The principles of a future programme of reform had been laid down in the manifesto of April 1702[86] in which the tsar called on foreigners – military officers, craftsmen and merchants – to enter his service or establish themselves in Russia. The phraseology of the text drawn up in German by the Livonian adventurer and 'projector' J. R. Patkul, newly commissioned by the tsar to engage army officers in the West, suggests that its underlying ideas were borrowed from the writings of the early cameralists. Many of the key expressions of that document will be seen to occur again, though not necessarily in the identical form, in the ordinances promulgated from 1711 by Peter I on matters connected with administration, justice and trade. 'Since Our accession' – so reads the manifesto –

'It has been Our foremost concern to govern Our lands in a manner that would bring home to Our subjects Our intention to ensure their welfare and increase. To this end We have endeavoured not only to promote trade, strengthen the internal security of the state and preserve it from all manner of dangers which might harm the common good, but also to institute good order [*Polizey*] and whatever else contributes to the improvement [*Cultur*] of a people in order that Our subjects may by and by become fit to form all manner of associations and exercise various skills along with other Christian and civilized peoples. Being aware, however, that Our subjects will be able to enjoy the fruits of these labours only in a state of complete security, We have not failed to give thought to the defence of Our frontiers as well as to the preservation of peace in the whole of Christendom and to the protection thereof from anyone who would venture to disturb it'

– a clear allusion to Charles XII. Hence, the manifesto continues, the tsar's decision to regularize the military estate, one of the main supports of all realms and governments. Since the general circumstances required that men, suited not only to the task of reorganizing the army but also to the instituting of all manner of knowledge that may contribute to the increase of the state, should be encouraged to come to Russia, the manifesto announced several measures concerning the entry of foreigners: the freedom of worship for non-Orthodox Christians and the establishment of a *Kriegs-Raths-Collegium* (a committee of the council of war) to exercise jurisdiction over all the foreign members of the military estate.

It may be noted in passing that the notion of the common good – one of the principal themes of the manifesto – was not alien to Russia. The resolution on the abolition of *méstnichestvo* passed by the assembly of the land in 1682 named as the reasons for the adoption of that measure the salvation of Christian souls, the common good of the people, the undying glory of the monarch and the increase of all blessings. In the Russian text of the manifesto, *Polizey-Wesen* (all matters relating to *Polizey*) – which was to contribute to the diffusion of *Cultur* – is rendered inaccurately as 'the condition of government' for the simple reason that the Russian vocabulary of the day could offer no equivalent of this rather imprecise Gallo-Germanic term. In its strict and narrow sense *la police* or *Polizey* was only one of the objects of law and government (the other ones according to Adam Smith being justice, revenue and arms). Dr Johnson defined 'police'[87] as the regulation and the government of a city or country as regards the inhabitants. The political writers of the late seventeenth and early eighteenth century use the word in a broader sense and opine that 'police' should redound to the inhabitants' well-being and prosperity defined as 'the common good'. A state whose policies were successfully applied to this end was eventually to be known as a *Polizeystaat*.

The ideal *Polizeystaat*, by regulating the conduct of the individual would enable him to enjoy happiness in its highest attainable aspects: spiritual, physical and material. So commendable were the objects of *toutes les lois de la police* and so well-intentioned were its executants supposed to be that to put any formal restriction on the extent of their authority would have seemed self-contradictory. On the other hand, the absence of any such limits made the promotion of the common good liable to abuse by a ruler on the grounds of *raison d'état*. Thus Lamare in 1705 took the common good to mean the sum of the well-being of the individual members of society but Louis XIV thought differently and dismissed any idea of a contradiction between the interests of the people and those of the ruler as false and imaginary: 'Those interests are in fact one . . ., the security of the subjects derives from their obedience.'[88] The problem was as old as political theory itself. Aristotle saw the careful management of the public funds as a way in which a tyrant could cleverly begin to play the part of royalty so that he should be regarded as a disinterested protector and husbander not of his own resources but of the nation's. The cameralist writers resolved the contradiction by equating the common good with a broader solidarity and in consequence took it for granted that the welfare of the subjects was the foundation of the happiness (meaning the success) of the prince as a ruler. The prosperity of a ruler which did not derive from the well-being of his subjects could not last.[89]

To attribute the terminology of the appeal and the intentions stated in it solely to Patkul, implying thereby that Tsar Peter merely put his signature to the document, would be to overlook the intensely personal character of his rule and the attention paid by him to the smallest detail of any ordinance published in his name. No student of the Petrine revolution who has familiarized himself with this particular piece of evidence would wish to argue that for a long time the tsar lacked a programme of reform or consistency in its execution. The presence in the tsar's library of possibly two works by cameralist authors shows that he took an interest in the ideas of their school in the early years of the eighteenth century. One is the *Fürstliche Machtkunst oder unerschöpfliche Goldgrube, wodurch ein Fürst sich mächtig und seine Unterthanen reich machen kann*, by von Klenck (Halle, 1702). With it went a manuscript translation into Russian of this work which Small calls 'the shorter catechism of mercantilism'. The other is a manuscript translation, probably of the book by Becher mentioned earlier, the *Politische Discurs*.[90]

What Peter I did lack in 1702 and in the subsequent decade was not vision but favourable circumstances, expert collaborators and the prestige that derives from success in war. Once he had retrieved his fortunes in 1709 he took full advantage of the improvement in his position and began, girder by girder, to erect the framework of the new system, introducing a permanent establishment and uniform pay for the army, creating the Senate and the office of *óber-fiskál* (chief fiscal officer or investigator) in 1711, multiplying the number of fiscal officers in 1714. Slowly at first, the service state was tightening its grip on society and at the same time rationalizing its methods of government. In 1711 the tsar's servants were required to take an oath in which they swore to abide by the law, to be loyal to the sovereign and to the state as a whole, and to safeguard the interests of both in 'the collection of tax, the enrolment of men and the like'. The people were to be reasoned with in the first instance. That is why so many of Tsar Peter's ordinances begin with a sentence or paragraph which explains their intent. Three years later the tsar ordained that *ukázy* on matters of general concern to his subjects should be published and put on sale for the information of 'all'. It is clear from *The Book of Poverty and Wealth* that Pososhkóv had no knowledge of this ordinance and, provincial that he was, did not keep himself informed about current legislation.[91]

In the preceding decade the relations between Peter I and his subjects had deteriorated as a result of the exigencies brought about by the war. Increasing taxation, conscription for the army and for public works and the retrieval of the peasants who were trying to escape from these and other hardships caused widespread discontent and awakened old hatreds, especially among the *strel'tsý* and the Old Believers. Twice was the tsar's government obliged, in addition to conducting a foreign war, to quell outbreaks of popular revolt brought about by the harshness of its policies. The first, the rebellion in the town and the region of Astrakhan, was sparked off by the arbitrary conduct of the local *voevóda* T. I. Rzhévskii and his assistants, some of whom were foreigners. Many of the complaints voiced by members of the local population, a motley assemblage of *strel'tsý* (most of whom were also part-time traders and craftsmen), merchants, *posádskie liúdi*, casual workers, Russians and non-Russians both old-established and newly arrived, are identical with the grievances registered by Pososhkóv: the heavy and increasing burden of a variety of obligatory services, tolls, levies, rents and petty imposts, the punishment of defaulters by *pravëzh*,[92] malfeasance, corruption, the high price of salt. Rzhévskii, later to be put to death by the rebels, caused particular resentment by the imposition of fines on the wearers of Russian dress and beards as a means of enforcing the adoption of the Western style of attire and appearance. The blame for these and other un-popular measures, including a reduction in the remuneration of the *strel'tsý*, was laid on the boyars and the foreigners. It was conveniently believed that Tsar Peter was no longer in control of the government and had perhaps disappeared. He must therefore be replaced with an unquestionably 'good' tsar and 'good' officials. It was the duty of the insurgents to fight for the Christian faith and for the sovereign. It took a Field Marshal, B. P. Sheremétev, and a division of troops, some of which had to be moved from the northern theatre, to quell this last urban rising under the old regime.

The disturbances in the delta of the Volga had hardly died down when, in October 1708, disorders broke out in the area around the mouth of the Don and spread rapidly to the entire basin of the middle course of that river and its tributaries: the Sévernyi Donéts, the lower Medvéditsa, the Buzulúk, the lower Khopër and the Bitiúg. The Bulávin uprising, as it came to be known from the name of its leader (until his death in July 1708), the Cossack Kondrátii Bulávin, was a Cossack mutiny, actively supported by the local populace. This heterogeneous mass of settlers, composed for the most part of *posádskie liúdi*, peasants, labourers of uncertain social origin and military deserters, had been driven from central Russia or the neighbouring Ukraine by exorbitant taxation, compulsory services exacted at will by private landowners or the state and the wrongdoings of officialdom. The Cossacks regarded the right to harbour fugitives as one of their most precious privileges. For decades they had welcomed people, who as well as offering their labour, brought with them gifts of goods, money and liquor. But the state which was just then mustering all its resources to check the advance of the Swedish army could ill afford the disappearance of so many able-bodied men and taxpayers.

The immediate cause of the outbreak was the brutal conduct of the search-party under Lieutenant-Colonel Iu. V. Dolgorúkii which had been sent to Cherkássk to seek out and repatriate all fugitives. The rebels, whose strength had been put at no less than 20,000, declared their intention to strike at the princes, boyars, landlords, corrupt officials, farmers and 'advancers' of the tsar's revenue, clerks and military officers. The professed aim of the leaders of the insurrection was to march on Moscow in order to put an end to all abuse of authority. Those of the insurgents who, like Bulávin himself, were Old Believers, wished for the restoration of the 'old faith'. Peter I's obvious unwillingness to make any concessions to the rebels ruled out any affirmation of his 'goodness' or any direct appeal to his mercy. None was shown to the men whose actions had endangered the security of the state and necessitated the formation of an anti-insurrectionary force numbering some 36,000 regular and auxiliary troops. They were treated with the thoroughgoing harshness which the tsar reserved for all real or suspected rebels. In June 1708 he ordered the destruction of all newly established Cossack settlements and allowed only those on the Don, as far north as Donétsk, to be spared. The instructions were carried out by the punitive expeditions under the command of Major V. V. Dolgorúkii and the *voevóda* of Kazan, Prince P. I. Khovánskii, who also took this opportunity to execute several hundred rebels. At the end of the year the territories inhabited by the Don Cossacks were incorporated in the *gubérniia* of Azóv and brought under closer control of the central authorities. The volume of migration to the south was in consequence reduced. The revolt on the Don was followed by sporadic outbreaks of unrest among the peasants of central Russia in 1708 and 1710.

The revolt of Bulávin coincided with the high point of the rebellion of the Bashkirs who inhabited the vast territory to the south of Ufá, bounded by the Káma and the Urals and divided by the Bélaia. The outbreak was caused by the brutality of the measures taken by the authorities to break the resistance of the population to the increased demands made on it by the 'advancers of the tsar's revenue' in their pursuit of money, men and horses for his army. The Bashkirs had for several decades resented the intrusion into their midst of Russian landholders and peasant colonists. It was on them that the rebels in their raids inflicted plunder, arson and murder. In the early months of 1708 Kazan was thought to be in danger from a rebel army. The leaders of the revolt, for the most part local headmen and mullahs, were suspected of acting in collusion with Bulávin. The rising was suppressed almost in its entirety in the spring and summer of 1708 by a militia of *dvoriáne* under the command of Prince P. I. Khovánskii assisted by a force of Kalmyk auxiliaries.[93]

From 1709, the year of Poltáva, Tsar Peter's record of military success, broken only by the disaster on the Pruth, contributed an admixture of charisma to the character of his rule. He enjoyed by now a deserved reputation for being above and outside the common run of men and was never a respecter of persons or of traditions or institutions any more than he was a sufferer of fools. He differed from Weber's typical charismatic ruler in the sense that he valued rather than despised rules and regulations, but ran true to type inasmuch as rather than settle the succession to the throne by specific provision, he reserved, in 1722, the right to appoint his own successor. Being a soldier by vocation rather than in virtue of his status, he put his trust in discipline and revelled in organized activity; he loved to see a place for every man and every man in his place, acting in accordance with official instructions set out in black and white. His ruthless corrective methods encouraged Frederick William I of Prussia to punish his own disobedient and recalcitrant servants *auf gut russisch*.[94] It seemed natural that a uniformed autocrat should wish to extend the orderliness and consistency of the drill manual to the entire system of civil government in Russia by setting in motion that self-winding and self-correcting administrative clockwork which was held to be the heart of the well-regulated state. Once the impulse had been given, the tsar's authority – previously delegated to congeries of glorified personal servants – would pass to a body of sworn professional officials. The public conduct of those 'pillars of the modern state and of the modern economy'[95] instead of following individual preference would conform to abstract norms and would be determined by detailed regulations.

It will become apparent presently that in one more respect Peter I failed to behave like the Weberian prototype: so far from showing a fine disregard for economic considerations he strove, with the aid of his native and foreign advisers, to secure the material resources required for the military preparedness and the administration of his state through the development of trade and industry. In giving a rational grounding to the exercise of authority on his behalf, Peter I, the future Father of the Fatherland, did not impair the patrimonial character of his rule or cast doubt on its divine derivation, nor did he in introducing the bureaucratic mode of government intend to alter the nature of the service state. Rather, he wished to bring it to perfection so that it could stand comparison with the absolute monarchies of the West. Such was the nature of the service state that its all-powerful ruler could with comparative ease convert it into a modern *Polizeystaat* ostensibly dedicated to a more benevolent purpose than the mere rendering of service to the sovereign. The ideal of the common good had already been derided and exposed as a trick by

German pamphleteers and was still to be denounced by Rousseau as an abuse, a pretext, a scourge for use against the people. Peter I invoked it solemnly and probably in good faith but in his mind identified it with what he considered to be the best interests of the state. The contrast or contradiction between the loftiness of his aspirations and the uncouthness of his proceedings was to be commented on during his visit to Paris in 1717.[96]

The ordinances issued by Peter I during the critical period between the Pruth expedition of 1711 and the operations in Finland in 1714 show that he attached as much importance to the repression of crimes committed against the state – the abuse of authority and malversation – as he did to positive action in the exercise of thrift, the collection of money, the mustering of young *dvoriáne* for military service and the development of trade with the East. From March 1711 the duty – unspecified at first – to protect the interests of the state from the misdeeds committed by its subjects from non-political motives fell to the *fiskály* – investigators – 'for all matters'. It was the duty of the local fiscal officers, under the direction of their chief – the *óber-fiskál* – who was attached to the Senate, to act on information laid by the common informer and, correspondingly, the duty of the Senate to act on the information supplied by the *óber-fiskál* to its judicial sub-department (or chamber), the *Rasprávnaia paláta* (which took over the judicial functions of the boyar *dúma*). Assuming that in the eyes of his counsellors the interests of the state were as self-evident as in his own, the tsar instructed the Senate in April 1713 to explain to the people at large the meaning of these interests, commanding at the same time that crimes against them be punished without mercy by death and confiscation of property. The conduct of some of the senators themselves, however, fell far below the high standards prescribed by the tsar two years previously for the holders of public office. The *óber-fiskál* A. Ia. Nésterov complained to the tsar that some members of the Senate were engaged in defrauding his treasury under the names of men of straw. Thus senator P. M. Apráksin was accused of a number of 'fiscal' offences: secretly buying a consignment of flax in Pskov for export without payment of toll or duty, transferring from the *gubérniia* of Archangel to that of Kazan 'a large number of peasants' without the knowledge of the authorities, under-assessing for tax purposes 'out of friendship' the lands of an unidentified secret councillor Dolgorúkov. In 1712 when the 'fiscals' were subordinated to the Senate, the senators refused to take any action against officials whom the 'fiscals' had accused of having committed irregularities. The 'fiscals' brought their reports to the Senate only to be met with angry taunts and recriminations, some senators calling them knaves and gutter-magistrates. When in July 1713 it came to the tsar's notice that the Senate had so far failed to take action on a single report sent in by 'fiscals' on matters of major importance, the tsar warned the senators: 'If by 1 November you do not punish such criminals without mercy and respect of persons you yourselves will suffer the punishment due to them.'[97]

In 1714 the duties and official grades of the 'fiscals' were more closely defined. Their task was to investigate all matters of public concern arising from the infringement of laws, rules and regulations: bribery, embezzlement, anything whatever that might be contrary to the interests of the state, as well as matters relating to ordinary persons in which no proceedings would otherwise be instituted. Having found evidence of abuses such as peculation, corruption, the evasion of state service on the part of *dvoriáne* or – to use a modern phrase – economic crimes such as illicit distilling or private trading in goods covered by a government monopoly, or crimes of violence, the 'fiscal' reported the results of his investigations to higher authority without taking any further action himself. In addition it was the 'fiscal's' duty to be present at judicial and other official proceedings such as tendering for government contracts, the valuation of Crown estates before a change of tenant or of private property before its confiscation. Some 'fiscals' were appointed against their will; amongst the least willing were those who made up the contingent which the *posádskie liúdi* were obliged to supply for service in that capacity, on the principle that a social class is most effectively spied on by its own members. After 1718 any tax due from such 'fiscals' was to be paid by the other members of the *posád*. In his work the 'fiscal' relied on information furnished by a network of carefully selected informers who presumably shared with their principals the sole reward for a 'fiscal's' labours: one half of the fines collected from the wrongdoers, real or suspected, de-nounced by him.

By December 1714, however, the tsar could see that neither moral exhortation nor physical surveillance had succeeded in improving the conduct of his officials and that fraud and abuse had in fact been multiplying. Those responsible had been trying somehow to justify their actions by arguing that these were not specifically prohibited. It did not, apparently, occur to them, observed the tsar, that any act which might cause harm and material damage to the state was a crime. In order to rule out such excuses all men in charge of any public concerns whatever were henceforth prohibited from accepting gratuities or deducting a commission on the handling of state funds or on revenue collection in the form of profits from sales, purchases, contracts or any services whatever. Salaries and fees for work executed, to be charged in accordance with present or future regulations, were to be the only legitimate recompense of officials. The emblematic phrase about the citadel of public good or justice (*právda*) being sapped by self-seeking wrongdoers, struck out from the draft of this ordinance, also occurs in an earlier one of the same year and was conjured up in the tsar's mind in its final form in 1722 by the continuing misdeeds of his subjects. Thus a new phase had opened in the arduous process of cleansing and rationalizing the administration of the service state with its malign tradition of allowing private gain to compensate for the lack of fair or regular reward for public service. The most flagrant abuses were committed in the provincial administration.[98]

Here the highest post, that of *voevóda* (prefect), was as a rule bestowed by the tsar for fairly short periods on men of high rank in recompense for their military exploits. In theory the *voevóda* received a salary but in practice, neither its amount nor its source being clearly defined, he retained for his own benefit a share of the revenue for the collection of which he was responsible and pocketed such gratuities as came his way. By the first decade of the eighteenth century the system had undergone a further change. Perry asserts that the prefects held their commissions for three years only and received no salary; on the contrary, it was customary for the *voevóda* to pay a premium of up to 4,000 roubles to the head of the *prikáz* responsible for the province in question. Despite this outlay the *voevódy* were still known to enrich themselves during their term of office. This profit was derived from the gratuities willingly or unwillingly given by the local inhabitants in return for favours received, exemptions granted or simply business attended to rather than neglected. By analogy, the lower ranks of the official hierarchy – the clerks and scribes who did not hold land of the tsar – were allowed to supplement their meagre salaries by charging fees for services performed in the offices of their superiors for the benefit of suppliants or of contesting parties.[99]

The first public body to act on the principle of paying its members a fixed and regular salary was the army. This extension of the practice of remunerating landholding *dvoriáne* whilst on active service was made necessary by changed circumstances: service had become virtually permanent and many of the newly commissioned officers were landless. The pay and establishment roll for the army was promulgated in 1711; in 1715 the same treatment, though from different motives, was applied to the provincial administration. In the interests of probity salaries were fixed for its entire staff, from the governor to the clerk in the office of the lowest executive officer; at the same time the arbitrary imposition of any dues in supplementation of such salaries was declared illegal and punishable by death. The funds required for the payment of salaries were to be obtained through an impost of 10 kopecks per rural holding (*grívennye dén'gi*) specially decreed for the purpose. The general process of bureaucratization had already been accelerated by the tsar's ordinance of 4 April 1714 which laid down the procedure for collective and formal, or collegiate, decision-making in all official business by a majority vote – the very essence of impersonal and rational bureaucratic practice, held to be manifestly superior to the arbitrariness and unreliability of individuals acting in isolation.[100]

It is against the background of these early ordinances relating to the intended transition from an arbitrary and corrupt to a bureaucratic and honest style of government that one should examine the much more widely known ordinance of 23 March 1714 on the mode of inheritance. This *ukáz* represents Peter I's only venture in social engineering; if successful it would, however, have affected not so much the social stratification as the occupational structure of the service state, for here too the tsar's intention was not to alter its character but to improve its performance by bringing out its potentialities. The institution of service was still closely connected with land tenure but the colonization of the southern and south-eastern borderlands and the growing number of transactions in land, combined with the inconsistency of successive enactments on the rights of landlords, gave rise to confusion and discontent.

The beginning of the joint reign of tsars Peter and Iván provided the landholders with an opportunity to obtain a ruling on the subject from the tsars and the *dúma*. An *ukáz* promulgated in 1690 declared: a *pomést'e* may be assigned, leased or exchanged, and a *vótchina* may be sold or mortgaged and peasants may be transferred by their landlord from one *vótchina* or *pomést'e* to another, as well as from his *vótchina* to his *pomést'e*. Once a peasant has been transferred he may not be recalled to his previous habitation by a new holder of the estate from which he was moved (unless that estate be a *vótchina* given as a dowry). The legal difference in the nature of the authority of a *poméshchik* and that of a *vótchinnik* over the peasants on his land was thus becoming as tenuous as the practical difference between being a *poméshchik* or a *vótchinnik*, especially as many hereditary men of service held both types of estate. Nevertheless, it remained official policy to distinguish between the grants of *vótchiny* and the apportionment of *pomést'ia*, both of which were still regarded as land held on service tenure. A reminder to that effect was uttered in 1701 when a high offical speaking on behalf of the tsar declared: 'In the state of Muscovy the *sluzhílye liúdi* render service in respect of land while the peasants on the sovereign's land and on the Crown demesne perform labour services and pay dues in kind.'[101] By this time, however, the *poméshchiki* were apt to regard the estates held by them as belonging to them and to their families, and sales of *pomést'ia* in the guise of unequal exchanges were apparently a common occurrence.

But in law the possession of a *pomést'e* bestowed on an individual to enable him to render service did not carry the same hereditary right as that vested in a *vótchina* granted for services rendered previously and settled on a family (*rod*). It is therefore natural to regard the ordinance of 23 March 1714 as a formal and final abolition of the obsolete and artificial distinction between the *pomést'e* and the *vótchina* and hence as something on a par with an act of allodification. In point of fact it was nothing of the sort; what the *ukáz* achieved was not the assimilation of the *pomést'e* to the *vótchina* but a union of two hitherto unconnected features – first, the regulation of the mode of inheritance within the family (*rod*) as prescribed in 1679 for the ancestral *vótchina* and the *vótchina* granted for service and, second, the ancient ban on the alienation of *pomést'ia* by sale or mortgage, save in an extremity. The product of this marriage was a hybrid: 'immovable property'. Urban property – messuages and shops – was subsumed in this novel concept together with landed estates. The tsar's intention in making the match was not to strengthen the traditionally weak property rights of his subjects, for such a course would have been prejudicial to the interests of the state, but rather to ensure that its requirements were met in full. It mattered little if the property rights of landholders and of prospective inheritors of real estate were to be weakened in consequence.

Peter I's decision on this highly controversial point was preceded by intermittent consideration over a long period. He had expressed an interest in the western European institution of primogeniture at the turn of the century; in 1711 he had called for information about Western systems of inheritance and the division of the immovable and personal property of parents among their children. The instructions accompanying the *ukáz* of 1714 show how determined Peter I was to enforce its implementation, knowing that 'accursed quibblers' were in the habit of frustrating all *ukázy* with their tricks. Any particular difficulty that might arise from the division of immovable property was to be referred to the Senate and dealt with in supplementary rules. Under the new law a parent was obliged to devise the whole of his or her immovable property to a son or, if he (or she) had no son, to a daughter and to divide his (or her) movable property among the other children. Immovable property in the possession of a childless person was allowed to pass only to his (or her) relatives.

In an extensive preamble to the *ukáz* the tsar explained the principal reasons for its promulgation: the harm done to the interests of the state as well as to the tsar's subjects (the peasants) and the decline caused by the subdivision of land through inheritance. His professed aim in introducing the new measure was threefold: by preserving large estates, and thus restricting the number of landlords, to make it easier for the peasants to satisfy the needs of their masters and to pay tax to the tsar, to prevent the decline of notable landed families and to induce unproductive landholders to exert themselves for the benefit of the state. 'Idleness', says the tsar, given as he was to moralizing, and on this occasion misquoting the Scriptures, 'is the root of all evil.'[102] The dispossessed sons will be compelled to earn their living by service, 'study' (leading to the practice of a skill or profession), trade and the like. Any such fresh start will benefit the state. Perhaps the most pressing though undeclared reason for the promulgation of the *ukáz* was the need to create a reserve contingent of 'cadets' for the army and for the future civil service. Since neither the learned professions nor trade were as yet developed enough to absorb even small numbers of young men, many 'cadets', not necessarily *dvoriáne*, were to be deprived of their traditional means of support. An ordinance issued three weeks later, possibly after the tsar had reflected on the extreme harshness of this aspect of the new mode of inheritance, drives home the point. A 'cadet' who has earned money with which he wishes to buy an estate (*derévnia*) or a shop may do so after a period of service: seven years in the army, ten in the civil service, fifteen in trade or in a profession. 'But he who has not done any of these things may never buy any land, even unto death.' In 1716 the tsar, no doubt under pressure from those to whom the new law had brought hardship, mitigated its severity by allowing widowers and widows with issue to inherit a quarter of one another's movable and immovable property.

The long-standing formal connection between state service and land tenure was thus broken but the principle that service was the duty of all *dvoriáne* was maintained and eight years later reinforced by the Table of Ranks. As the landless 'cadets' were soon to discover, they were obliged to serve whilst forgoing the benefits enjoyed by their landed brothers. Landed property – the *vótchina* and the *pomést'e* alike (both terms survived into the ninth decade of the century; Pososhkóv uses the generic term *derévnia*, 'a village') – came to be regarded as hereditary rewards for services rendered to the sovereign and the state in the past rather than as a form of remuneration for work being done in the present which was now to be rewarded with pay in the army or by a salary in the civil service. Such a system of remuneration was both more practical and more economical than settling real estate on men whose descendants might render service of disproportionately small worth, provided that the tsar's treasury always had the necessary amount of cash in hand. As has been seen, it was envisaged that a part of the money thus received would be spent on the purchase of land after the recipients had completed the requisite term of service.

Peter I appears to have made only a few gifts of land from the Crown demesne after 1711; he continued, however, to give away escheats and confiscated estates but ruled that they must not be assigned to petitioners without his personal instructions. An ordinance published soon after his death, in 1726, stipulated that only officers with a long and meritorious record of active service would be allowed to petition the sovereign for the grant of such estates. On the other hand, permission received by the hereditary men of service in the borderlands under the *Ulozhénie* (Chapter 16, article 40) to occupy additional portions of land in the steppe remained in force (at any rate in the areas to the west of the middle Volga) with the result that the lands to the south of the Sýzran' line on the Úza, the upper Khopër and the upper Medvéditsa were colonized in the reign of Peter. In order to protect the population of these areas from the incursion of Tatar and Kalmyk bands, Pánshin Gorodók on the Don and Tsarítsyn on the Volga were linked by a new defensive line built between 1718 and 1720. It is remarkable but seldom realized that this process of domestic colonization in the south should have continued in parallel with the conquest of foreign territory in the north. The distribution of any landed estates whatever by the *Vótchinnaia kollégiia* was finally prohibited in 1736 by the Empress Anne.[103]

At the time of the promulgation of the ordinance on the mode of inheritance the tsar's attention was still concentrated on the war and was to remain so for another four years. The summer of 1717 saw the disintegration of the northern alliance and the opening of preliminary peace negotiations between Russia and Sweden. These led to the inconclusive congress of plenipotentiaries of the two countries which began on Åland in May 1718, Russia being represented by Brius and Osterman. On 30 November of that year, at the siege of Frederiksten in Norway, a bullet fired by 'a dubious hand' removed from the scene Peter I's indomitable and unpredictable adversary. The political propaganda of the period spoke of Charles XII as another Simon Magus and of the Tsarevich Alekséi as another Absalom. In reality Peter I's heir apparent, though disaffected and backward-looking was a moral weakling and a rebel only in spirit. He had been deprived of the succession to the throne in February 1718 and was under sentence of death for high treason when he died in July of that year. The death of Alekséi Petróvich, whether accidental or contrived, removed from the tsar's mind the obsessive fear of an eventual relapse of the new Russia into the traditional ways of unreformed Muscovy with the active encouragement of his first-born.[104]

The knowledge that the two men capable of frustrating his designs or undoing his work were no more seems to have prompted Tsar Peter to embark on the comprehensive programme of reform which he had had in mind since 1715 or even earlier. On 22 December 1718 OS (1 January 1719 NS) Peter I issued an ordinance forbidding his subjects to address to the tsar petitions concerned with matters which should be dealt with by the more appropriate departments of state. The contents of this *ukáz* are far weightier than its subject would suggest. The preamble complains of the competing demands on the tsar's attention of a large variety of items of business concerning individuals as well as the state (and inadvertently points to the drawbacks of personal rule).

The document itself somewhat unexpectedly illustrates the tsar's attitude towards the basic problems of government and contains a significant self-assessment of his record as soldier and statesman. Characteristically, the relevant section of the document declares: 'There is only one person to whom petitions are addressed, yet in how many military and other exacting tasks that person is engrossed is well known to all. And even if it were otherwise, how could one man give his attention to so many petitioners? Verily an angel would not be equal to such a task, for even an angel's movements are circumscribed and if he is in one place he cannot be in another. Nevertheless, despite the heavy burden imposed on His Majesty by a hard-fought war, a war which he had not only to conduct but in which at the same time he was obliged to train his men afresh and to draw up military regulations and articles of war, his efforts have, with God's help, been rewarded with success. Everyone knows how greatly superior the present army is to its predecessor and what results it has achieved. And now that these things have been put to rights His Majesty, having the interests of the people at heart, has not relaxed his efforts but, being alive to the need for equitable civil government, is graciously striving to put this in equally good order. To which end in place of the *prikázy* [the existing departments of state], colleges are being established, that is to say committees of many persons whose presidents (or chairmen) will not have the same power as the senior officials of old who did as they pleased.'[105]

This measure which brings to its logical conclusion the rule laid down in 1714 on collective or collegiate decision-making may well owe its origin to the opinion conveyed to Tsar Peter by Leibniz in 1711 in terms which came closer to poetry than to philosophy. 'God', he wrote (probably in 1711), 'being the God of order governs all with His invisible hand wisely and methodically. The gods of this world being the counterparts of the divine authority of God must model their system of government on His. Experience has shown that the condition of a country can only be improved through the establishment of sound colleges. As in a clock one wheel has to be set in motion by another, so in the great clockwork of the state must one college drive another and provided that everything is in a condition of correct proportion and proper harmony, it can only follow that the hands of wisdom will point to joyful hours for the country.'[106]

The establishment of colleges had been advised in 1688 by the cameralist writer Becher as the administrative mechanism best suited to putting his recommendations into practice. The first record of the tsar's intention to establish a college is dated 12 January 1712; in April 1715 Leibniz was being informed that His Majesty had resolved to establish colleges of war, navigation, trade, justice and finance. At the end of that year Fick was sent to Sweden (under a false name) to acquaint himself with, and to report on, the laws, institutions and economic organization of that country. Analogous instructions were issued to P. I. Iaguzhínskii (probably in connection with his diplomatic missions to Denmark in 1715 and 1716) and to A. P. Veselóvskii who was appointed the tsar's resident in Vienna in 1715. In that year the tsar decided that the colleges were to be staffed by men of learning skilled in the law; at the end of 1717 the personnel of the colleges was determined.

The collegiate system was to guarantee the trustworthiness and efficiency of the central government. The eleven colleges or boards – of war, admiralty, foreign affairs, mines, manufactories, trade, revenue, expenditure, audit (suppressed in 1722), justice and *vótchiny* – were to assume their duties at the beginning of 1719 under the direction and control of the Senate and in gear with the outer administrative cogwheels in the provinces. The colleges were at first housed in a block built in 1714 under the supervision of Domenico Trezzini but were to find permanent quarters in another building specially designed by the same architect. The work began in 1722 and was completed ten years later. Trezzini's masterpiece – twelve units in red brick connected by an external gallery and framed by pilasters clad in white stone – is the embodiment of Peter the Great's wish to concentrate and harmonize the work of the new central departments of state. But the remote location of St Petersburg (later compared by a contemporary of Diderot's to an imaginary animal's heart placed at the tip of a finger) prevented complete centralization. Moscow still retained much of its former importance and was the seat not only of the college of manufactories but also of the subsidiary offices (*kontóry*) of the other colleges.[107]

The standard descriptions of the administrative organization of Peter the Great's Russia tend to omit a vital link in the chain of command – the *kabinét* or the tsar's personal office which was established in 1704. After 1711 its purpose was to keep the tsar in touch with the Senate and later also with those colleges (especially the Boards of Mines and of Manufactories) over which he wished to exercise direct control. The omission is understandable; to include the *kabinét* in any such account would be to spoil the impression of rationality and harmony created by the *ensemble* of the Senate and the colleges with their subordinate agencies. Within this scheme the *kabinét* was an anomaly; it survived the administrative reforms because neither it nor its efficient and self-effacing secretary, A. V. Makárov (1675–1750), could be dispensed with. The *kabinét* had no official status, its functions were not clearly defined but it had substantial sums at its disposal, especially after the revenue from the salt monopoly was allocated to it in 1715. Most of this money was used to meet state needs for which the appropriate *prikázy* or colleges were unable to raise the necessary cash at short notice; the rest covered the tsar's personal and domestic expenses. The failure to distinguish between the pecuniary resources of the sovereign, of his court and of government departments may be seen as a legacy of the patrimonial system under which the ruler and his ministers were financed from the same chest.[108]

The *Generál'nyi Reglament* (General Regulation), promulgated in 1720, laid down the rules for the dispatch of business by all officials in the colleges and in their subordinate agencies. The declared purpose of these institutions was to conduct the tsar's government in an orderly manner; correctly to estimate and apportion his revenues; for the benefit of his faithful subjects to improve the dispensation of justice and the usefulness of civic institutions; to maintain his army and navy in a state of preparedness; to promote trade, handicrafts and manufactories; to regulate tolls and tariffs; to increase and expand the extraction of minerals and generally to supply any other needs. Most of the aims set out in the *Generál'nyi Reglament* are identical with those of the *Polizeystaat* visualized by the German cameralists. In designing its Russian variety the tsar was ready, as a general rule, to copy the best models to be found in other Christian lands; in practice Peter and his advisers, impressed by the duration and effectiveness of the resistance offered by Sweden to a coalition of enemies superior in human and material resources, tended to follow the Swedish example.

Pososhkóv's treatise shows clearly enough that the tsar's attempt to transform officials of the Muscovite stamp into modern civil servants by paying them salaries commensurate with their duties failed in its aim. The reasons for this failure were to some extent financial. The salaries which were low to begin with had to be reduced on grounds of economy and proved to be inadequate, all the more so as they were paid irregularly or only after repeated demands. In the end they came to be regarded – preposterously – as mere supplements to such contributions as could be squeezed out of the population. With the introduction of the poll-tax in 1723, the collection of the special impost of 10 kopecks per rural holding was replaced by deductions for administrative costs from certain categories of local imposts (yet to be named) to be made after the tax had been collected in full. In consequence the lower officials who had been forbidden to charge fees for the transaction of official business found themselves without means of support and were allowed to resume their traditional practices.[109]

As if to provide for such a situation, the *Generál'nyi Reglâment* laid down the rule that officials in the colleges would be allowed to collect casual fees from members of the public for work done on their behalf. Regulations to govern this procedure were to be promulgated in due course. Pending their publication (which did not come about) it was convenient to assume that the higher officials of the colleges would in any case show themselves to be incorruptible and disinterested. Thus the Regulation for the *Shtats-kontóra* (Board of Expenditure) allowed its principal officials (under another article of the *Generál'nyi Reglâment*) on certain days to receive petitioners, to give each one every possible assistance and take prompt action in order to deprive the subordinate officials of grounds for accepting gratuities from the lowly, the poor and the oppressed. This personal touch was to be applied in an impersonal setting; in 1717 the office rather than the official's private residence had been designated as the proper place for making such representations. There are no grounds for supposing that any of these tell-tale regulations or any other similar measures were at all effective. On the contrary, all the evidence suggests that the majority of the tsar's servants, underpaid and habituated to corruption as they were, continued to eke out their livelihood by bribery or extortion and that Peter the Great's passion for probity in public life remained ungratified.

The defects of the Russian judicial system, castigated by Pososhkóv, did not escape the notice of foreign observers. Perry, who had been an unsuccessful litigant in England before leaving for Russia, had a poor opinion of Russian justice: 'There being no juries in that country, nor counsel admitted to plead, as in England . . . the will of the judge pretending to take some statute for his guide, decides the law as he pleases', and again: 'the bribery of the judges is the first step to go upon; money is known to be taken on both sides and generally he who bids highest carries the cause. Which occasions a . . . saying among the people . . . that God is high and the tsar is far off.' In 1711 Juel noted acidly that generally in dealing with Russians one must resort to gratuities – drink and gifts – the law and justice having no effect whatever.[110]

Peter I had a highly developed sense of natural justice and an even keener respect for the law, but unlike his father, Alekséi Mikháilovich, he did not go down in history as a legislator. On two occasions, at the turn of the century and towards the end of his reign, he ordered a revision of the Code (*Ulozhénie*) of 1649 but even the relatively simple task of repealing those of its provisions which had been rendered obsolete by more recent enactments was never accomplished. The tsar's approach to the law was entirely pragmatic. Peter I, as his actions show, distinguished clearly enough between civil, military and ecclesiastical jurisdiction but, unlike Pososhkóv, had no firm views on the subject of legal procedure: his preference swung, pendulum-like, from the accusatory to the inquisitorial method in 1697 and back to the accusatory in 1723. His greatest achievement as a legislator lay, characteristically, in the sphere of military law.[111]

The prime object of the *Artíkul Vóinskii* (the Articles of War) promulgated in 1715 was to regulate the conduct of the members of the tsar's armed forces. The *Artíkul* also prescribes punishments for crimes which are not necessarily connected with the performance of military duties but could be committed by any civilian and lays down general rules of procedure for the trial of criminal cases. For these reasons the *Artíkul* may be, and apparently was, regarded as a general code of criminal law. The tsar's *ukáz* which decreed the publication and distribution of the *Artíkul* declared that it was also intended for the guidance of civil officials whenever their activities were connected with those of the military. Although the decree in question does not specifically prescribe the application of the *Artíkul Vóinskii* by civil courts to the civil population, there is good reason to believe that in Peter I's reign and in the subsequent decade the *Artíkul* was used in this way, and that in consequence at certain times certain areas of Russia found themselves under military law. The *Artíkul Vóinskii* also had its effect on the general administration of criminal justice. It is not too rash to hazard the guess that military officers whose duties entailed the exercise of judicial authority in a civil or in a military capacity, when faced with the choice between applying the *Artíkul Vóinskii* or the *Ulozhénie*, would decide in favour of the former. The punishments laid down by the *Artíkul* were less severe than those prescribed by the *Ulozhénie* and, moreover, its sentences were liable to review and mitigation. Quite unexpected but wholly typical of Tsar Peter's mentality and the nature of his regime at that time is the inclusion in the *Artíkul* of some fundamental enactments pertaining to administrative and constitutional law. These include, in the form of a gloss, the definition of the tsar's prerogative as that of an autocratic monarch who is not responsible for his actions to any one on earth but has the power and authority to govern his state and territories as a Christian monarch in accordance with his own will and judgment.[112]

The difference between the administration of justice and administration pure and simple does not seem to have been any more clear-cut in Tsar Peter's mind than it was in the understanding of the majority of his subjects. Like Pososhkóv, the tsar uses the term *sud'iá* in its double meaning of 'justicer' and 'magistrate'. It was probably as a means of protecting his subjects from the rapacity and arbitrariness of officialdom, rather than from any wish to contribute to the elaboration of a constitutional principle, that Peter I, perhaps on the advice of foreign experts, made a determined but abortive effort to bring about a separation in the exercise of the two powers in the provincial administration. In 1719 he instructed the *voevódy* (prefects) – as the principal administrative officers of the newly defined forty-five subdivisions (*províntsii*) of the eleven *gubérnii* were portentously named – not to meddle in the dispensation of justice. The 'lower' (*nízhnie*) courts (also designated as 'provincial') established in 1719, constituted in the principal towns on a collegiate basis but in minor localities consisting of a single judge, were deliberately separated from the administration. However, as a result of a severe shortage of men fit to dispense justice (in 1721 40 per cent of the offices in the judiciary were unfilled and probably remained so), the principle of separation could not be adhered to in the setting up of the courts of higher instance – the eleven *nadvórnye sudý*,[113] established in 1719 (and reduced to ten in 1722) which from the beginning sat under the chairmanship of a senior official in the local administration – a governor or a vice-governor.

In 1722 after such important figures as Ménshikov and F. M. Apráksin had attacked the principle of separation, known to have been adopted from the Swedish judicial system, as artificial and unworkable, the tsar reversed this policy. The tier of 'lower' courts was suppressed and judicial authority was formally reunited with the administrative in the hands of the *voevóda* of each province who, in company with one or two assessors, henceforth constituted the 'provincial' court in its new form. The competence of that court, in relation to which the *nadvórnyi sud* was the next higher instance, was limited – thus it lacked the power to impose a sentence of death or banishment with forced labour (*kátorga*). In towns 200 or more miles distant from the seat of a *voevóda*, and of a provincial court, the *voevóda*, if he saw fit, could establish a judicial commissioner. In the event of one of the parties in a lawsuit wishing to appeal against a sentence of the *nadvórnyi sud* or if that court itself wished to refer to a higher one – as it frequently did – recourse was had to the *Iustíts-kollégiia* which was at once a court of law and the department responsible for the administration of the law courts and the dispensation of justice in general.

The highest court of appeal was the Senate which exercised authority over the entire judiciary on behalf of the tsar in whose person the supreme judicial power was vested. The edict which in 1711 had brought the Senate into being, instructed the senators to ensure the dispensation of justice without fear or favour and to punish judges who abused the law. All the categories of law courts described above dispensed justice in both civil and criminal cases to all the tsar's subjects but with so many exceptions that they finally defeated the original intention of creating a self-contained judiciary system in the provinces. Thus, as things finally stood in about 1721, the clergy, the inhabitants of ecclesiastical estates, the townspeople (*posádskie liúdi*), the merchants and the manufacturers were answerable respectively to the Holy Synod, the *Glávnyi magistrát* (Board of Civic Administration) or the local *magistráty* (municipalities), the Board of Trade and the Board of Manufactories. The complaints of aggrieved taxpayers were heard by the *Kámer-kollégiia* (Board of Revenue). The colleges (boards) and various other government departments (*kantseliárii*) naturally considered it their duty to provide jails on their premises for the custody of detainees before they were tried by the officers of the college acting in their traditionally dual capacity as official and judge (*sud'iá*). The investigations conducted by the *Iustíts-kollégiia* often entailed the use of torture and any misdeeds committed by that college were in turn investigated by the Senate in the same manner.

The persisting connection between justice and administration did not make for probity or efficiency. The *voevódy*, expert though they may have been in the practice of extortion, lacked the means of enforcing the decisions of the courts over which they presided and of executing their orders relating to civil cases; at the same time the *nadvórnye sudý* displayed a surprising degree of independence from superior authority. The *Iustíts-kollégiia* complained through the proper channels to the Senate of the irregularities committed by these courts and of their refusal to pay the fines imposed on their members by the *Iustíts-kollégiia*. The real sufferers were the litigants, many of whom found a direct approach – if need be accompanied by a bribe – to a courtier or a high official more effective than going to law. At the end of the reign of Peter half the cases which had for some time been under examination by the *nadvórnye sudý* were still unresolved; some of these proceedings were formally closed in the reign of Catherine II with the relevant papers being consigned to the archives 'for perpetual oblivion'. The judicial system set up by Peter I has been justly censured by Pososhkóv and others for being dilatory, weak, corrupt and open to interference by persons of influence. Its structure was elaborate but its scope limited since many sections of the population were exempt, and the peasants of private landowners excluded, from its jurisdiction; it failed to serve the purpose for which it was created and to observe the principles which it was intended to uphold: 'to seek the truth, be just in passing judgment, to protect the poor and helpless on behalf of His Majesty without respect of persons'.[114]

'How shall the state be governed if the laws are found to be inoperative?' This rhetorical question asked by the tsar in December 1718 was equally pertinent to the conditions prevailing in Russia at the end of the period of judiciary and administrative reform. In the eyes of the tsar contempt of the law, being insidious, was more dangerous than treason, for it might lead to the disintegration of the state, a point which he elaborated in 1723 when he drew a distinction between 'private' and 'state' offences: 'He who commits a transgression in his official capacity causes harm to the entire state.' 'Having been driven to commit such a transgression, by some vice or other, or by the wish to win favour or, worst of all, by cupidity, a man tries to drag all his colleagues in his wake, whereupon discipline must break down, for a wicked chief is in no position to punish his subordinates. Dissoluteness and impunity follow, the people suffer even greater detriment, other officials fall into temptation and gradually all come to act with impunity, bring the people to ruin and arouse the wrath of God.' The final outcome could well be the downfall of the state. Crimes against the state must therefore be punished in the same way as treason, that is by death.

In Russia, the tsar complained in his ordinance of 17 April 1722, 'many' were striving to undermine the citadel of justice – *právda* – of which he regarded himself as the keeper and remarked ruefully that it was futile to publish laws if they were to be ignored or treated like a pack of playing cards from which a choice can be made to match one's convenience. According to an anonymous polemical writer of the period, in Muscovy, before the bearded magistrates sitting in their appropriate places, stood a crucifix or an icon and lay copies of the New Testament, the *Kórmchaia Kníga*[115] and sacred books by St Cyril of Alexandria, St John Chrysostom and St Ephraem Syrus. A confirmed secularizer like Tsar Peter had no use for such symbols of the sacerdotal nature of acts of justice. In the closing sentences of the same ordinance he decreed that in all seats of executive and judicial authority a notice-board should be placed displaying a copy of that very *ukáz*. Its central portion, in terms suggestive of much bitterness and exasperation, commands the observance of the civil law, prohibits official decisions contrary to the provision of statutory regulations and forbids the submission to the tsar of reports intended to elicit from him rulings which would be inconsistent with previous ordinances. Nevertheless, in regulating the public conduct of his subjects Peter the Great continued to invoke Judaeo-Christian moral standards. In 1723 one of the two further notices to be mounted on the same stand was to instruct magistrates how to behave with decorum in their offices, for 'The judgment is God's' (Deut. 1.17) and 'Cursed is he who does the work of the Lord with slackness' (Jer. 48.10). The other notice was to enjoin on magistrates the observance of the public law as their first and foremost task.

In the context of the *ukáz* of 1722 justice is synonymous with the internal security of the state for the preservation of which the tsar consistently applied the harshest and most extreme measures; incapable of instituting the rule of law he resorted to the rule of fear. The use of physical terror by the *Preobrazhénskii príkaz*, established in 1686, whose miscellaneous activities included the prevention and suppression of political crime, and by the *Táinaia kantseliáriia* established in the course of the enquiry into the conduct of the Tsarevich Alekséi Petróvich in 1718 and concerned solely with the detection of treason or evil designs against the life and person of the sovereign, bears no direct relation to the contents of *The Book of Poverty and Wealth*. It is worth remembering, however, that both departments have a place in the biography of its author who underwent interrogation by the first and eventually died a prisoner of the second.

For the much-needed assistance in the protection of its interests the state looked to the private informer. The two edicts in which the tsar invites delation in speech (1713) and in writing (1715) promise not only impunity but also 'great favour' to those who as true Christians and faithful servants of their sovereign and fatherland will submit reports on matters of moment. Peter I never ceased to believe in the value of a *donós* – confidential denunciation – and towards the end of his reign, in 1722, formulated the maxim: it is better to err by delation than by silence. Those professional informers, the fiscal officers, of whom there were about 180 at that time, were universally feared, hated and despised; few of them could boast a blameless record and it was said that the 'fiscals' perpetrated as many misdeeds themselves as they detected in others.[116]

The question who, in these circumstances, was to have custody of the custodians themselves, Tsar Peter answered in the same year in a characteristically brief and somewhat cryptic fiat: Let there be attached to the Senate a procurator-general (*generál-prokurór*) and a supreme procurator (*óber-prokurór*); likewise a procurator in each college (including, from 1722, the Synod), whose duty it will be to report to the procurator-general; let there also be attached to the Senate a *reketméister*.[117] Just as it was the duty of the *reketméister* to correct the errors and make good the omissions of the judicial bodies, so it was the duty of the procurator-general to attend the meetings of the Senate and ensure that, in the performance of their duties, the senators abided by the appropriate regulations and ordinances and, further, that business was dealt with not merely on paper but in fact. The tsar suspected that irregularities were being committed behind the back of the procurator-general but the activities of the procurators in the colleges appear to have resulted in greater efficiency. The procurator-general was to direct the work of all the procurators and exercise general supervision over the activities of the 'fiscals'.

Originally responsible to the Senate, the *fiskalitét* – or body of fiscal officers – was in 1719 subordinated to the *Iustíts-kollégiia* and, finally, in 1722, absorbed by the *prokuratúra*. The 'fiscals' in the colleges and high courts (*nadvórnye sudý*) were placed under the immediate authority of the procurators appointed to the same bodies but still encouraged to bypass their immediate superiors in the mixed hierarchy of 'fiscals' and procurators by forwarding their reports to a higher official level. In 1723 the 'fiscals' were given military rank, no doubt in order to raise their status and improve their morale which must have been severely shaken by the execution in 1722 of the *óber-fiskál* (supreme fiscal officer) A. Ia. Nésterov for accepting bribes from some of his own underlings.

But the *prokuratúra* was not the apex of the human pyramid of mutual custodians. When men or communications failed, as they frequently did, the tsar's instructions were not obeyed and corrective action had to be taken, or when some special or confidential mission had to be carried out, the guards were called in – a private soldier or else a small detachment under the command of a non-commissioned officer or an officer from the *Preobrazhénskii* or the *Semënovskii* regiment. For about a year before the appointment of the procurator-general a Guards officer supervised the sessions of the Senate; in the 1720s when the efficiency and reliability of the provincial administration were falling short of the tsar's expectations, Guards officers were sent to look over the shoulders of the *voevódy*; at various times between 1713 and 1724 about ten *maiórskie rozysknýe kantseliárii*, under a major of the Guards, conducted special enquiries into actions or intentions likely to threaten the security of the state or the life of the sovereign, suspected malversation and similar matters. In an over-quoted phrase, possibly of Aristotelian origin, the tsar defined the procurator-general as 'our eye and steward in affairs of state'.[118] The procurator-general, responsible like his deputy, the supreme procurator, to the tsar alone, was the time-keeper of the senators, the progress-chaser of the upper ranks of the administration and the whipper-in of those two packs of watch-dogs, the 'fiscals' and the procurators set over the entire bureaucracy. These observers – including to some extent the *reketméister* – together with the rest of the civil and judicial administration – the observed – (numbering in all about 2,500 men) made up what has been termed a system of organized mistrust and brings to mind Swift's Kingdom of Tribnia where 'the Bulk of the People consisted wholly of Discoverers, Witnesses, Informers, Accusers, Prosecutors, Evidences, Swearers; together with their several subservient and subaltern Instruments; all under the Colour, the Conduct and pay of Ministers and their Deputies'.[119]

So well organized was the system and so acute the mistrust that the infamous Nésterov was brought to justice by the procurator-general P. I. Iaguzhínskii despite having been a protégé of the supreme procurator G. G. Skorniakóv-Písarev. In general, however, despite repeated efforts, some half-hearted as in the matter of the revision of the law code of 1649, some strenuous as in the instance of the reform of the judiciary, to bestow on the tsar's subjects the benefits of *Polizey*, his government not only failed to establish good order and promote public morality but, as we learn from Pososhkóv, did not even succeed in protecting the persons of his people from murder or their property from theft and organized brigandage. Taken as a whole, the Petrine system of domestic administration in its final, albeit unfinished, form comes closer to the modern police state or a military dictatorship than to the early eighteenth-century ideal of the *Polizeystaat*. Many of the new Russian institutions resembled those of Sweden in name but not in spirit or in performance. Sweden, like Russia, but with fewer resources at her command, had to find the money and the men and to produce the equipment needed to carry on the war. The economic régime of Görtz between 1715 and 1718 directed to that purpose may have been ruthless but it was also effective without resorting to intimidation and physical repression.[120]

With the death of Charles XII in November 1718 the negotiations in Åland which might have led to a treaty of peace and alliance between the late king and Peter I were doomed to failure but were not broken off until mid-September 1719. Peter I remained willing to make peace but only on his own terms, that is, by holding on to his territorial gains from Viborg and Kexholm in the north to Riga in the west. The annexation of this territory would given him the virtual monopoly of the naval stores required by the British navy, a situation which George I and Lord Stanhope, the Secretary of State for the North, were determined to prevent. But the tsar, by skilfully combining diplomatic activity in Berlin, Vienna and Paris with renewed acts of war against Sweden, succeeded in fending off British interference and forcing the Swedes to come to terms with him in bipartite negotiations. In November 1720 the two parties agreed to begin talks and in May 1721 the peace conference began its work at Nystad on the Finnish coast; the tsar was again represented by Brius and Osterman. Meanwhile the war continued. In August a Russian expeditionary force was standing by to invade Sweden if her representatives at Nystad continued to drag out the negotiations. But the conference ended on 30 August OS (19 September NS) with the signing of a peace treaty. The tsar remained in triumphant and permanent possession of Livonia, Estonia (with the islands of Ösel and Dagö), Ingria and eastern Karelia with Viborg and the surrounding territory. Russia agreed to pay Sweden 2 million rix-dollars[121] by way of compensation for the loss of Livonia. By her peace treaties with Hanover (November 1719), Prussia (January 1720) and Denmark (June 1720), Sweden had already lost her other overseas possessions, keeping only Rügen, Stralsund and Wismar.[122]

On 21 October 1721 (OS) the Senate in consultation with the Holy Synod resolved on behalf of the Russian people to request the monarch who by his single-handed direction had brought his state and his people to such great power, well-being and glory, to accept the style of Father of the Fatherland, All-Russian Emperor, Peter the Great. On the next day in the cathedral church of the Holy Trinity in St Petersburg, after the celebration of the liturgy, the reading of the peace treaty and the sermon preached by the Archbishop of Pskov (Feofán Prokopóvich), the chancellor, Count G. I. Golóvkin, gave an address in which he spoke of the tsar's faithful subjects as having been led by him from the shades of obscurity onto the stage of world fame and begged the tsar to assume the title which was being offered to him. Peter's speech of acceptance, brief but packed with meaning, was followed by a service of thanksgiving, the firing of a salute and a final prayer offered by the metropolitan of Riazán' (Stefán Iavórskii). The ceremony had also a deeper significance inasmuch as it confirmed the charismatic character of the tsar's personality and rule. The neo-classical style of its setting disproved the prophecy according to which after Moscow the Third Rome (Byzantium having been the second) there was not to be a fourth: the Emperor and Pontifex Maximus, newly installed in a city named after St Peter, was master of many provinces, counselled by a Senate and protected by the Imperial guard.

The description of the emperor as Father of the Fatherland was in full keeping with Tsar Peter's supremely patrimonial form of government. After defining his authority as absolute and reserving the right to exercise it as he saw fit in 1716, he had carried it to its furthest extreme in 1718 by depriving the Tsarevich Alekséi of the succession to the throne. In 1722 in the *ukáz* on the succession he went as far as to draw a parallel between property in private families and the dominion of the tsar (*gosudárstvo*). Reminding his subjects of the provision of the law of 1714 under which the father chose any one of his sons as the sole inheritor of his immovable property, he ordained that henceforth it would be in the power of the ruling sovereign to name as his successor whomsoever he would and, should that person prove unworthy, to deprive him of the succession. That procedure would prevent the recurrence of a conflict between the monarch and his heir apparent similar to that which had arisen between Peter I and the late tsarevich. Thus an enactment which, although drastic, had been rationally conceived and was intended to result in some desirable social consequences was extended from the sphere of private to that of constitutional law and used to make the tsar's authority even less rational and more arbitrary.

The *ukáz* on the succession was an irrational and retrograde measure, more reminiscent of oriental than of enlightened despotism, however hard the tsar's apologist and semi-official political theorist Feofán (Prokopóvich, bishop of Pskov) tried to justify it by borrowing his arguments from Grotius, Hobbes and Pufendorf. Irony had the last word, for in the end the tsar omitted to settle the succession on the future Catherine I. The general direction of the tsar's policy, however, remained unchanged; it was still his aim to ground the system of government on reason and its efficacy on bureaucratic discipline. These principles were applied not only in the reorganization and functioning of the central and provincial administrative bodies already described but also, in the same year of 1722, in the appointment, grading and promotion of officials. The new system was embodied in the Table of Ranks (*Tábel' o rángakh*) promulgated at the end of January 1722.[123]

Since the abolition of *méstnichestvo* forty years earlier official Russia had lacked a formal hierarchy. This pause made it easier for Tsar Peter to spurn convention and indulge his patrimonial authority to the full in civil and military appointments. In wartime, during the Azóv campaigns and especially in the critical first half of the northern war, he singled out for promotion any man who showed the necessary aptitude and inspired confidence regardless of his low social origins or foreign extraction. To cite but a few examples: François Lefort (1656–99), born in Geneva, entered the tsar's service in 1678, was promoted lieutenant-colonel in 1690, major-general in 1695, admiral in 1696; A. D. Ménshikov (1673–1729), sometimes described as the tsar's *alter ego*, the son of a court stable-man, was engaged as a servant by Lefort, handed over as an orderly to the tsar in 1686, appointed bombardier in 1693, major-general in 1704, created a prince in 1707; Ia. V. Brius (Bruce) (1670–1735), an ensign in 1687, was appointed major-general in the artillery and acting master of the ordnance in 1700, confirmed in that post in 1711 and created a count in 1721; P. P. Shafírov (1664–1739), of Jewish extraction, worked as a translator in the *prikáz* of foreign affairs from 1691, accompanied the tsar on his travels in 1697–8, was successively appointed secretary to F. A. Golovín in that dignitary's capacity as chancellor in charge of foreign affairs, privy councillor in 1709, deputy chancellor (for foreign affairs) in 1710 and created a baron in the same year; S. L. Raguzínskii-Vladislávich (1670?–1738) a native of Serbia, served as the tsar's diplomatic agent in Turkey from the end of the seventeenth century till 1708 when he entered the *prikáz* of foreign affairs, and was appointed court councillor in 1710; P. I. Iaguzhínskii (1683–1736), the son of the organist at the Lutheran church in Moscow, entered the Preobrazhénskii (guards) regiment in 1701, attended the tsar as an orderly, was promoted captain in 1710, colonel in 1711, major-general in 1717, took part in the Åland negotiations with Brius and Osterman in 1718–19, was appointed procurator-general of the Senate in 1722; A. I. Osterman (1686–1747) was born at Bochum, entered the tsar's service in 1703, was engaged as a translator by the *prikáz* of foreign affairs in 1708, appointed secretary in 1711, privy councillor in 1720 and in 1721 created a baron for his part in the peace negotiations with Sweden.

These men and others like them owed their emergence and rapid advancement to the unusual circumstances of the day as did Catherine I. The daughter of a Lithuanian peasant, employed as a servant in the household of pastor Ernst Glück, she was taken prisoner after the capture of Marienburg (in Livonia) in 1702, was Ménshikov's mistress before she was claimed by the tsar and became by turns his concubine, wife (1714), consort (1724) and successor.[124]

At a time when in the army commissioning from the ranks for gallantry was a common occurrence and the war effort was at its peak, the tsar gave priority to military officers and preference to military service. In 1712 he decreed that 'each and every *dvorianín* of whatever family will on all occasions pay respect and give precedence to an officer'; the only officially recognized forms of service rendered by the *dvoriáne* were military service or training or an official appointment. Yet despite these changes the old code of precedence was apparently still being observed in the new administrative bodies by those whom it had favoured before: the descendants of high-born dignitaries. Tsar Peter by contrast is known in 1719 to have spoken in favour of replacing *méstnichestvo* by a business-like consistency in the treatment of all officials and in favour of appointments based on qualifications. A modernized service state could not be expected to operate without a clearly defined civil and military hierarchy, and three months later work on the Table of Ranks was put in hand. Regulations of this nature which were in force in the countries of northern Europe provided a useful model but in the work of adapting it to Russian needs the Muscovite tradition was also taken into account. The final revision of the draft was carried out under the personal direction of the tsar. The definitive text bears witness to his militaristic sympathies and scale of values; as a scheme which found a place for each and every one of the tsar's men of service, now formally designated as *dvoriáne*, it would have satisfied even the most critical martinet. Thanks to the tsar the primacy of military over civil ranks was perpetuated and it was he who adjusted the entire official hierarchy comprising 262 designations – 126 in the army and navy, 94 in the civil service and 42 at court – to the ladder of promotion in the army ranging from ensign to field marshal.

The heading of the Table of Ranks phrased by the tsar himself states that those in the same category have seniority according to the time of their appointment but the military officers (irrespective of the time of appointment) are superior to all others in the same category. The Table shows (without any written reference to the fact) that officers in the Guards, that *corps d'élite* of the office-bearers of the service state, enjoyed a seniority of two ranks above the officers in the other regiments. The tsar also decreed that all the civil servants should receive the same pay as their military counterparts but two years later the shortage of funds caused him to abandon this principle. As well as laying down a comprehensive code of precedence the Table establishes a uniform and consistent system of promotion by making ingenious use of three concepts: the status of *dvorianín* (*dvoriánstvo*), hereditary or personal ('life') office or dignity (*chin*) and rank or category (*rang, klass*).

The principal criterion in awarding rank was meritorious service and especial credit was given for service rendered under arms in view of its arduousness but some concessions were made to pedigree. Thus the tsar was willing to allow the sons of men of high birth and standing to be accorded due honour at court but refused to confer upon them any rank which they had not earned by service. On the other hand, 'members of the armed forces who are not *dvoriáne* by origin but who win promotion to the rank of officer are *dvoriáne*, as are their children born thereafter' (but in the absence of further issue one son born previously and designated by the father inherited his status). Further, the legitimate issue and subsequent descendants of Russians or foreigners who were or had been (temporarily) placed in one of the first eight ranks were to enjoy the same regard and advantages as the best and oldest *dvoriánstvo* (in the collective sense) even if they were of low birth. By implication the civilians in the lower categories were only *dvoriáne* for life but even that is not clearly stated. This deliberate distinction between hereditary and personal *dvoriánstvo* is not far removed from that between the men of service 'by descent' and the enlisted men of service in the seventeenth century.

Thus the Table created anew something of a hereditary caste of men of service consisting of all ranks in categories I to VIII (in descending order), together with the holders of military ranks only in the remaining six categories. If after Peter the Great's death the administrative structure designed by him had been maintained at full strength, these lower echelons would have constituted – in accordance with the intention of the law of 1714 – a component of a professional class. In its essence the Table of Ranks was designed to improve and to continue the time-honoured practice of exacting a full measure of obligatory and permanent service from the established and approved hereditary *dvoriáne* whilst ensuring a supply of fresh blood from outside. But the opportunity of social advancement which at the turn of the century the tsar had offered to outsiders and foreigners – whether talented upstarts or military and technical specialists – was now restricted to the soldiery and to the trained administrators needed in the colleges. Entry into the *kollégii* at the bottom of the ladder was reserved for young *dvoriáne* who were to join the civil service as *iúnkers*, provided they had received the necessary education. If they had not, they were to acquire it during their term of apprenticeship as titular *iúnkers*. This opening was obviously intended as an alternative to service in the army for those sons of landed *dvoriáne* to whom their fathers, under the law of 1714, had not bequeathed any part of their estates. No stigma was to attach to those who chose to live by the quill rather than by the sword, for no other access was to be open to the higher ranks in the civil service and to ministerial dignity.

It is hard to judge whether the new statutory system of co-optation to, and promotion within, the *dvoriánstvo* offered more or fewer opportunities of acquiring the status of *dvorianín* to one who was not born into that degree. According to Kotoshíkhin such advancement had not been uncommon in his day. An undoubted difference between the old and the new organization of state service is the lack of any formal tie between the duties discharged by the office-bearers listed in the Table and land tenure. The hereditary *dvoriáne* were bound to serve the tsar in virtue of their status – it was literally a case of *noblesse oblige* – and conversely others acquired the status of *dvorianín*, hereditary or personal, in virtue of service. The Table refers to the advantage and honour of being a *dvorianín* but does not confirm the traditional right of the tsar's servants (shared with the Church) to own land inhabited by peasants or the privilege of exemption from the poll-tax. Nor does it mention the endowment of men of service with *pomést'ia*. Although, as we have seen, this practice was still in use (and the petitioning for *pomést'ia* was not yet prohibited) its survival was contrary to the obvious if tacit intention of the tsar that landed estates, when not granted by him outright, should be inherited or bought.

It is at this point that a tacit policy of allodification becomes discernible. One piece of evidence supports this observation. In the seventeenth century the function of the *Poméstnyi prikáz* (Office of *pomést'ia*) had been to apportion land to men of service, to supervise transactions in land and peasants between holders of *pomést'ia*, as well as changes in the ownership of *vótchiny*, and to adjudicate upon disputes concerning *pomést'ia* and *vótchiny*. In December 1718 the *Poméstnyi prikáz* was transferred to the *Iustíts-kollégiia* and at some point during the next two years came to be designated as the *Kontóra* or *Kantseliáriia vótchinnykh del* – the bureau for matters concerning *vótchiny*. In January 1721 the bureau was separated from the *Iustíts-kollégiia* and constituted a separate board – *Vótchinnaia kollégiia* – with instructions to deal with all matters, litigious as well as uncontroversial, concerning landed estates, and to carry out surveying work. The choice for the new board of a title drawing attention to the patrimonial rather than the official character of landed estates could hardly have been fortuitous.[125]

The staffing of the civil service and the orderly advancement of its officers caused much concern to the authors of the Table. Its rules introduced a system of progressive promotion based on seniority and length of service. In order to avoid injustice being done to those military officers who had earned their rank by giving many years of service, the promotion of civil officers was regulated by the notional pace of promotion in the army. Realistically, however, the Table allowed also for promotion out of turn in recognition of meritorious service.

The complement of the Table of Ranks is to be found in the tsar's instructions for the holder of the newly created office of chief herald (*gerol'dméister*) published in February 1722 upon the establishment of that office. The chief herald was concerned with the symbolism of armorial bearings and the ramifications of family trees only in so far as he was responsible for the issue of patents of nobility and the registration of grants of arms. By far his most important function was to keep records of all *dvoriáne* showing which of them were fit and due for state service and how they were employed, as well as to maintain a register of births and deaths of their children. A *dvorianín* whose services were no longer required for the duties originally assigned to him was not to be allowed to skulk at home but was to be sent to the herald for nomination to another post. The *gerol'dméister* was evidently intended to be much more a taskmaster than a master of ceremonies. As was to be expected from the references both in the General Regulation (*Generál'nyi Regl"ament*) and in the Table of Ranks to the training of *iúnkers* in the colleges, the duties of the herald extended also to the scholastic sphere. Young *dvoriáne* destined for the civil service were to receive instruction in jurisprudence, economics, public administration and commerce under the supervision of the chief herald. This introductory course of study was to be followed by a term of apprenticeship abroad. Although elaborate, the scheme was only provisional, pending the establishment of an academy, since the existing schools could not supply the service state with trained bureaucrats.

To young *dvoriáne* who had mastered 'that which appertains to the administrative procedure in the colleges' the Table of Ranks awarded a bonus by equating their acquisition of such knowledge with notional years of service in the army as non-commissioned officers. The equivalence of service with study had been introduced in the early years of the reign of Peter. From 1714, in implementation of the law on the mode of inheritance of that year, the tsar used the traditional muster (*smotr*, carried out by or on behalf of the sovereign and first recorded in 1556) to assign young *dvoriáne* to one or the other form of duty. As the number of schools and teachers was still inadequate, those who did not have the good fortune to be chosen for schooling in Russia or abroad had little chance of acquiring any but the most rudimentary education. Even at the beginning of the last decade of the reign of Peter, many young *dvoriáne*, having been taught at home by the local sacristan, could only just read and only a few could write.[126]

The Slavonic Greek and Latin Academy after a promising start – it had 180 pupils in 1689 – began to decline towards the end of the century but was revived by the *de facto* head of the hierarchy, Stefán Iavórskii. Under his 'protectorate' the Academy was expanded, staffed with teachers brought over from the Kiev Academy, and the curriculum was Latinized. In 1710 it had 147 pupils drawn from a variety of social categories (except the peasantry). Despite the tsar's ordinance of 1708 which required the sons of priests and deacons to attend 'the Greek and Latin schools' their number in the Academy was not disproportionately high.

The Academy was not the only school in Moscow under clerical control. The Jesuits, after being banished from Russia in 1689, were allowed to return in 1698 and to resume the teaching of Russian students. By 1701 they had in their boarding school over thirty pupils including, apparently, many sons of Russian dignitaries as well as some Lutheran boys. The success of the Jesuits caused Iavórskii to propose that non-Orthodox teachers should not be allowed to take Orthodox pupils and that Russians should be obliged to send their sons to Orthodox schools – in other words, to the Academy. But the Jesuits were doing valuable work by teaching Latin, mathematics, German and military science so that the tsar was unwilling to bring to an end 'something which had begun so well', despite a further admonition, in 1705, from the Patriarch of Constantinople.

By that time, however, the Jesuits (who were to remain in Russia until their second expulsion in 1719) had lost most of their Russian pupils. The diminution in the popularity of the Jesuit school may well have been connected with the opening in 1705 of the so-called German school under the direction of a Lutheran pastor, Ernst Glück, with generous support from the tsar's treasury. Glück died in the same year, but his successors continued his work until 1715. At its peak, in 1711, the school had seven teachers and seventy-seven pupils many of whom were maintained by grants from official funds. The German school or 'Gymnasium', as it is sometimes called, taught Greek, Latin and modern languages (including Swedish), as well as geography, ethics, politics, rhetoric, arithmetic, deportment and riding. Little is known about the two other language schools in Moscow. The existence of the Italian school under Ioaníkii and Sofrónii Likhúdy (Licudi) seems to have coincided with the decline of the Moscow Academy at the end of the seventeenth century. A Greek school established or revived by Sofrónii Licudi in 1708 was eventually joined to the Academy in 1724 or 1725. In places other than Moscow (excluding the Ukraine) elementary education was provided by the episcopal schools at Toból'sk (from 1703 or 1704), Rostóv (between 1702 and 1709), Nóvgorod (from 1706) and Smolensk (between 1714 and 1718). The Nóvgorod school, established by the metropolitan Job, was the creation of the brothers Likhúdy after their relegation from Moscow in 1704 and ranked higher than the other two as it also provided instruction in Greek, Latin, logic and rhetoric for the more advanced pupils.[127]

The polite education available in Moscow was of practical use only in so far as it produced linguists for the *prikáz* of foreign affairs and prepared young *dvoriáne* for a period of further study or training abroad. But in the initial phase of the Great Northern War the most pressing educational concern was to organize the training of technicians – gunners, military engineers, seamen and navigators. This need was met by the setting up in Moscow in 1701 of a School of Mathematics and Navigation modelled on the Royal Mathematical School at Christ's Hospital in London. Its principal purpose was to train instructors in mathematics and navigation and to prepare qualified seamen, but it also turned out engineers, architects and artillerists as well as all manner of teachers, administrators and craftsmen. In the preparatory division Russian and ciphering (arithmetic) were taught; the abler pupils moved on to the naval division where they learnt English, algebra, geometry, trigonometry, astronomy, navigation and surveying. By 1703 the school had 200 pupils, in 1711 it slightly exceeded its complement of 500, in 1715 it had 427. The social origins of the pupils were diverse and at first fairly evenly balanced but by 1715 the sons of *dvoriáne* and of other men of service predominated. Somewhat later schools for navigators were established also at Nóvgorod, Narva and Reval. Other schools founded before 1715 likewise served the needs of the armed forces and the shortage of specialists continued to be so acute that little attention was paid to the social origins of the entrants. The Artillery School established in 1701 trained principally non-commissioned artificers rather than officers as no more than a dozen pupils ever reached the upper division of the school. The total number rose from 180 in 1701 to 300 in 1704 but by 1707 fell to 136.

In 1712 the upper division of the Artillery School was converted into a separate School of Engineering. In 1713 this new school was instructed to add to its twenty-three pupils a further seventy-seven, drawn from sundry social categories, including *dvoriáne* with up to fifty peasant holdings on their land. The Artillery School remained in being but by 1719 was on the point of dissolution. The curriculum of the School of Engineering comprised arithmetic, geometry and fortification. In 1719 all the seventy-four pupils in the School of Engineering were moved to another, higher engineering school or training company (under the command of Lieutenant-Colonel de Colong) newly established in St Petersburg, and were replaced with one hundred new entrants. The training of engineers in Moscow came to an end with the transfer to St Petersburg of this last contingent of pupils. The school at St Petersburg enjoyed a certain prestige and attracted the sons of some prominent *dvoriáne*. The need for organized medical care was likewise the product of war. In 1697 fifty surgeons were recruited in Amsterdam for service with the army and particularly with the navy; many years went by before regular medical training could begin in Russia. The ordinance establishing a medical school under the direction of Dr Nicholas Bidloo, a native of Holland, was promulgated in 1706. The enrolment of students began in 1708. Ten students took their final examination in 1712 and a further ten in 1719. The last 'vocational' school to be established under Peter I (in 1721) was a training centre to which scribes (*pod'iáchie*) were to be sent to master the skills of their trade: arithmetic, bookkeeping and handwriting. A more leisurely and also more expensive method of producing specialists was to send young men who had spent a year or more with the Jesuits or in the 'Gymnasium' or at the Moscow Academy to western Europe as apprentices or trainees.

In 1715 the dozen or so pupils still remaining in the 'Gymnasium' no longer justified its existence and the school was closed; the six teachers were transferred to the Senate, presumably for administrative duties. In the same year the seafaring and navigation division of the School of Mathematics and Navigation – 305 pupils and two teachers, Henry Farquharson and Stephen Gwyn – was transferred to St Petersburg to form the nucleus of a Naval Academy, superior in status both to the School of Mathematics and to the Academy in Moscow and comprising also a company of *gardes de la marine*. This crossing of the English tradition of naval education with the French was due to the person of the director (until 1717) of the new Academy, the baron de Saint-Hilaire. The curriculum of the Academy as published in 1719 lists arithmetic, geometry, navigation, artillery, fortification, geography, drawing, painting, musketry, fencing and some astronomy. The concluding sentence of the ordinance calls for suitable teachers to be engaged to give the necessary instruction, implying that not all of these subjects were actually being taught. An *ukáz* issued in December 1715 commanded that henceforth the sons of all persons of quality over the age of 10 were to be sent to the Naval Academy and none was to be sent to foreign lands. It appears that the persons in question obeyed the order: by 1718 the 300 places were filled and another 500 pupils attended the preparatory division of the Academy.

Although, being compulsory, education was in most cases free of charge since the pupils in any school established under official auspices received a maintenance allowance from the tsar's treasury, it was unpopular because it did not bear much relation to the abilities and inclinations of the students. When volunteers could not be found, recruits were raised for education just as they were for the armed forces or for pioneering work. Truancy was punished with the same severity as absence without leave from the army, but pupils defected from the schools just as peasants ran away from the landed estates and soldiers deserted from their regiments.[128]

The period between January 1714 and December 1715 was a critical one in the development of the tsar's educational policy. By reason of the nature of the service state education was necessarily related to the wider question of the fitness and availability for service of the *dvoriáne* which was the subject of the ordinance of 23 March 1714 on the mode of inheritance. An *ukáz* published on 20 January of that year ruled that the sons of all hereditary men of service and of men employed in the central and provincial administration must learn arithmetic and geometry (the ability to read and write thus being somewhat optimistically assumed). Instruction in these subjects was to be given by pupils of the Moscow School of Mathematics and Navigation deputed for the purpose to the *gubérnii.* Under a later *ukáz* the necessary accommodation was to be provided by the bishops and the monastic houses. What makes these ordinances so striking is not the element of compulsion, for the tsar had long assigned *dvoriáne* young and old to service or study (and in 1710 he had for the second time ordered the sons of parish clergy to attend 'the Greek and Latin schools', with the added threat of being drafted into the army), but the emphasis on numeracy and the nature of the penalty to be inflicted on the dunces: 'licence to marry will not be granted to those who have not learnt these things'. As far as the service state was concerned pre-marital instruction was to be derived from Magnítskii's *Arithmetic.* The responsibility for the application of this rule was laid on the bishops. The last and isolated phrase in the *ukáz*: 'On primacy' (i.e. primogeniture) shows that in the mind of the tsar, as in reality, education received from, and land held of, the state were associated with the paramount requirement of service.

The *ukáz* on the mode of inheritance followed two months later and in July 1715, in fulfilment of the decision taken in January 1714, the tsar forbade young *dvoriáne* to enter the Moscow Academy in preference to learning arithmetic and geometry at home or at the School of Mathematics and Navigation. Pupils at the Academy who had committed this offence and were over 16 years of age were condemned to three years of 'the galleys' – in this instance hard labour in leg-irons in the docks of St Petersburg, an alternative form of state service. However, in December 1715, soon after the establishment of the Naval Academy, the tsar changed his mind (the capacity to do so was recognized by the *Ecclesiastical Regulation* of 1721 as 'the mark of a wise man') and introduced two new principles – segregation and centralization – into his scheme for the education of the sons of the men of service, thereby nullifying and reversing his original policy: the pupils of the new Naval Academy, unlike those of the Moscow School, were to be admitted solely on grounds of parentage. In January 1716 the tsar expressly excluded *dvoriáne* from the members of social categories – clerks, scribes and 'men of other stations' – whose sons were to receive instruction in the new 'ciphering' schools to be set up in the provinces. It followed by implication that from now on the sons of *dvoriáne* were to attend only the naval or military schools in Moscow or St Petersburg. By November 1719 the only 'ciphering' school to have any pupils, twenty-five to be precise, was the one at Iaroslávl'.

When this state of affairs came to light governors and *voevódy* received orders to fill the schools immediately, without further delay. Many sons of clergy, of *posádskie liúdi* and of lower officials were dragged away from their homes to be kept in confinement and drilled in arithmetic and geometry by some half-baked alumnus of the Moscow School with little else to keep up their spirits than the prospect of being allowed to marry on the successful completion of their course. Out of 1,389 young men herded into the schoolroom between 1719 and 1722 only ninety-three received the necessary certificate from their teachers but there is no evidence to show that the matrimonial state was denied to the rejected candidates. The use of physical force in a cause so fanciful as the advancement of education raised a cry of protest from the *posádskie liúdi*. The townspeople complained to the tsar of boys between the ages of 10 and 15 being sent to distant towns and held under arrest. Normally, said the petition, such boys learn their father's trade and begin to try their hand at business; many of the subjects taught in schools they learn at home but if they are taken away to school they will be unable to gain a knowledge of trade. The fathers pay tolls and taxes in the course of their business and render service to the tsar. If they lose the help of their sons business will decline and the tsar's revenue will suffer.

The tsar allowed himself to be persuaded by these arguments. As it seemed that the sons of *posádskie liúdi* were capable of exercising their economic and administrative functions without receiving a school education he resolved that they were not to be sent to school against their will but were to be admitted if they so wished. On analogous grounds there could be no case at all for educating the peasants (though Pososhkóv thought otherwise). The degree of literacy among the *posádskie liúdi* still seemed fairly high although in Moscow at the end of the seventeenth century there had been a marked difference in this respect between the prosperous *gostínaia sótnia* with 9 per cent of (male) illiterates and two less well-to-do communities with 37 and 58 per cent. The Regulation of the Board of Civic Administration (*Glávnyi Magistrát*) promulgated in 1721 spoke of the great need for academies and schools as well as of the beneficial effects of education on the people and instructed the *magistrát* of each town to set up schools for the teaching of reading, writing and arithmetic. This injunction was repeated in 1724 with a rather stronger emphasis on the contribution of education to public utility and moral improvement but again the legislator was content to leave the initiative to the ineffectual municipalities.[129]

The *Ecclesiastical Regulation* published in 1721 instructed bishops to have in their houses or attached to their houses schools for the children of priests and others who were aspiring to the priesthood. This directive alone provided the sons of clergy and of other persons subject to the authority of the newly established Holy Synod with a valid excuse for leaving the 'ciphering schools' by the dozen well before all the diocesan schools were actually set up and before the tsar, in 1723, laid down the rules concerning the education of the sons of active parish clergy: when of school age they were to be sent to school willy-nilly in the hope that the quality of the clergy would thereby be improved. In this way education (or the lack of education) was added to hereditary status or occupation and answerability in law as a distinguishing feature of each caste-like group under the authority of the service state: clergy, *dvoriáne*, lower officials, *posádskie liúdi*, peasants. As a result of the exodus of the sons of clergy, the twenty-nine 'ciphering' schools diminished in size and importance but continued to function for another twenty years or so side by side with the diocesan schools. In addition to those already in existence (in Russia, excluding the Ukraine) some thirteen episcopal schools were established between 1721 and 1725. The school at Nóvgorod, amalgamated with the local 'ciphering' school, assumed the role of something like a teachers' training college. The Moscow Academy, probably by reason of the growing proportion of sons of clergy among its pupils, was subordinated to the *Monastýrskii prikáz* in 1718 and subsequently to the Holy Synod.[130]

As long ago as 1698 or 1699 Peter I in an interview with the Patriarch Adrian, had expressed the wish to have in Russia a school from which young men could in the ordinary course of events enter all useful walks of life – the service of the Church and of the state, the army and the professions (architecture, medicine).

The educational needs of the army and of the Church at the elementary level had been satisfied, the *Ecclesiastical Regulation* of 1721 proposed the establishment of an ecclesiastical academy, but neither the civil service nor the professions were adequately provided for. The combined effect of obligatory education for the sons of *dvoriáne*, of the law on the mode of inheritance, of the Table of Ranks and of the instructions for the chief herald was not strong enough to produce the requisite number of officials for the colleges. The restriction of appointments in the colleges to one third of the number of sons in each family proved superfluous: few if any young *dvoriáne* showed a wish to take up a career in the higher civil service.

The tsar was again obliged to resort to compulsion and in 1724 he instructed the Senate to pluck one hundred such young men from 'the various academies' and assign them to the colleges for training in administrative procedure. The gap in the educational structure was to be filled by the foundation of a secular academy in St Petersburg where, as the tsar put it, languages and other subjects would be taught and books translated. Like its location, the annual income of 24,912 roubles assigned to it (being the equivalent of the revenues from the customs in the formerly Swedish towns of Narva, Dorpat, Pernau and Arensburg in the island of Ösel) was part of the fruits of victory over Sweden. The proposals for the establishment of an academy, approved by the tsar in an ordinance published in January 1724, make no direct reference to the immediate practical considerations to which it owed its origin. In 1722 the tsar himself had ordered the chief herald to organize a course of instruction for the young *dvoriáne* selected for the civil service, pending the establishment of an academy. This had been formally recommended by Fick in 1718 in order that all appointments, civil and military, in the colleges, *gubérnii*, courts of law, chancelleries, municipalities, etc., might be filled with His Majesty's native subjects.

In their closely reasoned comparison between an academy and a university the authors of the detailed proposal submitted to the tsar rise to so exalted a level of abstract argument that for a while they lose sight of the essentially utilitarian purpose of the new institution, but they come down to earth again when they state that the Academy must be suited to the conditions obtaining in Russia. It must therefore not only bring glory to the state but also benefit the people through teaching and the dissemination of knowledge. One institution must do what in other countries is done by three: contribute to knowledge, teach students and train teachers. The tsar gave his assent to the proposals but did not live to witness, in 1725, the inauguration of the activities of the Academy.

Peter the Great did not reform the Russian educational system since no such system existed, nor did he bring one into being, but he did oblige the rising generation of clergy and *dvoriáne* – the joint progenitors of the future intelligentsia – to learn to read, write and count. The effect of this command was as radical and as far-reaching as any of Peter's major and successful reforms. The decision was forced on him by political considerations and by practical needs. A literate and numerate *dvoriánstvo* enabled the service state to win and maintain its position as a European power; a literate clergy strengthened the authority of the Church as the spiritual auxiliary of the state.[131]

The *Ecclesiastical Regulation* (*Dukhóvnyi Regláment*), ratified in February 1721, fitted the hierarchy into the framework of the service state by reorganizing the administration of the Russian Church and defining the responsibilities of its clergy. The scope and intention of the *Ecclesiastical Regulation* put it on a par with the other regulatory enactments which came to fruition in the same period: the General Regulation for the conduct of business by officials in the colleges and their subordinate agencies of February 1720, the equally ambitious though foredoomed Regulation of the Board of Civic Administration of January 1721 and the Table of Ranks of January 1722.

From the earliest years of his reign the tsar had tended to classify the clergy as a *chin* – one of the services or orders in the state – alongside the armed forces and the civil administration. This tendency, first made apparent in the course of the interview (already mentioned) between the tsar and the Patriarch Adrian, found its final expression in the preamble to the *Ecclesiastical Regulation*: 'Perceiving much disorder and great deficiency in the affairs of the ecclesiastical estate and having been granted much success in the reformation of the military order and of the civil service, we should not neglect the regulation also of the clerical estate.'

For a tsar to instruct the Church in the conduct of its affairs was to usurp the function of an ecclesiastical council (*sobór*). The preamble glosses over this irregularity by trying to create the impression that '*sobórnoe pravítel'stvo*' – conciliar government – is equivalent to a 'spiritual college'. It was Leibniz who in his memorandum on colleges had recommended the establishment also of a 'religious', that is ecclesiastical, college and this was the name given in the *Regulation* to the new administrative body. Three weeks later it received the more dignified style of Most Holy Ruling Synod and its status was raised to a level corresponding to that of the Senate. In their oath of allegiance the members of the college (Synod) swore to act in all things according to the provisions of the *Regulation* and to be loyal subjects and servants of the tsar and of the tsaritsa and, after him, of his legitimate successors. The designation of the tsar as the '*kráinii sud'iá*' of the college or Synod should be interpreted in the traditional Muscovite sense of ultimate or supreme governor or magistrate rather than 'judge' since, as Gradóvskii points out, administrators also dispensed justice (and many a *prikáz* was also a jail). In the Synodal, formerly the Patriarch's, palace in Moscow a throne was to be installed for His Imperial Majesty under a canopy of fine velvet with gold trimmings. There was no mention of a throne for the president of the Synod comparable to that which the Patriarch had occupied during the coronation ceremony side by side with the tsar in the Uspénskii cathedral in Moscow. This new piece of scenery conveniently illustrates the fundamental aim of the *Regulation* which was the very opposite of 'spiritual' (*dukhóvnyi*), namely to subordinate the Church to the state and to turn it into an instrument of worldly policy. Only a relationship of this kind could have inspired the laconic comparison in the *Regulation* of anathema to a punishment similar to death and of the interdict to the placing of a person under arrest. The *Supplement* of the *Regulation*, published in February 1722, required all newly ordained priests to take an oath of loyalty to the sovereign and to promise to disclose 'all opposition'.

The *Regulation* is divided into three parts. The first comprises a definition of an ecclesiastical college – 'not some faction but a body of individuals assembled for the sake of the common good' – and an exposition of the reasons for establishing it: from a conciliar administration the country need have no fear of a single head of the Church, 'a second sovereign, a power equal to the ruler or even greater than he'. This is a thinly veiled allusion to the Patriarch Níkon, although the examples pointed to are the history of the Eastern Empire after Justinian and the conflict between the Pope and the Emperor in the West.

The second part defines the scope of the administrative authority of the college: common matters – worship and doctrine – and matters pertaining to bishops, priests and monks, teachers and students in ecclesiastical institutions, preachers and laymen. Much space is devoted under this head by the principal draftsman of the *Regulation*, Feofán (Prokopóvich), bishop of Pskov, to the question of the religious education of the people and the training for the ministry of their pastors which the *Regulation* considers to be inadequate. In 1710 the Danish envoy, Just Juel, had noted that the tsar deplored the ignorance and backwardness of the Russian clergy and their consequent incapacity to give spiritual guidance to the people. Juel himself was of the opinion that most Russians knew nothing of their religion and that no more than one out of five could read the Lord's Prayer. It is safe to assume that the tsar's complaint on this point was not the last. It was certainly not the first. In the interview with the Patriarch Adrian (already mentioned) Peter I had objected to the ordination of priests who could barely read or write. The next twenty years do not seem to have brought much improvement, for even the *Regulation* speaks of the coarseness from which the clergy were to be delivered, and of their ignorance. For this reason the *Regulation* imposed on the bishops the duty to establish and maintain – with the income from their estates – diocesan schools for the sons of clergy and others. In addition the *Regulation* recommended the establishment of a seminary to which boys were to be admitted between the ages of 10 and 15. Some of the entrants were eventually to be chosen for rapid preferment. An ecclesiastical academy, too, was to be founded but this part of the plan was abandoned. A Slavonic or 'grammar' school was duly established at the St Alexander-Névskii monastery by its archimandrite Feodósii (Ianóvskii) in 1721 and in 1725 named the Slavonic Greek and Latin Seminary. In addition, also in 1721, Prokopóvich in his own residence in St Petersburg organized a school for orphans and sons of indigent parents where Scripture, Church Slavonic, Russian, Greek, Latin and some 'modern' subjects were taught.

The final section of this (the second) part concerns itself with laymen in so far as they were subordinate to the spiritual administration. Every Christian must hear Orthodox instruction from his pastors and receive Holy Communion often, at least once a year. 'If a Christian appears to abstain from Holy Communion a great deal, he thereby reveals himself to be . . . a schismatic.' The directives given to the clergy by the civil authorities in 1716 and 1718 were now reiterated and clarified: priests were to report parishioners who stayed away from Communion to the bishops and the bishops in turn to the civil authorities.

Part III treats of the duties and responsibilities of the college (Synod) which was to consist of eleven members drawn from the higher orders of the ministry including the bishops. Like several of the other colleges it exercised jurisdiction over the particular social category corresponding to its scope, acting as an ecclesiastical court of appeal empowered to reverse the judgment passed by bishops on clerics or on inhabitants of ecclesiastical estates. The Holy Synod exercised general jurisdiction over all members of the clergy in the first instance. Clerics were to be handed over to the civil authorities only on charges of felony or crimes against the state, after being unfrocked by the Synod. In civil actions they were answerable before the appropriate college – the Board of Trade in commercial matters, or the *Kámer-kollégiia* in fiscal matters. Thus after a period during which (despite the existence of the *Monastýrskii prikáz*) clerics had suffered the indignity of being hauled before all manner of *prikázy* and *kantseliárii* they regained some degree of the immunity from civil jurisdiction which had been granted to them in 1669. On the other hand, some offences previously tried by ecclesiastical courts, including blasphemy committed in public and 'persistent display of non-conformity', were now subject to the jurisdiction of the civil authorities. The process of secularization of Russian society was thus associated with the constant increase in the power of the state. In the *Supplement* to the *Regulation* detailed rules were laid down for the reformation of the parish clergy and of monastic life. The section on monasteries recommends the amalgamation of small houses so that communities should not number fewer than thirty monks. No new monasteries were to be built without the consent of the Synod.

As well as introducing new measures the *Ecclesiastical Regulation* sanctioned and consolidated those which had been introduced piecemeal during the two preceding decades and had stood the test of time. In at least one respect, that of the ecclesiastical landed estates, the *Regulation* consummates a policy favoured by Iván IV and finally laid down in the *Code* of Alekséi Mikháilovich. Iván IV had forbidden men of service to make gifts to large monasteries lest service to the sovereign be curtailed and land go out of service. The *Code* of 1649 forbade the monasteries and the clergy to acquire any more *vótchiny* by any means whatever but Tsar Alekséi himself later not only made gifts of land to monasteries and to the Patriarch but also made provision for the allocation of estates (*pomést'ia*) to the clergy in the south-eastern borderlands. At the same time, however, by putting an end to the exemption of the monasteries from the payment of tolls and taxes in respect of their economic activities and by requesting financial contributions from the monasteries in times of need, he helped to establish the notion that it was the monasteries that were under an obligation to the state rather than vice versa. Peter I erected this notion into a principle, acted on it consistently and never ceased to show his hostility towards monasticism.[132]

The Patriarch Adrian was still alive in 1696 when Tsar Peter directed the *prikáz* of the tsar's palace to supply information about the annual expenditure of monasteries and episcopal households and forbade further spending on building without the tsar's consent. In 1698 the tsar instructed the *voevóda* of Verkhotúr'e (in western Siberia) not to pay any stipends to heads of monasteries which held *pomést'ia* and made the general observation that monasteries levied not a little grain and money from the peasants on monastic lands, but where this money went and how it was spent, nobody knew. In 1699 the tsar decreed that no remuneration in cash or kind was to be paid to any members of the clergy, regular or secular, who were in possession of land or any other source of income. An *ukáz* issued in 1701 decreed that monks were to receive a uniform stipend in money and grain.

In October 1700 the Patriarch died and in January 1701 a department of state for church affairs in all their aspects – religious, judicial and economic – was established under the familiar name of *Monastýrskii prikáz*. Its scope and powers were more extensive than those of its earlier namesake and its principal purpose, too, was different: to release the grip of the dead hand on ecclesiastical property and seize control of the income derived from it. The *prikáz* was to take over the administration of the estates belonging to the Patriarch, the bishops and the monasteries in order to subject them to the regular collection of ordinary taxes and, in due course, of special imposts and levies. A part of the net revenue was to be retained to meet the essential needs of the hierarchy, the rest was to be allocated to purposes traditionally associated with the social function of the Church – education and corporal works of mercy; any surplus was to be handed over to the tsar's treasury to subsidize the cost of the war. The special imposts levied on the section of the population answerable to the *Monastýrskii prikáz* were many and various and give the impression of having been exceptionally heavy. Thus a regiment of dragoons formed in 1706 was to be recruited and maintained entirely from the revenues of the *prikáz*. Since priests and deacons were exempt from conscription it fell to them to contribute (in grain) towards the cost of the pay of the dragoon regiments in which they would otherwise be serving together with the majority of conscripts. In 1707 the urban clergy were ordered to supply the dragoons with one horse (or its equivalent in cash) for every 300 households in their parishes. Both taxes were gathered annually until 1724.

In the early years of its renewed existence the *Monastýrskii prikáz* was charged with the care of destitute vagrants. These economic casualties of everyday life were soon outnumbered by sick, wounded and crippled soldiers and the wives or widows of soldiers without means of support. From 1706 the responsibility for the placing of war victims in hospices rested with the *Monastýrskii prikáz*. Gradually the *prikáz* was called upon to provide for the armed forces a regular though rudimentary medical and social service. From 1709 it was directly responsible for the management of hospices; in 1712 this growing burden was eased somewhat by the *prikáz* being relieved of the care of ordinary paupers in Moscow; in 1714 the fee for solemnizing marriages was doubled and allocated to the upkeep of hospitals ('*lazarettos*') and the maintenance of invalids in hospices or monasteries; from 1719 permanently disabled soldiers and sailors were placed in monasteries; in 1723 the tsar ruled that if the necessary room or funds were lacking the admission of novices to monasteries was to be suspended. The hospital and the hospital school, as well as the other schools in Moscow (except the naval and military ones) were supported from funds provided by the *Monastýrskii prikáz*, and so was the printing press.

The *prikáz* – when it was not overridden by other authorities – also dispensed justice in civil and criminal cases to all the persons, whether laymen or clerics, subordinate to it; but any such persons proceeded against members of other social groups in *prikázy* or courts appropriate to the status of the defendant. In its handling of ecclesiastical property the *prikáz* was often moved by considerations other than the best interests of the Church. Monastic estates were unceremoniously handed over to other departments, assigned to military units, sequestrated on behalf of the tsar or granted in perpetuity to deserving individuals. In 1710 the *prikáz* attempted to take over entirely the administration of some ecclesiastical estates together with their revenues; fixed maintenance grants were allocated to eighty monasteries and stipends to fifteen out of the twenty-eight bishops, but the experiment proved unsuccessful; the episcopal estates were handed back to the bishops in 1716 and monastic estates were likewise being restored even before 1720. In that year the process of reversion was officially sanctioned subject to the payment of tax and the discharge of financial obligations previously imposed by the secular authorities, such as the maintenance of the diocesan schools.

In 1720, when the *Monastýrskii prikáz* was temporarily suppressed and its fiscal functions were taken over by the *Kámer-kollégiia*, the number of holdings (*dvorý*) on ecclesiastical estates was estimated at about 150,000. This figure is hard to reconcile with that of 118,000 given above for 1678. Either the figures are incorrect, or the assumption that the amount of land held by the hierarchy declined sharply during the subsequent twenty years or so is false. Throughout his reign, having made the rule that monasteries must not acquire any more land, Peter I broke it only in exceptional circumstances, as when he allocated some estates confiscated from Mazepa for the upkeep of the monastery of the Transfiguration at Rzhíshchev in the region of Kiev. The monastery of St Alexander Névskii and of the Holy Trinity, founded in St Petersburg between 1710 and 1712, was endowed with land detached from other monasteries. In his attempt to reduce the number of clergy – which he considered to be excessive – the tsar was less successful. The exemption from the poll-tax covered not only active and officially attested priests but also their sons who could be expected in due course to present themselves for ordination. In consequence, although after Peter the Great's death the number of churches did not increase greatly – from 15,761 in 1722 to 16,901 in 1738, – the number of clergy rose disproportionately in the same period from 61,111 to 124,923. The number of monks and nuns on the other hand fell from 25,207 to 14,282.

After being suppressed in 1720 the *Monastýrskii prikáz* was revived for the second time upon the establishment of the Holy Synod. As one of the several agencies set up by the Synod with a view to rationalizing the central ecclesiastical administration, the *prikáz* continued to collect taxes and supply services from the estates under its control, to assign military invalids to monasteries and again provided hospices for the poor. Its judicial functions were restricted to civil jurisdiction over the secular inhabitants of ecclesiastical estates – employees and peasants. The process of assimilating the organization of the central bodies of the ecclesiastical to those of the civil administration moved into the next stage in 1724 when the *Monastýrskii prikáz* was replaced by a *Kámer-kontóra* of the Holy Synod 'after the model of the *Kámer-kollégiia*' (Board of Revenue). In 1726 the administration of ecclesiastical estates was delegated to a *Kollégiia èkonómii* under the Synod.[133]

The protests voiced by individuals at all levels of the hierarchy were too isolated to prevent the clergy as a whole from acquiescing in the changes introduced into the Church by the tsar and by the *Monastýrskii prikáz*. By 1711 Peter I was able to declare that he considered himself fortunate in having in one respect excelled Louis XIV: 'I have imposed peace and obedience on my clergy.' Three years before he had curtly informed Stefán (Iavórskii), the metropolitan of Riazán', that Mazepa, having abandoned Orthodoxy (which was not the case), had defected to the Swedish heretics, and ordered Stefán to anathematize the hetman. The anathematization of enemies of the state under pressure from the Crown had a long history in Russia and so Mazepa duly joined the company of Timoféi Ankudínov (the self-styled son of Vasílii Shúiskii), the false Dimítrii and Stepán Rázin. All four were solemnly cursed on the first Sunday in Lent, Ankudínov and Rázin till 1766, Dimítrii and Mazepa till 1869. In 1712, in a sermon, Iavórskii protested against the offensive conduct of the fiscal officers who exercised so much power over him and his judicial *prikáz* that, without having any evidence to support their calumnies, they were free to dishonour and denounce any cleric they pleased and to do so with impunity. 'What kind of a law is that?', asked Iavórskii, and in a letter addressed to the tsar he made his point quite clear: 'I said that the presence of fiscal officers in an episcopal court was both unwonted and improper.' But the metropolitan's wish to lay down his office and retire to a monastery was not granted and Stefán continued to bow to the tsar's will. The creation, in 1721, of purely ecclesiastical fiscal officers under chief inquisitors in Moscow and St Petersburg and inquisitors in the provinces may have owed something to this passage of arms.[134]

Soon the tsar himself began to encroach on strictly ecclesiastical territory. In 1714, two years before making literacy a prerequisite of marriage for the pupils of the ciphering schools, he ruled that the sons of *dvoriáne* must not marry before the age of 20 and their daughters before the age of 17. As if in anticipation of the official pronouncement of 1721 John Perry described the tsar as the Head and Governor of his Church as early as 1716; in the same year the tsar justified the description by instructing the metropolitan of Riazán' to add some points to the oath taken by the bishops on their consecration and to have those who were already in office sworn in again. The seven points do not form a coherent whole but merely list those abuses which the tsar considered to be in urgent need of correction, namely: arbitrary and collective excommunication; the lack of gentleness and persuasiveness in the treatment of the opponents of Holy Church (in other words the Old Believers, an attitude soon to be abandoned by the tsar himself); the tendency of monks to wander from monastery to monastery and even to lodge in private houses; the multiplication of priests, monks and other clergy in excess of genuine need; the failure of bishops to carry out regular visitations and to stamp out dissent; superstition and the performance of irregular rites; interference of the hierarchy in secular affairs. The ordinance on the duties of the chief inquisitor issued by the Synod in 1721 shows its overlord's continuing lack of confidence in the bishops who were evidently suspected of all kinds of misdemeanour, dereliction of duty and abuse of authority such as simony, favouritism, money-grubbing, embezzlement and the toleration of schismatics. After the *Ecclesiastical Regulation* had formally proclaimed the tsar the supreme governor of the Church he threatened any person who would dare to oppose the statute on the succession to the throne with capital punishment and anathema and interfered in such sacerdotal matters as the length of the marriage service and the style of icons.

The clergy, on the other hand, were expected to submit to the interference of the civil power as well as to perform a variety of ancillary duties for the secular authorities. As far as Peter I was concerned a church was a place where the word of God is heard and the will of the tsar announced by the reading of ordinances from the pulpit. In 1710 parish priests were expected to testify that no young *dvoriáne* liable for service or runaway peasants were hiding in their parishes; in 1716 the clergy were commanded to supply to the civil authorities the names of men and women who did not go to confession at least once a year and could therefore be suspected of being Old Believers. The parish priest was thus cast in the double role of ghostly father and government informer. His position was made even more invidious when the *Supplement* to the *Ecclesiastical Regulation* ordered priests to inform the authorities also of a penitent's intention to commit an act of treason or rebellion against the sovereign or the state. An ordinance promulgated in 1719 ordered the priest of each parish to be present at the collection of the poll-tax (by the *zémskii komissár*) and to testify that all the tax had been collected; from 1724 the document granting leave of absence to a peasant could, in place of his landlord (*poméshchik*), be issued by a bailiff or by the parish priest.

During the formal vacancy in the patriarchal see the authority exercised by Tsar Peter within the Church was similar to that of a Byzantine emperor who, in virtue of his unique position as the chief representative of the laity, the embodiment of civil power and the secular counterpart of the patriarch, was bound to enforce and maintain first and foremost all that is set out in the Holy Scriptures. In 1721, the year in which the *Ecclesiastical Regulation* was pro-mulgated, this attitude was changed to an Erastian approach to the relationship between Church and state. In July of that year, as if to prepare the doctrinal ground for subjecting the Church to the authority of the tsar, his chief adviser on ecclesiastical affairs, Feofán (Prokopóvich), bishop of Pskov, published a treatise in which he obliquely described the tsar's position as that of 'episcopus episcoporum' on the grounds that the supremacy of the sovereign was instituted by God over the spiritual as well as over the secular order. This new interpre-tation of the tsar's status may, after a pause, have encouraged Peter I to try his hand at church history and theology and, with the aid of an ecclesiastical 'ghost' (almost certainly Prokopóvich), to pontificate at some length on the subject of monachism in a veritable diatribe cast in the form of an ordinance promulgated in January 1724. The examination of the evidence leads the tsar to the grudging conclusion that monasteries are desirable in so far as they accommodate those who genuinely seek the monastic life. From among their number bishops are appointed, for such is the ancient custom. The tsar took this opportunity formally to reserve for himself the final decision in the future appointment of bishops and abbots. He denounced the taking of monastic vows by peasants as a threefold dereliction of their obligations: in relation to their own households, the state and their landlords (*poméshchiki*). The majority of monks being wastrels and idlers, a way had to be found to make their life pleasing to God and no longer a disgrace in the eyes of men. Service to the destitute, to the aged and to orphans was the answer.[135]

In 1722 the tsar appointed an *óber-prokurór* with instructions to supervise the proceedings of the Synod just as the *generál-prokurór* supervised those of the Senate. The first holder of the office was Colonel I. V. Bóltin, hitherto the commander of a dragoon regiment. The appearance of this uniformed figure amongst the bearded and cassocked members of the Synod may not have come as a shock to those who recalled the presence in the ecclesiastical administration before 1667 of laymen designated by the tsar. The first *óber-prokurór* failed to exercise the high degree of vigilance expected of him by the service state. In 1725 it became known that the archbishop of Nóvgorod and vice-president of the Synod Feodósii (Ianóvskii) was complaining of the late tsar's tyranny over the Church and of the exclusion of the Synod from state affairs. For having omitted to lay information against Feodósii, Bóltin was relegated to Siberia 'without duties to perform'.[136]

The numerous references in the *Ecclesiastical Regulation* to the Old Believers show how perturbed the authorities were at the continuing existence of the schism and give some idea of the measures adopted to bring it under control. The reintegration of the schismatics 'envenomed to fury by coarseness and ignorance' is listed together with the health and glory of the all-powerful monarch, seasonable weather and abundant harvests as an intention of public prayers to be offered by the bishops in the course of their visitations. Recurrent abstention from Holy Communion was, as before, to be taken as the mark of a crypto-schismatic. The bishops were to order the parish priests to report to them the names of such abstainers who could then be required to declare under oath that they were true sons of the Church and condemned 'all the schismatic cohorts to be found throughout Russia'. Ordinands must likewise reprobate all schismatic sects, swear not to turn a blind eye to any Old Believers in their parishes and to inform the civil authorities of any sign of disloyalty to the Church and state. Any person who harboured teachers of schismatic doctrines or gave alms to schismatic hermitages could properly be suspected of being an Old Believer himself. Any matters arising from the denunciation of a schismatic were to be dealt with by the Ecclesiastical College (i.e. the Synod). All schismatics were implacable foes of the state and of the sovereign and no schismatic must therefore be appointed to any position of authority, however modest. In other words, dissent from the official church amounted to opposition to the service state and could not be tolerated.

It was clear from these elaborate instructions that Old Belief was no nearer to extinction than it had been in the previous reign when Sófia Alekséevna had threatened any heretics who refused to renounce their beliefs under torture with burning at the stake and their harbourers with the knout and banishment.

Many possible victims of this onslaught forestalled the authorities by setting fire to themselves, others sought refuge in remote corners of the land or abroad, on Polish or Swedish territory.

The adherents of Old Belief which, it will be recalled, was the product of a schism, were themselves, from about 1685, divided into two broad groups – the *popóvtsy* and the *bespopóvtsy* or sacerdotalists and non-sacerdotalists (both of which were soon to split into sects in their turn). The first group preserved the sacraments and for their administration used priests who came over from the official Church; the second, having severed all links with the Church, kept only baptism and confession, the one administered, the other heard, by laymen.

The Old Believers' expectations of the second coming of Christ and of the end of the world were not fulfilled in the Apocalyptic year of 1660 nor yet again in 1701. In the following year the tsar ordered his subjects to shear off their beards. This ominous assault on one of the most cherished symbols of the Muscovite way of life caused particular distress to the Old Believers. After the outbreak of the war with Sweden, as the tsar's military machine and the construction of St Petersburg swallowed up seemingly unending quantities of treasure and human lives, it was borne in on some mystically minded Old Believers that the reign of Antichrist had already begun in spirit and that the downfall of the new Babylon was at hand. From Tsar Peter's point of view at that time and even later, the Old Believers were simply religious dissenters. As champion and defender of the Church the tsar was in duty bound to protect it from heresy but Peter I was disinclined to engage in religious persecution. 'Let them live' was the phrase he is said to have used in 1704 in speaking about the community on the Vyg. No allusion seems to have been intended to the practice of self-cremation which he was later to condemn in the most emphatic terms.

But in the long run a clash was inevitable. The policy of modernization which the tsar resumed in 1714 ran entirely counter to the wishes of the Old Believers who longed for the restoration of the Muscovite tradition in state and Church yet were witnessing the very opposite. They now believed – together with some conservatively minded conformist church-goers – that Antichrist was none other than Tsar Peter himself. If that was the case then the body of Old Believers – backward-gazing, suspicious of the hierarchy and of officialdom and inclined towards self-government – was the antithesis of the Russian Empire in the making. In the eyes of the powers that be the schismatics, though dispersed and heterogeneous, constituted the only identifiable movement of political dissent in the country. Old Belief, heterodox in politics as well as in religion, appealed to the victims and opponents of the presiding deity of the new Babylon. Many of those who left its precincts to join the Old Believers in the wilderness were as strongly actuated by their dissatisfaction with the new order as they were attached or attracted to the old ritual. The Old Believers' determination to resist change found expression in word and deed. As anonymous flysheets circulated in Moscow thousands of potential taxpayers and recruits continued to flee from the central areas to the periphery, hundreds chose to set fire to themselves rather than fall into the hands of the tsar's officials.

The population at large could not be relied upon to support the authorities in their efforts to stamp out Old Belief. Indeed, many members of the official Church were sympathetic towards the Old Believers and willing to protect them for a consideration or disinterestedly, not least because their way of life, free from official constraint and marked by a high degree of solidarity and self-reliance, presented an alternative to the acceptance of the straitjacket of bureaucratic rule. The tsar was now obliged to prevent the schismatics from gaining even more ground but acted with restraint. In accordance with the advice offered by Pitirím, the superior of the Pereiaslávskii monastery (at Pereiaslávl'-Zalésskii) and a former Old Believer, the Church through its clergy was to use persuasion to bring the Old Believers back into the fold while the civil authorities were to apply the fiscal screw.

Some time in 1714 Peter I approved the principle of doubling the rate of tax levied on Old Believers everywhere but near the borders. The appropriate ordinance was interpreted as covering the Old Believer settlements in the region of Starodúb as well as those on the Vyg, not far from the Swedish frontier. In his treatment of both communities the tsar had adopted a tolerant attitude but not entirely from disinterested motives. The members of the Vyg community, in exchange for not being molested, supplied iron ore (and later also limestone) to the works at Povenéts at the head of Lake Onéga; the Old Believers at Starodúb had to be humoured because they occupied an area whose strategic importance became apparent during Charles XII's eastward advance in September 1708. They could have shown their dissatisfaction at that moment by moving across the border to reinforce the community of émigré dissenters at Vétka.

Before a tax could be collected at the double rate it was necessary to identify those who were to pay it. To this end in 1716 the parish priests were instructed to draw up lists of those among their parishioners whom they knew to be Old Believers, as well as those who did not go to confession at least once a year. The lists had to be returned to the *prikáz* of Church affairs (*tserkóvnykh del*) in Moscow and did not serve fiscal ends alone. Armed with this information the functionaries of the Office for the Investigation of Schismatic Affairs (*Rozysknáia raskól'nich'ikh del kantseliáriia*, established in 1716) would seek out unregistered Old Believers as well as those who refused to pay the double tax and without trial inflict on them imprisonment, torture, the knout, excision of the nostrils and terms of banishment with hard labour (*kátorga*). The unenviable responsibility of pronouncing on the heterodoxy or orthodoxy of a man's religion lay with the parish priest in his character of father confessor. Those of his parishioners who did not go to confession regularly incurred a fine as did couples who contracted a marriage outside the official Church. Evidently the civil authorities were not bound by the tsar's recommendation to the bishops to exercise mildness in dealing with Old Believers and it was not long before Peter I himself changed his attitude.

From 1718 the *posádskie liúdi* were no longer allowed to nominate Old Believers for the higher official duties, such as the collection of revenue which they were obliged to render to the state. The reason for this ban was not that such men were considered to be dishonest but that they were apparently given to using positions of authority to exert pressure on members of the established Church and on converted Old Believers to hinder the work of conversion.

These adverse circumstances, however, so far from making the schismatics see the error of their ways, confirmed them in their belief in the righteousness of their cause. The non-conformists declared the census ordered in 1719 in preparation for the introduction of the poll-tax to be anti-Christian and called on the people at large not to allow themselves to be registered but to flee from the command of Antichrist. The efforts of the hierarchy to bring the Old Believers back into the fold were neither persistent nor widespread enough to be successful. The outstanding exception in this respect was the aforementioned Pitirím. As bishop of Nízhnii Nóvgorod from 1719 he was credited with the conversion of over 100,000 Old Believers in his eparchy by 1724. In the same year he was rewarded for his pains by being advanced to the dignity of archbishop. The total number of Old Believers towards the end of the reign of Peter I cannot even be estimated because although out of twenty-two dioceses nineteen did respond to the Synod's request to supply lists of schismatics, only four returns appear to have been at all reliable. Besides, the lists could not have thrown any light on the number of unregistered Old Believers who had been driven underground.

In the spring of 1722 the Synod drew up a programme for the reintegration of the schismatics by the use of systematic repression and discrimination. Communities of Old Believers were to be forcibly deprived of their priests or religious teachers; schismatic priests were forbidden to administer baptism and the children of Old Believers were to be baptized into the official Church; the validity of marriages contracted by old Believers outside the official Church was not to be recognized. The programme did not differ in its essence from the earlier treatment of the *raskól'niki* by the hierarchy under Peter I but it was carried out by the Synod with such vigour and intensity that it again assumed the proportions of persecution. The agencies instrumental in this campaign were the Office of Inquisitional Affairs (*Prikáz inkvizitsiónnykh del*, established in 1721 in St Petersburg but later moved to Moscow) which took over from the *prikáz* of Church affairs the responsibility for the supervision of ecclesiastical persons, and the already mentioned Office for the Investigation of Schismatic Affairs in Moscow, succeeded in 1725 by a bureau named *Raskól'nicheskaia kontóra.* The means of coercion remained the same: torture, corporal punishment, *kátorga.* The tsar and the Synod vied with one another in devising new means of breaking the morale of the Old Believers. In 1721 the Synod conceived the idea of ordering the entire population to take an oath of orthodoxy and treating all recusants as schismatics, but it abandoned the scheme in 1723; in 1722 the tsar ordered all Old Believers and their wives to wear a distinctive and grotesque attire.

Harassed and humiliated though they were, the Old Believers remained steadfast in their refusal to conform to the practices of the established Church. Their resistance could not but be regarded as a continuing threat to the security of the service state and mistaken for one of the principal causes of the prevailing disaffection of which it was a major symptom. The Synod took care not to hurl any invectives at the Old Believers themselves and reserved its strictures for their religious teachers, 'obdurate men', guilty of leading astray simple-minded folk for their own sordid gain.[137]

IV

The Economic Base

Taxation

The ravages of tax collection. Its organization. Peter's attitude towards the peasants and agriculture. Criticism of the Board of Revenue and of the poll-tax. The poll-tax and the census (1715–24). The revision of the census by the military (1721–4). The militarization of the government. The effect of the poll-tax on the urban communities. The Glávnyi Magistrát *or Board of Civic Administration (1721). The fruits of the Petrine* Polizeystaat.

Pososhkóv was as much concerned with the sources of spiritual as of material wealth and it is to these that we must now turn. One of the aims of good government or government for the common good by means of the collegiate system and its appendages was to create conditions in which revenue could be raised without ruining the population and putting large sections of it to flight. Perry observes that in Russia 'the reckoning value of any village or estate is not according to the extent of land that belongs to it but to the number of inhabitants or slaves there are upon it'.[138] Land without peasants was as useless to the *poméshchik* – the landlord – whose needs they supplied in labour and in kind as it was to the tsar, who knew as well as his officials that 'when the peasants flee and desert the land, the tsar's revenue falls short in consequence'. Yet desertion was the only effective defence that the taxpaying categories of the population – the peasants and the *posádskie liúdi* – could put up against excessive taxation by the state, exploitation by the landlord or his steward and the extortion and malfeasance practised by officialdom. In the countryside the tsar's revenue and the condition of his subjects suffered as much harm from the activities of the predatory and outlandishly named *landráty* and their assistants (among whom, according to Weber, an honest collector was as rare as a four-leaved clover) as they had experienced from 'the vitiated temper and injudicious administration of the boyars' observed by Perry in the previous decade. In Moscow the exaction of taxes and services drove many *posádskie liúdi*, especially the poorer ones, from their quarters and caused them to seek powerful patrons or change their occupations.

Thus the process of internal migration which had begun in the seventeenth century continued to gather momentum and absorbed ever greater numbers. Peasants were fleeing in their thousands, often in large parties, even from places in the basin of the Oká and in the region to the south of the middle Volga which in the later seventeenth century had been populated by runaways. Of the 353,000 male migrants in the first two decades of the eighteenth century 200,000 or 54 per cent are believed to have been runaways. The new migrants took refuge with landlords who were less demanding and, above all, able to offer more effective protection from the tax-collector; or removed to the Ukraine, to the outlying regions of the south-east or to the Urals (south-western Siberia); or else took to a life of casual employment, begging or brigandage in town or country, beyond the reach of legitimate authority. The ironworks in the Urals also attracted many 'disaffected *posádskie liúdi*'.

Whilst physical mobility produced a certain degree of social mobility and, in strictly numerical terms, one region's loss was another's gain, depopulation left agricultural land lying fallow, endangered public security and depleted the ranks of the taxpayers. As may be seen from the instructions for the prevention of depopulation issued to the new administrative officers in the provinces, the tsar's government realized that its pecuniary difficulties, when not caused by irresponsible landlords, were to a large extent of its own making and capable of being overcome by its own efforts. There is good reason to believe that the tsar's aides who in the decisive year of 1719 began to reshape the judiciary and the civil administration were acting on the assumption that once the new system had been set in motion and animated by the spirit of *Polizey* – that soul of civil government – it would in the natural course of events create conditions conducive to good husbandry. It is clear, however, from the evidence supplied by Pososhkóv that despite their many determined efforts, the central authorities did not succeed in satisfying the basic condition of effective government which is the exercise of adequate control over its own agents in the provinces. In their inefficiency the colleges or boards in charge of financial affairs resembled a free-running engine.[139]

Out of the eleven colleges functioning in 1720 two – the War Office and the Admiralty – were heavy spenders of revenue and three were concerned with its collection – the *Kámer-kollégiia* (Board of Revenue), the *Shtáts-kontór-kollégiia* (Board of State Expenditure) and the *Revizión-kollégiia* (Board of the Audit). To this number should be added the *Glávnyi magistrát* or Board of Civic Administration which collected the taxes and assigned the services due from the urban population (*posádskie liúdi*). The functions of the three first-named colleges were closely interconnected. In theory at any rate the *Kámer-kollégiia* examined the estimates of expenditure prepared by the *Shtáts-kontór-kollégiia* and after careful scrutiny of the needs of the other government departments assigned to them various portions of the moneys accumulated in the coffers of the collectors-cum-treasurers – the *rent-méisters* in each province. The task of the *Revizión-kollégiia* was to examine the accounts of the *Kámer-kollégiia* and *Shtáts-kontór-kollégiia* and exercise general control over the whole sphere of financial administration.

The *Kámer-kollégiia*'s appointed agent in each district was the *zémskii komissár*. His task – to name only his principal duties – was to impose all taxes and services due from the population, to collect all revenues except customs and excise and hand over the proceeds to the *rent-méister*, to account each month and at the end of each year for these sums to the *zémskaia kontóra* (the agency of the *Kámer-kollégiia* in each province), to raise conscripts for the army or for public works, to maintain roads and bridges and to police the countryside, if necessary with the aid of special constables elected by the peasantry. The *zémskii komissár*'s instructions (which were incomplete, having never been supplemented with the promised additions) forbade him to take any part in the administration of justice but in practice it was he who settled any disputes arising from the restitution of runaway peasants to their rightful masters. The *zémskii komissár* was in turn responsible to the *kamerír*, the supervisor of the collection of revenue in each province, likewise appointed by the *Kámer-kollégiia* and the administrative head of the *zémskaia kontóra* mentioned above. The *kamerír* acted in co-operation with the local *voevóda* (prefect) or *gubernátor* (governor) and, among other things, ensured that the army garrisons in the province received their pay and provisions; he also superintended the purchase of food and forage for the army as a whole.

The involvement of the *Kámer-kollégiia* through its officers in the administration of rural areas (but not of the towns which were shortly to come under the aegis of the *Glávnyi Magistrát*) emphasizes the essentially fiscal purpose of the newly reformed administrative machine whose ultimate object was to furnish the armed forces with money, supplies and men. Its smooth running was to be ensured by regulations drawn up for the guidance of officials in the provinces and in their subdivisions and, apart from day-to-day instructions, by an elaborate system of bookkeeping and accounting which Pososhkóv condemned as unnecessarily cumbersome. The model as a whole with its theoretical premises and practical aims lay beyond his purview and was probably beyond his grasp, but he saw clearly enough and describes vividly the ruinous and wasteful operations of the agents of the *Kámer-kollégiia* in the countryside.

In the peasants, whose wealth Pososhkóv identifies with that of the tsar and his realm, Peter I saw little more than a source of revenue and regarded the land principally as a place for quartering troops; he underestimated the economic potential of agriculture and paid little attention to its improvement. Only in the hungry year of 1723 did he order the establishment of a special office in the *Kámer-kollégiia* with instructions to compile and submit annual reports on the state of the harvest in various parts of the country, to inquire into the possibility of setting up corn magazines from which the people could be supplied in times of shortage and to encourage the peasants to fertilize their soil more liberally and to grow more grain. In the previous year the tsar had found it necessary to order the *Kámer-kollégiia* to set an upper limit on the price of foodstuffs. There is no evidence to show that any of these measures bettered the lot of the rural population. It is all the more surprising to find the tsar declaring in 1724, evidently after a change of heart, that just as the arteries nourish the human body, so the countrymen nourish the state and must therefore be cared for and not overburdened.

Although the Regulation of the *Kámer-kollégiia* gives the impression of having been drawn up (in December 1719) in accordance with the principles of cameral science, it was severely criticized some four years later by a member of that board, one Kochius, for its failure to give an adequate notion of cameral matters as a whole, to distinguish between their various categories and different needs with regard to organization, administration and accounting, to prescribe any procedure or lay down any priorities and, finally, to instruct in their duties those for whose guidance it was intended. Kochius believed that the inadequacy of the Regulation and the consequent lack of method in the workings of the *Kámer-kollégiia* were to blame for the already noticeable decline in its status and the reduction in the range of its functions, some of which had been taken over by other government departments and by the army.

The real reasons, however, for the disappointment experienced by Kochius and his colleagues were rather more complex than mere administrative mismanagement. The preamble of the Regulation of the *Kámer-kollégiia* asserts – no doubt with the tsar's acquiescence – that no fiscal burden is unbearable provided that the state which imposes it observes the principles of equity (*právda*), uniformity and appropriateness in the management of its taxation and expenditure. No taxpayer must be compelled to pay more or to be allowed to pay less than he ought, lest the oppressed poor abandon their dwellings and ploughlands, thereby causing a disastrous decrease in the public revenue – a view also expressed independently by Pososhkóv. The same document declares that a cadastral survey, that is, a survey of the country's human as well as material resources, is the sole true and correct basis of all taxation and expenditure. Moreover, the Regulation affirms, the physical nature of, and the conditions peculiar to, the various provinces must be taken into account in assessing the paying capacity of their inhabitants. Kochius makes essentially the same point in saying that a direct tax should be proportionate to the taxpayer's income and the same belief underlies Pososhkóv's argument in favour of a general land-tax. Both writers, the first by implication, the second explicitly, were attacking the *podúshnaia pódat'* or poll-tax which, after much preparatory work, was collected for the first time in 1724.[140]

The *podúshnaia pódat'* fits Montesquieu's description of a capitation tax as being more proper to servitude than to freedom. It appears to have been the tsar's own answer to the problem of raising the funds required for the upkeep of his armed forces without at the same time overburdening the taxpayer. The character of the poll-tax underlines the discrepancy between the enlightened intentions of the Regulation of the *Kámer-kollégiia* and the actual policy of the government, between the ideals of the disciples of the cameralists and the brutal pragmatism of the head of the service state. The fundamental economic question which never ceased to preoccupy the tsar and his advisers was not how to spare the taxpayer but at first how to pay for the war – and later how to dispose and maintain the army in peacetime. The tsar began to cast about for a solution of this problem in 1715, well before he had come to envisage a wholly collegiate system of administration. The disadvantage of the *podvórnoe oblozhénie*, the system of taxation by household and landholding, had long become obvious; as Pososhkóv points out, the *dvor* was not an absolute unit but one whose size depended on a variety of circumstances, including the arbitrary decision of a particular landlord. As early as 1714 the then *óber-fiskál* A. Ia. Nésterov advised the division of the required sum by the number of taxpayers; in 1715 the tsar instructed General Ia. V. Brius to discover how these things were done in Sweden. In 1717 references appear in the tsar's papers to the provision of quarters as well as to the payment of a contribution by the population. In November 1718 the following edict was promulgated: 'Calculate how many peasants are required to support one private soldier and the proportionate number of officers and NCO's in each regiment, taking an average figure, i.e., not more than is possible and not less than is proper.' Thus the poll-tax was born, descended directly from the traditional Muscovite method of levying the required sum on one or more categories of the population, regardless of the paying capacity of the individuals concerned, and distantly related to the Swedish system of *Roteringsvärk* under which evenly sized groups of the rural population assumed responsibility for recruiting and maintaining the rank and file of the infantry. The Petrine system had the virtue of simplicity but, as it later turned out, only the semblance of fairness.

According to the results of the most recent researches the total population of Russia in 1719 numbered 14.9 million. To this figure should be added the 500,000 inhabitants of the Baltic territories and the 100,000 non-Russians in Siberia. It is estimated that the total of 14.9 million was made up of 13 million peasants, 600,000 townspeople and 1,300,000 landholders, clergy and military personnel. Tsar Peter's government lacked this information.

Before the new system could be put into effect a census had to be taken of all male peasants and *posádskie liúdi* with the double object of compiling a tax roll and ascertaining the number of peasants in each region so as to match the quantity of troops to be quartered there with the size of the host population. On this score too the new administrative organization was found wanting inasmuch as it failed to complete the census by January 1720, as instructed. This time-limit was later extended to July but by the end of 1720 the work was still unfinished despite the tsar's command to chain the dilatory compilers of the return to their desks. In January 1721 in anticipation of the peace with Sweden two regiments were quartered by way of experiment in the province of Nóvgorod but the necessary statistical data were still lacking. The census, nominally completed in the spring of the same year, was found to be grossly inaccurate because many landlords had resorted to the traditional practice of concealing large numbers of peasants on their estates from the returning officers.

Thereupon, in May 1721, the tsar ordered a revision (*revíziia*) of the census by the local governors and *voevódy*. In January 1722, however, in order to save time, he assigned the combined task of revising the census and encamping the troops in the country to the generals of the army and a few civilian dignitaries with the assistance of a large staff of regimental officers. The work should have been completed by the end of 1723 but only in May 1724 was the total of 5,401,042 male peasants arrived at. On this basis the tax payable by the peasants on private estates was now fixed at 74 kopecks a head instead of the originally estimated and provisionally charged rate of 80 kopecks. The 'state' peasants (as those who held their land direct of the Crown were now called) were to pay a consolidated tax of 1 rouble 14 kopecks a head; both rates, as will be seen, were soon to be reduced. The 169,424 male *posádskie liúdi* paid 1 rouble 20 kopecks a head.

As the first 'revision', the name under which the census came eventually to be known, was no mere statistical survey but entailed the detection of secreted 'souls', an investigation into the circumstances of their concealment and the punishment of those responsible, the enumerators arrogated to themselves many of the functions appertaining to the local judicial and administrative officers. On the strength of orders received from the *Voénnaia kollégiia* (Board of War) they would impose their authority on governors and *voevódy*; at the bidding of the Senate they would investigate the failure of these officers and of the collectors of revenue to carry out the instructions of the *Shtáts-kontóra* (Board of State Expenditure) and in some places to dismiss an officer appointed by the *Kámer-kollégiia* (Board of the Revenue) in order to replace him with a local *dvorianín*. In this way, having from the importance of their 'capital task' (*glávnoe délo*) acquired a taste for civil power, the commanders of the encamped regiments made havoc in their military districts of the elaborate administrative organization set up with so much care only a few years earlier. As M. M. Bogoslóvskii has shown, in the last two or three years of Peter the Great's reign the narrow fiscal purpose of the *revíziia* debased the aims and darkened the horizons of the planners of the Petrine *Polizeystaat*. By the time Tsar Peter and his critical admirer, Pososhkóv, were ready to depart this world, the urban and rural inhabitants of the now fifty provinces of the Russian Empire, so far from enjoying the benefits of a well-regulated state were living under a military regime, occupied, laid under contribution and governed by the army and liable to be tried under military law. Peter the Great was not the first monarch to invoke the common good at the precise time when he was establishing a standing army, but even if his endeavours to bring relief to his hard-pressed subjects were genuine, he achieved far greater success as supreme commander, paymaster and quartermaster than as Father of the Fatherland.

The poll-tax may have balanced Russia's state income and expenditure for the first time since 1701, but it did not bring relief to the taxpayers, distribute the tax burden more evenly or make for a more rational deployment of the financial resources of the state: the proceeds of the *podúshnaia pódat'*, instead of being pooled with revenue from other sources for disbursement by the *Shtáts-kontóra*, were handed over to the army for its own use. Contrary to the expectation held out by the tsar in 1718, the poll-tax did not consolidate all the taxes previously paid by the peasants and *posádskie liúdi*, nor did it substitute individual for collective payment. In practice each peasant or urban community was obliged to raise from its members the tax due in respect of all those shown on the roll of the most recent census, no matter whether they were alive or dead, present or absent, young or old, able-bodied or infirm.

The new revenue officials were not necessarily less given to embezzlement than the old. In 1724 three commissaries (*zémskie komissáry*) in the region of Lake Onéga collected the poll-tax for the first six months of that year at the rate of 54 instead of 34 kopecks per head and pocketed the difference totalling 1,775 roubles. For these and other offences the commissaries were sentenced to the confiscation of their personal property and to death by hanging. Judging by the tsar's earlier observations on the subject of malversation it is unlikely that this incident was the only one of its kind. The part which the *podúshnaia pódat'* was ultimately destined to play in the system of serfdom by determining the position of the peasants on private estates as that of payers, and that of the landlords as collectors or at any rate guarantors, of the poll-tax could not have been foreseen by its originator or even by one of its earliest detractors, Pososhkóv, who denounced it as 'soul-killing'.[141]

One consequence of the census – if it was as immediate and as thoroughgoing as Bogoslóvskii suggests – should have met with Pososhkóv's approval, since it corresponded closely to a measure put forward in the *The Book of Poverty and Wealth*. The revisers cleared the *posády* (urban communities) of outsiders, for the most part soldiers of all ranks, who had been engaging in trade on the side but being exempt by virtue of their official status from the tax levied on the *posádskie liúdi*, were able to compete on favourable and unfair terms with the local tradespeople. The intrusion of such interlopers caused the authorities rather less concern than the exodus from the *posád* during the turbulent years of the Great Northern War of those 'who did not wish to render service and pay tax together with the rest'.[142]

The *Regulation* of the *Glávnyi magistrát* (Board of Civic Administration) promulgated early in 1721 more than once compares Russia's urban communities to a 'tumbledown edifice' and announces the tsar's decision to restore to the merchants, traders and artisans their sense of corporate identity by assigning them to guilds. The first of these in order of importance was to consist of bankers (as yet non-existent), prominent merchants, members of the professions and master craftsmen; the second of petty traders and artisans. The lowest strata of the *posád*, unskilled and hired workers, were to remain incorporate. The tone of the edict which in January 1722 commanded brigadier Prince Iu. Iu. Trubetskói and his associate, the merchant I. I. Isáev, to establish in St Petersburg the *Glávnyi magistrát* (Board of Civic Administration) (of which Trubetskói had already been appointed *óber-prezidént*) within five to six months or be condemned to exile with hard labour did not augur well for the spirit of the new institution. Although the *Glávnyi magistrát* is not commonly associated with the reforms set in train in 1719, being, like the other colleges or boards, endowed with certain judicial powers and functioning under the supervision of the Senate, it played an important part in the new and improved system of government. Indeed it is in the *Regulation* of the *Glávnyi magistrát* that the Russian definition of *Polizey* is to be found. The task of the *Glávnyi magistrát* was to establish *magistráty* in all principal towns, to ensure the dispensation of justice to their members, to maintain public order among them, to collect the tax due from them and deliver it as the *Kamer-kollégiia* might direct, to promote trade and handicrafts and to establish craft guilds.

A subsequent edict (apparently unknown to Pososhkóv who has much to say about workmanship) laid down stringent rules for the control of the quality of articles offered for sale: each was henceforth to be distinguished by the maker's own trade mark. Although, declares the *Regulation*, the dispensation of justice in all *gubérnii* and provinces is conducted and supervised by the *Iustíts-kollégiia*, nevertheless, since 'the tradesmen and artisans in the towns have not so far enjoyed any special protection and, what is more, most of them have been brought to ruin by all manner of wrongs, ill-usage and excessive burdens and their numbers have in consequence dwindled considerably, much to the detriment of the revenue', such men shall be subject to the jurisdiction of the burgomaster (*burgomístr*) in small towns, of a bench of burgomasters in the principal towns and, in the ultimate instance, of the court of the *Glávnyi magistrát* in St Petersburg. In practice the task of the *Glávnyi magistrát* and of the *magistráty* in general was as much to police the towns as to regiment the *posádskie liúdi* for paying tax and rendering service to the state. The *Regulation* also declared in rather ambiguous terms that the presidents, burgomasters and councillors of the *magistráty* should be free of all state service and that in future the temporary unpaid duties performed by them would be discharged by permanent officials. Meanwhile, however, upon the request of any college addressed to the *Glávnyi magistrát* each local *magistrát* would appoint an appropriate number of suitably qualified men to perform services – sometimes entailing long periods of absence from home – such as the collection of revenue and similar tasks.

These duties – the subject of one of Pososhkóv's many complaints – were numerous and burdensome; Kízevetter lists no fewer than twelve connected with the collection of customs and excise, of tolls and charges for the concession of government monopolies, apart from routine work in the *magistráty* and the collection of the poll-tax from fellow members of the *posád*. The standard rate of 1 rouble 20 kopecks a head was to be adjusted by the officers of the *magistrát* with the assistance of the headmen of the various sections of the community in proportion, first, to the amount of property owned by each man, and second, to the size of his family, in order to ensure that everyone contributed to the total sum due in accordance with his means and that the poor – including the *pódlye liúdi* ('base' men, who had no formal status but were nevertheless obliged to pay tax) – were not wronged or overburdened. It may, however, be doubted whether in view of the traditional tendency to favour the rich at the expense of the poor and of the evidence collected by Kízevetter, these high-minded principles were ever put into practice. Apart from the doubtful benefits of this peculiar form of self-administration, the rewards bestowed on the *posádskie liúdi* for their labours, clerical and manual, in the service of the state were scant, amounting as they did to the protection from interlopers and – but only temporarily – to the commutation to a cash payment of the obligation to supply recruits for the army.

The *Regulation*, together with the Instruction for the *magistráty* of 1724, by making provision for the establishment of schools and craft guilds, the care of the old and infirm, the prevention of pauperism and vagabondage through setting the poor to work, the holding of fairs and the like, gave effect to many of the proposals put forward by the cameralist writers and Pososhkóv alike, but the tsar did not live long enough to enforce these measures and Pososhkóv died before he could witness their ineffectiveness. The city fathers in the *magistráty* (which were as remote from any *Magistrát* in the true sense of the term as the *Rátusha* of 1699 had been from a *Rathaus*) had little time to spare for the practice of bourgeois virtues or the promotion of civic welfare. The façade of the 'tumbledown edifice' had been reconstructed in the Germanic style in accordance with the demands of *Polizey* but within its walls the new institution showed, like the rest, a tendency to revive old administrative practices and social relationships. After the completion of Pososhkóv's *Book of Poverty and Wealth* as much as during the author's lifetime the 'sound' men of substance, in the fulfilment of their duties, fleeced and disciplined their fellow citizens on behalf of the central government with undiminished vigour even though they themselves often suffered brutal ill-treatment at the hands of the military. In a private capacity the rich and powerful continued to ride the poor and defenceless with impunity. The original division of the urban population into two 'guilds' or categories according to wealth and social standing rather than on an occupational basis was upset by the rapid absorption of the artisans into the so-called craft guilds – *tsékhi* – established in 1722. Before long the *posádskie liúdi* fell naturally into three categories, reminiscent of the gradation of the previous era: the merchants of three degrees, the artisans and the unskilled workers (including market gardeners). The freedom of movement of the members of the *posád* was severely restricted: they were not allowed to travel without a pass or a passport issued by the local *magistrát*. Numbered and registered according to their skills as well as tethered, they were liable to be conscripted for public works or called up for official service more promptly than before.[143]

Assuming that it had been Peter I's own intention, as well as that of some of his counsellors, to make Russia into a *Polizeystaat*, it must be owned that he failed in that aim.[144] In their efforts the tsar and his cameralistically inclined advisers were hindered by the legacy of Muscovite administrative practice which combined corruption with inefficiency as well as by those very economic difficulties, aggravated by the war, which the new system was intended to overcome. Where the tsar did succeed was in making more people render more service and pay more tax than before. Perhaps against his own will he brought to perfection the Muscovite service state, the foundations of which had been laid by Iván IV. This success did not endear him to those of his subjects who did not have the chance of receiving rewards or favours for having distinguished themselves on the field of battle or in diplomacy or of making a fortune out of contracts for supplying the army and the navy.[145] The new Petrine empire, chronically short of men and resources, committed to a policy of protecting its gains, if necessary by further expansion, made heavy demands on all classes of society but offered little in return to the mass of the tsar's subjects by way of benefits, opportunities or incentives.

The society which towards the end of the first quarter of the eighteenth century began to emerge from a state of flux partly as a result of deliberate social engineering by means of enactments such as the law of inheritance of 1714 or the Table of Ranks of 1722, and partly in consequence of unexpected natural processes such as the social and economic changes engendered by the introduction of the poll-tax, did not allow the ordinary Russian much mobility or even freedom of physical movement. In theory (as has been seen) high birth no longer entitled a subject of the tsar to preferential treatment by the state. In practice the almost universal obligation to render service or pay tax to the state tended to keep the common man in the station into which he was born. By clearly stating the obligations to be discharged by the tsar's secular subjects –

dvoriáne, townspeople and bonded peasants – in the form of tax or service, the regulations for the poll-tax and the Table of Ranks contributed to the simplification of Russia's social structure. The four distinct orders – priestly, serving, trading and agricultural – merely envisaged in the seventeenth century as 'arrayed to do the tsar's bidding'[146] – had become a reality. Slaves (*kholópy*) of various denominations were classed as serfs and so were those formerly enrolled men of service (or their descendants) who had not succeeded in acquiring the status of *dvorianín*.

The peasants on the estates of the *poméshchiki* suffered most – or benefited least – from the reforms of Peter since they remained legally bound to their masters and the obligation to pay the poll-tax, in Miliukóv's words, 'tightened the knot of serfdom'.[147] A peasant could, with his landlord's permission, obtain official leave to work away from his village but for limited periods only. Unlike a peasant who left one landlord for another without permission, a runaway who before May 1724 found work in a manufactory could be kept there for the benefit of the owner of the works though possibly against his own will. If, however, he was fortunate enough to learn a trade in one of the metallurgical works in the Urals, state-owned or private, and his work was adjudged indispensable, he was allowed, before the expiry of his leave of absence, to buy his freedom from his landlord for the sum of 50 roubles. A peasant could further – if released by his landlord – be admitted into an urban community (*posád*) in order to trade or ply a craft, provided that his working capital was worth at least 500 roubles, or 300 roubles if he was enterprising enough to carry his goods to the new and distant capital city and port of St Petersburg. A peasant who resided in the *posád*, however, remained a peasant (as did his descendants) and was subject to double taxation: he paid the poll-tax both in his native village and, at the rate of 40 kopecks, in the *posád*. A *posádskii chelovék* could only change his occupation or place of work with the permission of the authorities and – if he wished to absent himself in this connection for a limited period – with the consent of his fellow taxpayers, neither of which was easily granted. Nevertheless, despite the steps taken by the government to bring the stray members of the *posády* back to the fold and to keep them there, a small number of *posádskie liúdi* found their way into the lower ranks of the civil administration, into manufactories or even into the Church. Only conscription for military service, which, incidentally, offered the chance of promotion from the ranks, severed a peasant or a *posádskii chelovék* and his family from their native community, in most cases for good.

The constraints imposed by the Petrine service state on social mobility (outside the armed forces) were reinforced by further restrictions on the physical freedom of movement of individuals. No person anywhere was allowed to move from one town to another or from one village to another without a written pass made out by his superiors. The object of this injunction, issued in

1719, was as much to suppress brigandage as to tie the taxpayers and potential recruits to the places where they could most easily be found by the tax-collector and the recruiting officer. 'No one is to be allowed to wander about without [i.e. instead of rendering] service' declared an *ukáz* promulgated in 1722. The more detailed regulations published in 1724 also served the interests of landlords inasmuch as they prevented the peasants from deserting their holdings.[148]

It may be noted in passing that Pososhkóv in his *Book of Poverty and Wealth* raised no objection to the caste-bound nature of Russian society but protested only against the usurpation of the privileges or immunities of one social category by members of another. On the point of freedom of movement he approves of the passport system and the restrictions imposed on the lower strata of the population as an effective means of preventing crime.

The tsar, with his military turn of mind, firmly believed in rewarding meritorious service interpreted in the widest sense – economic usefulness included – for the economist in him recognized the need to create in Russia a middle class in the Western style, more numerous, more heterogeneous and better educated than the caste-like order of the *posádskie liúdi*. Accordingly the law on the mode of inheritance (1714) encourages the younger sons of *dvoriáne* to earn their livelihood in government service, in a learned or useful profession or in trade; the *Regulation* of the *Glávnyi magistrát* dangles the prize of *shliakhétstvo* – the status of *dvorianín* – before those who have displayed assiduousness, zeal and honesty in the service of the *magistrát*; a momentous edict issued in 1721 allows men engaged in trade – *kupétskie liúdi* – who have set up manufactories to buy land, not in order, however, to turn them into country squires but so as to provide them with the necessary manpower.

As to general economic development, Peter I presumably adhered to the optimistic opinion expressed in the *Regulation* of the *Glávnyi magistrát* published in his name in January 1721 that given God's help and good *Polizey* the wealth of each town has – to translate the original wording into the idiom of the present day – its own dynamic capacity for spontaneous growth, derived from seaborne traffic, freedom of trade and skill in manufacturing. The formula taken as a whole is more appropriate to a seafaring republic than to a continental empire but the essence of its first clause does not differ fundamentally from the views expressed by Pososhkóv in his *Book of Poverty and Wealth* and announced in its subtitle. It was later in the same year that the tsar urged the élite of his fellow countrymen to labour for the advantage and benefit of all. The cost, however, of maintaining and extending even further his newly founded empire ruled out any real possibility of reconciling the economic interests of the state with those of the peasants and the *posádskie liúdi*, just as the exigencies of war had done in the preceding period. Before any thought could be given to the enrichment of the tsar's subjects, the means had to be devised of supplementing the revenue from taxation with income from other sources in order to meet the current needs of the state.[149]

Industry and Trade

The need for and development of native manufactories. The production of cloth. Manufacturers allowed to buy landed estates (1721). The Regulation of the Board of Manufactories (1723). Some social effects of industrial development. The protective customs tariff of 1724. Prosperity to be achieved through foreign trade. The Board of Trade (1715). Trade with Persia. War with Persia (1722–3). Endeavours to expand trade with southern Europe.

The tsar saw the answer to financial difficulties in self-sufficiency coupled with a favourable balance of payments, a policy which he formulated in his elliptical style about 1722: 'Make use at home [for manufacturing] of all the things from which imported goods are made; sell for money rather than exchange for goods', as a means of increasing the supply of silver currency. The mint-houses were constantly offering to buy silver in any form for coining into roubles and the custom-houses were assiduously collecting duty from foreign merchants in *efímki* (rix-dollars), as was the tsar's treasury from the sale of monopoly goods such as tar or Russia leather and of grain bought specially for the purpose. The *efímki* thus acquired were used for recoinage, spent on specialist services rendered by foreigners in Russia or abroad or transferred to eastern Europe, mostly in cash, to meet the expenses incurred there by the tsar's armies, his diplomatic agents and his court on its travels. As the Russian currency, silver and copper, was being debased, so silver tended to disappear from circulation. Melting down and hoarding by local inhabitants may well have accounted for a proportion of the drain but officially the blame was first laid on the activities of foreign merchants and in 1714 the export of all silver was forbidden. The principle which Peter the Great discovered for himself towards the end of his reign was expressed a generation later by Frederick the Great with typical conciseness and clarity: 'Le fondement du commerce et des manufactures est d'empêcher l'argent de sortir, en fabriquant chez soi toutes les choses qu'on prenait autrefois à l'étranger.'[150]

The policy of charging the state with the management of trade and industry, direct until about the end of the second decade of the century and later indirect, through the appropriate colleges, had the twofold advantage of saving as well as earning silver currency. By comparison with its modest and halting beginnings in the preceding period the development of Russian industry in the first quarter of the eighteenth century was so rapid and extensive that it is no extravagance to refer to it as a manufactorial revolution. By 1725 there were to be found in Russia (apart from the state ordnance works) some 178 industrial works located around and near St Petersburg (including Sestrorétsk), at Olónets near the south-eastern shore of Lake Ládoga, at Petrozavódsk on the north-western shore of Lake Onéga and in central Russia in the circle marked by the towns of

Moscow, Túla, Riazán', Nízhnii Nóvgorod, Kostromá, Iaroslávl' and Tver'. The new copper and iron works were located in the central Urals. No more than fifteen establishments dated from the preceding century; the total figure was made up of forty iron and armaments works, fifteen copper works, thirteen gunpowder-mills, seven shipyards, twenty-three saw-mills, nine linen and sailcloth factories, thirteen tanneries, six glass works, fifteen woollen factories, three silk-mills, six passementerie factories and six paper-mills; the remaining twenty-two fall into sundry categories, including sugar-refining and dye-making.

The great majority of these works were founded by the government or on its initiative but before the end of Peter I's reign about half the total number were in private hands. The size of these enterprises ranged from very large to very small; one of the largest textile factories is known to have operated 300 looms and to have employed 1,362 hands, skilled and unskilled; Pososhkóv's small factory was to have a complement of eight or ten looms and between sixteen and twenty full-time workmen. The total labour force employed by Russian industry in this period has not, to my knowledge, been estimated but it is known that in the 1720s some 31,380 'state' peasants were 'ascribed' by the authorities to the various works for auxiliary duties. Save the last mentioned, all these figures, like the rest of the data relating to the subject of industrial development in this period, are neither final nor reliable and must be treated with caution, especially as they are seldom accompanied by information about the profitability of the various concerns or the quality and usefulness of the goods produced by them. It is, however, clear even from these incomplete data that the principal function of industry in this period was to supply the tsar's army with firearms of all calibres, ammunition, side-arms, uniforms, boots, tents, saddlery, harness, etc., and his navy with men of war. The duties performed by the Russian – as distinguished from the foreign – officials of the *Manufaktúr-kollégiia* (Board of Manufactories) in 1722 illustrate the close connection between the tsar's industrial policy and the military needs of the state. Most of these men were army officers and nearly all were engaged in supervising the production of military supplies up and down the country. The industrial sector of the Russian economy in this period constituted a command system in its purest form – that of military command.[151]

In view of the strategic importance of the metallurgical industries the tsar evidently considered it both safer and more convenient to entrust them to the management of specialists in his service rather than to hand them over as going concerns to private entrepreneurs. In this respect the ironmaster Nikíta Demídych Antúf'ev (1656–1725), later known as Demídov, who in 1702 took over the Nev'iánskii *zavód* (works) in the Urals, was a notable exception. In handing over the works to Demídov the tsar characteristically enjoined him 'to set aside all self-interest and desire for excessive enrichment, to work with the utmost devotion and care, bearing in mind the hour of his death, and to seek not so much his advantage as that of His Majesty'. In time, however, the tsar came to lower his high moral tone: in an official utterance made in 1719 on the kindred subject of mining he commends the profit motive in that industry for its social value and stresses the need to guarantee the security of ownership to those who have gone to the trouble of establishing new mines. The tsar had every reason to be satisfied with the rapid resurgence of his country's metallurgical and armament industries, their many deficiencies notwithstanding. Russia continued to import arms in diminishing quantities until at least as late as 1715 but by 1724 she was exporting iron to England. Its competitive price reflects the cheapness of the cost of production in the Urals; its high quality was due as much to the nature of the local ore as to the efforts of the native and foreign craftsmen under the direction from 1722 of Georg Wilhelm (Vilim Ivánovich) Henin (1676–1750). The smelting of copper at Olónets had ceased by 1715 and the amount produced during the subsequent decade in the Urals was far too small to satisfy the needs of the Mint which had to be supplied with copper, as well as with gold and silver, from overseas.[152]

When, in 1714, the tsar began to pursue more or less methodically the policy of 'manufacturing manufacturers',[153] he confined it to branches in which, given the necessary help and stimulus, individuals or associations of individuals – the *kompánii* favoured by the tsar on account of their greater viability – were most likely to succeed and acquire an appetite for profitable expansion: wool, linen, leather, paper, glass. Private enterprise in the genuine sense of the term was the exception rather than the rule; over the next twelve years the tsar had the opportunity to observe and deplore the reluctance of those of his subjects who possessed the necessary capital to venture into manufacturing. 'Although other nations look askance at our manufactories, not enough progress has been made, not enough volunteers have come forward.'[154] Despite the unwillingness of Russians to turn themselves into industrialists and especially to invest their capital in *kompánii*, the policy of handing over manufactories initially established by the government to such associations or to particular entrepreneurs was pursued fairly consistently. As a result by 1722, the year in which the Board of Manufactories and Mines (*Berg- i Manufaktúr-kollégiia*), established in 1717, was divided into two separate departments, only five such establishments remained under the direct control of the *Manufaktúr-kollégiia*. The cost of this policy whose object was educational as much as economic – to delegate responsibility, to teach management, to stimulate enterprise – has not been calculated but it may be doubted whether it greatly contributed to Russia's self-sufficiency or saved the government any expense. The woollen manufactories in particular, despite the spectacular success achieved in breeding sheep in the Ukraine and in southern Russia, had still to be supplied with raw material, craftsmen and items of equipment from abroad. Furthermore, even after the whole procedure for the administration of government aid to industry was regularized by the *Regulation* of the *Manufaktúr-kollégiia* promulgated in 1723, the government continued to lavish subsidies, usually disguised as loans, on many of these concerns.[155]

The *Moskóvskii Sukónnyi Dvor* (Moscow Cloth Yard) established by the government in 1704 was handed over in 1720 to a 'company' of merchants under the management of the merchant V. P. Shchególin who had been associated with it since 1712. The participation of one of the associates nominated by the tsar had to be secured by a file of soldiers detailed from the Moscow garrison. 'The reluctant sons of Old Muscovy being marched into the Modern Age' would have been a fitting caption for this *tableau vivant*. The Moscow Cloth Yard was a typical product of Peter the Great's manufactorial revolution. Every stage of the factory's history as well as the character and organization of its production were determined by the needs of a government bent on developing its native resources. By 1718 it was producing as much kersey as was needed for clothing the garrison regiments and lining the uniforms of the field regiments. However, for reasons which are not altogether clear but would seem to be connected with the vested interests of foreign suppliers, the military commissariat[156] did not place its orders with the Moscow factory whose stock kept piling up until the tsar prohibited the importation of kerseys from overseas. On the other hand, the demand for soldiers' cloth – a more substantial fabric – could not be met from native production. The company for trade with Russia established in Berlin in 1724 was to reap the benefit from this deficiency. The majority of the merchants, courtiers or grandees who turned to manufacturing in this period did so under pressure from the tsar. Those who acted on their own initiative lost no opportunity to point out to him that they were moved by a spirit of self-sacrifice and by a sense of duty. Peter I in his turn rewarded the public services rendered by the entrepreneur and subsequently the director of the state-owned linen factory, Jan Tammes, alias Iván Pávlovich Tames, by granting him a rank in the official hierarchy; in 1720 the tsar conferred on Antúf'ev the status of hereditary *dvorianín* under the new family name of Demídov.[157]

The genuine difficulties – including an acute shortage of hands – under which these industrial pioneers laboured made it at once necessary and relatively easy for the tsar to put an end to the time-honoured and envied association between the status of *dvorianín* and the right to hold or own land. The decree, already referred to, which was promulgated in 1721 allowed all manufacturers, 'men of commerce' as well as *dvoriáne*, to buy landed estates for the sole and specific purpose of providing themselves with a reservoir of auxiliary labour, but few took advantage of this permission under Peter I. 'State' peasants were assigned to private manufactories only by way of exception.[158]

The *Regulation* of the *Manufaktúr-kollégiia* promulgated in 1723 speaks frankly of the effort and expense demanded by the initial stages of setting up a manufactory; its provisions codify the principles which the tsar and his aides had followed somewhat haphazardly since 1718. The professed task of the *kollégiia* was to promote the establishment in Russia, again for the common good and benefit of all the tsar's subjects, of such manufactories and works as were to be found in other lands and especially of those for which raw materials were available in Russia. The *kollégiia* would favour their founders with the appropriate privileges which, however, would not be exclusive, for the *Regulation* recognized the value of competition between different makers of the same product. The permission granted to manufacturers to acquire land and peasants was reaffirmed, as was the exemption, likewise granted in 1721, of *posádskie liúdi* engaged in manufacturing from rendering state service. At the same time the *Regulation* took the further logical step of exempting those manufacturers who were *posádskie* (except for any criminal offences and acts against the security of the state committed by them) from the jurisdiction of the *Glávnyi magistrát* and placing them under that of the *Manufaktúr-kollégiia*. All established manufacturers were declared eligible for exemption from the payment of tolls as well as of customs duties.

The permission granted by article 7 of the *Regulation* to every person irrespective of his rank or social condition to establish a factory did not elicit any comment from the author of *The Book of Poverty and Wealth*, even though it must have been the publicity given in accordance with the tsar's command to the generous provision of aid and advice to aspiring industrialists that eventually prompted him to benefit from this opportunity. At the request of the *Manufaktúr-kollégiia* economic aid was to be granted by the Senate to concerns which had been established by the government and were later handed over to associations (*kompánii*) whose prospects were considered promising in order that they might improve rather than decline. Loans payable in advance were promised only to foreigners who wished to avail themselves of the tsar's open invitation to establish manufactories in Russia but no such volunteers are known to have come forward. Foreign master craftsmen would be obliged by the *kollégiia* to take on Russian apprentices. But the participants – willing or unwilling – in manufacturing associations (*kompánii*) were obliged from the outset to add their own contribution in cash, however modest, to the fixed capital provided by the state. Where Pososhkóv was seeking credit, the tsar was seeking investment. The tsar's subjects who had not yet acquired the habit of investing large amounts of capital were to be encouraged by kindly treatment to set up in manufacturing on a small scale in the first instance; if a man prospered he could expand his business, if he failed he did not risk a heavy loss.[159]

The tsar's industrial policy had already led to the enrichment of a small number of merchants, including some who were of peasant origin, and of a few professional entrepreneurs such as Tames, but the permission granted to men of all ranks and social conditions to engage in industrial enterprise did not result in the emergence of a fresh contingent of manufacturers from the lower ranks of the urban section of the population; in that respect Pososhkóv, who had already greatly improved his standing, was something of an exception. Instead, the exemption of the manufacturers of various kinds from the jurisdiction of the *Glávnyi magistrát* (under which its *Regulation* had originally placed them) and their subordination to the *Manufaktúr-kollégiia*, created under the authority of that college a new though unnamed category of industrial beneficiaries of the state. Like the class of rich merchants from which most of them sprang, the big manufacturers exploited their immediate social inferiors and, by preventing their economic advancement, exercised an inhibiting effect on the development in Russia of a middle class in the Western style. Nor did the growth of manufactories undermine the institution of serfdom which, as has been seen, the authorities ingeniously adapted to the requirements of industry.[160]

Having brought into being such a variety of industries the tsar took steps to protect their existence by means of a new and comprehensive customs tariff promulgated in January 1724. The change was long overdue as no fundamental revision of the New Trade Regulation had been carried out since its coming into force in 1667[161] and the regulations published in 1720 were only provisional. The principle applied in determining the amount of duty to be paid on goods imported into Russia seems to have been inspired by a desire for autarchy coupled with a fear of foreign competition. Customs duty, assessed either *ad valorem* on the basis of current prices or *pro tanto*, was imposed at the rate of 12½, 25 or 37½ per cent in direct proportion to the state of development of a particular industry with the intention of giving the maximum of protection to the most highly developed manufactories. Duty, however, being payable in rix-dollars (*efímki*) at the official (and artificial) rate of 50 kopecks to the rix-dollar and the market value of the rix-dollar being slightly more than double that amount, the effective rate of duty was rather more than twice the nominal rate.

Accordingly on sailcloth, table-cloths and napkins, silk fabrics, taffeta, ribbons and bonnets, refined wax, starch, potash, vitriol, turpentine, bar iron, needles and parchment, all of which were regarded as being produced in sufficient quantities in Russia, the duty was 75 per cent of the value of the goods; on velvet, fine bays, Dutch linen, silver wire and thread and on playing cards 50 per cent; on sundry woollen fabrics (with the exception of [soldiers'?] cloth on which the duty remained between 4 and 8 per cent), silk mixtures, dressed hides, fringeing, gloves, writing paper, arms made from steel and on glass bottles, 25 per cent. The effective rate of duty levied on luxury goods was 20 per cent, on objects of everyday use and household goods, 10 per cent. The effective duty charged on exports was, as before, moderate, about 3 per cent, with the exception of linen and linen yarn which a rate of 75 per cent kept on the home market for the benefit of native manufacturers, causing the dissatisfaction of spinners and foreign customers. The tariff applied to the ports on the White Sea, to Narva, St Petersburg and Viborg but not the Livonian and Estonian ports where, under the terms of the peace treaty with Sweden of 1721, the existing and less stringent tariff remained in force. Goods imported into those provinces were not allowed into other parts of Russia; the transit trade between Riga and Poland was exempt from the new tariff which did, however, come into force along the rest of the Russo-Polish frontier. In order to attract export goods to St Petersburg a surcharge of 25 per cent was added to the rate of duty levied at Archangel, with the exception, however, of the native products, such as timber and tar, of the inland areas.

Considering that as a result of the conquest of Livonia, Estonia, Ingria and a part of Karelia the tsar had the virtual monopoly of naval stores in Europe, it is on the face of it surprising that he should not have taken advantage of this situation by laying a high duty on their export. It must, however, be borne in mind first that the market price of exports from the Baltic area was affected by the payment of duty in the Sound, and secondly, that in Russia under the new tariff, foreign exporters paid duty in rix-dollars calculated at an official and arbitrary rate of exchange. This rigging of the exchange rate alone constituted an increase in the rate of customs duty and the manner of its collection shows that the object of the new tariff was not only protective to the point of being prohibitive but also fiscal: to collect the maximum amount of silver currency for the tsar's treasury by the cheapest possible means.

Russian trade and shipping too were protected by the tariff. The duty charged on goods exported by Russian merchants in foreign ships was allowed a reduction of 5 per cent and collected in rix-dollars (or in Russian money at the penal rate of 1 rouble 25 kopecks to the rix-dollar). On Russian goods exported in Russian bottoms the rate of duty was reduced by two-thirds (but at Archangel only by half), and payment was to be collected in Russian money at the rate of 90 kopecks for each nominal rix-dollar. Goods brought home by returning Russian ships were liable to import duty at rates reduced by half at Archangel and by two thirds at other Russian ports, likewise in Russian money, provided that the value of such imports did not exceed the value of the goods originally exported plus a profit of 25 per cent. On any return over and above those limits duty was to be levied at the full rate and in rix-dollars calculated at 50 kopecks apiece. By reason of this restriction the provision relating to goods imported in Russian-owned ships would have exposed the over-protected native manufactories to a certain degree of competition rather than, as has been suggested, defeated the protectionist object of the tariff altogether. The whole eventuality, however, remained theoretical since the number of Russian merchants who exported goods in their own ships was extremely small.[162]

The mercantilistic tenet that a country or at any rate its monarch grows rich by foreign trade seems to have been accepted in Russian ruling circles since the days of A. L. Ordýn-Nashchókin who was in charge of Alekséi Mikháilovich's foreign and economic policy between 1665 and 1672. The cognate notion that trade follows the flag dominated the strategic schemes of Peter I.[162]

Throughout his reign Tsar Peter may be seen to have pursued one overriding and all-embracing aim: to extend the frontiers of Russia to the Baltic, the Black Sea and along the western shore of the Caspian, and to join these three seas together by a system of waterways – the Volga, the Neva and the Don, interconnected by canals. Once 'a union of those rivers' had been accomplished the tsar would be in a position to divert the course of East-West trade from Asia Minor and the Mediterranean so as to make Russia its thoroughfare, St Petersburg its terminal point and his subjects its carriers and middlemen. This ambitious and visionary programme is no figment of the historical imagination; it was stated in outline by the tsar himself during his visit to The Hague in 1697, a year after he had taken Azóv from the Turks, and amplified in Vienna in 1698 by his unofficial envoy B. P. Sheremétev.

In later years Peter I chose to present his conquest of the Baltic seaboard and his creation of a Russian navy as objectives marked out by his predecessors – Iván IV and Alekséi Mikháilovich – and blessed by Providence, but these pious tributes do not disparage the boldness and farsightedness of a design which, taken in its entirety, was only completed in the Soviet era with the opening of the Volga-Don canal in 1952. This junction of the seas by water was forestalled in the second half of the nineteenth century by the construction of a railway system which by 1875 had connected the Baltic with the Black Sea and in the 1890s was extended to the Caspian and beyond. In Peter's lifetime only the first stage was carried out: in 1709 the Výshne-Vólotskii (Tvéretskii) canal linked the river Tsna, a tributary of the Msta – further connected to the Neva by the Vólkhov and Lake Ládoga – to the Tvertsá, a tributary of the Volga. The possibility of completing the network by means of a waterway between the White Sea and the Baltic was adumbrated in 1702 when the tsar brought some naval craft over land and water from Soróka on the White Sea into the Neva roughly along the route now partly covered by the canal built between 1930 and 1933 'by tens of thousands of enemies of the state, helped by only thirty-seven G.P.U. officers'.[163]

As has been seen, the *Blitzkrieg* against Sweden begun in 1700 in implementation of the tsar's scheme did not succeed and developed into the Great Northern War which dragged on until 1721. In 1711 Peter I was obliged to hand back Azóv to the Sultan but as early as 1710 it was thought that he would wish to annex the Persian province of Gilan (presumably together with the intermediate provinces of Dagestan and Shirvan) in order to lay his hands on the raw silk produced in that province. Seven years earlier he had founded St Petersburg. In 1704 in order to allay the apprehension that was being felt in the west over his intentions in the Baltic the tsar declared that he did not want a navy, only a few convoy vessels and cruisers to protect his ports, those 'arteries', as he graphically put it, 'that cause a country's heart to beat more soundly and more profitably'.[164] The number of foreign ships that anchored at St Petersburg was one in 1703, sixteen in 1714, 108 in 1724, but during the first ten years of the future new capital's existence Archangel continued to handle the bulk of Russia's trade with the West and would for long have maintained its predominance had not the tsar from 1713 officially directed to St Petersburg varying proportions of nearly all Russian goods destined for the ports of western Europe. In 1719 that quota was fixed at one third of the total.[165]

Peter I's practice of making extensive use of the tsar's prerogative to monopolize the trade in particular commodities gave his treasury a considerable share in, and a high degree of control over, the sale of those Russian goods that were in especial demand in the West. In 1706 the English envoy Charles Whitworth, perhaps echoing Dr Samuel Collins's description of Alekséi Mikháilovich as 'the first merchant of his realm', reported: 'the Court here is turned quite merchant and not content with engrossing the best commodities of their own country . . . which they buy at low rates . . . [and sell] to the English and Dutch at great profit, they are now further encroaching on the foreign trade and buying up whatever is wanted abroad under the name of particular merchants who are only paid their commission but the gain and the risk is the tsar's'.[166] By 1714 the list of monopoly goods comprised potash, weidash, tar, hemp, hempseed oil, linseed, tallow, isinglass, caviar, wheat, Siberian rhubarb, hog's bristle and Russia leather. Whenever practicable customs duty was raised in the much needed *efímki*. In 1705 and 1706 English merchants were compelled to exchange a certain amount of rix-dollars for Russian money in proportion to the amount of hemp bought by them. In 1706 the merchant Dimítrii Solov'ëv was appointed the tsar's commercial agent at Amsterdam; his function was to sell on the most favourable terms the monopoly goods purchased and dispatched from Archangel by his brother Ósip, and to use the proceeds in accordance with the tsar's instructions. In this way in 1715 400,000 rix-dollars were put at his disposal at Hamburg in payment for Russian commodities delivered to Amsterdam.

It has been calculated that in 1710 at the annual fair at Archangel the foreign merchants bought 1,463,700 roubles' worth of Russian goods but that the monopoly goods accounted for only 2.5 per cent of that sum. In view of what has just been said about the continuing engrossment by the Crown of many commodities which previously had not been subject to any restriction, and considering the increasing importance of St Petersburg as a trading centre, it would be a mistake to regard the figures for 1710 as typical of the whole pattern of trade between Russia and western Europe during any period inclusive of that year. A well-informed foreign observer writing in 1710 on the same subject of foreign trade (whose volume, however, he overestimated by putting the annual turnover at Archangel at over 4 million roubles) suggested that the tsar's treasury had a share in the sale of goods not yet designated as monopolies but already treated as such and that the same was true of his boyars. In consequence, the same writer points out, the merchants who actually sell the goods, being mere middlemen, gain least, since they lack the means to trade on their own account and are merely factors who travel to the fair to conclude contracts with the foreigners on behalf of the tsar and boyars at whose mercy they find themselves. Thus it is that no Russian merchant, however rich he may be, cuts much of a figure but lives in a meanly furnished wooden house which no boyar will be tempted to seize. In 1711 the tsar himself expressed concern at the damage that the purchase of monopoly goods (at prices fixed by the authorities) might cause to the condition of the merchants and of the peasantry.[167]

The permission granted in 1711 to persons of any rank whatever to engage in trade, subject to payment of the appropriate dues, was calculated to raise more revenue from trade but, as may be seen from Pososhkóv's comments on the subject and the tsar's own eventual change of policy, did not improve the lot of the merchants and the *posádskie liúdi* who were again to suffer from what they regarded as the unfair competition of interlopers. The ordinance in question had its origins in the often quoted nine-point directive issued by the tsar to the Senate at a critical time – March 1711 – when Russia was facing the danger of being obliged to fight the Turks as well as the Swedes while suffering from an acute shortage of funds – and 'money', the mercantilist tsar reminded his senators, 'is the lifeblood of war'.[168] It is clear from the context of this dictum and from the supplementary resolutions of the Senate that Peter I and his advisers saw in Russia's internal and foreign trade, including that with Persia and China, a rich and as yet insufficiently exploited source of revenue.[169]

In the regulation of trade as much as in all other spheres of the tsar's government, 1719 was the turning-point. In March of that year, with the promulgation of the first instruction for the Board of Trade (*Kommérts-kollégiia*) a commercial policy was laid down and fitted into the general scheme of the emergent *Polizeystaat* in the spirit of Louis XIV's preamble to his ordinance concerning the navy: 'Nous avons cru que pour achever le bonheur de nos sujets il ne restait plus qu'à leur procurer l'abondance par la facilité et l'augmentation du commerce qui est une des principales sources de la félicité des peuples.' The Russian translation made about 1714 for the benefit of the tsar and his advisers renders to perfection the majestic and hollow phraseology of this document.[170]

Under the tsar's new ordinance Russian merchants were to be encouraged to build ships and man them with Russian sailors, and to be granted relief in the discharge of customs duties; the flow of trade was to be regulated and eased, and Russians and foreigners engaged in trade were to be enabled to enter and leave the country without restriction. In April 1719 'out of concern for the merchants of Russia' the tsar abolished all trading monopolies except – as a precaution against deforestation – for potash and weidash, but did not fail soon afterwards to impose an additional toll on the purchase for export of commodities formerly covered by the Crown monopoly. In 1721 at the official ceremony held in the cathedral church of the Holy Trinity in St Petersburg to mark the conclusion of the victorious peace with Sweden the tsar spoke as if he expected the development of trade to improve the lot of the people at large. This may be seen from the full version of his address to the senators: they must endeavour to take advantage of the opportunities now offered by the opening of trade – direct and indirect – with foreign countries in order to bring relief to the common people (*naród*). Presumably the tsar expected that the revenue from trade would allow some relief in taxation. An ordinance issued in the hungry year of 1723 shows that Peter the Great nevertheless continued to associate any increase in state revenue procured by the *Kámer-kollégiia* and the *Kommérts-kollégiia* precisely with the oppression of the common people (*tiágost' liudskáia*) and was searching as earnestly as the author of *The Book of Poverty and Wealth* for a way of removing the cause of this dilemma.[171]

More than a decade before, in 1712, at the suggestion of an unidentified adviser the tsar had considered the establishment of a separate government department, a college (one of the earliest recorded uses of the term in Russian) to deal with all matters concerning trade. The committee set up to discuss the question did not go beyond making suggestions (soon found to be impracticable) for reducing the customs tariff in the Baltic ports recently captured from the Swedes, but does not appear to have been instrumental in the setting on foot of the *Kommérts-kollégiia* which entered on its activities in St Petersburg in 1715. In the course of the discussions and the preparatory work carried out before the promulgation of the tsar's first instruction for that Board in 1719, the memoranda submitted by foreign experts draw attention to the need to resolve such practical questions as the collection of information about prices and tariffs as well as about treaties and regulations relating to trade in other countries, the connection between trade and industry and the relations between the corresponding government departments. But in 1715 the institutionalization of trade was as yet a distant prospect; the tsar's use of Russia's trade with the Dutch and the English as a fund for continually supplying himself with fresh means to continue the war with Sweden prompted a hostile pamphleteer to resurrect and hurl at him the epithet 'principal merchant of his realm'[172] – a thrust aimed at his monopolistic practices.

Peter I's wish, indeed his dominant aim, if correctly attributed to him by the intelligencer writing from St Petersburg in August 1716,[173] 'to bring prosperity to his dominions through trade' would indicate the beginning of a shift from a purely fiscal and monopolistic commercial policy (made necessary by the war) to a broader aim of general economic improvement. Hence, the same anonymous writer continues, the large number of warehouses and dwelling houses under construction in St Petersburg. The tsar, he says, intends to establish direct trade relations with the countries of western Europe by way of the Baltic; on the other hand, he wishes to increase his trade with the Asiatic countries, he wishes the communication between Europe and Asia to be kept up through Petersburg and to draw a profit from it. The writer notes that two caravans travel each year from Astrakhan to Persia, that the volume of trade between Russia and Persia grows year by year and brings in a profit of 200 per cent. The revenue from this trade in customs duty the writer puts at 70,000 rix-dollars a year. It is certain, he notes, that raw silk from Persia is sold at Petersburg 30 per cent more cheaply than in Smyrna. That is why the tsar intends to manufacture silk imported from Persia by employing workers to be recruited in France and Italy. This plan, if carried out, would gravely prejudice the interests of the Dutch merchants who each year bring to Archangel gold and silver brocades worth more than 1,500,000 rix-dollars (the figure seems grossly exaggerated but the fact is confirmed by Pososhkóv) made with silk which for the most part they have bought from the Russians themselves; the Dutch sell these fabrics or barter them for Russian goods.

The writer of the report is aware of the tsar's intention to establish trade relations with the great Mogul and the Emperor of China and of his wish to find a trade route to China by way of the lands inhabited by the Uzbeks which would be shorter than the one in use at the time. The report refers to Captain (Aleksándr Bekóvich) Cherkásskii's military expedition to the Caspian (1716–17) and names as its ultimate goal the discovery of a new route by land and water from the eastern shore of that sea (via Khiva and Bokhara) to India; it does not, however, mention A. P. Volýnskii's embassy to Isfahan between 1715 and 1718 or its subsidiary object which was to investigate the possibility of establishing trade relations with Bokhara and India through Persia. The commissioning in 1719 of two naval officers, Captain-Lieutenant K. Verden (van or von Werden) and Lieutenant F. I. Soimónov, to map the western and southern shores of the Caspian completes the picture of the tsar as merchant adventurer-in-chief and explains his interest in geographical discovery. The extensive report compiled in the summer of 1715 by the British diplomatic agent George Mackenzie[174] throws some further light on the reasoning behind all this activity: the tsar did not see with indifference that his country should be owing a (trade) balance to any other even in such 'superfluities' as silk. Other sources speak of the tsar's intention that the imports from China and Persia, added to the production of the silk manufactory recently established in St Petersburg, should by 1720 or 1721 at the latest satisfy the entire Russian demand for silk fabrics. The whole of the nascent Russian silk industry was to draw its supplies of raw silk from Persia and to depend on western Europe only for the recruitment of skilled workers. The tsar's 'chiefest and fixed desire' was to trade directly, either by himself or through his subjects, 'with all foreign parts' but his long-standing ambition to bring prosperity to his country by trade could not be realized until he had secured a commercial and strategic bridgehead on the Caspian.[175]

Peter the Great's war with Persia, begun in the summer of 1722, aroused the highest expectations among his advisers: the revenue from the provinces of Gilan and Shirvan alone was estimated at 2,250,000 roubles a year and the area was rich not only in silk but also in wool, cotton, natural dyes, spices, fruit and wine. Lord Carteret, Secretary of State for the North, who as His Majesty's ambassador in Stockholm had come to share the Swedes' fear of Russia, was filled with alarm at the fate that would befall the Turks (to say nothing of the Levant Company and the East India Company of London) 'if the Czar possess himself securely of the Country which he has in view, for in that case he will make himself absolute Master of the Silk Trade by intercepting that Commodity before it comes to them, and they will fare little better if that prince should proceed no further than to open a secure passage into his Country for the Silks and Manufactures of Persia and India'. If the communication which the tsar proposes between Russia and Persia and India 'be once settled', wrote Carteret, 'the Czar's boasted project of opening a Persian and an India trade in the Baltick will no longer be looked upon as vain'.[176] The Persian war ended more swiftly than its northern counterpart but just as successfully, with Russia's annexation in 1723 of the coastal strip between Tarki and a point 100 km to the north of Astrabad.

The tsar wasted no time in seizing the opportunities created by the virtual completion of his grand design and its mercantilistic preconception soon became apparent. Some time after the end of the Persian campaign, having made up his mind that the *Kommérts-kollégiia* must not only watch over trade but promote its expansion, he drew that Board's attention to the large variety of choice goods other than silk that might be brought to the Baltic ports from Persia for re-export westwards – petroleum, saffron, dried and salted fruit, nuts, dates and cypress wood (and in passing, with characteristic mastery of detail, pointed to saffron as an essential ingredient of Polish cookery). The tsar further ordained that in the expectation of high profits, trade with France, Spain and Portugal should be developed, that exports should be carried in Russian ships, that young traders and artisans should be sent to the West to learn commerce and that there should never be fewer than fifteen such apprentices abroad. Almost immediately afterwards a Lieutenant Alekséev was appointed Russian consul at Bordeaux with instructions to penetrate the French market by competing with, and if necessary undercutting, the trading nations established there and to set on foot direct trade between the two countries. At the same time a mission was sent to Cadiz with similar instructions including the establishment of a consulate.

In the autumn of 1721 it had been thought that the tsar would travel to France, Spain and Italy to conclude trade treaties with those countries in person but the tsar's interest in the establishment of regular trade relations with southern Europe dates from 1716, the year in which he appointed one Pëtr Beklemíshev his commercial agent in Venice. In 1718 Beklemíshev handled the sale for the benefit of the tsar's treasury of a consignment of wax, Russia leather, iron and tar.[177] In the summer of 1721 Beklemíshev was active in Cadiz, and reported to the Senate on the methods of interloping the trade between Spain and America and on the possibility of smuggling gold and silver coin out of Spain for use at a profit in the Levant. The desirability of selling Russian goods in Spain for Mexican and Spanish silver had been pointed out earlier by one of Tsar Peter's advisers and eventually found its way into his clearly formulated policy of 'taking payment in money rather than in goods.'[178] For the object in opening a trade with Spain was not to put money into the pockets of Russian merchants but to meet the treasury's continuing shortage of silver which grew even more acute after 1721 since under the terms of the treaty of Nystad Russia had to pay Sweden 1.5 million rix-dollars between 1722 and 1724. In 1720 the tsar was willing to allow the Compagnie d'Occident under the direction of the notorious financier John Law to mine gold and silver in Russia in return for a royalty of 10 per cent payable in kind to the tsar's treasury, plus a commission on all sales. The Compagnie d'Occident went bankrupt and by December 1720 Law was ruined and disgraced but the tsar seems never to have despaired of finding an Eldorado, if not within his own dominions then in the West or in the East: among the aims of the expeditions to Central Asia, whether based on Astrakhan or on Toból'sk, was the discovery of gold.[179]

All things considered, late in 1723 it looked as though the fears expressed four years earlier by the Russophobe Carteret (on that occasion writing from Stockholm) were about to be justified: it was still notorious that the tsar could sail half as cheaply again as any other nation since he gave his men much less pay, that provisions were exceedingly cheap in his country, that he likewise had all the materials of shipping at home for nothing and that the building of ships cost him nothing, 'the common labourer having no wages, only victuals'. It could still be assumed that the merchants would on that account 'necessarily freight his ships before either the Danish or Swedish which will breed up his people to be seamen'.[180] But in fact such fears were as groundless in 1723 as they had been in 1719. The unwillingness of the tsar's subjects to turn merchant adventurers and form trading companies brought home to him the need for 'compulsion' in that sphere, as in all others, 'when dealing with newcomers'. Intimidation too had its role to play in the development of trade; the members of the *Kommérts-kollégiia* were to be rewarded for loyalty and devotion but 'severely punished' for slackness.[181]

In 1724 the tsar spoke in a milder tone and in surprisingly maternal language: since it was well known that 'our people' (*náshi liúdi*) would never undertake anything without being driven, the Board of Trade must guide and oversee them in all things as a mother does with a child until it can fend for itself.[182] The usual stern paternalism, however, had the last word: the *dvoriáne* were to subscribe to the capital of the company for trade with Spain, each according to his rank. But nothing further was heard of these schemes which, incidentally, suggest that the tsar regarded investment in trade and industry as a public duty of the members of all the propertied classes. The ships and crews were provided by the navy and the goods were put up partly by the treasury and partly by individual merchants under strong pressure from the authorities. The three ships which sailed from Reval in May 1725 for Cadiz where they anchored in August were registered as merchantmen and carried about 16 tonnes of sailcloth and canvas, 17 tonnes of hemp, 22 tonnes of cable, 28 tonnes of Uralian iron bars and 27 tonnes of ammunition as well as some anchors, wax, Russia leather and other goods.[183]

V

The Aftermath

Public reaction to the death of Peter (1725). Stocktaking by Catherine I and the Supreme Privy Council. Relaxation in the conditions of service of the dvoriáne. *The law on the mode of inheritance of 1714 amended (1725). The formal link between service and land ownership partly restored. Changes in the system of state security. Retrospect: the success of 'policy', the failure of* Polizey.

In January 1725 upon the death of Tsar Peter his relict had been proclaimed Empress to the cheers and drum-beats of the guards regiments which had surrounded the palace and burst into the council chamber. Peter the Great was not universally mourned by his subjects. According to an English eye-witness, John Deane, many of the chief dignitaries and members of old noble families 'whose estates are almost ruined and they themselves quite wearied at the hurry the late tsar kept them in during his life . . . being naturally strangers to public spirit' were 'in their hearts really glad' that their 'good monarch' was dead and, Deane adds, 'I neither saw a tear nor heard a sigh at the mention of his name from any Russian while I was there.' George Tilson, who had been Under-Secretary for the North since 1708, took a more detached and far-sighted view of Russia. In March 1725 he wrote to Whitworth about the new Empress: 'if she proves a . . . Semiramis of Muscovy and polishes with mildness what the Czar began so roughly, that country may grow still more renowned and your old friends the Muscovites make a handsome figure on the stage of the world, for certainly the Czar has laid foundations for a mighty superstructure'. It was not the first but the second Catherine who was to win fame as the Semiramis of the North, though the latter part of the prediction brings credit to the observer.[184]

The stocktaking of the late tsar's political and economic legacy, carried out by his widow and successor, Catherine I, together with her associates, the members of the Supreme Privy Council (*Verkhóvnyi táinyi sovét*), may not have taken long to complete but nearly two years elapsed before their findings were set out in a draft ordinance. The contents of this document, significantly omitted from the *Collection of the Laws of the Russian Empire*, may come as something of a revelation to the student of Russian history who has allowed himself to be hoodwinked by the panegyrical lamentations of a Feofán Prokopóvich or dazzled by Iván Kiríllov's statistical picture of the flourishing condition of the Russian state in 1727. The opening paragraph of the ukase in question blandly states that nearly all public concerns, spiritual as well as secular, are in poor case and in need of immediate improvement, and remarks: 'However hard my late consort may have tried to institute good order in all things and to frame suitable regulations in the hope that good order would follow of its own accord, this has not come about.' One may infer from this avowal of Catherine I's, as well as from Deane's comments, that Russia in January 1727 was not in the 'strong and sound condition' that Peter the Great had declared it to be in October 1721 and that the principal achievements of his reign were indeed, as the tsar himself put it on the same occasion, due to his 'single-handed direction'. The survey which follows speaks, without making much effort to distinguish between cause and effect, of the excessive burden of taxation and its inequitable distribution, of abuses and irregularities committed in the collection of revenue – especially of the poll-tax – , of peasants fleeing from their villages to Poland and to Siberia, of a general shortage of money, the bad state of the Mint, stagnation in trade, the lack of information about state income and expenditure, an overblown, costly and predatory bureaucracy – 'ten officials in place of one now give orders to the peasants' – , of the disadvantages of quartering the army in the countryside and of the arrears in the pay owing to some regiments and battalions. An indictment such as that might have come from the pen of Pososhkóv himself; it certainly confirms the veracity of his own account of the state of Russia and dispels any possible doubts as to its relevance to the last years of Tsar Peter's reign.[185]

The members of Catherine I's Supreme Privy Council seem to have had little use for Peter the Great's domestic policies or their underlying principles such as the moral and legal obligation of service to the state, the rule of law, an institutionalized administration, the distinction between the judiciary and the executive in regional government and between total revenue and particularized expenditure in finance. These principles the tsar had often felt himself obliged to sacrifice to expediency or financial necessity but the empress's councillors did not attribute the unsatisfactory state of Russia to the failure of Tsar Peter's attempt to put theory into practice but rather to that attempt itself, so that the perhaps inevitable reaction to the Petrine revolution resulted in a gradual but fairly swift dismantling or remoulding of many of the new institutions during the short reigns of Catherine I (1725–7) and Peter II (1727–30).

In the first place the Council faced the familiar question of how to maintain an expensive bureaucracy and a standing army without overburdening the people. The expectations aroused by the Persian campaign had not been fulfilled: the waterways of Russia did not become the commercial crossroads of Eurasia at a vast profit to the tsar's treasury, and the revenue from the newly annexed provinces was not even enough to cover the cost of the military occupation. (In 1732 Russia restored to Persia the provinces south of Baku –

Gilan, Mazanderan and Astrabad – and in 1735 Shirvan and the area between Tarki and Derbent.) At home the receipts from the poll-tax were overdue but the strong-arm methods used by the military administration to exact payment from the peasants caused them to abscond and diminished the number of actual taxpayers. The draft ordinance asked whether some better method of financing the army could not be devised? In reply it was unable to point to any remedy other than deferring the date of payment of the poll-tax until September 1727, confirming the reduction in the rate from 74 to 70 kopecks a head made in February 1725 and allowing the army regiments to accept payment of the tax in kind. In addition in 1727 (and again in 1728) one third of the annual payment was remitted; the collection was handed over to the local *voevóda* and the full participation of the military authorities in the process was dispensed with for the time being. The removal of the army units from country districts to garrison towns or their vicinity, set in train forthwith, was likewise intended to ease the plight of the peasantry. The diminution in the revenue from the poll-tax could not, for fear of loss of prestige, be allowed to result in any drastic reduction in the size of the army, but whenever practicable soldiers of all ranks who as *dvoriáne* had other means of support were sent home on extended leave and for every two such soldiers one officer, native or foreign, who did not own land was discharged. In the reign of Catherine I the navy was kept up to strength, a few warships and about eighty galleys were built, but in the subsequent period expenditure on the navy was reduced, the dockyards were virtually abandoned and long-distance cruises were forbidden on grounds of economy.

Even in Tsar Peter's lifetime it was becoming apparent that his treasury could not afford to pay the multitude of civil servants required to run the new administrative system. In 1719 an order of priority had to be established for paying the armed forces and the civil service; the army and the navy came first and the other ranks had precedence of the officers. In 1723 the field army received only a fraction of its pay. Vockerodt maintains that the salaries of the native Russians in the civil service were generally modest and that most Russian ministers, senators and high officials did not receive any pay. He does not explain that such dignitaries held of the tsar estates which were inherited or newly granted, or both. In 1724 A. I. Osterman, a foreigner, had not yet received any land but his salary as vice-president of the College of Foreign Affairs was not paid regularly.

It is not clear how many foreigners were discharged from the civil service in the interests of economy but their departure may well have been the signal for a return to homelier and cheaper methods of administration. The colleges retained their presidents and vice-presidents but the number of assessors was reduced from four to two, as was the number of councillors; furthermore, it was laid down that in alternate years half the members of each college would withdraw to the country in order to attend to their peasants and estates and save the treasury the cost of their salaries. The principle of collegiate administration was thus abandoned, for no one would have argued that *tres faciunt collegium* in the administrative sense of the term. The device itself, like the extended leave granted to *dvoriáne* from the army, indicates a tendency to equate husbandry and the maintenance of fiscal discipline – since the landlord was now personally responsible for the orderly payment of the poll-tax by the peasants on his estate – with the civil or military service ordained by the Table of Ranks.

A further saving in administrative costs was effected by paying salaries only to the presidents, vice-presidents, assessors and councillors of the *Glávnyi magistrát* (Board of Civic Administration) before its abolition in 1727, the *Iustíts-kollégiia* and the *Vótchinnaia kollégiia* (concerned with matters pertaining to landed estates). The inferior officials in these colleges, as well as in the *nadvórnye sudý* (high courts, likewise to be abolished in 1727) and in the *magistráty* (municipalities which, it will be recalled, performed also a judicial function), were to find their recompense in *pro rata* payments made by litigants or petitioners as had been the practice in the *prikázy* of old. The principle laid down by the tsar in 1714 that persons in official positions should subsist entirely on their salaries supplemented with fees was thus finally relinquished.

No less fundamental changes were made in the number and function of colleges. The scope of the *Kámer-kollégiia* (Board of Revenue) and *Shtáts-kontóra* (Board of State Expenditure) had already been reduced towards the end of Tsar Peter's reign by the introduction of the poll-tax and by the fiscal activities of the army; the Supreme Privy Council, having found that there was little left to do for revenue officers in the provinces, in 1726 suppressed the post of *rentméister* (or collector of taxes responsible to the *Shtáts-kontóra*) and added his duties to those of the *kamerír* (or supervisor of the collection of revenue in all provinces except those of St Petersburg, Moscow and Toból'sk) until that office too was suppressed (except in Livonia and Estonia) in 1727; also in 1726 the *Shtáts-kontóra* was merged with the *Kámer-kollégiia*, only, however, to be restored as a separate college in 1730. In 1731 when it was found that the *Kámer-kollégiia* had, through negligence and connivance, allowed the collection of revenue to fall behind, its Regulation (which had already been decried some ten years earlier) was thoroughly revised, but as it had never acquired the function of a policy-making ministry of economic affairs in Tsar Peter's lifetime it could hardly have done so after his death. From 1731 it was strictly and formally subordinated to the Senate. The *Manufaktúr-kollégiia* was abolished in 1727 and its work was divided between the *Kommérts-kollégiia* and a special office for manufactories attached to the Senate. The consulates at Cadiz and Bordeaux were abolished in 1727. Upon the suppression of the *Berg-kollégiia* (Board of Mines) in 1731 and four years earlier that of the *Glávnyi magistrát* (Board of Civic Administration), their functions were taken over by the *Kommérts-kollégiia* until the restoration, under the Empress Elizabeth, of the *Berg- i manufaktúr-kollégiia* as a combined ministry in 1742 and of the *Glávnyi magistrát* in 1743.

De-rationalization at the centre was paralleled by the return to a Muscovite style of government in provincial Russia. This entailed the disappearance of any vestige of distinction between administration pure and simple and the administration of justice. The year 1727 also saw something like a restoration of the *voevóda* to his former status; he was endowed with the judicial powers hitherto exercised by the *nadvórnyi sud* (high court) and his administrative authority was extended to cover also the local municipalities, but unlike his seventeenth-century prototype he was subordinated to one of the eleven provincial governors (*gubernátory*). Of all the Empress Catherine I's associates only Count P. A. Tolstói used this opportunity to raise the question of reforming the judicature by a revision of the *Code* of 1649. The institutions borrowed by Tsar Peter from the Swedish monarchy were defeated by the Muscovite administrative tradition almost as decisively as the Swedes had been beaten by the Russians at Poltáva in 1709.[186]

The curtailment of the apparatus of the well-regulated service state was quickly followed, under pressure from the *dvoriánstvo*, by measures which tended towards their emancipation from the *patria potestas* of the autocrat. The terms of service which Peter the Great had sought to keep unconditional were altered; gradually, instead of merit being rewarded, privilege was conferred on status. From 1724 the *zémskii komissár* was no longer officially appointed but (nominally) elected by the local *dvoriáne*. After the death of Tsar Peter these officers do not appear to have been active and in 1727 when the *voevódy*, each one assisted by a senior army officer, were charged with the general task of collecting the poll-tax, it became necessary on the same occasion to make the landholder (or his agent) personally responsible for the payment of the poll-tax from the peasants on his land to the extent of obliging him to make up any shortfall. This measure was not an innovation but rather a revival or wholesale and mandatory application in a stringent form of an earlier fiscal practice. *Dvoriáne* could render valuable service to the state on their home territory without having to be uprooted for an indefinite period of service elsewhere. In December 1736 the length of state service rendered by a *dvorianín* was reduced from a lifetime to twenty-five years and one son (or brother) in each family was exempted from service so as to enable him to manage the family estate. Five years earlier the *pomést'e* and the *vótchina* had both been formally designated as 'immovable property' alias *vótchiny*, with the implication of absolute ownership. The same ordinance restored the right of fathers to bequeath equal shares of their land and chattels to their children whilst making due provision for the maintenance of their widows and the dowering of their daughters.[187]

The reform of the mode of inheritance by means of the law of 1714 had patently failed in its purpose. It did not result in the creation of a body of young men who, having been cut off by their fathers with mere chattels and having before them the prospect of being eventually allowed to acquire a piece of real property, would be eager to rise in the army, in the civil service, in a profession or in trade. Among the *dvoriáne* the inheritors of real estate and the 'cadets' alike were enrolled for service in the lower ranks of the army or the navy, the only difference between the two kinds of inheritor being that the 'cadets' who had forfeited their right to inherit land regarded their plight as a double disaster. The amendment in the law introduced in 1725 whereby 'cadets' were allowed to buy landed estates upon taking up service did not appreciably alleviate their lot. Published after the death of Peter the Great, it went some way towards restoring the traditional link between service and land ownership which the late tsar had intended to sever for the sake of social utility, but seems to have passed unnoticed. If the social consequences of the law of 1714 were disappointing, its economic effects were harmful. In the division of an estate grain and livestock were treated as movables and separated from the land. In order to be able to continue to treat their offspring equally, parents raised cash with which to make gifts to their children and did so either by overtaxing the peasants on their land or by selling parcels of the estate on the sly to the detriment of its viability. A parent could also evade the law by making provision in his will for the repayment to a child of a fictitious debt, which could only be discharged through the sale of land, inevitably at a loss. A further amendment made in 1730 sought to obviate these abuses by allowing parents to distribute all their possessions among their children.[188]

The elaborate and oppressive system set up by the mistrustful tsar to spy on his subjects and enforce probity and efficiency on the part of his civil servants was discarded in 1727. The much-hated *fiskály* were discharged; the *prokuratúra* was virtually abolished: the *prokuróry* were declared 'unnecessary' but retained in the colleges as councillors; the office of *generál-prokurór* was left in abeyance until 1730; that of the *óber-prokurór* of the Senate was spared and to its holder were assigned the duties of the *reketméister* despite the incompatibility of the two functions until the restoration of that office in 1730. The abolition in 1729 of the inquisitional *Preobrazhénskii prikáz* deprived the dwindling *Polizeystaat* of that weapon which in Tsar Peter's day had consistently foreshadowed the panoply of the modern police state, but the Secret Chancellery, abolished in 1729, was restored in 1731 under the name of *Kantseliáriia táinykh rozysknýkh del.*[189]

The one minor official body to be created was the *Komíssiia o kommértsii* established in 1727 'out of concern for the plight of the merchant community and for its improvement'.[190] The scope of the commission's activity was wider than its designation would suggest to a person living in a modern industrial society. Its enquiries covered overseas trade as well as native manufactories, including the customs tariff only recently instituted for their protection, and revealed that the supply of certain categories of home-produced goods on which import duty was being levied at the highest rate was inadequate, that their quality was poor and their price excessive. The dye known as Venetian lake (*bakán*) was said to be worthless – it turned from cerise to yellow within three days; the Russian needles were unfit for use and foreign ones were unobtainable. The silk industry had failed to develop despite the annexation of the Caspian littoral which, it will be recalled, had been undertaken – apart from other considerations – with the object of securing an abundant supply of raw silk. The prohibitive rates of duty directed against the importation of these and other goods, supposedly manufactured at home in sufficient quantities, led to their being smuggled into Russia without any benefit to the treasury; moreover, the heavy incidence of customs duty deterred Russia's foreign customers, merchants from England, Holland and Hamburg who were exporters out of, as well as importers into, Russia.

Too harsh and too extreme, the tariff of 1724 was the least successful of Peter I's economic measures. Reductions in the tariff had to be made as early as 1726; in 1727 the import duty on luxury goods for personal use (*galanteréiia*) was lowered from 20 per cent to 10 per cent, the export duty on linen yarn from 75 to 10 per cent: in 1731 the revision of the whole tariff was completed after two years of work. Imported goods which could be obtained from manufactories in Russia were now liable to a duty of 20 per cent, whereas goods which were not manufactured in Russia or manufactured only in small quantities but were not indispensable to the state paid 10 per cent. The official ratio of 50 kopecks to one rix-dollar remained, however, the basis for the calculation of percentages. Equally harmful in some of its long-term effects was the compulsory diversion of a large share of Russia's northern export trade from Archangel to St Petersburg. The economic stagnation that ensued in the basin of the Dviná resulted in the impoverishment of the local population and in its professed inability to pay the poll-tax. In 1727 the restrictions on trade at Archangel were removed but in order to enable St Petersburg to compete with Archangel the rate of the internal toll was raised at Archangel from 5 to 7 per cent and reduced at St Petersburg from 5 to 3 per cent.[191]

By 1725, the year of his death, Peter the Great had raised his country to the rank of a great military and naval power, provided it with an industrial base of its own, extended its frontiers to the shores of the Baltic and of the Caspian, given it a new capital, recast its central administration, subordinated the Church to the state, imposed full-time state service and promotion by merit on the *dvoriánstvo* and effected a revolution in the dress, manners and education of the topmost stratum of society. Peter the Great's Russia may legitimately be, and indeed was, seen by contemporaries as transformed, even if it is mistakenly regarded by uncritical students as reformed. For although Peter's epic exploits were rewarded with a vast increase in Russia's territory, prestige and power, these gains were achieved at an enormous expense of human life and of capital without producing any appreciable return in the form of practical improvement. Russia did not capture the transit trade between East and West; the legal, administrative and fiscal reforms failed to produce the results expected of them and where they did lead to, or augur, greater efficiency, the running costs of the new institutions were found to be excessive.

The striking contradiction between the success of 'policy' abroad and the relative failure of 'police' at home, to use Dr Johnson's terminology, is not, however, irreconcilable; the one explains the other. Peter I overstrained Russia's human and material resources; the allocation of the bulk of the revenue to military needs during the war with Sweden proved to be a necessity also in peacetime and stood at 70 per cent in 1724, only 8 per cent less than in 1701. It would have been no great consolation to the taxpayer to learn that the reorganization of public finance carried out under Peter the Great enabled Russia in 1724 to keep up an army of 130,000 men, a Baltic navy of 34 ships of the line, 15 frigates, 77 galleys and 26 other craft and a Caspian flotilla of about 80 craft for an outlay not more than 275 per cent higher than in 1701 when the army effectives numbered about 36,000 men and the Azóv fleet consisted of ten ships of the line, two galleys and six other craft. In 1727 Catherine I, whilst recognizing that a reduction in state spending was desirable, considered it dangerous as much as to think of cutting down the expenditure on the army and on the navy, 'those main bulwarks of the state'.[192] As the necessary means could not be raised through taxation, it was decided to create them by minting five-kopeck coins to the nominal value of at least 2 million roubles. The savings were achieved by virtually dismantling the mechanism of the Petrine *Polizeystaat.* The task of reconstructing it fell to the great tsar's more distant successors. Had Pososhkóv been allowed to live to witness the work of de-molition carried out by Catherine I and her councillors he would have applauded their action which to a large extent, though unwittingly, answered his call for a return to Muscovite administrative and fiscal practice.[193]

The Book of Poverty and Wealth as a Reflection on the Reforms of Peter the Great

When, in 1704, Pososhkóv first pondered on the personal conduct of his fellow countrymen and on the state of Russian society he found the clergy, regular as well as secular, to be unsound and inactive; as for the rest of the picture he did not know of a single walk of life that was not blighted in some way or other, whether in civil or military affairs, in trade or in handicrafts, down to the very beggars idly loitering about the streets. In 1724, after Tsar Peter had devoted ten years of unremitting effort to the modernization of the state, Pososhkóv did not find any great improvement in the condition of Russia but with the self-confidence and optimism common to all 'projectors' he believed that he himself had devised an economic model that would reconcile the needs of the tsar's treasury with those of his subjects.

If another plan still seemed necessary it was because neither territorial expansion nor closer contact with the West through St Petersburg as a centre of trade and culture, nor yet the reorganization of the central and provincial administration begun early in 1719, in fact none of the great changes effected by Peter I in the last years of his reign were matched by any significant or obvious improvement in the welfare of the common people. On the contrary, by raising the status of his country to that of a great power, the tsar entered into commitments which, no doubt to his disappointment and to the bewilderment of Pososhkóv, could be met only at the expense of the well-being of his subjects. But however deficient these policies may have been and however short of their initiator's expectations they may have fallen, Pososhkóv personally derived more benefit than he suffered harm from their consequences. If Pososhkóv who in 1708 or 1710 still called himself 'an agriculturalist',[194] even though in later life he came to be known as a 'man of commerce' – *kupétskii chelovék* – was a peasant at all, he was a *paysan parvenu*. His ascent in the social scale and rise from competency to riches were due directly to the opportunities created for enterprising members of the lower orders by Tsar Peter's policy of territorial and economic expansion. In writing his treatise he appears to have been moved by a disinterested wish to demonstrate the causes and the needlessness of poverty and to show how a superfluity of wealth could be attained. The purity of his motives, however, is blemished by an unfortunate tendency to denounce before the tsar certain individuals whose misdeeds appear to have escaped the notice of the authorities.[195] His *Book of Poverty and Wealth* as well as containing elements of delation – a *donós* – also owes something to the tradition of petitioning the sovereign in a *chelobítnaia* for the redress of wrongs suffered by the writer or by the group whose cause he is pleading.[196]

In waging war the tsar had acted from economic motives, seeking not so much territorial aggrandizement as a coastline, successively on the Sea of Azóv, the Baltic and the Caspian, from which he could engage in oversea trade. The enrichment of both ruler and subject was the ultimate aim but the immediate cost in human and material terms was high. The best that Peter I could hope for in these circumstances was not to overburden the people with economic demands on the part of the state. In this respect he was more realistic than Pososhkóv who aimed higher than the mere alleviation of poverty and set his sights on instant enrichment. For a traditionalist this is a strikingly novel attitude which contrasts sharply with the fatalistic older notion that 'the rich grow richer and the poor grow poorer' and with the resignation that emanates from the answers to the twin pseudo-riddle: 'Who is all-wise?' – 'The rich man.' 'Who is a fool?' – 'The poor man.'[197] Pososhkóv's other unexpected characteristic is his eagerness for change but this does not prevent him from judging the condition of Russia at the end of the first quarter of the eighteenth century by the standards of the previous epoch. For it is a commonplace that Peter the Great rebuilt the military and bureaucratic superstructure of Muscovy without effecting a fundamental change in the mentality and social attitudes of the great majority of his subjects, including the modest traders, skilled artisans and richer peasants for whom Pososhkóv speaks and whose interests he defends. The outlook of the schismatic community shows this very clearly. Owing to a general lack of schooling in the new way of life – secular, productive, efficient, rational, socially useful – to which Peter aspired on behalf of his people, their habits of thought, conduct and language were still those of the late Muscovite period.[198]

The ideals cherished by Pososhkóv and Tsar Peter, therefore, differ as widely as Moscow and St Petersburg were apart in character and distance. At one extreme was the *Polizeystaat*, the Erastian bureaucracy, the well-regulated state which Peter I had marked out as his aim in his middle years; at the other a Mammonistic, puritan, Orthodox *Basileia* dedicated to the search for *právda* – righteousness, justice, truth – proper to the Kingdom of God and alone capable of uprooting the inveterate injustice of which Pososhkóv complains so bitterly. Although both men recognized the need to institute the rule of law and to enrich the population in order to meet the needs of the state, and although the idea of *právda* – an all-embracing political concept not unknown in the medieval

West – has something in common with the ideal of the common good so often invoked in the tsar's decrees, Peter the Great's sense of justice, however profound and sincere, was a subjective one. It was not greatly concerned with individual justice and not at all with social justice but principally with the justice (*právda*) 'of the monarch's will', the will to enforce social discipline and political obedience. The two concepts of state and Church were as incompatible as their origins were different. Tsar Peter did not share Pososhkóv's unitary view of God, man and the world; had he not abandoned this traditional attitude he would have been unwilling to draw a distinction between things spiritual and things temporal and, having established it as a principle, to subordinate the Church to the state and religion to politics.[199]

Although generally classified as a work on economics, *The Book of Poverty and Wealth* also carried a political message as bold as its attack on poverty. Conveyed obliquely and incidentally[200] rather than delivered in the form of a sustained argument, it suggests that the government of which the tsar is supposedly the all-powerful head is in fact exercised and mismanaged by the *dvoriáne* who connive at one another's misdeeds. The tsar would therefore be well advised to dispense with the services of the traditional élite and turn for support to men of humble origins. The advice is based on Pososhkóv's personal experience and corresponds to the prejudices and affinities of his own social group. It also confirms, against the writer's intentions, the need for the creation in Russia of an impartial and efficient bureaucracy in the cameralist style. What is more remarkable is that by making his suggestion Pososhkóv calls in question the reliability of the *dvoriáne* as the executive class of the Russian service state and lays himself open to retaliation from that very quarter.

About the machinery of government Pososhkóv has little to say. He shows direct knowledge of the judicial system, the local administration and the organization of the collection of revenue but writes in ignorance of many official measures relating to trade, industry and public administration, some of which were formally announced. As early as 1714 Tsar Peter, partly in order to be seen to be taking his subjects into his confidence and partly in order to preclude any excuses for their ignorance of the new laws, had decreed that ordinances of general concern should be printed and put on sale for the information of 'all'. The order was carried out, the *ukázy* in question were printed in St Petersburg or Moscow[201] but it is obvious that a remote provincial like Pososhkóv had no opportunity of buying them as they came out. In any event if, as he maintains, he wrote *The Book of Poverty and Wealth* between February 1721 and February 1724, he could hardly have taken account of the latest legislation which included such fundamental enactments as the Regulations of the Board of Civic Administration (*Glávnyi magistrát*, 1721), of the Board of Manufactories (1723), of the Board of Trade (1724), the *Ecclesiastical Regulation* (1721), the Customs Tariff (1724) and the Table of Ranks (1722). Besides, the task of making a judgment based on the printed documents alone would have been beyond Pososhkóv's intellectual capacity. Except for the last-mentioned, all six enactments deal with matters which are examined in Pososhkóv's treatise. Without therefore being a critique of the reforms of Peter the Great, *The Book of Poverty and Wealth* is a reflection on their timeliness and, to some extent, on their effectiveness. They may have forestalled some of Pososhkóv's proposals but as they did not, even in the long term, bring about the economic improvement desired by Pososhkóv, they cannot be said to have disarmed his strictures.

The value of Pososhkóv's book as a view of the social and economic problems of Petrine Russia from the level of the urban community and as an illustration of the entrepreneurial mentality at work in the conditions of early capitalism does not need to be stressed afresh. The gaps in the picture are filled by this Introduction and by the Commentaries which, where appropriate, juxtapose the existent state of affairs, the handling of it by official action and the homespun and pedantic prescriptions of Pososhkóv. It will be seen that in their own primitive way these can be as fanciful as the complex Utopia of the tsar's bureaucrats.

Notes to Introduction

1 515, Preface.
2 767, p. 165.
3 664, pp. 238, 242, 247–8, 253.
4 684, vol. vii, pp. 397–436. For Strahlenberg see also 169.
5 762, Preface to vol. i. For Weber see also 128.
6 272, pp. 511–56; 286, pp. 1–118; 362, pp. 66, 78, 104–5.
7 515, pp. 53–4.
8 515, pp. 247–80. For other contemporary descriptions of Russia see 105; 175; 270; 286; 612; 723, vol. ii, pp. 586–92, vol. iii, pp. 621–52.
9 For Pososhkóv see Bibliography, items 1–26.
10 See 72, pp. 469–71.
11 See 9 (Tsarevskii's edition), pt ii, pp. 57, 290–322.
12 *PSZ* IV 1776 11 March 1700. 4 (1951 edition), p. 381, note 47; 20, pp. 537–8; 207, pp. 41–53; 649, p. 146; Chapter 9, p. 352.
13 For Avraámii see 74; 255, pp. 78–87. *Stárets*: a monk of mature age and long experience who directs the novices in a monastery; also a spiritual counsellor of laymen.
14 *PSZ* III 1673 23 Jan. 1699.
15 See 63.
16 See 20, pp. 529–31.
17 See 322; 629; 630.
18 Reckoned at 30 × 80 sazhens. See Table of Weights and Measures, p. 433.
19 *PSZ* VIII 5633 25 Oct. 1730. See also 4 (1951 edition), p. 325; 7, col. 1427; 18, pp. 66–7; 568, p. 279; 646, vol. xviii, p. 596.
20 *PSZ* VII 4717 11 May 1725. 18, p. 76; 695.
21 373, p. 406; Chapter 7, pp. 317, 321. For the origins of this idea see 562, p. 41.
22 628, pp. 192, 591.
23 Christopher Polhem was a follower of Becher. See 215, p. 100; 310, pp. 9–19, 73, 75; 593, p. 17.
24 628, pp. 6, 18, 152–3.
25 For cameralism and mercantilism see 17; 34; 68; 92; 93; 95; 106; 126; 165; 178; 189; 196; 225; 263; 279; 281; 295; 345; 373, pp. 371, 705 (for Faust ab Aschaffenburg); 447; 518, p. 89; 562, p. 41; 598; 628, pp. 142, 148, 152, 167–8, 173–4, 192, 591; 653; 672, pp. 178–90; 724.
26 See 504.
27 See Chapter 3 pp. 224, 229 and Chapter 9, p. 364.
28 286, p. 17.
29 373, pp. 589–90.
30 *AAE* IV no. 111, 15 May 1659, pp. 151–6; *AI* V no. 10, 13 Sept. 1676, pp. 18–20, no. 125, 1 July 1685, p. 214; *Ulozhénie*, Chapter 11, articles 6, 21, 89, pp. 52–71; 194; 231, pp. 17–38; 348, pp. 376–80, 411–17, 434, 447; 363, pp. 107–10, 158; 383, pp. 362–402; 449, pp. 106–16; 459, pp. 210, 261–2; 477, pp. 174, 396, 424; 500, pp. 150, 157; 501, pp. 200–1; 550; 572, vol. i, pp. 271–2, 643, 888–9, vol. ii,

pp. 1380, 1561; 573, vol. i, pp. 380–2, 387, 502–30; 763, pp. 275–7; 765, pp. 615–53; 766, pp. 68–70, 287–8. For the tsar as monopolist and for the sources of his revenue see also 108, pp. 607–8 and 166, pp. 59–61, 112. For craft corporations see Commentary on Chapter 5.

31 *PSZ* II 832 25 Aug. 1680, 890 26 Aug. 1681, article 1. 324, vol. i, pp. 60, 144–8.

32 81, pp. 105, 115–16, 119; 211; 277; 278; 414; 415.

33 *Ulozhénie*, Chapter 11, articles 1–2. 152; 306; 370; 429; 448; 609, pp. 571–2; 634; 691.

34 See 89; 113; 133; 135; 393; 475; 476; 477, pp. 228, 279–80, 341, 515; 634, vol. i, pp. 211–64, 277–312, 314–43, 515; 703, p. 65.

35 *Ulozhénie*, Chapter 19, article 3.

36 Ibid., articles 1–5, 8, 9, 11, 13. 174; 192; 474; 477, pp. 151, 200–1; 753.

37 380, pp. 199, 226; 477, p. 146; 691, pp. 321, 385.

38 For *pomést'ia* and *vótchiny* under the *Ulozhénie* see: *Ulozhénie*, Chapter 16 and especially articles 2, 5, 7, 8–10, 13, 16–18, 21, 24–8, 40, 46–8, 51, 53, 57, 60–2, 69 (also *PRP* VI, Commentary, pp. 222–4, 226, 237, 239) and cf. Chapter 17, articles 2, 4–10, 13, 18, 37, 41–2, 46–8; *PRP* VI, Commentary, pp. 266–7, 277. Subsequent ordinances concerning land until the end of the century: *PSZ* I 583 22 July 1674, II 633 10 March 1676, 644 24 May 1676, 700 10 Aug. 1677, 702 20 Aug. 1677, 725 31 May 1678, 764 19 June 1679, 765 19 June 1679, 860 28 Jan. 1681, 1074 April 1684, 1114 28 March 1685, 1116 1 April 1685, 1256 26 July 1687, 1391, 1690 (undated). On landholding in general see: *PRP* VI p. 262; 31; 146, p. 288 (Chancellor visited Russia in 1533); 260, p. 247; 300, p. 4; 305, pp. 1–2, 24, 38–9; 326, p. 311 and Notes, pp. 228–9; 363, pp. 107–10; 380, pp. 199, 226; 385; 459, pp. 125–88, 141–7, 191–261, 201–10; 499; 530, pp. 268–9; 579, pp. 51–3; 587; 661, pp. 138–48, 164–5, 180, 191–2, 194; 662; 745, pp. 426, 431.

39 477, pp. 143, 150.

40 *Sluzhílye liúdi po otéchestvu*, i.e. those who had a hereditary place in the system of precedence and, as a rule, were landholders in their own right.

41 See *Ulozhénie*, Chapter 13; *PRP* VI, Commentary, pp. 187–9; *Ulozhénie*, Chapter 17, article 42, Chapter 19, article 3. 634, vol. i, pp. 228–32; 786, p. 71; 796, pp. 53–4.

42 *Ulozhénie*, preamble; *PRP* VI, p. 21; 346, pp. 516–17.

43 635, pp. 231–8. For the Church generally in this period see: *AAE* IV no. 204, article 4, 15 May 1675, pp. 259–63; *PRP* VII pp. 365, 381; *PSZ* I 442 22 Jan. 1669, 711 19 Dec. 1677. 115, pp. 100–13; 197, pp. 322–9; 258, pp. 43–78, 93, 95, 101, 107; 259; 260, p. 243; 264; 324, vol. i, pp. 170, 236, vol. ii, pp. 130, 133, 147, 170, 203, 205; 488; 671; 712; 752; 792.

44 The musketeers who made up the garrison of Moscow.

45 See 329; 469, pp. 122–30; 477, pp. 300, 317, 320–3, 328, 331–2; 566; 670; 676.

46 See *Ulozhénie*, preamble.

47 See *Ulozhénie*, Chapter 16, articles 1–6, 21, 24–8, 41–50 (permitted quantities of land). 69, vol. i, pp. 295–7, vol. ii, pp. 415, 437, 440, 445–6, 451, 459, 476, 487–9; 171, pp. 107–34; 299, pp. 4, 5, 16, 21, 38–9, 286–7; 305, pp. 39, 141–7 (land held by boyars); 385, p. 113; 459, pp. 201–10; 465; 477, pp. 140–3, 149, 157, 228–9; 365, 790; 485; 501, pp. 108–14; 519, pp. 19, 22, 27; 606; *SIE*, vol. 5 under *Zaséchnaia chertá*; 749; 776.

48 412, pp. 83–5, 124–52; 477, pp. 264, 270, 308.

49 *Ulozhénie*, Chapter 11, article 2, Chapter 16, article 40; *PRP* VI, Commentary, p. 234. 305, pp. 9–10, 35; 393; 459, pp. 144–5; 477, pp. 50–1, 140, 143, 154–5, 279–80, 439; 472; 473; 476; 631, pp. 94–175.

50 *PSZ* II 744 Dec. 1678; *Ulozhénie*, Chapter 20, articles 1–3. 39; 84; 114; 181; 363, p. 42; 477, pp. 140, 379; 501, pp. 209–11.

51 352, vol. iii, pp. 72–4.

52 646, vol. xvi, p. 546.

53 155, pp. 133–55; 274, vol. i, p. 54; 319; 352, vol. iii, pp. 72–4; 379, p. 454; 431; 477, pp. 156, 448, 450; 487; 526; 619; 758.

54 See 401; 477, pp. 496–540, 687–93; 479, pp. 85–104; 769. For trade with the West see above, note 32.

55 352, vol. iii, corrected in Kliuchevskii, *Kurs russkoi istorii*, vol. iii, second edition, M–Petrograd, 1923, pp. 293, 471, in accordance with 442, p. 286.

56 474, pp. 88–9; 477, pp. 149, 162, 200–1, 350; 747, pp. 27–9.

57 See 35, pp. 35, 39, 41–2; 36, pp. 92–130, 150–4, 160–72, 179–81, map no. 1; 73; 89; 90; 91, pp. 590, 613; 100, pp. 102, 107; 117, pp. 269, 278–82; 238; 336; 359; 379, pp. 461, 466; 477, pp. 452, 454, 467; 534; 580; 594, vol. i, pp. 140–1; 663, pp. 21, 26–8, 48, 50–1; 673; 780, pp. 154–5.

58 166, p. 128.

59 New Trade Regulations (*PSZ* I 408 22 April 1667), preamble.

60 For higher figures in 1689 and 1692 and the highest figure of all so far: 95,122 roubles in 1700, see 379, pp. 54–8, 400.

61 *PSZ* I 408 Apr. 1667 (*Nóvyi Torgóvyi Ustáv* = New Trade Regulations, incomplete, includes *Ustáv v tsárstvennom gráde Moskvé*, a set of regulations for foreign merchants), supplemented by *PSZ* II 873 June 1681; *SGGD* III no. 158, 1653 (*Ustávnaia tamózhennaia grámota*, customs tariff), IV no. 55, 7 May 1667 (a full text of the New Trade Regulations). 36, pp. 135–50; 89; 52–71; 91, pp. 590, 613; 108, pp. 607–8; 156, pp. 174, 403–49; 158, pp. 102–26, 125–6, 288; 166, p. 128; 286, p. 75; 338, pp. 317–19; 363, pp. 128, 152, 158; 410, pp. 31–2; 477, pp. 138–9, 257, 424, 427–9, 431, 434; 612, p. 320; 698, pp. 116–26.

62 613, vol. i, p. 2.

63 *AI* V no. 48, 21 Oct. 1679, pp. 72–5. 155, pp. 180, 182; 383, pp. 25, 27, 283–98, 303–13, 349–50; 442, pp. 95, 97–8, 210, note 5; 444, pp. 92–7; 477, pp. 234, 263, 328, 422–3, 447–8; 638; 719, pp. 221–3.

64 *PSZ* II 633 10 March 1676, 700 10 Aug. 1677, 764 19 June 1679, 765 19 June 1679, 1116 1 Apr. 1685; *Ulozhénie*, Chapter 16, article 3; *PRP* VI, Commentary, p. 234. 477, pp. 146–7; 501, pp. 185, 193–5.

65 The office which handled the collection of direct taxes from the urban population engaged in trade and handicrafts, and from 1680 also the levying of tolls and of the royalties from the sale of liquor.

66 72, pp. 552, 554; 114; 115; 135; 180; 181; 182; 183; 197, pp. 115–43, 295–316; 219; 363, pp. 97–137, 113, 167, 173; 442, p. 98; 477, pp. 368, 372–82, 405; 515, pp. 189–90; 531; 737; *SIE*, vol. 15 under *Chéti*.

67 44; 87; 156, pp. 74–362; 197, pp. 295–316; 477, pp. 384–94; 737.

68 *Ulozhénie*, Chapter 10, article 2. 116; 152, pp. 187, 212–74, 319–36, 351–4, 372–81; 171, pp. 175–220; 173; 257; 334; 346, pp. 401–8, 414, 426, 432, 438–44; 477, pp. 340, 348–54, 360–6, 405; 785, pp. 237, 240, 283.

69 601, pp. 50, 64.

70 113; 134; 136; 138; 335; 477, pp. 325–43; 479.
71 57; 64; 72; 75, pp. 162–3 (Baklanova considers the data used and the calculations made by earlier writers on the subject of literacy to be unreliable and merely notes a gradual and general improvement in this respect during the seventeenth century); 119, vol. iii, pp. 263–6; 323, p. 2; 324, vol. i, pp. 47–8; 361, pp. 21, 24, 31, 34, 68–77; 477, pp. 555–8; 535, pp. 127–8, 132, 155, 157; 553; 581; 582; 588; 635; 637, pp. 6, 12, 17, 24; 643; 682; 775; *RBS*, vol. 8 under 'Ioakím.'
72 See Section III p. 71.
73 119, vol. iii, pp. 212, 215, 221–4; 613, vol. i, pp. 6–7.
74 35, pp. 47–54; 101, p. 23; 119, vol. i, pp. 360–5, vol. iii, pp. 147–53; 515, p. 147; 578.
75 *PSZ* IV 1820 23 Dec. 1700; 101, pp. 22–3; 119, vol. iii, p. 346; 155, p. 93; 314, p. 347 (the number of recruits given here by Beskrovnyi differs slightly from that quoted by Rabinovich, 'Formirovanie . . .' 556, pp. 226–8); 613, vol. i, pp. 5–7; 660; 788, pp. 60–1, 69–70.
76 For the collection of taxes see note 30 above. With regard to 'self-government' see the titles of 120 and 343. Kizevetter (343, p. 61) recognizes the self-contradiction, Lappo-Danilevskii (383, pp. 318, 349–50) notes a gradual deterioration in the character of 'self-government'.
77 *PSZ* III 1674 30 Jan. 1699, 1683 16 March 1699, 1686 30 May 1699 (article 6 for the status of the *Rátusha*), 1687 May 1699, 1704 20 Oct. 1699, 1718 17 Nov. 1699. 119, vol. iii, pp. 248, 250–3, 331, 333.
78 400; 515, pp. 30–4, 140–1; 686.
79 *PSZ* IV 1818 16 Dec. 1700; 1829 21 Jan. 1701, 1834 31 Dec. 1701, 1876 7 Nov. 1701. 170, pp. 113–24; 258, pp. 121–35; 286, vol. i, pp. 136–7; 733, vol. i, pp. 110–12.
80 4 (1951 edition), p. 268; 217, p. 43; 280, pp. 153, 155; 613 vol. i, pp. 23–4.
81 *DP* II no. 506, 12 June 1712, pp. 409–11; *PSZ* IV 2240 31 Dec. 1709. 38, vol. ii, pp. 42–7; 155, pp. 93–4; 242, pp. 253–5; 344, pp. 52–3; 358, pp. 16–26; 383, pp. 377–402; 392, p. 23; 419, pp. 77–90; 522, pp. 57–62; 541, pp. 18, 33–46, 128; 740, pp. 94–5; *ES* vol. 48 under *Posókha.*
82 PRP VIII, pp. 36–41; *PSZ* IV 2028 9 Feb. 1705, 2036 20 Feb. 1705, 2127 18 Dec. 1706, 2218 18 Dec. 1708, 2321 22 Feb. 1711, 2412 31 July 1711, 2456 10 Dec. 1711, 2496 1 March 1712, V 2879 28 Jan. 1715; *ZA* no. 48, 24 Apr. 1713, p. 206. 59; 66; 101, pp. 23, 25–9, 32; 118, p. 497; 314, pp. 324–5, 347–9; 442, pp. 258, 266–9, 279, 281, 293, 306; 477, pp. 421–2; 504, pp. 130–1; 515, pp. 252–3, 266–7; 568, pp. 119–20; 762, vol. ii, pp. 40–3.
83 104; 314, pp. 501–9; 280, pp. 290–306.
84 *PB* I no. 125, 20 Oct. 1696, pp. 111–13; *PRP* VIII, pp. 42–3, 211–15; *PSZ* IV 2321 22 Feb. 1711, 2331 5 March 1711, VI 3978 27 Apr. 1722. 59; 60; 119, vol. iii, pp. 250–4, vol. iv, pp. 238–58, 244–6; 229, pp. 295–326; 346, pp. 407–8, 435–8; 523; 528; 657, pp. 35–9, 54–8.
85 BL, Additional MS 37363 ff. 87–88v. (Tatar raids); *Sb. RIO*, vol. 11, pp. 96–7. 40, pp. 90–3; 41, pp. 158–61; 121, pp. 197–8; 127, pp. 34–8, 94–6; 280, pp. 384–9; 286, p. 57; 314, pp. 528–38, 560–7; 378; 541, pp. 34–46; 613, vol. i, pp. 334–5, 375.
86 *PSZ* IV 1910 16 Apr. 1702.
87 309 under Police.
88 381, vol. i, Preface and p. 4; 413, vol. i, p. 56.

89 *PB* II no. 421, 16 Apr. 1702, pp. 39–52, 337–40; *SGGD* IV, no. 130, 12 Jan. 1682, p. 401; *ZA* no. 21, 3 Dec. 1714, p. 42. 61, Book 5, Chapter 11, p. 467; 145, pp. 12–25; 220, pp. 116, 122, 125–6; 291, pp. 75–6; 413, vol. i, Preface; 436, pp. 180–1; 437; 558; 559; 628, pp. 16, 58, 83, 142, 193, 202; 639, pp. 3, 154; 651; 770; 787, pp. 49–50.

90 92; 112, nos. 167, 217, 219, 949; 345; 628, pp. 171–2. See also M. N. Murzanova, E. I. Bobrova, and V. A. Petrov, *Istoricheskii ocherk i obzor fondov rukopisnogo otdela Biblioteki Akademii Nauk*, pt 1, M–L, 1956, pp. 58, 259, 411. The *Fürstliche Machtkunst* has also been attributed to Freiherr Asanius Christoph von Marenholz, *Geheimrat* at Hanover. See H. W. Rotermund, ed., *Fortsetzung und Ergänzungen zu Christian Gottlieb Jöchers Gelehrten-Lexikon*, vol. iv, Bremen, 1813, under Marenholz. A Swedish translation of the *Machtkunst* was published in 1723; see 593, p. 29.

91 *PRP* VIII, pp. 44, 47, 51–4; *PSZ* IV 2319 11 Feb. 1711, 2329 2 March 1711, 2330 2 March 1711, 2331 5 March 1711, V 2785 16 March 1714, 2786 17 March 1714; *ZA*, p. xxxv, pp. 51, 93, 107, 119, 143 (random examples).

92 See Commentary on Chapter 3.

93 *PB* VI, no. 1852 6 July 1707, pp. 9–10, VII, 1, no. 2453 28 June 1708, pp. 223–4; *PSZ* IV 2218 18 Dec. 1708. 65; 133, pp. 119–24, 128, 130–1, 136–7, 140–1, 149; 154; 250, pp. 57–9, 64, 71–6, 81, 101, 170, 179–81, 207, 298–302, 309–15; 391; 392; 533, pp. 45, 70, 75, 85, 86, 88, 95, 97, 102, 107–8, 111–12, 119, 123, 138, 140–1, 152, 191, 198; 700, pp. 399–409.

94 597, p. 649.

95 764, p. 3.

96 BL, Additional MS 20365 f. 217v. (report from Paris); *PSZ* VI 3893 3 Feb. 1722 (the succession to the throne); *ZA* no. 330, p. 270 (undated and unattributed memorandum on the collegiate system of government); 436, pp. 159–60; 547, pp. 23–38, 76–93; 574, p. 258; 765, pp. 138–9, 140–8; 767, p. 192.

97 *ZA* no. 244, March 1711, p. 203, no. 249, 2 July 1713, pp. 206–7.

98 *PRP* VIII, pp. 21–2, 46–7, 50–4, 122–5, 164; *PSZ* IV 2330 2 March 1711, 2331 5 March 1711, V 2786 17 March 1714, 3211 19 July 1718, VI 3602 28 June 1720, 3721 28 Jan. 1721; *ZA* no. 14, 24 Apr. 1713, p. 38, no. 176, 25 Oct. 1723, pp. 129–32 (crimes against the state), pp. 328–36 (1710–14). 58; 118, pp. 295–317; 275, pp. 104–12; 344, pp. 189, 345; 628, p. 42; 646, vol. xvi, p. 495.

99 8 (1893 edition), pp. 172–4, 179; 118, pp. 229, 259–60; 156, pp. 84, 311; 286, p. 116; 343, pp. 70, 74; 477, pp. 389–90; 515, pp. 189–90; Chapter 3, pp. 226–7.

100 *PSZ* IV 2319 19 Feb. 1711, V 2673 24 Apr. 1713, 2786 17 March 1714, 2871 24 Dec. 1714, 2879 28 Jan. 1715. 118, pp. 260–1; 179, p. 230.

101 *PSZ* IV 1857 20 June 1701.

102 Or perhaps quoting a Byzantine tag. See 62, p. 400.

103 *PRP* VII, pp. 35–180, 237–67, VIII, pp. 11, 205, 208, 223–4, 246–53; *PSZ* II 764 15 June 1679, 765 15 July [?] 1679, 1370 17 Apr. 1690, 1391 1690, IV 1857 20 June 1701, 2158 21 Sept. 1707, 2231 2 Apr. 1707, 2467 16 Jan. 1712, 2667 24 Apr. 1713, V 2789 23 March 1714, 2796 14 Apr. 1714, 2804 4 May 1714, 3013 15 Apr. 1716, VII 4722 28 May 1725, 4938 20 July 1726, VIII 5658 9 Dec. 1730, 5717 17 March 1731, XXII 21 Apr. 1785, article 21, XXVIII 21, 536 26 Nov. 1804 citing the unpublished ordinance of 31 March 1736; *ZA* no. 2 13 July (year not given), p. 29, no. 11, 17 March 1711, p. 37. 243, p. 324; 261, p. 111; 302, pp. 65–9;

314, p. 189; 512, vol. ii, p. 535, note; 504, pp. 50–4; 549, p. 31; 557, pp. 162–3; 625, pp. 4–5, 378–82; 704, p. 110; 723, vol. i, Appendix 12, pp. 390–9; 745, pp. 439, 487. The figures given by Ustrialov (723) and Indova (302) respectively do not tally in all cases, moreover they refer to different periods. The correct total of *dvorý* (households) given away from the Crown demesne between 1700 and 1711 is 12,611.

104 *PRP* VIII, p. 205; *ZA* nos 218–21, pp. 163–70. 121, pp. 202–21; 170, p. 149; 227, pp. 92, 108; 267, pp. 16, 276; 280, pp. 501–6; 314, pp. 577–81, 421–9; 372, p. 102; 471, pp. 59–62; 723, vol. vi.

105 *PSZ* V 3261 22 Dec. 1717.

106 *ZA* no. 330, pp. 269–71 (undated). 244, pp. 364–9.

107 *PRP* VIII, pp. 62–5, 106; *PSZ* V 2791 4 Apr. 1714, 3129 11 Dec. 1717, 3255 12 Dec. 1718, 3261 22 Dec. 1718; *Sb. RIO*, vol. 11, pp. 364, 386; *ZA* no. 27, 13 Nov. 1715, p. 45, no. 29, 13 Dec. 1715, p. 29, no. 32, 16 Dec. 1715, p. 47, no. 247, 16 Jan. 1712, p. 205, no. 264 (undated), p. 219. 145, pp. 13–23; 190, p. 178; 244, pp. 332, 364–9; 279, pp. 84–6; 301; 314, pp. 297–303, 756; 518, pp. 52–93; 528; 628, pp. 125, 149; 657, pp. 43, 81.

108 *ZA*, pp. 5–6, no. 222, 1 Jan. 1721, pp. 170–3. 28, p. 32; 226, pp. 12, 36–7, 53, 58–82, 87, 90, 92, 97–8, 103–5, 128, 173, 198–9, 200, 205, 209, 212–13, 218, 228, 231, 270; 504, pp. 66–7; 765, p. 604.

109 *PRP* VIII, pp. 117 (specifically), 72–121; *PSZ* V 2871 24 Dec. 1714, 2879 28 Jan. 1715, 3078 3 Apr. 1717, 3303 12 Feb. 1719, article 25, VI 3534 28 Feb. 1720, articles 19, 20, 39, VII 4597 13 Nov. 1724; *Sb. RIO*, vol. 11, pp. 386, 538; *ZA* no. 262, 11 Dec. 1717, p. 217. 118, pp. 260–1, 269, 294; 124, pp. 32–3, 59–60; 286, p. 116; 518, pp. 52–93; 705.

110 514; 515, pp. 141–3, 188–9; 612, p. 343.

111 *PRP* VIII, pp. 208, 567–9; *PSZ* V 2828 15 June 1714. 314, pp. 398–9; 424, p. 82; 684, vol. i, p. 87.

112 *PRP* VIII, pp. 267–70, 279–80, 290, 292–4, 296–300, 325, 319–456 (Articles of War); *PSZ* V 3006 30 March 1716, 3010 10 Apr. 1716, VI 3531 23 Feb. 1720, VII 4389 9 Dec. 1723; *ZA* no. 38, 10 Apr. 1716, pp. 52–3. 48; 218; 512, vol. ii, no. 292, pp. 346– 7, no. 299, p. 349, no. 321, pp. 364–6. The *Ustáv Vóinskii* or Military Statute published in 1716 comprises the *Artíkul Vóinskii* of 1715.

113 From the German *Hofgericht*, court of appeal.

114 118, p. 246, with an incorrect reference to *PSZ* VII 4344 5 Nov. 1723. In relation to the foregoing passage: *PRP* VIII, pp. 22, 69, 190; *PSZ* IV 2165 20 Oct. 1707, 2330 2 March 1711, V 2673 24 Apr. 1713, 3244 26 Nov. 1718, 3282 15 Jan. 1719, 3294 Jan. 1719, 3295 Jan. 1719, 3344 8 Apr. 1719, 3453 10 Nov. 1719, VI 3824 1 Sept. 1721, 3917 12 March 1722, 3935 4 Apr. 1722, VII 4530 4 June 1724; *ZA* nos. 386–90, pp. 382–6, 1722–4. 60; 118, pp. 173, 185–8, 203–10, 221–3, 246, 229–49, 272, 455; 258, p. 287; 314, p. 326; 441, pp. 41–50; 518, pp. 223–331; 657, pp. 91–3; 731, p. 84.

115 The canonical collection of ecclesiastical laws analogous to the Byzantine *Nomokanon*. Cf. note 41 above.

116 *PRP* VIII, pp. 60, 208–10, 218; *PSZ* V 2673 24 Apr. 1713, 2726 23 Oct. 1713, 2877 25 Jan. 1715, VI 3970 17 Apr. 1722, VII 4422 20 Jan. 1724, 4507 20 May 1724, 4436 22 Jan. 1724. 18, pp. 32–4; 58, pp. 71–80; 118, pp. 295–307; 341; 607, vol. i, p. 230; 731, p. 60.

117 A Germanized form of *Maître des requêtes*.

118 61, Book III, Chapter 11, Section 9, p. 269.
119 Jonathan Swift, *Gulliver's Travels*, Part III, A Voyage to Laputa, Chapter 6.
120 *PRP* VIII, pp. 23, 122, 152, 164–5, 172–6, 213, 217–19; *PSZ* VI 3534 28 Feb.
   1720, 3581 13 May 1720, 3602 28 June 1720, 3721 28 Jan. 1721, 3877 12 Jan.
   1722, 3880 18 Jan. 1722, 3900 5 Feb. 1722, 3979 27 Apr. 1722, 3981 27 Apr.
   1722, VII 4507 28 May 1724; *ZA* no. 271, 2 June 1718, pp. 225–6, no. 322, 22 Jan.
   1724, p. 263, nos. 335–341, 1721–4, pp. 300–18, nos. 355–66, 1720–4, pp. 337–
   50. 58, pp.74–6, 78; 118, pp. 295, 307, 311, 313, 320–1; 179, pp. 222–4; 226, p.
   201; 405; 453, pp. 266, 271–2, 286; 512, vol. ii, no. 515, p. 564; 730, pp 28–75;
   731, pp. 1–26, 51–5, 60–88; Chapter 6 below.
121 Under a secret separate article paid in *Kurant-taler* and therefore at the actual cost
   of 1.5 million roubles. See 464, p. 481.
122 121, pp. 222, 226; 227, pp. 200–485; 314, pp. 581–90; 400, p. 30; 442, p. 494; 464,
   pp. 335, 415, 441, 460, 481; 571, pp. 181–2.
123 *PRP* VIII, pp. 166–70, 179–207, 490; *PSZ* VI 3840 22 Oct. 1721, 3890 24 Jan.
   1722, 3893 5 Feb. 1722. For the Table of Ranks see pp. 77–8.
124 See entries in *RBS*; 109; 199; 356; 493.
125 148; *PRP* VIII, pp. 179–203; *PSZ* IV 1910 16 Apr. 1702, 2466 15 Jan. 1712, 2467
   16 Jan. 1712, 3255 12 Dec. 1718, V 3384 4 June 1719, VI 3534 28 Feb. 1720,
   Chapter 36; 3705 16 Jan. 1721, 3881 18 Jan. 1721, 3845 10 Nov. 1721, VII 4449
   31 Jan. 1724, 4588 11 Nov. 1714, article 9, 4613 12 Dec. 1724. 223, pp. 26–36,
   62–71, 74–7; 245, pp. 222–33, 235–41; 363, p. 42; 435; 436; 477, p. 369; 557, pp.
   146–53; 683, p. 32; 704, p. 105; 706, pp. 48–109, 254.
126 *PB* I, no. 139, 25 Feb. 1697, pp. 134, 611; *PRP* IV, p. 3, VIII, p. 391; *PSZ* IV 2942
   23 Feb. 1712; 2497 15 March 1712, V 2762 20 Jan. 1714, 2771 4 Feb. 1714, 2778
   28 Feb. 1714, 2789 24 March 1714, article iii, 2845 26 Sept. 1714, 2968 20 Dec.
   1714, VI 3631 23 Aug. 1720, 3890 20 Jan. 1722, article 14, 537, nos 184, 185, pp.
   199–201. 155, p. 79; 176, p. 18; 481; 482; 501, pp. 241–6; 744, pp. 203, 220.
127 *PSZ* IV 2816 18 Jan. 1708, V 3356 18 Apr. 1719. 234, pp. 317–24; 442, p. 633;
   536; 567; 629, pp. 299–301, 351–62, 375–89; 637, pp. 80–1, 86–7; 744, p. 275;
   787, pp. i–xviii; 791, pp. 20–3, 27–8, 38.
128 *PSZ* IV 2476 16 Jan. 1712, V 2937 10 Oct. 1715, 2971 28 Dec. 1715, 3276 11 Jan.
   1719, VI 3845 10 Nov. 1721; *Sb. RIO*, vol. 11, pp. 146, 302. 32, pp. 208–9; 101,
   pp. 172–6; 124, pp. 241–51; 286, pp. 47–8, 51, 56; 612, pp. 325, 327; 314, pp.
   655–67; 404, pp. 1–11; 483; 515, pp. 213–14, 278; 736, pp. 20, 29, 49; 744, pp. 16,
   31, 38–9, 131–5, 220, 284–6, 288, 291; 787, pp. 192–3; 795.
129 *PSZ* IV 2186 January 1708, 2308 11 Nov. 1710, V 2762 20 Jan. 1714, 2775 26 Feb.
   1714, 2778 28 Feb. 1714, 2968 20 Dec. 1715, 2971 28 Dec. 1715, 2979 18 Jan.
   1716, 3447 6 Nov. 1719, VI 3575 30 Apr. 1720, 3708 16 Jan. 1721, Chapter 21,
   VII 4624 1724 (undated), article 33; *Sb. RIO*, vol. 11, p. 302. 118, vol. i, p. 265;
   423; 451, p. 33; 736, p. 24; 744, pp. 14, 17–18, 20–3, 32, 34, 36, 111–12, 203;
   Chapter 7, pp. 307, 313.
130 *PSZ* VI 3741 16 Feb. 1721, 3718 14 Feb. 1721, 3896 5 Feb. 1722, VII 4291 1
   Sept. 1723. 450, pp. 20, 33–9, 58; 637, p. 87; 744, pp. 13–14, 23, 30, 35–6, 101,
   117, 141, 297, 299, 305. See also Commentary on Chapter 1.
131 *PSZ* V 3208 11 June 1718, VI 3896 5 Feb. 1722, VII 4443 28 Jan. 1724, 4457 5
   Feb. 1724; *ZA* no. 4, pp. 33–4, undated, no. 269, 9 May 1718, pp. 222–5, point 2,
   cf. p. 270. 42, pp. 297–8; 577, Appendix, pp. 3–7, 18–26.

132 *AI* I, no. 154, item 19, 15 Jan. 1581, p. 270; *ODD* I, no. XLI, pp. CCCCXLVIII–CCCCLII, undated; *Ulozhénie*, Chapter 17, article 42; *PRP* VI, Commentary p. 275; *PSZ* I 442 22 Jan. 1669, V 2991 8 Feb. 1716 (cp. 504, p. 50), 3183 16 March 1718, 3602 28 Feb. 1720, VI 3708 16 Jan. 1721, 3734 14 Feb. 1721, 3761 15 March 1721, VI 3854 19 Nov. 1721, 3963 12 Apr. 1722, 4022 May 1722, 4081 4 Sept. 1722. 160, pp. 631–4, 723–7; 170, pp. 165–218, 184, 304–5; 244, pp. 365–6; 258, pp. 104–20; 260, pp. 343–5; 264, p. 399; 402; 451, pp. 3–6, 9, 10, 12, 20–1, 26, 33–43, 47–8, 53, 80–2; 477, pp. 161–2, 789–90; 512, vol. i, p. 112; 586; 612, p. 88; 727; 791, pp. 90–140.

133 *AAE* IV no. 315, Dec. 1696, pp. 466–7; *PSZ* I 442 22 Jan. 1669, III 1664, 1698 (undated), IV 1829 21 Jan. 1701, 1876 7 Nov. 1701, 1886 30 Dec. 1701, 2142 17 March 1707, 2248 29 Jan. 1710, 2249 9 Feb. 1710, 2352 25 Apr. 1711, 2477 31 Jan. 1712, V 2841 3 June 1714, 3026 11 June 1716, 3409 29 July 1719, VI 3576 3 May 1720, 3962 12 Apr. 1722, 4035 17 June 1722, 4081 4 Sept. 1722, VII 4183 8 March 1723, 4186 11 March 1723, 4515 29 May 1724, 4567 18 Sept. 1724, 4632 14 Jan. 1725, 4919 12 July 1726, 4959 26 Sept. 1726. 170, pp. 125, 138,141–2, 245–8; 258, pp. 170–1, 175–7, 186–95, 240, 220–67, 289–90, Appendix, pp. 19–23; 259; 260, p. 158; 641, pp. 709–10; 760, p. 372.

134 *The Spectator*, no. 139, 9 August 1711; *PSZ* IV 2414 11 Aug. 1711, VI 3870, 1721 (undated). 86, pp. 353, 361, 366; 450; 466, pp. 242, 247; 723, vol. vi, pp. 29–32.

135 *PSZ* IV 2271 15 June 1710, 2414 11 Aug. 1711, V 2789 23 March 1714, article 5, 2985 22 Jan. 1716, 2991 8 Feb. 1716, 3294 Jan. 1719, article 27, 3445 30 Oct.1719, VI 3870, 1721 (undated), 3893 5 Feb. 1722, 4052 16 July 1722, 4079 31 Aug. 1722, VII 4550 31 Jan. 1724, 4533 26 June 1724, article 13; *ZA* no. 36, 22 Jan. 1716, p. 51, no. 166, 14 Feb. 1723. 82, pp. 90, 194; 512, vol. ii, no. 477, p. 579; 515, p. 207; 733, vol. ii, Section 3, no. 10, pp. 3–20 (pp. 12–13).

136 *PSZ* VI 4036 13 June 1722. 110, pp. 39, 89; 258, pp. 78–9; 733, vol. i, pp. xxiv–xxv; *RBS* vol. 3 under 'Bóltin, I. V.'.

137 *AAE* IV, no. 284, 7 Apr. 1685, pp. 419–22; *PSZ* IV 2015 16 Jan. 1705, 2991 8 Feb. 1716, 2996 18 Feb. 1716, 3169 17 Feb. 1718, 3340 24 March 1719, VI 3547 14 March 1720, 3662 17 Oct. 1720, 3854 19 Nov. 1721, 3870, 1721 (undated), 3925 3 Apr. 1722, 3966 13 Apr. 1722, 4009 15 May 1722, 4034 12 June 1722, 4036 13 June 1722, 4052 16 July 1722, VII 4596 13 Nov. 1724, 4635 15 Jan. 1725; *ZA* no. 36, 22 Jan. 1719, p. 51, no. 374, 25 Jan. 1715, pp. 362–3. 170, p. 193; 172, pp. 68, 70, 75; 221, vol. i, pp. 269–312, Appendix, p. 307, vol. ii, pp. 157–85, Appendix, pp. 59–107; 328, pp. 222–3; 406; 451, pp. 28, 31, 48–50, 53, 59, 67–70; 458, pp. 10, 12; 468; 469, pp. 133–77 and particularly 137, 151–7, 162–3, 166–7, 169, 171; 560; 607; 609; 623, pp. 192, 211; 636; 728; 733, vol. i, pp. xvi–xxiii, vol. ii, pp. 114–23; *ES*, vol. 46 under 'Pitirím'; *RBS* vol. 3 under 'Bóltin, I. V.'.

138 515, pp. 248, 258.

139 *PSZ* V 2846 28 Sept. 1714, 3294 Jan. 1719, article 31, VI 3709 16 Jan. 1721, Chapter 10, VII 4518 29 May 1724; *ZA* no. 82, 10 Feb. 1720, pp. 79–80, no. 97, p. 88 [1721?]. 118, p. 342; 247, pp. 173, 202, 211, 213, 216, 218; 286, pp. 43–4, 50; 343, pp. 63–4; 355, pp. 70–9, 219–36, 243–56; 442, pp. 203, 404–5; 504, p. 125; 512, vol. i, p. 497; 729; 747, pp. 90, 134, 166; 779, pp. 148–51, 160, 168–74; 781, pp. 22, 24, 26.

140 *PSZ* V 3295 Jan. 1719, 3296 7 Jan. 1719, 3303 13 Feb. 1719, 3466 11 Dec. 1719, VI 4127 4 Dec. 1722, VII 4175 27 Feb. 1723; *ZA* no. 134 27 Apr. 1722, Section 9,

pp. 553–81, Section 10, pp. 589–602. 118, pp. 130, 139–40, 148, 160; 420, p. 10; 442, pp. 506–7, 515; 512, vol. i, p. 214; 518, pp. 140–222, 176–7; 657, pp. 93–7, 110; Chapter 7, pp. 317–8, 321, Chapter 8, pp. 323–4, Chapter 9, pp. 356, 366.

141 *PSZ* V 3245 26 Nov. 1718, 3287 22 Jan. 1719, VI 3660 16 Oct. 1720, VII 4503 19 May 1724, 4512 22 May 1724, 4533 26 June 1724, 4826 24 Jan. 1726; *ZA* no. 26, 18 Oct. 1715, p. 45, no. 42, p. 54 [1717]. 27, pp. 268–74, 286; 47, pp. 101–5; 118, pp. 141, 326–8, 331, 351, 364, 384–5, 397, 402–3; 195, p. 71; 314, p. 327; 344, pp. 81, 405–6; 350, p. 327; 432, p. 76–85; 436, pp. 180–1; 442, pp. 473–9, 499, 515; Montesquieu, *De l'esprit des lois*, Book 13, Chapter 4; 504, pp. 107–8; 654; 718, pp. 157, 162; 719, p. 231; 747, pp. 27–9; Chapter 8 below.

142 *PSZ* VI 3708 16 Jan. 1721, Chapters 3, 4; 118, pp. 340–1.

143 *PRP* VIII, pp. 150–2; *PSZ* VI 3520 13 Feb. 1720, 3708 16 Jan. 1721, 3980 27 Apr. 1722, VII 4550 17 Aug. 1724, 4624, 1724 (undated); *Sb. RIO*, vol. 11, pp. 386, 449. 191, p. 240; 343, pp. 132, 154, 171–5, 322, 326, 422, 615–17, 797–8; 646, vol. xvi, p. 488.

144 For Tsar Peter's economic policy see 132; 397; 497; 652; 675.

145 162, vol. i, pt 1, p. 31; 645; 783, pp. 92, 116, 395.

146 477, p. 395.

147 442, p. 545.

148 *Ulozhénie*, Chapter 19, article 19; *PSZ* V 3445 30 Oct. 1719, VI 4023 1 June 1722, 4055 18 July 1722, VII 4237 28 May 1723, 4312 17 Sept. 1723, 4518 29 May 1724, 4533 26 June 1724, articles 13, 15, 4622 22 Dec. 1724, 4736 14 June 1725; *ZA* no. 15, 13 Dec. 1713. 46; 332; 344, pp. 12, 48, 64–8; 646, vol. xvi, p. 488; 696.

149 *PSZ* V 2789 23 March 1714, VI 3708 16 Jan. 1721, 3711 18 Jan. 1721, 3840 22 Oct. 1721; Chapter 6 below.

150 761, p. 24. In relation to the foregoing passage: BL, Additional MS 37359, Whitworth to St John 17 Nov. 1711; *DP* III, 1, no. 212, 30 March 1713, p. 176; *DPV*, vol. 4, p. 42; *DDPV*, vol. 7, p. 179, vol. 10, pp. 265, 295–6, 371, vol. 11, pp. 204, 234, 237; *PB*, XI, 1, no. 4290, 2 March 1711, p. 102, p. 410; *PSZ* III 1519 5 Oct. 1695, IV 2330 2 March 1711, 2349 13 Apr. 1711, 2351 23 Apr. 1711, 2357 May 1711, 2361 16 May 1711, 2371 12 June 1711 (full text in *DP* I, no. 134, p. 130), 2383 21 June 1711, 2393 3 July 1711, 2426 17 Sept. 1711, 2432 28 Sept. 1711, 2601 4 Nov. 1712, 2764 27 Jan. 1714, 2793 6 Apr. 1714, 3441 27 Oct. 1719, 3456 11 Dec. 1719, Chapter 19, VI 3748 28 Feb. 1721, article 5, VII 4348 8 Nov. 1723; *Sb. RIO*, vol. 11, pp. 44, 96, 288, 312–13, 325, 338, 352, 359, vol. 39, pp. 49, 110, 262; 55, vol. ii, p. 42; *ZA* no. 152, p. 118 [1720]. 159, pp. 31–2; 226, pp. 61, 65–6, 110, 114, 118, 175, 196, 214, 221–2, 225–6; 442, pp. 153, 164–5, 360–4, 631, 639; 649; 726, pp. 27–31, 49.

151 *AI* V, no. 267, 10 May 1697, pp. 487–91; *PSZ* V 3086 8 June 1717, 3174 26 Feb. 1718, 3176 Feb. 1718, 3351 23 Apr. 1719, VI 3526 17 Feb. 1720. 18, pp. 72–3; 38, vol. i, pp. 307–16; 67, pp. 58–9; 100, pp. 110–26; 107; 123, p. 97; 124, pp. 183, 186; 208, pp. 867–9; 217, p. 52; 224; 230; 246; 268, pp. 26–55; 313; 314, pp. 87–126; 384; 407; 408, pp. 73–8; 439; 455; 496; 508; 509; 515, pp. 247, 268; 539; 645, pp. 137–42; 699, pp. 7–78; 711; 734; 739; 755; 757; 780, pp. 9–15, 39–42, 49–51, 86, 154–5; 782, p. 133; 784.

152 50; *DP* I no. 59, 23 Apr. 1711, p. 36, III, no. 1234, 13 Dec. 1713, pp. 1356–8; *PSZ* V 3464 10 Dec. 1719, VII 4237 28 May 1723; *Sb. RIO*, vol. 11, pp. 539–44, vol. 39, p. 464, vol. 79, p. 382. 58, p. 72; 99; 124, pp. 198, 202; 153; 226, pp. 72, 93–5, 98,

Appendices 4–5; 285; 289; 312, p. 189 (transportation of iron from Siberia); 313, pp. 23–4, 42, 52–5, 124; 327, pp. 196–8, 204; 366, note 11; 494, pp. 324–5 (transportation of iron from Siberia); 496, pp. 56, 76–8; 515, p. 247.

153 Karl Marx, *Capital*, vol. i, Book 1, Chapter 24, Section 6.

154 *PSZ* VII 4345 5 Nov. 1723.

155 *PSZ* V 3464 10 Dec. 1719, VII 4345 5 Nov. 1723, article 1, 4378 3 Dec. 1723, 4381 3 Dec. 1723; *Sb.RIO*, vol. 11, p. 161, vol. 69, pp. 34–7; *ZA* no. 265, 15 Dec. 1717, p. 220. 67, pp. 62, 201, 255–64; 286, p. 12; 314, p. 299; 384, pp. 30–2, 49, 50, 60; 408, pp. 93–4; 515, p. 268; 739, pp. xxxi, 65, 74, 78–9, 86.

156 For the establishment of the *krigs-kommissariát* see *PSZ* IV 2412 31 July 1711, 2456 10 Dec. 1711, 2457 11 Dec. 1711.

157 *PSZ* VI 3708 16 Jan. 1721, Chapter 6. 327, p. 204; 746, p. 15.

158 *PSZ* V 3158 8 Feb. 1718, 3162 14 Feb. 1718, 3176 Feb. 1718, VI 3549 18 March 1720, 3711 18 Jan. 1721, 4408 13 Jan. 1724, 4487 28 March 1724. 384, p. 44; 455; 596; 711, p. 18; 730, pp. 56–60; 739, pp. xxviii, xxxvi, 39–41; 743, vol. ii, pp. 20–1, 23; 782, pp. 123, 133–7.

159 *PSZ* VI 3710 17 Jan. 1721, VII 4378 3 Dec. 1723. 67, pp. 91–100.

160 67, pp. 161–2; 314, p. 108; 315.

161 For the New Trade Regulations see above, pp. 31–2.

162 *PSZ* II 873 1 June 1681, IV 1749 2 Feb. 1700, VI 3672 10 Nov. 1720, 3959 11 Apr. 1722,VII 4348 8 Nov. 1723, 4415 14 Jan. 1724, 4452 31 Jan. 1724, 4453 31 Jan. 1724, 4466 6 Feb. 1724, 4475 15 Feb. 1724, XLV (*Kniga tarifov*), pp. 1–123; *Sb. RIO*, vol. 40, p. 254; *ZA* no. 153, p. 118 (undated). 129, p. 141, n. 1; 162, vol. ii, pt 2, p. 60; 290, p. 212; 367; 400, p. 30; 410, pp. 33, 47–67 and especially p. 63, 74–5, Appendix, pp. 3–7; 480, pp. 124–51; 561. The tariff was drafted by one Bacon, a councillor at the Board of Trade. See *RBS*, vol. 12, p. 408 under 'Osterman, A. I.'.

163 PRO, State Papers Russia, SP 43/1 ff. 58–61 (intelligence from St Petersburg 10 Aug. 1716); *PSZ* VI 3485 13 Jan. 1720, preamble; *Sb. RIO*, vol.11, p. 57. 90; 159; 237; 286, p. 84; 314, p. 151; 400, p. 7; 613, vol. i, pp. 49–50; 674, pp. 3, 46–9; 768, p. x.

164 *PB* III, no. 624, 7 or 8 Feb. 1704, pp. 29–31.

165 *PSZ* V 2730 16 Nov. 1713, 3115 15 Nov. 1717. 270, pp. 22–4; 389, p. 219; 480; 600, vol. i, pp. 54–6; 615, Appendix, pp. 25–34; 686.

166 *Sb. RIO*, vol. 39, p. 262; 166, p. 61.

167 78, pp. 11, 26, 42, 58; *DDPV*, vol. 10, p. 296; *PSZ* III 1700 6 Oct. 1699, IV 2426 17 Sept. 1711, articles 5, 6: *Sb. RIO*, vol. 39, pp. 45, 110. 270, p. 24; 316; 357; 365; 366, p. 117; 442, pp. 164–5; 515, pp. 248–9.

168 *PSZ* IV 2330 2 March 1711, article 3. Or, rather, 'the sinews of war', Cicero's phrase in *Philippic* V, 2, 5, revived by the cameralists. Cf. 628, p. 42.

169 *PB* XI, 1, no. 4290, 2 March 1711, pp. 409–14; *PSZ* IV 2330 2 March 1711, 2327 13 March 1711, 2349 13 Apr. 1711, 2433 1 Oct. 1711.

170 *ZA* no. 19, 1714, p. 42, no. 76, p. 75.

171 *PRP* VIII p. 169; *PSZ* V 2793 6 April 1714, 3318 3 March 1719, 3428 10 Oct. 1719, VI 3840 22 Oct. 1721, VII 4453 31 Jan. 1724; *ZA* no. 169, 10 May 1723, p. 126. 518, pp. 357–67.

172 54, p. 19.

173 PRO SP 43/1, ff. 58–61.

174 PRO SP 91 107 ff. 1–31. 339.

175 *PRP* VIII pp. 147–8, 151 (the questionnaire for the description of towns, appended to *PSZ* VI 3708 16 Jan. 1721); *PSZ* V 3089 8 June 1717, 3318 3 March 1719, 3357 22 Apr. 1719, 3639 3 Sept. 1720; *ZA* no. 247, 18 Jan. 1712, p. 205. 49; 97; 140; 143, pp. 82–3; 249; 384, pp. 27–30, 34–5; 390, pp. 102–27, 161–7, 208–28; 409, pp. 85–7; 422, pp. 28–30, 76–81; 443; 508, pp. 304–7.
176 BL. Additional MS 22518 ff. 109–112v., Carteret to Stanyan, 5 Jan. 1722/3.
177 For trade between Russia and Venice which both sides were eager to develop in the years 1711–24 see Archivio di Stato di Venezia, Cinque Savi alla Mercanzia, Diversorum busta 348, no. 43; busta 349, nos 119, 121; busta 355, no. 3314; Deliberazioni del Senato Terra, Registro, 1716 II, no. 272, ff. 645–6. I owe this information to the kindness of Professor Brian Pullan. See further 78, pp. 74, 80, 91, 96–7; 163, vol. ii, p. 173.
178 *PSZ* VII 4348 4 Nov. 1723, article 1.
179 575, vol. 1, p. 332, *Sb. RIO*, vol. 11, pp. 290–1, 409–11. 143, pp. 56–60; 375; 376, pp. 340–5; 377; 422, p. 18; 464, p. 481; 605, pp. 115–68; 708, pp. 65–7; 714, vol. i, pp. 28, 86–107, 109–49.
180 492, vol. ii, p. 331.
181 *PSZ* VII 4348 8 Nov. 1723.
182 *PSZ* VII 4540 4 Aug. 1724.
183 376, p. 350; 693, pp. 19–22.
184 PRO SP 91 107, Captain John Deane's account of affairs in Russia, June–July 1725, unpaged; BL, Additional MS 37397 ff. 77–8, Tilson to Whitworth 22 March 1725. 342.
185 *PSZ* VII 5084 22 May 1727, cf. *PSZ* VI 3840 22 Oct. 1721. 340; 513; 546.
186 *PSZ* V 2871 24 Dec. 1714, 4503 19 May 1724, 4595 13 Nov. 1724, 4650 8 Feb. 1725, 4654 12 Feb. 1725, 4659 19 Feb. 1725, 4897 2 June 1726, 4928 15 July 1726, 4928 15 July 1726, 4934 16 July 1726, 5016 24 Feb. 1727, 5017 24 Feb. 1727, 5033 15 March 1727, 5039 20 March 1727, 5142 18 Aug. 1727, VIII 5300 30 June 1728, 5626 20 Oct. 1730; *Sb. RIO*, vol. 11, pp. 386, 538, 563; vol. 49, pp. 89–90, 240–2, vol. 69, p. 389; *ZA* no. 311, 9 Feb. 1723, p. 256. 37, pp. 119, 169, 202, 279, 306; 79, p. 306; 118, pp. 435, 461, 466, 477, 481–8, 490, 488–505; 150, pp. 15–18; 232; 238; 286, p. 116; 297; 304; 386, pp. 370–1; 422, p. 242; 442, pp. 500–7, 509, 517–18; 502, pp. 388–9, 393, 395; 507; 513, p. 93; 548, p. 34; 654, pp. 28–31; 706, pp. 253–5; 741, p. 345.
187 *PSZ* VII 4533 26 June 1724, article 11, 4536 26 June 1724, 5017 24 Feb. 1727, 5033 15 March 1727, VIII 5300 30 June 1728, 5717 17 March 1731, IX 7142 31 Dec. 1736. 118, pp. 414, 431; 386, pp. 370–1; 477, pp. 417, 420; 654, pp. 28–31; 759, pp. 5, 6.
188 *PSZ* V 2789 23 March 1714, VII 4722 28 May 1725, VIII 5653 9 Dec. 1730.
189 *PSZ* VIII 5625 20 Oct. 1730. 37, pp. 71, 75, 143; 58, p.80; 341; 507, p. 9.
190 *Sb. RIO*, vol. 63, p. 610.
191 *Sb. RIO*, vol. 55, pp. 290–3, vol. 56, pp. 311–12, 611, vol. 63, pp. 13–16, vol. 69, pp. 543–9. 297, p. 272; 364; 410, pp. 68, 70–2, 76–9; 502, p. 398; 714, vol. ii, pp. cv, cxv; 741, p. 318.
192 *PSZ* VII 5003 26 Jan. 1727.
193 79, pp. 296–7, 306–7; 129, p. 164; 304; 314, pp. 363, 387, 390–3 (disregarding the different proportions between the various items of expenditure given on p. 383); 351, pp. 230–1; 432, pp. 85–9; 442, pp. 141, 497; 735, pp. 15, 48.

194 7, col. 1427.
195 Choglokóv, Músin-Púshkin, Pustóshkin, Unkóvskii, Ushakóv, Zolotarëv. See Chapter 3 below. The 'affair of the Choglokóvs' is also alluded to in *Sb. RIO*, vol. 11, p. 265. *PSZ* V 2845 26 Sept. 1714 ordered that the estates and possessions of evaders of service be given to those who had laid information against them.
196 *PSZ* V 3261 22 Dec. 1718. 226, pp. 81, 87.
197 618, pp. 401–2.
198 See above, pp. 95–9.
199 *PSZ* VI 3978 27 Apr. 1722, article 4. 77, pp. 59–60; 82, p. 195; 248; 545.
200 Especially in Chapter 3.
201 *PSZ* V 2785 26 March 1714. 144; 512, vol. ii, p. 562.

Iván Pososhkóv

The Book of
Poverty and Wealth

OR

an Exposition
showing
how Needless Poverty arises
and
how Wealth may be caused to increase
abundantly

Preface

Commentary

It may be seen from the dedication, the preface and the extended title that the precise theme of Pososhkóv's treatise is not so much poverty and wealth as needless insufficiency which can and should be replaced with abundant riches. Only incidentally is he concerned with individual poverty or with the poor as a social category. His principal purpose is to put forward measures that will result in the preservation of existing resources through the avoidance of waste and in the creation of additional wealth. This will enable the tsar to raise enough revenue without causing privation to his people.

The minimum figure named by Pososhkóv is 6 million roubles, the maximum figure 9 million. This estimate together with the suggestion that the taxes collected during the war fell short of its cost would indicate that Pososhkóv knew something of the actual amount of money required and of the difficulties experienced by the authorities in trying to make ends meet even in peacetime. It is probably no coincidence that both figures are divisible by three which Pososhkóv regards as a mystical number. A calculating believer, Pososhkóv is seldom content with a purely rational argument. The residual asceticism which forms part of his sense of values does not allow him to recognize personal enrichment as the sole end of man's economic action or to approve of luxury. The spiritual riches that spring from righteousness are held superior and luxury stands condemned on moral as well as economic grounds.

The title of the work may well have been borrowed from a sermon by St John Chrysostom[1] on the same subject. Such acquaintance as Pososhkóv may have had with Chrysostom's work may have confirmed him in his dislike of luxury but did not make him an adversary of wealth or of the rich. It is rather the association of wealth with power and the abuse of both by individuals that arouse his indignation.

Preface

(13)* I, unworthy servant of His Majesty, herein set forth my views on the gathering of the Tsar's revenues. For it behoves loyal servants of His Majesty to use their best endeavours both to gather these revenues and to ensure that no part of them is wasted to no avail; moreover to keep a close eye not only on the revenue itself but also on those sources from which it springs, to the end that wealth may nowhere lie idle nor be wasted to no purpose.

Likewise they should with unabating zeal labour for the enrichment of the whole people, to the end that all should eschew purposeless expense, be more moderate in their use of spirituous liquors and be in their dress sober rather than gaudy, so that they may not be reduced to poverty by inordinate ostentation in their own dress and more particularly in that of their wives and children, but rather attain to that measure of affluence which is appropriate to their degree.

For a realm is not rich by virtue of great sums lying amassed in its treasury nor yet because His Majesty's counsellors are robed in cloth-of-gold. Only that (14) realm is truly rich wherein each and every man is rich, within his own compass, with the domestic wealth of his native land, and not merely in his outward apparel and its adornment. For it is not we who grow rich by adding fripperies to our dress: those countries grow rich whence we import such fripperies, whereas our substance is wasted by acquiring them.

More than for material riches we must all take thought also for our immaterial riches, that is, for righteousness. The Father of Righteousness is God and righteousness greatly multiples wealth and glory and delivers us from death; whereas the Devil is the father of unrighteousness, and unrighteousness not merely cannot enrich us but even whittles away the wealth that we have, reduces us to penury and brings us to death.

The Lord God himself said: 'Seek ye first the Kingdom of God and his righteousness,' and added, saying, 'then all these things shall be added unto you' – that is to say, wealth and glory. With these words of Our Lord in mind it behoves us particularly to seek righteousness. And when righteousness shall be firmly established among us our land of Russia shall surely grow in wealth and esteem.

---

* The numbers in parentheses in the left-hand margin refer to the pages of the text in Kafengauz's edition of 1951.

For herein lies the true ornament and glory and well-gotten wealth of a realm, namely that righteousness be implanted and firmly established both among the great and the lowly, and that all shall dwell together in amity, rich and poor alike. Thus shall all conditions of men be content with what they have according to their station since righteousness forbids us to injure our neighbour and love enjoins us to help one another in our need. And so shall all be enriched and the Tsar's treasury shall be filled to overflowing; and if there should be need to impose any further tax all will pay it with a good grace.

And if by virtue of the grace and autocratic power received by him from God our great Sovereign Peter Alekséevich should see fit to give effect to all the proposals which I put forward herein, I am persuaded that his treasury will always be filled to overflowing even without the imposition of further taxes. And so I dare to hope that, God willing, the imposts at present levied on the peasants may even be reduced.

As I see it, to have a full treasury is no great and difficult matter since our Sovereign can, like God, always do what he desires by the exercise of his power. But it is a great and difficult matter to enrich a whole people since this can in no wise be done without first implanting righteousness and extirpating oppressors, malefactors, brigands and robbers of every sort, both overt and covert.

I shall treat first of ecclesiastical matters, next of military and other secular affairs and lastly of the revenue due to the Sovereign and the soundest, most profitable and most dependable manner of levying it.

The CLERGY are the pillar and bulwark of piety and of man's salvation, for without priests no man can by any means attain to the Kingdom of Heaven. They are our pastors, our fathers, our leaders. Yet their ability to read and understand the necessary books leaves much to be desired. I do not know why it should be so but I am bound to say – since there is no avoiding it (albeit I am loath to put it into words lest I should incur episcopal censure) – that I see the cause in the shortcomings of our bishops, for they leave the matter of ordinations in the hands of their underlings. The latter accept bribes from the ordinands, make them learn two or three psalms by heart which they then recite to the bishop; the ordinands rattle them off in a clear and intelligible manner and so the bishop ordains them without being aware of the deception. Consequently many priests cannot read or write as well as they should, and in my view, even if a candidate has passed through a school he should still be examined as to his capacity to comprehend and expound what he has read and only then be ordained. Those who have received schooling but still show no such capacity should, in my opinion, on no account be ordained. One must look for wisdom and judgment in a priest over and above his training in order that he may be a true pastor of his spiritual flock. If our priests (whether in town or countryside) had more understanding it would be impossible for the schismatics to multiply among the people – indeed the schism would never have occurred in the first place.

This is the subject of the First Chapter.

The common soldiers are the defence and strong bulwark of the realm; yet their officers and those in charge of military affairs do nothing to ensure that their men are well provided with all things and do not go hungry or cold. It is the soldiers' common complaint that they suffer great hardship for some do not receive as much as thirty kopecks a month. How can they live on that, provide themselves with greatcoat, gauntlets and other necessaries and also feed themselves? If a soldier has to live in such straits will he not inevitably steal and desert? It is privation that drives him not only to desertion but also to the point of treason; as a traitor he will be fighting against his own comrades.

The well-being of both infantry and dragoons should be most carefully studied and all necessary measures taken to ensure that they are adequately fed and clothed. If this is done they will serve all the better. This is true of both our senior regiments and more recent and newly raised regiments: none must go hungry or cold.

Whether it is in accordance with some Western Articles of War or with the notions of our own officers, it is scarcely right that they should provide the soldiers with uniforms and subsequently recover the cost by stoppages out of pay; in this way some men receive less than thirty kopecks a month. I believe that His Imperial Majesty is not fully aware of this, so I discuss it at greater length in the Second Chapter on MILITARY AFFAIRS.

(17) It has been the custom of Russian magistrates to allow a multitude of petitioners all to be present together in their offices, so many that sometimes a man without influence cannot gain a hearing. Moreover, it is their custom to commit great numbers to prison without deciding their cases; the prisoners are then sent out in chains into the streets to beg. Thereby the name of Russia is brought into dishonour since in no country will there be found so great a number of prisoners as in ours. And this is due solely to laxity on the part of the magistrates.

This matter is developed in the Third Chapter on JUSTICE and the LAW.

TRADE in Russia is carried on most dishonestly. Merchants deceive and cheat one another; they conceal bad wares under good and sell bad instead of good; they demand unjust prices and entirely fail to act together for their common good – rather they prey on one another and so all are ruined. Moreover they do not attempt to act in concert in dealings with foreigners but buy goods from foreigners without consulting with their fellows.

Yet how vital a matter is trade! Magistrates should exercise unstinting care over the merchants' affairs. Trade enriches every realm; no realm, not even the least, can exist without them. Therefore it behoves us to take special care of them to protect them from abuses, that they may not be harmed by anyone nor be reduced to penury but zealously work for the benefit of His Majesty by the increase of their substance.

This matter is developed in the Fourth Chapter.

Nor are things as they should be in our craftsmen's workshops. When a person binds himself apprentice to a master and the term of his apprenticeship is fixed, even if the master does not shirk but teaches his pupil quickly, the apprentice will try to leave before the expiration of the full term and set up for himself; and as his work will not be of the quality of a master's he will charge lower prices and so put the master-craftsmen at a disadvantage. That is why there is no excellent CRAFTSMANSHIP to be found in Russia.

This is the subject of the Fifth Chapter.

Russia has more BRIGANDS than any other country. Not only are there bands of ten or twenty but even of a hundred and two hundred and more. Our country can by no means grow rich until they are extirpated. This is entirely due to the faultiness of our dispensation of justice, for when a thief or brigand is apprehended he is thrown into prison; he may well be subjected to torture but will still be kept there and fed for ten years or more. In the course of such a long period many have found means to escape and resume a life of crime more heinous than before. Others have been set free by the magistrates, instead of being put to death, and have returned to their former practices, so in expectation of the like treatment in the future they have continued to commit crimes without fear of retribution.

The Sixth Chapter treats of their extirpation.

It is also important not to forget the PEASANTRY, to protect them from ruin and abuse, and not to allow them to be idle that they may not through laziness be reduced in the end to poverty. For those peasants who live in the grain-growing parts should not remain idle in winter but work either in the forests or at handicrafts at home; others should be employed as carriers. None should remain idle and consume their winter stores of food without working and thereby waste their days. Those peasants who do not own good horses and therefore cannot be hired as carriers should seek useful work, either for wages or for their keep, and on no account remain idle.

This is elaborated in the Seventh Chapter.

The LANDOWNERS break up their estates, both during their lifetime and on the death of their kindred, into many small lots; they may divide one piece of land into ten parcels or more. This custom is most obnoxious and leads to nothing but disputes and trouble and even murder.

It is not merely wrong but highly injurious that a reliable land survey has not yet been made. What a great amount of land our Monarch has in his possession and yet it brings in no revenue at all! The *dvoriáne* buy up more and more land and let it out on rent and thus collect a large income yearly in rents; yet they do not pay a single farthing a year to His Majesty.

This is discussed at length in Chapter Eight.

(20)   The Russian Empire covers a vast space and is very populous, yet the revenues which reach His Majesty's treasury are anything but abundant; so much so that in time of war they are quite insufficient to cover the cost of waging the war. The extent of its lands is so great that it cannot even be calculated, yet no special tax is levied on land at all. Whereas if even quite a small tax were imposed on it, so that no one enjoyed the use of land scot-free, it would bring in a million and, moreover, would be constant. Land would thus become our great Monarch's most abundant source of revenue and never fail him. And if the system of taxation were thoroughly reformed and the tax-collectors did their work aright His Majesty would find his treasury receipts adequate even without further levies; there would be a yearly excess of two or three millions in the treasury.

This is the subject of the Chapter on the TSAR'S INTEREST.

My exposition therefore contains nine chapters, all of which aim at the establishment of righteousness and the eradication of all injustice and lawlessness. And if God shall graciously look down from on high with favour on all these nine chapters and the zealous will of our Emperor be exercised here below, not only will his treasury be filled to overflowing but also the whole people will grow rich and many enmities will cease. And if the principles set forth in these nine chapters are accepted and become firmly established among us wealth shall flow like a river year by year, never ceasing and never changing.

CHAPTER 1. Of the Clergy

Commentary

The part of the priesthood in the process of economic improvement. – The deficient state of the Church and of the clergy. – Lack of preparation for the priesthood. – The study of Church Slavonic grammar as a remedy against the spread of Old Belief. – Pososhkóv's Manifest Mirror *directed against the schismatics. Similar works by other authors. – Improvement in the provision of schools for the sons of clergy 1721–5. – The preparation of ordinands. – The* Ecclesiastical Regulation *of 1721 anticipates Pososhkóv's proposals. The remuneration of the parish priests. Their material circumstances. – The successional character of the ministry. – Pososhkóv's proposals for an ecclesiastical tithe. – The tsar's share in the responsibility for the relief of poverty transferred to the Church.*

Such connection as exists between the subject of this chapter and the main theme of Pososhkóv's treatise – the economic condition of Russia – is to be found in the role of the priesthood as assigned to it in the author's Preface.[1] Ideally, in the spiritual life of the people the priests are the guardians of all piety and the instruments of individual salvation; in social and economic relations they exercise a moderating influence by restraining covetousness and replacing hostility between the rich and the poor with mutual Christian love and the contentment of all with their natural stations. The adoption by society of the corresponding attitudes of deference and submissiveness would presumably lay the ethical foundations for the process of economic improvement envisaged in the subsequent chapters.

In reality the standing of the Church which was to lead the people in that direction was diminished by the vacancy in the office of Patriarch and its strength was impaired by the continuing conflict with the Old Believers.[2] Furthermore, the organization and administration of the Church lacked cohesion and effective management. Shchápov has pointed out the unequal size and inadequate number of dioceses (or eparchies) and the uneven distribution of churches in relation to the number of inhabitants as well as a shortage of clergy in some places and a surplus in others. He has also drawn attention to the length of time – in some cases two years or longer – for which episcopal vacancies were left unfilled. Thus for example in 1718 there were no archbishops at Kiev, Nóvgorod, Toból'sk, Smolensk or Kolómna while those at

Ústiug and at Viátka were considered to be too old. Only some of these failings were remedied by the reform of 1721.[3]

Pososhkóv attributes the schism (as he had already done in his first letter to the head of the hierarchy, Stefán, written in 1703 or 1704)[4] to the ignorance of the principles of the Christian religion among the people and this in turn to the inability of the clergy, untutored and engrossed in tilling the soil or simply sunk in sloth, to give the necessary instruction to their flock. His observations on this subject raise some fundamental questions about the character of religious culture in Russia at that time.

These deficiencies of the clergy which were also due to their lack of preparation for the priesthood had long given cause for concern. Traditionally, among the secular clergy, sons tended to succeed their fathers in all grades of the ministry so that for the most part the education of the clergy children was nothing other than the education of future priests. The synod of 1551 resolved that in all towns the clergy should establish schools to which they, as well as the local inhabitants, would send their children to be taught reading, writing and singing and to receive spiritual instruction. No mention was made of the countryside.[5] The synod of 1667 put the matter more emphatically: all priests were, with full diligence, to teach their children reading and writing and the fear and worship of God so that they might be worthy to enter the priesthood in succession to their fathers. Livings must not be traded and thus fall into the hands of village ignoramuses who hardly know how to tend cattle, let alone human beings. Revolt and schism in the Church follow from this.[6]

Pososhkóv argues in much the same terms. From a self-evident concern for the promotion of common linguistic standards and correct usage he recommends the study of Church Slavonic grammar. The less obvious connection between ignorance of grammar and the growth of Old Belief, but one which may well have been at the back of Pososhkóv's mind, had already been pointed out by Simeon of Pólotsk who maintained that the inability to follow punctuation marks allowed the misconstruction of sacred writings by amateur exegetists of the schismatic persuasion.[7] A similar view was expressed by the printer Fëdor Polikárpov in his preface to the 1721 edition of Melétii Smotrítskii's grammar of Church Slavonic.[8] Grammars were indeed in short supply. Smotrítskii's Church Slavonic grammar, first published in Lithuania in 1619, had not been reprinted in Russia since the Moscow edition of 1648,[9] Ludolf's *Grammatica Russica* was written for non-Russian students of the vernacular and only 300 copies of it were printed in Oxford in 1696; Kopijewitz's *Manuductio* of 1706 was again intended for non-Russians and in any case inadequate.[10] In 1723, however, 1,200 copies of a Church Slavonic grammar compiled by the subdeacon Fëdor Maksímov were printed in St Petersburg by order of the tsar and with the blessing of the Holy Synod.[11] The 'officials' or 'collators' (*správshchiki*) of the printing house in Moscow whose task consisted primarily in watching over the correctness of the texts of the liturgical books could not, incidentally, have taken any initiative in the matter of the production of new service-books; any such steps could only have been taken by the Church authorities. At the time when Pososhkóv was writing *The Book of Poverty and Wealth* the Moscow printing house was understaffed and had only two 'collators', both young and inexperienced.[12]

As to the other weapons to be used in the fight against the schism, Pososhkóv's own treatise, *The Manifest Mirror* (*Zérkalo ochevídnoe*),[13] was intended for all Christians, those who had fallen away as well as those who had not, but especially for those whom the 'unclean mouthings' of the schismatics had led into doubt. The outspoken author promises those Orthodox Christians who have not yet fallen into the schism a double benefit from frequently and diligently gazing into his *Mirror*: they will perceive the falsity of the teachings of the schismatics and, having done so, will spit in their eyes. With great vehemence and frequent reference to biblical and patristic texts Pososhkóv brands the schismatics as sons of the devil and forerunners of Antichrist and vindicates the doctrine of the official Church. Outside it and without the agency of its priests there can be no salvation. As Old Belief springs from ignorance the remedy against it lies in education. This rational piece of advice counterbalances the *Mirror's* own admixture of ignorance and superstition. Its other merit is the perception of Old Belief as a popular movement of distrust and discontent directed against authority in general and deriving its momentum from the mass of the people – monks, priests of little understanding and simple, uneducated peasants.[14] The final chapter deals with the heresy of iconoclasm and attacks those who, in Pososhkóv's opinion, have revived it, chiefly the Lutherans and the Calvinists.[15]

The other polemical works referred to by Pososhkóv in this chapter are the following: *An Enquiry into the schismatic . . . faith* by Dimítrii, metropolitan of Rostóv and Iaroslávl' (canonized in 1757), written in 1708–9 but not published until 1745; *The Sling prepared against questions put by the schismatics . . .* by Pitirím, archbishop of Nízhnii Nóvgorod (St Petersburg, 1721), and *The Rock of Faith* by Stefán (Iavórskii), metropolitan of Riazán' and Múrom, directed against Protestantism, finished in 1716, published in 1728.[16]

In suggesting that the reign of Peter had not brought about any improvement in the education of the clergy Pososhkóv's account is misleading. The tsar repeatedly ordered the clergy to look to the education of their sons[17] and spasmodic progress was made in the period 1700–21 when schools were established by bishops permanently or temporarily in six places (Chernígov, Kazan, Nóvgorod, Rostóv, Smolensk, Toból'sk). After the promulgation of the *Ecclesiastical Regulation*, in the period 1721–5, a considerable advance was achieved with about thirteen episcopal or diocesan schools established or re-established (at Bélgorod, Irkútsk, Kazan, Kholmogóry, Kolómna, Nízhnii

Nóvgorod, Pskov, St Petersburg, Súzdal', Riazán', Tvér', Vólogda, Viátka).[18] Each school drew up a curriculum in accordance with its teaching capacity and financial resources. For the subsistence of the pupils at the episcopal schools the larger monasteries were required under the *Ecclesiastical Regulation*[19] to hand over one twentieth, and the churches one thirtieth, of their grain harvest but when the crop failed delivery was withheld. The total number of pupils, not all of whom were sons of clergy, in the episcopal and other ecclesiastical schools in Russia and the Ukraine in the years 1726–7 may be put at about 2,260.[20] Despite the shortcomings of these establishments, and in some cases the prolonged intervals in their activity, they deserve honourable mention for having given origin to the ecclesiastical seminaries which first came into being in the 1730s.[21]

On the other hand, Pososhkóv's criticism that the examination of candidates for the priesthood did not go beyond a cursory test in reading and singing given by the local bishop (or, in the Patriarch's eparchy, by the Patriarch) is generally regarded as justified. Elementary instruction was given to newly ordained priests in the performance of the offices of the Church in Moscow on behalf of the Patriarch by a parish priest, elsewhere by a priest in the bishop's household. The last Patriarch, Adrian (1690–1700), as if to make up for the lack of formal training for the priesthood, arranged for every newly installed priest to receive, with his letter of installation, printed instructions concerning his sacerdotal duties which he was to learn by heart, as well as a copy of a compilation entitled *Of the Priesthood*.[22] It is hard to see of what practical use these ancient texts could be to the barely literate rustic priests described by Pososhkóv. In 1705, using the channel of the anachronistically styled Ecclesiastical Office (*Dukhóvnyi prikáz*) of the Patriarch, Peter I decreed that Holy Orders were to be conferred only on men who were educated and fully literate but in the absence of an adequate school system the command could only have remained a dead letter.[23]

The value of this chapter as a commentary on the state of the Russian Church in the final years of the reign of Peter is much diminished by the lack of any reference to the *Ecclesiastical Regulation* (*Dukhóvnyi Reglámeni*) of 1721,[24] many of whose provisions were intended to remedy the very deficiencies and abuses exposed by Pososhkóv. Indeed in many respects the *Regulation* forestalls Pososhkóv's proposals. It requires that the laity be instructed by its pastors in the principal dogmas of the Orthodox religion and also that all the faithful make confession and receive the Eucharist at least once a year. In stressing the importance of education for the priesthood and the laity the *Regulation* finds it necessary to prove the point that learning is not the cause of heresy and that, on the contrary, 'where the light of learning is extinguished, there cannot be good order in the Church'.[25] Formal education for the sons of priests is made compulsory; no priest may be ordained who has not received instruction in an episcopal school. Pending the establishment of such schools candidates for the priesthood were to read books on the faith and Christian law. Begging was to be eradicated. The aged and chronically sick were to be housed in hospices to be built by the richer monasteries. As to the form of remuneration received by the clergy, the *Regulation* realistically refrains from ordaining any change in the existing system but merely requires the conclusion of a written agreement between the parishioners and their priest to define the amount of his stipend (*rúga*) or the area of his glebe. In addition a sum payable to each priest was to be determined so that as far as possible he should be self-sufficient, and should not solicit any reward for the performance of rites.[26] Needless to say neither these nor any of the other commands produced instant results so that Pososhkóv's strictures lost nothing of their relevance. In speaking of the recent improvement, under official pressure, in attendance at church, Pososhkóv perhaps has in mind the *ukáz* of 'the Emperor and Autocrat . . . issued from the Holy Synod' on the keeping by the clergy of registers of attendance at confession and the imposition of fines for non-attendance, on the duty of the clergy to ensure that their parishioners go to church on feast days, etc.[27]

The material circumstances of the country priesthood were in one respect even worse than Pososhkóv's description leads one to believe because the amount of land allotted to particular churches was often not large enough to support a priest and his family.[28] The allocation to churches of pieces of land from adjacent estates (*pomést'ia* or *vótchiny*) was first made obligatory at the time of the land survey of 1620. The injunction, after being cancelled in 1676, was revived in 1680 and repeated in 1684. The standard size of such holdings was fixed at 10, 15 or 20 *chéti* (or *chétverti*, about 5.6, 8.4 or 11.2 hectares) in each of three fields according to the size of the estate from which the land was taken.[29] It would not appear that these instructions were carried out strictly or generally.

The notion conveyed by Pososhkóv that in the country parish priests, apart from any income they may have received in offerings for the performance of rites, subsisted only by tilling the land is not entirely correct. Thus in the northern eparchy of Kholmogóry some priests also received portions of grain (*rúga*) from their parishioners and the church land was sometimes worked by the villagers. In some places in the northern regions the priests eked out their income with casual earnings derived from handicrafts or from supplying the bishop's household with timber and tar. Elsewhere too the priest whose church was not endowed with land would receive from his parishioners a contribution in grain (*rúga*) the amount of which might be related to the area of land worked by them or fixed by mutual agreement. The latter system inclined the parishioners to make an annual contract with the contender who accepted the lowest possible terms, thus creating a relationship which inevitably weakened the authority of the local bishop over the country clergy. The number of village churches to receive a *rúga* in money or in grain or in both forms from the tsar was very small; urban churches and the monasteries were more fortunate in this respect. Pososhkóv does not mention the gifts from the parishioners to the priest of butter, eggs and other farm produce made in the spring during the Fast of the Apostles and again in the autumn.[30]

With regard to the successional character of the ministry, Pososhkóv takes the view that priests should be chosen for their qualities rather than by reason of their descent whereas the *Ecclesiastical Regulation* allows a priest to place one kinsman as a cleric in his parish.[31] As the ecclesiastical counterpart of such bureaucratic textbooks as the *General Regulation* (for all administrative colleges and other government departments) or the *Regulation of the Board of Civic Administration* (*Glávnyi Magistrát*),[32] the *Ecclesiastical Regulation* could hardly endorse Pososhkóv's view that sons of priests who were found to be unsuited to Holy Orders should be directed into the civil administration but a better illustration of Pososhkóv's scale of values would be hard to find.

In suggesting that the clergy should be remunerated with a tithe Pososhkóv assumes that the peasants will not find this new fiscal obligation burdensome. His proposal for a secular tithe is elaborated in Chapter 9. The ecclesiastical tithe, fanciful though it may seem, also had an advocate in one of Tsar Peter's high officials, A. P. Volýnskii. The instruction to his steward written in 1725 orders him, among other things, each year to collect one tenth of all produce and increase on his master's estate, to sell it and with the proceeds to pay stipends to the priests and minor clergy, to buy vestments and plate for the churches and to spend the remainder on the support of the old, the sick and the infirm.[33] It seems unlikely that these orders were carried out to the letter.

Faced with the intractable problem of pauperism Pososhkóv makes the same unrealistic proposal: the residue of the income from the ecclesiastical tithe is to be used for the relief of mendicants, wanderers and the destitute sick. By this time the old methods of alleviating distress by dispensing alms to the poor and housing the homeless in cells clustered around a church[34] were clearly no longer equal to a task made even harder by the material damage and dislocation caused by the Great Northern War.

Traditionally almsgiving was regarded first and foremost as an act of Christian piety; the recipients of charity were seen as the younger brothers of the Redeemer. The most substantial contribution to the relief of poverty was made by the tsar and the Patriarch by distributing gifts, feeding mendicants on certain days of the year and providing hospices for the sick, the old and the infirm. Their example was followed by the bishops, the richer monasteries and churches and by private individuals. But by the later seventeenth century the voluntary system with its religious motivation was beginning to break down under the strain of the demands made upon it. In Moscow only a small proportion of the needy found shelter in the hospices, the rich were being taunted for their hard-heartedness towards the poor and the state demanded more charitable activity of the Church.[35] In 1678 Tsar Fëdor Alekséevich, presumably for reasons of economy, tried to transfer the responsibility for the entire relief of the paupers, hitherto supported at the expense of his household, to the Patriarch (Ioakím). In the upshot the Patriarch assumed the major part of the burden but the tsar continued to provide for the sick and the wanderers. In 1681 Ioakím called on the clergy as a whole to give shelter to the poor and sick but to put the lazy and healthy to work.[36] Thus the course was set out upon, later to be followed by Peter I, of assigning to the Church the task of organizing the relief of the deserving poor[37] and the distinction was drawn between genuine hardship and social parasitism. When in 1700 Peter found that the Tsaritsa Márfa Matvéevna fed 300 beggars for five consecutive days each year in the Kremlin in memory of her late husband, Fëdor Alekséevich, and that his other female relations offered similar hospitality to a further thousand or so at the total cost of 143 roubles, he forbade the beggars the palace and ordered the money to be distributed among those who begged in the streets.[38] By so doing he formally dissociated the tsar and his family from the practice of ritual distribution of charity. Pososhkóv returns to the subject of pauperism in Chapters 3 and 5. A digression on the monastic estate relevant to this chapter occurs in Chapter 4.

CHAPTER 1

Of the Clergy

(21)   If there continue to be among the clergy men without education and proficiency in Holy Writ, uninstructed in the fundamentals of the Christian faith and without understanding of the will of God; moreover, if any are drunkards or prone to any other kind of excess or misconduct, then our pure Christian faith will be wholly corrupted and emptied of meaning, and men will fall away from the ancient unity of our faith into divers sects and all kinds of heretical beliefs.

A great part of the Russian people has already fallen into mortal heresies owing to the laxity of the priesthood. For many have strayed into the way of perdition; few are those who still adhere to our ancient faith. Thus, in Nóvgorod scarcely one in a hundred will be found still holding to the ancient faith. Although there are many priests in the town they do not bestir themselves to save the people from perdition and to guide them on the right way, and there are even some priests who condone their ways; and so the churches stand empty. Up to the present year (1723) the churches have been so empty that scarcely two or three true worshippers would be found there even on a Sunday. But now, thanks be to God,

(22)   little by little the people are beginning to go to church again, in obedience to the Metropolitan's order.[1] Where there were formerly only two or three in church, there is now a congregation of two or three dozen on Sundays, and even more on the great festivals; but this is due to fear, not to a true change of heart. These people will all soon cease to attend church, as before, unless further measures are taken, for the heresy of the schismatics has taken strong root among them.

This evil is entirely due to the priests for they are too ignorant to save themselves from the Lutheran and Roman heresies, and even from the most foolish beliefs of the schismatics; whereas it is their priestly duty to denounce these things and teach the people how to order their lives and escape the bottomless pit of Hell. But the priests either cannot or dare not be steadfast in their faith, or else they are mercenary or indifferent. O Lord my God, do not hold these words of mine in judgment against me, that I have dared to write disparagingly of the spiritual counsellors set over me. I myself am in nothing perfect either before God or before my Sovereign, or before the people; holding the convictions that I do, I merely conceived the hope that God might cause some improvement to come of this exposition of mine.

In Moscow I met a priest, of the great house of the boyar Lev Kiríllovich Narýshkin,[2] who could not even give a sound answer to a question put to him by a Tatar woman. What then could a mere country parish priest say, a man ignorant of the fundamental tenets of the Christian faith?

Since there are such shortcomings in the priesthood it behoves us to exert ourselves most earnestly to ensure that our priests should be the mainstay of true religion, a bulwark against heresies, a defence against the wolves of Hell, and should be able to turn the people of God away from the gates of damnation. Priests should be like Christ's Apostles: they should have no thought for their own well-being, or for riches, or for what they eat, but only for the salvation of human souls. For God shall hold them to account for all lost souls.

For the improvement of the priesthood it seems to me that His Imperial Majesty should take steps to have a grammar composed, ensuring that all is fairly and correctly set forth, together with the best possible commentary; and let it be sufficiently detailed for every obscure point to be clearly explained, so that the reader can learn all the cases and declensions, even without a teacher. And when so corrected, it should be printed in an edition of five or six thousand copies – perhaps ten thousand.

Some five or six thousand copies of a grammar have just been printed in Moscow, but the printers (God help them!) printed the book so poorly that it is impossible to make head or tail of the rules of orthography from it or to master them without the help of a teacher. What is more, they have used paper of the worst quality, which is good for nothing but rough drafts (at a pinch you might print calendars on that sort of paper, since they are only intended to last for one year). But a grammar is an important and permanent thing; it should be printed on the best paper so as to last.

Commodious schools should be built in every diocese, to which all the sons of priests, deacons, subdeacons and sacristans should be sent, from the age of ten, both from the town and the country churches of each district. Should any fathers be unwilling to let their sons attend school, the boys must be taken there willy-nilly, to be taught their grammar and the other branches of book-learning.

And here an inviolable rule must be laid down: any who have not had this schooling nor learnt their grammar shall not be ordained priests and deacons. Further, any clerks in minor orders who aspire to the priesthood, even if they have already attained the age of thirty, shall attend the schools; as they will not have come to learn under compulsion they will progress fast in their studies, and they will be able to complete them in two or three years, since they will be working of their own free will and be eager to learn. Those who gain a firm grasp of Grammar, and are still young enough, should be put through Rhetoric too, and even Philosophy;[3] such men will be suitable not only for the priesthood but even for a bishopric and can become teachers in their turn.

In this way the whole of Russia can become better educated in the space of not too many years. It is only the beginning which is difficult in such a great and glorious

task: once begun it will progress of itself, since intelligent and clever people take
to learning grammar and the other disciplines willingly and with pleasure.

If it is generally understood that ordination will be refused to those who have
not been educated in these schools, there will be no way for anyone aspiring to
Holy Orders to avoid this schooling; and so I believe that ordinands will vie with
one another in acquiring the necessary learning. Likewise if no one be appointed archimandrite[4] or abbot of a monastery without having had this
schooling, many monks will also apply themselves to acquiring Grammar and
the comprehension of books. The latter, as well as a knowledge of Grammar,
should be demanded of those of riper years. So it is most necessary that monks
should go to school to learn there, under a teacher of religion, to be initiated
into all matters pertaining to religion and the fear of God, to learn to interpret
the Scriptures and to acquire all the habits of a godly and sober life and skill in
disputations.

When they have mastered Grammar and acquired all other kinds of wisdom
and a thorough knowledge of Holy Scripture, pupils of these schools will be
able to counter the arguments not only of the schismatics but also of the
Lutherans and Romans and to silence them, seeing that all these have turned
away from true Christianity and wander, like wild goats, in impenetrable
thickets and in steep places difficult to climb. And so far have they strayed that
they cannot find their way back to the true religion.

Once priests' sons and other clerks have learnt their Grammar and acquired
a mastery of book-learning they will the more diligently care for their flocks so
that the wolves of Hell shall not scatter them in terror.

But at present there are indeed many priests who, far from converting anyone
from unbelief to faith, do not even know the meaning of the word 'faith'; nor is
that all – there are some who do not know how to conduct the church services
(26)   correctly. Nor is there any means to find this out: the officials of the Printing
House have grown fat with much drinking and rich living and have no inclination to print a clear compendium of all the church services so that anyone
can discover how each one is to be conducted. Thus only the priest who has
served a fairly long time in a cathedral church or as assistant to a competent
priest is capable of conducting the services correctly. No one who has not spent
much time under such direction can hope to do so merely from books.

It would be best to print the order of every service clearly in the service books
so that even an ordinary layman can understand how each service is to be
conducted, whereas at present many priests conduct them by guesswork,
according to their own lights. And it is not at all a good thing that this should be
so; this uncertainty leads to so much disagreement, even in the town churches,
that one is surprised at nothing in the country ones. So for perfect conduct of
the church services detailed rubrics must be given in small print in the
service-books directing how a particular service or rite is to be begun, carried

through and completed. If all this is clearly set forth every service will be conducted in an identical manner not only in the town churches but also in the country ones.

It will be impossible to achieve this perfect conduct of the church services unless two things are done: detailed rubrics for each office must be printed and teachers proficient in Grammar, monks as well as secular clergy, must be sent to the schools that have been built, and lay teachers also who are likewise skilled in book-learning, proficient in the offices of the whole Church year, well-versed in Holy Writ and able to expound all the difficult words.

The teachers of Grammar should give instruction before dinner, that is, in the forenoon. And in the afternoon the other teachers, who are proficient in Divinity, should teach their pupils the fear and reverence of God, and reading and ceremonial; further, how to know God, how to worship Him and to address one's prayers to Him, and with what awe the Holy Liturgy is to be conducted, how to raise one's understanding to God in the ritual of the Liturgy, and how to watch over one's spiritual flock, so that the wolves of Hell may not snatch them from the pasture. Moreover, the pupils should be provided with books to read in both alphabets, the ecclesiastical and the civil,[5] and also historical works. Therefore it will be necessary to print a considerable quantity of Bibles and to send half a dozen copies to each school; and also copies of the *Margarít*,[6] selections from the Church Fathers, the Gospels with commentary, the homilies on the Acts of the Apostles and the Lives of the Saints,[7] together with the *Menologies*[8] and other books required for the services. Thus the pupils will learn at school all the offices of the church and their correct performance, before their ordination.

To confirm them in their faith and preserve them from the errors of the Lutherans and Calvinists and from other enemies of Orthodoxy, as many copies as requisite must be printed of *The Rock of Faith*, composed by His Grace Stefán Iavórskii, Metropolitan of Riazán', of blessed memory; let half a dozen copies be sent to every school and let those who aspire to the priesthood commit this most precious *Rock* to memory so that they may be able to quote the right answer in rebuttal of any argument; and likewise shall monks do who are desirous of living a holy life. And those who reach the dignity of episcopal rank should have this holy *Rock* upon their lips even more than a priest so that by their words they may break the jaws of the heretics with this same *Rock*.

For exposing schismatics we need the books entitled *The Enquiry* and *The Manifest Mirror*, which expose the perversions of the schismatics and clearly demonstrate all their errors, and also the book called *The Sling*, to chase them far away with spiritual stones shot from that same sling and to consign them to oblivion, so that they may not creep into the sheepfold of Christ's flock nor harm Christ's sheep. And if the aforesaid *Enquiry*, *Sling* and *Mirror* are accepted for printing, half a dozen copies of each should be sent to every school.

It would also be advantageous to print accounts of various other heretical beliefs – the Roman, the Uniate, the Armenian and such early extinct heresies as the Arian, the Nestorian, the Apollinarian, the Eutychian, the Severian[9] and so forth, so that our pastors should be familiar with all these wily weapons of the Devil and know how to counter them. If our priests know the arguments of all these heretical beliefs and understand how to expose them and how to protect themselves from them, they can likewise protect their flocks from these wolves of Hell. If they themselves have no thorough knowledge of these heresies how can they detect them in others? That is why the Holy Apostle Paul wrote 'for there must be also heresies among you'.[10] It is clear that he wrote this in order that we, by recognizing heresies, may be able to expose them and defeat them with their own weapons, and may be on our guard against them.

Pupils should read their books without haste and with the greatest attention so as to understand and remember what they read. And if any pupils do not read clearly, those who instruct them in reading must give them constant encouragement and help in reading intelligibly, and expound whatever they have not grasped. The instructor shall test each pupil separately on the books which they are reading, shall take note of his ability to recite by heart and shall keep a record in his class-book of each pupil's attainments. If any pupil fails to repeat correctly from memory he must be punished and made to study the text afresh. And if after reading it a second time he still cannot remember what he has read, then it is plain that he is not apt for the priesthood.

Those who read clearly and are seen to have a good memory shall be given the books of the church year to read, to wit the *Menologies*, the *Triodion* and the
(29)   *Oktoechos*[11] and so on, as used in the church services. And I believe it would be a good thing to give them chronicles to read too so that they may know about all that has happened in the past.

Further, the pupils should practise writing for an hour or so in the evenings after their reading class, so that all may be able to read and to write well both the formal and the cursive hand.

On Sundays they shall be ordered to hold disputations among themselves on subjects out of Holy Writ. And both teachers shall listen and note each pupil's intelligence and knowledge of Holy Writ and skill in argument; a record shall be kept of all this for future reference, and furthermore a note of each one's predilections, whether for the sacred or the secular. Any pupil whose inclinations are towards sacred matters and who capably expounds the sacred texts should be singled out and be given books to read about the priestly office; he must be the more diligently instructed how to care for the flock of Christ's sheep and his spiritual children in that flock.

And if the book entitled *The Paternal Testament*,[12] which I wrote for my son Nicholas, be accepted for printing, then it would be well to recommend it to all ordinands since therein is set out among other things how a priest should perform his sacred duties. It sets forth not only how a priest, but also a simple monk, should live, and how on becoming an archimandrite he should care for the brethren and order his life; it rehearses the duties of a bishop; it shows how to extirpate the schismatics; how the laity may live a godly life and instruct their children so that they may be a credit to their father, live in love together, do what is right, love God and pray to Him and find favour with Him. All these things are set out therein so far as God has granted me ability to understand them.

When there is a vacancy for a priest in a parish one of these pupils shall be sent as incumbent, not thanks to family connections nor yet on account of the wealth of the parish or the wishes of the parishioners but with regard only to his understanding and his true worthiness for the priesthood. And both his teachers shall attest to the worthiness of the candidate that he is suitable for ordination.

And word should be sent to all bishops not to ordain any candidate without such a testimonial from his teachers. I cannot approve the present method by which the bishops test candidates: for the bishop's assistants accept gifts from the candidate, make him learn certain psalms by heart and then, having marked them in advance, see to it that he reads these same psalms to the bishop. Finding that he reads the Psalter with accuracy and intelligence, the bishop supposes that all his reading is of the same quality and so ordains him priest. In this way assistants lead their own bishops into wrongdoing.

I warned my son of this practice and wrote in that same *Testament* that, should he become a bishop, he must not rely on his assistants for the testing of candidates but must test each one in person; he should not give them the Psalter to read from but unfamiliar books, and should then examine them by word of mouth. It is easy to judge different capacities from an examination of this kind. When I was in Nóvgorod in 1720 I met a newly ordained deacon who could not read a single page of the Gospels during the service without making half a dozen mistakes. He was serving in the cathedral of St Nicholas the Miracle-worker. He had to be sent home.

A monk who aspires to the rank of archimandrite should be most thoroughly questioned by the bishop on his understanding of Holy Writ and whether he proposes to care for the brethren committed to his charge so that when he appears before God he may say 'Here am I and also the children whom Thou hast given me' – or whether he is merely concerned with his own salvation. In the latter case he is unworthy to be appointed archimandrite, for an archimandrite must have care not only for his monks but also for all the laymen under him and lead their steps in the way of salvation. And care must be taken to ensure that no aspirant to the rank of archimandrite is covetous for possessions, or addicted to drink, or inclined to fornication in order that as archimandrite he may not disgrace his position. Therefore enquiry should first be made of the brethren of his monastery and then of the laymen within its precincts. And if all praise him he should be raised to that rank provided that he has an adequate knowledge of Holy Writ.

And I warned my son in my *Testament* that a newly ordained priest who is not perfect in all the ritual must never be promoted from a subordinate position, so that no charges on account of the shortcomings of the priest may be made against his bishop.

In this *Testament* I also described (so far as God has given me ability) the priest's office in detail – how he should order all things, confess his spiritual children, care for the rich and the poor. For this reason I believe that my *Testament* will be very useful for the improvement of the priesthood. And if the son of the incumbent at any church wishes to succeed his father but shall be deemed unsuitable for ordination by his instructors, he must be refused even if there is a petition in his favour. Such priests' sons should be relegated to secular employment, while those who are unreceptive to book-learning but pious and God-fearing may receive minor orders as subdeacons and sacristans. Those of somewhat higher attainment may be made deacons. But choose for the priesthood only those of proven worth, learned in Scripture and humble in character, that the same may be a light to the world, and not darkness. And (32) those worthy of ordination, be they even the sons of sacristans or peasants, shall receive a cure of souls, but not by virtue of their father's position nor by influence. However, anyone who is equal to the task as to his faculties but unworthy as to his character, shall not be admitted to the priesthood nor to any other ecclesiastical office, but rather given employment in the offices of government or in any other capacity whatever excepting Holy Orders. And if anyone is otherwise of excellent character but prone to drink he shall on no account be chosen for the priesthood, for drunkenness is a grave fault in a priest and undesirable too in those in minor orders. It is harmful not only in newly ordained priests but also in those who have already grown old in the priesthood. The following rule should therefore be laid down: if any priest gets drunk and then in the street or in any public place shouts unbecomingly or swears or uses foul language or fights with anyone or sings songs, he shall be arrested and brought before the episcopal consistory. For such unbecoming conduct he shall be punished with labour on episcopal or monastic estates and further with a fine or unfrocking, or as the bishops may decide, as a warning that priests and deacons must not drink to excess. So if by any mischance a priest has got drunk, let him go to some private place and sleep it off; let it on no account be seen by the people that he is drunk. And if any priest or deacon, or worse still a monk, goes and drinks in a tavern or an inn he should receive double punishment so as not to bring shame on the spiritual estate.

If then the clergy can cure themselves of such unbecoming conduct it will be like a new light shining in Russia. Thus they must be trained above all to inculcate piety and true faith among their spiritual children at Confession, to teach them how to stand firm in these so as not to be led astray by any Lutheran (33) or Roman wiles, and to avoid discussion with schismatics since they do not know how to argue with them. And at Confession they should also teach the people the right way to pray to God, how to revere the holy icons and what honour to accord them; to render due reverence to the spiritual estate; how to pray for our Sovereign and for all Christians; how to live in amity with friends and neighbours; on what strict principles to bring up their children and how to teach them the fear of God so that parents, having engendered children in the flesh, may not consign the souls put into them by God to eternal damnation; and how to be loving towards their kin and all fellow men and to do wrong to no one: for we are all brothers in Christ.

To this end priests should exhort all their spiritual flock, whether in the towns or the countryside, to teach their young children to read and write and train them in good behaviour and forbid them most strictly to loiter or play in the streets. In order that this admonition may never be forgotten but that all parents may bring up their children in the fear of God, priests should reiterate it at every Confession.

If the life of the clergy is ordered thus enlightenment will shine forth among the whole people, for all will as it were awake from sleep under such perfect and loving care of their spiritual guides, seeing that all will fully understand how to know God, how to pray to Him, how to worship God's saints and call on them for help, and how to live a truly Christian life.

Thus then must our spiritual pastors care for their flocks so that all men may live a righteous life. Far from appropriating things that do not belong to them they should not even covet anything belonging to their neighbour; if anyone comes upon something lying in his path he should try to find out who dropped it or have it taken to an appropriate place; and what men would not wish done unto themselves let them by no means do unto others, or even desire that it might be done. If all men, even those in secular life, lived thus they would not be far from the Kingdom of Heaven.

4)   Further, let it be enacted that priests and other clergy in the countryside shall no longer have to plough their land and mow their meadows, but concern themselves with the church services and their pastoral duties, and that in place of land they shall be maintained by a tithe of all the produce of the *dvoriáne* and peasants of their parish. Priests at Confession should then earnestly impress on their spiritual children that they must offer without fail (neither holding anything back nor grudging any part thereof) this tenth part of all produce set aside for their use, whether corn, meat, eggs or other food, and must bring it to the church for the subsistence of the priests and other clergy and of the poor who depend on that church. They must likewise set aside as the Sovereign's due a tithe of whatever quantity of grain or cattle or anything else is destined for sale. And confessors must earnestly exhort their spiritual children not to keep back anything. If they act righteously in setting aside a tithe for God and another for the Tsar, God will bless them with abundance in all things, so that they shall be

like the Jews of the Old Dispensation who likewise gave a tithe of all their increase.

I am without information as to what is done in other Christian lands in this matter, namely, how the clergy of country parishes are maintained, but I know full well that in Russia they subsist on their own toil and are scarcely to be distinguished from the peasantry. The peasant bends to his plough and so does the priest, the peasant swings his scythe and so does the priest, while Holy Church and pastoral duties are neglected. Because of this many Christians die not only without the consolation of the last sacrament but even without repentance and absolution, as if they were mere animals. And I do not know how this can be put right; the clergy have no stipend from the Sovereign, they receive no offerings from the laity, and God knows how they should subsist. So I put forward the following proposal: let a tithe be levied on the parishioners of every church so that they offer for the benefit of the clergy one tenth part or even one twentieth, as shall be ordained in this matter by the Sovereign and the (35) episcopacy, of what they set aside for their own consumption. In this way the clergy would be adequately maintained without land. This is only right, seeing that they are the servants of God and it is meet for them (in Our Lord's words) to receive their nourishment from the Church and not by working the land. Whereas if a priest has to labour in the fields, Holy Church must be false to herself and lose her flock. If it is improper for a priest to work the land it is no less improper for him to engage in any form of trade, or follow any craft, to the detriment of the services of the Church and of his pastoral duties, seeing that priests are separated from the laity for the service of God and therefore it is not meet for them to occupy themselves with anything but the church services and their pastoral duties. And so by God's command they should be maintained by the faithful, and not by working the land or by the exercise of a craft. And whenever there is no service in church or other ministration to perform they should be occupying themselves with reading the Scriptures or writing something conducive to man's salvation or to the glory of the Church.

For the Lord God Himself in the very earliest days of the priesthood, when he brought Israel up out of the land of Egypt into the Promised Land, commanded the land to be divided by lot among all the Israelites but forbade the giving of land to the priests and acolytes,[13] manifestly in order that they should be diligent in their religious duties; and He commanded them to be maintained by the Church and not by labouring on the land. How much the more then is it meet under the New Dispensation for our priests to concern themselves only with the service of the Church, since men's souls too have now been entrusted to them. But in our land the parish priests are burdened with tilling the soil and so have less concern for their ecclesiastical duties than for their land, and pastoral duties have fallen into neglect. Hence a vast number of Christians die without opportunity for repentance and the last Sacrament. For the country priests are quite simple folk; they grow up in the country and understand nothing but the ways of the countryside. They do not understand at all that they will have to answer before God for every lost soul,[14] nor do they know what value God puts upon a human soul.

If anyone takes exception to what I have said on the grounds that I have written all this in disparagement and criticism of the priesthood, God is my witness that I write it not at all to disparage but to correct. I myself am not without fear that I have touched on a matter too great for me; nevertheless God's will be done. He knows all the reasons for my presumption. And if our Sovereign shall deign in pursuance of God's command to free our priests from work on the land, then an ordinance of His Imperial Majesty should lay it down that landowners as well as peasants (whether on private, Crown, episcopal or monastic domains) shall all set aside a tithe of the corn destined for their own use and deliver it from their barns at threshing time to the clergy. And so shall they do invariably all the days of their life that God may bless them and give them increase in all things. Even if this should appear onerous at first, when they have grown accustomed to it and God's blessing has descended upon them, making their fields fertile, they will forget all the hardship.

And if any part of the corn set aside for the priests and other clergy shall remain unconsumed, it shall be used to feed the poor and the stranger.[15]

Further, hospitals and almshouses should be built for the sick poor both in the towns and in the countryside, appropriate to the size of the parish, and they should be fed there on this surplus, or as the Sovereign shall direct. As for the land which is now held and cultivated by the clergy, I think it should be leased out and churches and hospitals for the poor built with the income therefrom. And whatever corn a landowner or peasant has for sale, a tithe of it must be set aside as the Sovereign's due. Likewise in respect of all cattle destined for sale, one tenth of the price shall be set aside for our Sovereign. And one tenth part of any animal used for food shall likewise be taken to the church for the support of the clergy and to the almshouses. Similarly a tithe of all honey, butter, fish, eggs and other produce consumed at home shall invariably be set aside for the church, and likewise, as the Sovereign's due, a tithe of all that is sold. By doing thus we shall become like the pious Jews of old, for we shall be giving a tithe to God and a tithe to the Tsar of all our increase, and the priests and other clergy will be thereby adequately supported without the need to work their own land. And from the fees for special services and other ministrations the clergy will maintain their dwellings and apparel.

If it were so done, the priests would be able to celebrate matins and a liturgy every day and also be free at all times for special requirements. Acting thus the priests will become perfect servants of God and intercessors for the Sovereign and all the people. As things are now among the country clergy, even if there are two or three priests for one church, not many services are held. Happening to be in the parish of Ustréka where the church had three priests and a deacon, I found that there was a liturgy only on two days at Eastertide. The inhabitants said that there had never been more than one liturgy in Holy Week before and that it was due to fear of me that there were two. I stayed there throughout Holy Week and it was in no way different from an ordinary week – there was neither liturgy nor vespers nor matins. In the case of churches with only one priest, I imagine he will not celebrate more than a couple of dozen liturgies a year, for if he neglects his land he will starve.

So because priests must spend their time in cultivating their land the houses of God stand like bare barns where no praise of God is heard and Christian people are dying no whit different from beasts because of the same.

(38)

The country priests cannot be told apart from peasants: peasant and priest alike plough and mow. And on a feast day when it would be proper for them to be in church praising God, the priests will be off with the peasants preparing kilns, and when they should be celebrating the liturgy all the clergy are busy threshing their corn. With their lives full of mundane cares, far from tending Christ's flock, they cannot even care for their own souls.

But if God shall provide for them as set out above there will always be divine service in the holy churches and the priests will devote themselves to the care of their flock and no longer only to their land. And when the service is over a priest should read books and visit his flock in their homes, to see whether in their daily lives they are correctly following his direction and have not sinned in any way. Thus a priest should each month visit all those under his spiritual care and fortify them, that they may be mindful of what they were taught at Confession and perform without fail what he has commanded. And on these visits he should on no account partake of any kind of refreshment since he has come for the better supervision of his flock and not to fulful some special ministration. Let such priests be like the Holy Apostles, so that by their visitations they may guide the people to salvation with no thought of reward. And those to whom God has given skill with the pen should in their leisure time copy the chant-books and sell them to those desirous of possessing them. And if they are summoned anywhere for special ministration they must abandon everything else and go with dispatch to do what is required of them. By so doing all the country priests would excel as pastors and light would shine upon the life of the peasantry.

But the cure of souls as it is today is exceedingly imperfect and there is great reason to fear that God will exact retribution from our prelates, seeing that even those priests who live in the towns do not clearly recognize wherein lies sin and wherein salvation. Hence they do not exhort their parishioners to repentance and do not instruct them how to follow the way of salvation, and so many people perish in ignorance.

(39)

Indeed I have met many old men, even about Moscow, who are aged sixty and upwards but have never been to Confession, not because they are schismatics but because their priests do not oblige them to come. The custom among the peasantry has been not to go to Confession until one was old, and so some died unshriven, if they died young. This was due to nothing but the laxity of the clergy. The disorder into which our lives have thus fallen is too terrible to contemplate. But all these things can be put right by command of our Sovereign and the exertions of the Holy Synod. What grave dangers both the Tsar and the bishops incur if they continue to neglect such a great and momentous matter, for in the words of the holy prophet Ezekiel: 'thus cried the Holy Spirit, that God shall exact retribution for all lost souls at the hands of those who were set over them to govern them'.[16] Therefore does God's very threat inspire dread; and both spiritual and secular powers must exert themselves to the utmost to right these abuses and to escape this fate, namely that God shall exact retribution for the lost souls at the hands of those set over them to govern them.

My opinion then is based on my belief that damnation or salvation for each of us lies in the hands of our priests. If they are without understanding so will their flocks also be without understanding; if they lead a righteous and holy life all their flock will likewise have understanding and come near unto holiness. For through their ministry the people may be filled with all righteousness, stand fast in the Christian faith and preserve their souls from everlasting damnation; and under their firm guidance all shall – by God's grace – come nigh to the Kingdom of Heaven.

And when the priests have perfected themselves in knowledge and have acquired the habits of virtue and good conduct, an end must be made to their present repulsive and patched clothing. Whether in town or country, priests and deacons must be forbidden to wear filthy and tattered clothing; nor must they wear grey or white undyed hodden. If it is beyond a priest's means to buy foreign cloth he should have his garments made of kersey,[17] and if this too is impossible he should use hodden dyed crimson or blue. Priests must wear long cassocks with wide sleeves.

Priests and deacons should not go about improperly dressed for they are the servants of God and stand before the altar offering sacrifices for the Sovereign and all Christians. In view of their closeness to God, the Lord God Himself commanded even under the Old Dispensation that both priests and acolytes shall celebrate in clean garments. How much the more then does it behove our clergy in the New Dispensation of Grace to observe cleanliness in all things – in body as in soul, and likewise in their apparel and in the whole ordering of their lives, that they may be set apart from ordinary folk alike in their life and in their dress – and this not only in their outer but also in their inner clothing and in all their apparel. Their headgear should be round, trimmed with beaver or fox; their boots should be low with round toe-caps and they should on no account wear *lápti*[18] anywhere. The practice of approaching God's altar in *lápti* must

40)

be utterly prohibited, for those who do so do not merely detract from their sacred office but also from the reverence due to God. For it is in reverence to God that priests have been commanded to celebrate at His altar in rich vestments. In virtue whereof some priests don a gold vestment to celebrate in, yet on their feet they have nothing but patched *lápti*, caked in filth, and their under-robe is no less repulsive. Who will not be amazed at this mixing of gold with mould, when he sees a priest so arrayed? If it behoves us to carry out our Sovereign's commands conscientiously, how much the more so then those of God. A priest should always be sober and have a gracious word to say to everyone; his expression should be humble, his step unhurried. And he should never say to others things which are of no profit to them but only what is for their good. If they so do, priests shall be like unto the Apostles of Christ; all will reverence them for their conduct and will joyfully give them what is prescribed for their livelihood.

(41)

So in this matter let it be as His Imperial Majesty shall think good, either according to what I have proposed or as anyone else may amend. Amen.

CHAPTER 2. Of Military Affairs

Commentary

Pososhkóv lacks first-hand knowledge of this subject. – The cost-effectiveness of a large army and of dense infantry fire. – The musket and its use. – The Russian flintlock. – The difficulty of maintaining the new Russian army in peacetime. – The inadequacy of a soldier's pay. – Deductions from pay towards the cost of equipment. – The guards favoured. – Provisioning of the army before and after 1721. – Discontent in the army. – Desertion. – The punishment of deserters. – Unruly behaviour of the soldiery. – The remedy: a unitary system of justice.

In this chapter Pososhkóv tries to bring up to date the memorandum *On the Conduct of Military Affairs* which he wrote in 1700. At that time Pososhkóv described himself as an agriculturalist and pleaded ignorance of military matters. However, by reason of his indirect connection with the Arsenal in Moscow, he was better informed about things military at the beginning of the Great Northern War than at its end, by which time the Russian army was second to none in the whole of northern and eastern Europe. Self-opinionated and persistent 'projector' that he was, Pososhkóv takes this opportunity to renew his proposal – which the tsar had rejected in 1697 – for a mobile barrier of muskets mounted on *chevaux-de-frise*.[1]

The arguments which underlie these reflections of an amateur strategist are relevant to his general theme in so far as they concern the tsar's financial resources. This concern is even more apparent in the memorandum just mentioned. Pososhkóv is of the opinion that a comparatively small force, highly trained, well equipped and adequately paid is both cheaper and more effective than an ill-armed and underfed standing army. He believes that soldiers should shoot in order to kill rather than to impress; the prevailing practice of using massed units of infantry six (or four) ranks deep to fire simultaneous or successive volleys[2] seems to him an idle display since it costs powder and ammunition but does not cause any loss of life to the enemy.

Pososhkóv harks back to the wars with the Turks and their Tatar auxiliaries of the seventies and eighties of the previous century. In the incident described in the memorandum on military affairs to illustrate the same point, 'the Tatars did not even look at the Russians who were thundering away to no purpose'.[3] But after 1689 the Russians did not fight any more pitched battles with the

Tatars and in the Great Northern War, after the initial débâcle at Narva, the Russians proved a match for the Swedes within less than a year.[4]

In the north, as elsewhere in early eighteenth-century Europe, the performance of hand firearms was judged by their mechanical reliability and the rate at which they could be fired rather than by their accuracy and range. The longest distance at which it was considered worth trying to hit a man with a shot from a French musket was 100 metres. Tsar Peter was evidently aware of the imperfection of the musket and of its use. About 1708 he ruled that recruits should be instructed in effective, unhurried firing. They should load their guns without haste 'for we often observe bullets fired from muskets hissing as if they were rockets . . . All this is caused by haste which is not at all necessary in this business and indeed harmful.'[5] He was referring to various unauthorized methods of loading resorted to by soldiers who were eager to ease their task and speed up the rate of fire. On the other hand, Pososhkóv's suggestion that mounted troops could best achieve superiority by accurate fire was contrary to Peter's intention that the Russian dragoons should learn to use side-arms in the final assault on the enemy.[6]

The flintlock made for the use of the Russian infantry according to the specifications laid down in 1715 weighed 5.74 kg, had a barrel 19.8 mm in calibre 101.6 cm long, and a fixable bayonet. It fired one to two shots a minute, its maximum range was 300 paces and its effectiveness 15 per cent at between 250 and 300 paces and 40 per cent at 100 paces under rifle range conditions. The musket carried by the dragoons was lighter, 4.91 kg, its 17.3 mm calibre barrel shorter, 45.7 cm. Its range was 100 to 120 metres and it fired no more than one shot per minute.[7] It is obvious from the performance of these and similar weapons available in Europe at the time that before Pososhkóv's proposals could be put into effect great technical advances would have had to be made. Pososhkóv's ideal army would be smaller and cheaper to maintain than the army of the day; this would make it possible to increase the soldiers' pay and to give special rewards for marksmanship.

The system of recruitment for Peter's army was as brutal as it was unfair. The oral poetry of the period laments in heart-rending tones the ill-starred and miserable lot of the recruit;[8] the prosaic Pososhkóv does not allow emotion to dim his perception of the economic and social difficulties created by the appearance in the midst of Russian society of a greatly enlarged military establishment without an adequate financial base. Unwittingly perhaps he puts his finger on the chief economic problem of the last quinquennium of the reign of Peter, that of supplying and paying a standing army in peacetime.[9] The poll-tax did not provide the solution; as has already been said, it quickly became apparent that the answer did not lie in determining the cost of the upkeep of the army with a view to collecting the requisite amount of money from the taxpayer.[10] However fast a national economy may have been developing in

Russia at the time it is nevertheless clear that neither the administrative nor the monetary nor yet the transport system was equal to the basic task of feeding the men and the horses.

The annual pay of a common soldier was 12 roubles a year in the cavalry and 10 roubles a year in the infantry. In addition he was entitled to a 'portion' consisting of flour, groats, salt and – except on garrison service – meat, calculated in 1720 to be worth 5 roubles 74 kopecks a year on the basis of prices officially approved at that time. The 'ration' of oats and hay for a horse was worth only slightly less, 5 roubles and 70 kopecks, and covered no more than the six months outside the grazing period. Pososhkóv's comment on this proportion, had he known of it, can be imagined. He estimated that the cost of feeding and clothing a civilian for one year was at least 6 roubles.[11] It would appear that from the outset the amount of money allowed for the various items was not enough to buy the prescribed quantities of food. Thus the prices allowed for flour and oats were respectively 1 rouble 50 kopecks and 50 kopecks per *chétvert*, whereas the prices current in St Petersburg in 1719 were 2 roubles 70 kopecks for flour and 1 rouble for oats. On active service the troops fared better at the expense of the local population, the basic daily portion for the army being two pounds of bread, one pound of meat, two measures (*chárki*) of spirits and a gallon of beer.[12]

From a soldier's nominal pay 5 roubles were deducted towards the cost of the eventual replacement of his equipment[13] but Pososhkóv points out that the men had to provide some of the items of clothing themselves. In 1712 the supply of equipment was entrusted to a government department (*Mundírnaia kantse-liáriia*) in Moscow, ultimately to be incorporated with the College or Board of War.[14] The guards appear to have received preferential treatment. Long service or good conduct in the ranks of the Preobrazhénskii and the Semënovskii regiments were rewarded with double pay. On one occasion, in 1711, the tsar instructed the Senate that the cost of making the uniforms for the guards regiments should be met out of general funds rather than from stoppages of pay.[15]

Between 1712 and 1721 the army had been supplied with provisions under contracts made by the commissariat with private suppliers; from 1721 food and forage were raised direct from the taxpayer wholly or partly instead of cash, with the delivery and storage handled by the army. Three years later, after the hungry year of 1723, the army was simply rusticated, that is, quartered in the countryside, and there lived in such barracks as it was able to put up, collecting food and fodder for the most part in place of the poll-tax. This system has the appearance of a desperate measure but it is admittedly possible that from 1720 the service state deliberately bypassed the market and had recourse to what John Hicks calls the Revenue Economy[16] because in this way it could dictate the prices which it had laid down for foodstuffs in 1720, perhaps in extension of the principle contained in articles 21 and 25 of Chapter 7 of the *Code* of 1649.[17] It is also possible that the contract system began to break down about that time owing to the shortage of silver money and the depreciation of the copper coinage. Neither of the methods of direct collection of tax by those for whose subsistence it was intended, introduced successively in 1721 and 1724, achieved the desired twofold result of distributing more evenly the fiscal burden incumbent on the population whilst securing an adequate supply of food and fodder for the army. That of 1724 was partially abolished in 1725 after Peter's death but restored for six years in 1730.[18]

The harsh conditions of military service described by Pososhkóv evidently had an adverse effect on morale and discipline in the army. Low and unpunctual pay was one of the causes of discontent. In the spring of 1706 at Mogilëv some 3,000 recruits, driven to desperation, raised a cry at the tsar: 'Righteous sovereign, give us our pay!' The necessary money did not arrive until the autumn.[19] About 1715 an anonymous letter of warning addressed to Tsar Peter by a marine stationed in St Petersburg complained bitterly of service without respite – manning the galleys in the summer and working in the shipyards in the winter – and of pay that would not buy enough food or clothing. The tsar was reproached personally with having sacrificed 'a million lives' in St Petersburg and established for show a costly and futile bureaucracy. 'We have seen', says the letter, 'great abundance in many foreign parts, whereas at home the land has been laid waste by an out-and-out war. Is the tsar the wise man he is made out to be? He has brought us to ruin and does not know how to govern us. We shall combine with the army in Finland and rise in revolt to redress the wrongs suffered by the people.'[20] The numerical strength of Tsar Peter's army was continually diminished by mass desertion, especially in the years preceding the battle of Poltáva (1709). It was the Russian peasant's traditional reaction to unsatisfactory material conditions which the danger to life and limb made even more repellent. Between 1705 and 1709 no fewer than 10,000 men deserted each year. The flight of soldiers from the army also affected public security because the deserters tended to form gangs of thieves and robbers. The sanctions reserved for deserters at different times during the Great Northern War were extremely harsh but mitigated now and again in order to spare lives which the army could ill afford to lose. In 1700 the general rule was laid down: deserters were to be punished in a way that would deter others from doing the same. From January 1705 one out of every three deserters was to be hanged, the other two were to receive the knout and to be sent into exile with hard labour for life. However, in August of the same year the tsar ruled that only the instigators should be hanged or, if none was found, one man out of ten. The rest were to be given the knout and returned to their units. Artices 94 and 95 of Chapter 12 of the Articles of War of 1715 established death by hanging 'on the nearest tree' as the penalty for all acts of desertion, but in 1717 article 95 was amended on the grounds that it had originally followed the practice of other states where soldiers were not conscripted by ordinance but served for hire.[21] From now on deserters in their first year of service were to run the gauntlet for three consecutive days; if they deserted for a second time or after their first year of service they were to receive the knout, have their nostrils torn out in front of their regiment and be sent to public or industrial works to labour there in perpetuity. A court martial was also to punish those who had harboured or fed a deserter. In 1720 the death penalty was restored for deserters who on giving themselves up had been pardoned but had run away again. A succession of ordinances during the reign of Peter promised a complete acquittal to deserters who gave themselves up by a prescribed date which was often extended. The ways in which such deserters were treated varied: some suffered only minor punishments while others languished in gaol for long periods awaiting trial. This was no inducement to follow their example.[22]

The behaviour of soldiers in quarters was supposed to be regulated by Chapter 11 of the Articles of War of 1715 but it is clear that excesses against the civilian population were committed with impunity.[23] Hence Pososhkóv's plea for a judicial system that would be common to all. This proposal runs counter to the inclination of the service state, reformed or unreformed, to assign the administration of justice in civil cases to whatever authority, ecclesiastical, military or civil, was charged with the regulation of the activities proper to the occupation and place in society of the persons concerned. Thus in later years of the reign of Peter townspeople were placed under the jurisdiction of the Board of Civic Administration (*Glávnyi Magistrát*), manufacturers under that of the Board of Manufactories, ecclesiastics under that of the Synod.[24] But the whole subject belongs more properly to the next chapter.

CHAPTER 2

Of Military Affairs

(42) Soldiers who have not learnt to observe the Articles of War[1] in all respects, who are not well trained in the use of their arms and whose marksmanship is poor, will not give a good account of themselves in war nor be formidable to the enemy. Moreover, if they are poorly fed, their quality will be altogether low. There are rumours that some soldiers do not even receive as much as thirty kopecks' pay a month. I suppose that no one dares to inform His Majesty of their indigence; he is, I imagine, led to believe that they are all well fed and contented. Some half-dozen years ago a new recruit at Výshnii Volochók received, after stoppage, twenty kopecks as his month's pay. On being handed the money he drew a knife and slashed himself in the belly; manifestly it was not joy that made him act so as to endanger even his own life. The reason for his action was that he was so poorly paid. I presume that the officers never make an honest report about such things to His Majesty. In view of all this, and seeing that they are not properly fed, the troops give indifferent service in battle since a soldier marching on an empty stomach will stumble over a straw instead of hotly

(44) pursuing the enemy over obstacles and streams. A hungry man is like an aspen leaf which quivers in the slightest breeze. A hungry man is a bad workman; how then can he be a good soldier? I have actually heard soldiers say that they would be glad to be killed. So what useful service can such men give, who do not want to kill the enemy but would rather be killed themselves in the hope of finding relief in death from the hardships of this life? Yet given that soldiers are well found and well trained, officers and men alike must not be granted too much freedom to act as they please or else their military worth will still be small. For if anything in the army is not to their liking there is much danger that they will prove troublesome: licence never leads to anything but trouble.

In their billets both infantrymen and dragoons behave so wildly and commit such outrages that they are beyond reckoning, and where their officers are quartered the men behave even worse: they burn firewood recklessly, and if it runs short go and cut down such trees as they need. And if they are told that according to His Majesty's ordinance they may only burn their own wood, they will merely behave the more outrageously. This makes many people wish that they were not householders.

Nor is there any court where redress can be obtained for these outrages; though military courts are harsh it is hard to get a hearing in them since they are far from the common people. Not only is it hard for such people to gain access to them but even a military person will think twice about trying to obtain redress against someone of higher rank.

In 1721 Captain I. M. Nevel'skói of the Preobrazhénskii regiment[2] was sent to Nóvgorod to trace some stolen silk goods which had been sent from Moscow to Nóvgorod for sale. A certain Nóvgorod townsman, Peter Terént'ev, was accused of complicity in this affair, but only in one deposition, and I myself had nothing whatever to do with it. Yet Nevel'skói had Peter taken to his quarters and kept him there under arrest for more than two weeks. And despite Peter's innocence Nevel'skói also sent his clerk with a party of soldiers to seal all Peter's goods and turned me out of Peter's back room. And my wife said: 'Show us your authority for turning us out of the house and putting all our possessions under seal.' And the soldiers forcibly dragged her out of the room and tried to turn us off the premises altogether, but we resisted and would not go. So Nevel'skói threatened us in the following terms: 'If you don't clear out I'll come myself and throw you right out into the street and drag your wife out by the hair.' So my wife, fearing injury and such a great indignity, spent more than two weeks in various other houses. Now I was living in this house of Peter's by the orders of the Governor, Prince Iu. Ia. Khilkóv.

This Captain Nevel'skói passed for a good and reasonable man yet even he committed such outrages. And Peter waited on him with a gift. The Captain then unsealed his possessions but not mine; naturally he hoped to extract the like from me too. Prince Khilkóv had the greatest difficulty in persuading him to remove the seals and the guard.

Likewise in that same year, when Colonel D. L. Porétskii was in Nóvgorod in the office of the provincial court, he reviled me in the most abusive language, called me a rogue and threatened to run me through, but I am not aware of having done anything to merit such treatment. And these abusive and threatening words were uttered in the very judges' chambers; however, there were no judges there at the time, only the deputy clerk of the court, Roman Sémikov. Both he and the other clerks and many gentlemen present heard the abuse and threats. So next morning I presented a petition to the judges to examine the colonel in the matter of his abusive and threatening words. But Porétski did not appear for examination, saying that he was answerable only to the Board of War and did not propose to appear before a local court. So I did not obtain justice although I am a man of some position. How then shall a man obtain justice who is of even less account than myself? If you have complaints to make against the outrages of the military, make them to God alone!

Now if the same justice were dispensed to all without favour – to ordinary civilian and officer alike – then the soldiery would give up their high-handed ways – albeit unwillingly – and behave with propriety towards men of all conditions and do no offence to anyone, as now, whether in billets or on the march. So if all troops, both infantry and dragoons, ceased to act contrary to His Majesty's commands and to commit outrages but set themselves to be on good terms with all men, and if their officers too practised such obedience and were on good terms with all men, and further if in all foot regiments the men were sufficiently well drilled for them not to be thrown into confusion by any enemy, then in battle they would be like a stone wall.

If the men can handle their arms expertly, maintain the hammers and flints of their muskets in proper trim (so that there is never a misfire), keep the weapon clean inside and out and the barrel true,[3] then the musket will be very reliable, accurate in aim and effective in battle. Moreover, if they do not shoot wildly (as they do now) but at the target, so that neither bullet nor powder is wasted, and if they learn to shoot from the shoulder accurately enough to hit a horseman galloping from the field, then such soldiers will be most fearsome in battle, and that not only on land but also in naval engagements.

For naval warfare young soldiers should be trained to hit the target without fail when shooting from the shoulder; they will then be able to do the same even when embarked in small boats in rough seas.[4] If they can learn to do that, fighting at sea would be held in the greatest honour and would, I am sure, make us most glorious and redoubtable throughout the world.

(47)   Further, if soldiers were also to carry a very sharp side-arm no little advantage would ensue therefrom, for once it penetrates into a man's guts or other internal organs, he will be beyond medical aid and sure to die. Whereas even if one pierces a man right through the belly with a blunt weapon the wound can be healed as it will not have damaged the guts. But a really sharp weapon makes a mortal wound.

In my opinion such soldiers might well receive higher pay than at present: I would propose sixteen roubles a year for the ordinary private soldier and for those who can hit a cap at fifty yards without fail, when firing from the shoulder, twenty roubles a year, so that others may be encouraged by their example to acquire the same skill. And if they can also hit a moving target without fail they might be given twenty-five roubles a year since such men are worth two or three who have not this skill. If a thousand such soldiers fired on closing with the enemy in a land battle, at the lowest reckoning some five hundred or six hundred of the enemy would fall and so, however high the enemy's spirit, he would falter and could not but turn tail. I believe that the enemy without staying for a second volley would turn his thoughts to flight.

It is said in praise of the Finns that they are so steady in battle that if one man is killed another immediately takes his place in the line. There is nothing remarkable about this: if there are only one or two casualties among a hundred men there is no point in filling the gaps. But if fifty or sixty are killed out of a hundred, I do not see how even these famous Finns could replace them. And if they do not then take to flight but firmly stand their ground and await a second volley, there will be no one left to flee; all will fall on the spot.

I do not know by what long-established military tradition it has become the sole accepted practice for all to fire at once as if from a single gun. That kind of drill is all very well on an exercise or at a gay banquet but it is of no use in the bloody banquet of war. For war is not in jest but in earnest; there must be no waste of powder or shot – every bit of them must be used to the best effect. I have heard foreigners say with approval such things as: 'The engagement was so fierce that the men were under fire for some six hours on end but neither side could dislodge the other.' If that is the Western way let them keep it. God grant that we Russians earn rather this sort of praise: 'It is no use fighting the Russians; with one volley they do for more than half of you.' A battle of that kind will not last six hours but just one minute. If God grants our Russian troops to be so well trained that not a single man wastes a single shot, then given ten thousand such men I am certain that no one would dare to engage us even with twenty thousand: any enemy would flee headlong from us as from a wild beast.

At Azóv the Tatars attacked Swart's regiment[5] and on the orders of their colonel the men all fired together in one volley in the Western manner; the whole regiment did not even kill as many as a dozen of the enemy. Seeing that the Russians then set about reloading, the Tatars quickly charged, giving them no chance to reload, and chased them like sheep back to their own territory together with their colonel. Now if they had not wasted their fire, but only half of them had fired at a time while the other half withheld their fire, they would not have been routed like sheep. And if all of them had been accurate marksmen they would have killed at the lowest estimate two hundred or three hundred of the enemy and the Tatars would not have had the courage to charge a whole regiment. If they had killed five hundred or six hundred the enemy would have taken to his heels and disappeared for good. The Tatars are brave enough as long as casualties are not high but when they lose a couple of hundred men they lose heart, for they like to win without loss to themselves.

In my young days when I was at Pénza the local troops discovered that I was a very good marksman and said to me (these are their very words): 'Stay here for the season and we won't be afraid of the Tatars.' I replied that I could do nothing against them single-handed but they said: 'You are an excellent shot and never waste a bullet. The Tatars are pressing us hard and we cannot kill any of them; but we see that you can even hit a bird on the wing. Skirmishers[6] come forth from their side and ride about at a range of thirty yards; yet all we can do is stand there pointing our guns at them. Now if you killed even one of them they would stop harrying us like this, and if you killed two or three they would all make off for good.'

Bearing this in mind, if we could, with God's help, recruit ten or twenty thousand such troops I am sure that all our enemies would take fright. Moreover, if we were to equip these troops with *chevaux de frise* on which guns have been mounted, these could open fire at two hundred and fifty yards while the enemy was still closing in and inflict casualties on the covering troops which advance ahead of the main body. And when they have closed to seventy yards they should again be met by fire from these guns, and any that survive this salvo should be picked off by our troops with their muskets; and any that still survive should be bayonetted in close combat. If they attempt to flee, our dragoons should likewise dispatch them with their muskets.

Infantry equipped with these weapons should be supported by mounted troops at least one thousand strong, capable of firing at the trot or canter at any target, whether ahead, on either flank or behind; a mere thousand such men will be worth in action more than ten thousand. Indeed they would be more effective than twenty thousand because I do not know who could stand up to such troops. Far from remaining under fire (as now) for a whole day, the enemy will have had enough of it in a quarter of an hour. I can well imagine that they would not stand even two volleys, and the survivors would all think of nothing but saving their skins.

If then with God's help we could recruit five or six thousand such troops there would be no point in maintaining and feeding fifty thousand cavalry[7] to no purpose. And if both infantry and cavalry do not waste their fire it will be difficult for the enemy even to take to flight in face of them; still less will they dare to come to grips with such troops. Our men must have the best and most accurate firearms. The mounted soldiers should be equipped with a musket, a pair of long pistols and a pair of short ones; also they should carry at the saddle by the leg[8] a very sharp lance with a shaft eight or nine feet long. They should wear a red uniform since they are men of fire: as a small fire burns much wood, so also these. Given open and unencumbered country a small body of them can defeat, with God's help, a large force. In open country ten thousand such troops would be worth fifty thousand ordinary ones.

As for those men who are not such expert marksmen that they never waste a bullet, it is no less necessary to take good care of them and see that they do not lack food and clothing. For one hears so often that some do not even receive as much as thirty kopecks' pay a month. How can a man get along on that, how will he procure himself a greatcoat and other necessaries, what will he buy his food with? In such straits is he not bound to steal and desert? It is necessity that leads to desertion, and some will even be apt to turn traitor.

Infantry and dragoons must be well cared for and great attention must be paid, even when in quarters, that they do not go short of adequate food and clothing. In the field they must be even better found so that they may serve with a will. If all their wants are satisfied they will do their duty all the better – and

(50)

this is no less true of the best regiments than of the less good or those newly raised. If all are satisfied in the matter of food and clothing, all will serve with a will.

Nor does it seem to me at all proper, even if adopted from Western practice, that a private soldier of foot or horse should receive a uniform and that the whole cost of it should then be recovered month by month out of his pay. How can a soldier help being reduced to great straits by such stoppages? His pay is at the rate of only ninety kopecks a month, and after stoppages he actually receives only thirty kopecks or less. How can he possibly buy greatcoat, cap, gauntlets and stockings or leg-bands out of such a small sum? I think that the practice of stoppages should be given up and also a soldier's pay should be increased by ten kopecks a month, so that he may have enough for his needs. It seems to me that troops would serve with much more will and zeal if the practice of stoppages were given up.

I myself saw a soldier in St Petersburg buy two kopecks' worth of meat in the last week before Lent, saying: 'I'd like just to get a taste of meat before the Fast begins.' Is it not the height of indigence to have been eating nothing but dry bread during the whole period when meat is allowed? And if the same indigence prevails in the field, then service must bear hard upon the men. I am sure that if they were adequately fed and clothed they would be twice as effective. What sort of a soldier is a man who is hungry and cold and goes about hunched up, full of complaints at the conditions of his service?

If any infantryman or dragoon should be guilty of misconduct and desert despite being well fed, he must be caught and questioned as to why he deserted. If it was to avoid service let him be executed, or alternatively brand a cross (or some other mark) on his forehead so that he may be known to all as a deserter. He will not desert again in future because no one anywhere will admit him into his home with such a mark on him, nor give him any work. Thereafter, should he again be found away from his regiment, let him be arrested and sent bound before a court martial; and then the sentence shall be death. But if the arrested soldier says that he deserted because of ill-treatment by an officer, then the matter must be investigated. If the ill-treatment is proved the officer must be punished and the soldier shall escape branding. For many infantrymen and dragoons complain of receiving very bad treatment from their officers, yet the latter are not brought to book.

All conditions of men would live together in greater charity if His Majesty were to decree that the same justice shall apply alike to peasant and merchant (whether poor or rich), soldier and officer (without any exception, be he colonel or general). And if His Majesty were further to decree that courts should be near enough at hand for everyone (be he even of low degree) to have easy access to them to bring a case against either a civilian or a soldier, then officers would not only cease to ill-treat their men but would cease to oppress the peasantry also. If they see that the dispensation of justice is both upright and impartial the officers will one and all give up their habitual arrogance and high-handed and oppressive ways; they will treat all conditions of men charitably and behave well in billets; they will not do what they are forbidden to do and will not continue to ignore His Majesty's commands; the same though they may appear, they will be changed in heart. They will show consideration to all men so that anyone will be glad to accept soldiers in his home as if they were his own kin. It seems to me that no court can be fair in which a civilian has to obtain redress from a soldier for an injury done to him by a soldier, and likewise from one officer for an injury done by another. There is an old saying that 'dog does not eat dog'. For it is obvious that a soldier will never inform against a fellow soldier, and officers as a matter of course do not give away a brother officer or a soldier, quite contrary to their attitude towards civilians. For in the nature of things blood is thicker than water; they are bound to back one another up, because this time it is Tom who is in trouble but next time it will be Dick and so they cannot help treating one another with partiality.

However, if the courts are to remain as at present, separate for soldiers and civilians, at least let all come under a single superior court and be in all matters subject to it; then justice may be done. Even so in order to achieve impartial justice it is essential that the judges be independent – neither soldiers nor officers themselves – so that justice may be meted out to all men without favour.

(53)   The judges should receive the most stringent instructions never to show favour to any man, and not to condemn even a mere peasant unjustly when he is innocent, nor to dare to ignore his complaint.

In the case of soldiers the law hitherto has been applied as follows: soldiers who have committed murder or rapine are held to be guiltless and the victim to be in the wrong. Though a man may catch a soldier red-handed this will do him no good, for even if he brings the soldier before the court with clear evidence of guilt it will be himself who will be beaten. A servant recovered a horse of mine yet the horse was confiscated and Captain Mávrin had my servant beaten, saying: 'Why are you holding up the convoy? You should go to St Petersburg to get your horse back; they would give you judgment there.' But that court was far off and the issue uncertain; the horse cost me only four roubles and to present a complaint there would have come to more than the horse was worth. True, the horse in question was in the hands of a carter, not a soldier, but of one employed on officer's business; yet again I did not pursue my rights in the matter.

Another consideration: it seems to me not at all an admirable procedure that one soldier should have to present a complaint against another to military officers. If his complaint is against someone of the same rank as himself he will obtain redress for certain but if it is against an officer the thing is out of the question; he will not get redress in any circumstances but will be fobbed off. A person who is not very insistent will be put off with false promises; anyone who persists in his complaint will be pressed into various duties until he is heartily sick of the whole matter. And that is poor justice. Therefore everything must be done to secure true justice, so that no one need complain to God nor harbour any grievance against the courts. Let no one have to invoke God's help, let every man obtain true justice and all wrong-doing receive judgment on this earth and not be left to our Heavenly Judge.

If then courts of justice in Russia are made fair and within reach of all, men will no longer need to invoke divine justice upon one another but everyone will receive judgment and reward according to his deserts in this life.

CHAPTER 3. Of Justice and the Law

Commentary

Peter the Great's sense of justice akin to Pososhkóv's. – The measures against the prevailing state of near-lawlessness. – Changes in judicial procedure (1697, 1723). – The 'general perquisition' (povál'nyi óbysk) remains open to abuse. – Attempts to revise the Code of 1649. The commission of 1720. – Pososhkóv's request for a legislative assembly. – Pososhkóv the aggrieved landlord and master of peasants. – The treatment of runaway peasants under the Code of 1649. – The illegal migrations of peasants continue into the eighteenth century. – The measures against peasant flights 1721–4. – Pososhkóv's contribution to this subject. – Passes for peasants working away from home in use by 1683, made obligatory in 1719. – The dereliction of duty by men of service. – The musters and general inspections of dvoriáne held by Peter I. – The punishment of absentees. – The economic damage done by the malfunctioning of the judicial system as seen by Pososhkóv. – 'The riches of the people are the riches of the tsar.' – Economic activity hampered by old-established practices. – The futility of pravëzh which continues despite the tsar's prohibition (1718). – Credit difficult to obtain and arrange. – The regularization of the procedure for drawing up legal documents. – The provision of sureties. – Mendicant pauperism condemned by Pososhkóv and combated by Peter I. – The question of the cost of maintaining prisoners in jail.

The subject of this chapter,[1] longer and rather more incoherent than the rest, is justice in its broadest sense, extending from the punishment of crime to the economic consequences of inequity. Since in Peter I's Russia, despite his somewhat half-hearted endeavours to separate the judicial from the administrative power,[2] justice was dispensed by the higher officials, the subject involves the author in an examination of the manner in which the country is governed. Many deficiencies come to light, all of which can be seen to result in impoverishment, both individual and collective. Pososhkóv's verdict on the system of government established by Peter is adverse in the extreme. His sense of justice is outraged by a regime which is based on service but allows the rich and powerful to evade their duties and to spurn the law at the expense of their inferiors.

As an Orthodox Christian Pososhkóv believes in the divine nature of justice – *právda*[3] – of which the final act will be the Last Judgment. Meanwhile practical secular considerations demand that equity should prevail. Always something of a puritan, he sets a social value on thrift – a penny saved is a penny gained – for the public as much as for the private purse. Without directly invoking the authority of St Paul[4] he insists that consumption must be justified by productive labour. In identifying the economic interests of the individual with those of the realm as a whole he comes close to the teaching of the cameralists.[5] However cheerless the picture that Pososhkóv paints of Peter the Great's Russia may be, he is not a pessimist but, like his sovereign, is actuated by a savage kind of optimism. Both see man as corrigible rather than perfectible and put their trust in printed laws, rules and regulations, barbed with the threat of punishment.[6] This affinity extends further. The tsar too believed in the divine nature of justice as dispensed by his executive officers. 'The judgment', he said, echoing the Old Testament, 'is God's.'[7] In 1699 he ordained that instructions issued on his behalf from the *Rátusha* should bear a stamp showing a hand thrust out of a cloud and holding a pair of scales. The device was to read: 'The eye of the ruler beholds justice.'[8]

What the tsar saw in reality was a state of affairs bordering on lawlessness. The *ukáz* which altered the character of the process at law speaks of the deliberate dragging out of proceedings, of innocent men of no standing brought to ruin while the guilty gain time and pettifoggers prosper. The statement was repeated in a similar context in 1700;[9] Pososhkóv took up the same theme some twenty years later. His strictures testify to the failure of Peter's repeated efforts to reform the law code, the judicature and judicial procedure. The tsar resorted to corrective remedies in 1722 by establishing the offices of *generál-prokurór* (whose duties corresponded closely, indeed literally, to those of the 'faithful eye of the tsar' visualized by Pososhkóv) and of *reketméister*[10] but Pososhkóv does not appear to have been aware of the activities of either officer.

Like Pososhkóv the tsar had long attributed the prevailing state of lawlessness to the lack of an up-to-date code of law and to the want of order in the judicial process. In 1697 there arose from a case of breach of the peace a particularly flagrant instance of a groundless counter-accusation combined with perjury. The tsar, incensed, ordered a change in the process at law in all causes from the accusatory and mixed method to the inquisitorial.[11] The 'Brief Description of the Process at Law' which forms part of the Articles of War published in 1715 applies the principles laid down in 1697 to military law but it appears that eventually, for a period, the 'Description' was used in criminal proceedings by the civil as well as the military authorities. It deals almost exclusively with the constitution of a court of law and the conduct of trials.[12] In the ordinance on the due form of processes at law published in 1723 the Emperor, without admitting the failure of the method instituted in 1697, states that in the courts much superfluous talk is allowed and much unnecessary writing is done. Nor should any distinction be drawn, as was done formerly, between adjudication (viz. the accusatory method) and investigation (the inquisitorial method). There is only one process at law (the mixed type) from which, however, crimes against the state are excepted.[13] The rules laid down in this ordinance revived in a modified form the accusatory procedure which had been set aside by the ordinance of 1697 and by the 'Brief Description' of 1715 but by reason of its sketchiness, the ordinance superseded the *Code* of 1649 and even the 'Brief Description' (assuming that it was used in civilian courts) only in so far as it obviously repealed their provisions. The object of the new provision was, as before, to speed up judicial proceedings and prevent barratry and pettifoggery. The ordinance prescribed a point-by-point interrogation of each party, preceded by due notice and followed by the formal approval by both sides of a written summary of the evidence. These and similar provisions of earlier and later date concerning appellate procedure and the right of an accused person to challenge a judge on grounds of possible prejudice do not appear to have had any beneficial effect on the way in which justice was dispensed. Equally useless, judging by Pososhkóv's account, were the tsar's instructions of 1719 and 1720 exhorting all magistrates to administer justice speedily and equitably.[14] The ordinance of 1723 may also have been intended for the guidance of the commission formed in 1720 for the revision of the *Code*.

The new rules for the observance of the due process of law introduced in 1723 did not affect the traditional form of judicial investigation – the general perquisition (*povál'nyi óbysk*) – condemned in such strong terms by Pososhkóv. Perquisitions were carried out by persons of trust designated for the purpose by the authorities in criminal cases as a matter of course and in civil cases at the request of the contesting parties. A minor perquisition consisted in the questioning of the inhabitants of the place of residence of the accused or defendant, a major or general perquisition, which Pososhkóv had in mind, examined the population of a given locality within a radius of 3 or 4 versts in civil, and up to 15 or 20 versts in criminal cases. The point at issue was decided by a majority of depositions in favour of or against one of the parties. The rules for the conduct of perquisitions were amended in the interests of fairness by the *Code* of 1649 and again by the novels of 1669. The ordinance of 1691 issued in the names of the tsars Peter and Ivan sought to eradicate the worst faults in the procedure followed in carrying out perquisitions: the questioning of groups rather than of individuals one by one, the swearing of depositions in the absence of the officer in charge of the investigation and the signing of blank forms by the deponents, obviously to no effect. In 1724 the conduct of perquisitions was included in the duties of the junior officer in the local administration, the *zémskii kommisár*.[15]

The changes that had occurred in society and had been effected in the law by the novels introduced in 1669, 1676 and 1677[16] made a revision of the *Code* of

Alekséi Mikháilovich imperative. Tsar Peter was fully aware of this necessity even before the mass of ordinances and regulations enacted by him was to make it more acute still. In February 1700 he appointed a commission with instructions to bring up to date those sections of the *Code* of 1649 which subsequent legislation had rendered obsolete. The work was completed in 1703 only to be shelved although the draft was kept up to date until 1705.[17] In 1714 the state of confusion resulting from the existence of contradictory laws obliged the tsar to order all magistrates to base their decisions on the *Code* of 1649 alone, regardless of the novels or any particular ordinances except in matters of which no mention was made in the *Code*, pending its revision.[18] But at some point during the next few years he gave up this intention and at the end of 1719 ordered the Senate to attend readings of the Swedish code so that the draft of a new Russian code could be ready towards the end of October. Any articles that were found to be unsuited to 'our people' were to be replaced with articles from the *Code* of Alekséi Mikháilovich or new ones; articles in that *Code* which were 'weightier' than those in its Swedish counterpart were to be preserved.[19]

The task of the commission appointed for this purpose by the Senate in 1720 was therefore to adapt rather than adopt the Swedish code, supplemented by the statutes of the seventeenth century on the conduct of trials and the execution of verdicts and by the laws of the formerly Swedish provinces of Livonia and Estonia.[20] The work was completed in 1725 but only after the Emperor's death. The draft was divided into four books of ninety-six chapters and about 2,000 articles. Book 1 was devoted to judicial procedure in general, Book 2 to evidence, including the use of torture as a means of obtaining proof in criminal cases, Book 3 to crimes and their punishment; Book 4 constituted a civil code and was divided into five sections: Land Economy (including the status of bondmen), Contracts, the Care of Minors, Marriage, Wills and Inheritance.[21] Had Peter the Great lived longer, approved the draft and promulgated the new code (which would have resolved most of Pososhkóv's grievances), he would have gone down in history as a lawgiver as well as an empire-builder.

Pososhkóv's request that the draft of a new code be discussed and approved in a free vote by a popular assembly was not as bold or as novel as it appears to be although the concept is not of a kind to have commended itself to the autocrat and those who exercised authority on his behalf. The *Ulozhénie* had been approved by the sovereign in consultation with the 'hallowed assembly' of the higher clergy, the *dúma* of boyars and the members of the drafting commission but it has been established that the petitions submitted by representatives of the social groups – men of service, merchants and *posádskie liúdi* of lower standing (traders and artisans) – were taken into account in the drawing up of certain sections of the *Code*, especially Chapters 11 (Of the laws concerning peasants) and 19 (Of the *posádskie liúdi*).[22] It may be taken for granted that Tsar

Peter would not have invited public discussion of the draft code. Pososhkóv's use of the expression 'a free voice' suggests some knowledge on his part of the Polish parliament where each deputy reserved the right to speak and vote as he saw fit.[23]

In spite of having won for himself a social position of some consequence, Pososhkóv continued to regard himself as one of the injured and deprived. But not all his reverses of fortune, such as they were, could be blamed on the high and mighty *dvoriáne* and their allegedly vested interest in injustice. Pososhkóv complains that some of his peasants absconded in 1722; in the summer of 1725 some more were to wander off, others to eat up their allowance of grain whilst refusing to work for him.[24] And yet when it came to the question of land ownership a *dvorianín* might well have regarded him as a trespasser, but Pososhkóv evidently felt no qualms about owning populated agricultural land, some of which had no connection with his activities as a manufacturer. The *Ulozhénie* (Chapters 17, article 41 and 19, article 15) clearly intended that such ownership should be restricted to men of service. The ordinance of 18 January 1721 extended it to manufacturers but only in order to supply them with labour.[25]

The *Ulozhénie* ordains that upon a request for delivery granted by a judicial authority a runaway (peasant) must be returned forthwith to the estate of his rightful landlord. Holders of *pomést'ia* and owners of *vótchiny* were entitled to compensation for any tax paid in respect of the absentee and for the loss of his services at the rate of 10 roubles a head for each year of absence from the person who had harboured their man. This oblique abolition of the five-year period of limitation on the retrieval of runaways marks the final stage in the process, begun at the end of the fifteenth century, of attaching the peasants to the estates on which they lived and worked.[26] But legally to bind them to the land was one thing, to keep them on it bodily was another.

From the early 1660s until the end of the century peasants absconded constantly, singly, in families or in groups and sometimes in numbers that assumed the proportions of an exodus. The area to suffer most from the resultant depopulation was that to the east of Moscow, between the lower Kliáz'ma and the middle Oká. The fugitives made principally for the south-east – the left bank of the middle Volga – and for the south. The migrants were attracted by the opportunities of advancement and acquisition of land that military service on the frontier presented to enlisted men or by the comparatively favourable conditions of employment offered on the large estates belonging to boyars and other men of rank and influence in Moscow. The distance covered by emigrant families was not necessarily so great as to put them completely beyond the reach of a search party. In the last two decades of the century fresh waves of migrants swept into the area of the middle Don.[27] The tsar's government in its inability to reconcile the collective or group interests of the *dvoriáne* with the need to populate and guard the frontier by turns granted immunity to fugitive settlers and gave in to the landholders' demands for repressive measures to be taken on their behalf.

The harshness of these measures was due to the growing inclination to treat the harbouring of fugitives, who often indulged in robbery, wanton destruction, violence and arson, as a crime rather than a tort. This view seems to have gained general acceptance in Pososhkóv's middle years. Evasion itself was not prohibited by the *Code* of 1649 and therefore no punishment was prescribed for it but very soon successive ordinances ordered the flogging of retrieved runaways. In the early 1660s the government adopted the practice of periodically sending to particular areas special officers (*sýshchiki*) with instructions to seek out evaders. In 1683 the liability for harbouring fugitives was raised to a punitive level – 20 roubles a head by way of compensation, plus the provision of transport for the runaway's return, as first laid down in 1661.

Cases concerning runaways were specifically included in the ordinance of 1697, already mentioned, which changed the mode of judicial procedure from the accusatory to the inquisitorial. By incorporating this point in the detailed instruction to search officers issued in the following year the tsar's government made clear its intention henceforth to assume the initiative in the process of retrieval from its very outset. The new procedure, if it was ever adopted, seems to have been abandoned during the crisis brought about by the outbreak of the Great Northern War. When men had to be hurriedly conscripted for military and labour service there was no time to pay attention to the legitimacy of their habitation. The hardships created by the exigencies of the war intensified migration, driving increasing numbers of peasants and their families into the remoter parts of the country. In the army the rigour of military discipline led to continuous desertions.[28] The authorities ordered the return of all runaways in 1702, forbade once more the harbouring of evaders in 1704, repeated their injunctions in 1706. Also in 1706 they acknowledged that their orders were being ignored and instructed the chief local administrative officers, the *voevódy*, to carry out searches on the spot and have the runaways returned to their landlords but the drain continued just the same. During the remaining years of the war the tsar and the Senate did not show any great firmness in this matter, because they either could not or would not use any sanctions against those who broke the ban on harbouring runaways repeated yet again in 1715.[29]

The first detailed ordinance on the subject in the eighteenth century was promulgated in 1721, the final year of the Great Northern War. The fine to be paid by the harbourer was still 20 roubles a head but was to be threefold if the evaders were not sent back within eighteen months. The landlord's factor (or bailiff) was to be held responsible for any delay, punished with flogging and banishment with hard labour (*kátorga*); on Crown and ecclesiastical estates the stewards were to pay the threefold fine or be flogged and sent to do forced labour in public or industrial works.[30] In future the fine for harbouring for one year was to be 100 roubles a head for a male and 50 for a female peasant. If documentary evidence proved that a landowner had instructed his factor to receive runaways, all his property was to be confiscated and handed over to the rightful landlord of the runaway. Bailiffs and headmen were encouraged by the promise of a reward to report the presence of runaways to the authorities. For harbouring evaders on their own account the factors of landlords were to be given the knout; stewards and headmen on the estates belonging to the tsar's demesne and on those formerly owned by the Patriarch were to pay 100 roubles for each male and 50 for each female peasant harboured and to be similarly punished. The latter provision was extended in 1722 to factors of private landlords – *vótchinniki* and *poméshchiki*. All evaders on being returned to their place of origin were to receive the knout as a warning to others. The same ordinance, issued in clarification of that of 1721, explained that in cases where there was evidence that the bailiff and headmen had received runaways without their master's authority and had harboured them without his knowledge the master was not liable to the payment of compensation to the rightful landlord. It should be noted that this concession, made for the benefit of the absentee owners of very large estates, considerably reduced the extent of the loophole opened in 1698 by an ordinance which ruled that evidence of any authority having been given by boyars and the like to their factors to admit fugitives was merely to be reported to the tsar.[31] The supplementary ordinance also deals with complications resulting from marriages contracted by absconders and the birth of infants, from the possible flight of the landlord's factors and from the state of dereliction of a runaway's place of origin. Peasants who refused to reveal their place of origin even under torture were to be sent to St Petersburg before being settled on His Majesty's lands at his discretion. The *ukáz* further lays down rules for allowing agricultural labourers to work for hire in another locality and attempts to enforce in full the provisions of the earlier ordinance with regard to the restitution of runaways. It appears that some harbourers did not provide the means of conveyance for their return but simply turned them out, stripping them of their chattels and grain. The runaways thereupon did not return to their former masters but fled to outlying places near the south-western frontier with Poland or to Poland itself. Landlords who were found guilty of such practices were to be ordered to pay additional compensation to the rightful landlord at the rate of 100 roubles for each male peasant. Factors or bailiffs who had broken the regulations on their own initiative were to be flogged, to have their nostrils cut out and to be sent to do hard labour in public or industrial works. In 1723 peasants were reported to be fleeing from many districts to Poland and across other borders with their wives, families and possessions. Orders were therefore given to establish frontier posts in order to stop the fugitives, have them flogged and sent back to their rightful landlords.

Any leaders among the fugitives were to be given the knout and sent into banishment with hard labour. By 1724 the urge to run away, no doubt, among other things, from the poll-tax, appears to have become endemic. The instructions given to the military commanders of the districts in which the army was quartered were preventive as well as punitive. Measures were to be taken to ensure that no escapes occurred; peasants who were alleged to be preparing to run away were to be apprehended and punished. Those who succeeded in making their escape and were caught were to be handed over to the local *voevóda*; a landlord or his factor who received runaways was to pay a fine at the rate of 5 roubles per man per month over and above the compensation to the rightful landlord.[32]

These four successive enactments show that the tsar, on behalf of the service state, had not only resumed the initiative in compelling runaways to return to their original masters but had gone as far as attempting to keep the peasants bodily tied to their native soil. The success of these measures, if success there was, was no more than partial: between 1719 and 1727 the number of absentee peasants was put at 200,000.[33]

The cold inhumanity of these *ukázy* is matched by Pososhkóv's indifference to the plight of his immediate social inferiors. The shortage of labour and the dearth of taxpayers stifled compassion, nor were cameralistic or 'enlightened' ideas allowed to bear on the life of rural Russia. Pososhkóv sees the ordinances of 1721 and 1722 (which he treats as one) as a contrivance wrought by 'the lords' for their own advantage and to the detriment of humbler folk, indeed he is under the (erroneous) impression that the law ordered only some landlords to return the runaways who had settled on their land. It is not out of the question that this was in fact the way in which the ordinance was applied. Pososhkóv's recommendations for a 'just' law on the subject of runaways includes a fundamental proposal for the exculpation of the landlord's factors whom the ordinance of 1722 put in the position of potential scapegoats. Pososhkóv's other useful contribution to the issue is to point to the confusion which apparently existed between receiving a fugitive and hiring a labourer for a limited period. The *Code* of 1649 (Chapter 11, article 32) allowed this practice which, however, was often a disguised form of evasion.[34]

Passes from wardens (*sótskie*) and similar documents issued to peasants who were working away from home were in use by 1683.[35] In 1719 as a measure against brigandage all taxpaying members of the urban and rural population who wanted to absent themselves from their dwelling-places were required to obtain written permission from their superiors.[36]

Pososhkóv's resentment against the privileged and prosperous harbourers of evaders was exacerbated by the conviction that they themselves were evading their obligation to render military service to the tsar. In naming Pustóshkin, Zolotarëv and others, Pososhkóv was, strictly speaking, committing an act of denunciation, although it is questionable whether he was doing so in the expectation of earning a reward. These men, like many others, almost certainly owed their sheltered existence to bribery. Men of service were called up as circumstances required only by categories, not individually, since an adequate system of records and communication was lacking. Thus the central authorities as a rule knew only those who under the pressure of the more reliable and less corrupt local officials obeyed the call. For particulars of absentees they had to turn to informers; the detection of shirkers belonged to the duties of the 'fiscals'.[37] On one occasion the *óberfiskál* Nésterov boasted of having tracked down over a thousand men of service who had failed to report for duty.[38] Pososhkóv's allusion to the *Code* of 1649 in connection with the evasion of service is not entirely appropriate because articles 115–20 of Chapter 10 which no doubt he had in mind were concerned with summonses issued to defendants in private suits. Failure to appear in court in response to the third summons resulted in a judgement by default.

In order to ensure a sufficient supply of manpower Peter I took personal charge of the inspection of men of service which previously had been carried out by the tsar's commissioners in the provinces. The musters held by him in 1704, 1706, 1711, 1712, 1713, 1714, 1716, 1718 and 1720 were partial inasmuch as they concentrated on one or more specified categories. In 1704, 1712, 1713 and 1714 adolescents were inspected before becoming liable for service at the age of 15 and selected for prospective service in the guards, in field or garrison regiments, for schooling at home or apprenticeship abroad. Two general inspections were held, one in 1715, the other in two stages, in 1721 and 1722. One of the objects of the muster held in 1722 in St Petersburg was to find judges for the new law courts, officials for the *kollégii* and for administrative posts in the provinces. The Choglokóv brothers may well have been among those appointed on that occasion.[39]

From 1704 the penalty for failure to report for inspection or for service was the irreversible confiscation of the defaulter's land; in 1714 the tsar ruled that their estates (*pomést'ia* and *vótchiny*) should be awarded to the person who had denounced them.[40] The frequency with which these threats were uttered arouses suspicion as to their effectiveness. Absenteeism had been one of the notable failings of the Muscovite army in the seventeenth century; the first quarter of the eighteenth did not see a significant improvement.[41] The re-formed service state, staffed as it was with many more officials, including the *fiskály*, was still incapable of achieving full mobilization for war, let alone exacting government service in peacetime. The all-powerful autocrat de-manded service but was impotent when faced with disobedience. As com-pulsion was out of the question and the use of the death penalty would have alienated even further the very social group on which the tsar's exercise of his authority depended, he had to be satisfied with holding out the prospect of what he himself described as 'political death' – outlawry, with the symbolic acts of drumming out and nailing the printed lists of the condemned to the gallows in a public place.[42]

The loss and under-use of manpower caused by the illicit migration of peasants and the evasion of service by *dvoriáne* was associated in Pososhkóv's mind with the financial losses suffered by individuals in consequence of the malfunctioning of the judicial system and by the adherence of the authorities to certain archaic juridical and administrative practices and formalities. It has been seen that since 1711 Tsar Peter had taken great pains to institute the rule of law in Russia[43] but Pososhkóv's survey shows that these endeavours had not resulted in any obvious improvement. Pososhkóv, the entrepreneur in a hurry to grow rich, begrudged the time spent in judicial proceedings that were always slow and, as often as not, useless or unwarranted and, above all, wasteful. It is in this context that Pososhkóv, in an aphoristic aside, first[44] equates the riches of the people with the riches of the tsar. Hobbes had said it before: 'The riches, power and honour of the monarch arise only from the riches, strength and reputation of his subjects.'[45] The cameralists of the later seventeenth century had put forward the same view. Whether Pososhkóv was quoting from hearsay or was prompted by the spirit of the age is an open question.[46]

Of the institutions condemned by Pososhkóv, the most futile and the most barbarous was that of *pravĕzh*, thus described by Giles Fletcher writing in about 1590: 'This *Praueush* or Righter is a place near to the office where such as have sentence passed against them, and refuse to pay that which is adjudged are beaten with great cudgels on the shins and calves of their legs. Every forenoon from eight to eleven they are set on the *praueush* and beat in this sort till the money be paid. The afternoon and night time they are kept in chains by the Sergeant except they put in sufficient sureties for their appearance at the *Praueush* at the hour appointed . . . If after years of standing on the *Praueush* the party will not, or lack the wherewithal to satisfy his creditor, it is lawful for him to sell his wife and children outright for a certain term of years.'[47] In Pososhkóv's day the authorities used *pravĕzh* to enforce the settlement of private debts and the payment to the tsar's treasury of sums overdue from tax-gatherers and farmers of various sources of revenue. Pososhkóv's statement that a debt of 10,000 roubles is redeemed by a hundred months (i.e. eight years and four months, not nine years and two months) of *pravĕzh* is an ironical interpretation of the first part of article 261 of Chapter 10 of the *Code* of 1649 which lays down the rule of one month of *pravĕzh* for every hundred roubles of debt. But the law does not ordain physical retribution as a complete alternative to the repayment of a debt. After allowing for a period of grace it provides for the compulsory sale of goods and chattels and of land, followed by the recovery of any balance still outstanding. Only insolvent men of service of higher rank and their bondmen as substitutes for their masters were to be subjected to coercive *pravĕzh*; debts owed by *strel'tsý* could be settled through deductions from their pay, other men of service of inferior rank were to be handed over to their creditors to repay their liabilities with their labour priced at statutory rates.[48]

In the early years of his reign Peter did not appear to have had any objection to *pravëzh*, unless it be that he considered it too mild a punishment, since in 1700 he commanded that an initial period of *pravëzh* should be followed by the knout and *kátorga* (banishment with hard labour). In 1717, however, he felt 'moved by his conscience' to point out to the Senate that *pravëzh* was 'ruinous to the state and offensive to God'. In 1718 he decreed that, instead of being subjected to *pravëzh*, public and private debtors alike should be obliged to discharge their debts by working at the rate of one rouble a month a head, men in public works and women in the spinning house. But by 1722 the Senate appears to have forgotten the prohibition as in an ordinance of that year it deprecates the detention in custody or subjection to *pravëzh* only in relation to solvent debtors. This would corroborate Pososhkóv's account which suggests that *pravëzh* was still being applied even though officially it had been abolished,[49] and would explain why another and final abolition was found to be necessary in the reign of Catherine II.

In the absence of any established system of credit, loans were difficult to obtain and awkward to arrange. Public opinion, still strongly influenced by the teachings of the Church, frowned on money-lending so that those who were willing to lend at what was necessarily a high rate of interest did not want it to be known that they were doing so. Loan agreements had to be entered into by means of officially registered deeds and guaranteed by sureties, a procedure which Pososhkóv finds unnecessarily cumbrous. In his account of Russia written in 1666 Kotoshíkhin refers to loans made to private persons by the Siberian *prikáz* from the proceeds of the sale of pelts. An *ukáz* promulgated in 1669 forbade the granting of such loans from funds held by *prikázy* but Pososhkóv implies that the practice still survived.[50]

Peter I began to regularize the procedure for drawing up legal documents to validate all manner of economic transactions at the end of 1699, within twelve months of introducing stamp duty 'for the filling of the tsar's treasury and the greater validity of deeds'.[51] In 1701 he altered an earlier order for all such documents to be drawn up in the appropriate *prikázy* and established a separate office of deeds (*krepostnýkh del*). Its seat was a building in the Ivánovskaia square in the Kremlin where in earlier days the services of specialist clerks could be obtained privately. Such clerks were also to be found in the chief provincial towns. In 1711 a 'chamber' (*paláta*) was set up in Moscow for drawing up deeds in transactions between merchants and inhabitants of tax-exempt areas in Moscow. From 1719 matters relating to the making of deeds were handled by the Board of Justice (*Iustíts-kollégiia*) in St Petersburg and in the *gubérnii* by special commissioners under the direction of the courts of higher instance (*nadvórnye sudý*).[52] Many such transactions involved the provision of sureties. The mistrustful service state demanded such guarantees as proof of its subjects' capacity and willingness to meet the obligations imposed upon them as its servants or resulting from contracts and judicial proceedings to which the state was a party and from measures taken for the protection of public order.[53]

As a taxpayer and a man who on moral and economic grounds preached the gospel of work, Pososhkóv took the strongest exception to the spectacle of conspicuous waste presented by begging, whether by mendicants or by prisoners. The mendicant poor (*níshchie*) played a distinctive part in Russian religious life by providing the pious Christians with the opportunity to exercise the virtue of charity. The people took it for granted that 'the pauper is fed by the rich man and the rich man is saved by the pauper's prayers'.[54]

In his *Paternal Testament*[55] Pososhkóv, recognizing mendicant pauperism as a way of life, drew up something like a code of conduct for those whom adverse circumstances obliged to live on charity. In the present book, resigned to the continuing presence of the destitute even in an improved society, he consigns them and confines them to the poorhouse.

Peter I from his earliest days as tsar showed a marked lack of sympathy for all beggars and especially those who were able-bodied but idle. In 1691 he threatened with the knout and banishment to Siberia all those who made themselves out to be blind or crippled. A further *ukáz* published in 1694 was directed against beggars of any origin but especially monks and nuns and priests without a living. All were to be returned whence they came. Later ordinances on the same subject sought to apply the same principles in a period when, largely as a result of the Great Northern War, the number of paupers seems to have increased to such an extent that many of them remained permanently homeless. Able-bodied beggars, including monks and nuns, were to be apprehended and employed in public works or returned to their places of origin, those who were unfit were to be placed in hospices and hospitals. On at least one occasion the tsar found it politic to subsidize the welfare activities of the Church: in 1712 he ordered that the cost of the construction of a church hospice at Kazan and of the maintenance of its inmates be met from public funds.[56] But the trafficking of prayers for alms continued, much to the tsar's displeasure. In 1718 he prohibited almsgiving on pain of a fine of 5 roubles on the first occasion and 10 on the second.[57] In 1721 the *Ecclesiastical Regulation* instructed the newly established Holy Synod to regularize the giving of alms. A long paragraph full of sidelights on the daily life of mendicants denounces hale and slothful beggars as repugnant to God and harmful to the fatherland and accuses their benefactors of aggravating the shortage of grain by countenancing consumption unmatched by production. The blunt language and the angry tone of the passage suggest that the key phrases had been uttered by the tsar himself.[58] Pososhkóv shares these opinions and sentiments but knows that almsgiving cannot be stopped by law.

Only in the last five years of his reign did Peter the Great try to reduce the cost of maintaining prisoners in jails. At the end of 1720 he decreed that an accused person who had not been charged with any criminal act was to be kept in prison at the expense of the plaintiff who would be required to pay one kopeck per day per person in Moscow and two in St Petersburg. In 1722 a rider was added: if no payments were being received the prisoner would be sent home after a higher court had been informed. Later in the same year it was decreed that prisoners who were being held on charges preferred by the state were to be employed in public works and paid three kopecks a day or sent begging into the streets chained together, one gang or more from each place of detention. It would appear that when the benefit of his treasury was at stake the tsar did not object to begging. The proceeds were to be divided among the prisoners. The rate of payment for the maintenance of prisoners detained in consequence of private proceedings was now to be two kopecks a head everywhere. Overdue payments were to be doubled; nothing further was said about releasing such prisoners and they were not allowed to beg. In 1724 magistrates were instructed not to keep prisoners in jail for long periods.[59] It is clear from Pososhkóv's observations that these ordinances were not known to him and did not have any perceptible effect on the state of the prisons.

CHAPTER 3

Of Justice and the Law

God is righteousness and therefore He loves righteousness. If a man desires to please God he must be righteous in all his actions. It behoves all magistrates then, above all others, to adhere to righteousness, not merely in their actions but also in their words – never to utter falsehoods but to say that which conforms to truth.

Since magistrates dispense justice in the name of the Tsar and justice is acknowledged to be of God, it behoves them to pursue nothing more earnestly than the Truth, that they may not offend God or the Tsar. If a judge dispenses justice inequitably he will receive from the Tsar temporal punishment, but from God eternal punishment both in body and soul.

But if he dispenses perfectly equitable and impartial justice according to the true facts, alike towards the rich and prominent as towards the poorest and most obscure man, then he will receive from the Tsar honour and glory and from God grace and the Kingdom of Heaven. For if he shall act unrighteously neither fasting nor prayer shall save him, since he is like unto that liar, the Devil. But if he shall act righteously he shall be like unto God, since God is righteousness itself. Indeed, a judge who never errs in his judgments shall find that to be just is of more avail to him than fasting and prayer; for it is written, 'Righteousness delivers from death'.[1]

A judge should not ask of God anything more than that He may make it plain to him how to render true judgment between the faithful, that he may not in his ignorance condemn the innocent or acquit the guilty.

It is beyond my poor wits to conceive how perfect justice may be attained but I venture to put forward some suggestions here in writing, in so far as God grants me understanding. Only I do not do so without trepidation because I am a person of little account, untutored in scholarly matters and utterly without knowledge of how to write well. I am but a simple man; nevertheless, under God's will, I have ventured to expound my views in simple language.

In the first place I put forward the following opinion as regards the dispensation of justice. When a man is appointed by His Imperial Majesty to the magistrature he should request a priest to keep an all-night vigil and to sing a liturgy and a service of intercession to God our Heavenly Father on his behalf. And in these prayers he should implore God with tears to grant the magistrate enlightenment in his duties and to guide him to determine correctly innocence and guilt in all cases. And in the exercise of his office it behoves the magistrate to place himself wholly in God's hands, so that he may not give way to temptation or by straying from the path of probity fall into any[2] pitfalls.

It would be no bad thing if every day, on rising, he were devoutly to recite the newly composed hymn to God our Heavenly Father,[3] praying that the business of his court may be regulated according to the will of God and that God may not lead him into any temptation but keep him from any evil deed.

It should be his invariable practice, on taking his seat in court, first of all to order all prisoners to be brought before him and ask them severally of what they are accused, and to learn the facts of the case from the clerk who has charge of it. If a case is a trivial one he should deal with it at once; but if it is impossible to do so, he should order the accused to be released against sureties or in his own recognizance to appear when summoned, or else to be placed in charge of a constable,[4] and set a time for each accused to appear before the court. For to have to appear in court every day is mere waste of time and unnecessary protraction: each case should be called for a set time. Moreover, no one should be present during the hearing except those concerned. The judge should record the terms of bail of each prisoner in order that he may try each case on the set date; and he must keep most strictly to this order so as not to bring blame on himself.

(56)

So every day a judge should review the roll of prisoners to see that no one is kept in custody unnecessarily. From time immemorial the practice has been widespread that a man may be committed to prison without the judge's knowledge by some clerk of the court or constable, and may remain there a long time even though he is innocent. If any judge fails to prevent this he shall be answerable in the superior court which will be created to deal with unjust magistrates. Up to the present it has not been the custom for judges themselves to review the prisoners or to examine their cases without the need for constant goading; the clerks merely call over the names in order to make sure that all are present, not to deal with their cases, and thus many innocent men remain in prison and starve.

In 1717 I saw myself a great gentleman's retainer bring a man of his master's before the office of state at Preobrazhénskoe,[5] since he had 'invoked the name of the Sovereign'.[6] Prince Fëdor Iúr'evich Romodánovskii[7] questioned him as to the offence and he answered: 'I wanted to serve my Sovereign as a soldier but my master had me put in chains, and that is why I invoked the name of the Sovereign.' So Prince Fëdor Iúr'evich sent him off to the army and the man who brought him in was put in prison and remained there some fifteen weeks, from Lent to St Peter's Day;[8] only then did an attorney appear and obtain his release in a recognizance. But correctly speaking he should not have been kept in custody a single day nor was there any reason to require a recognizance of

(58)

him. All such practices are inventions of the officials and cause much loss to the people by wrongful detention and by exacting needless sureties; if there is no case against a man there is no reason to bind him by a recognizance.

These things are commonly done in all offices of state. In 1719 the investigator Istléniev took two carpenters away from their work under the toll-collector at Ustréka for not having passports,[9] and sent them off to Nóvgorod. And there the judge Iván Miakínin[10] committed them to prison. One of them died a year later and the other remained in prison for two years and by the skin of his teeth regained his liberty in his own recognizance. A great many common people perish without a hearing in such ways.

There is no man more excellent and judicious than Prince D. M. Golítsyn,[11] yet in 1719 (in St Petersburg) I petitioned him for permission to build a distillery and for a licence to supply vodka for sale[12] but he had me put under arrest for no known reason. I remained in custody for a whole week and began to get impatient at being there so long without knowing why. On the eve of the Lady Day fast I asked the corporal of the guard to inform the Prince of my case and Prince Golítsyn said: 'Has he been in custody long?' And the corporal said: 'A whole week, Sir.' And he at once ordered my release. Now I am not entirely without position, I think, and Prince Golítsyn knows me personally; yet I was detained for a whole week for no reason at all. How much worse is the case of a man of no account who will be arrested and forgotten about. In this way a great number of innocent folk languish in prison and die there before their time. In small towns too many *dvoriáne* have their servants and peasants taken into custody. For this reason rolls should be kept of the prisoners both in the offices of state and in the chief towns to ensure that no man is held in the custody of such an office or in the town gaol unless his name appears on such a roll. And if on calling over the roll anyone should be present whose name has not been duly entered on it, then the person who put him under arrest without due form should receive severe punishment in order that such a thing shall not occur again. In the case of prisoners of long standing, if the judge cannot find time to review them every day because of much work, he should at least do so every second or third day; and if that too is not practicable, then he must do so without fail once a week, preferably on Mondays. Those prisoners who are in the custody of offices of state shall be inspected there; but the judges shall go to the gaols to inspect the prisoners and ascertain whether there is anyone there whose name is not on the official roll, or whether there is anyone registered who has escaped.

I am truly astounded that judges are in the habit of holding men in prison for five or six years or more. If judges and governors were to inspect the new prisoners daily this would no longer happen and there would be no possibility of an innocent man being imprisoned or kept in custody.

In my opinion every judge should have a list of all his cases and read it over every day. He should urge the clerks not to wait for litigants to importune them but to ensure that a case be prepared for hearing and not left in abeyance. And when a case is ready for trial the judge and his colleagues must hear it without waiting to be urged again by plaintiff and defendant to deal with it. A judge must bear in mind that he must not let a single day pass in vain without having decided some case on his list; and when he has heard it he must give his judgment at once so that the common people are not troubled by any unnecessary dilatoriness.

In my view a case should be prepared for hearing as follows. The clerk who has made the abstract of the evidence should sign it with the words: 'I, so-and-so, have made this abstract and the plaintiff's case has merit on the following points . . . Or if the plaintiff is in the wrong and the defendant in the right, then the clerk should proceed in the same way stating why the defendant is right and the other party wrong. When trying a case a judge must diligently separate truth from untruth and for his own better understanding make a summary of the case, setting forth all the rights and wrongs of the matter. Then, with this summary to hand, he shall examine the clerk's finding and see whom he

(60)   considers to be in the right. If the clerk's finding coincides with that of the judge, all well and good; and if the clerk's finding is more reasonable and more correct, he must be shown regard. If his findings are correct in half a dozen or a dozen cases he should be promoted in rank. But if the clerk has found contrary to justice he must receive condign punishment, and if his judgment was deliberately partial he must receive severe physical punishment and his salary must be reduced. And if he puts his name to an unjust judgment a second time he shall be liable to the death penalty.

When any man, be he rich or very poor, submits a complaint about an offence done to him or about any other matter, then, in my humble opinion, the judge should accept the complaint, make a note of the date of submission, but before passing it on for entering in the records read it carefully himself so as to memorize the facts. And when he has examined the complaint in detail he should take the complainant to a private place and question him thus: 'My friend, you have submitted a complaint about an offence against you. Is this a true complaint against the other party?' And if he says: 'It is entirely true', then the judge shall say: 'For the Lord's sake take care not to fall into a snare and into great loss, and what is worse than personal loss, into sin, that you may not be condemned at the Second Coming of Our Lord by His righteous judgment.' And he should further say: 'Sometimes we judge rightly and sometimes wrongly, for we cannot see into men's hearts, but at the Last Day it will be not our fallible judgment but judgment both perfect and right; all deceit and all truth will be made plain, and not only great things but even the most minute matter will be made manifest, for God Himself, who sees into our hearts, will be the judge. The Holy Apostle Paul says: "It is a fearful thing to fall into the hands of the living God."[13] Therefore, my friend, take thought that you do not bring divine judgment upon yourself. We must be in great fear of divine judgment for God is no respecter of persons but looks at the deed itself. So even if you do injury to this man but are deemed right in our court, our judgment in your favour will in such a case tell greatly to your disadvantage at the Last Judgment; and moreover you will have led us into sin too.'

'Further, if you are in any way at fault yourself with respect to this man and you grind him down, trusting to your superior influence, then you will damn yourself irredeemably. For even if you then repent it shall nought avail you. Therefore take heed now, that you may not commit yourself to eternal perdition. Which of us is not in sin before God and at fault before our Sovereign? Let us then try not to fall out between ourselves: for the Lord's sake do not take part in any great quarrel, do not add injury to injury nor be the cause of further harm to your opponent. Even if you are in the right you will not come out of it without loss, and if you are in the wrong you will not only have caused your opponent loss but also you will have fallen into a deep pit of your own making. For all the losses which he may declare shall be forthwith exacted from you, and you will also have to pay the fees due to the Crown and those due to the officials of the court. Go now and take counsel with men of good repute; it would be better to settle the matter out of court on any terms, even if they are to your own disadvantage.'

And the judge shall retain the complaint in his own hands until a settlement has been drawn up. Then the judge shall send for the defendant, and when the man is brought before him he shall question him as to where his fault lay with respect to the other party and adjure him on oath to tell the whole truth, how the matter arose and what passed. If the defendant pleads guilty judgment shall be entered against him in the record, but in view of his admission of guilt he must be shown indulgence so that mutual differences may be composed and great losses on both sides prevented. If he pleads guilty to only one part of the charge and as to the rest now asserts on oath that the accusations made against him were groundless, then the judge must examine the plaintiff more minutely and seek out the truth by all the means at his disposal. And if the facts are as the defendant claims it may be taken as proven that the plaintiff's case was a malicious one.

But if the defendant does not admit himself in the wrong after such solemn adjuration and reaffirms on oath that he knows nothing of the matter and that the plaintiff has accused him without justification, all that he says must be taken down and the judge must subject the defendant to a searching examination to the best of his ability at the time.

If the defendant resorts to equivocation the details of his deposition will reveal whether he spoke the truth or not on the first occasion. And if he is found to be in the wrong he must be adjured once again most solemnly to consider his best interests by making a settlement.

If it proves that the plaintiff's case is without merit and that his action was vexatious, he must be compelled to settle so that he may not do harm either to the defendant or to himself, and both parties must compose their quarrel without further enquiry, so that neither may suffer unnecessary loss. But if either plaintiff or defendant continues obdurate and is unwilling to settle, to him one must say: 'Well and good if you prove to be in the right; but if you prove to be in the wrong you will not receive the slightest mercy from us. Nevertheless, even if justice is wholly on your side it is better to settle before incurring great losses, since even a bad peace is better than a just war; therefore love one another. Do you not know that where there is love there is God, but where there is enmity there is the Devil?' Then three or four days' grace shall be granted to the parties and if they arrive at a settlement they shall both appear before the judge and apprise him thereof. And the terms of their settlement shall be recorded in a book kept for this purpose. The record shall state the facts of their case in full (not in summary), and both parties shall sign this record. The complaint may then be torn up and returned to the complainant. And both parties shall pay into court such fees as may be laid down for a voluntary settlement, and the judge (or the governor) shall attest their signatures in the book and the receipt of the said fees. If any parties fail to agree a full examination shall be conducted (as laid down) before a judge, and the latter shall hear and take note of the nature of the accusation and question both parties and extract the truth. For, given sufficiently full depositions, the true and the false will become manifest.

(63)   If one party is a person of power and position and has a ready tongue, whereas the other is a poor man or one who is not poor but tongue-tied or of feeble understanding, the judge must have no scruples about giving judgment against the powerful party if the merits of the case prove to lie with a poor plaintiff or defendant, or alternatively with one who is inarticulate though not poor. And if either party by his verbosity does not give his opponent an opportunity to vindicate himself then, for the love of God, the inarticulate speaker must be given every assistance and the powerful must not be allowed to get the better of him. Since justice is called divine it must be administered in such a way that it shall be like divine justice, that is, impartial. And the plaintiffs and defendants shall appear in court or at interrogations in person, and not be represented by hired advocates since all such merely obscure the truth with their quibbling and prolixity and make the innocent appear guilty and the guilty innocent. They so obscure the truth that even the judges cannot make head or tail of their speeches. Whereas if a man is no quibbler himself and no quibbling advocate interferes, he will keep closer to the truth; and if he does utter any falsehood his confusion will reveal it. For this reason guilt or innocence is more likely to be determined correctly without the intervention of advocates. There-fore each party must be able to give his evidence without being confused by his opponent and without the clerk of the record hurrying him or entering into

arguments – nothing of the kind; let each party state his case as best he can, provided always that he does not introduce extraneous and irrelevant matters.

When an interrogation is in process and the two parties are confronted and set about accusing one another, the judge must have before him the notes of the case made in his chambers at the time of the first hearing and observe carefully whether plaintiff or defendant strays from his previous testimony. If anyone varies his testimony from what he said when he was examined alone the new testimony must be looked into even more minutely than the former in order to arrive at the truth. And if the deposition of an inarticulate speaker agrees with his earlier one, whereas that of a ready speaker proves to be different, all possible assistance must be afforded to the former and the powerful party must not be allowed to browbeat him or do him injury of any kind.

Should any person from outside intervene during an interrogation and start prompting one of the parties, he must be put under arrest. If his prompting had no malicious intention he shall be fined; but if it was deliberate and premeditated further proceedings shall be taken against him.

In view of this it is advisable to have special rooms in every court-house where no stranger is admitted during an interrogation and the judge is not subject to interruption. The judge himself must act as attorney for the injured party and be a severe and unmerciful judge towards the offender. He must judge so fairly that even if a close relation of his is brought before the court and found guilty, he does not spare him in any way, in order that the Lord God at His Second Coming may not overturn the judgment and the judge himself be condemned to eternal torment for his unjust judgment.

If litigants call in any third party in corroboration, whether jointly or separately, the truthfulness of such evidence must be established with all diligence and care in amplification of the court records, since error is nowhere more rampant than in witnesses' testimony.

As for the accursed 'general perquisitions', Satan presides over them: there is no trace of God's truth in them. The depositions of the witnesses are not written down at the time, yet the clergy of the place who have neither seen nor heard any of those whose testimony is invoked then sign the depositions as a true record. In order to eradicate all those prevarications which make for injustice signed statements should first be taken from witnesses (as is the practice in offices of state); the clerks should not interrupt nor put words into their mouths but allow them to tell their story in their own way. Whatever witnesses say – good or bad, concordant or discrepant – should be taken down word for word and they should sign their statements. And the clerk or secretary should there and then countersign these statements so that the witnesses cannot change them subsequently. If anyone says: 'The same goes for me', let it appear in the record that he said: 'I subscribe exactly to what the previous witness said.'

So if anyone invokes a 'general perquisition' signed depositions should be

taken down in full on the spot as used to be done. And when these depositions
are received in court, orders should be given to produce two or three of the said
witnesses from different villages, or in the case of a specially extensive enquiry,
one witness in every ten, so as to provide reliable evidence. When the witnesses
appear in the court-house the judge who has received and studied the depositions shall take one of the said witnesses into his chambers, bring him before
the icon of Our Lord and say: 'My friend, you have been picked as a witness.
Give me your account as if you were standing before Christ at his Second
Coming, and take heed that you do not utter a single false word. If you lie you
will bring yourself to perdition, so be advised and see to it that you neither add
nor subtract, but relate exactly what you saw. I tell you that if you lie to me and
give an untruthful account out of friendship or for a bribe, the person who
induced you to lie shall incur a fine and in accordance with the recent Imperial
decree you will be beheaded for bearing false witness.[14] And your head will be
impaled and displayed to the sight of all and sundry at the entrance to the
court-house as a permanent warning to other false witnesses (and the heads of
all such false witnesses shall similarly be impaled in a row). All their goods shall
be forfeit to the Crown and their wives and children shall be sent to hard labour
in perpetuity. Therefore take thought for yourself and your family. If you have
made any false statement to the clerk correct yourself now and tell me the whole
truth – exactly what you saw or heard and from whom, or whether you only
heard all this from the person who named you as a witness. If you tell me the
whole truth now you will escape execution and will be forgiven for any false
statement which you made to the clerk.'

(66)   If anyone then admits to the judge that he bore false witness at the instigation
of the party who called him, both the false witness and the man who suborned
him shall be deemed equally culpable and shall receive equal punishment. And
after the infliction of severe physical punishment they shall be branded on the
face and arm as false witnesses. And if they bear false witness again they shall
be executed forthwith.

Anyone who pleads guilty in any such case shall be accorded a reduction in
the severity of his punishment. A special book shall be reserved for all those
cases in which a plea of guilty has been entered, so that each one can be
referred to at a moment's notice, even if it be after a lapse of ten years. And if
anyone is later convicted of the same offence he shall receive the penalty to be
prescribed by the law. Should any person not admit his guilt before the judge in
chambers but begin to contradict himself, he must be subjected to a most
searching examination under every possible head to discover how long ago the
incident took place; whether his companions whose names appear in the record
were all present; whether they arrived before or after him or all at the same
time; where they came from and where they met; how it all began and how it
ended; at what time of the day or night the offence was committed and in what

building or yard or other place whatsoever. And if in a building, then whereabouts in it – in the 'place of honour'[15] or near the door or by the stove or at table; whether the suspect and his companions were sitting or standing; whether the hour was early or late; whether the weather was good or bad at the time; and afterwards the manner of their parting – which of them left first, or who remained with him, or whether they all left together; how many of them there were, and whether he knows all or none of them.

The interrogator shall with all the skill at his command examine the witnesses in the most minute detail and the testimony of each one shall be taken down in full precisely as he gives it, because there is always a great deal of false witness in any given body of testimony and falsehoods can be readily exposed by such exhaustive interrogations. A witness shall be taken into a private place after interrogation. Each witness shall be kept apart after interrogation so that he cannot communicate with anyone else. The next witness shall then be taken and questioned in the same way. No other person should be present during the interrogation except the clerk who will keep the record. If the witness can read and write he shall sign his statement, but if not he shall make his mark so that there can be no argument subsequently. But if it should happen that a witness under interrogation succeeds in passing word to his companions with intent to falsify the evidence, he must then be further examined under torture to establish the reason for his having communicated with them.

However many witnesses there may be they must all be interrogated in the same way. Should some of them fail to present themselves none shall be interrogated until all are present. By such a minute investigation all truth and falsehood will be laid bare. Should any of the witnesses be liars their false evidence cannot remain undetected, whatever their ingenuity. Even two witnesses were unable to conceal their lies from Daniel the prophet, and for their lies both were put to death.[16] So in a case where there are half a dozen witnesses, even if they all learnt by rote for a whole year what each was to say, they could not establish false evidence but their deceit would be detected.

If, however, there should happen to be only a single witness, he should likewise first be examined by the clerk (as is the practice in offices of state) and then (as described above) taken into the judge's chambers and submitted to an equally searching examination, or rather to an even more searching one, as God may guide and judge, since it is most difficult to arrive at the truth on the strength of one person's testimony alone. But a witness of this kind should be kept in custody after examination and the person in whose favour his evidence lies should be brought into chambers and examined, following precisely the same order as in the case of the witness, without omitting any details; rather the questions should go into even more minute detail, in order that the whole truth may be arrived at on the strength of the testimony of one witness only. And the party on whose behalf the testimony was given should be asked about this witness – whether the witness joined him before or after the opposing party, and where he sat or stood on arrival, and whether he left in the company of the opponent, or before or after him. If the plaintiff or defendant contradicts himself in his testimony the said witness should be brought in again and the contradiction explained to him; and he should be most solemnly adjured to tell the exact truth without being subjected to torture. And if he admits that he was induced to give this false evidence, then (as explained above) guilt shall lie equally on the person who suborned him and on himself for collusion in the falsehood.

If it proves impossible to arrive at a conclusion on the grounds of these interrogations, the person accused by the witness shall be brought into chambers. If he admits his guilt on being confronted with such a direct accusation then that is the end of the matter. But if he does not and swears that the witness is making a false accusation against him, he must be submitted to a detailed examination, again following the same order, so as to arrive at the truth, viz. how the two parties met at the time in question; how the witness happened to be there; whether he arrived after or before the other party. He must relate the beginning and end and whole course of the affair exactly as it was. And if his account reveals discrepancies compared with that of the third man, the witness shall be brought back into chambers and subjected to a second examination, but this time in a different order, with particular regard to the discrepancies. If he becomes confused and his answers are now different he shall be taken forthwith to the torture-chamber and further examined, at first under imminent threat of torture. If it is shown that he bore false witness for the sake of friend or family, and not as a hireling, then it seems to me he should escape the death penalty but receive most severe physical punishment according to the law. And he shall be branded not only on the arm but also on the face so that all may know that he bore false witness and that no one may trust him.

(69)   When such investigatory examinations are in progress the judge should also sit in the afternoons so that he can put his questions in all sorts of different orders without being pressed for time. He need not conduct his examination exactly as described here but rather as the case and occasion may require, that is, with full knowledge of the facts and not mechanically (for here I can only give general indications, without knowledge of a particular case; the above is just an example of the way to proceed). When embarking on a case every judge must pray to God for grace that he may be given wisdom to reach the truth and recognize falsehood. No one who is not concerned shall be admitted to the courtroom during the hearing of a case lest they interfere with the examination.

When the examination of plaintiff, defendant and witnesses has been completed and the truth is manifest, the proceedings must be concluded at once so that people are not ruined or made to suffer unnecessary hardship by the case being allowed to drag on. Further, those who are condemned to death must not be kept in custody for a long time – not more than a week or ten days, during which time they may fast and pray and repent of their sins. But any of them who prove to be blasphemers,[17] who treat Christ's body and life-giving blood as unclean things and with foul curses call them the abomination of desolation, must not be allowed to live even another day. They shall be taken from the torture-chamber straight to execution, since even in the days of Moses God Himself ordered such men to be put to death. If any such blasphemer shall request time for repentance he must not be believed, since for his like there is no repentance. For the Lord God Himself said with His own lips: 'The blasphemy against the Holy Ghost shall not be forgiven unto men, neither in this world, nor in the world to come.'[18]

Blasphemers[19] have manifestly blasphemed against the Holy Ghost if they pour scorn on the operation of the Holy Ghost and diminish or deny His divine power, alleging that in our time the Holy Ghost no longer descends nor is present during divine service. For all blasphemers are minions of the Devil. Whatever the Devil says is a lie and blasphemers are in no wise different: whatever they say is all lies; as their tenets are false so are all their words false. If any persons – clerical or lay – shall take their part and request that the lives of certain of these blasphemers be spared, pledging themselves that such a man is wholly repentant and will in future adhere without prevarication to our ancient Orthodox faith, this must be recorded explicitly in a written undertaking, to wit, that so-and-so will never blaspheme again nor entice the pious from their ancient faith to his new heresies, but on the contrary will try to bring back into the true and original Christian faith those of his former associates who have fallen away from a life of piety. Anyone whom he persuades to repentance shall be made to swear an affidavit in this sense. But if he fails to redeem anyone from error it follows that his own repentance was spurious and those who stood surety for him shall incur a fine, and he shall be imprisoned for life or, indeed, executed. Anyone who, having repented, continues to spread erroneous beliefs shall on no account be given any further stay of execution and his sureties shall also be fined and beaten.

In my opinion there is no sense in putting brigands to the torture more than three times; their imprisonment would be unduly prolonged by such repeated applications of torture. There is no need to keep a criminal a long time in prison: the longer he remains there the more harm he will do. Any malefactor who has given identical answers under torture from beginning to end shall be asked once more, when brought to the place of execution, if what he said was the truth. And if he says the same again in the face of death he shall be executed and any others whom he has brought under suspicion shall be summoned and examined as may be deemed expedient, even after his execution.

For if such summary justice be meted out to criminals it will inspire more terror in them than any horrible manner of death, since a brigand who is caught knows that there will be no escape for him and that the end of his life is at hand: once you are caught you are lost. Such men consider long imprisonment to be very lenient treatment and even banishment with hard labour now does little to deter them since they escape even from that. But if it is known that the whole matter will be wound up within a week criminals of every description will be seized with terror.

When a criminal is arrested and there is already another in the prison who has been there a long time, the new prisoner must on no account be put in with the other without first being examined. Let him be kept apart so that he may not communicate with anyone else. It is not advisable to put such men together, even after examination, because many come out with the whole truth on arrest and admit to their crimes, whereas after the old prisoners have had time to work on the new they will try to exculpate themselves and will not admit their guilt even under the threat of torture. In this way some succeed in regaining their freedom.

If thieves name certain others living in the same house as their accomplices every room in it must be thoroughly searched to see if there is any garment or other object which does not belong to the occupant. If anyone is found to possess such a compromising object no further witness should be needed to establish the man's guilt. But if no such object is found his neighbours must be closely questioned whether they know of any robbery committed by him and be adjured to tell all without concealment. And they must be told: 'If you know of any robbery and fail to declare it and it later comes to light that you knew of it you will die the same death as the thief.'

If the man's close neighbours have nothing to say, then the more distant ones should be questioned, and if these also say that he is an honest man he shall be branded[20] upon the arm with a mark signifying that he has been under suspicion, and he shall be released. But if other thieves subsequently accuse him let him be put to the torture.

If the officer sent to apprehend criminals shows any sort of leniency towards them and this is discovered, then in my opinion he is worthy of death.

In my view if newly arrested criminals were taken off to the torture-chamber immediately after being questioned, so as not to have time to invent a plausible story, their minds will still be confused and they will speak more truthfully; whereas if they have time to reflect they will not tell the whole truth. If any criminal admits his guilt when first questioned but is obstinate under torture, he must be subjected to a more severe degree of torture to make him reveal who induced him to exculpate himself. And when he names the person, the latter must be apprehended and severely tortured until he says why he induced the other to exculpate himself; and he shall receive the most severe physical punishment.

Those criminals whose lives are spared should not simply be set free but, after receiving due physical punishment, be branded on both arms and on the

(72)

face so that all may clearly see what their crime was. And if any one of them subsequently be implicated even to a small degree in a similar crime it shall be certain death for him.

Another matter: magistrates must take great pains to ensure that the gaols are not always full of prisoners. It would be a good thing if they were empty. It is no credit to them that they have many men in prison – on the contrary, it is the greatest possible credit if they have none.

As with prisoners, it is much to a magistrate's credit not to have a crowd of petitioners waiting about his offices. I cannot see what virtue there is in having so many petitioners crowding the offices that no one can gain access to him. It were best if only two or three, or at most half a dozen persons, were present before the magistrate at a time, namely those concerned in a given case; whereas all those not concerned should discreetly remove themselves. Thus they would neither get in the way of the genuine petitioners nor hamper the magistrate in his enquiry. In my opinion magistrates should ensure that no strangers should loiter about in their presence or about the clerk's desks.

All clerks should be given the most stringent instructions on no account to drag out the affairs of petitioners unnecessarily. Every magistrate should keep a close watch on his clerks to see that they do nothing without precise orders. If an extract or the like has to be prepared every clerk must say when he will have it ready and tell the petitioner to come back at that time and on no account to wait about the offices in the meanwhile. In confirmation a clerk should give the petitioner a note stating by what time he will have the matter ready. If a clerk fails to do so by the time stated and the petitioner presents the note to the magistrate, the latter shall summon the clerk in question and ask him why he has not completed the work in accordance with his promise. If he can produce a clear and reasonable justification for his failure – not mere wilful delay on his part – he shall be granted further time. But if he still does not get the work done by the promised time he must be punished and fined.

If matters are so ordered in every office, then the whole building will never be thronged with waiting petitioners; they will remain at their work instead of waiting about to no good purpose – merchants will be about their business, artisans will ply their trade; and thus the whole people will benefit.

No gratuity shall be accepted from plaintiffs or defendants since a bribe blinds even a wise man. For if a judge has received gifts from one of the parties he will do all he can to further that man's cause and to prejudice that of his opponent, and so the case will never be tried fairly but inevitably with a bias towards the one party. For this reason a judge must never accept even the most trifling consideration so as not to sin before God and his Sovereign by rendering unjust judgment.

If a man comes before the judge and stands speechless, the judge must himself ask him in a gentle voice to put his case. When he has told it the case

3)

should be given preference before that of an importunate person, since many people are by nature modest and bashful and even in cases of dire distress have no one to help them and do not dare to press their own interest. Therefore a man of this character must be helped in every way, and if right is on his side he must all the more be given a helping hand since glib advocates easily get the better of such tongue-tied people and their prolixity obfuscates the right-eousness of an inarticulate cause. And if a poor man prefers a complaint against anyone on chancing to meet a magistrate and the sum at issue is small (less than a rouble), then if possible the matter should be settled out of hand so that the man need not be dragged into court.

(74)

The judge must follow not merely with his ears but with his whole mind all cases which reach a hearing; his associates too must all give their full attention to the case. During the hearing the Bench must not allow anyone to come near with any irrelevant matter nor discuss any other matter with strangers so that the judges may not be distracted from the case in hand. The case must be so carefully tried that no other judge can later upset the judgment. Above all it behoves a judge to be in great fear lest God shall reverse his judgment and commit him to eternal torment for his injustice.

When the whole record has been read through the presiding judge must not yet declare for either party but keep to himself what conclusion he has reached. Only when his associates have signed their opinions and he has examined them shall he declare his own. If their opinions agree with his, the clerks' opinions shall then be read, and if they are in agreement too there is no need for any further deliberations but judgment shall be delivered accordingly. But if there is a conflict of opinions the matter must be discussed further even if this entails reading the whole record through again; the point of disagreement must be discussed at length and after careful consideration judgment delivered in accordance with the opinions which prove to be more correct.

In delivering judgment the clerks must sign the verdict first, then the associate judges and last of all the presiding judge, so that nothing can be added to or subtracted from it afterwards.

(75)

And if any case remains doubtful and defies solution the transcript should be sent to another specially convened board consisting of the most experienced and learned clerks. This board shall be instructed to make a summary of the case and, after due consideration thereof, submit a full report together with a summary, and record its opinion at the end of the report. If it still proves impossible to come to a definite conclusion with the help of this report, I am inclined to think that, despite the prohibition in our ancient laws against receiving any further evidence (whether in the form of petitions or charges) after the proceedings in court have been concluded, far from refusing such further evidence, depositions in amplification should be taken from those concerned, even against their will, so that the case can be decided without ambiguity. Alternatively a retrial should be ordered to ensure that the case is settled without miscarriage of justice.

If any clerk perversely puts his hand to an opinion with intent to make the innocent party culpable or to exculpate the guilty, or to perpetrate any kind of falsification, whether tending to the culpability of the innocent or the exoneration of the guilty, he must be most minutely questioned and the judge and his associates must carefully examine and clarify the matter. If his dishonesty and trickery are proved he shall be examined under torture to ascertain why he so acted. Conversely if a clerk has arrived at the whole truth of a case his salary should be increased and he should be raised in estimation above his fellows for having solved a case which the judges had failed to solve and clearly demonstrated where the truth of the matter lay.

And if any plaintiff or defendant tries to dispute the sentence of the court without justification he should be made to pay double fees and costs for his vexatious objection. And if he disputes the sentence a second time, he should pay four times these amounts and also suffer further punishment for contempt of court.[21]

I for my part rate the administration of justice and the judge's office extremely highly – above all other callings. Therefore no man of limited understanding nor even one of great gifts should aspire to the judiciary or other high public office but should by every possible means endeavour to refuse such an office since it is most onerous.

It may seem a matter of no great consequence that soldiers are sent from the chief towns into the country to fetch *dvoriáne* or persons of any other degree, when no more than a few pence are at stake. Yet those summoned may easily suffer a loss of two or three roubles, and sometimes as much as a dozen, greatly to the detriment of our people. Even if it is some quite trivial enquiry officials will not put it off till a suitable time but send for anyone they need on the spur of the moment. It does not occur to them to send someone to take a deposition or to take down answers to questions in writing on the matter at issue: officials know no better than to have such people brought all the way to the town to answer any question whatever. If a person lives a hundred or more versts from the town this will cost him two or three roubles, and at times when travel is difficult the expenses may amount to five or six roubles; if a person happens to live five or six hundred versts away he will be lucky if it is less than ten roubles. But the officials take no account of the losses of others; they consult only their own convenience and ignore the inconvenience that they cause to others. And if they send for a man just when there is important work to be done they may deprive him of his whole livelihood.

These summonses cause a great deal of distress to people but magistrates pay not the slightest attention to safeguarding the interests of His Majesty's subjects and protecting them from loss. Yet he who truly desires to promote the interests of His Imperial Majesty should have more care for the Tsar's subjects than for himself and ensure that they are not reduced to penury; and he should therefore avoid causing them any loss whatever. Every magistrate must exercise perpetual vigilance over the people and constantly be zealous to render true justice and not to anger or ruin anyone. But as things are the magistrates do not make the least effort to protect the people from loss.

(77)   Another matter: Do those in high authority consider it right that three or four years running peremptory orders were sent out from the office of the governor of St Petersburg to all revenue officials and their subordinates employed in and about Nóvgorod, summoning them to the capital to render account? Thus they would make the journey three or four years running or even more and stay there between two and three months, and each of them would be twenty or thirty roubles out of pocket before returning home. And those who made the journey five or six years running, I know for sure, used to get through something like a hundred roubles, not counting gratuities which might come to another hundred. All this is most ruinous to the people and conduces to their impoverishment. If an audit is necessary there is no point in putting it off from year to year; if it is not necessary there is no sense in dragging them all that way. Surely it would be best for the audit to be done in the town where the official serves. Nor should it be done ten years in arrear; the local magistrates should do it without delay on receipt of the cash- and account-books. In that way the work of temporary servants of His Majesty would be made easier and they could render account without difficulty since all the details would still be fresh in their minds. But ten years later – I do not see how an accurate audit could be made; this is nothing but a source of perquisites for the officials in St Petersburg. Given immediate accounting the temporary officials' pockets would not suffer at all, and on the termination of his appointment each would resume his ordinary occupation and so merchants would never be brought to permanent impoverishment by this procedure.

In Western countries the well-being of men of divers occupations, in particular that of the merchants, is carefully fostered and so the merchants in those parts are very rich. But our magistrates have no care for persons at all and by their callousness impoverish the whole realm. For if the people are rich so is their country, and if the people are poor their country cannot be accounted rich. I cannot conceive by what reasoning our magistrates see fit to do nothing to benefit the realm but only look to their own ephemeral fortunes; their way of
(78)   benefiting the realm is to waste thousands of roubles to no purpose. If for any reason a person's goods are distrained on behalf of His Majesty they might as well be thrown into the fire, for when they have been deposited in custody of a court they are kept under lock and key for a year or more before a valuation is made. Thus a sable coat that was worth some five hundred roubles is not worth even five by the time it is taken out, all perished. Therefore let a rule be made

that, if such a thing happens on the authority of any magistrate, restitution for the perished goods shall be made by those magistrates who allowed it to happen; they would then take due care willy-nilly. It is their present ways that cause the needless and irretrievable loss of such property. Magistrates must take the greatest care to ensure that no property whatever, wherever it may be, is allowed to go to waste without good reason, for all the riches that people possess make up the sum of the riches of the realm, just as impoverishment of the people equals the impoverishment of the realm. Nor can I understand why magistrates so harass the tax-gatherers and other collectors of revenue and relentlessly keep demanding the payment of arrears. If someone has either by some misunderstanding spent a sum that belongs to the Tsar's treasury or misappropriated funds and cannot make the sum good at the audit, it seems to me that an undertaking should be required of him to repay it by a given time. If he says he will repay it soon, all well and good. If he promises repayment within a year or a couple of years, what need is there for relentless harrying? Rather he should be made to pay interest on the sum as may be determined.

In this way benefit accrues to our Sovereign and at the same time the people are neither harmed nor kept away from their occupations. Whereas such relentless demands for restitution cause manifest ruin to peasants and merchants alike and exhaust the realm instead of harvesting its treasure.

But His Majesty's revenue will suffer no diminution provided that the collection is not carried out ruthlessly. Every sum will come to hand in the fullness of time whereas ruthless exaction of payment is not taxation but ruination. If a deficiency is discovered in any man's accounts written notice should merely be sent to the appropriate Board in St Petersburg in order that it may have a clear record of what arrears are outstanding and against whom.

79)   In this way great benefit will accrue to His Majesty's treasury and it will be a source of pride to our country that no man will be ruined or reduced to poverty, nor his household suffer harm. As the law stood until recently to cover a man's debt his home and goods are seized, valued at a half or a third, or even a tenth of their true worth, and sold; and so he is utterly ruined.

Now by His Majesty's new ordinance interest of ten per cent a year is to be paid on all such arrears.[22] Thus His Majesty's treasury will not merely be conserved but augmented and the people will be protected and suffer no harm. If any persons who hold concessions from His Majesty for taverns or anything else fall behind in their payments, there is no need at all to take action against them or their guarantors because this very delay will actually benefit the Tsar's revenue. Whereas by such summonses magistrates cause great losses to those engaged in any trade and thereby do not further His Majesty's interests but merely harm them. For this reason magistrates should take the greatest pains to ascertain whether any such matter is really important and urgent, and if not, let it be postponed. Let them use their wits to ensure that His Majesty profits from every possible source and that no loss is incurred needlessly.

If any person requires a sum of money for a venture the treasury should advance it to him on application, only making sure that he is trustworthy; and a special register should be kept for such loans. I think it quite wrong that any agreement[23] to supply His Majesty's government with goods or to receive money or goods from his treasury should be concluded at the Office of Deeds. Rather let the recipient sign his name in this special register and his guarantors and witnesses after him, according to custom. For that the Sovereign should enter into a contract with those who are his natural servants is most improper and ill becomes the Tsar's honour. Contracts are properly made by subjects

(80)   between one another, to ensure that, if one party breaks it, the other may go to law and seek redress. Now it is improper for the Sovereign to seek redress at law against his own subjects. If any man is in default all his goods may be seized and not only his goods – our Sovereign has power of life and death over his subjects. Therefore the Sovereign should not bind himself by contract with any of his own subjects; were he to sign such a document he would himself be equally bound by it.

Anyone who receives a loan of ten thousand or a hundred thousand roubles from the treasury must acknowledge receipt thereof in the special register. Provided that he is a free agent his guarantors will as a matter of course sign with him; but no witnesses need sign seeing that a magistrate will attest the document. In this way the completion of the loan will be greatly expedited since the formalities can be accomplished on the very same day that it is required. Nor is it really necessary in any commercial transaction to have a contract drawn up in the Office of Deeds for the handing over of the goods for it is the preparation of such contracts that causes great delay. How much better is the practice current in other parts of Christendom, and even among the infidel Moslems of the Turkish Empire, where not merely in transactions to the value of a hundred roubles but even ten thousand roubles and upwards documents like ours covering many pages are not required: the recipient merely signs his name in acknowledgment – that is sufficient guarantee – and writes a couple of lines instead of our whole sheet. However, until dishonesty is rooted out among us it will be necessary for safety's sake for guarantors and witnesses alike to append their signatures below that of the borrower. Moreover, agreements between merchants should be concluded within a day, which would be to the great advantage of them all; whereas, as things are, there are always great delays in the Office of Deeds. This causes unnecessary expense and hampers trade.

I believe that our most vital need is for the rule of law; once that principle can be established all will shrink from unrighteous actions. Fair and impartial dispensation of justice is the foundation of all well-being, and once that is laid it must follow that His Majesty's revenues will be doubled. To achieve this a new

1) code of law ought to be compiled with full provision for every kind of case. Unless such a digest be made there can be no rule of law, since now each judge has his own notions and gives judgment as he pleases, whereas he should be so furnished that he may give a correct decision even if he is a man of no great understanding.

In order to establish a just code of laws a complete collection should first be made comprising the old *Code*, recent civil and military laws (whether printed or manuscript) and recent and older Novels. Abstracts should be made of all judgments delivered in previous cases, in all courts and offices of state, for which no provision was made either in the old *Code* or in any Novel. And taking all such judgments into account new articles should be drafted so that similar cases can in future be decided out of hand and not sent up to the Senate. Let there be clear, well-arranged laws providing for every possible case.

To our own body of law, both ancient and recent, should be added material from foreign codes. Any articles in foreign codes that can be seen to suit our practice should be extracted and incorporated in our code. And that it may be the more perfect, the Turkish Code[24] should also be translated into Slavonic and an abstract made of the rules therein which regulate judicial procedure and the application of civil laws; and anything appropriate to our circumstances should be adopted from them. For I have heard it said that in all matters of government they have clear and fair rules – more so than in the West. In consequence all matters are speedily and justly dealt with among them; there is no waste of paper, as with us, no unnecessary loss of livelihood and, most important of all, the merchants are protected and fairly treated.

For the drafting of this new code let there be chosen two or three representatives from among divines of outstanding wisdom, learned in the Scriptures and from among laymen experienced in all affairs of law and government: that
2) is, men of high rank who are without arrogance and who have the interests of men of all conditions at heart; men of lower degree without self-importance; officials of proven ability; wise and justice-loving *dvoriáne*; merchants of wide experience in affairs; military officers who are lovers of justice, experienced and seasoned in the service; boyars' retainers[25] who are men of affairs and fiscal officers. And I think it would be of some advantage to include a number of peasants of intelligence who have served as village headmen and wardens, with a wide knowledge of practical matters. I have observed that there are intelligent people even among the Mordvá,[26] so must there not be such among our peasantry too? When this commission has drafted the new code the whole people shall make known their views thereon with a free voice, without any compulsion, so that the proposed text may contain nothing offensive or oppressive (through ignorance of their way of life) either to high or low, rich or poor, great or small, or indeed to the peasantry. When it has received the full approbation of all concerned the text shall be submitted to His Imperial Majesty

so that he may peruse it with all his wisdom and acumen. And those articles that seem good to him shall stand but those that he deems inappropriate shall be rejected or amended, as seems advisable. Many will disapprove of this proposal of mine, alleging that I am trying to detract from His Majesty's autocratic power in thus seeking the views of the people. But this is not so; my aim is the pure essence of justice – that every man should be able to examine his own interests to see whether there is anything in the proposed new articles that is objectionable as being contrary to true justice. If anyone finds an unjust article of this kind he should not hesitate to draw attention in writing to the injustice and without fear of the consequences ask for the text to be amended, since each of us is best aware of where his own shoe pinches. Consequently all should (83) review what affects themselves before the final text has been drawn up; once that has been done, no one can do anything more about it. This opportunity is given in order that there may not be any complaints afterwards against the authors of the new code. Likewise a free expression of views thereon is necessary in order that none shall find fault with any of its articles but everyone shall have safeguarded his own interests, and also that no one shall be able to make objections subsequently but that the text shall be inviolate for all time.

Law-making of this kind is a matter of the highest import and it must be done so judiciously that no person of whatever degree can undermine it. That is why it cannot be achieved without taking counsel of all and allowing a free voice to the people, since God has not given any one man perfect understanding in all matters but has caused wisdom to be divided into many small portions, to each man his capacity – to one much, to another less. Yet there is no man to whom God has given none at all, and the particular wisdom that God has given to one of limited understanding He has not given to the clever. Therefore even the wisest of us must not be arrogant and puffed up by his own cleverness, nor must the less intelligent be despised; they too should be consulted since God often makes known His purposes through simple men and therefore it is all the more perilous to despise them.

Thus it is very right and proper that for the establishment of a just code the opinion of all should be consulted. Even if achieved by the arduous labours of a commission on behalf of all, yet it should not be immediately printed but first put to the test of practice. If no ill effects appear in its application it may be allowed to stand, but if a fault appears in any article it must be reconsidered and amended. It would therefore be advisable to apply the new code in the courts for two or three years using manuscript copies or printed booklets; thus many of its articles will have been proved in practice while it is still under consideration.

(84)   If any other such task is undertaken in a similar spirit of humility and philanthropy God Himself will certainly be with it and guide it towards perfection, for God is always with the humble and turns His face from the proud and arrogant.

Now the dispensation of justice is of all things the most holy and pleasing to God. Therefore we must exert our best efforts to make the judgment rendered in the name of the Tsar like unto that of God. For God is the righteous judge of us all: at His judgment-seat there is no partiality. Therefore let there be none at the judgment-seat of the Tsar. God is a just judge and therefore demands justice of men. And I firmly believe that the love of justice is more necessary in a Sovereign than fasting and prayer.

May it please His Imperial Majesty, guided by his own natural wisdom and the grace of God, to direct that a new and comprehensive law code be compiled from the old *Code* and much other matter, and to give consideration to these fruits of my modest wit. If any of my proposals are deemed worthy of acceptance let them be incorporated in the Code. Then, after trial, when it has proved itself in many difficult and unusual cases, let a great many copies of the Code be printed so that there may be one not only in every town but also in every village and that all may read it, learn the will of His Imperial Majesty, do nothing contrary to his will and eschew all unrighteous deeds. At the beginning of the Code a table of contents shall be provided, arranged both in alphabetical order and by subjects, so that anyone may find rapidly and easily the law on any point and a complete ruling thereon. As long as all forms of government whatever together with the administration of justice do not rest on a comprehensive written code which lays down the principles of their exercise, and as long as these are not observed in practice with undeviating exactitude, the true dispensation of justice will never be attained, try as one may.

85) Even when such a foundation has been laid, it should in my opinion be supported by a strict, unalterable ordinance, viz.: Any servant of His Majesty in a court of high or low instance, in town or country, be he noble or of humble birth, a principal or a subordinate, or for that matter any other person in authority or his deputy, and above all any official investigator or fiscal officer who commits an arbitrary act in contravention of the new Code (even if he only infringes some minor article) shall be put to death forthwith, as the law provides.

Also, as a further safeguard against any departure from strict justice, judges and officials must not accept requests addressed to them by anyone whatever. Even if a man who has done meritorious service should relapse into the bad old ways and, relying on his past services, commit an oppressive act against another (of however little account he may be), yet there shall be no deviation from the law in his case and he shall for his wrongdoing incur the prescribed penalty; his past services shall not be taken into acount in the determination of his guilt. In this way there shall be no infringement of the Code or abuse in its application. If, however, any man inadvertently transgresses the law and there is good reason to relax the full severity of the law in his case, he shall be branded upon the arm; but if he is found guilty of the same offence again the full penalty shall be imposed on him without mitigation. If the dispensation of justice is so maintained for five or six years, strict and inviolate, one and all will take heed of the warning, the man of low degree and humble birth as much as the man of high degree and noble birth or one who has attained high degree through meritorious service. No longer will they commit oppressive acts as they are wont to do but they will beware of committing any injustice and zealously practise righteousness.

As a further safeguard in all matters pertaining to justice and government there should be set up a special office to ensure that magistrates do not depart a hair's breadth from the rule of law. The head of this office shall be a man in the closest confidence of the Tsar and utterly loyal to him. He must be the Tsar's 'eye' – a trustworthy eye – and rank above all judges and officials; he shall keep (86)   a strict watch on officials[27] of all kinds and have to fear no one but God and His Majesty. All shall have free access to his office; he himself shall be without arrogance or harshness, condescending to all manner of men. He shall visit all the Boards of government in turn (presumably not every day but as time allows) to see how each official is doing his work and look into any irregularities and any complaints made against the officials. Similarly he shall make the round of all courts of law and enquire of the litigants whether any one of them is being treated wrongfully or with undue delay, whether judgment has been given against anyone contrary to the provisions of the Code, and whether any judge or clerk has accepted any consideration over and above what is proper. In all Boards of government and offices printed notices shall be displayed as follows: If any magistrate or clerk commits an injustice in the course of his duties, recourse may be had to the said special office and all shall there receive redress.

Likewise, if any person of high standing has committed an oppressive act towards a poor man, or a magistrate or military officer towards a common soldier or trooper, and the victim has not found redress, he may seek protection there. And if any magistrate or commissioner or fiscal officer commits any act of injustice or injures the interests of the treasury by embezzlement or care-lessness, and anyone has true information thereof, he should report the matter to this special office without hesitation or fear; for even if the informant's complaint is against his own master or commanding officer, however in-fluential, the office of the special commissioner will on no account hand him over. Provided the information is true and the report was not made on mere guesswork or hearsay but in full knowledge of the facts, informers shall receive a substantial reward for such information.

It were best for His Majesty to cease paying judges and all his servants in the public offices of state a salary in money and in kind in order that our Sovereign Lord's treasury be not needlessly diminished by this charge. I reckon that (87)   something like twenty or thirty thousand roubles is paid out yearly to all such servants of His Majesty, but it is a total waste and disappears without return because there is little that they will do for nothing; and even if they were to do something for nothing what advantage would there be in that to our Sovereign? It seems to me that their livelihood would be best secured by the payment of fees for work done at fixed rates.[28] It should be laid down what proportion of his fee for judging a case the judge should receive from the winning and losing parties respectively; what commission should be allowed on the collection of moneys for the treasury and similarly on the conveyance of all grants made by His Majesty, on commercial transactions and the placing of contracts, and what fees should be charged for preparing extracts of various kinds, viz. from ordinances, deeds or memoranda. This procedure must be so firmly established as not to exclude even the most trivial piece of work – nothing must be done *gratis*, but the exact fee charged, as laid down. Under this new regulation all will pay gladly and the officials themselves will do their work the more willingly and no longer deliberately cause delays, for if an official completes his work by the time stipulated he will receive the full fee prescribed, but if not, only the half, and if he is grossly dilatory he will lose the whole fee. So every clerk will work expeditiously to the great advantage of the interested parties.

It follows that the fee to be paid for every transaction must be prescribed by regulation whether it concerns one rouble or many thousands, and everyone will be remunerated according to the work he has done and never exact a farthing more than what is prescribed.

If anyone takes more – however little – than the prescribed fee he shall be fined at the rate of one rouble for each kopeck in excess. And the man who offers money in excess of what is prescribed shall likewise be fined at the same rate. In this way no one will be unfairly charged for work done in an office of state; the two parties to a case and any other client whatever will know exactly what fee is due and to whom. Thus no transaction will be subject to deliberate protraction but every official will be prompt in his own interests. However, as a further safeguard, the following regulation should be applied to all matters: if any official spins out over three days a matter which requires only one day he shall receive nothing for his pains; if a fortnight, he shall receive immediate punishment. Similarly in important matters which cannot be dealt with in less than a week, if he takes a fortnight, only half the fee shall be paid; if a month, nothing; if he takes six weeks he shall be beaten without mercy.[29] The amount of work and therefore the number of days needed shall be estimated for all kinds of business. As true evidence thereof the clerk shall give each client a note stating on what date he undertakes to have it ready. If he has not done so by the time stated he shall incur the appropriate penalty. If he is punctual the full fee for the work shall be paid; if he exceeds the limit by an equal amount, half the fee; but if the delay is twice as much he shall receive nothing. And for delays exceeding this he shall receive immediate punishment.

And in this matter all magistrates shall receive the most solemn warning not to accept any gratuities over and above the sum laid down for the work. For if such a prohibition on the giving and accepting of gratuities is not made they will not be satisfied with the prescribed fees but will exact more than ever, just as at present officials at the Office of Deeds demand half a rouble or more in respect of transactions that are worth a mere ten kopecks. Consequently in the work of the Office of Deeds it shall likewise be laid down what fee is to be charged for preparing a given document, and the treasury shall receive only the fixed duty on all such documents. The fee for engrossing documents shall be abolished; the copyist and the superintendent shall in person receive the appropriate fees for their work, as prescribed. If the clerk has the document ready on the same day he shall receive the full fee, but if he takes two days, only half. If he takes three days he shall receive nothing but hand over the documents without payment. And if anyone demands a fee (whether the full sum or not) after taking three days over the work he shall be fined a hundred times the amount due.

(89)

Not only all contracts but official papers and letters of every kind should be written with fifty or more lines to a page. It is most astonishing that the whole world except ourselves writes small; little wonder that all the neighbouring countries cannot meet our demands for paper. If saving paper seems a trivial matter to others it does not seem so to me, because our large writing and extravagance causes a total loss to the realm of some ten thousand roubles a year.[30] Although Western countries manufacture their own paper and are richer than we are, yet they use it with the greatest economy. They are sparing in their use of paper and indeed of all kinds of things and they are rich just because they know how to live sparingly. Whereas we are still heedless, and as long as we take no pains to use both imported and home-made goods sparingly we shall never be rich.

To discourage excessive payments to officials and the excessive use of paper, notices should be printed and displayed in all Boards of govenment and in all court-houses for all to read and be warned against any unnecessary expense whether to themselves or to others. The bee is quite a small insect; it does not gather its honey by the jugful but in tiny droplets, yet the bees in their multitude gather many tons. Likewise with the gathering of the wealth of a realm: if all live sparingly and neither commit any extravagance nor allow anything whatever to go to waste, that realm can indeed grow very rich.

(90)

But, to resume, if anyone is tempted to accept more than he should a second time he shall incur a double fine (i.e. at the rate of two hundred roubles for one rouble) and beating with the knout on a tackle,[31] and for the third offence he shall either be executed or sent to the mines for life.

Should any judge act contrary to the new Code not for a bribe but out of favour or complaisance he must suffer the penalty as laid down and no mercy shall be shown him. But if anyone accepts a bribe to infringe the new Code I consider that his house should be ransacked and then left vacant for several years and a notice displayed declaring his crime – that for infringing the Code the owner has suffered the penalty of his crime and his house has been abandoned; that no one now lives there but it is left to mice and bats to inhabit.[32] A punishment of that kind will be remembered for generations.

For if magistrates of all degrees are not punished and heavily fined there will be no way to establish[33] righteousness and the rule of law even if a just code is in force. Even if many magistrates have to be removed in order that justice may be well and truly established, so be it. I think that this cannot be achieved without some sacrifice and, to put it frankly, it cannot be done without removing a couple of hundred magistrates since the habit of dishonesty is inveterate among us in Russia. I doubt whether we can eradicate this vicious habit without making an example of this kind. For if a piece of land reverts to grass you cannot sow it with wheat until the top growth has been burnt off. Similarly, a strongly ingrained bad habit among the people must be eradicated by strong measures. In my view this is the only way to bring about the rule of law not only in the courts but in all government.

1) However, rather than expose magistrates of high birth to severe punishment it would be better, if the rule of law is to be established, to make appointments from the outset among those of lower degree, in particular from among experienced and God-fearing subordinate officials. There should be appointed to sit with them, as appropriate, retired military officers and merchants known for the sharpness of their intelligence. If any such fail in their duty no one will be likely, in view of their low birth, to take their part and try to justify them. Moreover, they themselves will be more circumspect than men of high birth; for the latter take little notice of what the law ordains but do just as they please in their natural arrogance.

These magistrates of low degree should be given such standing as will make them secure from fear of any person except God and the Tsar: they should carry out their duties strictly in accordance with His Imperial Majesty's new Code, without attempting to be wise on their own account or adding or subtracting one jot or tittle from what is laid down. And if any of them should find the Code wanting in any detail he should bring the matter to His Imperial Majesty's attention before the Code appears in print.

Should no such officials be found fit for appointment as magistrates they should be chosen from the petty *dvoriáne* – men who are quick-witted, experienced and God-fearing. They must know full well that immediate execution will follow any infringement or abuse of the new Code, so that they may be ever mindful of death in the performance of their duties.

In this way, if God watches over us and sends His help, the rule of law may be established here in Russia too. It is much to our discredit that not only other Christian peoples but even the Muslims dispense justice fairly, yet although we have a religion that is holy, pure and renowned throughout the world, our judicial procedure is worthless. Whatever laws His Imperial Majesty promulgates are all set at naught and everyone continues in the bad old ways.

(92) Until the rule of law is established in Russia and is firmly and universally rooted among us no measures applied for the remedy of abuses[34] as in other countries will have any effect. Likewise we shall never acquire a good name since all the nastiness and want of principle among us is due to deficiencies in the law and in the dispensation thereof and also to short-sighted government. It is to shortcomings in the law and to this alone that the prevalence of brigandage and all other kinds of crime among the people is due. Peasants abandon their homes to flee from injustice and many parts of Russia are deserted solely as a consequence of such great shortcomings in our laws. Whatever disasters befall us are all due to injustice.

Justice and its fair dispensation cannot be achieved (in my view) either by leniency or severity, nor by appointing renegades[35] to high office among us, nor by any other such devices. First must come the special compilation of an unalterable Code covering all matters both great and small. For the old laws are all out of date and, moreover, have been distorted by unjust judges. If God shall look down with favour upon this matter and send His holy aid, and if the revised Code sets out exemplary decisions for all manner of cases separately, even a judge of no great attainments will be able to arrive at a just decision. Without such a fundamental Code nothing effective can be done in the interests of justice.

For even as a high building cannot stand firm without a firm foundation, so true justice can in no wise be established without a fundamental Code, seeing that injustice is so strongly entrenched among us. The strong will ever oppress the weak: in the end the unscrupulous ruin the defenceless, and although magistrates are well aware of wilful oppression by powerful and litigious men they do not dare to check them. Thus it is exceedingly difficult to establish the rule of law. It will admittedly be difficult to dispense justice to all, but I think it will be even more difficult to establish a fundamental code of laws, since the powerful who have been accustomed to oppress others will not submit to it of their own accord but will rather make every possible difficulty in order not to be

(93) hampered by the rule of law. And so they will do their utmost to continue oppressing and ruining the poor and defenceless as hitherto. Should any who are opposed to the rule of law become known before the task of revision is begun they must be removed by one means or another so that they may not hinder the setting on foot of this great task.

There is no way of introducing and establishing perfect justice without a revision of the old laws. For it is no easy matter to wean from injustice those who govern us and to inculcate a sense of justice in them, seeing that the habit of injustice is so deep-rooted and ingrained in them. From the first to the last they have become venal and weak; some take bribes, others quail before the powerful or the litigious; some go in fear lest, if another in the future occupies their present position of authority, he will not treat them with like indulgence. So it comes about that the Tsar's affairs do not prosper as they should: judicial investigations are not carried out faithfully and His Imperial Majesty's ordinances remain a dead letter, for all servants of His Majesty from among the *dvoriáne* act with partiality towards their own kind. They dare to exercise their authority only over defenceless folk and lack the courage to say 'no' to prominent *dvoriáne*. So they do just as they please and thus all manner of affairs of state are brought into disarray.

For instance, although orders have been sent repeatedly to all chief towns concerning the duties of youths and younger children of *dvoriáne*, even when any such young person is summoned by name he is not sent off immediately but only at the third time of asking (as allowed under the old *Code*), and then only if no means can be found of evading the order. Many of these young *dvoriáne* have disobeyed and flouted His Imperial Majesty's orders in this way for so long that they are now well past the age of manhood and continue to live on their estates without ever having lifted a finger in his service.

It seems to me most strange not to obey the Tsar's order, as also that the old *Code* should have explicitly allowed an order to be repeated three times, a concession that was nothing but conniving with rogues and others who contemn the Tsar's majesty. But now it should be done thus: if anyone does not obey the first summons, the second shall carry a fine equal to the sum in litigation and the plaintiff shall be entitled to his costs (as may be laid down) from the moment of the second summons.

Further, if His Imperial Majesty sends a military or other emissary with an order for a certain person to appear and that person goes into hiding or refuses compliance or disappears on the way, this shall be deemed an offence liable to a fine from the very moment of the first summons and the plaintiff shall be entitled to recover his costs from that same moment and the whole sum in dispute shall be awarded to him without further trial or the appearance of the parties in court. In this way the very first summons will strike such fear into the recipient that he will speed hotfoot to answer it and there will be no more waiting for a third summons to be sent.

The old law has been unduly indulgent towards the *dvoriáne*. Thus in the district of Ustréka there is a certain *dvorianín*, Fëdor Mokéevich Pustóshkin, who is already of advanced years and yet has never lifted a finger to serve His Majesty in any capacity. Whatever peremptory summonses have been sent to him, nobody has succeeded in laying hands on him: some he bought off with gifts, and whenever this did not work he would feign grave illness or madness and drool into his beard. By such subterfuges he has caused some emissaries to let him go again when they were already on their way back with him, and as soon as they were out of sight he would give up the pretence of madness and on reaching home rage like a lion. Although he has performed no service whatever for His Imperial Majesty beyond living in idleness, his neighbours go in constant dread of him. He has raised four sons, the youngest of whom is seventeen, but up to the year 1719 nobody could induce them to present themselves for service. However, in that year two of them were enrolled (I do not know the circumstances). Nevertheless, all of them still live at home more than half the time – those who were enrolled as well as those who were not – but how they spend their time I cannot say.

This is the way that a very large number of the *dvoriáne*, not merely this Pustóshkin, spend their lives. I met another such *dvorianín* in the district of Aléksin, Iván Vasíl'evich Zolotarëv by name, who when at home terrified his

(95) neighbours as if he were a lion, and when on service behaved worse than a nanny-goat. He failed to wriggle out of the summons for the Crimean campaign[36] so he sent an impoverished *dvorianín* in his stead, Temiriázev by name, whom he furnished with a retainer and a horse of his own. This man then served under his name while he himself remained at home and continued to range the countryside attended by half a dozen[37] henchmen, doing violence to his neighbours. I am astounded at the behaviour of these people. It is of course common knowledge that all commanders in the army are money-grubbers: they accept bribes from such people and turn a blind eye.

The above is true not only of the provincial *dvoriáne* but even of those who serve in respect of estates in the Moscow region and go by the name of *tsaredvórtsy*:[38] the majority of them too deceive His Majesty. When their turn for service comes round some apply to join search-parties for deserters and, on receiving the commission, go off to their estates and stay there till the hostilities are over. Others enrol as inspectors for confiscating liquor distilled illegally in private dwellings; and so, by finding themselves all sorts of trivial employment of this kind, they live through the period of hostilities.

You have but to look around nowadays to find a vast number of malingerers variously employed. One of them would be a match for five of the enemy, yet, having found himself some lucrative place, he goes on quietly piling up a fortune; such men procure themselves appointment as commissioners, *chétvershchiki*,[39] vice-commissioners, magistrates, or to other high official positions, and so lead an easy life and enrich themselves. Thus it is the poor *dvoriáne* who serve His Majesty in the wars and with very little respite too – some serve for twenty or thirty years; whereas the rich ones find ways of being discharged from the service after serving only five or six years and of procuring some profitable place, and having once achieved this so continue for the rest of their lives. For example, Sergéi Stepánovich Unkóvskii only served for some five years in the armed forces; he then procured a lucrative place and has been living on that for the past fifteen years or so. At the moment he is commissioner at Ustréka and feathering his nest nicely. He can hardly be forty even now – a

giant of a man who could render first-rate service and might well serve in the
'Giants'[40] were he not too tall even for that. Yet here is a man who left the
service when he was not much over twenty.

Indeed, wherever one looks, it is apparent that His Majesty has no truly
zealous servants. The ways of all his counsellors are crooked: they exempt those
who ought to serve and oblige those to serve who are least capable of doing so.
The official in charge of the saddlery in Nóvgorod is a certain Iván Ivánovich
Ushakóv. When I met him in 1710 in this capacity he was just over twenty years
of age; he is now just over thirty and still has little notion of the meaning of
service. His uncle, too, Iván Naúmovich Ushakóv, has enjoyed a civil post for
over ten years now, yet a man like him is still good for a dozen or more years
under arms. So the rich wriggle out of service, the poor and the old have to
serve, and men of substance are unwilling to serve, even if they are young. The
sons of I. A. Músin-Púshkin, Marko and Grigórii, were enrolled in the
Preobrazhénskii Regiment but no sooner had they reported for duty than they
were given leave to take up civil posts when they were still in their early
twenties. They will hold these year in year out until their dying day. I can only
suppose that His Majesty is not fully apprised of this practice. Yet this is what
all those in authority do – they allow vigorous young men to leave the armed
forces. Even if His Majesty's approval is sought for this the application will be
inaccurate or misleading; as soon as the officials have wheedled His Majesty's
verbal assent out of him they take the matter into their own hands and, I
imagine, go as far as stating in the official order that so-and-so has been
granted indefinite leave or has been assigned to some particular duty by His
Majesty's express command. And far from rendering to His Majesty the service
due to him these young men settle down to a life of idleness and indulgence in
the chief town to which they have been sent and not only have they no
experience of field service but virtually none, I should suppose, even of guard
duties. Enjoying a lucrative place they learn how to make money instead of
soldiering and so spend their whole lives without having seen service. Neither
they themselves nor the officials who released them show the least concern that
these young men should learn the art of war (that is, how to defeat the enemy);
instead they are only allowed to learn how to make their fortunes and evade all
service under arms.

For some time now many *dvoriáne* have succeeded in evading service, found
themselves a place and make a lucrative living thereby. Here is a clear case: it is
reported of two brothers in the district of Ustréka, Román and Sergéi, the sons
of Iván Choglokóv, that they have never seen service but somehow obtained
appointments as magistrates. One held office for some three years at Zheléznaia
Ústiuzhna, the other at Výshnii Volochók; and they declared self-importantly
that they had received these appointments by His Majesty's personal command.
Consequently everyone went in fear of them and made no resistance to their

oppressive acts; no one dared to contradict them. But since the recent inspection held in Moscow their appointments have for some reason been called in question. While they were there they petitioned to be reappointed but without success; it is common knowledge that all their wiles availed them nothing. I cannot believe that His Majesty did in fact give civil appointments to such sturdy young men who had never seen service. It is a matter of common observation that His Majesty does not make such appointments for nothing but only as a reward for meritorious service rendered over many years. Now the service that these young men could render would be worth that of ten men seeing that they are so sturdy themselves and also that, being rich, they could maintain in their own retinue a number of *dvoriáne* without means.

It is not at all advantageous for His Majesty when such vigorous and rich men in the prime of life live at home while the poor and puny are called to the colours. The feeble and hungry can render only poor service. It amazes me that, despite all our Monarch's endeavours and his threats of merciless punishment, those in authority will not give up their bad ways. For they still keep a multitude of such sturdy youngsters under their patronage, some under their personal protection, others about their persons, ostensibly engaged in the service of the Sovereign but in fact as a way of avoiding service under arms for as long as possible. Some also are registered for service but on one pretext or another go off home and remain there. Therefore it seems to me that it would be no bad thing for His Majesty to promulgate an ordinance to the effect that when a man returns home on leave from military or other duties, his neighbours must all (98) demand to see his leave pass. If he has no such document for the said term he must be sent to the nearest chief town under guard. If the pass shows the length of time for his stay at home his neighbours must see to it that he does not outstay his leave even by a single day. And if any man is found by his neighbours to be without a pass or with a pass that shows that he has overstayed his leave, and they keep quiet about it, they must be fined for their failure to report the matter.

There are some *dvoriáne* who have not been enrolled for service and indeed have never served in any capacity. Sometimes such men, by some dodge or other, procure themselves positions of authority. Should anyone, whatever his standing (be he gentleman or bondman, cleric or peasant), lay a true information that such a *dvorianín* has been favoured with an appointment as magistrate, commissioner, or to any similar post, or again, that a *dvorianín* is living at home and enjoying the services of his peasants without having rendered service of any kind to His Majesty, then let the peasants of all such *dvoriáne* be taken away from them and handed over to those who do serve His Majesty. And the informant shall be given a quarter, or even a half, of the defaulter's land and peasants as an incentive to zeal in informing against such idlers.

If such an ordinance were printed in quantity and distributed not merely in all the chief towns but also throughout the countryside, with orders that the sacristans read it aloud to all present at the end of divine service on three or four consecutive Sundays, then everyone will know this ordinance of His Imperial Majesty and will not conceal idlers; all such malingering *dvoriáne* and their children could thus be exposed within a year.

If the Lord God were to send us His help in eradicating the ingrained dishonesty of magistrates, fiscal officers and other officials, the concerns of private persons would benefit no less than those of the Tsar.

I am of the opinion that even if the most extreme punishment were meted out to magistrates of all degrees, unless the old law code is repealed and a new general regulation drawn up, justice can never be attained in public administration. We can all see how our great Monarch is trying to achieve this but has little success because there are too few like-minded men to help him. For if there are only a dozen to pull uphill with him but millions to drag downwards, how can his great work go forward? Even if he punishes one man severely a hundred more are ready to step into that man's place. So endeavour as he may, so long as the old ways have not been given up, he will surely find himself left in the lurch.[41]

An antiquated system of dispensing justice can no more be put right without taking it apart and examining each separate detail than an ancient building can be renovated without taking it to pieces, examining each separate member and removing all rotten parts from it. In relation to justice the task of putting the laws to rights is not a matter for one man alone but for many wise heads called together for the purpose of making sound every old part that is rotten or warped, however small. For legislation is a weighty matter. The Lord God Himself did not introduce the New Dispensation without setting aside the Old. But when He had set aside the Old then He set up the New and so it took firm root, so that the gates of Hell cannot prevail against it. Likewise the rule of law will never be infringed once all the ancient injustices have been cut out for good and all. The multitude of new laws which are being promulgated now have little effect for inveterate injustice defeats them all. Thus it comes about that he who can oppress his neighbour with impunity will continue to do so just as before and, as before, there is no redress at law for the weaker against the stronger.

Despite the severer provisions of the recent ordinance on runaway peasants it will not bring about much improvement since the ordinance affects only people of little substance and does not touch the powerful. The latter will not hand over those peasants who are already in their hands and they will continue to harbour any who come to them in future. For example, five or six peasants ran away from me but found themselves a new home notwithstanding the said ordinance. They ran away on 9 June 1722, so it is now more than a year ago and there they still are. If people took due notice of the ordinance no one would have dared to take them in. Runaway peasants should be dealt with in such a

(100)   way that all the gentry, whether of great or of little substance, cease to harbour such persons. Instead, the matter should be dealt with as set out below, whether the gentry like it or not. But what the great landowners have contrived in the above-mentioned law is laughable: who would credit that they enacted that all ordinary folk are to return runaway peasants to their rightful owners together with a payment of twenty roubles for each year that the peasant has been harboured by them, and that for this they are to provide the carriage them-selves? Whereas the gentry have made things easy for themselves: the law provides that if any runaway peasants have come into the possession of any landowner through his factor or his headman[42] and were taken on without a written order of the landowner in question, the factor or headman shall be flogged but no fine shall be exacted from the landowner. And so there has come about a quite open migration: these great landowners have settled runaway peasants to make whole large villages in the downstream regions and borderlands;[43] some of these villages consist of two or three hundred house-holds or more. And it is surely only a fabrication on the part of the landowner to assert that such a large settlement can be established without the knowledge of the master. In my opinion such powerful men should be fined double compared with the poorer. So the peasants live in those villages in complete security; and if the rightful owner gets wind of their whereabouts the most he can do is take a furtive look at them but he cannot hope to get them back. The local governors do not even dare to send their men into such estates; moreover, the factor or headman who accepted the peasants may have died long before so there is no one who can be flogged for the crime. Clearly this ordinance has been drawn in flagrant contradiction to true justice.

The ordinance would be acceptable if it applied equally to the rich and the poor and had been drafted in sufficient detail, stating clearly in what circum-stances a case of harbouring entitles the rightful master to compensation amounting to a hundred roubles, twenty roubles, or none at all. In my humble opinion if this ordinance is not amended much harm will come to ordinary people and many *dvoriáne* of little substance, and merchants too will surely be ruined. For if any such person takes on a man without knowing that he is a runaway, to work only for a week or a month for a wage, or (let us say) as a

(101)   herdsman on his lands just for the summer season (without any thought of keeping him permanently), the man's master will receive his compensation of a hundred roubles and moreover will be able to enter a claim for any amount he likes against the man who employed the peasant in respect of chattels removed by the runaway. Many will be brought to ruin through no fault of their own by the application of this law.

It seems to me that this matter should be dealt with as follows: if any person harbours a runaway with intent to employ him permanently as a peasant to work on his land or in his household or as a landless peasant,[44] the landowner on whose estate the man is found shall be liable to pay compensation irrespective of whether it was the landowner himself or his factor or headman who took him in; for if you own the land you must take the blame. The factor or headman is innocent since he did not accept the runaway on his own account but on behalf of his master; thus the blame attaches to the master and not to his agent. It cannot be admitted that a factor or headman can take on anyone independently of his master's will.

Likewise, it is in every way proper that a merchant who takes on any runaway permanently and not temporarily, should be liable to pay the compensation of a hundred roubles even if the man has been with him for less than a week.

Any person who tries to gain possession by force of another's peasant or household servant should, in my opinion, be fined even more heavily than a mere harbourer of runaway peasants.

If anyone hires a man for a year without obtaining the necessary document from the Office of Deeds, it will be enough for him to pay twenty roubles since he did not take on the man in permanent ownership but merely for a period of time in consideration of a wage. But if anyone hires a man for a day or a week to work in his house or elsewhere, there is no need for a formal document in respect of such employment. No fine whatever should be incurred since these men have been hired for such a short time. For if compensation has to be paid in respect of men hired only by the day, the week or the month, universal hardship will follow. The proper way to deal with the matter is this: peasants of all kinds shall, as used to be the case, be strictly forbidden to leave their homes for any other place (even in the capacity of carters), whether for a year or even a week, without obtaining a duly signed pass from their warden; and this shall apply equally to peasants on Crown, episcopal,[45] and monastic lands. Likewise, the peasants of the private landowners shall not go anywhere without possessing a pass in due form. Thus if any man hired for a wage has such a document his employer shall be free of any pecuniary liability.

In my opinion justice demands that the question of runaway peasants should be dealt with in a way that is equally fair to the rich and powerful and to the poor and defenceless. Nor can I propose anything fairer than what follows.

Landowners of every description, great and small, shall send instructions to the factors and headmen on all their estates, whether ancient ones or ones newly acquired, whether in the central provinces or downstream or on new land in the border regions, to send off under escort without delay all extraneous persons, whether recent arrivals or not (including such as may have been there fifty years or more). They shall be returned with their wives, children and grandchildren to their original masters. There will be no need for compensation of a hundred roubles (or even a hundred kopecks) for every year's absence provided that they are sent back with all their movable possessions; this will quite satisfy their former master.

(102)

A year's grace or more should be given for making this restitution so that all landowners (whatever their means) may be able to do so without fail. If His Majesty issues an ordinance to this effect the rightful masters will welcome it and will be grateful even if they receive no compensation; and all these landowners would soon rid their estates of such aliens down to the last person, whether male or female. If after the time allowed for restitution any landowner deliberately retains any such persons (be they many or just a single one), young children not excepted, and the matter is brought to light, he shall be fined a hundred roubles for a female and two hundred roubles for a male, and the factor and headman shall receive fifty strokes of the knout and all the peasants ten strokes for this concealment. If this were done all would in future pay heed to His Majesty's orders and not attempt to hold back what is demanded of them.

(103)   In my view the effect of such an ordinance would be that even highly placed personages would not try to retain any runaway peasants who have long been in their possession but (I trust) would also take warning for the future. Not only the masters themselves but also their factors and peasants would all conform to the law. Further, if any person does not comply with the order to restore such aliens but either drowns them or does them to death by any other means, for each such man ten shall be demanded.[46] And if the new master appropriates the goods and chattels of the peasants in question he shall make tenfold restitution to their original masters. In this way, I believe, all runaway peasants would be restored to their rightful masters and could occupy vacant land all over Russia, so much so that in some parts the arrival of these newcomers would more than fill the land.

The high and mighty will naturally be aggrieved at the mere obligation to return such peasants together with their families, goods and chattels even without having to pay any compensation. I am sure that they will make an outcry about it. It has been easy for them to argue that under the present ordinance it is only the small landowners who must restore the runaways with their families and also pay the compensation, whereas they themselves, I know, will grudge even providing the carriage. I therefore expect that they will try every means to dispute this measure so as to frustrate the whole of the proposal, for they love to make others carry their burdens.

If the restitution of runaway peasants is not carried out in the way I have put forward I fear that there will be no end to the matter of restoring them to their former places and resettling them on the now vacant land. If any further indulgence is shown towards powerful personages in the matter of restoring runaways they will cling to all those who have been with them for a long time and will even continue taking on new ones. It is such high-handedness that prevents the establishment of the rule of law among us.

A measure which orders the return without compensation of what does not belong to one scarcely seems very harsh, yet the high and mighty will look upon it as a great outrage.

If then an ordinance were to be enacted by His Majesty to the effect that all persons, high and low alike, shall return all runaways with their wives, children and grandchildren, I am convinced that vacant land on all estates would be settled again within a year, and further that these people would be able to occupy other hitherto uncultivated land. His Majesty's revenue will increase greatly as a result of the occupation of all this vacant land and with the increase of the population trade will expand.

Thus there remain only those runaways who have escaped abroad. If His Majesty were to issue a command to be sent also to landowners in foreign parts, they, I believe, would not be disobedient to His Majesty but would all return as many such runaways as they may have. Some of these may have taken service with foreign monarchs; the said kings and princes[47] will least want to quarrel with His Majesty over runaways and will send back as many as they may have with a better grace than our own magnates. And as regards estates in the Ukraine, an expedition could be dispatched to round up such runaways.

The old law code runs thus: if anyone, with malicious intent to cause loss, lays a false complaint and if it be established that the same is false, he shall be charged at the rate of one *grívna* a day for all the costs incurred and the time consumed.[48] Yet anyone who is a genuine plaintiff likewise has to pay the same *grívna* a day, whether the sum at issue is one rouble, a hundred, a thousand or ten thousand roubles. What justice is there in this ancient ordinance? Rightly considered, everything should be in proportion. It should be laid down explicitly how much is to be charged per day where the amount at issue is one rouble or ten or likewise a hundred, a thousand or many thousands of roubles. Accordingly the daily costs in a given action should be determined in accordance with the pleadings and in the light of similar cases that were brought in good faith.

If any person brings a vexatious action with malicious intent to cause loss and it is clearly proved that this is so, there must be no compunction about mulcting him of the same sum as that which he was trying to obtain and about giving it to the party he was suing. And the costs, also calculated in proportion to the sum in dispute, shall be exacted from the plaintiff and given to the defendant; indeed, the barrator should be fined double to discourage him and his like from doing the same again.

Again, as the law stands, a person convicted of debts to the amount of ten thousand roubles shall suffer *pravëzh* for a hundred months – that is nine years and two months in all [*sic*]. And when the defaulter has suffered the full penalty he will petition to be allowed a period of grace to collect the money and the time allowed for this is the same length of time as the *pravëzh*. All these delays result in little satisfaction for the plaintiff. This procedure has proved to be a most notorious incentive to fraud and litigation.

It seems to me that both these provisions of the old *Code* should be repealed and that it should be enacted that, irrespective of the sum at issue, a defendant shall be obliged upon conviction to declare by what date he will repay the money. If the plaintiff is willing to grant a delay for the discharge of the debt then he has the right to determine how long this delay shall be, even if it be as much as a year. But as a general rule no more than a week's grace should be given to repay a debt of a hundred roubles, ten weeks for a thousand, and for greater or lesser sums in proportion.

If, however, the debtor says that he has not the wherewithal to pay, an inventory should be made of all his possessions, movable and immovable, their value appraised, and orders should be given for them to be sold at a profit. The valuers should be told that they must put a proper value on the goods. If they value at only half the true value they shall be flogged for their dishonest valuation; if they value too high, they shall themselves be obliged to accept the goods at that valuation and the money so collected shall be given to the plaintiff.

Again, the present ordinance concerning beggars is not altogether sound inasmuch as it lays down that those who give them alms shall be fined. But that is not the way to be rid of beggars. It cannot be done, all the more so as the ordinance contradicts God's commands: whereas God ordained almsgiving our magistrates impose fines for it. But almsgiving ought not to be fined. Rather His Majesty should decree that all beggars should be arrested and questioned to determine what kind of persons they may be and where they come from – peasants, traders, artisans and so forth. And in accordance with their de-(106)   claration they shall be sent back to wherever they came from. Yet instead of this, those who give them alms are fined.

The matter would be better dealt with thus: all beggars who are in poor health, crippled or very old should be allowed to end their days in peace, but it should be the duty of any person to seize healthy peasant beggars of either sex and their children, whether in town or countryside, if the law so order it. Anyone who sees a healthy beggar should seize him and bring him[49] before the authorities and they shall record the place where he was caught. This done, the authorities shall hand him over to the man who brought him in. If the latter, however, does not accept him, the beggar, whoever his master may formerly have been, shall be handed over in full possession to anyone who asks for him. If no one does so such beggars should be drafted to some public works or other. The moment the *dvoriáne* hear of this ordinance they will instantly retrieve any beggars who belong to them and never let them go begging again. In this way, within one year or less there would be no more vagrants in the countryside nor beggars in the streets.

For there are many landowners who keep their peasants and servants working at home all summer but send them off in the winter with orders to beg in the streets. And if one of them in the course of his wanderings is hired to do some work and receives payment for it, his master, on learning that he stayed in one place for a month or two as a hired worker, will allege that he ran away and, having notified the authorities, will make a claim in accordance with the law for compensation against the man who hired his peasant. This practice causes great loss not only to merchants but also to the *dvoriáne*.

Again, some traders and artisans are such lazy wretches that although they have a roof over their heads they have no desire either to trade or to work, but instead roam about begging. Others put on fetters and pretend to be prisoners; and when they have collected enough alms fill their bellies in idleness at home. Yet others engage in trade or exercise a craft themselves but send their children out begging. Such beggars should be severely punished, if the charge is proved, so that they may not eat the bread of idleness.

07) If anyone cannot make a livelihood by his own exertions he should become a hired labourer or servant and have all his children apprenticed so that they may learn a trade and thereby help to support their father. Begging teaches them nothing but how to become thieves and idlers: such people are like the weevils which make nothing but merely devour the bread that we have made.

Likewise, our magistrates keep the prisons full and the prisoners do not work but just live there and consume bread like so many weevils. The magistrates should not dismiss as unimportant this grave matter of beggars and prisoners; on the contrary, both the magistrates themselves and their subordinates should make it their most earnest concern to ensure that no man may waste his life and eat the bread of idleness. God did not give us bread to this end, that we should consume it like the weevils and turn it into dust. Rather should we profit God, our Sovereign, our neighbours and ourselves in return for the bread we eat, that we may not be like unto the unprofitable weevil which turns everything into mere dust and brings not the slightest advantage but only harm to mankind.

I reckon that there must be something like twenty or thirty thousand or more beggars and prisoners in all the towns and villages of Russia. They must consume yearly not less than fifty or sixty thousand *chétverti* of corn. Assuming that one has to allow for each at the very lowest estimate six roubles a year for bread, other food and clothing, it follows that these parasites each year turn into dust something like two hundred thousand roubles' worth of treasure. This huge waste is incurred solely through the laxity of His Majesty's servants. When it comes to taxes they will make a man's life a misery for the sake of a few kopecks, yet they show complete indifference when many thousands of roubles are wasted unnecessarily. They do not consider how they might contribute to the increase of the wealth of our realm but are concerned only with the sums that pass through their hands and these they regard as a net gain; that is their conception of 'profit'. But they are quite blind and indifferent to all the harm

08) that is done to the people and, what is more, the enormous loss which His Majesty himself suffers by their exactions.

The most prudential principle of tax collection is that those entrusted with it should endeavour to fill His Majesty's treasury without ruining the people. All those in authority should not merely collect what is due but also ensure that nothing goes to waste anywhere; that no one shall eat bread which he has not earned but that all shall work and that their labours shall be fruitful. All those who govern us call themselves zealous and loyal servants of His Majesty. Yet if we look at them with an unprejudiced eye it becomes manifest that their supposedly zealous deeds run contrary to the notion of a zealous servant whose duty it is not only to husband what is gathered in the form of revenue but equally to have due regard for wealth which is not so gathered, in order that nothing whatever may go to waste and that no man spends his days in vain.

A careful watch should be kept on all manner of material possessions, whether in His Majesty's coffers or in private hands of rich and poor alike, so that nothing of this kind shall anywhere go to waste or be squandered. The official who has this in mind will be a true contributor to the wealth of the realm.

Every servant of the Tsar set over any province or office of state who truly desires to serve His Majesty well must eschew intemperance and rather than lead a life of pleasure or devote too much time to the chase, bend all his energies to expediting the business in hand so that those who are under arrest in an office of state or in a gaol do not remain there longer than necessary and thus eat bread which they have not earned but return to their work. Those who are found to deserve death for their crimes should on no account be kept long in suspense and fed to no purpose but should be promptly executed.

An eye must be kept on all taverns to see that they are not the resort of idle and penniless riff-raff. Any such persons who are capable of work should be made to give an undertaking that they will not engage in any nefarious activity, nor gamble nor help to harbour any rogues; thus no man will be without work.

(109)   Those who have been condemned to any form of physical punishment must on no account be detained for even a single day lest they waste their time to no purpose. As for those who are to be sent to work in the mines or to other hard labour, they too should not be held in custody longer than necessary: let them be branded with a permanent or temporary brandmark and be sent off each to his place without delay, so that they are not maintained in idleness.

Every person in authority should regard it as part of his duties to ensure that no one subject to his authority shall idle about to no purpose and that young children shall not on any account be playing at knucklebones or with tops or at any other such games in the streets (except on holidays) and still more that youths shall not do any wanton damage nor engage in egg-cracking.[50] No man, of whatever station (including *dvoriáne*), shall distil grain without written permission.[51] *Dvoriáne* must keep a vigilant eye on their peasants and give most stringent orders to their factors and headmen not to allow any peasant to over-indulge in liquor at any season of the year. Neither older nor younger children should be allowed to idle about: some should be put to school and others taught one of the crafts practised among the peasantry. Those who are too young to handle an axe should learn to spin yarn and, when they have mastered this, they should be sent to the linen manufactories to work in winter for a wage or for their keep. In the summer they will be engaged in field work. He who has been inured to hard work in his youth will not be a good-for-nothing in later life.

Here is another matter where there is room for improvement. People are thrown into prison[52] for the most trivial misdemeanours, or even when they are quite innocent, the intention being to detain them for a matter of hours but they are soon forgotten and may still be there a year later. To avoid this, every magistrate must without fail inspect all his prisoners every day by having them all in person brought before him. This would prevent clerks and constables from putting a person in prison for the sake of what they may earn in services to the prisoner. When inspecting the prisoners the magistrate must himself question all those newly committed about the charge on which they have been arrested. If the charge is a trivial one he should settle the matter out of hand, so that the accused may return to the exercise of his trade instead of kicking his heels in custody.

If all magistrates were to carry out their duties in this way, reviewing the prisoners every day and dispensing summary justice, prisons would no longer be needed. It is the inaction of magistrates which is the cause of so much wrong and ruin in our land, whereby many perish needlessly; for many die in prison or before their time of starvation and want.

With regard to prisoners in custody it seems to me that the following rules might be followed: the case of a man arrested on a criminal charge should be settled within a week or at most two; in civil cases no one should be held in custody longer than twenty-four hours. If a magistrate holds someone longer than twenty-four hours in a civil case he shall provide the prisoner's food at his own expense. Given these rules magistrates would not keep people in custody for long periods as they do at present. An end must also be made to the practice of allowing prisoners in fetters to beg for alms in the streets. Truly it is a shameful thing nowadays that you still have to fight your way through crowds of beggars and prisoners in fetters.

It has long been the accepted practice that when ten or twenty guarantors stand surety in the sum of a thousand roubles for a loan, either between private persons or from the Tsar's treasury, the terms of the loan must provide that the money may be recovered either from the borrower or from such of the guarantors as are at hand. Hence, if a borrower defaults the creditors pick on whichever of the guarantors is the most prosperous, and if he does not succeed in standing up for himself, exact the whole sum from this one person and bring him to utter ruin. Many a lender is unaccommodating: when repayment falls due but the borrower is unable to pay, he does not even grant a week's grace but hales all the guarantors before the authorities and, the case going against them, all are utterly ruined. If they cannot produce the money forthwith the possessions of all are at once distrained, valued at less than a half of their true worth and all sold for a song. In this way the guarantors are ruined and then turned out into the streets. This practice leads to many a good man being (111) reduced to beggary, and this is tantamount to bringing ruin on the whole realm. Now if it were provided that guarantors may only enter into a surety in proportion to their substance it would follow that even in the case of a large loan – a thousand or several thousands – each guarantor would be answerable strictly in accordance with his means: that is to say, if a man can pay a thousand roubles he should stand surety for no more than this sum and should record in writing in his own hand that he is standing surety for a thousand roubles; but those who have not a thousand roubles to spare should each stand surety in proportion to their means, one for a hundred roubles, another for more or less. And he who cannot pay more than ten roubles as his share should set down his name for ten roubles and, in the event of the borrower's defaulting on his repayment, this guarantor shall not be liable for more than ten roubles. Thus each guarantor shall pay only that sum to which he has put his name. By this ordinance no man who has offered himself as a surety would risk ruin and men would therefore perform this office the more willingly.

The old *Code* laid down imprisonment for three or four years or longer on conviction of certain crimes. I have become convinced that this provision is most ill-conceived. Rather than keep a man in gaol for half a dozen years and starve him to death, give him some speedy punishment or inflict a fine. It is wrong to waste the days of a man's life. A man who has his freedom can provide for half a dozen or more other people besides himself; lying in gaol he cannot even provide for himself but, like the weevil, will eat bread and unprofitably turn it into dust.

In 1718 an apprentice glazier of the Iamburg glass factory,[53] Iván Semënov, was arrested in Nóvgorod for making himself a passport in his own handwriting. He was twice put to the question to find out whether he had forged passports or other documents for anyone else. No evidence was obtained of any forgery except of this one passport for himself, yet he was thrown into prison although it was evident that he had committed no other crime. And he was kept in prison for three years by the orders of Iván Miakínin who naturally would not set him (112) at liberty because the apprentice had nothing to give him as a bribe and the said Miakínin is a money-grubber who has never done anything for love. In his eyes justice is always on the side of him who has most to offer; this administrator of justice has sought not justice but money. So the man remained in prison one month short of five years as a result of this rank miscarriage of justice and the whole of those five years were lost to him. If Miakínin had not been mercenary and had set Semënov free after inflicting the prescribed punishment Semënov's work would have brought a profit of two or three hundred roubles to the realm. Instead he remained in prison and ate the bread of idleness; and all that bread was so much waste.

If we wish to set all these matters wholly to rights we must beseech all-bountiful God, who loves mankind, in His mercy to visit our endeavours with His divine favour. Putting our trust in God's will, it behoves us, if we desire to establish the rule of law, first of all to draw up a code which makes precise provision for the correct judgment of all manner of cases both grave and trivial. It must be so drawn up that no judge is obliged to decide a case according to his own lights; rather the code shall specify the conditions for conviction or acquittal in every kind of case: which offences shall be dealt with harshly and which leniently so that by consulting the code a judge even of modest understanding may decide any kind of case correctly.

CHAPTER 4. Of the Merchants

Commentary

The place of the trader in the social hierarchy. – Trading as the preserve of the posádskie liúdi. – Restrictions on trading by peasants relaxed in 1711. – The interests of the landlords protected (1714). – The terms on which a peasant might enter a posád. – Business conduct judged by ethical standards. Fair trading as understood by Pososhkóv who advocates a price war with Russia's foreign trading partners. – Peter I's commercial policy. The Board of Trade (Kommérts-kollégiia). The Bírzha (exchange) in St Petersburg. – Pososhkóv on Russian prices. – The high cost of imports. – Russia's balance of trade in 1726. – Pososhkóv on costume and class. – Tsar Peter's sumptuary regulations. – The growing demand for cloth, civilian and military. – Efforts to manufacture more cloth in Russia. – Silk-weaving. – Pososhkóv's wish to reconcile enrichment with salvation.

In speaking of the trader as the auxiliary of the warrior Pososhkóv no doubt had in mind the part played by traders in supplying the tsar's army during the Great Northern War.[1] It soon becomes apparent, however, that this partnership between the taxpaying inhabitants of urban areas and the scot-free military often degenerated into commercial rivalry. Pososhkóv shows that the *posádskie liúdi* still formed a distinct, cohesive and exclusive social category in fact as well as in law but, despite their economic usefulness, found themselves at a disadvantage in relation not only to the military but also to other social groups. In revealing the great diversity in the social origins of the traders in this period, postwar research[2] has confirmed the substance of the one-sided case made by Pososhkóv who maintains that the soundness of the exchequer depends on the prosperity of the trader and this in turn is assisted by the security and exclusiveness of his social and economic status. His place in the social hierarchy and his economic role deserve therefore to be carefully protected. This protection, originally accorded by articles 4, 15, 16 and 17 of Chapter 19 of the *Code* of 1649, was revived in 1721 with the intention, professed in the preamble to the Statute or Regulation of the *Glávnyi magistrát* (Board of Civic Administration), to rebuild 'the tumbledown edifice of the trading community'.[3] The underlying principles were, as before, exclusiveness, cohesion and an obvious identity, suited to the requirements of the service state and approved of by the conservative Pososhkóv.

Trading by unauthorized persons was traditionally held to subject the *po-sádskie liúdi* to unfair competition since the interlopers were apparently able to trade without paying toll or bearing what should have been their share of the taxes paid and services rendered by the *posád*.[4] In the ideal society envisaged by Pososhkóv, where each caste busied itself in the spirit of *právda* with its proper occupation within the bounds laid down by the tsar, competitive trading, fair or unfair, was out of place. Trade was to be reserved to the officially recognized native commercial confraternity instinct with brotherly love. This is what Pososhkóv means by free trade – not free for all but open to members of only one social category, unhindered by competition whether native or foreign. The Western merchant, however unwelcome, had long been a part of the Muscovite economic scene and his legal status was well established,[5] although Pososhkóv evidently did not think that it was too late to displace him. The case against trading by members of social categories other than the *posádskie liúdi* and the lower ranks of the military men of service, including the *strel'tsý*, was a much stronger one. In fact such activities, being contrary to the provisions of the *Code* of 1649, required official sanction.

Several ordinances issued between 1699 and 1700 allowed peasants to trade on condition that they entered a *posád* and duly shared its obligations.[6] Such entry, however, was not effected at will but controlled by the *Rátusha* and, presumably, later by the *Glávnyi magistrát* (Board of Civic Administration). No reference was made in these *ukázy* to the relationship between the peasant and his landlord. In 1711, owing to the acute shortage of funds experienced by the government, the restrictions on trading were relaxed in the expectation that more and more open trading would increase the revenue from the toll of 5 per cent (*rublëvaia póshlina*) levied on the purchase price of goods.[7] In addition, a proportional tax was to (but never did) replace the annual levy of 10 per cent (*desiátaia den'gá*) on working capital.[8] The contentious question of the relations between peasant and landlord seems to have come to a head in 1714 and obliged the authorities to intervene, at least to the extent of declaring their attitude. An ordinance of that year ruled that peasants engaged in trade must remain subject to, and pay the dues required by, their landlords or else stop trading.[9] The tsar's resolutions on some points submitted to him by the *Magistrát* of Moscow in 1723[10] settled the matter in relation to all the parties concerned on the principle laid down in 1714 (and also propounded by Po-soshkóv) with one important addition: a man who wished to enter a *posád* must produce evidence of being able to do at least 500 roubles' worth of trade. This considerable sum (Pososhkóv stipulates 100 or 200) could be reduced to 300 only for those who traded to the new port of St Petersburg. A peasant who entered a *posád* on these conditions was still obliged to pay the poll-tax at the rate of 80 kopecks in his native village, as well as to pay the customary dues to his landlord. These provisions furnished the officers in charge of the census which accompanied the introduction of the poll-tax with a set of rules for screening the population of the *posády*. As Bogoslovskii points out, the eviction and transfer of persons who were not by law entitled to reside in urban areas or engage in trade were similar to those which followed the promulgation of the *Code* of 1649.[11] The point bears repeating that for all its novelty the poll-tax was calculated to fit, and therefore to preserve, the traditional social divisions of the taxpaying part of the population.

The conditions for entering a *posád* were so stringent that the number of peasants to take advantage of them was small. In 1724 only 33 such entries were recorded in the province (*gubérniia*) of St Petersburg and a total of 369 for the provinces of Smolensk, Archangel and Nízhnii Nóvgorod.[12] Pososhkóv does not seem to have been aware of any of these regulations.

In examining the state of trade in Russia Pososhkóv, as is his wont, judges business conduct by ethical standards. Economic failure is accordingly seen as an act of divine justice: dishonesty is punished with personal ruin which eventually leads to general impoverishment. Salvation, at once spiritual and economic, lies in the observance of Christian justice (právda, δικαιοσύνη, *justitia*) associated by Pososhkóv with a notion of the just price not unlike that which the medieval scholastics and canonists developed in the West. It is not altogether surprising that in Pososhkóv's pragmatic mind the idea of natural justice did not need to undergo 'a long and tortuous evolution before it could be rationally related to such practical matters as buying and selling'.[13] Pososhkóv does not attempt a definition of what he calls 'the true and proper price' but merely implies that it is the current market price undistorted by cheating. Here his intuition and knowledge of Scripture bring him close to the essence of the doctrine propounded by the schoolmen; on the other hand, his recommendation that the fair prices should be permanently enforced by officials differs diametrically from Western medieval theory and practice. In the West it was held that the most effective way of combating such abuses as engrossing, forestalling and regrating committed with a view to driving up prices was to restore free competition by excluding the middleman. The public authorities would encourage or compel the peasants to sell their produce direct to the consumer.[14] In Muscovy the office of overseer set over a fixed number of the tsar's subjects for one administrative purpose or another, and referred to by Pososhkóv in this context, was traditional, but official price control was unknown, with one exception. Under Chapter 7, articles 21 and 25 of the *Code* of 1649, in times of scarcity and high prices soldiers on active service could ask the tsar's permission to buy surplus food and forage from private individuals at prices which would be fixed below those charged in the market.[15]

When it comes to reforming the relations between Russian merchants and their foreign customers Pososhkóv abandons his attitude of Christian righteousness for one of secular militancy. He would like to see his countrymen, acting in concert, wage something like a constant price war on the foreigners. The tactics of boycott and collective cornering recommended by him show little understanding of the interplay of supply and demand but do reveal the narrowness of his outlook. Not that Pososhkóv was alone in believing that his country being, unlike the rest, potentially self-sufficient, could prosper in economic isolation from its neighbours and other foreign nations. A number of French, English and Spanish writers on economics in the seventeenth century were under the same delusion with regard to their own countries.[16]

Unlike Pososhkóv, Tsar Peter consistently overlooked the plight of the small domestic trader. All his strategic designs and many of the enactments promulgated in the last decade of his reign make it clear that his sights were set higher, on the expansion of foreign trade. The task itself was to be discharged by the Board of Trade (*Kommérts-kollégiia*), established in 1716 principally with foreign trade in mind. The two successive sets of regulations issued by the tsar instructed the Board to further the development of all trade and to ensure that it was carried out in a free and orderly manner, without undue restriction or abuse such as profiteering. But the principal function of the president of the college – the closest approximation to Pososhkóv's 'supreme commander of commerce' – was to promote foreign trade on terms favourable to Russia whilst watching over the security of foreign as well as of native merchants. The tsar, irrespective of his plans (of which more presently) for putting an end to the importation of textiles, went out of his way to induce foreign merchants to settle in St Petersburg. To this end he granted them freedom of movement into and out of Russia, protection from excessive taxation and onerous services, and special juridical status. The application of these safeguards rested with the *Kommérts-kollégiia*.[17]

In St Petersburg the day-to-day dealings between Russian and foreign merchants had long been assisted by the exchange or *Bírzha* established in 1704 as a place where trade contracts could be made through brokers and bills of exchange drawn. Its usefulness was evidently proven because the Regulation of the Board of Civic Administration (*Reglament Glávnogo magistráta*) of 1721 provided for the establishment of exchanges in all principal trading resorts. The original exchange was moved from its rough and ready quarters to a larger building which was replaced by another in 1724. Information about the prices of Russian grain was already available at the *Bírzha* in 1723 when the tsar ordered the regular publication of printed lists showing the prices of local commodities as well as of those current in other European centres of maritime trade.[18]

Pososhkóv does not appear to have heard of the *Bírzha*. His rancour towards foreign traders and his mistrust of them were no doubt exacerbated by the tiresome tendency of the foreigners to adjust the price of their goods to the constantly falling value of the rouble in relation to the rix-dollar and the florin.

The Russian prices cited by Pososhkóv in this chapter, in so far as it has been possible to verify them, correspond roughly with those given elsewhere. In northern and western Europe the movements of the prices of the articles in question do not show the same upward tendency.[19] It is worth noting that Pososhkóv regards the ducat and the rix-dollar as imported goods rather than as means of payment. He returns to the subject of money in Chapter 9.

Pososhkóv is also aware of a connection between the high cost of imported and, for the most part, 'superfluous', goods and the low price of raw materials, in other words, the unfavourable terms on which Russia was trading. At the same time he assumes that all the money spent on expensive imports, whether by individuals or by the government literally disappears from the country, thus diminishing the sum total of its wealth. A loss incurred in this way would, in rational terms, be described as an adverse balance of trade. In the final years of Peter's reign Russia is said to have had a favourable trade balance but its full details are not known. The usually quoted figure of 1,103,300 roubles for 1726 represents no more than the gross excess of the value of exports over imports through Archangel and Petersburg only, to the exclusion of the other Baltic ports and of the whole of Russia's Eastern trade. In the ports newly conquered from Sweden customs duties were charged in accordance with local regulations on goods passing into and out of other parts of the Russian Empire. Riga in particular continued to serve as a centre of two-way trade between its vast White Russian and Ukrainian hinterland (which was partly under Russian and partly under Polish rule) and western Europe. For Riga in 1726 Seménov gives the value of exports as 1,550,000 roubles and that of imports as 540,000 roubles. His balance-sheet does not, as it ought, 200 years after the publication of Sir Thomas Mun's *England's Treasure*, take into account any invisible items or government purchases such as those of the precious metals imported for the Mint duty-free (and presumably therefore not shown in the customs registers). Nor is it known whether any apparent exports were not in fact repayments of debts incurred earlier. If any of these suppositions are justified then the true balance in Russia's favour may well not have been so large in 1726. In earlier years, especially at the height of the Great Northern War when the expense of feeding and clothing troops was incurred abroad, the balance was doubtless such as to account for Pososhkóv's apprehensions and the tsar's counter-measures.[20]

Pososhkóv's disapproval of luxury probably springs from a combination of puritanical frugality, natural or acquired, with the traditional notion that no one should consume more than befits his social status. Each man should know his place in society, show it in his dress and keep it until he is officially allowed to change it. The disquisition on apparel leads Pososhkóv into a digression on the monastic estate which should be treated as a postscript to Chapter 1 (Of the Clergy).

Tsar Peter, too, a man of simple habits, disapproved of conspicuous consumption. His visit to Paris in 1717 convinced him that luxury would be the undoing of France[21] and alerted him to the existence of a similar danger in Russia. His own predilection for the western European way of life had already stimulated in those of his subjects who were able to enjoy the fruits of his victories an appetite for expensive consumer imports. The list is long: tapestries, carpets, furniture, cut glass, silk fabrics, muslin, English cloth, hats, shoes, pipes and tobacco, French and Rhenish wines, tea, fruit, spices, sugar, molasses and lamp oil were all on sale in St Petersburg. The economic consequences, real or imaginary, of this growing demand – overspending by individuals and the efflux of money – were evidently giving rise to anxiety. The use of gold and silver for the ornamentation of dress seems to have caused the tsar especial concern, not only because these precious metals had to be imported but also because they were the cause of unnecessary and excessive spending by individuals. The rot, it seemed, could be prevented by producing some of these goods more cheaply at home whilst restricting the general demand for them. The final point of the Table of Ranks recognizes that the eminence and dignity of rank require the support of appropriate trappings but points out that men may be brought to ruin by living above their rank and role. Each person should therefore have such dress, carriage and livery as his station requires.

This admonition of the tsar's which was to be invoked in the prohibitions of 1740 and 1742 does not differ in its essence from the sumptuary regulations proposed by Pososhkóv who may well have been familiar with the principle propounded by the ecclesiastical synod of 1551: 'Let every one be attired as befits his condition.'[22]

It will be recalled that in 1700 Peter commanded those of his subjects who were living and working in Moscow and in other towns to wear clothes and shoes in the Western style. As the order was repeated at intervals until the end of Peter I's reign, it is evident that it was not obeyed instantly and it would therefore be inaccurate to speak of a sartorial revolution. As well as being gradual, the change was one of appearance rather than substance: the cloth of various kinds which Muscovy had been importing from western Europe since the middle of the sixteenth century was now cut to a pattern more appropriate to its provenance. If Vockerodt is right in maintaining that a 'German' coat required twice as much material as a Russian one – which is surprising because the Muscovite upper garments were long and ample – then perhaps after 1699 the amount of cloth imported for sale to private persons may have risen somewhat. Greater by far was the constant increase in the amount of cloth required for the army which according to Whitworth was reclothed every two years. The cloth was supplied under contract by foreign merchants in return for cash, almost certainly silver, of which the government was constantly short. The remedy lay in making more cloth in Russia. As early as 1712 the tsar decreed that cloth should be manufactured in more than one place in Russia so that within five years no more soldiers' cloth should be imported from overseas.[23] Pososhkóv does not seem to have been aware of this aim. The authorities were also trying as hard as Pososhkóv would have wanted them to, to beat down the foreign, principally English, contractors, but were hindered by the inadequacy of the Russian output and, one may guess, by vested interests of long standing. The production of cloth for civilian wear too was encouraged by the government by means of expensive subsidies in cash or kind. Calamanco was especially favoured and chosen by Pososhkóv himself as the variety to be made in his factory.[24]

The tsar was as anxious as Pososhkóv to effect a reduction in the amount of money spent by individuals on silk fabrics manufactured in the West but was not as ready in his ordinances on the subject to state his reasons, probably for fear of ruffling the foreign merchants engaged in this trade. In a spirit of unbounded optimism engendered in all probability by misleading advice, the tsar in 1719 named 1720 and in 1720, 1721 as the year in which native manufactories, supplemented by imports from Persia and China, would meet the total demand for silk and lamé fabrics in Russia.[25] By that time the silk factory established in 1717 under pressure from the tsar by three grandees, F. M. Apráksin, P. P. Shafírov and P. A. Tolstói, was already in difficulties caused by lack of capital and shortage of raw material. The silk-mill founded in the same year by the merchant M. Evréinov had, by 1722, produced goods to the value of nearly 40,000 roubles of which it had sold only 1,800 roubles' worth. The works set up in 1714 at the prompting of the tsar by A. Ia. Miliútin seem to have fared rather better.[26]

In the last paragraph of this chapter Pososhkóv who, in his *Paternal Testament*, had advised his son to prefer spiritual to temporal treasure and to seek only moderate wealth, abandons all ascetic pretence and wishes for enrichment in this world followed by salvation in the next. It does not occur to him that making the best of both worlds means serving God and Mammon, a propensity of which he considers himself to be innocent.[27]

CHAPTER 4

Of the Merchants

13) The merchants must not be treated as if they were of no account since no
country, whether great or small, can subsist without them. The merchants and
the military work in partnership: the military wage war, the merchants support
them and furnish them with everything necessary.

Therefore unstinting care is due to them. Just as there can be no soul without
a body, so the military cannot do their duty without the merchants. The military
cannot exist without the merchants nor the merchants thrive without the
military.

Now it is true that a realm is enlarged by the actions of the military, yet it is
the merchants who work for its adornment. Therefore the merchants must be
carefully protected from all oppressors so that no harm may be done to them by
the military or any other of the Tsar's servants. There are many people of little
understanding who consider merchants to be of no account, despise them and
treat them badly without good reason yet nowhere in the world is there any
calling to which the merchant is not of some use.

So it behoves us to watch over our merchants, to ensure that they suffer no
harm at the hands of interlopers and equally that they do not harm one another;
further, men of other callings should not on any account be allowed to intrude
into their number or interfere in any way in their affairs. Rather let the
14) merchants trade freely so that they may both prosper themselves and enlarge
this source of His Majesty's revenue.

If our Russian merchants were given freedom in their trade so that they
suffered no kind of interference at the hands of either men of other callings or
the foreigner, then His Majesty's revenue from trade would be of quite another
order. I am convinced that this revenue would be doubled or trebled since, as
things are now, a good half is lost through the actions of interlopers from other
countries.

If anyone but a merchant (be he a councillor of His Majesty, an officer, a
dvorianín, an official, a member of the clergy or a peasant) wishes to engage in
trade let him first relinquish that state and enrol as a merchant; then he may
trade in his own right and not on the sly, and engage in any kind of commerce
he likes, paying all the appropriate taxes and tolls on an equal footing with all
the established merchants. Nor should he then, as now, engage in secret and

illicit transactions, that is, without the approval of an official charged with the supervision of trade, nor withhold any part of the taxes due.

Each estate must conduct itself fittingly so as not to fall into sin before God or commit a fault in the eyes of the Sovereign. Let every man be known for what he really is: if a warrior, then a true warrior; if of some other calling, then let him devote himself wholly to that.

The Lord God Himself said: 'No man can serve two masters.'[1] Hence a warrior (or indeed a person in any walk of life) must conduct himself as befits that calling and not intrude into some other sphere; for if a warrior insinuates himself among the merchants he must needs be false to his profession of arms. Moreover Our Saviour Himself said: 'For where your treasure is there will your heart be also.'[2] And St Paul the Apostle says: 'No man that warreth entangleth himself with the affairs of this life; that he may please him who hath chosen him to be a soldier.'[3] Even among the common people there is current a very similar saying: choose one or the other – either to trade or to make war.

(116)   Therefore a soldier or person of any other calling must not engage in trade; but if he feels so inclined he must enrol himself as a merchant.

Unless steps are taken to remove all those interloping merchants who are properly gentry, civil or military officers or peasants, our merchants can never know true prosperity nor can the revenue from their transactions have any means of increase.

May the Lord God so order things in this land of Russia that all those in authority perform their duties with diligence and refrain from meddling in trade, but rather protect the merchants from interlopers. So also with the military: neither officers nor men should meddle in trade or harm the merchants in any way but rather attend to their own profession of arms. Similarly officials should confine themselves to their proper duties and on no account meddle in trade; craftsmen must make their living by their craft and not thrust themselves into trade; peasants must devote themselves to their own work and not encroach upon that of the merchants. If a peasant has goods worth about a hundred roubles to trade with he must enrol himself on the list of merchants, whatever kind of peasant he may be – whether he belongs to the Sovereign or his consort, the metropolitan[4] or a monastery, a senator or a *dvorianín* – or indeed any other kind. Even if such a peasant is ordered to go on living in the same place as before he must nevertheless no longer till the soil and must cease to count as a peasant. He must count as a merchant, come under the authority of the Board of Civic Administration and either pay the petty imposts[5] as they occur on his own transactions or pay in one sum his proportionate share of the tax due from any one kind of trade: whichever he does he must pay without fail.

Dvoriáne should for their own sakes keep a vigilant eye on their peasants and instruct their factors and headmen on no account to let them dabble in trade

nor remain in unprofitable idleness either in summer or in winter, but always to
17) be about their work. The peasants must not encroach on the sphere of the
merchants by engaging in any trade whatever and likewise their masters must
not engage in any sort of trade.

If a peasant is rich enough let him rent vacant land, sow grain thereon and
sell the surplus crop. But he must not himself buy from other peasants even the
smallest quantity with a view to profit. If he buys even a single *osmína* and
another peasant (or even the seller) reports the matter to the custom-house
then the said illicit dealer shall be fined one hundred *osmíny* and the informer
receive a reward of ten *osmíny*. Likewise, if anyone buys ten *chétverti* to sell
again, he shall be fined one thousand *chétverti* and the informant receive one
hundred *chétverti*.

If any peasant, whoever his master, wishes to engage in trade he should
present himself at the Board of Civic Administration and say: I have goods
worth a hundred or two hundred roubles or more (as the case may be) to trade
with; he may then be enrolled as a merchant as shall be laid down by His
Majesty's ordinance.

If God so order it that men of all callings go diligently about their own
business, then every kind of business will prosper and our merchants will grow
rich to a degree far beyond their present conception of riches. And the revenue
from the taxes on their trade will be not merely double but, I believe, three
times or more what it is at present.

At present there are boyars, *dvoriáne* and their dependants, officers, soldiers
and peasants all engaged in trade which thus escapes tax; moreover, under the
name of such people even the merchants do much business which also evades
tax. It is my belief that at present less than half the true amount of toll is in fact
collected; nor will the full amount ever be collected unless landowners and all
those in His Majesty's service are forbidden to trade altogether, since many
prominent people have a hand in trade and ordinary folk who do the same are
outside the authority of the Board of Civic Administration.

I know for certain that in the district of Nóvgorod alone there are something
18) like a couple of hundred peasants engaged in trade who do not pay a single
farthing in toll. And if the tax-gatherers attempt to collect such dues the
peasants' masters take their part and use force so that these officials go in fear
of their lives and dare not come near these peasants. Some of them are so rich
that they have in their possession goods worth five or six hundred roubles but
do not pay a single farthing to His Majesty. So if all these improvements were to
be put into effect the merchant estate would, as it were, be aroused from sleep.

Most wrong too is the inveterate lack of probity of merchants among themselves, for foreigners and Russians alike cheat one another and display wares
which appear to be of good quality but are bad below the surface. To some
goods of the worst quality they give a spurious look of excellence and thus sell

them at a higher price than is right. By such deceitful practices they cause great loss to gullible customers, cheating them as they do over weight and measure and price. But they do not consider such cheating a sin; their dishonest ways do great harm to the innocent.

In the long run these dishonest merchants come to grief through their dishonesty and fall into greater poverty, and so everyone suffers. Whereas if the honesty which befits Christians were to prevail among our merchants, wares of good quality would be sold as such, and similarly those of moderate or bad quality as such, and the true and proper price asked according to the quality of the goods, as determined for any particular article. Far from receiving an excessive price for anything no merchant would even ask it; he would cheat neither the old nor the young nor the ignorant but always act with perfect honesty in all matters. If this were so God's grace would shine forth on the merchant estate and His blessing would be upon them and their trade be hallowed.

To ensure such constant and unchanging just dealing among our merchants all markets should be provided with official overseers of different grades.[6] The office of the chief official or *sótskii* should have a round, whitewashed board set above the door, with the legend 'SÓTSKII' so that all can see it. The offices of the lower officials should have a similar board so that customers who have bought goods may know where to have them verified, to see whether the seller gave them good weight or measure and whether the right price was asked for goods of that quality.

If a seller asked a price above what was right he must be fined ten or twenty kopecks for every kopeck in excess and be punished with the rod or whip so that he will not do it again. But should he do the same again his fine and punishment shall be double. But if any person gives short weight or short measure, palms off goods other than those which the customer had chosen or sells bad quality for good, he shall incur more severe punishment and be fined ten times the value of the goods.

If overseers of any of the three grades condone any such irregularity on the part of a seller they shall be fined respectively ten times, fifty times or a hundred times the value of the goods and be given as many strokes of the knout as shall be laid down by the law.

The officials of the two higher grades shall be given the strictest instructions and warnings to keep unfailing watch on their subordinates and thus ensure that the latter do not condone any sharp practices among the merchants under their control, nor show any favour or put any temptations in their way[7] but avoid like the plague anything of the kind lest it reach the ears of higher authority. These subordinate officials must inspect all their shops to see that no inferior merchandise is made to appear good, but sold for what it really is – good as good, fair as fair, and bad as bad. They must ensure that all weighing and

(119)

measuring is exact;[8] that no one adds to or demands anything over and above the correct price for any article, but that the price demanded corresponds to its true worth. Also foreign materials, viz. woollen and silk stuffs and brocades, must be measured off and sold beginning with the outer end of the bolt and not from the inside.[9]

(120)   Every customer, whoever he may be – rich or poor, informed or ignorant – is entitled to the same fair dealing. Merchants must not accept, still less demand, a single kopeck in excess whether the sum in question is one or ten roubles.

In the interest of perfect fairness it would be no bad thing that there should be prescribed prices for every kind of merchandise, whether sold by weight or by length, so that in a market the price would be just the same in the last shop as in the first.

When a fine is imposed on anyone for any misdemeanour the overseer should not put off its collection until some other day; the offender must pay at the time of the offence. And all such fines must upon receipt be entered in the official register, and once a month the total sum collected must be forwarded to the appropriate office. No quantity of goods, great or small, should be sold to foreigners at fairs without permission from the official charged with the supervision of trade. If any dare to sell to foreigners any article whatsoever, even if its value is only one rouble, without the permission of the said supervisor, he shall be fined a hundredfold (one hundred roubles for one) and suffer as many strokes of the knout as shall be laid down, so that he may remember not to do the same again in future.

No one, be he rich or poor, should be allowed to send Russian goods abroad by sea or by land until a price has been set upon them with the permission of such supervisor and by common consent of the merchants concerned, thus ensuring that no one is treated unfairly.

When a foreigner agrees to buy a large or small quantity of Russian goods all the Russian merchants, whether rich or poor, should contribute to the quantity to be supplied, in proportion to their stock-in-trade, in such a way that no one shall be treated unfairly, be he rich or poor. But if any person does not desire to

121)   part with some of his stock when the sale of only a small quantity is in view, he may be allowed to do as he pleases. In this way all merchants will act together in amicable agreement and none will be able to offer a lower price than the rest. If a certain price is set upon an article by common consent foreigners will have to buy at that price, however unwillingly. But if the foreigners do not agree to buy our merchandise at the fixed price and try to have it reduced, then our rich merchants should themselves buy up all these goods from their fellows of smaller means. If the said merchants cannot buy up such goods for ready money the money should be advanced to them by the *Rátusha*[10] and they may then disperse. They should not bring any more of this kind of merchandise for sale until further orders, even if they have to wait for two or three years or more;

they should occupy themselves with some other business until such time as this trade is resumed with the foreigners. As long as foreign buyers will not accept our merchandise at the fixed price such goods should on no account be offered to foreigners, however small the quantity.

If the foreign merchants who try to force ours to fall in with their wishes (that is to say, will not entertain a higher price for our merchandise nor lower the price of theirs) break off negotiations and return home without buying, they must take away with them all the merchandise they have brought for sale. Unless an agreement has been reached they should not be permitted to unload and store it in warehouses even if they are willing to pay the storage charges two or three times over; nor should they be permitted to deposit their merchandise in any private homes. If they will not take our goods there is no object in their leaving theirs here; let them take them back to where they came from.

If they come again the next season we ought to add ten per cent (or twelve per cent, or whatever His Majesty may decree) to the price of our merchandise compared with that fixed the year before, to the advantage of our merchants and

(122)   to ensure that they do not lose any money. If the foreigners do not appear for two years the price must be increased again by as much as for the first year. And so for every year that they persist in their obstinacy the same percentage shall be added. Not the slightest concession shall be made in order that the capital invested in this merchandise may not lie dormant for the merchants but earn interest year by year. Even if, through the obduracy of the foreigners, the price of our own goods rises with all the added percentages to double the original price fixed, no concession shall be made; this price must thenceforward be adhered to by reason of their stubbornness.

Should the foreigners later relent and bring us their merchandise as before and bid for ours, nothing whatever shall be taken off the increased prices of our goods: they must be offered thenceforward at the higher price since the increase is entirely due to the foreigners' stubbornness. If they are unwilling to pay more for our goods they will remain with their own goods on their hands, whereas we, thanks be to God, are able to survive without theirs. But I believe that, for all their ingenuity in commercial and all other civil affairs, once they are aware of our merchants' inflexible rule on the matter of increased prices, they will not allow the price to double itself but agree to trade every year. Seeing our inflexibility they will abandon, however unwillingly, their habitual obstinacy and arrogance; for 'necessity knows no law'. As for us, even if they did not offer us any of their goods at all we could still survive, whereas they cannot last even for ten years without ours. That is why we must keep the whip hand over them, and they will have to be our obedient servants and treat us in all matters with deference instead of arrogance. Is it not then strange that they should come here with their trash and try to put a low price on our commodities which are essential to them, but for

(123)   theirs charge double what they are worth and sometimes more?

Nor is this all: they even presume to decide the value of our great Monarch's money, which should not concern them in any way. Let them rather decide the value of the money of their own monarchs, seeing that they exercise rule over their own rulers! Whereas our Emperor is his own master and if he so order in his own realm that a one-kopeck piece shall count as a ten-kopeck piece, it shall be so.[11] In this country His Majesty's authority empowers us to determine the price of imported merchandise. If the foreigners do not like it they need not sell at that price. A foreign merchant is free to agree to sell or not; we shall not take away his goods by force. But we can insist on refusing storage on shore for unsold or unsuitable goods; let them be taken back or kept on board.

It is high time that they gave up the arrogance which they have shown up to now. It was bad enough treating us in a high-handed manner in the days when our rulers did not personally concern themselves with trade but all was left in the hands of the boyars. In those times the foreigners who came here would slip a present of a couple of hundred roubles to persons of influence and make a profit of a million on a hundred roubles, since the boyars did not care a straw about the merchants and were quite ready to exchange the whole lot of them for a brass farthing. But now, thanks be to God, our Sovereign has looked into all this; foreigners can no longer use such underhand means for having things all their own way and to their own advantage.

So if foreign merchants in their obstinacy refuse to trade with us for two or three years (or even half a dozen) our merchants will reap an incalculable profit therefrom because foreign goods which used to cost a rouble here in Russia will now stand at half a rouble or less, whereas the price fixed for foreign buyers may on no account be reduced because of their obduracy, since the said price was so fixed precisely because of their intractability.

(124)   The foreigners have priced their own merchandise unreasonably high and thereby done us great wrong. As for the wrong done to them, that is not our fault but the fault of their own stubbornness. For this they have blamed our money, which is no concern of theirs. If our money goes to their country and no one there will accept a kopeck even at half its value, what is that to us? They are masters in their own house but here they have no power whatever; authority resides in our Monarch and by his gracious will we enjoy some freedom of action. Yet they have come here and by undervaluing our money have caused the price of all their own goods to increase. The gold ducat used to fetch 110 kopecks but now stands at two roubles; the rix-dollar[12] used to fetch fifty-four kopecks but now stands at eighty. A pood of copper formerly stood at three roubles but now stands at seven or eight; of tin, at a little over three roubles but now at more than six. Sulphur used to cost half a rouble the pood but now sells at three times as much. A ream of writing paper, formerly at eighty kopecks, now sells at two roubles. A crate of window glass could once be bought for three roubles but has now gone up to ten. The foreigners have doubled or trebled the

prices of all their goods and thereby hope to reduce Russia to poverty. Moreover, they make light of us by offering various liquors instead of essential commodities, and recommend them as 'most admirable and desirable'. They hope that by heeding such persuasive talk we shall buy more of them and thus part with more money. But what do we get out of this? We drink the stuff and pass it through or spew it out.

Again, we import glassware which we shall only break and throw away if we buy it. If we ourselves were to set up half a dozen glass works we could easily supply all foreign countries with the glassware they need. Therefore it behoves us to have a care what we are about so as not to be taken in by all this foreign talk. Whatever trash foreigners bring they strain every nerve to puff its merits in order to induce us to buy more from them. They are up to all kinds of tricks: they bring over their own bottled beer and sell it here at thirty kopecks a bottle,

(125)   whereas we could offer the same bottle at two or three kopecks.

Whether a high price is set on our goods or the reverse is entirely the will of our Sovereign: his decision shall be irrevocable.

It is most important that our merchants accept foreign merchandise only on terms which have received common approval and under the authority of the supervisor of trade, not as heretofore as each may decide for himself. Only those goods shall be accepted which are sound and of good quality: poor stuff must not be accepted. Our merchants should divide the goods purchased among themselves in proportion to their stock-in-trade by general and amicable agreement, so that no one is in any way unfairly treated.

If the foreigners try to add a surcharge to the price of such selected merchandise, none is to be accepted at the increased price but only at the appropriate price as agreed before the selection. If they will not give way and let the said merchandise go at this agreed price, we must refuse to proceed: let them take all their goods back. Inferior or useless merchandise must not on any account be accepted even at half-price lest they rate us as fools and jeer at us for getting the worst of the bargain.

Above all we must not buy either liquor which is merely drunk and passed through or vessels which get broken and thrown away. Glassware is something which we can very well export rather than import.[13] All kinds of goods which are fragile or spoil easily, such as foreign fabric-covered buttons, ought not to be taken even at half-price, since a person will need two or three sets of such buttons during the time that he wears a particular garment. Rather we should purchase strong brass buttons which are not soldered with tin (or, better still, not soldered at all) and are mounted on wooden moulds or else silvered pewter

(126)   buttons on tin shells. Likewise if instead of steel buttons anyone imports for sale buttons of pewter with a high content of bismuth, these should not be accepted either because they are too brittle. Only the most durable kinds must be taken which will outlast two or three garments: for example, black glass ones with

strong iron eyes are acceptable because they are most serviceable, do not tear the cloth, are very hard-wearing in use and not expensive. If they are made with really strong eyes they will outlast five or six garments in succession.

So also with all kinds of merchandise – the greatest care must be taken to see that it is durable. All kinds of silk brocades of durable quality may be accepted but those sorts which are made of inferior raw silk, such as certain damasks, satins and other silk fabrics, should not be accepted even at half-price, however patterned, and it must be forbidden for anyone to make garments of such stuffs because to do so is merely to throw money away.

No silk or for that matter woollen goods which are not sound and durable in wear – for example, stockings and certain other silk garments which do not last – should ever be accepted. Likewise ribbons which are very thin and of bad quality ought not to be accepted even if they are cheap, but only those which are strong: even if more expensive they will wear well. No ribbons ornamented with gold and silver tinsel should be accepted, as they are worthless and merely a waste of money.

Likewise we ought not to buy kerchiefs of Western or Persian silk fabric because they are nothing but a waste of money, being neither serviceable nor necessary. You have to give a rouble or a rouble and a half for one and use up two or three in a single year and as many the next year; a man of fashion will run through fifty such kerchiefs in ten years. Even at a rouble a piece he will have spent fifty roubles. Twenty or thirty thousand roubles a year are lost to our realm on such frippery. Linen is much more practical than silk for wiping the face or the nose. To use silk kerchiefs is nothing but to indulge one's vanity and to line the pockets of the foreigner. So if an embargo were put on silk kerchiefs they would cease to be in demand and everyone would continue to use linen ones as heretofore.

27)

We cannot expect foreigners to encourage us to live carefully and without waste; they naturally cry up anything which will bring them, but not us, a profit. Not only do they enrich themselves and their like through all their sharp practices but also drive us further towards poverty. Therefore it behoves us to be fully cognizant of all their ways, whether in commercial transactions, military affairs or matters of craftsmanship. We must not be gulled by their specious words but judge them by their deeds and that with a most watchful eye.

In all cases where a commodity is to be found in Russia we must be content to use our own and on no account to buy from abroad even at half the price – I mean such things as salt, iron, needles, mirrors, spectacles, window glass, hats, turpentine, glassware, children's toys, yellow and red ochre, green earth and Olónets clay.[14] Nor do I think that we need to import cloth for military uniforms: even if our Russian soldiers' cloth should be more expensive than the foreign, at least there is no drain of money out of the country. Therefore in this matter too we ought to rely on our own products so that the money may stay in

Russia. It is the duty not only of those who direct our commerce but also of all other servants of His Majesty to ensure that no purchases are made abroad of anything which is neither really necessary nor durable, but that we only buy those things which are durable and not obtainable here and which are indispensable to us. It is not with silk brocades that we should adorn ourselves but with honesty and education and Christian virtues and mutual love and un-
(128)   shakeable constancy, both in the exercise of our pure Christian faith and in all other matters. So adorned we shall be glorious not only on earth but also in Heaven.

Here is another thing very wrong with our merchants. If any person builds a fine residence for the use of himself and his family and runs into debt in doing so, his neighbours and associates take it amiss and procure the imposition of all sorts of heavy taxes and services on him instead of being the more well-disposed and grateful towards him for erecting a barrier to their advantage against the spread of fire and at the same time adding to the adornment of our country; this can only be called diabolical hatred. Rather should such a man be granted exemptions because he has stretched himself too far in building his house; yet instead of lightening his burden his neighbours do their best to ruin him.

In my opinion it would be a good thing for His Majesty to confirm by ordinance that anyone who builds himself a town residence shall be granted certain exemptions from tax for a term of five or six years or more. And during this period he shall not be chosen for any public service so as to give him time to put his affairs in order again and so that others, seeing this, may also be encouraged to build themselves houses.

Nor is it right, in my view, that many artisans and traders should dress in a style above their degree and their wives and children even more elaborately, wasting their substance through such ostentation. Here too I believe it would be wise to decree that each calling should have its own distinctive dress: artisans and trades-people, and likewise the merchants, should have their own, quite different from that of persons in His Majesty's military or civil employ. At present there is no way of telling from his dress to what station a person belongs, whether he is a townsman, an official, a gentleman or a bondman. Nor can one always tell such people apart from soldiers or even from His Majesty's commissaries. It would surely be a good thing if one could tell the station of one civilian from that of another by his dress, not only civilians from soldiers and commissaries.[15]

(129)   Merchants of the highest rank – those with property valued at between a thousand and ten thousand roubles – should wear coats of the crimson cloth which sells[16] at two roubles or more the arshin, and vests of various silk brocades but excluding any that are figured or spangled. Such people shall not be permitted to dress even their children in figured brocades. They should wear

silver-gilt buttons. Gold and silver braid and piping, and fabric-covered buttons should on no account be permitted even on their children's dress. As over-garment, all merchants should (I think) wear a coat reaching to the knee so that it will be longer than those worn in His Majesty's military service but shorter than that of the clergy. They should wear breeches of cloth or velvet[17] but on no account of any silk fabric. They must wear boots; on no account must they wear shoes. Their summer headgear shall be hats (which must be worn even if of fur); but they must not roll the brim after the manner of the military. Their winter headgear shall be caps with bands of fox or glutton fur, but on no account of sable. (Sable caps may be worn only by the chartered merchants engaged in foreign trade and by members of merchants' corporations[18] who own property worth more than ten thousand roubles.)

The middle ranks who own property worth between a hundred and a thousand roubles should wear coats of English cloth (at about one rouble[19] the arshin), vests of cotton or woollen cloth with buttons of solid silver or silvered copper.[20] In the summer they should wear straight-brimmed hats, in winter caps of fox and beaver fur but of a shape distinct from that of the superior rank, and be shod with boots.

And merchants of the lowest rank, who own property worth between ten and a hundred roubles, should dress in Russian cloth dyed blue or some other colour, either felted or not; but it must be dyed – undyed cloth is to be worn by handworkers and peasants.

30) Though such regulation of dress may seem to some a trivial matter I think it is important. In the first place it makes each calling distinct and so each person will know his station; secondly, it will prevent any undue expense among persons of each calling; thirdly, our country will benefit no little from it. Such a sumptuary regulation of dress will be, I imagine, hotly opposed by the for-eigners because their market for silk stuffs will be greatly reduced. In all this it shall be as His Majesty may determine. Each rank of merchants should receive its separate rules not only as to material but also as to cut, and the rules should be strict and unalterable for the future. Therefore they should be backed by fines and warnings that no one may be tempted to overstep his limits.

If any merchant has property worth a thousand roubles or more he should not demean himself but, rendering thanks unto God, should wear the dress appropriate to his degree. There are many people nowadays who have two or three thousand roubles yet go about in a grey coat, and conversely some with less than a hundred roubles who dress as if they had a thousand. It is only proper that those whose means are small should not indulge in vainglory but each man know his place.

If any man who is worth more than a thousand roubles does not wear the dress appropriate to the station of his fellows and anyone reports this (knowing what he is really worth) an inventory shall be made of all his property. And if it amounts to two or three thousand roubles he may keep two or three hundred, seeing that that was the rank which he preferred for himself, and all the excess over and above this shall be confiscated on behalf of His Majesty and the informant rewarded with one tenth part of the surplus. But if the inventory shows a total of only a little above a thousand roubles no penalty need be exacted for a discrepancy up to three hundred roubles, nor shall the informant receive any reward. But when the excess amounts to five hundred roubles or more the whole of this sum or even

(131) rather more shall be confiscated on behalf of His Majesty and the owner shall keep his thousand roubles or whatever lesser sum remains.

Again, if any man has clothes made for himself appropriate to a higher degree than his own, they shall (on information received) be taken away from him and given to the person who denounced the wearer of inappropriate garments. And the culprit must be punished to discourage him and others from doing the like again and from reducing his own means thereby. This may not be an important matter yet will considerably further the enrichment of our country, for no one will indulge in any wasteful expense.

If our great Sovereign determine the matter in this sense, severe fines and warnings must back up the regulation to make sure that everyone wears his prescribed dress not only in his place of residence but on journeys as well.

If anyone dons the clothes appropriate to a rank other than his own he shall be severely punished; moreover, if his conduct arouses suspicion a formal inquiry must be set on foot. In particular if it is a case of peasants who dress themselves up as boyars' retainers or even as gentlemen or as soldiers, then it is evident that they are trying to escape to a less toilsome life or to a life of brigandage.

It would be as well to regulate this matter of apparel in such a way that not only the outer garment but also the clothing underneath down to the very shirt shall be distinguishable and indicate a person's calling. Given such regulation men of every rank will be recognizable and no one will be able to lie his way into a different one; this should also, it seems to me, help to diminish disorderly behaviour. For there are many about nowadays who have assumed military dress and roam the streets doing as they please and no one dares to restrain them, supposing them to be genuine soldiers. The worst are those who disguise themselves as men of the Preobrazhénskii or Semënovskii regiments and by their behaviour bring disrepute on those who are in fact serving in them. Whereas, if all callings were to be so distinguished, anyone who behaved in a disorderly manner would at least disgrace only his own kind and it would also be easy to track down the culprit. It would also be desirable to introduce distinctive badges for all infantry and dragoon regiments so that it may be immediately apparent to what regiment any soldier (foot or mounted) belongs.

(132) Should it appear too difficult to make a regulation for all callings, it should at least become possible to distinguish between master and man in any passer-by. However, all this shall be as the will of God and of His Imperial Majesty may

determine. But it is most important to ensure that no one should wear[21] apparel or display ornaments thereon appropriate to a degree above his own.

Above all, it is unfitting that monks should wear silk garments, and most inappropriate that their cassocks should be of any kind of silk or satin. For they have renounced this world and all that is therein and it is fitting that everything worldly should be alien to them. They are living corpses – living only in God but dead in the eyes of the world. Therefore it behoves them to avoid even the slightest elaboration in their apparel, indeed to eschew any kind of secular adornment in all things; rather it behoves them to adorn themselves with holy living and all virtues, especially with humility and renunciation of the world that lies beyond the confines of their monasteries. Their calling imposes on them the wearing of the plainest possible garments of wollen cloth; the cut of the habit should be as simple as a sack and innocent of all ornament. Their undergarments should similarly be of the humblest material, that is sheep's wool, and on no account of sable, marten, fox or miniver. For throughout Russia monks spend something like twenty or thirty thousand roubles a year on such luxury, an expense which is quite unwarranted. It is not an ornament to our country nor will the world be any the better therefor; it is mere vainglory and a lure to loose women. There is nothing but sinfulness in such adornment.

I do not know the opinions of others on this matter but I am of the opinion that, far from dressing in silk, monks should not even have silk trimmings on their garments. A monk is one who is dead to the world. Further, they must on no account indulge in intoxicating liquor nor mix with the laity nor act as stewards of monastic estates. Rather let their life be confined to their monasteries and their churches. Let them not adorn their cells with any ornaments. It is also advisable that the timber of their cell walls should be left rough and that they should not keep young boys there, still less their own children.

A monk's life must be ordered quite differently. A monk has neither father nor mother, nor children nor relations; he is devoted wholly to God. He should not eat food that is too liberally sweetened or spiced or fried in much fat. On special occasions the rule may be relaxed and a small amount of butter used, but not so much as to make the food rich; likewise in the matter of intoxicating drink a very small quantity may be permitted but not enough to induce any feeling of inebriation. A monk should continually be at prayer or at work or engaged in contemplation. He must live in such a way that he be wholly in God and that God be continually in him. He should not only avoid eating rich food and indulging in meat (after the manner of the Lutherans) but also avoid fish except on permitted days. For all such things are part of the secular world, not of the monastery. When fish is permitted, the fish should not be prepared with much fat or spice but be cooked plainly; it is not in the least necessary to use any kind of condiment except salt. A monastery is a place of hardship and privation, not of luxury; that is why the monastic life is called angelic, since monks divide their time between singing the services and observing the Rule in their cells and are thus constantly engaged in fasting, prayer and contemplation.

The head of a monastery should be bound by the same rules of work and self-denial as all the other monks. He should eat the same food as all the brethren, from the senior monks on his council to the junior monks engaged in menial tasks, for this is the essence of the true coenobitic life. Likewise all must wear the same garments, unadorned, one in no particular differing from another. So let them labour in their monastery so that no visitor can tell what the rank of any monk may be.

(134)   When Christ lived on earth His raiment was (for our edification) without adornment nor had He any change of raiment; but having just one garment Himself He enjoined His disciples to follow His example. Christ also asked for plain food without flavouring. For when He entered into a certain village to visit the sisters of Lazarus, Mary sat down at Jesus' feet hearkening to His words, while Martha busied herself with preparing meat for Christ and serving it. And the Lord commended Mary who troubled not about the meat but sat and listened to His words, but to Martha He said: 'Martha, thou art careful and troubled about many things: but one thing is needful.'[22] What is this one thing needful? Manifestly He bade her provide just enough to satisfy. So also monks should only be provided with just enough to satisfy; let them not eat to excess that they may not feel heavy. Nor should they have any personal possessions whatever.

Living such a life they may be accounted true followers of Christ, inasmuch as they indulge in nothing for themselves but cleave only unto God, are continually engaged in fasting and prayer, eat no meat and deny themselves all comfort; and as Christ lived, so do they order their lives. Moreover, their life is without women, and indeed many of them are virgins; therefore it is most right and proper for them to be accounted true followers of Christ.

As for the Lutherans, I do not know on what grounds they can be called true followers of Christ. They live in bestial fashion, not in accordance with the Gospels, eating meat like dumb animals or the ignorant Mordvá. Not merely have they no right to give themselves such an exalted name but it is scarcely seemly for them to call themselves men; rather it would be just and proper to call them swine and their manner of life swinish and unchristian.

For the general benefit of the people not only the monks but also the merchants must be restrained from drunkenness and luxurious living. Above all the merchants must be dissuaded from indulging in foreign liquors: they must neither drink them themselves nor give them as gifts to others. I think that it would be as well to forbid all servants of the Tsar, civil and military – indeed all men of all callings – to touch foreign liquors and waste their money on them.

(135)   Those who want to make merry can do so well enough with beverages made in

Russia. Thus they would not spend so much money on liquor and better still not fall into the bad habit of drinking liquor imported from abroad. If anyone is giving a banquet, even for highly placed personages, let there not be so much as a whiff of foreign wines and spirits in the air. I make an exception of tobacco. It would, however, be well to introduce the cultivation and preparation of tobacco as it is done in foreign parts so that no money need leave Russia to pay for tobacco either. Instead let us regale one another with those things with which God has favoured our own land.

It is quite proper that resident foreigners should keep stocks of their own foreign liquors in their homes and offer such without payment to anyone they wish – as Rhenish, Alicante or Hungarian wines. But if a foreigner tries to sell them in the way of trade, he should, irrespective of quantity, be fined a hundredfold the value, and the rest of the stock found in his possession should be confiscated on behalf of His Majesty. Conversely, if a Russian invites foreigners to his house he should offer them Russian liquors and on no account spend even a small sum of money on foreign ones. Foreign wines and spirits should be bought only by senators and other close counsellors of His Majesty – that is, our richest men – but yet in moderation, that the expense may not be unduly great. This restriction may of course be set aside if anyone receives His Majesty in person; in the Tsar's presence the law is suspended. Foreign liquors merely pander to our vanity; they harm our prosperity and undermine our health. To pay for them we allow to pass out of Russia gold ducats and silver dollars and various commodities which the foreigners must have. In this way they add to their own wealth whereas we receive from abroad stuff fit only to be passed through or poured away; sometimes it may even make us vomit, harm our health and cut short our lives.

Yet God, in blessing, blessed us, the Russian people, with corn, and honey and a sufficiency of all good things to drink. We have different kinds of spirits beyond compute. We have excellent beer and admirable mead of the highest quality and purity, which are no whit inferior to Rhenish wines, indeed much better than the common sorts of Rhenish. We also have beverages flavoured with sweet cherries, raspberries, blackcurrants, blackberries and apples, including *karázin*[23] and flavoured mead.[24]

If, then, foreign liquors were not allowed in and orders were given to make our own mead of various kinds and flavours for sale in our inns, more liquor would be made than is at present imported.

Further, if tobacco manufactories were to be established here, we should, in order to ensure their good management and that the tobacco should be quite as good as that which we import, engage a master of this craft from abroad to teach us the right method. In this way we could produce enough tobacco to be able to send it abroad by shiploads. If we grew tobacco in Russia it would not cost more than one kopeck a pound, whereas foreign tobacco costs over thirty kopecks a

6)

pound. We have plenty of land suitable for its cultivation and this could be extended so as to yield a million roubles in revenue. We have a great deal of the kind of land on which it thrives; we could grow it in the country about all the downstream towns, especially Simbírsk, Samára, Pénza, Ínsar, Lómov, Mtsensk and Sarátov, Tsarítsyn, Astrakhan and Vorónezh, and also all about Kiev. In those districts one could get a yearly crop of a million poods.

If the cultivation of tobacco[25] were introduced and extended in Russia all the money that at present goes abroad to buy it would remain at home; and if we come to export it ourselves, then money will flow in to us from abroad.

If the culture of tobacco is established in Russia it follows that, whatever quantity of Russian liquors a man may drink and of home-made tobacco he may smoke, no part of the money he pays for that will leave the country; buying foreign liquors is tantamount to flinging money into the sea. However, in my opinion it is better to fling money into the sea than suffer it to go abroad to buy
(137)   foreign liquors. Someone will recover all the money from the water, but the money that has gone abroad to pay for the liquors will never come back to us but is lost for ever to the country.

In the interests of the prosperity of this realm all other foreign goods too must be bought with circumspection; only those should be bought which are quite indispensable. As for all their foreign gewgaws and gimcracks, they may keep them, lest riches be drained out of Russia to no purpose. We must be deaf to the insidious blandishments and all the boastfulness of the foreigners. We must keep our heads and buy from them only what is necessary for and advantageous to the prosperity of this realm; all things which bring us no advantage or which are not durable must on no account be purchased. It would be best to arrange for foreign merchants arriving at St Petersburg, Riga, Narva or Archangel to sell their merchandise before unloading it, whether in large parcels or small, but in any case before unloading; they should not be allowed to unload the cargo into yards or warehouses until the transactions have been concluded and all the duties paid. Thus such goods as shall not have been sold (whether because we did not require them or because they were offered at too high a price) can be taken away again without ever being unloaded. On no account must they be kept in this country.

If this were done foreigners would become much more friendly towards us and give up their present arrogant ways. We must be mightily determined to break the spirit of pride in them once and for all and bring them to a sense of due humility, so that it is they who are courting our favour, not we theirs. If we can insist that they shall not store their unsold merchandise in our warehouses they will become much more eager to sell, duty will be paid in full on all the goods and they will no longer keep up the practice of deferring payment.
(138)   It would be a good thing to ensure that all merchants help one another and do not allow any of their fellows to fall into penury. If they cannot put him on his

feet again with their own money, let him be granted a loan at interest from the revenues collected by the *Rátusha*[26] as his trade may require, so that no one engaged in trade may fall into poverty through any personal misfortune.

If all these things are so arranged for our merchants they will never be impoverished but year by year will prosper in their affairs and God in blessing will bless them for such brotherly love and will give them abundance in all things and salvation for their souls.

CHAPTER 5. Of the Craftsmen

Commentary

Need for improvement in the quality of native craftsmanship. – Apprenticeship in pre-Petrine Russia. – Guilds established in 1721. Their purpose administrative rather than vocational. – The craftsmen of Moscow and St Petersburg. – The ordinance of 1722 on craft guilds. – Foreign master craftsmen prized for their skills. – Invention neither encouraged nor protected. – The rules of icon painting. A superintendent for the reformation of religious painting appointed (1707). The ordinance of 1722 on this subject. – Pososhkóv's near-heterodox views on the style of icon painting. – The production and exportation of hemp and flax textiles. – Small private producers. Official control of the size of fabrics. The output of linen and canvas manufactories. Jan Tames's manufactory. His protectionist memorandum. The provisions of the tariff of 1724 concerning linen and canvas. – The value of the exports of hemp and flax higher than that of the products made from these materials. – Pososhkóv, the state-aided manufacturer. – The shortage of factory labour. Official restrictions placed on its mobility. – The use of women prisoners as factory hands. – Peter I and Pososhkóv on pauperism. – The cost of imported dyes. Prospecting for natural dyes encouraged. – The search for sulphur by Pososhkóv and others. – Petroleum. – Foreign doctors and apothecaries.

A further prerequisite of Russia's general enrichment, Pososhkóv asserts, is an improvement in the quality of native craftsmanship. No economic argument is advanced to support this view but we may guess that Pososhkóv, the home-made mercantilist, wanted to replace costly imports with products which could be made more cheaply and more profitably at home. The point which Pososhkóv does make is that if Russian craftsmen were properly trained in their skills, they could prosper as their foreign counterparts now do in their own countries and, he implies, in Russia. He therefore proposes that a new central authority be established to assume responsibility for the training and certification of apprentices. Pososhkóv looks to the tsar to meet this need by establishing official bodies whose function would be similar to that which the craft guilds of western Europe had performed in their heyday when they supervised the training of apprentices and exercised strict control over the quality of the goods produced by their members.

In Russia, before 1722, the only organization of craftsmen to bear any resemblance to a guild or corporation was that of the icon painters employed by the Armoury (*Oruzhéinaia Paláta*) in the Kremlin. The proficiency of the younger artists was periodically tested by their seniors who placed them in grades corresponding to their accomplishments.[1] Apprenticeship in the primitive form of domestic pupillage appears to have originated earlier and to have been fairly common in a variety of trades in later seventeenth-century Moscow. The relationship rested on a contract between the parents of the apprentice and the master as provided for in the *Code* of 1649.[2]

Peter I was fully aware of the need to bring about an improvement in the areas of production covered by this chapter. His determination to introduce into Russia a social organization copied from that of the cities of western Europe may be seen in his enactments relating to the government and activities of the urban population. The tsar first made a note of guilds as a matter in need of attention as early as 1715, but it was not until 1721 that Chapter 7 of the Regulation of the *Glávnyi Magistrát* (Board of Civic Administration) divided the inhabitants of towns into guilds or categories and decreed that each art and craft should have its own corporation or association of artisans, headed by aldermen, and its own book of statutes, rights and privileges.[3] The creation of autonomous and privileged corporations would, however, have been incompatible with the nature and purpose of the service state; the true object of this section of the Regulation was to establish an official body which would enable the authorities to exercise tighter fiscal and physical control over an as yet ill-defined and elusive social group which had barely taken root either in the old or in the new capital.

In Moscow the number of artisans registered in 1726 as members of corporations was 6,885. Of these about 3,973 (or 57.7 per cent) were newcomers from the country who had set up as shoemakers, tailors, furriers, carpenters, chandlers, victuallers, blacksmiths and goldsmiths. Of that number about 1,839 (or 46.3 per cent) were peasants on leave of absence granted by their masters or landlords. All were in a small way of business, with average earnings of perhaps not more than 5 or 6 roubles a year. St Petersburg towards the end of the reign of Peter had 2,500 registered artisans in private, as opposed to state, employment, including an unknown residue of the 1,417 craftsmen who had been forcibly transferred to the new capital from Moscow in 1711. Whether the ordinance of 27 April 1722 on craft guilds was intended to compel all craftsmen to join a corporation is not clear. The text contains an ambiguity: the interpolation which speaks of voluntary membership and forbids compulsion could be taken to refer either to foreign craftsmen only or to all craftsmen. The tenor of the four ordinances on the same subject promulgated later in the year indicates that, irrespective of the original intention, the final decision was in favour of compulsory membership.[4]

The prime and declared purpose of the ordinance of 1722 was to bring about an improvement in the poor quality of workmanship. The corporations were to admit members upon approval of their qualifications as master craftsmen and to issue testimonials to that effect to those who had been thus enrolled. It was the duty of the corporations to watch over the quality of the goods produced by all craftsmen, irrespective of whether they were or were not members of corporations, ensuring that the work of each and every one was done with the necessary degree of skill. Goods ready for sale were to bear the mark of the craftsman who made them, as well as the mark of approbation stamped by an alderman of the corporation. No goods were to be sold which were not branded in this way and aldermen who stamped shoddy goods were threatened with dire punishment. Goods which were not fit to be stamped were to be destroyed. It must be inferred from Pososhkóv's obvious ignorance of these regulations that they remained a dead letter. Master craftsmen were allowed to take on any number of apprentices (provided they were furnished with attestations showing that they were not runaways) for a term of at least seven years at the end of which they were to undergo examinations and receive certificates 'as in foreign lands'. Corporations (*tsékhi*) were to be established without delay in St Petersburg and Moscow and later also in other towns. These instructions were duly carried out but it is doubtful whether Pososhkóv had the time to judge such effect as they may have had.

The dearth of native master craftsmen must have been considerable since article 10 of the Regulation of the *Manufaktúr-kollégiia* of 1723 implies that 'the good and skilled' masters to be employed in works and manufactories were foreigners almost by definition. The same article requires them to train Russians and bring them to perfection so that in future they might work as master craftsmen themselves and that their products might redound to the fame of Russian industry.[5] From 1720 the contracts concluded on behalf of the Russian government with Dutch specialists obliged them to impart their skills to Russian apprentices or workmen.[6] Invention did not receive official encouragement, nor were inventors protected in Petrine Russia. Pososhkóv's suggestions in this connection show that he had a precise notion of the nature of patents of monopoly and their application in western Europe.[7]

For a man as deeply religious as Pososhkóv the icon, being both a vehicle of grace and an object of veneration, was the most precious product of human skill. As such it demanded the attention of qualified craftsmen working in accordance with traditional rules. As the mass medium of the Orthodox religion icons came under the scrutiny of the authorities and Pososhkóv was not alone in finding fault with the icons that were being produced at that time. The qualifications, or the lack of qualifications, of icon painters and the character of their work had caused concern in official quarters as early as 1707. In that year Iván Petróvich Zarudnói (alias Zarúdny or Zarúdnev) was appointed superintendent for the reformation of ecclesiastical painting, furnished with instructions by the ecclesiastical authorities and set over all icon painters in Russia. In 1710 his post was assigned to the Armoury in the Kremlin and he received further and more detailed instructions regarding the supervision and licensing of icon painters. Qualified artists were to be divided into three categories and receive certificates of competency; they were also to obtain stipends from the tsar. They were authorized to take on pupils who in turn were to be presented by their teachers for certification at the Armoury. It would appear from the next ordinance on the subject, published in 1722, that the intervening years had not brought any improvement. The rules laid down by the ecclesiastical synod of 1551 were still not being observed and had to be reiterated: icon painters must be of good moral character and possess a modicum of talent, they should aim at verisimilitude and conform to time-honoured models. Zarudnói was reappointed as supervisor of painters sacred and secular and authorized to examine the qualifications of icon painters and to license those approved by him to practise their art in Moscow. In the provinces skilled icon painters were to act as his deputies. With reference to canon 82 of the Trullan Synod of 692 rules were laid down forbidding the substitution, in icons, of symbols for figures: a lamb for the Saviour, a lion for St Mark, an ox for St Luke, an eagle for St John. Icons carved in wood (crucifixes excepted) or cast in metal were prohibited. The ordinance was to be published and no one was to be allowed to plead ignorance of its contents which evidently failed to reach Pososhkóv.[8] In both ordinances on icon painting, that of 1707 and that of 1722, the authority of the Church was associated with that of the tsar. Tsar Peter may have reduced the number of icons 'in his house' but was too well acquainted with the ritualistic nature of Russian religious life to allow his personal preferences to diminish his traditional role as champion, defender and vindicator of the Church.[9]

Pososhkóv's proposals for the guidance to be given to icon painters had little in common with the rules laid down by the Russian ecclesiastical synod of 1551, or that of 1666–7 which had first enjoined the appointment of a superintendent[10] or indeed with the instructions issued to Zarudnói. None of them was concerned with points of technical detail. These were to some extent dealt with by the manuscript manuals for icon painters (*pódlinniki*) which Pososhkóv does not mention. Instead he refers indirectly to a western European work which might be Dürer's *Vier Bücher von menschlicher Proportion*.[11] The drift of his remarks suggests that he considered the advice given by the manuals on the proportions of the human body to be inadequate; the reference to the naked body would confirm this supposition. Pososhkóv's insistence on the lifelike presentation of the human form may be due to nothing more than a general respect for the subject-matter of icons. Nevertheless, his spontaneous preference for the artistic style of western Europe comes dangerously close to heterodoxy; it is something of a surprise to find Pososhkóv setting naturalistic standards for religious painting at a time when the first generation of secular artists was only beginning to learn to draw from the nude in a life-class in St Petersburg.[12] A Muscovite purist in religion and politics, Pososhkóv was not incapable of sophistication.

The section on the manufacture of textiles has no connection with the digression on the painting of icons but is relevant to the stated subject of the chapter because it deals with the utilization of native resources, both human and material.

The question, raised by Pososhkóv as a pressing one, of the production and exportation of textiles woven from hemp and flax did in fact, in the last decade of Peter I's reign, receive the full attention of the authorities. The subject was a controversial one. In 1715 the tsar formed the opinion that the linen and canvas woven by Russian peasants and townspeople in lengths of ½ arshin by 9 or 10 or 11 *vershkí* were underpriced and that this put his subjects at a disadvantage in relation to the foreign purchasers of these fabrics. If, instead, he reasoned, they were made to the standard western European size of 1½ by 1¼ arshins, they would sell more profitably. In October 1715 he accordingly forbade the production of narrow pieces and decreed that only broad ones should be made. The producers, however, proved uncooperative, not only because of the expense involved in the installation of new equipment but also because in many cases the weaving was done by young children who could not handle large looms. Furthermore, the demand overseas for broad Russian fabrics was by no means proven. Thus in England narrow Russian linen was in demand among the poorer sections of the population precisely because it was cheap and was also bought by merchants for re-exportation to Spain, Italy and the East Indies. The ban was only temporarily lifted in 1718 and was repeated in 1720 and 1723. At least one consignment of narrow fabric was impounded before the tsar finally relented: the tariff of 1724 imposed a fractional export duty of 80 kopecks per 1,000 arshin on broad and narrow pieces alike.[13]

The other source of linen and hemp fabrics were the manufactories whose annual output at the end of the reign of Peter has been estimated at 1,200,000 arshins. Among their products the items in demand for export were sailcloth, ticking, canvas, shirtings, table-cloths and table-napkins.[14] This information is somewhat difficult to compare with the remarks made by Pososhkóv because he refers to various fabrics rather than articles and, moreover, in some cases uses the Russian form or translation of western European terms which to the English-speaking reader suggest a different material. Thus velour (*trip*) was made from silk or worsted, bombazine (*bumazéia*) was a worsted and silk or cotton and silk mixture but, judging by the use of this term in another context, was probably meant to stand for ticking.[15] Calico (*mitkál*), being made of cotton, is irrelevant; sailcloth, on the other hand, is very much to the point.

The large state-owned linen and sailcloth manufactory (*Khamóvnyi dvor*), built at Preobrazhénskoe near Moscow in 1696–7 and later expanded to a size which enabled it by 1725 to employ 1,362 workers, not only supplied the Russian fleet but also sold a part of its production on the open market, especially for export.[16] In addition, three out of the four privately owned sailcloth works were large enough to destine some of their output for sale overseas. The number of linen and canvas manufactories active in Russia at the end of the first quarter of the eighteenth century may be estimated at between ten and twelve.[17] The largest of these was established in 1711 at the tsar's command as a joint-stock company. From 1718, under the direction of the Dutch entrepreneur Jan Tammes or Iván Pávlovich Tames, it exported a part of its production. The same is probably true of that component of the same works which Tames took over and expanded after 1724 when the assets of the joint-stock company were divided among the partners, as well as of the linen works established jointly by Tames and the merchant Maksím Zatrapéznov or Zatrapéznyi at Iaroslávl' in 1722 (but later divided).[18]

Towards the end of Peter's reign his officials took a decidedly optimistic view of the condition and prospects of the linen and canvas industry. In 1721, at the request of Tames, the importation of linen of the Dutch type was prohibited in anticipation of its being produced in Russia. In his memorandum Tames argued in terms very close to those used by Pososhkóv: protected by customs barriers the people flourish and prosperous subjects are the adornment of the realm.[19] In 1723, in a joint session, the *Manufaktúr-kollégiia* and the *Kommérts-kollégiia* correctly adjudged the quantities of sailcloth and ticking produced in Russia to be large enough to leave a disposable surplus for export, and the amount of fine linen produced to be equal to home demand. In order to give manufacturers of these goods the necessary protection, the tariff of 1724 imposed import duties ranging from 25 to 75 per cent on household linen, sailcloth and ticking. A measure of which no doubt Pososhkóv would have approved was the export duty of 37½ per cent laid on all yarn in order to debar the foreign competitors of native manufacturers from a cheap source of raw materials.[20] In 1731, however, this regulation was found to be more damaging to the production of yarn than it was beneficial to the textile industry.[21]

Hemp was much in demand in western Europe for the production of sailcloth, cable and cordage. It had been virtually a Crown monopoly until the abolition in 1719 of the restrictions on the exportation of all such 'reserved' articles (except potash and weidash, in order to protect the country's stock of trees). At the same time, however, presumably to make up for any temporary loss of revenue, a surcharge was added to the export duty on the former 'reserved' goods.[22] Under the tariff of 1724 an export duty was to be charged on hemp at the rate of 27 kopecks per *bérkovets*. In relation to the selling price of 9 roubles per *bérkovets* this works out at 3 per cent. Compared to the exorbitant duty of 3 roubles per *bérkovets* proposed by Pososhkóv in Chapter 9, this rate gives the impression of having been calculated for revenue rather than for prohibition. The export duty of 45 kopecks per *bérkovets* of flax at the price of 12 roubles 50 kopecks was 3.6 per cent.[23] For want of information no comment can be made on the prices of the various textiles quoted by Pososhkóv with the exception of linen cambrics. Pososhkóv maintains that these should not sell at more than 60 kopecks per arshin whereas in 1724 the price charged by Tames appears to have been a mere 14 kopecks.[24]

Pososhkóv clearly underestimated the degree of development reached by Russia's linen and canvas manufactories and was unaware of the substantial contribution made by these industries to the country's foreign trade surplus. Exports via St Petersburg and Archangel in 1726 are said to have been worth 2,688,000 roubles. The value of linen and hemp fabrics made in Russia and exported in 1723 was officially estimated at 150,000 roubles; a report of the *Manufaktúr-kollégiia*, undated but clearly relating to the closing years of Peter's reign, speaks of 200,000 roubles. The quantities exported in that year via St Petersburg and Archangel only are said to have been 10,319,300 arshins of 'linen' fabrics, 7,747 pieces of sailcloth, 494,362 poods of hemp and 59,424 poods of flax. At a rough calculation, therefore, assuming the price of hemp to have been 9 roubles and that of flax 12 roubles 50 kopecks per *bérkovets*, the value of hemp and flax exported would have been 525,000 roubles,[25] considerably higher than that of the products made from these materials. This in the end bears out Pososhkóv's argument.

It may be interpolated at this point that the articles recommended by Pososhkóv as suitable for production in Siberia – wire, sheet metal and plate iron – were in fact being made by the state-owned metallurgical works in the Urals.[26]

As a manufacturer of woollen and linen stuffs, Pososhkóv was exceptionally fortunate to obtain state aid for his own works which comprised no more than eight or ten looms[27] since as a general rule the *Manufaktúr-kollégiia* was unwilling to subsidize small enterprises because it rightly considered them to be uneconomical.[28] Pososhkóv's appeal for official aid to individual master weavers, if heard, would certainly have gone unheeded.

Pososhkóv's remarks on the supply of labour have the merit of drawing attention to the difficulties experienced by manufacturers in mustering and keeping their hands.[29] Article 12 of the Regulation of the *Manufaktúr-kollégiia* of 1723[30] was intended to help the manufacturers to overcome these obstacles by restricting the mobility of labour. The application of the article rested on the assumption that the worker was bound to his employer by an agreement entered into for a definite number of years and could therefore be punished for a premature change of employment. Thus if a worker, already engaged by one employer, was hired by another, both he and the worker were liable to a fine of 100 roubles. If, however, the new employer acted unknowingly, the migrant was to be treated as a runaway and receive corporal punishment. One particular kind of labour, guaranteed against desertion, was supplied by the prisons. Between 1718 and 1721 five ordinances directed that women and girls imprisoned for criminal offences should, evidently for their correction, be sent to the spinning houses in Moscow and St Petersburg. It is also known that women prisoners were used as hands in Tames's linen factory in Moscow.[31] Pososhkóv could not have had much regard for this kind of work which he considers suitable for strays, paupers and outcasts of one sort or another although, rather as an afterthought, he presents it as offering the prospect of a career.

A comparison between Tsar Peter's and Pososhkóv's views on pauperism has already been made in the Commentary on Chapter 3 but the present context calls for a reference to the Instruction for the *Magistráty* (municipalities) issued in 1724, probably some time after Pososhkóv had completed his treatise. Article 32 of the Instruction links the question of pauperism to that of employment and shows yet again that, like Pososhkóv, Peter looked upon paupers as delinquents rather than as victims of social circumstances and saw the antidote to pauperism and vagrancy in compulsory and permanent employment. The article reads like a record of the tsar's own words, uttered with feeling: 'Many people neither have nor wish to have any skills by means of which they might earn a living and pay their taxes. In consequence, many live in extreme poverty; others, and perhaps the larger part, have taken to vagrancy of which nothing can come other than drunkenness and all manner of undesirable behaviour, and eventually robbery and theft. For this reason such people should be compelled to busy themselves with handicrafts or some work or other so that they may be turned away and restrained from such excesses. Skills and handicrafts should be multiplied in order that such vagrants may not loiter and remain idle in the guise of paupers.'[32]

Lastly, we turn to Pososhkóv's rather disconnected remarks on the desirability of discovering natural dyes and on the recruitment of doctors and apothecaries and to his account of his own discoveries. The building of St Petersburg and the production of textiles and of leather created an ever-growing demand for dyes and paints. In 1726 dyes worth 275,661 roubles were brought into Russia via St Petersburg and Archangel, accounting for somewhat over 17 per cent of the total value of imports through those places. Great savings could therefore have been made by producing dyes and paints in Russia.[33] The unsuccessful attempt at making Venetian lake has already been mentioned in the Introduction.[34] In 1716 the tsar gave orders for samples of imported dyes to be shown in all towns to encourage prospecting by the local population. Successful searchers were to receive rewards in money. The exhortation was repeated in 1723 in article 20 of the Regulation for the *Manufaktúr-kollégiia*. Sulphur was needed for making gunpowder of which it constituted 12 per cent by weight. Some sulphur was mined in Russia, principally at Sérgievsk on the river Sok,[35] but not enough to produce sufficient quantities of gunpowder for the army and navy. In 1705 the *Prikáz artillérii* (Department of Ordnance) experienced a constant shortage of sulphur. The time at which Pososhkóv made his find is hard to establish but it is possible that Peter's request, made early in 1709, for a sample of the sulphur newly discovered on the middle Volga near Samára had some connection with Pososhkóv's discovery. Mining began there in 1710 but only about 700 poods a year were produced. Not until 1714 was a deposit of sulphur found near Kazan, believed to be large enough to satisfy the country's entire need. These facts and Pososhkóv's testimony contrast strangely with Just Juel's remarks recorded in 1710 about the vast amount of gunpowder fired on ceremonial occasions 'for in Russia they prize gunpowder no more highly than sand and there is hardly to be found another country in Europe where it is made in such quantities'. In 1717 Peter I gave instructions for master craftsmen who were skilled in the handling of native sulphur to be engaged abroad. The reasons for which Pososhkóv chose not to offer to supply sulphur to the government under contract may or may not have been altruistic; it is certainly true that such contracts provided the opportunity of making a fortune.[36] Pososhkóv's discovery of petroleum was probably made on the river Sok and in that case is hardly likely to have been original as the existence of oil wells in that region had apparently been known locally for a long time. In Pososhkóv's day petroleum was used mostly as a remedy for chest diseases.[37]

Neither foreign doctors nor apothecaries – and in practice this meant doctors and apothecaries pure and simple – were absent from Russia but their number was small. Between 1700 and 1725, 150 medical practitioners were invited to come to Russia from other countries and at different times 31 doctors of medicine and 51 surgeons practised in Russia. In 1720, 129 surgeons were employed by the army. But according to a saying quoted by Juel[38] there were three doctors in Russia: the steam bath, vodka and garlic. Apart from the Crown pharmacy in Moscow there were eight pharmacies, all owned by foreigners, and twenty-two apothecaries, likewise foreigners.[39]

CHAPTER 5

Of the Craftsmen

39)   Without the appointment of a good director to give appropriate guidance our craftsmen cannot hope to prosper or acquire a good reputation but can only expect to live out their lives in penury and obscurity.

It is therefore necessary to promulgate an ordinance laying it down that those who have apprenticed themselves to a master must from the very beginning of their training remain in one place and serve out the agreed time under him, and may not leave their master even for a week (still less for a year) before that time is up, nor be absent from their own shop even after the termination of their apprenticeship without due discharge. If this were done our master craftsmen would not be in the sorry state that they are in now but become true masters of their craft.

Up to now apprentices have been in the habit of binding themselves to a master for five or six years but, after serving a year or two and learning very little, going away and setting up on their own. By charging lower prices they deprive their former masters of work and make them go hungry while still incapable of making a living for themselves. And so they drag out a wretched existence, being neither masters nor workmen.

I am told that in foreign countries there is a strict ordinance on this matter providing that if a man fails to complete the term of his apprenticeship by even a single day and goes away he can never be accepted as worthy. Further, if he serves his full term but fails to get a certificate from his master, no one (it is said) will take him on as a journeyman or again as an apprentice. Hence all their master craftsmen are worthy and admirable. But we have no such law forbidding apprentices to leave their masters before an agreed date and before they have fully learned their trade. That is why we can never have worthy craftsmen here.

Likewise, foreign laws lay it down that if a man invents a new method of his own or learns it from someone else and begins to make use of it (such work not having been produced by anyone before), the inventor has the sole right to it for his lifetime and others are not permitted to have any part in it until after his death. If the same were done in Russia we should surely have as many inventors as there are abroad. Many ingenious men would of their own accord set about inventing new things which would be profitable to them. As things are much talent goes to waste owing to the deficiencies of our civil laws. Surely an ordinance should be enacted providing that no one shall be allowed to share in any invention or method whatever as long as the inventor is alive.

Given such an ordinance many would come forward who now do not dare to make known their inventions because even testing the invention will bring them a loss. Indeed, if the test is successful, no sooner does the inventor set to work than others copy his invention and bring down its price. So without having found out anything for themselves they take away the livelihood of the inventor. To take my own case, I have five or six useful inventions to my credit but have not been allowed to profit from them and so they have all come to nothing. Therefore it is a matter of great importance to have a strict ordinance on the subject of inventors; many inventors would then come forward.

(141)   Similarly we need an ordinance for the regulation of all crafts enacting that each of them must have its overseers, in particular that of icon painters. A director should be set over all the crafts whose task it should be to keep a close watch on all the master craftsmen and overseers. He should be given quarters in which to carry on this work, which will be to ensure that every craftsman may exercise his craft with all the skill and care of which he is capable.

A strict ordinance on apprenticeship is needed to the effect that if any person is indentured to a master to learn a craft but leaves his master without a certificate (even if he has been a good pupil) he must be punished and sent to the army. Further, if any officer or other person in a position of authority extorts such a certificate for an apprentice from his master and the latter reports this to his superior, the false certificate shall be annulled and the instigator shall be fined as the law shall prescribe. Any apprentice who acquires the necessary proficiency but leaves without a certificate shall not be employed for any purpose but be sent to the army.

Given such a strict rule, that no one may leave before he has served his full apprenticeship and received his certificate, apprentices will stay where they are and apply themselves the more diligently to learning their craft, and masters likewise will teach them the more willingly. The effect of such an ordinance will be that apprentices will apply themselves well willy-nilly, and when they have fully learnt their craft and received their certificate from their master, they shall show their masterpiece and certificate to the chief supervisor of crafts. The said supervisor shall then decide whether any such person should continue in pupillage or become a journeyman under other masters, or whether he may set up as a master craftsman on his own. And as the supervisor decides, so shall it be.

If such an apprentice has acquired all the necessary skill and discretion and demonstrated these before the supervisor, his colleagues and other master craftsmen, and if his masterpiece is well and truly made and without blemish, the candidate shall be given full and formal permission to set up on his own and have his own workshop and accept apprentices.

2)   Every recognized master craftsman who has his own workshop shall also have his own mark and the overseers likewise shall each have their own marks. A master shall put his mark on every object which is made in his workshop and the overseer shall likewise put his mark on every piece of work that is submitted to him and passed as good.

Every recognized master craftsman shall keep a close eye on all his apprentices and journeymen to see that they do not bring any disrepute on his craft since these wares will all bear his mark. If any fault, either of material or workmanship, is found in an object the master whose mark it bears shall incur a fine. The fine levied shall be ten times the value of the object sold, except in the case of armourers. But if an armourer makes any kind of gun of iron that is too brittle or too soft and badly tempered, so that it explodes when fired, the master whose mark it bears shall be fined a hundred times the value of the piece and shall also receive physical punishment. However, if a gun is strong and of good workmanship yet does not shoot true, the fine shall be only tenfold. If anyone makes a gun with a bad firelock so that it will not fire, or a sword or sabre or lance or other side-arm without using the best natural steel for the edge, or of brittle metal, he shall be fined twentyfold. In the case of all other kinds of iron objects made for household use, if any are made of brittle metal, a fine of ten times the value shall be imposed. If a shopkeeper buys such articles for sale without observing their defects and sells them as sound, he too shall pay the fine as shall be laid down by regulations in the matter of the sale of inferior wares.

3)   So if craftsmen were prohibited from plying their craft as they please without conforming to any general regulation or submitting their wares to due inspection, all good craftsmen would prosper and be as highly considered as is now the case abroad. Foreign craftsmen are men no different from ourselves; but they draw strength from the ordinances that regulate their work and hence excel in craftsmanship. If our ordinances were to provide as firm a foundation our craftsmen would surely surpass the foreigners.

It should also be laid down that no craftsman from outside, be he native or foreign, be allowed to ply any craft in a given place without notifying the appropriate officials: but once he has been approved by the supervisor and his associates he should do as they decide.

If a foreign craftsman renowned in some important craft which is new to us comes to Russia, let him be given a workshop and a dozen or more apprentices to teach on the clear understanding that he will teach those pupils diligently and without keeping back any of his knowledge. If he instructs them with diligence so that they attain a skill comparable with his own, he shall be paid whatever sum was agreed upon and a premium to boot for having initiated them fully and taught them rapidly. He may then be allowed to return home with all honour so that other master craftsmen, on learning how well he has been rewarded, may be encouraged to journey hither and so promote all kinds of crafts in Russia.

But if any such foreigner wastes his time in idleness (as is the long-standing habit of foreigners), neglecting to teach his pupils – since he has come here merely to wheedle money out of us and then make off home again – and such deceitful intentions and conduct can be proved within six months of his arrival, let him be sent home with dishonour, taking no more than what he arrived with. We do not want him to spend his time here in idleness, nor do we want others, in the knowledge of this, to come to Russia in future with intent to deceive us.

Such pupils of theirs as prove apt and acquire mastery of a new craft, so that their work is as good as the foreign work, shall be declared master craftsmen and granted emoluments enough to ensure their prosperity.

(144)   Those of our governors who are Russians have a most unsound view of this matter, for they account their compatriots as of no worth and are unwilling to reward them so that they may live free of want. Such shabby treatment drives a man to stealing and all sorts of wrongdoing, and to the neglect of his craft. And such emoluments as are given are scarcely enough to keep body and soul together, being no more than five kopecks a day. Yet a man cannot even maintain himself on that; how then is he to maintain his wife and children save by letting them become beggars? All this cannot lead but to bad ways and bad craftsmanship.

In holding such views our governors cause our Sovereign great loss and no profit at all. They imagine that by not giving our craftsmen adequate emoluments they are doing something profitable to him whereas in fact they are doing him great harm. Indeed in all affairs whatever our governors will fight to the death for a mite but reck not at all the loss of a thousand roubles. By not giving adequate emoluments they take away from our people all ambition and zeal for excellence and prevent the increase of good craftmanship.

Those pupils who have not learned enough should be attached to those who have, so that they may complete their pupillage and acquire the necessary skill.

Above all other craftsmen the icon painters are most in need of careful instructions in their art; they must know to perfection the canon of proportions for persons of all ages and the appropriate representation of every kind of figure.

The icon painters too must have overseers set over them, the wisest and most experienced possible, to ensure that no incompetent person is admitted to their number. Any icon painters who are not fully competent must work under a master and must paint what he orders them to paint; and when they have acquired the requisite skill they may become masters in their turn. In my opinion it should be strictly forbidden for any icon painters to paint sacred icons without having been certified as masters and received a licence to exercise their craft.

(145)   Holy Writ says: Cursed be he who doeth the work of the Lord negligently.[1] Icon painting is eminently the work of God since icons are made for the worship of God and that worship ascends to God Himself.

But many paint so carelessly that some icons are terrible to behold. Some painters through their incompetence portray certain figures in such a way that living men with those proportions would be monsters. For instance, when drawing the Virgin they make the nose long and very thin, the neck long and slender, the fingers also long and very slender and the fingertips pointed such as no person ever had. You will not find that any part of the figure conforms to the proportions of a real person. Such drawing in a sacred image cannot but be an offence.

However, he who has always so painted in his ignorance, having no knowledge of the proportions of the human body, has not sinned and God will not hold it against him. For whether the figures are drawn in or out of proportion, the holiness of the icon does not reside in the quality of its painting; every icon is sanctified in the Lord's name. Yet it behoves us to ensure that icons are painted with the greatest possible care so that they may not contain errors in any particular. Further, if any saint is being depicted in an icon, the image of the Saviour shall also be depicted thereon, so that the icon may be sanctified in the name of Jesus Christ.

Granted that many of us know the proportions of the human form it is still necessary that we should have a Russian 'Painter's Manual' with drawings according to the Russian and not the Western manner, so that it may be clear to all. It should be arranged as follows: on the first page an adult naked man standing erect with outstretched arms, palms and fingers extended. A line shall be drawn from the heels to the crown of the head, and another line from the middle finger of the right hand to the middle finger of the left. The proportions shall be marked along these lines in *vershki* or in relation to the size of the human head or otherwise. On the following pages shall be given the whole sequence of figures, viz. on the first page a newborn child, on the second a one-year-old child, on the third one of two years; and so on for each year up to the age of twenty, by steps of two years between twenty and thirty years of age and by steps of five years from thirty to ninety. All these are to be nude figures. Then there shall be a second sequence of clothed figures standing and sitting and in various other postures. When it has been prepared the work shall be engraved on copper plates and printed in a thousand copies and distributed to all the chief towns and orders shall be given that all icon painters must use these models. The size should be in broadsheet.

All peasants in the countryside and other uneducated people (whether living in town or country) should be strictly forbidden from now on to paint icons without obtaining a licence. Daubers are to be found in the countryside who sell icons at three, two or even one kopeck a piece and paint them so badly that the figures have neither arms nor legs, just a trunk and head and with mere points for the eyes and mouth – and that is accepted as an icon. Hence it behoves us to exercise strict control over this craft above all other crafts.

The following matter also needs careful attention. We ought to introduce into Russia the manufacture of various fabrics made of flax and hemp, to wit, velours, bombazines, linen cambrics, calicoes, cotton cambrics, and sailcloth and other fabrics[2] which can be produced from our own raw materials. It is most necessary that such materials should be put to use here where they are grown. For if instead of exporting our raw flax and hemp we were to make them up here where they are grown, the fabrics would be two or three times cheaper than those manufactured abroad and thus our own people would benefit.

Therefore, to promote such manufactures an ordinance should be issued that all young and middle-aged vagrants be seized, inscribed on a register and put to work. Young children of both sexes should be taught the craft of spinning, adolescents that of weaving or bleaching or calendering, so that they may in due course become master craftsmen. I believe one could collect something between ten and twenty thousand such vagrants and, having built the necessary workshops, teach these good-for-nothings so as to extract a great deal of work from them. Rather than having to import fabrics made of our own materials it is we who should export manufactured fabrics abroad. Even if it appears unprofitable in the first few years and our products turn out to be more expensive than the foreign ones, we should not lose heart but persevere. Should it take five or six years to make such people into good craftsmen this need not cause despondency; for when they have become fully skilled the cost of teaching them will be recouped in a year or two.

(147)

Corn is dearer overseas than here, and food in general is much dearer. Foreigners buy our flax and hemp at a high price[3] and over and above that pay the marine insurance, customs dues twice over and various carriage charges. But they are not idle: they make up this raw flax and hemp, despite the high price paid, and they prosper by these manufactures, since they bring the manufactured fabrics back to us and sell them here at a high price: velours at sixty kopecks or more the arshin, linen cambrics at a hundred and twenty to a hundred and fifty kopecks and cotton cambrics at sixty kopecks to one rouble the arshin. Home-made linen cambrics would, I believe, scarcely sell at sixty kopecks the arshin and cotton cambrics at more than thirty kopecks. All fabrics made of flax or hemp could sell at less than half the price that we now pay the foreigner because corn and food are much cheaper here than abroad and we could buy our own raw flax and hemp at well below half the price which foreigners pay for these in their own country.

If then such things were set in train in Russia what point would there be in our selling raw flax and hemp to foreigners? Better to sell them the finished products – sailcloth and cordage and cambrics and calicoes, and receive in return rix-dollars and other things that we lack.

(148)

I believe we could produce enough of such fabrics to supply the whole of Europe and moreover offer them at prices much more attractive than those now prevailing. So rather than let foreigners enrich themselves by using our commodities it were better for us here in Russia to make a profitable living from our own products. Admittedly it will not be easy to establish the manufactories and set these industries in train but as soon as Russians have acquired the necessary skills and work has begun we shall assuredly be able to put such merchandise on the market at half the present price.

In the interests of the prosperity of the realm the Tsar's treasury should be the first to provide the necessary funds for the building of workshops for these purposes. This should be done on open spaces in those towns where corn and other food are cheapest, or in the region to the west of the river Oká, or wherever else may be suitable. The workers should be made subject to rent,[4] so that they may prosper and the treasury benefit at the same time.

Likewise in the case of other crafts which are profitable to the realm, where the masters have not the resources to build large manufactories themselves, funds should be advanced to them from the town taxes (or from any other source of revenue that His Majesty may direct) to build workshops so that all such enterprises may grow. Loans should be made not only for buildings but for all kinds of tools and stocks so that stocks can be built up at favourable times without running into the danger of excessive expense. The revenue officials should keep their eye on the borrowers to ensure that they do not spend these loans on useless things nor squander them on drink but apply the whole sum to its proper purpose. These subsidies and rents shall be paid over annually as the regulations may provide and depending on evidence of proper use.

Likewise we should procure craftsmen who know how to draw wire by using water-power and to make sheet metal and plate iron. No matter what the difficulties it is most necessary to procure such men and send them to our manufactories in Siberia to teach our people these skills.

Likewise we should procure craftsmen who know how to make plain and patterned velours, and also bombazines, and set up workshops for their manufacture and give them apprentices to teach so that they may instruct a dozen or a couple of dozen persons in these skills also.

If any person sets up any such works (so useful to the realm) by his own origination and at his own expense, he should receive permission to seize vagrant children of either sex to teach them his craft and once taught they shall remain with him in perpetuity; regardless of whom they may have belonged to formerly, whether they were peasants or household serfs, they shall remain with him in perpetuity. In this way there will be an end to beggars, vagrants and idlers; instead of loitering about in the streets they will all be turned into craftsmen. And when they have been fully taught and have become prosperous master craftsmen themselves our realm will benefit from their work and grow in renown.

It would also be advantageous to procure master dyers, skilled in the preparation of woad, indigo, cinnabar, azure, Venetian crimson and the ordinary kind, Venetian verdigris and the ordinary kind, vegetable yellow[5] and other dyes made by combination from potash, weidash,[6] copper, tin, lead, sulphur, chalk and other substances found in Russia. As for natural colouring matters, these must be diligently sought out by our own and foreign prospectors (familiar with them in their own lands). Let them discover deposits of such colouring matters and other useful minerals for the needs of pharmacy, dyeing and so on; and they should be promised a good reward for every such discovery.

Further, His Majesty should attract to his service such foreign military men and masters of certain arts, in particular doctors and apothecaries, as he deems sufficiently zealous and who are much travelled and consequently well versed in many subjects. It would also be advantageous to question merchants who have made journeys overseas. It causes me astonishment that in our land of Russia, which surely cannot be less in extent than the whole of Western Europe and comprises every kind of country – warm and cold zones, mountainous parts, various great lakes and a length of coastline impossible to estimate (for if you followed the coastline starting from the settlement on Kóla[7] you would not reach the other end in a whole year) – virtually no prospecting has been done for natural resources. I have not done much travelling myself yet even I who have no special knowledge have travelled to some purpose, for I have discovered a deposit of very pure natural sulphur, having the appearance of amber:

(150)   we have more of it than the whole of the rest of the world. I have also discovered the medical substance called pissasphalt:[8] I do not know how much there is of it abroad but one could extract at least a hundred poods here. I have also discovered a great quantity of petroleum, of yellow and red ochre (at least a thousand poods of each) and a deposit of Olónets clay.[9] I have no notion how many such things might not well be found in Russia; but we have not the knowledge, because we have not travelled overseas and are ignorant of the right places to search; and the foreigners who do know are not willing to tell us.

In all honesty, I did all that lay in my power but could make no headway. Prince Borís Alekséevich[10] promised me a reward for my sulphur mine, so great that – these were his very words – 'your children and grandchildren together will not be able to spend it all'. But all I received was a gift of fifty roubles! Yet I had in fact produced a profit of many thousands for His Majesty by this discovery of the sulphur and contributed not a little to our military power. If I had kept the matter to myself for the space of a year I could have made a profit of a thousand or two thousand roubles for myself, for I know that Prince Borís would have given me ten roubles a pood for it under contract. If I had kept it in my own hands for two or three years I could have made a great fortune out of it. But without thought for personal gain I announced the discovery because I saw that there was such a dearth of sulphur that it was being collected from private houses not by the pound but by the ounce, wherever it could be found, for the manufacture of gunpowder. When I brought three barrels of my sulphur to Moscow and gave them to Prince Borís the foreigners who visited him each took a sample and sent it home; understanding that they could not hinder our warlike preparations by denying us sulphur, their fellow countrymen began to export it to us again.

So even if I have received no benefit from this important discovery at least, God be praised, the needs of the army have been met.

CHAPTER 6. Of Brigandage

Commentary

Razbói – robbery with violence. – The efforts of the government to extirpate brigandage in the later seventeenth century. – The motives for brigandage. – Brigandage and its repression in the reign of Peter I. – The connection between taxation and public security as reflected in the proclamation of 1724. – The attitude of Pososhkóv towards organized crime and its punishment. – The police in Moscow and St Petersburg. – The honesty of the Old Believers.

The most common form of crime in Muscovite and Petrine Russia was *razbói* – robbery with violence, usually perpetrated by armed bands operating from a secret hiding-place. In the course of the seventeenth century, as the grip of the state and of the landlord on the peasantry tightened, to those who were bold enough to break the legal and economic ties that bound them to the soil brigandage offered sustenance and shelter, sometimes also prestige. With deep forests to hide in and vast plains to scour, the Russian countryside was well suited to the unending guerrilla waged by these public enemies against the rest of society. From the point of view of the authorities every gang of marauders was the possible rallying-point of a peasant revolt – but at no time since the establishment of the office for the investigation and punishment of crime (*Razbóinyi prikáz*) in 1555–6 did the government succeed in extirpating brigandage.[1]

Under the *Code* of 1649 (Chapter 21, Of matters concerning brigandage and theft) the punishment for an act of brigandage committed for the first time was the cutting off of the right ear and imprisonment for three years, followed by transportation to the south-western borders. The penalty for the same act committed for the second time as well as for any one act of brigandage accompanied by arson or murder was death. Thieves were punished by beating with the knout in a public place, imprisonment and the cutting off of an ear but the punishment for a third theft was death. During the subsequent three decades the degree and form of punishment for brigandage fluctuated between the extremes of harshness and comparative leniency – now death by beheading or hanging, now beating with the knout, the cutting off of a finger and banishment to Siberia for hard labour in perpetuity. Occasional intervention by the tsar or the Patriarch made for inconsistency in judicial procedure. In 1655 the Patriarch Níkon on behalf of the tsar (who was absent on campaign) offered free pardon to any self-confessed criminal; in 1663 the tsar himself commuted the impending death sentences of prisoners held on proven charges of robbery with violence to an exemplary punishment more cruel than death (and no less lethal) – the amputation of both feet and of the left hand. The severed extremities were to be nailed to trees on highways together with appropriately intimidating notices. When the death penalty for *razbói* was in force it was not necessarily applied in every case because apparently the tsar's officials were able to exercise their discretion in sentencing. Some lives were presumably spared in this way for hard labour in distant parts; the grisly balance was probably made up by those who died under the knout. Further and in some respects different provisions are contained in the novels (newly decreed articles) of 1669. Articles 17 and 18 of the section on brigandage (articles 17 to 75) rule that a (presumed) brigand who was not caught in the act should receive the same punishment as a first-time thief, namely the removal of two fingers and imprisonment for a fortnight for further investigation. But a brigand caught in the act or found to have committed earlier robberies, murder or arson was to be sentencd to death. A brief *ukáz* issued at the beginning of the regency of Sófia Alekséevna clearly recapitulated the penalties for brigandage and theft.[2]

The hostility of bandits to the established order as represented by officialdom and the great landlords, lay and ecclesiastical, is well attested but it is equally clear that most of them did not take to a life of violent crime in order to subvert the Church and state but rather to make a living at the expense of society. It is hard to see brigandage as a weapon in the class struggle when it is wielded by a gang composed of ten *poméshchiki* and their peasants or by another made up of two *poméshchiki* and their household servants or when it is directed by former villagers against their own kind as well as against the landlords.[3] Beyond the pale of society class barriers and loyalties lost their meaning. The brigands satisfied their needs by taking away from their victims what they themselves lacked: personal possessions, grain, cattle, horses, women, girls. They showed their feelings by indulging in wanton destruction: killing the remaining livestock, emptying the contents of granaries onto the village street. Main roads or waterways on which merchandise and government supplies were carried were among their habitual hunting grounds. In Moscow robberies were committed with alarming frequency. In 1709 Richard Grice, a teacher of mathematics at the School of Mathematics and Navigation, was killed by robbers prowling in the street at night. Just Juel, the Danish envoy, writing about Moscow in 1711, speaks of a plague of banditry: 'A man who goes out at night risks his life. In winter not a single night goes by without a murder or a robbery.' In Juel's part of the town sixteen people were killed during three months.[4]

In the reign of Peter brigandage continued to draw its strength from popular discontent with an unjust social system and to feed on the prevailing state of lawlessness. Conscription for military service in the Great Northern War created a new grievance and a fresh variety of runaway – the deserter. The ordinances on the subject of brigandage and desertion suggest that the authorities regarded every runaway recruit or soldier as a potential brigand.[5] The first ordinance of Peter I to be promulgated on the subject of *razbói* distinguished between robbery with and without murder. Brigands who were found guilty of murder were to be given the knout, branded on the cheek and sent to Azóv to do hard labour in perpetuity; in all other cases the *Code* of 1649 was to apply. The tsar's decision bears witness to the shortage of labour at Azóv as much as to his humaneness. The same preference for a sentence of hard labour rather than of death was shown in 1704 but in 1711 the *Code* of 1649 – which laid down the death penalty for repeated acts of robbery – and the novels of 1669 were brought back into force. Peter's grim and terse answers to questions put to him by his officials about the punishment of *razbói* in 1714 – 'without mercy', 'do not spare his life', 'death' – betray the anger aroused in him by brigands who had been spared but later ran away from hard labour in distant places and by his subjects who harboured criminals or deliberately withheld information which might have led to their capture. All were to be punished by death; for robbery without murder excision of the nostrils was added to banishment with hard labour. A further ordinance published in 1719 conveys a feeling of exasperation and strikes a note of urgency, almost of alarm. As if to reinforce his case the tsar cites the *Code* of 1649 and the novels of 1669 and invokes another ordinance (already mentioned) of the previous century, an unusual thing to do for a ruler who seldom looked back further than the beginning of his own reign. Brigands were to be detected, reported to the authorities and punished, not abetted. Those who gave themselves up would be spared even if they deserved death but those who did not yield would be executed. Officials everywhere were to testify under oath that the areas under their jurisdiction were clear of criminals, undesirable individuals and deserters; all vagrants were to be reported to higher authority, search parties of men of service were to be sent out to track down wanted men. Slackness in co-operation on the part of landlords and officials would be punished. Six months later yet another ordinance[6] spoke of havoc wrought, of churches attacked and pillaged so that not even the bare walls were left standing.

The connection between brigandage and the constant stream of internal migrants swelled by deserters from the army had long been apparent to the tsar. In December 1713, possibly accepting the advice contained in a memorandum submitted by one Iván Filíppov, he had made a note *pro memoria* not to allow people to move from one town to another without a passport or written permission to proceed.[7] Only now, in 1719, was the decision made to establish the passport system which was to regulate peasant migration until 1861. Search parties were to be sent out with orders to prosecute anyone who was found away from home without the appropriate document. But the expectation that the introduction of passes would prevent discontented and unreliable members of the population from turning to banditry was not realized, as may be seen from Pososhkóv's account and proposals. Those for the election of wardens reiterate some of the provisions contained in an ordinance promulgated in 1710.[8]

The institution of the poll-tax made the need to control the movements of the peasant population even more pressing. The proclamation of 1724 on the collection of the new tax brings out the connection between taxation and public security as it deals point by point with the interrelated matters of peasant flights, the harbouring of runaways, the extirpation of thieves and brigands and the granting of permission to peasants to work away from their villages. The responsibility for the repression of brigandage was laid on the colonel and other officers of the regiments quartered in the countryside. The penalty prescribed for failing to report the presence of brigands or failing to co-operate in their capture was severe corporal punishment (beating with the knout or rods), banishment with hard labour in perpetuity and the confiscation of movable and immovable property. Peasants were allowed to work for hire within a radius of 30 versts (32 km) of their abodes on obtaining written permission from their landlords and beyond that limit on obtaining in addition a pass from the local *zémskii komissár*. But they must not be accompanied by their families, wives or children and the period of absence must not exceed three years. Not all these provisions were entirely new; written permission from the landlord of a peasant who wanted temporarily to work elsewhere had already been alluded to in an *ukáz* issued in 1683.[9] Pososhkóv could not comment on the proclamation of 1724 as at the time of its publication he had already completed the manuscript of his book.

Pososhkóv's concern at the prevalence of organized crime and at the failure of the authorities to suppress it is understandable: an armed and destructive brigand is the antithesis of the peaceable and productive peasant, trader or manufacturer and the lack of security makes impossible any methodical accumulation of capital.

The punishments which Pososhkóv would like to see meted out to robbers are not the product of a frenzied and vindictive imagination but are consistent with Muscovite penal practice. The amputation of fingers (usually two from the left hand) went back several centuries but that of a hand (across the palm or below the wrist) only as far as the middle of the seventeenth century; branding was traditional though it was regarded as a means of identification of a convicted criminal rather than as a punishment in itself; hanging by the ribs was customary and was specifically prescribed for robbers by Peter I in 1719. Breaking on the wheel appears to have been introduced into Russia in the seventeenth century although it is not mentioned in the *Code* of 1649.[10]

Pososhkóv's view that in Russia petty crimes were not punished with the same severity as in western Europe is supported by Russian scholarly opinion of the later nineteenth century. In this respect Pososhkóv appears to have been more bloodthirsty than his countrymen who on the whole were disinclined to take human life unless commanded to do so by higher authority. Whether from religious or economic motives magistrates tended to make wide use of the sentences of imprisonment provided for under the *Code* of 1649. In France, to take a random and opposite example, the principle 'La prison n'est pas une peine' was observed until the Revolution.[11]

Only the names of the office of *generál-politsméister* established in 1718 in St Petersburg and that of *óber-politsméister* established in 1722 in Moscow suggest their possible relevance to the subject of this chapter.[12] In fact the instructions for these officers deal with the regulation of the public life and activities of large urban communities in their many aspects of which the prevention of crime is only one.

A great many of the inhabitants of the northern regions whom Pososhkóv commends for their respect for other people's property were Old Believers and, as such, renowned for their honesty[13] but Pososhkóv's hostility towards the schismatics would not have allowed him to point out this connection.

CHAPTER 6

Of Brigandage

51)   From of old many efforts have been made for the suppression of brigands and for their punishment, and many investigating officers have been sent out, such as Artémii Ogibálov, Evstignéi[1] Neélov and others like them, with orders to act ruthlessly. Nevertheless, no success was achieved thereby; brigands continued to abound and commit many crimes in all parts of the country (except in the northern coastal district and the lands beyond the river Onéga).[2] They plunder villages and hamlets without number and do people to death. Nor will there ever be an end to these brigands unless our present ways of maintaining law and order are improved and the very cause of brigandage is removed.

   There is no brigandage such as we have here in Russia in any Christian or Muslim state for the sole reason that those countries show no leniency whatever towards brigands: they are not kept long in prison; once arrested they are tried and sentenced there and then. In consequence people scarcely dare to lead a life of crime. Whereas here, when any criminal is caught we cannot bear to part with him: he is thrown into prison, fed as if he were an honest man and kept there for ten or twenty years. In the course of these long terms of imprisonment many succeed in escaping and then revert to an even more criminal way of life than before, and knowing what to expect they do so the more readily.

52)   But however many officers may be sent out they will never be able to stamp out brigandage without a change in our procedure. My view of how to stamp out thieves and brigands once and for all is as follows.

   Our Sovereign Lord should direct that an ordinance be sent to every part of his realm in words such as these: Wardens with authority over a hundred, fifty and ten persons respectively shall be appointed in all towns, quarters and settlements, whether inhabited by *dvoriáne*, officials,[3] the military, traders and artisans, post-drivers, foreigners or others, and further in all villages and hamlets, both large and small, whether owned by the Sovereign, the bishops and monasteries, private landowners or any other kind of person whatever. These wardens shall exercise authority alike over the masters and their servants and peasants. Each warden shall keep most strict watch over those under his charge to ensure that no one, not even a person of standing, shall leave home without the knowledge of his warden. If anyone has to make a journey he must obtain a passport duly stamped from his warden. These passports shall state in full where the person is going, for what purpose, for how long, and how many people are accompanying him, with their names.

Similarly in all great households wardens shall be appointed with authority over ten, fifty and one hundred men, chosen from among the boyars' serving-men to watch over all the retainers, and likewise from among the gentlemen to watch over one another. Not only these wardens but also all the gentlemen and their retainers should keep a close eye on one another to prevent anyone from absenting himself for any reason whatever without the knowledge of his warden, or going out during the night time.

When persons do go out with the knowledge of the warden or proceed on a journey with a passport, the said warden (of whichever rank) shall nevertheless keep a vigilant eye on them to ensure that they in fact go to the place for which permission was granted. Should they go anywhere else they must be brought back and prosecuted. This being so, if any such person is shown to be guilty of any theft or act of brigandage the neighbours who knew about it but kept silent shall incur the same penalty as the criminal himself. Likewise if any person steals anything from a great house all those members of the household who were privy (153) to the crime but kept silent shall receive the same punishment as the thief, and even those who knew nothing of it shall also be given as many strokes of the knout as may seem proper. Further, any warden (of whichever rank) who keeps silent about a theft known to him shall receive more severe treatment and harsher punishment than the criminal himself.

If the members of any such company under the authority of a warden, whatever their rank, do not obey him, he shall report to higher authority that they are insubordinate and are still absenting themselves without his knowledge and permission. The higher officials shall then send soldiers to arrest these mis-creants and, when the latter are brought before them, question them most closely as to the reason for their disobedience. If the testimony shows that their disobedience had nothing to do with any criminal activity they shall nevertheless be punished, as the law directs, for disobeying His Majesty's ordinance, in order to deter them from doing the like again.

Should they prove insubordinate a second time they must be examined in the torture-chamber. If it appears from the examination that they did not act in furtherance of some crime but set their wardens at naught merely out of inveterate wilfulness or defiance, they shall now receive a double punishment for this. In clear witness whereof they shall have one finger cut off each hand, or instead a brand-mark shall be made on the arm to indicate that they have been twice convicted. If any person shall be guilty of such misconduct a third time he shall receive triple punishment and his whole hand (or more) shall be cut off, as the law may direct.

But if it is proved that such disobedience was in furtherance of some crime, then the guilty person shall be punished by death even if it be his first offence, or perhaps suffer the severest physical punishment together with branding on the face and forearms,[4] so that all who see this may in future not dare to disregard the Sovereign's ordinance.

54)   If any person shall threaten to assault the warden set over him or abuse him with bad language, the dishonour shall be indemnified in tenfold measure and any injury done twentyfold.

Printed copies of the said ordinance must be sent out by express messenger to all towns – that is to say, two or three hundred copies more or less to each chief town depending on the number of villages and hamlets under its authority – so that each warden may have his own copy. The messengers shall hand over the copies of the ordinance to the governor or other appropriate official in person. The said official shall immediately cause the copies received to be distributed throughout his district, ensuring that the messengers shall deliver one to every village and hamlet without omission. On arrival in any village they shall take a census of all the males and shall choose wardens with authority over every ten persons and similarly over every fifty and hundred. In choosing these wardens the reckoning must not be by households but by the total number of persons of male sex. If there are ten males in one household then a warden must be chosen from their number; if twenty, then two such wardens. Wherever there is a remainder of one or more men after division into tens, these remaining males must be included in some other company of ten. When ten such wardens (with authority over ten persons) have been chosen, two of their number shall be appointed as the wardens with authority over fifty and one of them as the warden with authority over a hundred – these to be men of superior judgment.

When all these wardens have been chosen and their names entered in a register they shall be most solemnly adjured to carry out the Sovereign's decrees without deviation or mistake, and without fear or favour. Then the hundred-men[5] shall be called together and His Majesty's ordinance shall be read aloud to them two or three times over so that they shall all be familiar with it and remember it, and cannot later put forward a plea of ignorance. The printed copies, as the ordinance directs, shall then be handed over to the three senior wardens in the presence of all these men.

55)   When the copies of the ordinance have been so delivered the messengers shall most solemnly call upon the local headmen to declare whether there are any criminals, brigands, horse-thieves, burglars or runaways of any description in their district.[6] Moreover, should there be any persons who have come thither from elsewhere (whether foreigners or unattached persons of any kind) who are neither runaways nor natives of that place, the presence of all such persons must be declared, however long they may have been established there, and not a single name shall be concealed; for most severe physical punishment and a fine will be imposed for any false declaration. Likewise should the said headmen know of any such persons or of anyone who is harbouring a robber band on his premises in any

of the neighbouring districts, they shall make a full and detailed declaration thereof without holding anything back. If anyone deliberately conceals his knowledge of such robbers he shall be punished with death.

Therefore it is the duty of everyone to give such information without being intimidated by such criminals or by the landowners to whom they belong. If anyone protects such a person and it later becomes known through the wardens that he was well aware of such criminal activities but did not report them, he shall himself suffer punishment and that punishment shall be precisely the same as that of the malefactor himself. Likewise, if any wardens (of whichever rank) fail to report notorious criminals but some other person does so, these newly appointed wardens shall receive the same punishment for concealment as the local headman would receive.

Therefore the headmen must be most diligently questioned on this matter, that they may be more fearful of concealing such persons as the ordinance requires to be given up than of fire itself. If any person knows of any crime committed even by his own master or by his factor, or is aware that someone is secretly harbouring any strange persons whatever, he must on no account keep silent about it out of fear of such wicked men. For that will be the end of them – they will not enjoy their freedom much longer; once caught, their lives are forfeit. If anyone is guilty of such concealment that shall be the end of him once and for all. So, even if a man lays an information against his own brother living nearby that the latter was privy to such a matter but failed to report it, still the informant shall be rewarded and he who withheld the information shall be forthwith put to death.

A headman or peasant who admits that he has personally taken part in some act of brigandage or other crime in the company of his own master or his master's factor, shall be pardoned and merely branded upon the face so that he may be known in future; but the landowner or factor shall be put to death.

(156)

If the aforesaid messengers receive an identical report in several villages that a certain person has been committing acts of brigandage, on passing from these villages on to others they must first enquire, as before, of the local headman whether he knows of any persons who may have been the suspect's accomplices. And when they have made full enquiry about the district for which the headman is responsible, they must ask him further whether he knows of any malefactor in any other districts. But whether he has information to give of any such person or not, he must be directly questioned about the man who has already been denounced in the other villages. Even if the headman barely admits that he had heard a rumour of such a person but does not really know anything about it, this fact too shall be recorded.

On their return the messengers shall lay all these depositions before the provincial governor. The governor shall then send a strong detachment to apprehend those who have been denounced. On arrival the officer in command shall make a most thorough search of the houses belonging to the accused, to see whether there are any arms or clothing there which do not belong to them. Likewise, all other household objects should be examined and the officer should find out whether there are any secret hiding-places and any objects concealed therein. If any person is found to have such a compromising object in his possession it shall be deemed manifest without further investigation that the case against him is proved. However, when brought to the magistrate's chambers he shall be put to the question; and if he does not deny his guilt he shall receive sentence forthwith in accordance with the gravity of his offence.

But if he denies the charge he must be subjected to severe torture. He must be questioned about his accomplices and be forced to reveal in detail what places he frequented, where they all had their den and the names of any others who were privy to his crimes. Likewise such men must be questioned about other robber bands and, if they know of any, they must tell where these are to be found. If in the course of the investigation an accused person will not admit to murder or to crimes of robbery, whereas his neighbours solemnly swear that he is guilty of such, he shall receive sentence in conformity with the appropriate provision of the law.

If any notorious brigand, on learning of this severe and strict ordinance, shall of his own free will give himself up and submit a confession, he shall not be put to the torture and shall go free of punishment, even if he has committed murder or harboured a band of robbers or even been their leader, provided always that he gives an undertaking to refrain from such acts in future and reveals and names all his companions. But his accomplices shall all receive sentence in conformity with the law. He himself shall merely be branded on the cheek and arm so that all may know that he was a most notorious malefactor but has now repented; and so he shall be set free.

If he subsequently shows zeal towards His Majesty by detecting criminals, and brigands belonging to other bands are apprehended as a result of his zeal, he should also be rewarded therefor. But if he relapses after his repentance into his former criminal ways he shall be put to death by the most cruel possible means – breaking on the wheel or hanging by the ribs.

Orders shall be given to all wardens (of whichever rank) and to all the inhabitants of a place to keep a watch upon their neighbours. If anyone entertains guests at his table or overnight guests who are carrying no merchandise with them, the wardens should all go and enquire who the visitors are, whence they have come and where they are bound for. If this information is readily given each visitor should then be requested to show the passport given by his warden. And if he produces his passport without making difficulties and it agrees with the information which he gave, then the matter may rest there. But should the passport not accord with what the holder asserts or should he admit that the document is false, or worse still if he becomes evasive in his replies or takes up a

57)

truculent attitude, he shall be arrested, bound and brought to justice. If he resists arrest he must be taken by force if necessary; and if anyone is killed in consequence those making the arrest shall not be held responsible.

However, should it chance that such visitors are a large party and manifest suspicion falls upon them, word must be sent to the neighbouring villages to come and help in arresting them all. If any village fails to send help on receiving such a request, the headman or warden who failed to answer the summons shall be punished in accordance with the ordinance and all the peasants of that village shall be flogged. If it should happen that any headman or warden summons his men for this duty but they refuse to obey and do not go to help, no headman or other officer shall be liable to punishment but the men shall all be punished without delay for their disobedience, as shall be laid down.

(158)

Any such party of persons whose members prove to be honest and whose papers are in order, signed and sealed by their warden, but who nevertheless refuse to show them out of haughtiness and moreover resist the peasants who have been gathered against them, shall be arrested and brought to justice. If they admit their obstinacy before the magistrate and say that they would not show their passports merely because of their disdain for the peasantry, they shall be stripped and beaten with rods and a fine shall also be exacted from them, as may be determined.

To deal with such obstinate persons orders shall be given to each of the senior wardens of the neighbourhood to send every week three or four of their men to those villages which lie on the main highways. Likewise to deal with disturbers of the peace ten men from the various groups of a hundred shall be kept in readiness in the smaller villages along the highways, and twenty or more in the large ones (taking into consideration the number of travellers), to act as witnesses against violent disturbers of the peace and refractory persons, and also for the purpose of arresting brigands.

If the measures outlined above were to be introduced I believe that brigandage would die down within a year and that within two it would completely disappear. Only it is essential that those who are responsible for law and order adhere strictly to these rules omitting no part of them whatever. Then if the ordinance is not disobeyed I am persuaded that there will be no more brigandage here in Russia.

Even now there would not be so very many thieves and brigands if magistrates did not treat them with leniency. For on hearing that a thief or brigand has been caught they enquire whose peasant he is. And when they are informed that he belongs to a certain important personage, or to one not so important but who is a notorious barrator, or to one noted for his lavish hospitality, or again to a relation of the magistrate himself, they let the man go free (even without a bribe) so as to ingratiate themselves with his owner. Such peasants or house-serfs go on committing crimes with impunity, relying on the protection of their masters. Moreover, any brigands who have enough money use it to buy their immunity.

9)   In 1719 I was attending a provincial court presided over by Ivan Miakínin. A certain *dvorianín*, Skrýplev by name, was brought before him; he looked a decent enough man but had a chain round his neck and irons on his legs. So I asked what he was charged with and was told that the case against him was very grave and that he was unlikely to escape sentence of death. Yet when all else failed the pecuniary argument came to his rescue: His Honour the Judge discharged him without a stain on his character. On the way back to my distillery I enquired at Derzhkov Vólok about this Skrýplev and the local inhabitants said that he was a notorious trouble-maker and murderer and that he already had half a dozen murders on his conscience. Nevertheless our judges in their mercy had acquitted him.

    It is for this reason that it seems to me that it is even more important to put the fear of God into our judges and their clerks than into the thieves and brigands themselves. Clerks must cease showing leniency towards criminals and protecting them; it would then be difficult for a judge to acquit and discharge men worthy of death if he were no longer to receive recommendations in this sense from his clerk.

    To stamp out brigandage once and for all it would be better to repeal all the numerous ancient ordinances and to draw up a new and succinct one. Even if the ordinance for the suppression of brigandage promulgated by the Board of Justice in 1719 were revised and printed copies made with every care and distributed to all chief towns, it still would not be of the slightest avail. For brigandage flourishes everywhere just as before: villages are plundered and fired, peasants burnt to death. For this ordinance merely brings together all the ancient ordinances instead of being entirely new. The ancient laws provide that, when a brigand is caught, he shall be put to the torture three times and then once more when confronted with his accomplices. Thus it happens that some malefactors are taken to the torture-chamber ten and twenty times and are kept for years on end under such repeated torture; nothing but ill can come of their being thus kept in prison.

    Now if an apprehended thief or brigand were at once brought before a magistrate and put through a thorough and expert examination, he would soon 0) reveal whether he was in fact a criminal or not. At this point if he prevaricates and will not tell the whole truth he must be threatened with torture to induce him to make a clean breast of the whole matter. When he does confess his guilt he must be made to answer the following questions (allowing him to take his time): where and for how long he has been leading a life of crime; what places he frequented; where he has been keeping the stolen goods or whether he handed them over to someone else to keep for him; how he earned his living before taking to thievery; why he abandoned his proper livelihood; whether his master, or his master's factor or the neighbours know of his crimes; and similarly whether the headman or any of the wardens had any inkling of them. Should the man prove recalcitrant in the course of this detailed examination and refuse to make a full and frank confession he must at once be put to the torture. Even if it is already late in the day this must on no account be put off till the morrow lest he have any communication with other criminals already under arrest. Even if there are no such prisoners of long standing in the gaol the torture must still not be postponed till the next day in order that he may have no time to think up a tale. If he will not talk under torture he shall be put to the torture again the next morning, including the hot iron. And if even so he will not make a clean breast of his crimes despite the clear evidence against him, he shall be put to death without delay as the law prescribes.

In the case of a criminal who makes a complete confession before torture and admits all his misdeeds on his first examination (carried out as suggested above), torture can in my opinion be dispensed with; the man should rather be made ready for execution.

If it should prove that his master or the factor or any other person in authority knew of his criminal ways, the same procedure must be applied to such persons as to the criminal himself; indeed they should be punished even more harshly. Seeing this, others will take it to heart and in future no one will protect criminals of whom he has cognizance. Likewise those neighbours who knew someone to be a criminal and did not report the matter shall receive such punishment as the law prescribes.

If criminals make use of a man's house, carry out their depredations therefrom and share the proceeds with the householder, the latter, as harbourer of the band, shall be condemned together with them and put to death in accordance with the law.

(161) His house shall be razed to the ground and the site left vacant for several years so that all may know and remember clearly that the said house was a resort for criminals. Even small children will not forget such a warning.

When a criminal names all his associates in crime (whether in the course of examination or not) and reveals where they live, if they live not too far away they must be arrested at once (before the execution of the criminal). If the distance is a hundred versts or more, however, he must be put to death at once and the others arrested later, so that the course of justice is not held up by further delays.

It is reported that in foreign countries criminals are not held in custody for long periods but that as soon as their guilt is proved they are at once put to death. Moreover, hanging is the penalty not only for notorious acts of armed robbery with murder, but also for theft. That is why people do not dare to commit such crimes in those lands. In this country our ancient laws are much too lenient towards thieves, which is most unjust towards the victims of their depredations. A man is not hanged for petty theft nor even for the theft of a thousand roubles, and in consequence thieves here do not even greatly fear arrest. If all thieves and brigands were promptly put to death in this country as they are abroad, and the death penalty were imposed (without possibility of pardon or delay) for the petty crimes as well, this would be a really effective deterrent.

Nowadays the Devil has so multiplied robbers that if a peasant amasses as little as fifty or sixty roubles, those of the neighbourhood soon learn about it and come and wreak destruction on him and his home; they torture many people to death in their attempts to extort money. The neighbours hear and see all that happens and yet do not come to the help of the victims but give the robbers a free hand. For protection from such disasters our Sovereign should promulgate an entirely new ordinance addressed to all the peasantry to this effect: if henceforeward any persons enter a man's home with intent to commit robbery it shall be the duty not only of the other inhabitants of his village but also of the neighbouring villages and hamlets, and of the local landowners too, to come to his help whenever they hear a commotion or receive word of such. If they do not help to catch the robbers all those neighbours shall be given the knout, those living farther off less severely, those nearer at hand more severely. Further, they shall between them make restitution to the victim of twice the value of the loss which he has suffered at the hands of the robbers.

62)

My proposed new legislation for the complete suppression[7] of thieves, brigands and runaways will be difficult to apply only at first. It will require that no one may on any account travel further than ten versts from his own home without a permit, and at night not even visit another village a single verst away (or, if in a town, any other quarter of it). But even if this regulation is troublesome for a year or so it will work more smoothly once people have become used to it. Brigandage will be checked if such written permits are introduced since robbers do not appear out of thin air but must come from some village or other, where a man cannot help knowing all about his neighbour, what affairs he is engaged in and what journeys he makes. Nor do these criminals congregate in the open but in these very same villages, so their doings cannot possibly remain hidden from their neighbours. Hence it is right that the neighbours should receive the same punishment as the criminal, since they know all the facts – who lives by crime and who by honest trade – but do not report them.

So if a man knew that his neighbour would not keep silent on seeing his nefarious doings, country folk would not dare to take to brigandage; moreover, landowners would themselves have difficulty in going into hiding among their own peasants. Under this new law brigands would have no chance of increasing in numbers again. By the time the restriction on movement has been in force for a dozen years or so it may be possible to allow travel without permits again, provided always that the officials are strict in the execution of their duty and do not flout this new decree of His Majesty. For every matter of moment gains strength from being pursued with consistency.

There is no cause for us to be surprised that there is so little crime in foreign countries for even here in Russia this is true at any rate of our least fertile regions – I mean the northern coastal district and the lands beyond the river Onéga – where theft and robbery are unknown. If an inhabitant of those parts goes into the forest and begins to feel too warm he can take off his fur coat or kaftan and hang it up on a tree; it will still be there when he comes back. Or again, he can let loose

(163)   his colts into the woods in spring and only come back for them after Pokróv[8] when the frosts begin. Now why should this be so? Manifestly because the people in those parts will not tolerate thieves. If anyone is guilty of theft he is not thrown into prison but given a ducking. Where such strict customs prevail no one dares to take another man's property even if he finds it left lying about in the forest.

Passports

These passes should be made out by the wardens as follows.

A person who has to make a protracted stay in another town shall receive a passport on a whole or half sheet, stating in full where he has gone and for what purpose. If it has been made out by a warden over a hundred persons on his own authority it must bear his personal seal. If by a warden over fifty persons, it must likewise bear his seal; if by both together, it must bear the seals of both, as received by them from the governor. These seals shall be affixed to every pass by way of attestation at the end of the text in place of a signature.

All wardens shall keep a register of all such passes issued, giving names and places of destination. When the holder of a pass arrives at his destination he shall forthwith report to the local warden and the latter shall record his arrival in his register and enter on the pass the date thereof.

When the visitor has completed his business the chief warden shall enter on the pass details of how many days or weeks he stayed, where he came from and where he is bound for, and authenticate the entry with his seal. At the same time he shall record in his own register details of the man's visit, in particular the length of his stay. Wherever the bearer of the passport may go and whatever length of time he may spend in a given place, the local wardens must make such a record of his visit. Even if he only spends a single day at a place they must carry

(164)   out the whole of the above procedure and never in any circumstances let a person leave without making such an entry.

For those who are only going away for a short time, having some business in another district, the passes may be made out on a quarto or octavo sheet and the seal shall similarly be affixed directly below the text. There is no need to enter in the register passes valid for only three or four days. But if a person is leaving home for a week or two the pass must be entered in the register without fail since for one reason or another the bearer might not report again for a long time.

A person who reports anywhere without such a pass must be arrested and brought before a magistrate. Likewise any person who produces a pass which bears a seal other than that of the chief warden of his place of domicile (or any other incorrect seal) must be arrested and brought before a magistrate.

On return home the holder must hand back his passport to the warden who issued it and not keep it himself.

Even if this procedure may seem somewhat cumbersome at first it will not be any hardship once people have become used to it. Given such strict supervision I do not see how brigands could form bands and have their meeting-places in the villages and continue to commit robberies as hitherto. Even if they congregate in the woods they could not appear in any village without the necessary passes. Similarly it will be very difficult for deserters and runaways to move about, either alone or with their families: there will be no way for them to leave their domicile and all ways will be closed to them.

The ordinance must strictly enjoin wardens of all ranks that neither they themselves nor their men must on any account allow any person whatever – not excluding priests, monks and beggars – to spend the night in any dwelling without such a pass – nay, not even to come in and warm himself. Anyone who is impudent enough to try to do so shall be arrested and brought before a magistrate. Likewise if any person tries to skirt round a village or to slip by along byways, he shall be seized and brought before a magistrate without delay.

65) As regards the printing of these passports, every governor should reckon up how many wardens in all come under his authority and how many there are in each inhabited place. He must then order a good craftsman to make a separate seal for each such warden. On each seal shall appear the name of the district and of the place concerned, and no seal shall be identical with any other seal. These seals shall then be distributed to the wardens.

When a warden over a hundred persons makes out a pass he must, at the end of the text, seal it with his official seal; and similarly a warden with authority over fifty persons. In the course of time everyone will become familiar with these seals and recognise which is which. No one will be able to practise any deception, since although the chief wardens themselves will be changed every year, the seals of office will always remain the same.

CHAPTER 7. Of the Peasantry

Commentary

The causes and consequences of the poverty of the peasants. – The dvor *(holding) as a basis for taxation by the state and exactions by the landlord. – The value of payments per* dvor. *– Pososhkóv's equation: poor peasant – poor tsar. – The need to fix a firm basis for assessing the private income and public revenue from each* dvor. *– The ultimate responsibility for protecting the peasantry rests with the tsar, the true and permanent overlord of the peasants. – Pososhkóv's outmoded conception of the* pomést'ie *as a benefice. – Peter I's interest in the welfare of the peasants. Pososhkóv as advocate of peasant literacy. – His sympathy for the Mordvinians. – The need for the conservation of forests stressed by Pososhkóv and well understood by the tsar. His measures to that end. – Pososhkóv as planner of villages safe from fire. – Government safety measures already in force. – The size of Russian villages.*

This chapter examines the causes and consequences of the poverty of the peasants who, as taxpayers, were the principal source of the tsar's revenue. The views put forward here are developed in the next chapter; the two should be treated as one.

In the course of the seventeenth century the Muscovite state systematically reduced and simplified the basis on which taxes were imposed on the inhabitants of landed estates – *pomést'ia* and *vótchiny* – held by men of service. The survey of all the land and its inhabitants carried out at different times in different areas in the 1620s was revised in the 1630s with the aid of a new measuring unit – the *zhivúshchaia* or populated *chétvert*[1] – which made it possible to register for tax purposes all parcels of land, however small, as well as the number of peasant holdings located on them. After 1680 liability for tax was determined by the quantity of such holdings (in some cases mere households), known as *dvorý*. As a basis for taxation the *dvor* had the twofold advantage of being simple to register and of extending the incidence of tax to the landless peasants (*bobylí*); its chief drawback was the scope that it offered to tax evasion through the amalgamation by the landlord of previously separate *dvorý* in the manner described by Pososhkóv.[2] It was the professed wish of the government that the burden of tax should be evenly distributed in accordance with the paying capacity of the family groups in any given community so that the rich were not out of pocket in relation to the poor and the poor were not overburdened in relation to the rich.[3] But the great disparity between the various *dvorý* could not be evened out to any significant extent by a system of distribution which was habitually operated by the more prosperous, and therefore more powerful, members of the community for their own advantage.[4] The amalgamation of *dvorý* and perhaps an increase in the number of male peasants on private estates from 2.3 million in 1678 to 3.4 in 1719 might account for the rise per *dvor* of the dues, labour, produce, sometimes also money, exacted by the landlord from the peasants on his land.[5] The increase per male peasant, however, in the corresponding period was far less pronounced. The explanation of this disparity lies in the fact that the peasant on a private estate was the servant of two masters, of the landlord and of the state, who were competing with one another for his tribute which could not be augmented indefinitely. Iu. A. Tíkhonov has pointed out that between 1688 and 1725, in central Russia, the state secured for itself the lion's share of the total tribute. According to Tíkhonov, between 1688 and 1723 the tax paid annually in money (without any adjustment for its declining value) by a *dvor* increased fivefold – from 50 kopecks to 2 roubles 50 kopecks. A similar figure is given by Tróitskii. Assuming that the average number of male peasants per *dvor* was 4.25, a payment of 58 kopecks a head was still less than the poll-tax of 74 kopecks imposed in 1723. But there is an apparent discrepancy between these figures and those given in *Ocherki istorii SSSR*, where the total contribution per *dvor* between 1700 and 1725 comprising provisions, recruits – presumably calculated on the basis of commutation at the rate of 1 rouble 60 kopecks per man – , labourers, carriage, as well as payments in cash, is put at between 10 and 15 roubles per *dvor*.[6] Pososhkóv estimates the annual contribution per *dvor*, probably in cash alone, at 8 roubles. It is significant that whilst determining the poll-tax at 74 kopecks from each male peasant, the authorities should have estimated the value of the payments in kind and in money made by each peasant to his landlord, whether on the tsar's demesne, on ecclesiastical or on private estates, at only 40 kopecks a head. Strumílin considers that this figure represented the average payment but did not include the cost of grain and other provisions supplied by peasants to landlords residing in towns during the winter months.[7]

Pososhkóv for his part blames not the state but the landlord for the impoverishment of the peasants on privately held land. Oppressed and exploited as they were, they had in the end no remedy but to abandon their holdings. But daily boon-work as described by Pososhkóv was apparently exceptional: the normal stint was three days a week, precisely the amount worked on Pososhkóv's own land.[8] Time and again Pososhkóv repeats what was to him an axiom: poor peasant – poor tsar, and conversely: the wealth of the peasant is the wealth of the ruler.[9] Wealth is to be created, among other means, by establishing a firm basis for assessing the amount of tax due from each *dvor* to the state and the amount of labour, produce and money due to the lord. (Something like this was eventually done but only in the western provinces of the Empire and as late as 1847–8.)[10] Pososhkóv proposes to keep the *dvor* as the basic taxable unit; he reserves his arithmetical definition of a *dvor* for the next chapter where he relates its size to the quantity of land worked by its occupiers on the one hand and the amount of tax to be paid by them on the other. Unwittingly perhaps Pososhkóv reverts to the earlier concept of the populated *chétvert'* but without allowing for any difference in the quality of the soil as had been done in the seventeenth century.[11] He has no confidence in the poll-tax as a method of assessment or as a source of revenue and implies that it is doomed to failure. Here he was wrong because the poll-tax was not abolished in European Russia until 1887.

But the ultimate responsibility for protecting the peasantry, according to Pososhkóv, rests with the tsar whom he sees as their true and permanent overlord. This description should be read in conjunction with the aside in Chapter 9 which speaks of the soil under the very feet of the landlords as the property of the tsar, and with the attack in Chapter 3 on the *dvoriáne* who live at home and rule over peasants without rendering service to the tsar. Taken together, these three utterances give a synopsis of Pososhkóv's conception of the economic and legal essence of the service state: the tsar is the absolute owner of the land and its inhabitants, the landlords do not own the land in their possession any more than they own their persons. They are, moreover, servants of the tsar who gives them land temporarily for their subsistence. The consistency of Pososhkóv's theory suffers from being put forward piecemeal: the landlords have apparently forgotten that they do not own their estates but at the same time are mindful of their merely temporary sway over the peasants and for that reason pay little attention to their welfare. In reality the most effective reminders of the precarious nature of the ownership of landed estates were the confiscations of *pomést'ia* by the tsar as a punishment for offences committed by their holders in his service.[12]

Tsar Peter's tacit approval of the allodification of *pomést'ia* from about 1721 has already been noted in the Introduction. By the time at which Pososhkóv was finishing his treatise, his ultra-conservative notion of the *pomést'ie* as a benefice probably looked outmoded as well as one-sided, in view of the fact that he ignores the existence of *vótchiny*.

The tsar, towards the end of his reign, took rather more interest in the welfare of the peasants than did their immediate landlords but it is most unlikely that he would ever have taken the risk of interfering in the tense relations between landlord and peasant as Pososhkóv wanted him to do. The instruction for the *voevódy* of January 1719 shows Peter's concern at the conduct of some land-holders who bring their estates to ruin by imposing all manner of burdens on the peasants and in addition beat them and torment them so that they take to flight. The depopulation thus caused brings about a shortfall in the tsar's revenue. Such ruination must not be allowed to occur, and the devastators must be identified and ordered to hand over their estates to their nearest relations (rather than to the tsar, as Pososhkóv would have wished).[13] The style of this particular article suggests that the tsar had a hand in its drafting.[14] The same may be true of the article devoted to the balance of income and expenditure in the Regulation for the *Kámer-kollégiia* likewise completed in January 1719. The Board of Revenue was instructed to ensure that 'nobody should be burdened more than is proper, for otherwise the oppressed poor will leave their farms and eventually the revenue will decline and the weeping of the poor will call down the wrath of God on the whole state'.[15] Tsar Peter once more formally acknowledged the importance of the peasantry in 1724. Dissatisfied with the prolixity of the draft translation of A. W. von Hohberg's treatise on agriculture, *Georgica Curiosa*, he produced his own abbreviated version of the section on the official protection enjoyed by the peasants in antiquity: 'The husbandmen are the arteries of the state which is nourished by them as the body is fed by the arteries. For this reason they must be cared for and not burdened to excess but rather protected against all assault and damage.'[16] The generic statement is the tsar's own interpolation; the next sentence conveys the sense of the original and introduces the burden of the whole passage which is the proper treatment by an army of the peasant population on its own as well as on enemy territory. Peter took this opportunity to express his considered opinion on the importance of the peasantry but soon returned to the point.

In the chronic conflict between landlord and peasants Pososhkóv, without excusing any fecklessness on their part, deplores their wretched condition and their ignorance. Literacy was considered desirable by the tsar's government in religious instruction, state service and in the life of urban communities in general[17] but the enunciation of the idea that literacy could be used by the peasant as a weapon with which to defend himself against an oppressive landlord must have been seen by the authorities as an act bordering on incitement to disobedience. Only an enlightened landlord like A. P. Volýnskii (1689–1740) would instruct his steward to make arrangements for some peasant youths to be taught to read and write because, as he put it, the presence in each village of a small number of literate men was extremely necessary.[18]

Pososhkóv's sympathy for the downtrodden was broad enough to include the Mordvinians[19] (the aboriginal inhabitants of the area on the middle Volga to the north of Saránsk between the rivers Móksha and Súra), though not without discrimination since he recommends preferential treatment for those who have been converted to Christianity. Other memorialists too set store by the conversion of the non-Russian population to Orthodoxy. In 1723 a proposal concerning the Mordvinians and similar to Pososhkóv's was made by one Símonov. An abortive attempt to run a special school for converted children of non-Russian stock had been made in Kazan between 1707 and 1709 by the metropolitan of that province, Tíkhon. Tsar Peter had pointed out the need to evangelize the Mordvinians as early as 1698 or 1699. In 1724 he was sketching out a policy in relation to the Kalmyks: their chiefs should be attracted to Christianity with teaching and gifts.[20]

The tsar understood no less well than Pososhkóv the need to preserve Russia's forests from devastation and was no less eager than Pososhkóv to increase the stock of deciduous trees, with the difference that he favoured the oak rather than the hazel-nut. In 1701 an ordinance was promulgated forbidding the clearing of forests within 30 versts (some 32 km) of rivers but just over two decades went by without any effective action being taken. In 1722, for the protection and supervision of forests the office of *óber-val'dméister* was established under the direction of the Board of Admiralty.[21] The instructions for this officer issued in 1723 declared the oak 'everywhere' and the elm, the ash and any fir over 12 *vershkí* (about 53 cm) in diameter to be 'prohibited' or protected trees close to rivers down which timber could be floated: the Volga, the Oká, the Don, the Dnieper, the western Dviná and their tributaries, also by rivers which flow into the lakes Ládoga and Il'mén', within 50 versts (about 53 km) of both banks of large rivers and 30 versts (about 32 km) of small ones. The location of 'prohibited' trees was to be shown on special maps and forests were to be guarded by designated inhabitants of nearby villages and inspected regularly by local *val'dméisters* (foresters). Permission to fell protected trees to meet the needs of the Admiralty, the artillery and other official agencies had to be obtained from the *óber-val'dméister*, and on no account were such trees to be put up for sale or used for private purposes other than those listed in the *ukáz*. The felling of trees for the construction of merchant ships and river craft was allowed subject to certain specifications being observed. The export of masts was encouraged but made conditional on permission being given by the Admiralty and the felling being done under the supervision of the foresters. On the northern Dviná and on other rivers falling into the White Sea trees other than oak and large pines were exempt from the ban. The rest of the instruction deals with fire precautions, the supply of timber to industrial works and the imposition of fines for breaking the rules concerning the protection of trees and forests. The standard penalty was 5 roubles for each trunk, of which 2 roubles were to go to the tsar's treasury and 3 to the supervisor who spotted the culprit. Arson in forest or steppe was declared a capital crime. Article 20 deserves special mention because it indicates the degree of paternalism exercised or aspired to by the tsar's government: coffins must not be made from the trunks of pines or from boards of oak, elm or ash. Spruce, birch or alder should be used instead. There is no record of any corresponding regulation concerning cradles.[22]

The bureaucrat's desire to interfere with private concerns, no matter how trivial, for the sake of a general good, the cameralist's wish to prevent avoidable disaster or loss by the application of foresight and vigilance may have been new to Russia but were not alien to the prudential mentality of the author of *The Book of*

Poverty and Wealth. Pososhkóv the conservationist, the man of the trees, had also the makings of a planner, as may be seen from his proposal to build villages to a design that would save them from the ravaging effects of fire. Once again Pososhkóv was asking the tsar to do something which had already been the subject of official action though only on paper. An ordinance published in 1722 pointed out that village fires caused ruin and destitution. In future cottages were to be rebuilt in pairs with hemp patches planted in between to a distance of not less than 30 sazhens (about 64 metres). The barns were to be placed at the back of the cottages, with the drying kilns not less than 35 sazhens (about 75 metres) away so that in case of fire whole villages did not burn down from being crowded together. A further *ukáz* published two years later noted that the peasants continued to rebuild their cottages in the old way, notwithstanding the instructions issued in 1722 which were now reaffirmed. Landholders or their factors were not to allow cottages to be built close to one another.[23] It seems that both legislator and amateur planner were labouring for Utopia. It should be noted that contrary to the impression given by Pososhkóv who in this chapter speaks of twenty or thirty *dvorý* in one village, not many Russian villages consisted of more than a few cottages and streets.[24] In the seventeenth century the average was five and it may be doubted whether this number increased very much in the first quarter of the eighteenth.

CHAPTER 7

Of the Peasantry

(166)   The peasants live in poverty for no other reason than their own idleness, to which may be added the indifference of the authorities and harsh treatment and neglect at the hands of their masters.

But no peasant need ever be reduced to poverty if the following were done. The taxes which he pays to His Majesty should be in proportion to his landholding (that is, the amount of land cultivated by him on his own account) and be collected from him at a convenient time of year; further, the peasants' masters must cease the practice of demanding from them dues and labour beyond what is the just amount proportional to the peasants' landholding. Moreover, the landowners must keep a strict eye on their peasants to ensure that they do not idle but apply themselves to their work on all days other than Sundays and holidays.

If a peasant falls into slack ways he should be severely beaten, for once a peasant goes downhill he will never return to the path of duty but will surely fall away into brigandage and other like crimes.

In summer the peasant must cultivate his land with all due care and in the winter work in the woods, either to supply the needs of his family or else of others, (168)   thus making some profit for himself. If there is no profitable work that he can do at home he should go somewhere where hired labourers are needed, so as not to spend his time to no purpose. In this way no peasant need be reduced to poverty.

For the betterment of the peasants' lot attention should also be given to laying out their cottages in a different way so that they can live in greater comfort and security. For they sustain much loss by living too close together, since if one cottage catches fire the whole village is burnt down and sometimes not a single cottage is left standing. As a result a peasant may be left without corn or livestock and this reduces him to the most dire poverty. Such disasters would not occur if peasants did not huddle together in this way.

Steps must be taken to prevent this kind of disaster befalling them. They must be ordered to build their cottages farther apart, that is, not up against one another but with gaps between each pair. There must also be wide lanes between the rows, thirty sazhens broad, but, if space is short, never less than twenty sazhens, so that if one peasant's cottage catches fire all the neighbours can rush to fight it. If there are such free passages between the cottages there will be no difficulty in coming to the rescue from any direction and the neighbours will even be able to prevent any two cottages threatened by the fire from being completely burnt down, since they will no longer, as now, rush to put their own possessions in a place of safety but all help to save the cottage which is on fire. As things are at present neighbours can give no help when there is a fire because they all set about safeguarding their own possessions; even so not everything can be saved but all suffer some loss. Thus all are ruined and brought to destitution.

If our Sovereign, showing his concern for the peasantry, were to order that peasant cottages in all villages and hamlets shall be built in pairs, it must be made incumbent on all landowners to rebuild their villages as occasion offers (that is, little by little if not straight away), so that the cottages stand in pairs with an open space in 70) each direction, as here illustrated. If this principle were followed there would be no difficulty in the way of containing the fire and no cottage would be allowed to burn to the ground.

When clerks are sent out for the purposes of the census or the land survey, that would be the right moment to rebuild a whole village at one stroke and also to allot to each peasant his share of the land – a whole, half or quarter holding[1] in proportion to the size of his family. And let it be determined at the same time in proportion to this allotment of land both what taxes the peasants owe to His Majesty's treasury and also what other dues, to the end that no excessive burden is put upon any one peasant and that the poorer do not suffer at the expense of the richer ones but that all are fairly assessed in direct proportion to their landholdings.

Further, peasants suffer heavy losses at the hands of brigands. Supposing a village has a population of twenty or thirty households (or even a good deal more), if even quite a small party of brigands attacks a peasant in his cottage, subjects him to rough handling, sets fire to his house and loads his possessions quite openly on to carts, his neighbours will hear and see all that goes on but will not dare to come out of their own homes to the rescue of their neighbour. Because of this brigands do as they please and even torture many peasants to death. This is another reason why no peasant can become rich.

To obviate such disasters a strict order should be sent out to all villages and hamlets that if brigands attack a peasant and his fellow villagers do not go to his rescue nor attempt to arrest the brigands, they shall all be flogged and shall themselves make double restitution for whatever the brigands have taken, seeing that they made no effort to help. If brigands descend in large numbers so that it is beyond the capacity of the village to lay hold of them, the neighbours must run to the nearest villages round about and tell all the adult men to come, armed with firearms and 71) staves and clubs, to seize the brigands. If the peasants of any village fail to do so they shall be flogged and contribute to making up for the losses[2] suffered by the plundered village. And if anyone loses his life through their failure to come to the rescue a fine of fifty roubles (or more, as the law may prescribe) in respect of each man murdered shall be exacted from all those who did not go to the rescue.

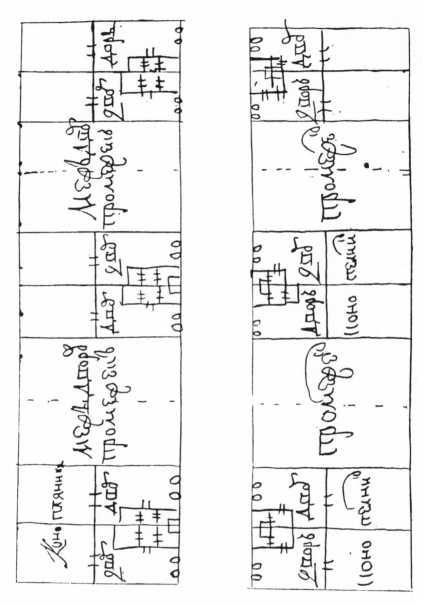

Pososhkov's model peasant holding (see pp. 310–11)

So if peasants could live together in such unity, always willing to help and support one another, brigands would never even think of risking such sudden raids to plunder and burn. And if the peasants behaved as befits a community, without doing injury to one another, they would want for nothing and be blessed in their lives.

The peasants also suffer no little hardship from a lack of literate men among them. A village of twenty or thirty families may not have a single literate man, so a stranger has but to flourish a written order before them, or even merely to state that he has such an order without producing it, and they will surely believe him. This causes the villagers unnecessary loss, since, like the blind, none of them sees or understands anything. Consequently many an impostor is able to do them great harm and they cannot question his actions. Similarly, those engaged in collecting taxes extract from them a great deal more than is due, and so the peasants suffer unnecessary loss.

To guard against this it would clearly be advisable to oblige peasants to send their children under the age of ten to the sacristan to be taught to read and, that learnt, also to write. It seems to me that it would be no bad thing to ensure that even in the smallest village all are able to read.[3] The peasants must receive strict injunctions to send their children to school without delay and to keep them there for three or four years. If during that time the children have not made any progress and, further, if the parents have failed to send to school such children as thereafter reach the right age, the parents must by one means or another coerced into remedying this. The young peasants who have learnt to read and write will be more useful not only to their masters in the management of their affairs but also to His Majesty in his service. They will be especially suitable as wardens. No one will be able to cheat the peasantry or extort anything from them in future.

I believe it would be advisable to extend this ordinance to the authorities in 'downstream' towns[4] so that the children of the Mordvá may also be educated, by force if necessary. Once educated they will themselves see the advantages of literacy. For soldiers, constables and clerks of all sorts descend upon them (even more than in the Russian villages), sometimes armed with a written order and sometimes not, and do what they will with them, since the Mordvá[5] are an illiterate folk with no one to look after their interests. So anyone can cheat them, demand what is not to be found in any order and extort payment by fair means or foul. But if their children are taught their letters, these literate ones will be in positions of authority among them and will not allow them to be oppressed as at present but protect their fellows from all kinds of wrongful treatment. Moreover, some of them will through their schooling learn the Holy Christian faith and desire to be baptized therein; and these educated ones will in the course of time bring their fellows also into the Christian faith. All of the Mordvá, Chuvásh or Cheremís[6] peoples who accept baptism must then be treated with due consideration by governors and all those in authority, who should in every way favour and protect them in preference to the unbaptized. The baptized must be treated with condescension in all things compared with the unbaptized, so that the latter may be envious of them.

His Majesty should direct the Russian peasants in those parts and the Mordvá people to live together in amity without doing injury to one another, and on no account to cut up for firewood timber suitable for building. They must not on any account cut down young timber for firewood on the edge of the steppes or, for that matter, in their own forests, with the exception of misshapen trees which are of no use for building. Any tree that falls should be removed, and when the (173)   saplings have grown to the thickness of a paling they may be cut and used for all domestic purposes.

If young wood establishes itself anywhere in the steppe regions, the local peasants must go every autumn and mow the grass for some dozen yards all round the wood so that in the spring steppe fires may not reach it and destroy it. I have seen many such young woods in the steppes, some the height of a man, others more than twice as tall, which had all been destroyed in steppe fires. But for these fires there would be extensive woods even on the edge of the steppes.

Again, once when I was at Chern and Mtsensk I saw young saplings no thicker than pea-stakes being cut down for firewood. To make one load a hundred or more trees had to be cut; yet there was plenty of dead wood lying about there. One mature tree will often provide ten or more loads of wood. The inhabitants should have confined themselves for the time being to gathering dead wood; if the young growth had been left to mature there would have been plenty for all.

In completely treeless parts far from sources of timber each of the inhabitants should set aside a dozen or more *desiatíny* of land near their village, plough it in the autumn and sow it with seeds of such forest trees[7] as birch, lime, maple, aspen, oak and elm, and also broadcast a couple of *chetverikí* of fresh ripe hazel nuts. When the seeds germinate the area must be protected from fire; and the ground must be kept clear the first year so that steppe grass does not smother the seedlings. In six or seven years' time the bushes from the hazel nuts that were sown will come into bearing, and in ten years' time will bear full crops; on good land they will be very fruitful. If everyone did this close to his own village all would have a plentiful supply of wood and nuts. Though they may find the work unrewarding to begin with, in the long run they will see the advantage of it.

As regards nuts it would be as well to make a strict ordinance that no one is to pick them before St Simon's Day[8] but allow them to ripen so that the kernel matures. Even if some mature earlier than September 1st in a particularly warm (174)   spot, no one shall dare to gather them before that day but only after September 1st when they begin to fall naturally. The gathering of the crop should be done by general agreement and on the advice of the local warden in such a way as to be fair to those with and without families alike.

A *chetverík* of such ripe nuts is better than ten times the quantity of unripe ones. Nowadays many people strip them all from the trees when they are still green without giving them time to ripen fully and thereby not only cause their neighbours to go hungry but also deprive themselves of sustenance, since they will hardly get as much for a *chétvert'* of unripe nuts as they could expect to be paid for a *chetverík* of ripe ones. They also reduce His Majesty's revenue since a *chetverík* of ripe nuts can be sold at forty kopecks or more, whereas no one would give that sum for even a *chétvert'* of unripe ones. So where the toll on the ripe nuts would have been a rouble, the unripe ones will not yield even ten kopecks. Moreover, anyone who buys the latter will derive no profit from them since they are valueless both for eating and for making oil. All that happens is that the dealers who buy them mix them with nuts of good quality and deceive the public by displaying the good ripe ones on top, and thereby fall into sin.

Ripe nuts bring some little profit to our realm since they are exported – to Persia, Sweden and elsewhere – whereas unripe ones are a complete loss. Therefore it is most necessary to prevent the premature gathering of nuts – let no one dare to pick any before St Simon's Day nor after that date begin their picking unless the warden has given permission and there is general agreement.

If anyone acts contrary to this ordinance and picks even a small quantity before St Simon's Day he shall be fined five roubles and beaten with rods. If any person brings to market nuts, whether fresh or dry, which have been gathered unripe so that the kernel is not mature, such nuts shall be confiscated on behalf of His Majesty. The seller shall be fined one rouble per *chetverík* (or as may be laid down). If they are very unripe, so that the kernel is less than half-size, he shall pay a double fine and the nuts shall be thrown away on to the river mud in the summertime and in the winter through a hole in the ice.

75) If any person catches another in the woods or on the road or in the village with freshly gathered nuts before September 1st, the nuts shall be given to the discoverer and the guilty person shall be fined at the rate of one rouble per *chetverík* (or, if less than a *chetverík*, then in proportion), and he shall be beaten to deter others from doing the same in the future. Should any factor, headman or warden show undue favour by not exacting the fine from someone caught doing this, or by exacting the fine without inflicting the physical punishment, or again try to bring pressure to bear on the discoverer in any way (even after the event), the said persons in authority shall, in accordance with the new regulation, be fined for contravening His Majesty's laws and shall be severely punished like all others who contravene them.

A similar regulation should be made about fishing to prevent the peasants from reducing to naught this part of His Majesty's revenue through their ignorance. In lakes and rivers where sparling[9] is not found it is inadvisable to allow the fishing of similar small fish. For, being unable to recognize sparling, the peasants catch instead all sorts of immature fish – young pike, ide, roach and especially immature perch. All these fish should be allowed a full year's growth; yet the peasants even take the fry when they are no larger than a grain of oats and by this practice reduce the stocks of fish in our rivers and lakes to nothing. When I was at Ustréka I took up a sample of the fry in a scoop and counted eighty-eight in it; a sample from a place where the fry was denser might have yielded two or three hundred. Now if these had been allowed to grow to yearling size what was in the scoop would have become enough to feed a whole family, and in two years' time the same would have produced twenty times that weight, not to mention the additional natural increase which the two-year-old fish would have produced. Caught and dried this fry will fetch twenty kopecks a *chetverík*, whereas after two years' growth the same fish would make at least ten loads and be worth not twenty kopecks but twenty roubles or more; and the toll on this would amount to more

(176)   than a rouble. So through this lack of forethought on the part of the peasants not only does His Majesty lose revenue but they themselves lose much good food.

Nowadays one hears many complaints that 'the fishing is not what it was', yet people do not understand why. The fishing has declined for no other reason than that the young fry is over-fished and so has no chance to mature. If in our cattle-rearing we were to use all the young calves for food we should have neither bulls nor cows. Similarly with fowls: if we were to eat all the chickens there would be no fowls left in a matter of two or three years. The case is no different with fish: small fish inevitably grow into large fish and if the small ones are removed there will be no large ones to be had.

So, in my opinion, the catching of all small fry (including immature sparling) should be prohibited even where sparling is found, and permission given to take only fish over a year old. Thus no more harm could be done to His Majesty's interest by this insensate practice, nor would the fishermen bring themselves and others to starvation by their indiscriminate fishing. If His Majesty were to give the matter his attention and strictly prohibit on pain of a fine or physical punishment the catching of immature fish (excepting always true native sparling), the stock of fish in our lakes and rivers would increase greatly.

I also advise the following measure. If any man brings to market any young undersized pike, carp, roach or perch (always excepting true sparling), whether fresh or dried, the fish shall be confiscated on behalf of His Majesty and given to invalid soldiers or paupers in almshouses, and the purveyor shall be fined whatever sum may be determined per *chetverík*. After such a law has been in force for a year people will cease to take immature fish. The order prohibiting the catching of immature fish and the making of fine mesh nets except for sparling must be sent in advance to all chief towns so that fines may be imposed for its contravention from the year next following.

(177)   If anyone catches even a small quantity of immature fish for his personal consumption and, being found in possession of the same, is brought before a magistrate, the fisherman shall be fined in accordance with the new law and one

quarter of the said fine together with the fish shall be given to the person who brought him to justice. Such fines will soon put a stop to private fishing of this kind.

Given such a regulation our stocks of fish will so increase in three or four years that there will be plenty for the whole country. And if the law is not broken in future we shall never be short of fish for all time. Even if fish then sells at half or a third of its present price the tax collected will be ten times as much or more, because the amount of fish sold will be enormous.

Again, it is surely not at all right that landowners should impose intolerable burdens on their peasants. For there exist masters so inhumane that during the busy season they do not allow their peasants a single day to work their own land. Thus the whole of the ploughing and mowing seasons are lost to them. Or else after receiving in full what is due from their peasants in rent[10] or supplies for the table, masters make further demands on them over and above this. By such extortions they drive the peasantry to destitution, and if they see that any peasant is becoming more prosperous they at once increase his dues. In these circumstances a peasant can never grow richer under such a master. Many *dvoriáne* say, 'don't let a peasant grow too long a fleece but keep him shorn short like a sheep'.[11] By acting so they impoverish the realm, since they fleece their peasants to such an extent that some have not even a single goat left and so in dire need they abandon their homes and flee to the new lands downstream or to the borderlands or even to foreign parts. In this way they make foreign lands more populous and leave their own deserted. And what concern is it of the landowners if a peasant is rich provided that he does not neglect his fieldwork, what concern if he has a thousand roubles or more provided that he commits no crimes and does not engage in illicit trade? A rich peasant is surely a credit to his master.

78) Landowners do not own their peasants in perpetuity; hence, being but temporary owners, they do not treat them with much care. The true owner of the peasants is our Sovereign, Autocrat of All the Russias. Therefore it behoves landowners not to ruin them but to take care of them in accordance with the Tsar's commands, so that our peasants should be proper peasants and not paupers. For the wealth of the peasantry is the wealth of the realm.

Therefore it seems to me that an ordinance should be drawn up defining what the landowners may exact from their peasants by way of rent or other dues, how many days a week the peasants should work for their masters and also what they should make for them by their handicraft, to the end that the rendering of their dues to the Sovereign and to their master shall not be too great a burden and that they may be able to feed themselves without difficulty. Those in authority must keep a close watch to ensure that masters do not impose any dues on their peasants over and above what is permitted by law, and do not reduce them to destitution.

All landowners, great and small, should therefore consult together on the subject of all dues and products of handicraft to which the master is entitled, and determine by common consent and with His Majesty's approval what dues should be imposed so that the burden on the peasantry may not be unduly heavy. It should be specifically laid down what sum of money is to be levied on a whole holding and on a half, quarter and eighth thereof respectively and what quantities each shall supply to the master's table; what amount of land on each whole holding or part thereof shall be ploughed and sown by the peasants, and the crop in due course reaped and threshed, on behalf of the master. Likewise cartage should be apportioned on the same principle so that each peasant contributes in proportion to his landholding and none is treated unfairly; in sum, so that it may not be a burden to him to pay all his dues to the Sovereign in full without falling into arrear.

If what is so agreed by general consent is then confirmed by Imperial decree and adhered to without fail thenceforward, the peasants will all eat their fill and some of them will grow rich to boot.

I have indeed given much consideration to the question of how the collection of the peasants' dues may best be carried out so as to be most profitable to His (179) Majesty and at the same time least burdensome to them. I have not found any principle fairer than to grade peasant 'households' according to the amount of land made over to each, that is, to the size of a peasants' holding and to the amount of grain which he sows on his land for his own use.

I do not know what our *dvoriáne* are thinking of. They are the peasants' masters and yet do not even know whom to call a peasant; nor have they any clear notion on what principle to reckon peasant holdings. They merely count the number of gates or enclosures, and some of them even go by the number of hearths. But even as the smoke of the hearth disappears into the air so all their calculations amount to nothing at all. Nor do I see any advantage in the method of counting souls; for the soul is an impalpable thing which cannot be grasped by our minds and upon which a value cannot be put; values can only be put on things of solid substance. The recent census gave a great deal of work, and, I should think, cost the treasury twenty thousand roubles or more. I venture to think that it was all labour in vain and wasted money for this form of tax will not come up to expectations. I shall treat in Chapter 9 of where a truly constant source of revenue is to be found.

As regards the peasants I believe it would be better to proceed thus. No master who has received his dues in full from a peasant shall demand of him anything further over and above that sum; nor shall he oppress him in any way but rather ensure that the peasant does not waste his time in idleness but works to the utmost of his powers for his own sustenance. Under such conditions a peasant, if he has enough sense, can become a man of some means.

If any peasant fails to do his ploughing, falls into idle ways and makes no provision for the future, it is the duty not only of the masters or their factors but also of the wardens to take steps to punish him severely, so that he does not become impoverished through his idleness nor take to crime or drink.

Even industrious peasants may suffer much hardship because no precise grading of their holdings has as yet been made. Certain great landowners count five or six or even ten dwellings as one household, so that these peasants have an easy time. Those of moderate means combine two or three dwellings into one with a common entrance and close the other entrances with fencing. These peasants also do not have too hard a time. But those landowners who are poor and without influence declare each peasant dwelling as a separate holding and those peasants consequently fall into permanent destitution under the intolerable burden of taxation. Thus the rich and powerful boyars protect only their own peasants from this burden but have no care for any others.

Therefore the first step towards the establishment of justice must be to define the peasant holding and what is to count as half, a quarter or an eighth of a holding. I am greatly amazed that despite the enormous number of landowners in Russia who are both rich and in positions of authority, they cannot meet together in conference and decide on a definition of the peasant holding, or a half or a quarter thereof, and what is to be understood by a whole holding or three quarters or one-and-a-quarter.

In those quarters of Moscow inhabited by artisans and traders in which a certain number of peasants also live, this matter is regulated sensibly: he who occupies a whole messuage pays tax on a whole one but he who occupies a half or a quarter pays tax in proportion. Whereas in the countryside the clerks of the land survey and of the census reckon as a single holding whatever dwelling has one entrance-gate. Whether there is one cottage within or half a dozen or ten, they record this simply as a single holding. This is contrary to all good sense as well as supremely unjust; it is unfair and ruinous to the poor and weak. Common sense demands that the peasant holding be not defined by such things as gates or hearths but by the amount of land held by a peasant family and by the amount of grain sown on that land.

In my opinion if a peasant is to be registered as occupying a whole holding he must be given enough ploughland to be able to sow every year four *chétverti* of rye and eight *chétverti* of spring corn and enough meadowland to provide twenty shocks[12] of hay for his own use.

If a peasant is allowed land insufficient to sow even one *chétvert'* of rye, such a holding must be reckoned as less than a quarter – perhaps as one sixth of a holding. Let each peasant's obligation be reckoned in proportion to the amount of land that he holds.

If a peasant has both the means and the enterprise to lease land from another landowner because his own master has allotted him too little, the land which he leases shall not be deemed to form part of his own holding even if he can sow ten *chétverti* or more on it; nor shall he pay any tax to His Majesty on it because this obligation will fall upon the owner of that land. The peasant shall not pay anything to his own master in respect of this additional land but only to the landowner who leases the land to him – either in cash or in sheaves of corn, as may have been agreed.

If any landowner sees that a peasant is well provided with seed corn and horses and freely hands over to him enough land to sow ten *chétverti* of rye in the autumn or twenty of spring corn together with enough meadowland to provide fifty shocks of hay, then the said peasant should be assessed at two-and-a-half holdings in respect of dues both to His Imperial Majesty and to his master. Thus all holdings are to be reckoned not by the number of entrance-gates or hearths but by the amount of land held and the area under crops. If this were done all over Russia there would be no unfair treatment either of rich or poor but each peasant would pay dues both to his Sovereign and to his master in proportion to his means. To protect the peasants against injustice it is imperative that every kind of due paid by them to their masters be likewise assessed in proportion to the amount of land held. The landowner shall not on any account exact from his peasants more than is due to him. Thus neither the demands of His Majesty nor those of the landowners will be intolerable to the peasantry. If things are ordered in this manner there will no longer be any reason for landowners to conceal, as hitherto, the true number of their peasant households,[13] since a landowner who deliberately registers whole holdings as halves, quarters or eighths will no longer be able to exact from these households more than is appropriate to the declared size of their land. A peasant will be paying dues both to the Tsar and to his master on the amount of land which he in fact holds and uses, and no more.

(182)

Should any landowner still register whole holdings as halves or less and pay tax accordingly, at the same time exacting dues from his peasants at the rate of whole holdings, and the abuse be brought to the notice of the authorities, the holdings in question (peasants included) shall be handed over to the informant. If the peasants refuse to submit to such extortion by their masters and themselves report the matter, the peasant who lays the information shall be given his freedom and fifty roubles in cash. But peasants who are aware that their master is demanding excessive dues from them and yet keep silent about it shall be given as many strokes of the knout as may be determined.

If a landowner settles any household serf, labourer, landless peasant or share-cropper[14] on a whole holding (or a half or a quarter), the correct dues must be levied upon him in respect of the land he holds, whoever he may be. In this way household serfs and the like will become taxpayers to the Sovereign no less than the peasantry proper and the rate of tax will not be intolerable to any of them since it will always be in proportion to the amount of land which goes with the household.

In this way His Majesty's revenue will greatly increase and if this principle is followed all over Russia the tax which falls on each household will be lighter for all to bear. As things are now some peasants are totally ruined by the taxes they have to pay whereas others escape scot-free.

The Tsar, it is my conviction, should be more zealous for the welfare of the peasants than their masters are, since the latter enjoy only temporary possession of their peasants, who belong to the Tsar in perpetuity and whose wealth is the wealth of the realm and whose poverty is the impoverishment thereof. Therefore (83) it is incumbent upon the Tsar to protect the interests of our merchants and peasants no less than those of high-born and military persons, so that none may grow destitute but all be prosperous in their several degrees.

If the matter of peasant households is regulated in the manner described the peasants' life will be no different whether their master be a man of great position or quite poor. Nor will they, as now, have any reason to take to flight, for life for them will be the same everywhere. And whether a peasant possesses a whole holding or less or more, the village must still be built on the plan of cottages in pairs with a garden on either side, as will be explained in Chapter 8. So laid out no village will be totally destroyed when there is a fire.

If any landowner oppresses his peasants by demanding of them dues or work above the fixed amount and the said peasants seek redress from the authorities, they shall be transferred from that master to His Majesty together with all their land. Being aware of this, even the most vicious landowner will keep himself in check and refrain from bringing his peasants to ruin.

There may be cases when a magistrate fails to make due investigation into such a complaint by peasants against their master and sends them back to him, or alternatively investigates the complaint but takes the landowner's side on all points and puts all the blame on the peasants. If the peasants then take the matter to a higher authority and there make good the case against their master and also bring an accusation against the magistrate, the latter shall not only be stripped of his possessions but also be deprived of his life. And so shall the wicked justicer perish miserably and the righteous one enjoy blessings in this world for his righteous judgment no less than in the world to come, for ever and ever, Amen.

CHAPTER 8. Of the Land

Commentary

The theme: taxation and its equitable basis – a reliable and up-to-date land survey. – Official policy in the matter of a land survey. – Surveying technique in Russia. – Pososhkóv's estimate of the area of taxable land. – The probable consequences of the general land-tax proposed by Pososhkóv.

This chapter continues and completes Pososhkóv's search for an equitable tax system. It lacks cohesion and the section on land measurement is overloaded with detail but the chapter is held together by its twofold theme which is that of taxation and its practical basis – a reliable and up-to-date land survey. The absence of such a survey also affects other aspects of land economy inasmuch as it prevents any fair or sensible division of land made necessary by legal circumstances or required for effective cultivation. To judge by the introductory paragraphs primogeniture, instituted in 1714 by the law on the mode of inheritance with the intention, among others, of putting a stop to the continual subdivision of landed estates by *dvoriáne*, was not universally observed.[1]

The need for a new survey had already been recognized by the tsar's cameralistic advisers who in this respect were ahead of Pososhkóv. Article 5 of the Regulation for the *Kámer-kollégiia* (Board of Revenue, 1719)[2] stated that the true basis for the determination and calculation of revenue raised from the land was a land register and instructed the Board to draw up such a register forthwith. According to the government servant and historian V. N. Tatíshchev (1686–1750) Peter I intended in 1719 to order the preparation of a general land survey based on the rules of geometry and the principles of equity but the official charged with the task was called away to other and more urgent duties and the project was abandoned at an early stage.[3] The adoption of the poll-tax obviated the need for a survey as far as the government was concerned. Only in the reign of Catherine II, in 1765, did work on a general survey begin.[4]

The technique of surveying used in Russia was primitive in the extreme. Fields were divided into the simplest geometrical figures – rectangles, trapezia, triangles – and measured with two lines, one 30 sazhens, the other 50 sazhens long, so as to produce the result in *desiatíny*. Where a holding was made up of three fields (autumn sowing, spring sowing, fallow), only one was measured and the area of each of the other two was assumed to be the same. But according to expert opinion the instructions issued to the surveyors in 1684[5] were so detailed that had they been followed, they would have resulted in a higher degree of accuracy than before (i.e. in 1646 and in 1678–9). The one element lacking in the recording of boundaries was the measurement of the angles between meeting lines. The use of the compass as recommended by Pososhkóv would have filled this gap. Recourse to the compass or the theodolite for measuring distances from a fixed point in recording boundaries had already been suggested in a memorandum submitted to the Senate in 1718.[6]

The advice now offered by the ever-optimistic Pososhkóv to the future army of surveyors is much more detailed than that included in the official instruction of 1684 and to some extent obscures the author's main intention which was to deliver a counter-blast to the poll-tax. In his calculations Pososhkóv not only proceeds by guess-work but is inconsistent into the bargain. In considering the total area of ploughland, meadowland and forest on which the proposed general land-tax is to be levied, he speaks first of 20 or 30 million *desiatíny* but next evidently has in mind 50 or 100 million *desiatíny* since those are the areas which, when taxed at the rate of 2 kopecks per *desiatína*, would produce the estimated sums of 1 or 2 million roubles. In point of fact in 1725 the area covered by arable was 41,848,000 hectares, that under pasture was 66,296,000 hectares and forests took up 213,958,000 hectares, a total of 322,102,000 hectares or about 294,965,000 *desiatíny*.[7] Nor are Pososhkóv's calculations correct. A tax of 6 kopecks on 20 or 30 million *desiatíny* would not produce 500,000 or 600,000 but 1,200,000 or 1,800,000 roubles.[8] Only one of his inspired guesses hits the mark. The total area of land – 294,965,000 *desiatíny* – taxed at the rate of 2 kopecks per *desiatína* would have produced 5,899,300 roubles and thus exceeded by 1,899,300 roubles the annual revenue expected from the poll-tax.[9]

Pososhkóv's general land-tax, to be paid by the rural landlords in relation to the amount of land in their possession and by all other householders in relation to the size of their *dvorý*, would not only have made the *poméshchiki* into taxpayers but would also have led to the regulation of the amount of boon-work and dues contributed by their peasants. Pososhkóv points out that some *poméshchiki* (all of whom he regards as mere beneficiaries) farm out large tracts of land without any of the profit reaped by them accruing to their overlord, the tsar. Tsar Peter, even if he did possess the capacity attributed to him by Pososhkóv, of accomplishing anything he chose to do, would hardly have set out on a course which in correcting the distribution of the fiscal burden would have disturbed the traditional division of the population into two categories: the common run of men who were required by the state to pay direct taxes and extraordinary contributions and to perform workaday duties, and the privileged who by reason of their service in the army, in the administration and at court were, together with the clergy, exempt from such impositions. Pososhkóv himself points to the main obstacle: the acquisitive habits of the haves.

CHAPTER 8

Of the Land

(184)   It seems to me not only a wrong but even a sinful practice that on the death of a landowner the members of his family divide all his land (with or without peasants living on it) into small parcels. A single field may thus be divided into many separate lots and so come under ten (or even many more) different owners.

And such is the confusion that one owner may receive ten *chétverti*, others two or three, another a single *chétvert'* (or even a half or an eighth),[1] and each one of them is determined to cultivate every strip that he receives, whether good or bad. Those who are able to fend for themselves can enter into possession and work the whole of their share, whereas those who are not fail to do so. So this kind of division leads to nothing but disagreement and trouble, and as a result many fields now under divided ownership are abandoned and revert to grass or woodland. To let such land go out of cultivation is to detract from His Majesty's interest since uncultivated land brings in no revenue.

Conversely a man who has sole ownership of a piece of land clears it, ploughs it and manures it, and so year by year even a poor piece of land will be improved; likewise he will mow all his hayfields. All this promotes His Majesty's interest.

These landowners not only divide unoccupied land[2] into many portions in this way but even land on which villages and hamlets stand. There is a village in the

(185)   province of Nóvgorod called Ustréka with some twenty peasant households belonging to seven different landowners; in some villages there are even more. With such a multiplicity of owners there must inevitably be quarrels and matters of contention.

To avoid this I think that the present way of breaking up an inheritance should be abandoned and instead both occupied and unoccupied land should be apportioned in undivided parcels as defined by known boundaries.

If such parcels of land cannot be kept undivided because of the large number of beneficiaries, then they should be offered at a valuation and any member of the family should be able to put down this sum and receive in return all such land for his own; and that is quite fair. If all the owner's kin are too poor to do this the land should be sold to any purchaser outside the family and the proceeds divided among the heirs in proportion to their shares. In this way not only will crimes be avoided[3] but there will be no occasion for dispute since even the smallest shares will receive proportionate compensation in cash.

There is also a very wrong practice on the part of all the clerks and revisers concerned with the land survey and the census. When making an inventory they record merely the names by which each (occupied or unoccupied) piece of land is known, how many *chétverti* of arable there are in each and how much meadow-land. Far from making any measurement or even seeing for themselves, they just record whatever the peasants tell them. Thus they will record a certain piece of land as consisting of one field of fifty *chétverti*[4] of seed corn plus two more fields of the same size,[5] but when it comes to sowing one of them it turns out that this amount is more than can be sown on all three fields together.

I myself have seen one such piece of land recorded as six *chétverti*, yet twenty *chétverti* of rye will sow one of its three fields alone and on the top of that there are more than three (square) *versts* of woodland. What but confusion can result from this sort of thing? A size and a name are entered for every piece of occupied or unoccupied land but no one troubles to record a description of the land, to state what other pieces of land surround it or precisely to define its boundaries. The result is a multitude of disputes and troubles. Some people, heedless of God's anger, will appropriate a piece of land, claiming it as their inalienable possession,[6] holy icon in hand, thereby incurring deadly sin. Small wonder then if it happens that when engaged in such misappropriation and the marking of a false boundary men are struck dead on the spot.

Common sense requires that all land of whatever kind be defined by immovable boundary marks. And if a river, stream or other immovable landmark does not form the boundary between two properties, then some other immovable mark must be chosen which cannot be destroyed. If there is nothing of the kind an immovable landmark can be made in some open spot, for instance a pit may be dug seven to ten feet deep and the same across, which is then filled with large boulders heaped up to form a cairn, well above ground level. This cairn can then be built up with earth to a height of a couple of yards and will provide an indestructible boundary mark. From this mark a measuring line should be run out straight along the boundary to the next corner. A nautical compass should be placed under the line and a record made of the angle between the line and compass north, and the length of the line from the cairn to the corner should likewise be recorded in sazhens.

If there is no suitable permanent landmark at the corner a pit should be dug some four or five feet deep and as much across and filled with stones or coals. Build this up into a mound a couple of yards high and, after making it firm, cover it with turves and plant half a dozen young trees upon it (trees three or four years old are very suitable). The same species of tree must be planted from first to last on all such mounds[7] as may be made round the piece of land. When another piece of land is measured out a different species of tree shall be planted on its mounds so that one set of boundaries shall be defined by birches, another by pines or firs or oaks or elms or aspens exclusively. But where one piece of land is contiguous to

(187)

another and so has a common boundary with such a newly surveyed area, with the result that the mounds along the common boundary are planted with the wrong kind of tree with respect to the piece to be surveyed, the record shall state the number of mounds already made which define the boundary and what kind of tree is planted on them; a second species of tree must not be mixed with these. At a point where the boundary of such a contiguous area diverges from the common line one of the existing mounds may be used if it is at that same point, and let the record show this; but if it diverges at a point between two mounds, then a mound shall be made near the existing boundary line – not actually on it but a couple of yards out – so as not to spoil it, and it shall be planted with the appropriate species of tree for that whole piece of land.

Any tree that dies must be replaced. In some two or three years' time (or even half a dozen), when the young trees have established themselves, each surveyor shall inspect all his boundaries to see whether any of them has suffered any damage. If the boundary marks are found to be damaged anywhere even a little, proceedings must be taken against the culprit and he must be severely punished in accordance with the law. And the trees must be looked over: the one which has taken and is growing away best should be left and the others removed. However, if two or three are growing well then all of them may be retained as circumstances suggest (provided that they are all of the same species) and the superfluous ones removed. Strict orders must be given for the remaining trees to be carefully tended and not harmed in any way. And if a tree of some other species establishes itself on the mound it must be removed and not allowed to grow lest such trees confuse the landmarks.

When the survey is being carried out the above-mentioned compass shall be placed under the measuring line to ascertain its direction with respect to a given landmark. The direction of the line shall be recorded as shown by the compass – east, south, west or north or the direction in degrees within the quadrant – that is, how many degrees south of east or east of south, and so on. The record shall show in sazhens the length of the straight lines forming the boundary from landmark to

(188)

landmark or from corner to corner and the direction (right or left) and angle of each change of direction.

If a boundary makes a curve anywhere and the one owner will not concede any ground to the other, the measuring line shall be laid straight from mound to mound and their distance apart measured, and also the greatest width of the curve from that base line; and all these figures shall be recorded. Wherever there is an old boundary along a river or stream that boundary shall remain the boundary. However, the measuring line must still be run out and a record made of the lengths of the straight lines from mound to mound, but where the old boundaries make curves they shall not be changed. The course which the measuring line followed in making the survey shall not be marked out with the plough but only a record kept of the angle at which the line lay.

Except where there are bulges the plough shall be passed two or three times up and down each side of the boundary as defined by the measuring line and the loose earth shall be thrown up on either side along the said boundary line and it shall be recorded what parcels of ground this boundary divides, to whom they belong and what name they go by. If any river, stream, ravine, dry gully or marsh lies across the boundary this too must be recorded – on what boundary line it lies and at what distance (in sazhens) from the nearest mound. And if a way passes across this land, it must be stated where it comes from and where it goes to, and also what landmark there is nearby – such as a large or small river, a large or small lake, or a marsh.

Every boundary shall be recorded in full detail so that it may remain immovable for all time and be free of all ambiguity. Even if this prove very laborious generation after generation would be able to live thereafter without any disputes. And if by God's grace this excellent work were carried through I think that it would be advisable to print a hundred copies or so of the survey and distribute them to all chief towns. If there should be a fire in one place the book would be to hand somewhere else and all the labour of the survey would not have been in vain. No one would any more be in doubt about any matter pertaining to land anywhere, but the book would be for everyone, as it were, a mirror of clarity.

Every piece of land shall be surveyed and recorded as follows. From a given point of origin the boundary runs (let us say) due east or due south or else there is

89) some deviation to the right or to the left of a cardinal point (state in what quarter of the compass and how many degrees right or left), and from the base point to the first mound the land on the right belongs to such and such a village or hamlet or is a part of such and such a piece of land, and on the left hand similarly there is such and such a piece of land (give the name). Provided that all the pieces of land contiguous to that which is being surveyed are recorded by name, the boundary line will be safe for ever from all alteration and not subject to any ambiguity, for it will be possible to trace any such boundary by means of its immovable landmarks, the compass bearings and the measurements from corner to corner and from mound to mound. When a piece of land has been surveyed all round and the last section of the line comes back to the point from which the survey started, the compass bearing of this last leg must likewise be included.

If a dispute arises about any boundary, the area of land concerned (how many *chétverti* of arable and how much meadowland) shall first be ascertained from the old land register and then the boundary of the said land shall be determined according to the method given above and an immutable boundary drawn round it.

After the boundaries of a given piece of land have been determined the measuring line shall also be run out across the middle of the said land between two of the fixed landmarks and so the total length of that land measured. Similarly it shall be measured across its breadth, starting from one of the mounds and ending at one on the far side or at some other fixed mark (using a long line). Place a quadrant at the point of intersection and note the difference between the right angle and the angle of intersection; and measure both the length and the breadth. At the same point of intersection a compass shall also be placed and a note made of the direction of north. This shall be shown on the chart by means of an arrow.

A scale chart of the land surveyed shall then be made, on broadsheets, showing all the details, viz. the separate distances (expressed in words, not figures) from mound to mound and from corner to corner or between any other kinds of landmark, together with the names of all the pieces of land contiguous to the one in question, and at what points each of them meets it. In the centre of the chart indicate the length and breadth of the said land by dotted lines joining those landmarks between which the line was stretched; and along the dotted lines write the length of the longer and shorter diameters in sazhens. If the chart is correctly drawn, anyone with a knowledge of survey work will be able to tell from it, without going to the place, how many *desiatíny* the piece of land contains and how many *chétverti* of arable it represents.

(190)

To this end every surveyor must prepare charts of every piece of land which he surveys, and every piece of land so surveyed, occupied or unoccupied, must be recorded on a separate chart. And it must be noted on the said charts at how many *chétverti* of grain each arable field is reckoned according to the old register and at how many shocks of hay each piece of meadow. When a surveyor has finished the survey of the area allotted to him he shall bind all his charts together into a book and deposit it in the Office of Estates[8] where it shall thenceforward be kept in a safe place for reference.

If the whole surface of Russia were surveyed in this way all disputes about land would cease. No one would be able to appropriate even a sazhen of what belongs to others but each would enjoy the possession of his land, poor though he be and exposed to legal trickery and high-handed practices.[9] The powerful would no longer be able as now to oppress the weak, even to the point of taking away all that they possess, and it will be obvious to all if someone appropriates what does not belong to him.

Further, if anyone attempts to obliterate a boundary or move a marker mound into another's land, all will be aware of it since it will not be possible to do so in a single day, nor single-handed, and so the deed will be plain for all to see. Even if someone were to succeed in so doing the facts can later be investigated; only in the event of the loss of all the charts and records could such a wrongful act succeed. That is why the survey must be printed in book form and several copies of the charts made, one set to be kept in Moscow, another in St Petersburg and a third in the chief town under whose jurisdiction the land in question lies.

Strict orders must be issued, on pain of heavy fines, that any such boundary line or lines (even if they come under a single ownership) shall on no account be ploughed over, nor any boundary or mound moved from one place to another, but that every boundary shall remain unalterably in its place for all time to come.

(191)

Further, similar immovable boundaries must be set up in the steppe-lands. The land shall be measured off according to the deed of grant and the area expressed in *desiatíny*. For the purpose of making a survey of the whole of the estate granted in the manner described above, a base point shall be chosen and from there the measuring line shall be run out straight, even for a whole verst or more, to a point of change in direction. The straight lines shall be expressed[10] always in sazhens. At every corner make a mound in the manner described above and then continue to run the line out straight to the next corner. In this way measure out the whole perimeter back to the base point. The trace of the line shall be marked out with the plough, the angles determined with the compass and charts made in the manner prescribed above. And if there is a wood nearby the mounds shall be planted with saplings as described above; but if young trees cannot be procured anywhere acorns may be collected and a dozen or so planted on each mound or in other cases the seed of elm, birch, maple or some other species. The records must show what kind of seeds have been scattered on a given set of mounds. When the perimeter of the estate has been established in the manner aforesaid the line shall be run across from corner to corner, since in the steppe areas many of the tracts to be surveyed will be rectangular so that no mounds will be needed except at the corners. And in the centre of the chart compass north shall be shown. The chart shall also state in figures the measurements of the whole perimeter and the position of the centre point.

All grants of land to great lords and to petty *dvoriáne* alike shall be accurately surveyed in this way and not as hitherto estimated by eye, so that the land marked out shall be neither more nor less than the grant. It is most important that in all such surveys the most accurate measurement in *chétverti* shall be obtained, so that if His Imperial Majesty should repeal the pernicious poll-tax and ordain in its stead a tax on land the latter may be defined at so much per *chétvert'*. In this way neither poor nor rich will suffer any injustice.

192) Previous surveys made by eye and guesswork credit one owner with five *chétverti* whereas he has as much as fifty, and another with twenty when five *chétverti* of grain are too much to sow the whole area. If the correct measurements were ascertained for all pieces of land no one would suffer any injustice.

Once the boundaries have been fixed by survey the rule must be strictly observed that no piece of land, whether occupied or not, shall be divided, as now, into many portions or even into two, but if anyone sells, mortgages or conveys as a gift any land, it must be the whole undivided parcel as defined in the survey.

Even if it takes a long time to carry out a complete survey of the kind proposed, once it is done it is done for good and will make for peace and quiet among landowners. The boundaries as defined by this survey must be final; not only shall the boundary lines be unalterable but neither shall any name be changed, and whatever designation has been current since time immemorial so shall it continue for all time. And if any property has to be broken up or distributed by official order on the occasion of a landowner's death or for any other reason, the division must be made in whole pieces of land of whatever nature as shown in the survey books, and nothing shall be added or subtracted from the boundaries shown therein.

If any person damage any boundary line or even alter the designation of any piece of land whatever, he shall be subject to a fine.

If a way passes across any land, it shall be marked off with the plough on either side in the same manner as any other boundary line. If it is a cart track it shall be allowed a width of three sazhens; if it is a local road – six sazhens; if it is one of the high roads to Moscow, twelve sazhens or more. There is no need to compute the area of roads (whether in *desiatíny* or *chétverti*) in the survey nor to reckon roads as part of any person's land, since any road, on whatever land it may be, is deemed to belong to His Majesty and not to any landowner. Consequently such land shall not be subject to the land-tax nor cultivated for any crop whatever. If our Great

(193) Emperor deign fully to follow my proposal and God look favourably on it from on high and visit it with His divine aid, the whole task could be completely carried through within no great term of years.

When all estates (of whatever category) have been surveyed, the land-tax on them shall be assessed as His Majesty may decree – at so much per year on each *chétvert'* or *desiatína* from every holder of land in Russia (other than land allotted to peasant households in the form of ploughland or meadow) – that is to say, this tax will fall on all kinds of land, woods and marshes held by the *dvoriáne*; since the peasants will be paying another tax on all the land held by them in accordance with the system of assessment described in Chapter 7. Such land must therefore be kept separate from that of the *dvoriáne*.

Taking a *desiatína* as an area of eighty by forty sazhens,[11] I think it would be possible to set the annual tax on a *desiatína* at eight kopecks for arable, six for meadowland, four for woodland and two kopecks for marsh. I reckon that the annual return would be two or three hundred thousand roubles or even a good deal higher. In this way the land-tax would provide a sure return: it would never diminish but only increase from year to year.

If anyone clears woodland to make new arable fields his tax would be increased accordingly. But if after clearing and cultivating he lets the said land go out of cultivation again, there is no call to demand the higher rate of tax on it since it will revert to woodland.

Similarly, if any person drain a marsh and turn it into meadow the higher rate of tax will be imposed. Therefore the Local Commissioners[12] shall make an annual inspection to see if anyone has increased the area of his arable or meadowland and add to his assessment accordingly. By this system no one will own land scot-free but all will make their contribution.

(194) Nowadays there is many a landowner with twenty or thirty pieces of land assessed at a thousand *chétverti* in all, who leases them for use as ploughland and

meadow. This brings him in a yearly income of fifty or sixty roubles, yet he does not pay a single farthing to His Majesty on them. Even a man of no consequence like myself owns some hundred and fifty *chétverti* and yet pays no tax whatever on them to His Majesty.

If all the land in Russia were to be accurately surveyed and calculated in *desiatíny* I believe the total would be twenty or thirty million *desiatíny* or more. Reckoning my land-tax in round figures at six kopecks per *desiatína*, the return would be [one million] five or six hundred thousand roubles. Moreover, no one would be able to conceal his obligation nor evade payment since the concealment of even a single *desiatína* would be impossible.

God created the land immovable; even if the possession of a piece of land passes from one person to another the land itself remains immovable. Hence if land is made the object of a tax, that too can be considered immovable and will certainly be gainful. If God look with favour upon it and send His help such a tax could be brought into effect within a reasonable time. Only the first year's work would be at all laborious: once the method of surveying with the compass and making the measurements has been mastered people would soon learn to make the scale charts. Even if, in the first year, only one skilled surveyor could be sent to carry out the work in each Government, it should be possible the next year to send ten, the third year perhaps as many as a hundred, since provided that it is laid down at the start exactly how the survey is to be carried out, many people can be trained to do it in a single month. The success of my scheme is in the hands of His Majesty: if he so wills, it can be carried through in a few years.

I reckon that the return of this land-tax will be about a hundred thousand roubles from each Government.[13] But I also reckon that people of consequence will do their best to hinder it because they are accustomed to do just as they please and are not so fond of giving as of receiving.

95)   I assume also that landowners are bound to make difficulties about my proposed system of taxing the peasants in proportion to the land held by each household. But if His Majesty can break down the inveterate obstinacy of the landowners then I am sure that the tax paid by each peasant household can be halved. At present one household pays about eight roubles or a little less; under the proposed system I think it would not be as much as four. If all the peasants as well as the *dvoriáne* pay tax in proportion to the amount of land which they hold such a tax will be much more dependable than the poll-tax and at the same time give a constant and high return.

The only difficulty in setting a tax on land is that it must first be all surveyed as outlined above, but once all the measurements (in *desiatíny*) have been established and the tax imposed in proportion, everyone will find it both convenient and simple. It is therefore advisable that the survey should include not only all the arable, meadow and woodland but also all marshes, large or small, and define them by suitable landmarks and their contiguity to other land. Separate charts should be made of all large tracts of marshland and the neighbouring landowners should be asked which of them is willing to consider a given marsh as part of his lands. The marsh should then be entered under his name.

And if the neighbouring landowners refuse the offer of such marshes they shall be deemed to be the property of the Sovereign and leased by his officials to anyone willing to accept them. But if there are small marshes on any estate they shall be entered as belonging to the owner of the said estate.

The boundaries of any such marshes which the landowners refuse to accept shall be determined as for other areas of land: mounds shall be made at the corners, as in other cases, and a balk thrown up all round with the plough; and note shall be made of the points at which the boundaries of other estates abut upon it. Those who have refused the offer of such marshland shall have no further right to enter it for any purpose whatever nor to pasture their livestock on it; the person to whom it has been leased or sold shall have the sole use of it.

(196)   Similarly a survey should be made of all plots occupied by peasants, *dvoriáne* and people of other stations in the countryside, and by merchants, other town-dwellers, clerks and other servants of His Majesty (not excluding even high officials) in the towns, and all these too should be assessed for tax so that nobody may live scot-free on His Majesty's land.

I believe that there must be some two or three million square versts or more all told within His Majesty's dominions in the hands of all the population, excluding only such steppe-lands and remote forests as have not been assigned to any owner, – indeed such an enormous quantity of land that any final computation of it is impossible. Yet our Sovereign receives not the slightest payment in return for it. Landowners lease their land and receive a considerable income therefrom without paying anything whatever to the Sovereign.

Every square verst [reckoned at 500×500 sazhens] contains $78\frac{1}{8}$ *desiatíny* [reckoned at 80×40 sazhens]. If one reckons a flat rate of two kopecks per *desiatína* on arable, meadow and marsh-land, this fixed land-tax will yield over a million roubles yearly. And this revenue will never decline but rather gradually rise with the clearing of woodland.

If God so disposes that our great Sovereign impose a universal tax on land-holdings, no one will occupy land for nothing as at present but all will be taxpayers in proportion to the amount of their holding. Furthermore, the size of the plot on which the peasant's dwelling stands should conform to certain exact and fixed rules and not be merely guessed by eye; so that if a peasant is deemed to occupy a taxable holding, then let his plot be of the right size.

I think that the plot should be some fifty or sixty sazhens in length (including the threshing floor); the width corresponding to a whole holding should be twelve sazhens, to a half-holding eight sazhens, to a quarter-holding six sazhens and to an eighth-holding four sazhens. The length is made the same in each case in order that the kilns for drying the grain be as far as possible away from all the dwellings.[14]

98)   The rate of tax (compounding all dues) on a whole holding should be set, I think, at three or four roubles a year or as may seem more appropriate after thorough consideration; a half-holding will pay half this amount, a quarter-holding a quarter, and so on in proportion. In this way no one will be unjustly treated and the burden of all will be bearable.

A whole holding should in my opinion comprise four *chétverti* of ploughland in each of the three fields,[15] and a half-holding two *chétverti*. Anyone who occupies a quarter-holding should receive one *chétvert'* in each of the three fields, so that he can sow his whole *chétvert'* of rye every season, or two *chétverti* of spring corn.[16] And to those who occupy one sixth or one eighth of a whole holding land should be invariably allotted in the same proportion. If any man is willing to take upon himself a higher burden of tax he shall receive more land (arable and meadow) in direct proportion to the increase, and this rule shall be observed invariably.

Similarly the landowners shall receive from the peasants their various dues including the number of work-days to be done on their land in accordance with the above proportions. In this way the peasants will be equal to all their work. And no landowner shall impose any further burden upon them over and above what is laid down so that the peasantry may not suffer impoverishment through such inordinate exactions. If all is so ordered and arranged the landowners will give up their many iniquitous practices such as counting two or three households as one. For the better prevention of such dishonesty by landowners and also for protection against fire, the buildings in all villages and hamlets must be disposed in pairs and not all huddled together as now, but never more than two cottages together. What was touched on in Chapter 7 in this connection is set out in more detail here with the appropriate measurements. If this is done it will be impossible to treat three or four households as one, nor will there be any point in so doing.

99)   When peasant holdings have been dealt with, town property should be surveyed and similarly assessed for tax according to the size of the messuage.

I think that such urban property, within or without the walls, belonging to merchants, officials and all manner of persons at present exempted from taxation, whether men of influence or not (with the sole exception of the clergy and their assistants), could be taxed at the rate of one quarter kopeck a year per square sazhen or perhaps at half this rate.

Likewise all market gardens and other plots on the outskirts of a town[17] on which vegetables are grown or which are laid out as orchards must be measured in square sazhens. I think that one kopeck per ten square sazhens could be levied on such plots.

It would not seem right to levy a duty on the produce of such vegetable gardens offered for sale in the market of the same town. Should the produce, however, be taken to some other town toll ought to be levied, and if any new duty is devised it too should be met.

I believe that it would be appropriate to set up a special office to deal with these

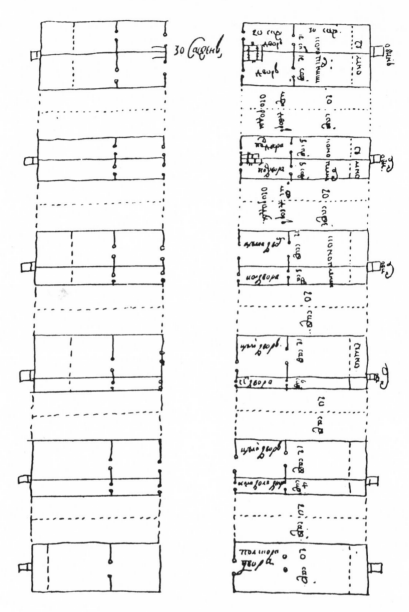

Pososhkov's model village (see p. 332)

important matters which concern land: there will be a great deal of work for such an office to do and the revenue which will pass through it will amount to a million roubles and be of the first importance. My land-tax is only difficult to introduce; once it has been introduced and is well established it will continue to flow unchanging as a river. The land was created immovable by God; therefore a land-tax, if God so wills, will also be immutable for ever and ever. Amen.

CHAPTER 9. Of the Tsar's Interest

Commentary

The fiscal nature of the tsar's interest. – Regalia and monopolies. – Internal tolls and duty on imports and exports. – Pososhkóv's suggestion for a single tax on all merchandise. – The kabák *(liquor monopoly) a social plague but profitable to the exchequer. – Peter I farms out the* kabák. *– Private distilling allowed (1716). – Ex-soldiers as collectors of toll and salesmen of liquor. – Changes effected in the liquor monopoly in 1713 and 1750 close to Pososhkóv's recommendations. – His proposal for a loan fund for entrepreneurs. – Customs duties haphazard before 1722. – Tariff policy laid down in 1720 aims at a favourable balance of trade. – The tariff of 1724. – Rates of duty suggested by Pososhkóv unrealistic. – Pososhkóv advocates increased profit from coinage. – The monetary operations of the government. – Abundance of copper coins of small denominations. – New monetary policy adopted in 1721. – Concern at the outflow of silver from Russia. – Effect of purchase of foreign silver for coinage on the balance of trade. – Sweden's monetary policy compared with Russia's. – Pososhkóv blames the foreigners for the rising prices of imported goods. – The production of salt in Russia. – The government takes control of the wholesale and retail sale of salt (1705). – The producers are invited to take charge of retail sales (1711) which they find uneconomic. – Salt in short supply. – The Kabinét takes over the collections of the revenue from the salt monopoly (1715). – The shortage continues. – Increase in the wholesale price allowed (1723). The monopoly, criticized by Pososhkóv, lifted in 1727 but restored in 1731). – Hypocrisy of the service state. – Scurvy not caused by lack of salt. – Revenue from tax on salt proposed by Pososhkóv would have been equal to the yield from the monopoly. – Tobacco in Russia: importation, production and sale. – Pososhkóv's anachronistic views on the ownership of land and peasants by* dvoriáne. *The financing of the current needs of the tsar.*

In this chapter Pososhkóv investigates in a desultory way the profitability of the revenue derived from indirect taxation. The sources designated as pertaining to 'the tsar's interest' comprise *regalia* such as the income from the production and sale of alcoholic beverages – particularly brandy and vodka but also beer and mead, from the management of taverns on behalf of the Crown, from the minting of coins and from the monopoly of salt and tobacco. The tax or toll on internal trade and the duty on imports and exports do not belong to the same category but are considered under the same head because the responsibility for their management as well as that of the *regalia* (except coinage) fell on the *posádskie liúdi* by way of obligatory and unpaid service.[1] Pososhkóv finds the existing methods of managing 'the tsar's interest' ineffectual and open to abuse. The improvements which he recommends are designed to cut out waste and increase profitability.

The system of internal tolls and the rates of duty on imports and exports had undergone little change since the promulgation of the Tolls and Customs Regulations (*Tamózhennyi ustáv*) of 1653 and the New Trade Regulations of 1667 (*Nóvyi torgóvyi ustáv*).[2] When the tolls were not collected by representatives elected for the purpose by the *posádskie liúdi* in fulfilment of their service obligations towards the state, they were farmed out to individuals together with the concession to produce and sell alcoholic beverages in return for a fixed annual rent. (Thus when Pososhkóv was farming the tolls at Ustréka, he was at the same time engaged in distilling and the sale of liquor.) Both methods were uneconomic; in addition, that of management by sworn government agents weighed heavily on the *posádskie liúdi,* but the government seemed unable to find any solution to this problem other than periodically going over from the one method to the other. In 1724 the takings from the production, sale and taxation of alcohol (1,185,510 roubles) amounted to about 18 per cent of the total revenue for that year (6,696,383 roubles), the receipts from tolls and customs (825,623 roubles) to about 12 per cent. The sum of 1,185,510 roubles does not include the 7,489 roubles collected from the branding of private stills (see below) but does comprise 342,893 roubles obtained from the surcharge of 10 kopecks per *vedró* on the retail sale of brandy, decreed in 1723. A tax at the rate of one kopeck for each *vedró* of spirits sold had been charged since 1705; the receipts from the new tax were to be shown separately.[3]

Many of Pososhkóv's recommendations are impracticable or confusing. Thus whereas he speaks of a single tax on all merchandise he is in fact proposing three distinct levies of which only the first and the third are alternatives. The first to be put forward is a purchase tax levied at source on goods bought for home consumption. The rate of 10 per cent – twice as high as the toll which it was to replace – might well bear too heavily on the first buyer, hence the elaborate scheme to enable him to borrow the necessary cash. The second, a tax on profit at resale, would be payable in addition to the first. The third is a duty recoverable by the Russian merchants who would include it in the price at which they sold the goods to the foreign merchant.

In 1704 in order to increase the revenue from internal trade a 'new and levelling' toll (*novouravnítel'naia póshlina*) was introduced. It extended the liability to toll at the rate of 5 per cent to goods bought by outsiders from countrymen and by inhabitants of the same town from one another. But this endeavour to collect toll wherever goods changed hands appears to have had an inhibiting effect on trade and was abandoned in 1714 without any explanation. It is therefore surprising that Pososhkóv should seek to reintroduce the principle of a universal toll on only slightly less burdensome terms. From 1704 toll was also charged on carts from which goods were sold in market places (in proportion to the area occupied) and on barges tied for the same purpose to moorings (at so much per craft). The first-named was abrogated in 1724 together with the tolls levied on steam baths in villages, beehives and the special imposts paid by priests and ecclesiastical attendants. The news of the abrogation had evidently not reached Pososhkóv or else he would have toned down his protest against the irksomeness and restrictiveness of these petty imposts.[4]

According to Križanić such foul, revolting and extraordinary drunkenness as that which he had witnessed in Russia was not to be found in the whole civilized world. The reason for this was the *kabák* or right reserved by the Crown to sell liquor to the public. The privileged few who by special permission were allowed to prepare their own drink but were compelled to consume it within a few days held celebrations under every possible pretext. The lower orders were allowed to drink only in the tsar's taverns which in all respects resembled pigsties. But there were not enough such taverns and the poor, when they had the opportunity, drank more than they could hold. The drink, Križanić adds, was vile and sold at a fiendish price.[5]

The *kabák*, then, was a social plague but it provided the tsar with a valuable source of revenue and the large-scale purveyor of liquor with the chance of making a fortune. In the seventeenth century this opportunity was not always open. Thus in 1681 the farming of the production and sale of alcohol by private individuals was officially prohibited. The ban proved to be ineffectual but the government used its monopoly to lay down official retail prices in various localities. So high were the profits on the sale of spirits – 40 kopecks ($66\frac{2}{3}$ per cent) on the wholesale price of one rouble and 140 kopecks ($233\frac{2}{3}$ per cent) on the retail price of two roubles per *vedró* (about 12.2 litres) – that the authorities could afford drastically to cut the price of liquor distilled by the managers of the tsar's taverns. This was done in 1681 to eliminate the competition from illegal sales and in 1699 in order to compete successfully with private contractors.[6]

In so far as the various ordinances show the tsar to have held any definite views on the subject he appears to have favoured a policy of gradually farming out the operations of the *kabák* as being likely to lead to a more dependable return than the use of the grudging, inefficient and corrupt services of the members of the *posád*. In 1705 Peter I ordered the farming out of the collection of the profit from the *kabák* (as well as of those toll-houses which collected under 1,000 roubles a year) wherever this was practicable. In 1707 the intentions of the government were defined more precisely: concessions were to be tendered for, and awarded to, bidders supported by trustworthy guarantees. As solvency was the principal consideration, offers from peasants on monastic and other lands were no longer to be considered.[7]

In order to safeguard the exclusive rights given by the Crown to its agents and concessionaires, the tsar tried for a long time to uphold the restriction on distilling to persons who had received official licences and – for domestic purposes only – to landholders. Under Peter I private persons were allowed to brew beer and make mead subject to the payment of a tax of 5 kopecks for one *chétverť* (about 210 litres) of beer and one pood (16.4 kg) of mead. Only in 1716 did the authorities give up the unequal struggle against the illicit production of alcohol by landholders and others. In that year an ambiguously worded *ukáz* allowed persons of all degrees, high and low, to distil spirits for their own domestic consumption as hitherto, and also under contract for the public taverns, subject to the payment of a tax of 25 kopecks per *vedró* of capacity on the vessels used for distilling and branded accordingly. Pososhkóv points out the actual and potential loss of revenue caused by this method of assessment. He implies that permission to set up stills had previously been given exclusively to *dvoriáne* who continued to take advantage of it to sell liquor to the public on their own land, thereby infringing the tsar's monopoly.[8]

One of the reasons for which the tsar wanted to hand over the *kabák* to concessionaires was his awareness of the burden which the collection of tolls and of the profit on the production and sale of liquor imposed on the *posádskie liúdi*. It was common knowledge that these unpaid auxiliary workers, selected by the authorities unless they were elected by the community, recouped themselves for time spent and income lost in their labours for the state by fleecing the customer. Moreover, the whole system was out of keeping with the professionalization which the administrative system was undergoing at the time. In 1722 the tsar ruled that the 'elected' *posádskie liúdi* in the service of his treasury would be replaced by super-annuated soldiers of all ranks. These men were to be assisted by Old Believers and such townsmen as still wore beards. The spectacle of the most reliable elements of the population yoked to the least trustworthy would have been curious to behold, had not the scheme turned out to be impracticable. The required ex-soldiers came forward slowly and in insufficient numbers, but even so the amount spent on their pay – 70,000 roubles a year – was considered excessive and they were discharged in 1727. As the sums due from the various collections of tolls and the profit from the *kabák* were calculated and fixed in advance by the government, not enough enterprising and relatively prosperous men like Pososhkóv were willing to run the risk of having to make good out of their own pockets a possible shortfall in their takings. In most places, therefore, the traditional system of management by the *posádskie liúdi* remained in force.[9]

The changes introduced in 1731 were not far removed from the recommendations which Pososhkóv makes in this chapter. Where it was not farmed out, the collection of toll and of the profit on the production and sale of liquor was to be delegated for not longer than one year at a time to elected members of the *posád*. Provision was made for remuneration in salaries and fees but no figures were specified.[10]

Pososhkóv's scheme for the production and sale of liquor on a national scale at uniform prices was not as unrealistic as it might seem seeing that such prices were actually introduced in 1750.[11] A distiller by trade and a puritan by conviction, Pososhkóv offers a convenient way of reconciling the moral benefits of sobriety with the needs of the tsar's treasury: higher prices, he believes, will in due course lead to higher profits accompanied by diminished consumption. The proposal that any takings from this source in excess of the estimated income should be used as a loan fund for large-scale entrepreneurs who are short of capital underlines the difficulties experienced at that time even by prosperous individuals in obtaining credit. The rate of interest charged by money-lenders was at least 12 to 15 per cent, in special circumstances it could reach between 20 and 24 per cent a year and higher rates were not unheard of. Pososhkóv's idea differs from the corresponding provision in the Regulation of the Board of Manufactories of 1723 (in all probability unknown to him) which offers financial aid only to existing manufactories and works operated by 'companies'. A scheme not unlike Pososhkóv's under which local traders of limited means were to be granted loans out of the receipts from indirect taxation had been devised and put into practice in 1665 by A. L. Ordýn-Nashchókin in his capacity as *voevóda* of Pskov.[12]

The customs duties collected at Archangel and later at St Petersburg until 1722 cannot be qualified as a tariff in the modern sense of the term because they did not constitute a system designed to operate as an instrument of economic policy. Even from a purely fiscal point of view the work done by the custom-house at Archangel was far from satisfactory. In a complaint addressed to the tsar in 1711 one Georg Metzel describes how, through bribery, fraud and conspiracy, duty was evaded at Archangel and toll inland. About this time a surcharge of half a rix-dollar in cash was added to the toll on goods imported by foreign merchants into Archangel. As in any case the charges which foreigners had to pay on imported goods by far exceeded those which were levied on Russians, arrangements were habitually made to have the goods imported in the name of a Russian man of straw or simply smuggled into the country – a practice known in English as 'colouring strangers' goods'. An earlier ordinance, promulgated in 1699, had decreed that on all imported alcoholic beverages (except communion wine), irrespective of whether they were intended for private use or sale, duty was to be paid in rix-dollars. The intention was purely fiscal and, in view of Pososhkóv's strictures, it may be doubted whether the rule diminished the consumption of imported wines and spirits.[13]

With these exceptions the regulations in force were essentially still those of 1667. The reply given by the Senate in 1716 to a query sent by the tsar from abroad about the rates of duty in Russian (as opposed to the formerly Swedish) ports stated that Russian goods bought for export by foreign merchants with money obtained from the sale of goods which they had imported from overseas were not liable to export duty because duty (in rix-dollars) had already been collected on the imported goods. Although well established, this was not a practice of which Pososhkóv approved and it may be that the tsar's advisers, similarly disposed, were contemplating the possibility of increasing the revenue from duty charged on goods exported from Russia. In 1719 the tsar declared an unrestricted trade in commodities which until then had been monopolized by the treasury (except potash and weidash), only to subject them within a few months to an extra duty. In April 1720 the duties at St Petersburg were reduced so as to favour that port and any Russian importers and exporters operating there. Russians were to pay 50 per cent less duty on exports than foreigners and no duty on imports bought with money obtained from the sale of Russian goods abroad. However, Russia still lacked a consistent tariff policy. It was not until August 1720 that a commission was appointed with instructions to draw up a tariff calculated to achieve a favourable balance of trade. In 1722 as a temporary measure the rates of duty in force at Riga were extended to all the other ports. The first set of proposals drawn up by the commission was rejected; those put forward in 1723 were revised and finally approved early in 1724. The provisions of the new tariff have been summarized in the Introduction. The importation of large quantities of alcohol seems to have caused as much concern to the commission as to Pososhkóv but it would appear that he had no knowledge of the special excise which was laid on French wine in 1723 at the rate of 2 roubles per *ánkerok* (Du. *ankertje*) of 38.8 litres, or of the general restriction imposed on the importation of French wine and brandy in 1724 with a view to replacing the latter with Russian spirits.[14]

The rates of duty on exports proposed by Pososhkóv bear little relation to those of 1724; some do not even appear to be based on any rational calculation. Thus Pososhkóv would consider a duty of 10 roubles per mast 'as under the old tariff' appropriate, whereas under that of 1724 (as recorded in the *Pólnoe Sobránie Zakónov*) the duty levied at St Petersburg on a mast measuring 20 inches in diameter would be 75 roubles. Conversely, the rates proposed by Pososhkóv for flax, tar and tallow are higher by a factor of at least six than those laid down in 1724 so that the comparison is not worth making. Pososhkóv, moreover, does not seem to have been aware of the disastrous disadvantage at which such high duties would have placed the producers of these commodities in the *Pomór'e*. On the other hand, the rates for Russia leather and grain (which was scarce in Russia at the time) as proposed by Pososhkóv and those laid down by the tariff of 1724 (according to Kózintseva) are not very far apart. In sum, although Pososhkóv knew the term, the concept of a tariff was beyond his grasp.[15]

In the last section of this chapter Pososhkóv examines the real and nominal value of the Russian coinage and puts forward proposals for increasing the profit derived by the Crown from the various mints. These at the end of Peter's reign were in a sorry state. The recoinage carried out between 1701 and 1709, principally of the silver money issued in Russia at various times in the last three or four decades of the seventeenth century, had produced a total profit of 4,439,722 roubles. In so far as the coins that were called in represented wealth accumulated by the tsar's subjects in the preceding period, the government was able during the critical phase of the Great Northern War to augment its current revenue by using those reserves. But in 1710 the profit made from recoinage was only 243,743 roubles and the war was by no means over. From 1711 the government through its purchasing chamber bought for the mint all the gold and silver it could find in the open market but the profit on the coinage of precious metals acquired in this way was low whereas that from the coinage of copper was at that time estimated at 150 per cent. In 1700 copper coins equivalent to half a kopeck and less had been reintroduced; the copper kopeck had appeared in 1704. Encouraged by the success of copper the Senate resolved that each year enough copper coins would be minted to put a 'profit' of 200,000 roubles at the disposal of the government. This policy, tantamount to the printing of unsecured banknotes with the inevitable inflationary effects, was followed in 1712 and also in 1713. The tsar raised the requirement for that year to 300,000 but the mints were only able to show a total gain of 371,000 roubles on the coining of copper money and the production of gold and silver money from bullion and old coins. By the beginning of 1714 the large amount of copper coins in circulation appears to have led to an increased demand for silver money, presumably for hoarding or melting down.

As to the silver coins, including the one-rouble piece introduced in 1704, their standard was in 1711 reduced from between 82 and 84 to 70 parts of fine metal in one Russian pound of 96 *zolotnikí* of about 4.27 grammes each, without any diminution in the weight of the coin. In this way the silver content of the one-rouble coin which had been on a par with the rix-dollar was brought into line with the lion-dollar of the better quality. The official reason given for making the change was the intention of the authorities to prevent foreigners from exporting roubles (presumably bought with copper or obtained from the sale of goods) to have them melted down abroad but the measure may also have been seen as a convenient way of increasing the profit from coinage. In 1718 the proportion of 70 : 96 was confirmed and extended to the ten-kopeck and half-rouble pieces. The production of the one-, three- and apparently also of the five-kopeck pieces (not mentioned in the relevant *ukáz*) was discontinued. As the population tended increasingly to make payments to the authorities in copper, it was not long before the government departments experienced a shortage of silver. Early in 1714, therefore, the tsar stopped the production of copper money but he could not prevent its being forged in vast quantities. In any case it would appear that the ban was presently either lifted or disregarded.[16]

Almost as soon as it began to suffer from a general shortage of funds, the government resorted to the customary expedient of reducing the weight of coins without altering their face value. Thus whereas in 1700–1 from one pood (16.4 kg) of copper 12 roubles 80 kopecks were minted, the corresponding ratio for 1702–3 was 1 : 15 r. 40 k., for 1704–18 1 : 20 r., for 1718–25 1 : 40 r., out of all proportion to the price of copper which from 1705 up to the time when Pososhkóv was discussing 'the tsar's interest' seems to have been more or less constant at about 7 roubles per pood (although it may have risen fairly steeply in the first quinquennium of the Russo-Swedish War). It has been calculated that between 1704 and 1717 at least two-and-a-half million roubles' worth of copper coins of small denominations – half, a quarter and one eighth of a kopeck – were produced. Between 1718 and 1723 half a million quarter-kopecks were minted although in a memorandum submitted to the tsar early in 1721 the Board of Mines (*Berg-kollégiia*) pointed out that as there was a great deal of money in circulation already there was no advantage in producing more even though this might seem to bring in a high profit for the Mint. But when the proportion of copper to silver money was too high, much harm was done to trade (apart from other drawbacks such as the excessive weight of copper coins and their poor resistance to fire). On this recommendation the tsar resolved that copper was to be used for quarter-kopecks only and fixed the ratio of copper to silver at 1 : 10. The resolution was not put into effect.[17]

According to the table (compiled by B. N. Mirónov) which shows the increase in the amount of money per head of population in eighteenth-century Russia in relation to the price of grain, between 1711 and 1720 the index of the amount of money rose by 113 points, whereas that of the price of grain rose by only 49 points (1701–10 = 100). It may well follow from these figures and from the opinion expressed by the Board of Mines that some sections of the population had copper cash to spare. This money would be spent whilst an unknown proportion of the silver money would have gone out of circulation, having been melted down, hoarded or smuggled out of the country. Pososhkóv does not complain of any stagnation in trade being caused by a lack of confidence in the copper currency, so it may be that the small trader and his customers were not troubled by such misgivings.

In response to the memorandum of the Board of Mines of 1721 the arrears due from the Mint to various government departments were cancelled and the terms on which the Mint supplied the departments with coins were revised. The policy of keeping the silver money, old and new, in Russia, was reaffirmed, the melting down of coins was prohibited and the ban on the exportation of gold and silver in coin and kind, reimposed in 1714 and repeated in 1719, was renewed. (The original prohibition, older in Russia than mercantilist doctrine, imposed in the second half of the sixteenth century, had been intended to prevent merchants from central Asia and the Near East from stripping Muscovy of precious metals. It seems that the introduction of the silver rouble, combined with the relatively higher price of silver in Turkey and central Asia, had revived or increased this undesirable tendency.) Old coins were to be exchanged for new ones at an official rate at the mint-houses. No duty was to be charged on imports from overseas of silver for the Mint which might cost as much as 976,000 roubles for 2,000 poods in one year. This picture justifies Pososhkóv's concern at the outflow of silver from Russia; the cost of the purchase of silver for the Mint should be taken into account in any analysis of the favourable balance of trade which Russia is said to have enjoyed at the end of the reign of Peter I when (in 1726) the exports through St Petersburg and Archangel were supposedly worth 2,688,000 roubles and the imports 1,585,500.[18] Whatever the value of the trade surplus may have been, it still did not make Russia rich. Moreover, the new empire was in a state of financial crisis which had been caused by the delay in the completion of the census and therefore in the collection of the poll-tax, a bad harvest and the coincidental obligation to pay a substantial cash indemnity to Sweden.[19]

In that country between 1715 and 1719, under the direction of Görtz, a series of ingenious financial measures had been adopted to deal with similar problems: the face value of the copper coins and silver dollars was increased, the silver dollars were called in, the copper pieces, if not exchanged for government bonds, were restamped to a lower value. These devices associated with a strict regulation of foreign trade enabled the Crown to find the where-withal to pay for the war. In Russia the tsar saw the remedy in the production of more copper money unaccompanied by any of the methods that had been applied in Sweden. In 1723 he ordered the issue of a further 500,000 five-kopeck pieces, lighter by half than 'the existing kopecks', but the operation was not completed in Peter's lifetime.[20]

Judging from the policy pursued by the one and the recommendations made by the other, neither the tsar nor Pososhkóv seems to have been aware of the circumstances which had brought about the monetary crisis of 1662. From 1654 the government had been issuing vast quantities of copper coins worth 1.2 per cent of their face value, in the expectation of making a 'profit' of just under 4 million roubles. In his memorandum on the coinage of 1708 or 1709 Pososhkóv argued that it was possible to maintain the face value of coins by striking them in a way that could not be imitated by forgers. Already at that time he regarded the ratio of 4 kopecks to one *zolotník* of copper as the appropriate one. The corresponding average intrinsic value of the copper coins specified in Chapter 9 is slightly higher – 5.4 per cent. The tsar's Mint did not sink quite so low although, as has been seen, by 1723 it contented itself with copper coins having an intrinsic value of 20 per cent, a steep decline from 60 per cent in 1718. Pososhkóv expected that the degree of debasement proposed by him would produce an annual 'profit' of 2 million roubles for an outlay of 80,000

(10,000 poods of copper at 8 roubles per pood), about ten times as much as the Mint was expected to yield in the last decade of the reign of Peter I. Earlier the profit from the restriking of foreign coins had been 41,702 roubles between 1684 and 1693, 80,944 in 1694, 86,421 in 1695 and for the whole period between 1701 and 1709, when the process consisted also in restriking old Russian silver coins and producing some new copper coins, 4,439,722.[21]

As a nominalist Pososhkóv had a kindred spirit in his rather better-informed and more enlightened English contemporary, Nicholas Barbon, who maintained that 'the stamp and effigy on the coin gives value to the money and makes it current', provided that certain limits are not exceeded. Pososhkóv's conception of the pure silver rouble, however, was inspired by the mystique of the tsar and autocrat. If coined, silver roubles of the standard suggested by him would not have been in circulation long before they had been buried, melted down or smuggled out of the country. The silver rouble which Pososhkóv associates with the reign of Ivan IV was not a coin of that denomination but only a unit of account which stood for 100 kopecks containing 92½ in 96 parts of fine silver.[22]

The connection between the steady devaluation of the Russian currency and rising prices was observed by John Perry who records that in the early years of the century the exchange rate for the rouble fell by between 30 and 40 per cent and 'the price of everything, more especially what there was occasion for from foreign parts, was soon advanced in proportion to the exchange'.[23] Pososhkóv blames the foreign merchants for adjusting in that way the prices of the goods imported by them and considers it possible to stop this movement by officially establishing a rate of exchange favourable to the rouble and by taking concerted retaliatory action against the foreigners. Earlier on[24] Pososhkóv gives the impression that he regards the ducat and the rix-dollar as expensive imported commodities rather than as value-tokens. In subsequently upbraiding the foreigner for similarly rating a coin according to its intrinsic value he shows a strange lack of consistency.

Though Russia was poor in silver she was rich in salt. In some areas it was obtained by simple methods: thus at Stáraia Rússa (near Nóvgorod), where some of the salt springs ran close to the surface, by skimming off the water; on the White Sea by boiling from sea water; to the south of Astrakhan by excavation from the bottom of salt lakes which were dry at certain times of the year. Elsewhere conduits had to be used to bring the brine to the surface before it could be boiled in large pans. This was the case in the numerous salt-works on the rivers Sukhóna, the lower Výchegda and the middle Káma, especially at Tót'ma, Velíkii Ústiug, Sol' Vychegódskaia, Iárensk and Sol' Kámskaia. Well over half the salt produced in Russia came from these north-eastern regions.

In January 1705 the tsar's treasury took over the retail sale of salt from the private middlemen and assigned it as a service to the *posádskie liúdi*. At the same time the producers were invited to contract with the authorities to supply salt to the public subject to the payment of toll, presumably still at the rate of 10 per cent as laid down specifically for salt in the Tolls and Customs Regulations (*Tamózhennyi ustáv*) of 1653. The retail price was to be double that at which the salt was bought from the wholesaler. The *posádskie liúdi* in their capacity as retailers were therefore nothing other than collectors of a purchase tax on salt. In 1706 the authorities drastically reduced its rate by fixing the treasury's share of the retail price at 12 kopecks per pood where that price was 24 kopecks or less and at half the retail price where it was higher. Between 1705 and 1709 the annual profit from the new monopoly was only about 150,000 roubles a year but it seems that by delaying the payments due to the suppliers it was possible to maintain a reserve cash fund of 300,000 roubles. The net gain, however, remained low and in 1711, at a time when the Senate was doing its utmost to increase the revenue, amounted to only 199,000 roubles. In that year the authorities, evidently displeased with the results of their trading operations, called on the producers to take over the retail sale of salt. The producers, however, did not find it possible to form a company for this purpose on the terms laid down by the government and, for their lack of co-operation, suffered a reduction in the prices paid to them – the larger ones by one kopeck per pood and the smaller ones by half a kopeck. The reduction brought down the profit made by the principal producer G. D. Stróganov to a mere 1/32 kopeck per pood. In 1706, according to an informer, it had been 2½ kopecks. Stróganov still found it worth his while or expedient to remain in business but the smaller producers could not afford to do so. By 1714 salt-works were being abandoned by the dozen and a shortage of salt was making itself felt. The production of salt at Stáraia Rússa had stopped in 1710 after the tsar had prohibited the burning of hardwood which he wanted to preserve for shipbuilding. Work was resumed in 1719 when the producers undertook not to use hardwood as fuel.[25]

Between October 1713 and January 1714 the authorities tried once more to farm out the sale of salt, this time to the merchants of six communities in central Russia but their representatives declined to accept the terms that were offered to them. In 1715 the appropriation of the revenue from the salt monopoly was taken over from the Senate by the *Kabinét* (the tsar's personal office)[26] but so far no connection has been established between this change and the subsequent rise in the receipts from the sale of salt. The total for the years 1715–24 was 5,978,486 roubles, the lowest annual figure being 544,664 for 1716 and the highest 659,527 for 1722.

The continuing shortage of salt enabled its unpaid distributors to recompense themselves for their pains by selling salt only in bulk, at least one pood (16.4 kg) at a time and for a consideration. The small customer who could not afford to bribe them was turned away. The tsar forbade this abuse under pain of death in 1722. The position of the suppliers showed no improvement. In 1723 the Stróganov brothers whose works in the region of Solikámsk accounted for about 60 per cent of the annual output of salt in the country petitioned the tsar to be relieved of the task of supplying salt which they found burdensome and uneconomical.[27] The tsar refused the request but allowed an increase in the wholesale price paid to the producers from 1½ kopecks to 9 kopecks per pood. In return the producers were obliged, from 1725, to supply a specified quantity of salt each year: the Stróganov family's contribution was to be a minimum of 3 million poods.[28]

In July 1727, 'for the sake of the common good', Peter II freed the sale of salt from official interference, subject to the payment of toll. To that extent, therefore, Pososhkóv's wish was granted but in 1731, the revenue from salt 'having fallen from 600,000 roubles a year to less than one third of that sum', the Empress Anne restored the monopoly.[29]

The previous history of the salt monopoly illustrates the ability of the reformed service state to compel the large suppliers to render service by producing salt at only a small profit and the *posádskie liúdi* to act as unpaid retailers. It also shows the readiness of the state to sacrifice the public good, to which it was officially wedded, to a solid fiscal advantage, even if such an advantage was attended by dire social and economic side-effects. Producers of salt might go out of business and the consumers – every man, woman and child in the realm – might in consequence be unable to salt fish and meat and pickle cabbage, but still the 50 per cent purchase tax would be levied on an essential commodity. For all the harmful effects of the deficiency of salt, scurvy, contrary to Pososhkóv's assertion, was not one of them. Although it was endemic in northern Russia at the time, it was caused not by the lack of salt but by the insufficiency of fresh fruit and vegetables.[30]

Pososhkóv was unable to calculate the yield from the excise on salt at the rate of 10 kopecks per pood proposed by him because he did not know how much salt was sold each year. Assuming that 60 per cent of the salt produced in Russia at the time can be attributed to the Stróganovs and recalling that in 1724 they were ordered to supply no less than 3 million poods a year, we may estimate the annual production at 5 million poods which would have yielded roughly 500,000 roubles in tax, about as much, therefore, as the monopoly.

To turn, finally, to tobacco. During John Perry's stay in Russia between 1698 and 1712 tobacco was still frowned upon as 'unclean and irreligious, a priest would not come into a room where it was smoked'[31] but it was nevertheless in constant demand. Between 1698 and 1704 the exclusive right to prepare and sell tobacco was vested in a company headed by the English merchant William Goodfellow. At the end of 1704 the tsar deprived the company of its privilege and the sale of tobacco was allowed on the same footing as that of alcoholic beverages, that is, in taverns, by licencees or sworn agents of the tsar's treasury. At that point the importation of tobacco appears to have passed into the hands of the Dutch. Good-quality tobacco was grown in the Ukraine and sold at half a kopeck per pound. The small team of craftsmen engaged in Holland on behalf of the tsar in 1716 was by 1717 occupied in the preparation of Ukrainian tobacco for sale in Russia but the venture did not bring a profit. According to Miliukóv a 'free' trade in tobacco was allowed on 23 April 1723 but this ordinance does not appear to have been published. A further ordinance to the same effect, allowing the sale of tobacco by all and sundry, was promulgated in 1727.[32]

The chapter also contains some revealing details and comments such as the information that work was paid for in liquor, the author's views on the way in which the obligations to render service affected the lives of the *posádskie liúdi* and above all his observations on land tenure which should be read in conjunction with Chapter 7 and the relevant section of the Commentary on that chapter.

In the present chapter Pososhkóv touches for the third and last time on the subject of the ownership of land and peasants by *dvoriáne*.[33] In his opinion the land which the *poméshchiki* presumed to own, and their own persons too, in fact belonged to the tsar. The institution of serfdom he regards as a feudal quid pro quo: the *poméshchik* is entitled to the services of the peasants who live on the land held by him so long as he himself renders service to the tsar. Peter I for his part had, by 1721, abandoned the strictly conditional conception of landownership which was still in force at the beginning of the century.[34] There is nothing in this or any other chapter to suggest that Pososhkóv was aware of the existence of the law on the mode of inheritance of 1714.[35] The cursory remark at the beginning of Chapter 8 gives the impression that the repeated divisions of land which Peter I wished to check by means of that measure continued in the subsequent decade.

No evidence has been found to confirm Pososhkóv's assertion that one half per cent of all revenue was applied to the current needs of the tsar. However, the same figure of half a kopeck for extraordinary expenses is quoted by the French envoy in St Petersburg, Jacques de Campredon, in a memorandum dated 1721.[36] A rule of this kind under which a percentage of state revenue is set aside for the personal use of the monarch, though arbitrary, would at least have been rational. In point of fact this particular area of financial administration was left untouched by bureaucratic reform and no effort was made to separate the state chest from the private purse. The extraordinary expenses incurred by the tsar in his private and official capacity alike were met out of moneys derived from a variety of sources and handled by his personal office, the *Kabinét*. This confusion between the private and the official sphere is characteristic of the dual nature of Peter I's government, at once bureaucratic and patrimonial.[37]

In this chapter as elsewhere, Pososhkóv shows his awareness of the existence of economic problems but, being unable to analyse them in economic terms so as to arrive at economic solutions, is reduced to invoking the intervention of the political authority. This finally involves him in an excursus on politics. The nature of the existing political system made superfluous any examination of the position of the individual in the state or of the purpose of government but it seemed unexceptionable to allude to the common good so often trumpeted by the tsar as the principal motive of his actions. Their validity, in Pososhkóv's view, was derived from the godlike attributes of the tsar. The comparison of the tsar to the Almighty and the references to godlike government and to the imposition of justice by the ruler may have been the last echoes to be heard in Russia of the advice offered to Justinian by the deacon Agapetus who states that in the authority attached to his dignity the king is like God who rules over all.[38] Rationality was not Pososhkóv's strong suit: his medieval outlook reduced economics to politics and politics to religion in conjunction with ethics. In the end, he tells us, material benefits flow from moral virtue.

CHAPTER 9

Of the Tsar's Interest[1]

(200)   The collection of the Tsar's revenue must be carried out in a fair and efficacious manner, that is, in such a way that no one is wronged but that all that is due to His Majesty is gathered in without bringing ruin on his realm thereby. For it is wrong that those who collect taxes for the Tsar should bring ruin on the people: if they truly wish to serve the interests of their Sovereign their first care in the collection of revenue will be to protect the people from ruin. The revenue collected in this spirit will be both abundant and certain. Moreover, the sums collected must be safeguarded so that no part of them be lost at any stage. Good husbandry goes hand in hand with tax-gathering, for where there is no husbandry the tax-collector's task is made the more difficult. Just as a leaky vessel can never be filled, so also with the collection of revenue: if the proceeds are not duly safeguarded the work of collection will not have been fruitful.

When I was in Nóvgorod in 1710, for example, I noticed that two warehouses in the market were full of harness and other military stores and the whole of it had been allowed to become rotten and useless and had to be shovelled out; goodness knows how many hundred roubles it was all worth. I suppose that a great deal of the Sovereign's treasure goes to waste through this sort of negligence, through the laxity of the commissaries responsible for stores and grain stocks in the various garrison towns and in the supply trains of our armies.

(201)   Of even more direct and serious effect are the losses in stocks of oak timber intended for building warships at St Petersburg. In 1717 I was travelling along Lake Ládoga[2] and saw large quantities of oak timber lying about on the shores and islands. Some of the beams were enormous, worth, I imagine, a hundred roubles apiece, and yet many of them were already half buried in the sand, some indeed scarcely visible. I imagine that the same state of affairs exists on other shores and islands and if the timber is still lying there much of it must surely have become rotten by now. Goodness knows what is the loss to the Tsar's treasury by such avoidable negligence. However grave such negligence may appear it is not as grave as the harm done by the timber purveyors themselves, for they cause great and incalculable harm to the vessels by supplying rotten[3] timber. For if a single such unsound beam chance to be in some vital spot of a vessel it will be the ruin of the whole vessel, and if there are a dozen or more such timbers in it the vessel is not worthy of the name of vessel at all.

A good sound ship is like the defences of a fortress; one built of rotten timber is worse than a wattle palisade. A palisade is not a strong defence in itself yet if it is well manned with troops the enemy cannot take the place easily; whereas no battle is needed to cause the loss of a vessel made of unsound oak – the battering of the sea is enough: the whole crew will perish without the need for any other enemy.

So important and vital is shipbuilding that only the very best and soundest fresh-cut timber must be selected for this purpose. Any tree which is apparently sound but whose wood is already darkened with age must on no account be used for shipbuilding since it is not strong enough. And if any tree has already begun to decay it is good for nothing but firewood.

(02) At St Petersburg I have seen timbers brought for shipbuilding which were no longer in a fit state to be split but merely disintegrated; if one tried to shape them a chip struck off would break into two or three fragments. It is quite useless to supply such timber for shipbuilding. In my opinion decayed timber is to be feared in shipbuilding more than fire because a fully fitted-out vessel costs, I suppose, about a hundred thousand roubles and may be lost through a few rotten timbers and with it all that the treasury has paid for, as well as many of its crew. For building warships raw oak timber of the best quality must be selected, after careful inspection; its tint must be blueish, not red. If a vessel is built of such oak it will be as if of iron, for even a musket-ball will hardly dent it. When such oak has fully dried out a ball will only penetrate into it to a depth of less than one inch; but it will go deeper into reddened oak and deeper still into rotten timber. Therefore any vessel which is built of such sound oak is worth more than twenty rotten ones, inasmuch as in the first place it stands up to musketry, in the second it is not affected by the impact of the water, and in the third it does not rot in water but becomes more resistant and has a life of fifty years or more. But a vessel made of rotten timber will not last even five years and all the work and money expended on it goes for nothing.

I think it would be better to build ships of sound pine rather than rotten oak. Under damp conditions the latter will not last as long as five years but will completely disintegrate and perish. When I was working at the Mint I had the presses in which the coins are struck mounted upon large oak blocks. These blocks were sunk in the ground to no more than half their height, yet within three years they had all perished. So I cramped sound oak beams together in
(03) pairs and set the presses on them and they have remained in perfect condition to the present day.

All the above shortcomings in the supply of oak timber are due to the ignorance of the foresters. For the foreign shipwrights working here do not care if the wood is of poor quality: their only concern is to display their superior skill and to pocket their pay for the work. Yet an honest craftsman would not consent to make anything with bad material.

All foreigners, whether craftsmen or military men in the service of His Majesty (nor are the foreign merchants any whit[4] different), are more concerned about their fellow countrymen than about us. I imagine that none of these Europeans is glad to see us building a navy; they want all the glory and riches for themselves and that we should be dependent on them. No doubt these people will be angry with me for writing this work and if they discover that I have written disparagingly about them in it they will do their utmost to find ways of refuting my charges. Time and again I have observed how selfish they are: they flatter us in everything and extract money from us yet at the same time by every kind of trick they try to keep us in poverty and obscurity. When His Majesty issued an order for the making of copper coins of precisely circular form there was not a single Russian or foreigner to be found who could construct the requisite press; it was only the foreigner George Frobus[5] who undertook to procure the necessary craftsmen from abroad. So seeing that the whole matter was hanging fire I took a hand in this unfamiliar matter and succeeded in getting the minting under way. Even if I thereby injured the reputation of the foreigners I suffered no harm in consequence. But now one cannot but go in fear of them, seeing that they are so numerous and might do me some injury for anything I said to their detriment.

It is impossible to put things right in the matter of unsuitable timber supplied for shipbuilding unless the present system of supply is changed and fines are imposed on the suppliers and inspectors.

(204)   It is clear to me that it should be done as follows. Those responsible for selecting the standing timber must order those who fell the trees first to inspect a tree to see if it is sound. And if it is healthy and shows no signs of decay, then a blaze shall be cut at a height of two sazhens or more above ground level and inspected when it has dried out. And if the tree is sound and healthy and fit for felling, and hard and solid enough to work, then it may be felled and cut to size. And when this has been done the timber must be inspected to see whether it is sound throughout. If no part has been damaged by frost and there are no other signs of decay the man who felled it shall put his mark on it. And whoever receives it from him shall likewise carefully examine it to make sure that there are no imperfections. If it is sound in all respects then the collector shall also put his mark upon it. And no beam or board shall be passed for shipbuilding without such marks.

If, after felling, any tree is found in the course of shaping to have been damaged by frost or to be decayed in any part and is too soft to be worked, such timber must be rejected and used for cooperage or purposes other than shipbuilding, or burnt for potash. However, if the rejected timber can be put to any good use, including the finishing of a vessel but not for its vital parts, then it may be passed, but without the mark of approval.

Further, the following safeguards must be observed in the supply of ship's timbers. If any such timber, whether large or small, proves on delivery to the shipyard to be unsound, it shall be set aside and not counted, and he whose mark is upon it shall supply at his own charges another such piece of timber, or two in place of one. And the woodmen who shaped it, put their mark on it and handed it over to the collector, shall be beaten with rods or the knout to ensure that they do not fell and shape unsuitable timber again in future. Under threat of such punishment they will never again fell or shape unsuitable timber or supply it for the building of warships.

(205)   If it prove impossible to obtain enough raw oak for shipbuilding, then, it seems to me, there is no sense in wasting money from the Tsar's treasury on oak timber, because inferior oak is in no way preferable to pine and its cost is out of all proportion to its value. I believe that for the same sum that would be spent on building a vessel of oak one could build three or even four of pine, and such a vessel would give scarcely less good service than one of oak. When saturated with water oak becomes like clay and is exceedingly sluggish to sail, whereas pine or fir is a great deal lighter. Moreover, firwood stands up to the buffeting of the seas better than oak of inferior quality.

I conceive that many people will challenge these words maintaining that pine cannot compare in strength with oak. This I do not deny, that the best raw oak is five or ten times better than pine, but reddened oak is scarcely any better and oak that has decayed is certainly worse even than fir.

I feel horror at daring to discuss such a high matter but my extreme concern has emboldened me to speak out. As God is my witness, I do so not for the sake of my personal advancement or advantage but solely out of that devotion which I feel towards His Majesty's authority. For so have I been since my youth and I would rather bring trouble upon myself than remain silent when I see something done that is harmful to this realm. Whatever may appear unworthy of credence in all nine chapters of this work of mine can be tested by further evidence and enquiry; but a truth-loving heart may judge of all these things better than any evidence.

Again, when I was in Nóvgorod in 1710 I saw cables being made for these same warships and they were being made out of such inferior hemp as to be quite useless. The cables were then tarred and taken to St Petersburg for fitting out the vessels. To put one's trust in such cables is to invite disaster. In view of such harmful practices it seems to me better that the Admiralty should receive the cables untarred and then test the quality of the hemp to ascertain how much (206)   shives it contains and whether it is sound or rotten. This can be done by unwinding some of the cable, whereas nothing can be judged from one already tarred. Once the cables have been inspected they can be tarred, and such cables will be reliable.

The anchor hawsers of a vessel are most important and vital parts and should be made of the very best quality hemp, since if the hawser is sound the ship is safe but if it is inferior then plain disaster faces both vessel and crew. If hawsers are still being made now of such poor quality hemp, it were better to run before the wind than to drop your anchors.

I must also say something about the practice of pressed labour.[6] Men sent on to St Petersburg (and other places) from the chief towns to labour there for a period of three months work for this length of time but there is nothing to show for it at the end. It is dispiriting to watch them at work since they think only of getting to the end of the day rather than seeing their work through to the end.

This might be put right as follows. Reliable and incorruptible overseers should be chosen for this work. They shall be given instructions to keep a watchful eye on everything and estimate how much work the labourers have accomplished during their three months' stretch. And they shall assign a similar amount of work to newly arrived labourers, or even increase it a little (taking into account the nature of the task) and say to them: 'this is your stint; should you get it done in one month it will count as your three months' stretch and you will be discharged'. And when their stint is completed let them be employed if they so desire on some other projects of His Majesty or seek work with private employers. But if they do not want further employment let them return home.

The overseers shall be commanded to observe these instructions under pain of heavy fines and physical punishment, it being made clear that if the labourers finish their allotted stint in one month the overseers must discharge them without so much as a day's delay and must not demand any consideration from them for so doing. If things were so arranged there would be good hope that many labourers would complete in one month the stint calculated to take them three months.

(207)   The discharge papers of those workmen who have completed their stint, even if it takes them less than one month, shall be marked 'three months' since they will have done the equivalent of three months' work. For if their discharge paper does not declare that they have done three months' work, the authorities of the place from which the workmen were sent will demand back the money paid to them.

If all the labourers sent from a particular place were to be divided into gangs instead of working as a single body, then any such gang on completing the stint allotted for three months could be discharged without delay, and so the other labourers seeing this example would press on with their work. And let all those who do not wish to work to a shorter date work out their full three months. In this way all parts of the work would be expedited.

So if it is made worth their while[7] all the labourers will apply themselves to their work the more willingly and the work itself will proceed more rapidly, for, once their stint is completed, they will even be willing to continue doing the same work for wages.

This method of prescribing a certain length of time for any piece of work should be applied not only to manual labourers but also to skilled craftsmen, whether natives or foreigners. Payment by the month should be abandoned in all cases and replaced by payment for a specified task. In this way every kind of work will be done more quickly. Here is an example which I noted at the Arsenal when A. A. Kurbátov[8] was one of the officials in charge there. A foreigner brought in a gun for which he had been making a wooden stock. It was quite plain, neither carved nor inlaid; yet he had taken four months over it and was almost certainly being paid more than ten roubles a month. Now, if the stock had been ordered on agreed terms the maker would have been paid, let us say, a hundred and fifty or even a hundred and twenty kopecks for it and he would have done the work in two or three days, not four months. And Kurbátov became very angry with him and said: 'The stock's not worth more than two roubles and it has cost us something like sixty.' Foreigners make no effort to complete work quickly but rather spin it out as long as they can; they care about nothing but their monthly salaries.

Again, there is much that is amiss with the collection of His Majesty's revenues, for people are always trying (as they say) to get two or three hides off one ox, whereas in sober truth they cannot even get a single hide off in one piece, and, try as they may, end up with nothing better than a lot of strips. This is most harmful to His Majesty's interest since by trying to extract more than is due they thereby lose the principal.

For the new Trade Regulations[9] lay it down that, when goods are brought to town for sale, the peasants who sell them shall pay toll at the rate of five kopecks per rouble and the purchasers at the rate of two-and-a-half kopecks per rouble on their ready money[10] and another two-and-a-half kopecks per rouble on the value of the goods purchased, thus making a total tax of ten kopecks per rouble. Goods removed and sold by them elsewhere are then subject to a further tax on resale of five kopecks per rouble. Thus the tax amounts to fifteen kopecks per rouble in all.

But nowadays, far from paying the prescribed fifteen kopecks, some goods are not paying even half a kopeck a rouble because many people buy goods brought to their doorstep and others go out into the countryside to buy. The first five kopecks, which should be levied on the peasants, are lost and your merchant will similarly sell to someone on the sly and so the second five kopecks are lost; and the second purchaser will take the goods away secretly to his own town and to his own shop or split them up among various shops. And so, as the whole of the goods will have been dispersed by retail sales, the third five kopecks of duty are also lost.

Again, if a merchant cannot secretly transport the goods that he has bought, he will procure a false certificate of duty paid made out in his own name, and the man who buys the goods from him will take them away for resale using the other man's certificate. If he succeeds in reselling the goods without paying the prescribed toll the certificate is brought back to where it was issued and somehow or other the toll-gatherer is suborned and the certificate is treated as

(208)

so much waste paper. Many such certificates are never entered in the records for this reason.

(209)   If a merchant is unable to sell the goods secretly, only the one levy of five kopecks on the final sale will have been paid but the others will have been wholly lost to the Tsar's treasury. If on the other hand anyone succeeds in disposing of goods secretly but cannot avoid producing a certificate of duty paid at the place where the goods were taken up, then he procures a certificate showing a very low value for the goods in some minor town or village with which the goods have no connection and compounds with the toll-gatherer to pay only two kopecks a rouble on this very small sum, which hardly comes to one kopeck a rouble on the real purchase price.

In this way instead of several separate levies at five kopecks each the revenue collected does not amount to half of a single such levy of five kopecks, that is, instead of fifteen kopecks in all it scarcely amounts to one kopeck per rouble. In consequence the revenue from this source cannot be large since so much of the duty has been evaded.

At present there are many ingenious minds inventing new taxes in an attempt to increase the revenue – the tax on market stalls, the poll-tax,[11] the tax on draught horses, mooring dues, the tax on boats according to length, bridge tolls, the tax on beehives, bath-houses, hides, barges and the tithe on the hire of carters. All this they choose to call 'petty items of revenue'.[12] But such trivial taxes can never fill the treasury; they merely cause great perturbation to the people. They are called 'petty items' and petty they are.

Another levy has been added to all these petty ones – one which is most offensive to His Majesty's dignity; one half per cent of all revenues is applied to the current needs of His Majesty,[13] our great Monarch and Emperor, glorious throughout the world. This levy seems to me more pernicious than all the other taxes; our Sovereign is pre-eminently an autocrat and his dignity must not be impaired by any of his subjects whatever, not least those about his person. Our Sovereign is like unto God: whatever he desires he may perform; and therefore he may cause his coffers to be full to overflowing and no lack of money may touch him.

(210)   My view is that all the above-mentioned long-standing and substantial taxes as well as all the petty new-fangled ones should be abolished and that there should be introduced in their stead one single most royal and just tax, one that was instituted even before the Incarnation of Our Lord, to wit the tithe; that is to say, there shall be taken ten kopecks in every rouble and not fifteen kopecks. And this shall be an invariable tax, subject to no alteration or exception at any time, so that every kind of merchandise shall pay this duty of ten kopecks per rouble once and once only; in no circumstances shall any further duty be exacted a second or third time on the same merchandise.

Some merchandise may not be sold within the year, but only in the next year or the year next but one; however, once the duty has been paid, at no later time shall a further payment of duty be exacted on the value of the said merchandise.

And if God so will, the life of the people will be made easier and His Majesty's revenue from a tithe of this kind will certainly be at least twice as great as at present, possibly as much as three times.

At present the multitude of different taxes impoverishes the people since the more different taxes there are, the more revenue officials there must be and each such official must have his own collectors and underlings, and all those who are enrolled for this service must necessarily abandon their own callings and make their living out of the self-same taxes which they are engaged in collecting. Hence the work of collection is never fruitful and the people all grow poorer. As for those who act as collectors, they do not abide by their oath but act dishonestly and steal the moneys which they are collecting in order to support themselves, some owing to the burden of service imposed upon them, others in defiance of their oath; but naturally by reason of their breach of faith they cannot prosper.

Moreover, when these collectors have served their term officials from the capital (or from the chief town) proceed to check their accounts and pluck them bare in the course of the audit which they succeed in dragging out for a year or two, thereby ruining them utterly.

In my opinion it would be better to lay down by ordinance precisely what all those taken for such service are entitled to for their subsistence so that they may not be tempted to break their oath but may eat the bread of righteousness. Similarly the officials from the capital should be given precise instructions on the amount to be collected from each local tax-gatherer, so that every man's bread may be blessed to him.

It goes very much contrary to what I am advising that, when men are chosen to serve as local revenue officials and as their subordinate collectors, they are made to take an oath[14] and swear solemnly that they will not appropriate anything whatever belonging to His Majesty and yet those chosen are the poorest of people. How can such a man remain honest if he cannot make a living without stealing? And so each and all fall into sin: the collectors yield to peculation in their need, their superiors know that they will do so from the very first day and yet force them to take the oath.

When any of them are caught peculating they are put to the question and given the knout and their homes are plundered, and they will also suffer in the next world for breaking their oath. In my opinion, provided it were possible for all these collectors to be supervised and (if need be) punished it would be better to forgo the oath; but if this cannot be done, better forgo the punishment and let God be their judge.

If the oath is retained, then the man should be questioned at the time (and a record kept) as to what he intends to live on when so employed and whether he can provide for his own subsistence. And if he says that he has not the wherewithal an emolument should be assigned to him for his subsistence. And if anyone, after being granted such emoluments, still misappropriates the money which he collects he must be severely punished. In view of this it is altogether preferable to give up the taking of oaths and all that goes with it and instead to assign by ordinance clearly defined emoluments for the local revenue officials and their subordinate collectors.

For all these reasons it seems to me, again, better entirely to give up the oath and all that goes with it and to retain only the physical punishment. It will be enough for the culprit to suffer pain for his fault in this world; he will be free at least of torment in the next.

In the matter of imposts it is evidently greatly preferable to make one single levy on all merchandise at the time of the first sale, for 'an ox can only be skinned once'. Likewise, a man must only be punished once for a given offence, either by man or by God.

(212)

As regards the salt traffic, I do not believe it to be advantageous that it should be a Crown monopoly. It would be better to allow free trade in this commodity and instead of taxing the retail price to impose a duty of ten kopecks on every pood sold[15] for the market, that is, on weight not on the retail price. Whatever the bulk buying price may be, even should it stand as low as two or three kopecks a pood, the same duty of ten kopecks a pood should still be levied, or more or less as His Majesty shall direct.

This duty shall be collected at the source, at the point where the salt is discharged for distribution. Each barge-load will yield some ten thousand roubles or more in revenue, lake-salt[16] and sea-salt alike. Even in cases when it is selling at one kopeck a pood the same duty shall be levied on the pood, as officially fixed. And all merchants shall be given certificates of clearance by the custom-house, so that they are then free to sell not only in the towns but also in the countryside, whether in Russian or alien parts,[17] or abroad, and no further duty of any kind shall be levied on the salt at any point. In this way the collection of the duty will always be secure: it can never be lost by accidents of water or fire. If a cargo of salt is lost by the sinking of a vessel or by fire the revenue will not suffer in the slightest.

Given free trade in salt many thousands of people will make an honest living therefrom and their bread will be blessed to them and not cursed, since they will be earning enough by their honest toil without the need to steal. Even if salt becomes cheaper than at present many will make their fortunes from it and the people will not contract scurvy from lack of salt and die a premature death. Whereas at present there is such a lack of salt in the countryside that many have to go without it in their food and so they contract scurvy and die. In some places the price is more than a rouble a pood owing to delays on the way, and even so salt is not always to be had. As a result there is much needless mortality from lack of it.

13) But if there were no monopoly and trade were free, no place would be without salt and His Majesty's treasury would receive a net revenue of a hundred roubles per thousand poods; nor would there be any need for an army of officials to manage the salt traffic. Nor would His Majesty have to supply barges, warehouses and workmen and guards, and cables and anchors and other gear, and carts for conveying the salt. The custom-house would manage the traffic alone and that only in those towns where the merchants would take up the salt for sale.

Wherever the merchants sell it retail no dues of any kind should be levied nor any further certificate required except that issued at the place of bulk purchase where the salt was taken up for distribution. So it is above all necessary that the certificate be made out at the source. Two records must be kept at the place where the salt was produced: one of extraction, the other of delivery; and the same applies to natural salt.[18]

The merchants shall take the salt wherever they wish once they have bought it and should there be a loss anywhere it is they who must bear it; His Majesty's revenue will always be secure. And so people will not, as now, contract scurvy and die prematurely for lack of salt because the merchants will take it round the villages themselves and not only sell it for cash but also barter it for grain, cattle and other things or even part with it on credit. Whereas His Majesty's factors and collectors of the due will not part with any salt except for cash even to the extent of a single kopeck's worth, and what is more they do not sell it everywhere, so that a person who wants to buy some may have to travel a hundred versts or more. As a result the less prosperous peasants all perish; and although many are dying for lack of salt nobody troubles to inform His Majesty of this. Even if high officials do know about it they show no concern for the health of the people.

Five or six thousand officials, or even more, are employed in collecting the salt dues – collectors and their subordinates, managers, workmen and inspectors – and all of them eat into that salt like weevils and thereby make
14) themselves a living. Whereas if there were a free trade in salt all these people would be plying a trade and thus making their living by their own exertions.

It would be as well to reckon up the gross profit from the sale of salt, the total expenses of all kinds, the net profit after all these expenses have been deducted and the total annual sale in poods. If duty is levied at ten kopecks per pood on all bulk sales, then given the total amount sold it will be clear what the total revenue will be. I believe that it would be no less than that now received from the retail sale of salt and there would be much less discontent and the people would be better fed.

The kind of duty on salt described above should be introduced also for other kinds of goods under exactly the same rule and fixed for all time. If all such duties were levied at the source as described, they could be dealt with by one and the same custom-house. If a man takes up any goods whatever at any place whatever, then no matter at what price the goods are bought (whether at market or on his own doorstep or in the countryside) he will no longer be able to evade the duty as at present. Whatever price he buys at, he must pay the duty in full, to wit ten kopecks per rouble. It will be quite impossible for him to avoid payment since he will not be allowed to carry the goods away without a certificate of duty paid; consequently, if he proceeds anywhere without such a certificate the goods will be confiscated on behalf of His Majesty without right of recovery. And if any person other than a revenue official discovers anyone carrying any goods whatever without a certificate of duty paid, and arrests him, he shall be rewarded with one tenth part of the said goods for making the arrest. In face of such strict measures no one will carry goods anywhere without having duly declared them.

(215) Any person who wants to be free to convey his merchandise elsewhere must declare it wherever it may have been bought. And the revenue official shall examine the said merchandise and enter on the certificate an exact description of all the goods as to weight, quantity and value, and likewise make an exact record in his register of the quantity and value of each item and of the amount of duty levied on each. Similarly he shall enter on the certificate the full details and the amount of duty levied, and not as heretofore just 'received as due'. Not merely every rouble but every fraction of a kopeck must be specifically recorded so that each payment of duty may be fully known.

If any merchant has not the wherewithal to pay the toll at that time, some known and trustworthy persons may be accepted as surety for the payment and in attestation thereof the guarantors shall put their signatures in the register. And merchants who receive certificates of duty paid under this kind of guarantee shall each and every one sign their names in the register and without such an entry and signatures no certificates shall on any account be issued. Whenever a merchant does not pay the dues at the time when he takes up the goods, the amount which he owes his guarantors and in duty shall not be entered on the certificate issued to him: it shall merely state that the duty has been levied (giving the amount in figures). But the officials shall record in their registers these debts and unpaid sums and the names of those standing surety for their payment, and further obtain a security to ensure that the payment of the duty is not, as now, continually postponed.

When merchandise of a kind that can be stamped is passed by the custom-house, it must all be marked with the official stamp. In the case of livestock (bulls and cows), each animal shall be branded with the amount in roubles (in figures) on the right haunch, that is to say, how many roubles have been paid for the animal, and any kopecks in excess of whole roubles shall similarly be branded in figures on the right shoulder. If any animal is bought at less than one rouble the amount shall be expressed in kopecks and likewise branded on the right shoulder. The same branding shall be applied to horses – roubles on the right haunch, kopecks on the right shoulder. In this way it will be impossible to buy or sell any cattle or horses without their having been duly branded and the

16) duty paid. And when livestock is so passed, the revenue officials shall enter all the details in their ledger – the number of each kind of animal and price of each; and for horses also their age and distinguishing marks.

If any person who buys livestock removes it without having it branded, it shall all be confiscated on behalf of His Majesty even if he has the necessary certificate. And when he sells such branded livestock anywhere, whether in town or countryside, and receives a price higher than the buying price, duty must be levied at the rate of ten kopecks per rouble on the profit from the transaction only, but on no account on the buying price. Similarly, if anyone makes a purchase and then resells to another, whether immediately or even several years later, duty shall be levied on the profit from the transaction but nothing further whatever may be levied on the original buying price.

When a merchant arrives in a town with certain goods or livestock and presents his certificate of duty paid the revenue officials shall copy the said certificate into their register in full and then examine the merchandise. If the certificate is found to be correct in all particulars the officials shall then levy a duty of ten per cent on any profit over and above the buying price. If, however, the merchant sells at the same price at which he bought or at a lower one, he has no duty to pay but shall pay the clerk a fee of one kopeck for making the entry and one kopeck also for checking the certificate.

Should any merchandise prove to be overweight to the extent of two or three poods per hundred the same uniform duty of ten per cent shall be levied on the excess. Similarly with respect to any merchandise, if the size shows an excess of up to three per cent the duty of ten per cent shall be levied on that excess. But if the excess weight, measure or quantity is more than three per cent, the excess shall be confiscated on behalf of His Majesty. And if any merchant buys anything in a secret manner without paying the duty, both the goods bought by him and the money received from him by the seller for the undeclared merchandise shall be forfeit to His Majesty and both parties to the transaction shall be stripped and beaten without mercy and the reason for the punishment recorded in the ledger. And if either is caught doing the same again, then the merchant's goods shall be confiscated and he shall pay a fine equal to double

17) the sum that he received and both shall receive as many strokes of the knout as may be determined.

If any seller shall sell merchandise on which duty has not been paid and then confess his fault and declare that the buyer knowingly bought such goods from him, the seller shall be exonerated, the merchandise bought shall be forfeit to

His Majesty and the buyer shall be fined. Conversely, if a buyer inform against a seller of the like offence, the money received by the seller shall be confiscated and he shall pay a fine, and the buyer shall not be punished. But if neither party confess that they entered into a clandestine agreement and some other person inform against them, both the goods and the money received shall be confiscated and a fine imposed. The informer shall receive one tenth part of the goods and both parties shall be punished as mentioned above, and in addition they shall be made to pay the money with which the informer is rewarded.

If anyone buys merchandise or exposes his own wares for sale without having registered them at the custom-house, paid the duty and received a certificate of duty paid, or (even if the duty has been paid and the certificate issued) without having had all or part of the wares stamped, then the merchandise which has been stamped may be sold but that which has not shall be forfeit to His Majesty.

If officials in town or countryside demand to see any person's certificate and he cannot show one, or else he has a certificate but the merchandise or livestock has not been duly stamped, then any merchandise not recorded on the certificate or not duly stamped shall be confiscated without right of recovery on behalf of His Majesty. An inventory shall be made and the goods sold to any willing buyer, and the sum obtained credited to the customs revenue.

If any revenue official or his subordinate observes any merchandise or grain being moved without a certificate or without the official stamp and fails to seize the same on behalf of His Majesty, the said official shall incur a double fine and double punishment.

Any merchandise acquired for despatch abroad by sea, or to China or other foreign countries overland, must likewise pay the same duty of ten per cent at the source, that is, at the point at which it is bought. In this case too the duty shall be collected in full and certificates of duty paid issued, so that no duty shall be payable even at the markets close to the frontier on the price paid at the source.

(218)

In respect of any merchandise which has been purchased by foreigners for export abroad, whether by sea or by land, all the present variety of petty levies shall be replaced by a fixed export duty, viz.: on ships' masts – ten roubles per piece (in accordance with the tariff formerly in force at Archangel); on scutched hemp and flax – three roubles per *bérkovets*; on pitch and tallow – four roubles; on Russia leather – five roubles per *bérkovets*, or whatever rate is deemed appropriate; on grain – a rouble or a rouble and a half per *bérkovets*. Similarly on all other merchandise, whatever its nature, a fixed export duty shall be imposed in place of all the various petty levies, as may seem appropriate, excepting always the duty paid on the purchase price at the source when the goods are taken up. But in the case of bar iron no export duty shall be imposed over and above the prime duty [of ten per cent].

The rate at which the export duty is to be levied on any kind of merchandise must be notified to all merchants in order that they may be duly apprised thereof and add it to their selling price when negotiating with foreigners, so that they may not incur any loss by having to pay the duty themselves. But if anyone does sell his goods without addition of the said export duty he shall himself be liable for the full amount of the duty. Further, such goods as foreigners have hitherto been in the habit of buying in certain inland towns, or contracting to buy at a certain price from the local inhabitants, shall be subject to the prime duty of ten per cent to be paid in accordance with the proposed regulation, in full at the source and at the time of the transaction.

The export duty shall be paid in full and without any exception whatever on all merchandise destined for export by sea or land, at the official rate. If any Russian or foreigner should succeed by some trick in removing any merchandise from those inland towns without a certificate of duty paid, the goods shall be confiscated on behalf of His Majesty without possibility of 9) exception or recovery, and shall be sold to any willing buyer. And the culprit shall pay a fine for evasion of duty equivalent to the value of the goods, or as may be determined by law.

If any person has merchandise remaining over which he has failed to sell for export and now wishes to sell at home, it shall be subject only to the resale duty but not to the export duty. Conversely, if he buys to sell at home and then sells to foreigners for export, the full export duty must be paid without fail by the merchant in question over and above the prime duty of ten per cent. And if any Russian proposes to take any merchandise abroad in person the full export duty must likewise be paid on it without exception.

Again it seems to me that the tax on spirits too is very badly administered and that His Majesty's revenue suffers much thereby. In the first place, the officials concerned are only temporary, being changed every year. Secondly, the liquor shops are kept in a bad state and the quality of the liquors served is extremely low. Thirdly, the price of a given liquor is not the same everywhere: liquor going under the same name is sold at one price in one town, at another elsewhere, and each town has its own price. Even that price is unsteady, being changed every year or even twice a year – here is unsteadiness indeed!

Our Tsar is not a merchant but an autocratic ruler. If he orders a thing to be so it must be so unalterably, without the least variation to one side or the other. Just as God rules the whole world so our sovereign exercises power in his realm, and his sovereign power wills that all things shall be invariable and praiseworthy. Just as weights and measures should be everywhere the same so prices should always be the same and invariable, whether in a year of plenty or dearth. Therefore the price of liquor should be the same in a place where grain is abundant as in one where none is grown. The quality of the liquor should not vary, nor should the price of a given quantity be altered but all these things should be maintained inviolate.

(220)   It is not at all a good thing that the officials in charge of the liquor revenue should be constantly changed; since even if an official has some previous acquaintance with taverns and knows what is expected of him, he will still not be able to perform his duty as he ought. An official appointed for the first time is sure to make a loss at every step since he does not know what various stocks he needs to provide and will buy everything at too high a price, and wherever he has the chance of making a profit he makes a loss. Whereas if the officials were permanent they would not incur such losses by paying too much on any transaction, but would buy all their supplies when they are cheap. If, for example, mead happens to be cheap in a given year they could lay in supplies for two years or even three. Similarly with drinking vessels; they could lay in at a favourable time such stock as is needed and would not have to pay too high a price for such supplies; they would know exactly what was required.

To improve this state of affairs these officials should be chosen from among men who are not too rich but of moderate means, provided that they are sensible, honest and capable and not drunkards, and such that one and all can testify that they are men of probity, zeal and good repute, and fit for the discharge of such duties. When they have been chosen they shall be given a yearly salary. If by their unflagging zeal they collect a sum in excess of the sum stipulated, they should be rewarded with a further payment at the rate of ten per cent on the excess so collected. This reward for collecting an excess amount shall be paid over to them out of the total sum collected and must be entered in the ledger in full detail, viz. how many payments of ten kopecks have been made to each man. Likewise if any man entrusted with the sale of liquor brings in a sum greater than the sale of the liquor assigned to him for the year would ordinarily produce, he may be given one half of the excess as a reward for his zeal. And the excess sum collected must be accurately entered in the ledger and below this entry a record shall forthwith be made of what part of the sum has been paid in reward to each such person.

The liquor revenue officials shall themselves draw their prime salaries (as
(221)   may be determined in each case) every year out of the moneys collected by them and keep a full record thereof in the ledger of outgoings. For if they have to apply to higher officials and accountants for their salaries, as is done now, equity will not be achieved: they will lie in order to obtain additional rewards.

If my proposals were adopted the liquor revenue would become extremely profitable because none of those responsible would pay too much for anything nor incur any unnecessary loss, nor do anything incompetently; and the sum allotted to them by way of salary would be recouped with interest. Indeed, the salaries might well be defrayed entirely from excess receipts and so the net revenue from the sale of liquor would remain intact and whatever is done will be done in a manner that is both profitable and dependable.

Again, His Majesty's best interests suffer a great deal because the landowners do not play their part in the collection of revenue but rather hinder it. Orders have been given, in accordance with His Majesty's command, to build taverns at convenient places and for the collectors of the excise and their subordinates to levy the liquor revenue there. Yet those that have already been built have been destroyed by the landowners and so collection has come to a standstill. Though an honest man and a true servant of His Majesty, V. D. Korchmín[19] has been much to blame in this respect. For a small tavern was established in the vicinity of Olónets and brought in a hundred roubles or more a year before he became the local landowner. Whereas now his bailiff does not allow liquor to be delivered there but stocks this shop which clearly belongs to His Majesty with liquor of Korchmín's own manufacture. This results in a loss to His Majesty of a hundred or more roubles a year. And some landowners go so far as to do violence to the collectors, remove the liquor and smash the crockery; by such disorderly conduct they have made themselves enemies instead of servants of their Sovereign. Far from being zealous for their Sovereign and furthering rather than hindering the collection of his revenue, these wretches have forgotten that the very land which they presume to own is not theirs but His Majesty's and that their persons are not their own but likewise his; and yet they feel no fear on account of their conduct.

222)   If the petty landowners do so much mischief what can we expect of the great ones? They will not allow anyone to set foot on their land, of which they are but the temporary owners, for the purveying of His Majesty's liquor. They have built their own taverns on their great estates, calling them 'kvass-houses', and openly sell beer under the name of kvass, and also carry on a clandestine trade in spirits.

Now the liquor revenue is a most ancient right of His Majesty, not of the landowners. If a stop were put once and for all to such wilful actions on the part of the landowners, and taverns were built at suitable places on all their estates, the revenue from liquor would go up by a hundred thousand roubles a year or more. If the *dvoriáne* were forbidden in accordance with His Majesty's present ordinance to distil spirits for sale and their licensed retorts and stills were suppressed, I believe that the sale of liquor would go up by two or three hundred thousand roubles a year.

If any of them, however great a magnate, were then to request that such 'kvass-houses' be not suppressed but that he be allowed to trade in beer on his own account as before, orders could be given for official agents to be appointed to manage this trade for a period of two to three years. If the profits prove to be satisfactory the landowners may thereafter bid for the right to farm this trade at an annually rising rent. But on no account must they be allowed to use their privileged position solely to their own advantage, since the land that they all use belongs to the Tsar, now and at all times, and is granted to the *poméshchiki* for their sustenance. Hence the Sovereign's sway over it is the greater and unlimited, theirs the less and limited in time. So not only should they not be dealers in liquor on their own account but also not be in possession of land without paying for it. And if any such person desire to deal in liquor let him bid for the right to do so; for the liquor revenue comes within His Majesty's interest and therefore no one must usurp it.[20]

Even the petty landowners distil spirits and sell them in their villages and some even bring them into the towns and sell them there – thereby doing great harm to the liquor revenue. But if the licensing of private stills were abolished members of the *dvoriánstvo* would cease also to engage in the sale of liquor.

(223)   I believe that it would be advantageous to pay salaries to all these officials. I am sure that this would lead to an increase in the revenue for the collection of which they are responsible. They must then bear the full responsibility together with the *magistráty*[21] and local chief revenue officials. The latter should keep a due watch on all kinds of revenue collection and at the end of the year they should audit the accounts of all the local collectors and verify their outgoings, so that as permanent officers these officials may not (as now) be subject to unnecessary vexation at the hands of officials from the capital.

The local chief revenue officials should each choose yearly suitable subordinates for all revenue collecting. And if any subordinate proves to be zealous and competent he may be granted a salary. If he gives satisfactory service for three or four years as a subordinate he may then be considered suitable for employment as a permanent official.

The permanent officials must be provided with full instructions point by point as to how they are to carry out their tasks. In particular they must be given precise instructions how to draw up their reports if these are to be of any practical value. They must comprise the total revenue of any kind collected in a given month, total outgoings and the amount of cash in hand.

To report every month on the quantity of liquor in stock and its actual or selling price is a quite needless burden on officials and a hindrance to good administration. At present they even make a weekly report, which merely results in a waste of liquor by reason of these frequent checks and needless payment to clerks; and all this causes a loss to His Majesty's treasury. In my opinion the reports should be limited to a monthly summary of accounts, so that the officers of the Board of Revenue may know the amount collected in any given form of revenue, the outgoings and the balance in hand. Such reports need not be more than three lines long, instead of three pages.

And the above officers shall consolidate all these summaries and submit to the Board one single report on a single sheet instead of a hundred separate (224)   ones. It will be much easier to tell from such a report the figures for receipts, outgoings and cash in hand; everything can be put under these three headings.

At present the officials in charge of the liquor revenue spend more time on their reports than on the collection of revenue. This is inevitable when the officials in the capital make insistent demands for detailed reports on the quantity of each kind of liquor sold each week and the quantity and value of the stock remaining for the next week. At the end of the month the officials again check the quantities of all liquors on hand so that they spend all their time preparing these reports to the detriment of their proper tasks.

These reports should be rendered only annually to provide a true record and to balance accounts at the end of the year, and not weekly. The report need only show what profit there has been to His Majesty's revenue and that there has been no loss in the revenue collected. And if any revenue official fails to conform with the instructions issued to him he shall be liable to a heavy fine together with such physical punishment and branding as may be determined. And if anyone embezzles His Majesty's revenue he shall suffer, if not death, first physical punishment and then branding upon the face, indicating that he shall be sent for life to the army for hard labour. Nor shall the chief revenue officials be exempt from a fine, to ensure that such men are not chosen for this service in future.

Prosperous merchants should on no account be appointed as revenue officials; they must apply themselves to their commerce and pay the duty on the profits thereof.

A man of industry in a large way who is short of ready money and applies for a loan out of current revenue to extend his affairs should be granted a loan of five or six hundred roubles, or a thousand or more (according to the nature of his business); let the affairs of our merchants be further extended and let those who venture grow rich. All chief towns shall be notified of the conditions for such loans so that the local chief revenue officials may advance money from the chest of the *Rátusha*[22] (two or three hundred roubles according to the nature of the venture) to those local men of commerce who own manufactories. And to such men as have established great manufactories for the making of cloth, linen, cotton, glass, iron and so forth, loans of a thousand roubles or more may be made for the extension of their ventures provided that they are men of good repute, honest and hardworking in their affairs and known not to be wastrels.

In such cases, in order that those borrowing the money shall not be burdened with any fees and expenses, the documents need not be drawn up in the Office of Deeds[23] but should be entered in an official register, for the borrowers will be paying a yearly interest on the loan at a rate to be determined. The borrower shall give a signed receipt for the money and his signature shall be witnessed by one or more guarantors. If a loan is made without due investigation of the borrower and the latter loses the borrowed money, the loss shall be made good not merely by his guarantors but by the whole of his community.

I think that interest of more than six per cent a year should not be taken on large ventures, seeing that they will be giving employment to a great number of people and thereby helping to increase His Majesty's revenue.

25)

If anyone wants a loan at short term (up to three months) for the purpose of buying merchandise, interest should be levied at the rate of one per cent per month.

The revenue collected in a given chief town shall not be transferred to any other place but a return shall be made to the Board of Revenue as to the amount of such moneys collected there in a given year. It shall not be used without express permission from the Board of Revenue for any other purpose than for loans of a few months' duration.

If His Majesty decides that the local revenue officials shall receive salaries, they must be chosen from men of moderate means; a rich man will not give the same service for a yearly salary of five hundred roubles as a poorer man for a hundred roubles. A rich man who is engaged in any branch of revenue collection will continue to give most of his attention to his own affairs, whereas a person who has no important affairs of his own will confine himself to his task and pay little attention to other matters. His thoughts will only run on how best to carry out the task assigned to him.

(226)

The whole method of collecting the liquor revenue needs, in my opinion, to be reformed in all its details.

The contractors should receive orders to purvey to all towns nothing but liquor of the best quality, that is, containing one third by weight of alcohol,[24] or in other words, such that one third part by weight will burn away and two thirds remain. The burning should be done in one operation without removing the liquid from the vessel in which it is being weighed. The liquor must be perfectly pure, showing no turbidity in a glass vessel and be free from odour.

The standard barrel[25] should be improved by making it larger, to hold thirty pounds of good quality liquor. When contractors bring liquor for distribution, any barrel whose contents are passed as satisfactory shall be weighed and then emptied and weighed again; this will clearly show how much liquor the barrel contained. By using this barrel as a measure there will be no loss of liquid and the whole transfusion will be expeditious and easy.[26] A hundred or so barrels could be dealt with in a single day and the retailer will gain much thereby, since he will not have to pollute any other buckets, basins or ladles with liquor, and no liquid will be lost.

The selling price of the liquor shall be fixed by His Majesty's command and not by private agreement. There has long been an iniquitous custom whereby liquor was sold at a higher price if the contractors had purveyed it at a higher price and at a lower one if they had obtained it cheaper themselves. In this way it was not even persons in high authority but those of the basest sort who determined the price, whereas by rights the price of liquor should be fixed by the Sovereign's decree and not by the will of mere peasants. It thus comes about that the price is not the same in every town and such a practice is in my opinion greatly at variance with the autocratic power of His Majesty.

(227)

Liquor must be sold at a uniform and unalterable price, the same everywhere. If the price of liquor is the same everywhere and the quality likewise uniform, the liquor revenue will benefit greatly since there will no longer be any advantage in conveying liquor from one place to another; it will be bought wherever the customer happens to be.

His Majesty should by his autocratic power decree that the selling price of liquor be unalterable in all Great Russian towns and villages (Siberia excepted) – the same in Moscow as in St Petersburg and the same in all towns and places. If it prove impossible to raise the price in the Ukraine it must be strictly forbidden for anyone – not only merchants, but also *dvoriáne* and officers – to buy spirits and tobacco there and convey them to the Great Russian towns and villages, without special permission. Should anyone bring back with him from those parts more than one barrel of spirits he shall pay a heavy fine and be severely beaten.

If any official of the liquor revenue adulterates the spirits on sale so that they fall below the standard quality, or accepts such from the contractors, he shall pay a heavy fine and be severely beaten.

So if these measures are introduced and maintained in full vigour there will be no call for anyone to convey liquor privately from one place to another because it will be of the same quality and price everywhere. And in consequence the liquor revenue will greatly increase in all towns and the expenses of transport will be less.

The official price of liquor shall be fixed at His Majesty's pleasure. This no one can know in advance but I should suppose that the price of one *vedró* of ordinary spirits might be set at three roubles and for sales of small quantities at twelve kopecks a pound. Even if the contract price were only fifty kopecks for one *vedró*, the retail price must on no account be lowered.[27]

(228) To make quite certain that the liquor is not being diluted with water the said officials shall keep in every liquor shop in all towns and villages a small pair of scales (suspended by iron chains) with which the alcohol content of one *zolotník* of spirits or vodka may be estimated by ignition. They shall also be provided with two identical perfectly clean pound or half-pound glass vessels of the kind made in Iámburg,[28] one containing a standard sample sealed by the Board of Revenue, the other empty. If any merchant's liquor or vodka appears to be of poor quality, the doubtful liquid shall be poured into the empty vessel and set beside the same sealed vessel and a comparison made in good light. If the former is identical in colour with the standard vessel then the liquor has not been diluted with water, but if its colour is different from the standard then there has been dilution. If the merchant or official is not satisfied by the accuracy of this test, then for complete certainty the doubtful liquid shall be tested on the above-mentioned scales, taking three measures thereof. In the case of spirits, if one measure is consumed when ignited there has been no

adulteration; in the case of vodka, if two measures are consumed (and therefore there remains one measure after igniting), there has likewise been no adulteration. If, however, in either case, the weight of the residue is greater, then the liquid has been adulterated. The spirits or vodka proved to have been adulterated shall then be sealed and taken to an officer of the Board of Revenue and the person responsible for the adulteration shall be severely punished as the law may determine. This method ensures that no spirits or vodka can by any means be adulterated with water or anything else.

If my proposals were adopted I believe that the revenue would increase by two or three hundred thousand roubles a year (or even more) compared with the present sum. Such an increase would be noticeable even in the first year and after that, I am sure, would become much larger; moreover, there would be less drunkenness among the people.

I do not know why many of those in high authority endeavour to make liquor as cheap as possible and encourage people to drink as much as possible, without reflecting that sober people, whatever their degree or calling, show greater (229) capacity in all that they do; in particular those engaged in trade or manufacture are likely to show more enterprise. Whereas drunkards do no good work, as may be seen even among some servants of His Majesty, to say nothing of the craftsmen. People are brought to dire impoverishment by drink, especially by the use of imported liquors; such excesses do no little damage to His Majesty's interests.

The *dvoriáne* have taken steps to be granted licensed stills and they pay an annual duty of only one rouble on a still with a capacity of four *vëdra*. They have persuaded His Majesty that his treasury will gain in revenue thereby but they have deceived him. Anyone can see that there would be more profit to the treasury if they did no distilling and distilleries were unknown among them. Through this system of licensing the *dvoriáne* have caused His Majesty a loss (rather than a profit) of some ten thousand roubles or more a year and have opened the doors to the practice of free distilling for their own advantage. For anyone who has a licensed still and pays one rouble a year for the right can produce yearly some three or four hundred *vëdra* of spirits; and if he sells it all he will get three or four hundred roubles for it, thereby causing His Majesty a loss of a hundred roubles or more a year on liquor sales against a payment of one single rouble.

The system of licensing has made it easy for distilling to be done also in unlicensed stills. In the district of Ustréka there are some hundred *dvoriáne*, I should say, and I was told by the Local Commissioner that he only had official cognizance of three licensed stills, yet all these *dvoriáne* were engaged in distilling in the woods and bottoms, or even in their own homes, giving out quite unashamedly that their stills were duly licensed. The result of this abuse is that the liquor revenue has much declined.

I suggest that licensing be abolished and that the *voevóda* in every chief town send out a subordinate with a posse of soldiers and a clerk with funds, with orders that all stills and pipes belonging to the *dvoriáne* be dismantled in the name of His Majesty and payment made for the copper at the market price, after extraction of all the tin, lead and other impurities, so that His Majesty may not suffer any unnecessary loss from all this.

(230)   All *dvoriáne* shall make a solemn declaration that they will on no account possess any distilling apparatus in future and, calling together their servants and peasants, shall inform them clearly of this so that they too may know all about it. If stills and pipes are discovered in anyone's possession again after the dismantling, the apparatus shall be confiscated and a fine of twenty-five roubles (or as may be determined) exacted from the offender, and for failing to report the matter every single one of his household servants shall be fined five roubles and every peasant two-and-a-half roubles. Should any servant or peasant discover any distilling apparatus in the possession of his master and report the matter, a reward shall be paid of five roubles to a servant and two-and-a-half roubles to a peasant, and the man shall receive his freedom.

To meet the needs of the *dvoriáne* it could be decreed that they are entitled to two or three *vëdra* of spirits yearly, according to their means and rank, at the contract price, and ten or twenty kopecks (or whatever sum is fixed) could be added to this price per *vedró* to cover ullage.

If the *dvoriáne* no longer make their own liquor they will themselves drink less, and they will not supply their own product to towns and inns nor make gifts to servants of His Majesty or payments to craftsmen for their work in the form of liquor.

I cannot see any virtue in heavy drinking or in causing others to get drunk. To my mind three or four glasses a day is enough to keep a person in good health, and perhaps as much again might be added when there is occasion for good cheer. But heavy drinking is anything but good; it merely impairs the faculties and health and leads to material loss and premature death. Anyone

231)   who becomes a habitual drunkard will ruin himself utterly. Every effort must therefore be made to reduce drunkenness among the people.

If it should be the Sovereign's will that the *dvoriáne* should be allowed to purchase liquor at the contract price from the taverns in the chief towns, then a tariff must be drawn up showing how many *vëdra* of liquor may be purchased yearly at this special price by persons of different ranks. This tariff shall be distributed to all chief towns with a nominal roll of all the *dvoriáne* resident in the district. Liquor shall then be sold to them yearly in the towns at the special price in conformity with this official tariff. If anyone wishes to buy more than his allowance he must do so at the full market price.

The officials of the liquor revenue shall keep special registers in the large taverns in all towns to record the quantity of liquor supplied to the *dvoriáne*, and all transactions shall be entered in detail and countersigned by the purchaser and by other *dvoriáne* as witnesses. These witnesses should append their signatures to the entry in order that no man may obtain his allowance twice over.

And at the end of the year an alphabetical list shall be made at the back of the register of the names of all the *dvoriáne* so that the entries relating to any one of them may be verified without any delay to see how much liquor he has purchased and who were his witnesses. These registers shall be forwarded to the Board of Revenue. If any *dvorianín* shall be proved to have bought more liquor than his allowance he shall pay a fine at the rate of twenty-five roubles for each *vedró* in excess and the witnesses shall each be fined five roubles (or such sum as may be determined).

If any *dvorianín* or officer takes up his full allowance (but no more) and then resells it to another he must pay the appropriate fine and the purchaser must also be fined the like amount without exception. If anyone buys liquor in this manner and then reports the matter to higher authority, the seller shall be fined but the purchaser shall be exempt and the liquor remain his in reward for the (232)   information. And if any liquor contractor, be he *dvorianín* or merchant, sells liquor or makes a present or even a loan thereof to anyone (not excluding servants of His Majesty) or accepts grain from anyone from which to distil liquor for his use he shall be fined twenty-five roubles per *vedró* and shall be punished according to the law.

The selling price of vodka shall be, for the inferior sort – six roubles a *vedró* (that is to say, twenty kopecks a pound), for the middling quality – twenty-five kopecks a pound, and for concentrated spirit for medicinal use (such as *spiritus cephalicus* and *spiritus apoplecticus*) which rates at twenty proof,[29] fifty kopecks a pound; and for preserving spirit containing sugar and for *spiritus mellis* and *elixir vitae regium* and for the fortifying *spiritus mastichinus*,[30] which all rate at sixteen proof – sixty kopecks a pound.

Plain concentrated mead (similar to Rhine wine) shall be sold at ninety kopecks the *vedró* (that is to say three kopecks a pound). Mead flavoured with raspberry, blackcurrant and the like, made from the fruit without added alcohol, shall sell at a hundred and twenty kopecks the *vedró* (that is to say, four kopecks a pound): but similar mead fortified with alcohol shall sell at one hundred and eighty kopecks the *vedró*, that is to say at six kopecks the pound. Plain natural mead[31] shall be sold at sixty kopecks the *vedró* (two kopecks a pound). Strong beer of the best quality shall be sold at sixty kopecks the *vedró* (two kopecks a pound); ordinary beer shall be forty-five kopecks the *vedró* (one-and-a-half kopecks a pound).

I think that the impost on all beers, ales, mead and the like might well be repealed since its collection is troublesome; moreover, the brewers are not honest. One will brew a *chétvert'* and only declare an *osmína*; another brews an *osmína* and declares half the quantity, all of which leads to wrong and sin. All of them brew two or three times as much beer as they declare; at most half the true amount is declared. Some of them are not even aware of the obligation to make such a declaration. No one gains by this system except the clerks; and His Majesty receives very little revenue from it.

33)   If this practice were discontinued people of all conditions would be able freely to brew their own beer and prepare mead without risk of confiscation. Moreover, they will not be in a hurry to drink up all that they make but exercise restraint. And for their health's sake they will drink more moderately; nor will they commit the sin of deceit since they will have no good reason to lie any more and to forswear themselves.

Instead of all these petty imposts and the duty on liquor there should be imposed a special duty on hops at the rate of four roubles a pood (that is to say, ten kopecks a pound). Neither rich nor poor, nor even members of the Senate itself, would then be able to avoid this payment. If they want beer they must necessarily buy the hops to make it. In this way men of all sorts and conditions will be making a contribution to His Majesty's revenue and will not drink their home-made brews scot-free.

If this proposal were adopted the revenue would be a hundred times the revenue brought in by the impost levied on the quantities declared since everyone would be paying duty in proportion to the quantity that he brews, even if it were a mere *chetverík*.

All chief towns shall be informed of His Majesty's ordinance so that all revenue officials throughout the towns and villages may be apprised thereof, to wit, that if any person is found in charge of hops (even if they belong to a great landowner) without a certificate of duty paid, the hops shall be forfeit to His Majesty without right of recovery. And if anyone brings in his hops for registration the details (including the owner's name) shall be entered in a register, and if the hops are for sale they must be carefully inspected to see if there is any sand or other secret adulterant therein, or whether there are hops of poor quality below the surface, or whether they are in too damp a condition. Hops that do not stand up to scrutiny shall be confiscated without compensation. But if no defect is found the trading duty of ten per cent shall be levied on the value of the hops and also the special duty of four roubles per pood. However, if the hops are not for public sale but for the personal use of some great landowner, they shall be subject only to the special duty of four roubles per pood and the quality of the hops need not be examined but they may be passed without

34)   further ado. They must, however, be weighed and the quantity entered in the register. A certificate shall then be issued authorizing their removal. The certificate shall clearly state that the said hops are not for sale and that the duty has been paid in full. But if the owner of any hops reserved for personal use subsequently decides to sell them, then he must pay the trading duty of ten per

cent on the market price of the goods in addition to the special duty on hops. And the officials shall record such duty collected on hops as a separate item.

If any hops rejected as defective are confiscated this shall be recorded in full in the register and the hops shall be offered to the taverns for what they will fetch, without payment of the special duty.

Similarly, the trading tax of ten per cent shall be paid on the market price of all honey offered for sale, as well as a further special duty of a hundred and twenty kopecks per pood. But anyone conveying honey for his private use or for the use of a landowner and not for sale, shall pay only the duty of a hundred and twenty kopecks a pood, and the details shall be entered in a register. This register should be separate from the merchants' registers. Thus all sums collected by any official in duty on hops and honey not for public sale shall be entered under a separate head; and all sums collected in duty from the merchants shall likewise be recorded separately, so that the total annual revenue from these duties on hops and honey under each head may be known. The officials alone shall be wholly responsible for the collection of the ten per cent duty and the special duty.

If any landowner refuses to pay the special duty on hops or honey the goods shall be seized in the name of His Majesty but the said officials shall pay the owner for the goods out of the appropriate revenue account at the market price as found in the merchants' registers, subtracting therefrom, however, the trading duty of ten per cent.

(235)   If anyone contracts to supply hops or honey, for example to His Majesty's court or to the taverns, the purveyors to the court should receive a patent from the court, and the purveyors to the taverns from the *kameríry*.[32] And the hops purchased anywhere by them shall be inspected by the revenue officials to ensure that the said hops are not too damp and do not contain any admixture nor any stalks or leaves. And if they are in perfect condition they shall be weighed and the trading duty of ten per cent levied on the price at which the purveyors bought them, but not the special duty; and a certificate shall be issued to that effect.

Similarly honey shall be inspected to make sure that there are no impurities or dead insects in it; and if it is sound the ten per cent duty shall be levied but not the special duty, and it shall be passed once it has been weighed and the certificate issued. The certificate shall state that the said goods have not been bought for resale but for the use of the court or the taverns. But if any hops or honey prove to contain impurities the goods shall be seized on behalf of His Majesty without right of recovery and the owner fined a sum equal to the value of the goods.

If any hops or honey have been submitted for inspection at the custom-house and have been granted a certificate but subsequently shopkeepers or others inspect them and find impurities in them, the person who issued the certificate shall be fined for aiding and abetting the seller.

From earliest times in Russia – in the days of the Great Princes and under our first Tsar Iván IV Vasíl'evich – our coinage used to be of the purest silver, refined over bone as is evident from those ancient coins which are still in circulation. But in the reign of Mikhaíl Fëdorovich they began to strike coins from melted down rix-dollars without refining the metal in this way. The foreigners even advise us to add a large proportion of copper to this silver for making coins of small denomination. Though myself a person of no account, I could not refrain from drawing attention to this vicious innovation. In 1718 I wrote a report for His Majesty on this subject to prove that such coinage is very apt to lead to fraud and is tantamount to an invitation to counterfeiters.[33] I waited upon A. V. Makárov[34] in the hope of submitting this report but was unable to present it to him on account of the strict guard about his person. He then left to take the waters and so the report remained on my hands. Subsequently I handed it to Egór Sergéev, the courier attached to his household, and requested him to present it to Alekséi Vasíl'evich at a suitable moment. But I do not know whether he ever did so. Consequently in this chapter devoted to His Majesty's interest I have thought good to rehearse again the matter of this most royal of revenues which proceeds entirely from the will of the Sovereign.

It is my considered opinion that our coinage deserves the most careful attention so that His Majesty's coffers may be filled and the people may derive no little benefit therefrom.

The minting of coins must be done with consummate wisdom so that the quality of the coinage may at all times be impeccable and that counterfeiting may not be possible. No change whatever should be allowed in this principle which must stand as firm as a rock. The coinage should be the responsibility not of one man but of acute and sober minds (it is no task for the flighty), to ensure that the coinage is sound and pure and admirable in every way.

In my view it were better that the silver content of the coinage be restored to its former fineness, in fact, that its fineness should not be exceeded in any other objects whatever.

Just as the Christian faith has been preserved in Russia in its purest state, without any taint of heresy, so our coinage should also be the purest in the world, free of all debasement, and such that it excel all foreign coinage and earn the praise of all both in the quality of the workmanship and in the fineness of the silver. And if our great Monarch, the Emperor of All the Russias, should see fit to have coins struck of a fineness equal or superior to that of our ancient coinage, they will be an object of praise also among all future generations.

Foreigners reckon the value of their coins according to the content of metal and not in accordance with the will of their kings; they honour silver and copper more than their Sovereign! But we revere our Monarch as we do God and are jealous for his honour and most zealously carry out his will. Therefore, on whatever thing we see His Majesty's superscription that thing we treat with all honour and respect. So if copper is to be marked with His Majesty's superscription, the purest copper must be used without admixture, and in the case of silver – it must be the purest silver without blemish. So also in the case of gold, it must be the most pure and noble gold such that it surpasses that of all other countries. I would have it here that the gold used in our ducats should be of a fineness superior to that of the *sultanín*,[35] so that the name of our Monarch may

(238)   be magnified throughout the world not only in his lifetime but also after his death. Such ducats would be in greater demand in all lands than the *sultanín* since the gold ducat is not intended for the purposes of trade or for the amassing of wealth but for the most eminent and everlasting glory of His Majesty.

I have seen Russian ducats which are of excellent design and fabric but intrinsically deficient, for the gold, not having been refined, is of insufficient purity so that the coins would not be suitable, as they should be, for turning into gold leaf without further refining.

As for our silver coins, although they ought not to be exported to other countries, they should still be struck from the purest silver, either as fine as or even finer than those struck in the reign of Iván IV, so that the name of our Monarch may be magnified unto all generations even among the country folk for the excellence of his silver coinage. These coins should be for circulation within Russia and should not on any account be exported. The ducat alone may be allowed out of the country.

Likewise our copper coins should be struck from pure copper without any admixture of silver, and should not be silvered so as to give an appearance of silver when they are new (whereas later on they are seen to be of copper); they must be made such that they remain unchanged for ever in the state that they issue from the Mint. Their face value shall not be, in the foreign manner, that of the actual value of the copper but as His Majesty shall decide. I think that copper coins of ten kopecks face value could contain one *zolotník* of copper, the three-kopeck piece half a *zolotník* and the one-kopeck piece a quarter of a *zolotník*.

If anyone objects: why should one *zolotník* of copper make indifferently four one-kopeck pieces to the face value of four kopecks, or two three-kopeck pieces to the face value of six kopecks, or one ten-kopeck piece to the face value of ten kopecks? I reply: we are not like the foreigners; our concern is not the value of the copper but the glory of our Tsar, copper is not so dear to us as is his name and style of Tsar. Therefore it is not the weight of copper in the coins that we take into account but His Majesty's superscription upon them.

The half-kopeck pieces of the first issue weighed one-and-a-half *zolotníkí*

(239)   which is much too heavy, so much so that they would not even be accepted as one-kopeck pieces; whereas even a coin weighing only one *zolotník* which has the value 'ten kopecks' shown on it can circulate as a ten-kopeck piece. Be advised therefore that in our country it is not the weight of metal that decides but the Tsar's will.

In foreign parts kings do not have as much power as the people and therefore these kings cannot give full effect to their own will; it is their subjects who have the real power, most of all the merchants. It is in the nature of their occupation that these merchants should regard a coin as a quantity of a commodity and the effigy of the king stamped on it as a guarantee that it does contain metal[36] precisely to the value stated on it.

But to our simple way of thinking it is not honour but dishonour to a monarch that the value of a coin should be its value as a commodity and not the value that the monarch puts on it. Those foreigners would like to bring it about that in Russia too the face value of all coins should correspond exactly to the intrinsic value of the metal, and therefore advocate an addition of silver to our copper coinage in order that the intrinsic value of the coin (that is, the content of metal) may correspond exactly to its face value as currency.

But I believe that this is not good advice at all for us since our Monarch is absolute and all-powerful, and no aristocrat or democrat. Therefore it is not the silver that we honour nor the copper that we value; it is His Imperial Majesty's word that bestows honour and authority.

So powerful is His Most Glorious Majesty's word among us that if he orders a copper coin of one *zolotník* weight to be stamped and issued with the denomination of one rouble it would circulate for ever without fluctuation at the value of one rouble.

Thus the chief vice of these adulterated coins, unacceptable to us as true and humble servants of His Majesty, is that His Majesty's word will be debased should the prevailing price of the metal[37] in the coin decline. The second vice is that the silver used in the billon is wasted to no purpose. The third vice is that the way will be wide open to counterfeiting, which indeed has already begun.

(240)   All ingenuity must be applied to the making of our coins so that not only His Majesty but also the whole people benefits thereby and that counterfeiting is made impossible. All of us must direct our thoughts and efforts to eradicating all wrongdoing and unrighteousness among our people and establishing righteousness and turning aside all possible disparagement of the Russian nation.

The above-mentioned coins of billon had no sooner been put into circulation than counterfeits appeared. I recognized the very same year, on examination, two one-kopeck pieces and one three-kopeck piece as counterfeits. I took them home, wrote a report on the matter and waited on A. V. Makárov for two whole days but did not succeed in presenting my report to him because at that time His Majesty was on his way to the Onéga lands[38] to take the waters. Seeing this I went back to Nóvgorod and so my report was put on one side.

If these billon coins are not withdrawn counterfeiting is bound to become widespread, whereas the way both to avoid this and to make a profit from the currency is to strike light coins of very pure copper.

If His Imperial Majesty were to deign so to order that, for the replenishment of his treasury and for the common good of the people, one *zolotník* of copper shall be made into four one-kopeck pieces, a pound of copper will make coins to the value of three roubles 84 kopecks and a pood 153 roubles 60 kopecks. Similarly if two three-kopeck coins are struck from one *zolotník*, a pound will make five roubles 76 kopecks and a pood 230 roubles 40 kopecks; and if one ten-kopeck piece is struck from one *zolotník*, the sum will be nine roubles 60 kopecks per pound and 384 roubles per pood. By this computation the profit per pood of copper, if turned into one-kopeck pieces, will be 140 roubles, into three-kopeck pieces – 220 roubles, into ten-kopeck pieces – 370 roubles.

(241)   So if 10,000 poods of copper are coined in one year, assuming that 5,000 poods are struck as one-kopeck pieces, the profit will be 700,000 roubles; and for 3,000 poods struck as three-kopeck pieces the profit will be 660,000 roubles; and for the remaining 2,000 poods as ten-kopeck pieces the profit will be 370,000 roubles. After all costs have been deducted the net profit on the 10,000 poods of copper will be 1,840,000 roubles.[39]

To put an end to counterfeiting the existing copper currency should be replaced by the sort described above; thus to the profit already made there will be added a profit of three or four millions or more. If the present coinage is not reformed it will be impossible to eradicate the abuses to which these coins give rise since many counterfeits have already appeared and if an end is not made of them, counterfeits will continue to be made in future; whereas it will be impossible to counterfeit the new coins either by means of casting or striking them.

Further, if all the small silver kopecks were called in and melted down by the dry method, i.e. over bone (rather than using acid), and restruck as rouble and half-rouble pieces, there would be considerable profit therefrom also.

What I have said concerns not only specie: every object which bears upon it the name of our Tsar should be of the greatest purity and excellence. That is why I also proposed that the quality and purity of the liquor to be stocked and sold in the pot-houses should be so high that it would be difficult to find the like in private houses. Similarly all other beverages purveyed in the Tsar's name should be of the best quality, far superior to home-made ones in taste and purity. Further, the rooms where people drink should be light and well-appointed and perfectly clean since the sale of liquor takes place in the Tsar's name. Such august patronage must receive honour and not dishonour. Measures must be taken in such places for the protection of customers who are

(242)   drunk and incapable and exposed to pilfering – which certainly is not the case at present. No dice-playing shall be allowed in taverns excepting only by the guards and watchmen.[40] All the vessels should be of good quality and clean. If any officer or soldier throws his beaker on the floor after drinking and smashes it, he must be fined and severely beaten so that such people do not disgrace a public house in this way again.

Taverns should be kept in such a way that anyone who happens to be passing, whether by day or by night, may enter and find refreshment there. Any wares bearing the Tsar's name must be superior to other similar wares. If any such wares are not superior to the same made by the common people, then they have no right to the Tsar's name; let merchants deal in such wares but not the Tsar.

The Tsar is our judge and his attributes are godlike. Therefore it would be wrong for any objects bearing the Tsar's name not to be superior to common ones. But before the Tsar's judgment-seat, as before God's, there is no distinction of rich or poor, strong or weak; justice is the same for all and so it is before God. If therefore the silver and copper coinage were reformed, and also the collection of toll and excise and the sale of liquor improved in the way that I have put forward, I am sure that the revenue would be at the very least three or four millions a year above what it is at present. If all the above matters are put on a correct and firm footing I am confident that, with God's grace, His Majesty's annual revenue will increase by five or six millions or more compared with the present time.

Should it become His Majesty's will that all the proposals which I have herein rehearsed be put into effect, to wit, those affecting the Clergy, Military Affairs, Justice, the Merchants, the Craftsmen, the stamping out of Brigandage and apprehension of runaways, the Land, the Peasantry, and easy ways of increasing His Majesty's revenue – then, with God's help, I can say with 243) confidence that our great land of Russia will be much improved both in its spiritual and its civil order, and not only will His Majesty's coffers be filled but also all the inhabitants of Russia will grow in riches and esteem. And if the art of war is also brought to perfection among us, Russians will not only gain great glory but become the terror of all neighbouring states. Amen.

Thus then I have set out, without holding anything back, this exposition of my views on the way to remove all injustices and imperfections, both great and small, and to implant true justice and righteousness, in so far as God has given me strength. I now submit it for the consideration of the one and only majestic 244) white eagle, acknowledged lover of justice, Peter the Great, Emperor of All the Russias, true autocrat and unshakeable pillar of strength.

God is my witness that I have not written all this for my own advantage but have been impelled thereto by my zeal. The flame of love for His Imperial Majesty became so ardent within me that no other preoccupations could quench it, for though this is not a lengthy work it has taken three years to complete by reason of my many other cares. Although I have made many drafts it has been seen by no one, for I have kept it strictly secret in order that my proposals should not become known among the people.

So now with all devotion I request that, in your mercy, my name may be kept secret from the high and mighty and from those who love not justice, for I have not spared them in what I have written. But may God's will and the exalted will of Your Majesty be done towards me. Amen.

For if any man desires to please God he cannot also serve Mammon. And in precisely the same way, if any man strives to serve the Tsar truly he cannot but incur the hatred of the selfish of this world.

I, Iván Pososhkóv, Your Majesty's most humble and unworthy servant, yet most zealous seeker after righteousness and justice, have composed this work, kept hidden from the public gaze, in three years' labour and now submit it to Your Imperial Majesty. Amen.

24 February, 1724.

Notes

Commentaries

Preface

1 440, vol. 63, pp. 637–46.

Chapter 1. Of the Clergy

1 See author's Preface, pp. 155–6.
2 See Introduction, pp. 22–3, 96–9.
3 *PSZ* II 898 27 Nov. 1681, V 3239 20 Nov. 1719, articles 3, 5. 170, p. 139; 607, pp. 351–68. For the reform of 1721 see 170, pp. 219–89 and Introduction, pp. 87–94.
4 7, p. 1430.
5 659, pp. 43, 93. Cf. 794, p. 169.
6 671, pp. 3, 31 (1667).
7 Quoted from the MS of 'Zhezl pravleniia . . .' ('The Rod of Governance . . .') published M, 1666, by A. Tsarevskii, *Pososhkov i ego sochineniia. . . ,* M, 1883, pp. 110–11. For Simeon see also Introduction, p. 40.
8 Quoted in 774, pt i, p. 68.
9 See 642 and 293.
10 Heinrich Wilhelm Ludolf, *Grammatica Russica*, Oxford, 1696. Elias Kopijewitz, *Manuductio in Grammaticam Sclavonico Rosseanam seu Moscoviticam*, Stolzenberg, 1706. See 715.
11 *Grammatika slavenskaia v krattse sobrannaia v Grekoslavenskoi shkole . . . v velikom Nove grade pri dome arkhiereiskom . . . Poveleniem . . . Tsaria . . . Petra Velikago, blagosloveniem . . . sviateishago . . . Sinoda*, SPg, 1723 (512, vol. ii, p. 594). For a description of Maksimov's grammar see 144, no. 194, pp. 261–4.
12 *RBS*, vol. 14, under Polikarpov, Fëdor Polikarpovich, p. 340.
13 See 9.
14 Tsarevskii, op. cit., pp. 121–6, 132–5 (quotations from the MS of the *Mirror*).
15 9, pt ii, pp. 140–317.
16 (1) Dimitrii (Rostovskii), *Rozysk o raskolnicheskoi brynskoi vere*, M, 1745 (the vast forests on the river Bryn' north-east of Briansk were a schismatic sanctuary). See 618, pp. 445–8. St Dimitrii (canonized in 1757) too attributed the schism to the misinterpretation of Holy Writ by uneducated amateur theologians.

(2) ... *Kniga* ... *imenuemaia prashchitsa, novosochinennaia protiv voprosov raskolnicheskikh.* ... , SPg, 1721 (512, vol. ii, p. 508).

(3) Stefan Iavorskii, metropolitan of Riazan', *Kamen' very*, M, 1728 (see *RBS*, vol. 19, p. 420).

17 *ZA* no. 5, undated, pp. 33–4; *PSZ* IV 15 Jan. 1708, 2308 11 Nov. 1710, 2352 25 Apr. 1711, articles 8–9, V 3447 6 Nov. 1719, VI 4021 31 May 1722, VII 4291 1 Sep. For the lack of education among the clergy see also 794, p. 168, and Introduction, p. 88.

18 791, pp. 18–27, 40–3, 90–140.

19 451, Supplement, p. 58; 517, p. 48.

20 512, vol. i, pp. 107–21.

21 *PSZ* VIII 5518 17 March 1730. 791, p. 46.

22 236, pp. 59–61; 617, pp. 204–7; 732, pp. 202–7. The book in question, *Kniga o sviashchenstve*, is attributed to St John Chrysostom because it includes his six sermons on the priesthood (see 440, tomus 48, pp. 621–92). It was first published in Lvov in 1614, next in Moscow in 1664 and reprinted in Moscow in 1705. See 320, p. 16; 647, p. 32.

23 170, p. 104; 618, p. 304.

24 First published in that year in SPg, reprinted with the Supplement in M in 1722 and in SPg in 1723. See 512, vol. ii, pp. 519–26, 591–2, with valuable comments. Cf. texts in *PSZ* VI 3719 25 Jan. 1721, 3734 14 Feb. 1721, 4022 May 1722.

25 451, pp. 162–6; 517, p. 74.

26 451, pp. 16, 23, 47, 63, 37, 58, 54, 81, 55, 58; 517, pp. 35–6, 63, 118, 172, 92, 158–9, 136, 219–20, 140–1.

27 *PSZ* VI 4052 16 July 1722.

28 635, p. 127.

29 *PSZ* I 633 10 March 1676, article 14, 700 10 Aug. 1677, article 18, II 832 25 Aug. 1680, article 4, 890 26 Aug. 1681, article 2, 1074 Apr. 1684, article 4. 617, p. 102. Three fields: autumn sowing, spring sowing and fallow.

30 *AI*, V, no. 122, undated, pp. 200–1. 732, pp. 162–6; 793.

31 451, p. 70.

32 *Ego Tsarskogo Velichestva generalnyi reglament ili ustav.* ... , SPg, 1720, also *PSZ* VI 3534 27 Feb. 1720. See 512, vol. ii, pp. 480, 515, 603; ... *Reglament ili ustav glavnogo magistrata*, SPg, 1721, also *PSZ* VI 3708 16 Jan. 1721.

33 759, pp. 15–16.

34 778.

35 563, pp. 140, 147–9, 154–5; 635, pp. 238–44.

36 *AAE* IV no. 228 30 Sep. 1678, pp. 314–15; *AI* V no. 75, pp. 108–17, Nov. 1681, p. 116. 98, pp. 86–100.

37 See Commentary on Chapter 3, p. 203, and also the ordinance of 3 June 1714 (*PSZ* V 2821) which commanded that fees for marriage licences issued by the bishops were to be used for the maintenance of hospitals for sick and wounded soldiers. On 14 December 1722 the Holy Synod decreed that the income from the sale of candles was to be applied to the building in church grounds of hospices for the destitute sick (144, no. 185, pp. 253–4).

38 773, pp. 181–2.

Chapter 2. Of Military Affairs

1 14; 18, pp. 34, 40, 49; 5, shorter version, p. 325.
2 294, pp. 10–11; 432, pp. 26, 28–9; 538, pp. 38–9, 43.
3 5, longer version, p. 262.
4 686, pp. 40–6.
5 432, pp. 29–30.
6 294, pp. 26–7, 64, 80; 388, pp. 32; 555, pp. 78, 85–6, 104–7; 565, pp. 93–4.
7 101, p. 94; 538, pp. 38, 43.
8 85, pp. xiv, xv, xxxviii; 101, pp. 22–33; 555, pp. 21–3.
9 432, pp. 76–87.
10 See Introduction, p. 104.
11 See Chapter 3, p. 241.
12 *PSZ* IV 2319 19 Feb. 1711, V 2642 30 Jan. 1713. 789, pp. 20–1. For army establishment pay lists see *PSZ* XLIII, SPg. 1830, pp. 1–44.
13 *PB* VIII, 1, no. 2530 5 Aug. 1708, pp. 65–7, VIII, 2, pp. 542–4, X no. 3572, 20 Jan. 1710, pp. 19, 470–1, no. 4121, 28 Nov. 1710, pp. 419, 756, XII, 1, no. 5024, 28 Feb. 1712, pp. 19, 281–2. 396, p. 13.
14 *Mundír* is derived from the French *monture* or the German *Montierung* (also *Mundierung*) and means equipment. *PSZ* IV 2467 16 Jan. 1712, article 7, 2524 15 May 1712, 2614 19 Dec. 1712, 2691 4 July 1713. 303; 442, p. 370; 645, pp. 142–3 (separate arrangements fot the purchase of cloth for the infantry); 657, pp. 86–7.
15 *PB* XI, 2, no. 4900 20 Nov. 1711, pp. 256, 571. 612, p. 230.
16 288, p. 24.
17 See Commentary on Chapter 4 below, p. 248.
18 *PSZ* VII 4533 26 June 1724. 432, pp. 78–89; 555, pp. 39–42.
19 *PB* IV, no. 1326, pp. 341–6 and also pp. 288, 282, 286, 1142; 216, p. xliii.
20 53.
21 *PSZ* V 3136 20 Dec. 1717.
22 *PRP* VIII, pp. 335–6, 340–3, 392–5, 403–8; *PSZ* IV 2019 19 Jan. 1705, 2031 10 Feb. 1705, 2068 24 Aug. 1705, 2467 16 Jan. 1712, 2876 18 Jan. 1715, 3006 30 March 1716, 3136 20 Dec. 1717, VI 3599 13 June 1720. 226, p. 89; 251; 555, p. 41.
23 *PRP* VIII, pp. 339–40, 400–1.
24 *PSZ* IV 2165 20 Oct. 1707. 118, Appendix, p. 20; 264, p. 399.

Chapter 3. Of Justice and the Law

1 Cf. 15.
2 See *PRP* VIII p. 69; *PSZ* V 2673 24 Apr. 1713, 3244 26 Nov. 1718, 3282 15 Jan. 1719, 3294 Jan. 1719, articles 5, 6, 3295, Jan. 1719, article 22, 3344 8 Apr. 1719. 118, p. 173; 265, vol. ii, p. 39; Introduction, pp. 69–70.
3 See 248 and Introduction, pp. 67–71.
4 II Thess. 3.10.
5 See Introduction, pp. 11–12.
6 Punishment or, more commonly, 'severe punishment', generally meant the knout. For a description of that instrument and the different ways in which it was administered see 694, p. 254 and 147, pp. 366, 371. Part 3, Chapter 2 of 'The Brief

Description of the Process at Law' of 1715 referred to below contains a broader definition of 'severe corporal punishment'. See also *PRP* VI, pp. 500–1 under *Chiniti nakazanie.*

7 Deut. 1.17 cf. *PSZ* III 1572 21 Feb. 1697, preamble, VII 4436 22 Jan. 1724.

8 *PSZ* III 1719 17 Nov. 1699.

9 *PSZ* III 1572 21 Feb. 1697. 51, p. 47.

10 *PSZ* VI 3900 5 Feb. 1722, 3979 27 Apr. 1722. See also Introduction, p. 72.

11 *PSZ* III 1572 21 Feb. 1697; *PRP* VIII 571–8; 197, pp. 537–45; 222, p. 3; 679, pp. 22, 70, 73–4; 788, pp. 44–6. The change was extended to ecclesiastical courts in 1705. See 618, Appendix, p. 35, article 55.

12 '*Kratkoe izobrazhenie protsessov. . .*', drafted by the *óber-audítor* (chief military judge) Ernst Friedrich Krompein (Krummbein?) and possibly first published in 1712. *PRP* VIII pp. 578–631; *PSZ* V 3006 30 March 1716. 112, p. 32.

13 *PRP* VIII, pp. 277, 292, 632–40; *PSZ* VII 4344 5 Nov. 1723; 745, p. 642.

14 Cf. *PSZ* IV 2330 2 March 1711, V 3290 23 Jan. 1719, 3298 4 Feb. 1719, 3608 8 July 1720.

15 *Ulozhénie*, Chapter 10, articles 156–9, 161–7, 175, Chapter 21, articles 29, 38–44, 95–6, 108–9, Chapter 17, article 51, Chapter 18, article 5; *PRP* VI, pp. 153–5, 411, 417–19, 425, 488; *PSZ* I 441 22 Jan. 1669, III 1412 9 Aug. 1691, VII 4536 26 June 1724; 197, pp. 407–13, 559–60.

16 *PRP* VI p. 433.

17 *PSZ* IV 1765 18 Feb 1700. 51; 119, vol. iv, pp. 88, 108–9, 192–243; 387, pp. 18, 20, 34–5.

18 *PSZ* V 2819 3 June 1714, 2828 15 June 1714.

19 *PSZ* V 3463 9 Dec. 1719, VI 3626 8 Aug. 1720. 755, pp. 225, 235; 518, pp. 343–4.

20 *ZA* no. 57 [end of 1718] p. 64, no. 74, 9 Dec. 1719, pp. 73–4; 427, p. 158.

21 427.

22 152, pp. 297–305, 376–80.

23 360, pt iv, pp. 179–80.

24 18, pp. 67, 190–3.

25 *PSZ* VI 3711 18 Jan. 1721. For Pososhkóv's status see Introduction, pp. 6, 9.

26 *Ulozhénie*, Chapter 11, articles 1–12; *PRP* VI pp. 163–8, 174–9.

27 477, p. 338; 428, p. 177.

28 See Introduction, pp. 100–1 and Commentary on Chapter 2.

29 *PSZ* II 985 1 Jan. 1683, III 1572 21 Feb. 1697, IV 1920 16 Nov. 1702, 1972 1 March 1704, 1980 30 Apr. 1704, 2092 16 Feb. 1706, 2174 2 Apr. 1707, 2891 28 Feb. 1715, 2910 20 May 1715. 428, pp. 22–5, 29, 34, 38, 40–2, 45, 48, 51, 53, 55, 58, 61, 67, 73–9, 112–14, 156, 175; 477, p. 180.

30 *PRP* VIII p. 317 ('the galleys').

31 *PSZ* III 1625 25 March 1698. 428, p. 78.

32 *PSZ* VI 3743 19 Feb. 1721, 3939 6 Apr. 1722, articles 7, 8, 3958 11 Apr. 1722, article 6, VII 4181 18 March 1723, 4371 22 Nov. 1723, 4533 26 June 1724, 4622 22 Dec. 1724.

33 314, pp. 176–7. The estimate seems a conservative one.

34 *PSZ* II 985 1 Jan. 1683.

35 332, pp. 21–3; 779, pp. 148–57.

36 *PSZ* V 3445 30 Oct. 1719. 779, p. 157.

37 See Introduction, pp. 58–9.

38 314, p. 198.
39 *PSZ* IV 1960 22 Jan. 1704, 2098 15 March 1706, 2111 11 July 1706, 2337 13 March 1711, 2466 15 Jan. 1712, 2497 5 March 1712, V 2625 9 Jan. 1713, 2663 4 Apr. 1713, 2685 1 June 1713, 2688 26 June 1713, 2771 4 Feb. 1714, 2845 26 Sep. 1714, 2988 26 Jan. 1716, VI 3631 23 Aug. 1720, 3810 30 July 1721, 3825 8 Sep. 1721, 3874 11 Jan. 1722, 3897 5 Feb. 1722.
40 *PSZ* V 2845 26 Sep. 1714.
41 *PB* XI, 1 no. 4290 2 March 1711, p. 102, XI, 2, pp. 410, 417. 501, pp. 167–9.
42 *PRP* VIII pp. 120, 342, 348; *PSZ* V 3006 30 March 1716 (Articles of War), Chapter 12, articles 98, 99, Chapter 15, article 123, VI 3534 28 Feb. 1720 (General Regulation), Chapter 53, VII 4460 5 Feb. 1724.
43 See Introduction, Section III under Judicial reform, The failure of the rule of law.
44 See also Chapter 7.
45 *Leviathan*, part 2, Chapter 19, Comparison of monarchy with sovereign assemblies.
46 See Introduction, pp. 11–12 and Chapter 7, note 11.
47 233, pp. 51–51v.; 187.
48 *Ulozhénie*, Chapter 10, articles 262–9.
49 *PSZ* IV 1805 15 July 1700, V 3080 16 Apr. 1717, 3140 15 Jan. 1718, VI 4091 13 Sep. 1722. 187, p. 166.
50 *PSZ* I 454 27 June 1669, IV 1833 30 Jan. 1701 (preamble). 363, p. 106; 20, p. 528. See also Commentary on Chapter 9 below with reference to loans out of receipts from indirect taxation.
51 *PSZ* III 1673 23 Jan. 1699.
52 *Ulozhénie*, Chapter 11, article 4; *PSZ* III 1732 9 Dec. 1699, IV 1740 1 Jan. 1700, 1833 30 Jan 1701, 1838 7 March 1701, 1848 7 Apr. 1701, 1953 15 Dec. 1703, 2446 31 Oct. 1711. 118, Appendix, p. 37; 790, pp. 83, 89, 92, 110–11, 119, 123, 125, 129–30.
53 467, pp. 112–27, 154–9, 170–1; 677, pp. 847–8.
54 347, p. 63; 551, p. 58.
55 8 (1893 edition), pp. 169–71.
56 552.
57 *PSZ* III 1424 30 Nov. 1691, 1489 14 March 1694, IV 2470 21 Jan. 1712, 2477 31 Jan. 1712, V 3172 2 Feb. 1718, 3213 20 June 1718, 3294 Jan. 1719, articles 19, 21.
58 *PSZ* VI 3945 6 Apr. 1722, 4047 9 July 1722. 451, pt 3, pp. 54–5.
59 *PSZ* I 328 25 Oct. 1662, VI 3685 12 Dec. 1720, 3928 4 Apr. 1722, 3940 6 Apr. 1722, 4091 13 Sep. 1722, 4111 17 Oct. 1722, VII 4530 4 June 4530.

Chapter 4. Of the Merchants

1 783, pp. 84–5, 116, 395.
2 252; 532, pp. 221–4; 604; 681; 707.
3 *PSZ* VI 3708 16 Jan. 1721.
4 344, p. 212.
5 678.
6 *PSZ* III 1666 1 Jan. 1699, 1706 27 Oct. 1699, 1723 24 Nov. 1699, 1775 11 March 1700.

7 *PSZ* IV 2327 2 March 1711, 2349 13 Apr. 1711, 2433 1 Oct. 1711.

8 *PSZ* IV 2084 March 1705. 162, vol. iv, pp. 114–15.

9 *PB* XI, 1, no. 4291, 2 March 1711, pp. 103, 414; XI, 2, no. 4719, 1 Sep. 1711, pp. 121, 423; *PSZ* IV 2770 4 Feb. 1714, 2799 9 Apr. 1714, 2812 12 May 1714. 344, p. 16.

10 *PSZ* VII 4312 27 Sep. 1723.

11 *PSZ* VII 4373 28 Nov. 1723. 118, pp. 340–3.

12 604, p. 204.

13 77, p. 59; cf. 248, p. 62.

14 570, pp. 428–9.

15 *PSZ* VI 4047 9 July 1722 (seasonal price changes allowed in Moscow); 344, p. 351; 530, p. 268; 667, pp. 287–310.

16 622, pp. 112–15.

17 *PSZ* V 3318 3 March 1719, VII 4453 31 Jan. 1724.

18 *PSZ* VI 3708 16 Jan. 1721, Chapters 18, 19. 693, pp. 5–7, 10.

19 129, p. 94; 226, pp. 2, 5, 12, 64–5; 416, vol. i. p. 77; 442, p. 361; 445, pp. 50–1; 515, p. 249; 540 vol. i, pp. 372–4, 382–3, 469, 518, 524, 548, 563, 565.

20 *PSZ* V 2793 6 Apr. 1714, 3441 29 Oct. 1719, VI 3748 28 Feb. 1721. 78, pp. 82–90; 139, nos 713, 717, 718, 722, 737; 314, p. 143; 452, pp. 208, 217; 600, vol. iii, pp. 23–6. See also Introduction, pp. 45, 112 and Commentaries on Chapters 5 and 9.

21 585, vol. 36, p. 387.

22 *PSZ* V 3127 17 Dec. 1717, 3144 19 Jan. 1718, VI 3890 24 Jan. 1722, article 19, XI 8301 17 Dec. 1740, 8680 11 Dec. 1742. 205, p. 240; 655, p. 310–11; 693, p. 24.

23 *PSZ* IV 1999 22 Dec. 1704, 2467 16 Jan. 1712, 2874 29 Dec. 1714, 2929 1 Sep. 1715, 3158 8 Feb. 1718, VI 4041 28 June 1722, VII 4256 28 June 1723. 286, p. 106; 613, vol. i, pp. 5–7; 762, vol. i, pp. 222, 224; 767, p. 210; 783, pp. 84–5.

24 *PSZ* V 2875 9 Jan. 1715, VII 4408 13 Jan. 1724, 4487 8 March 1724, 4787 11 Oct. 1725; *Sb.RIO* vol. 69, pp. 36–7, vol. 94, pp. 136–8; 18, pp. 71–2; 67, pp. 201–2; 123, p. 94. Calamanco: a woollen stuff of Flanders, glossy on the surface, woven with a satin twill and chequered in the warp so that the checks are seen on one side only. See also Introduction, pp. 114–5.

25 *PSZ* V 2793 6 Apr. 1714, 3357, 22 Apr. 1719, VI 3639 3 Sep. 1720.

26 *PSZ* V 3086 8 June 1717, 3176 Feb. 1718, 3357 22 Apr. 1719, VI 3639 3 Sep. 1720. 384, pp. 27–31, 34, 40, 59; 409, pp. 85, 82, 87, 93; 780, pp. 22, 54, 101, 109, 169–70.

27 8, 1893 edition, p. 116.

Chapter 5. Of the Craftsmen

1 446, p. 11.

2 *Ulozhénie*, Chapter 20, articles 45, 115. 71; 201; 603; 680.

3 *PSZ* VI 3708 16 Jan. 1721, Chapter 7; *ZA* no. 23 18 Feb. 1715, p. 43. 240; 510; 511.

4 *PSZ* IV 1752 13 Feb. 1700, 1972 1 March 1704, article 21, VI 3980 27 Apr. 1722, 4054 16 July 1722, 4066 31 July 1722, 4102 4 Oct. 1722, 4395 17 Dec. 1723. See also *Instruktsiia magistratam*, *PSZ* VII 4624, undated, articles 8, 14, 15; 490, pp. 377, 398; 591; 783, pp. 96–7.

5 *PSZ* VII 4378 3 Dec. 1723.
6 726, pp. 29–32.
7 543, pp. 3–24.
8 *ODD* II, 1, no. 42, cols 259–60; *PSZ* IV 2451 20 Nov. 1711, VI 4079 31 Aug. 1722, VII 4154 31 Jan. 1723. 659, Chapter 43, pp. 150–4; 205, pp. 82, 113–36, 209; 308, pp. 218–20; 446, p. 49; 512, vol. ii, p. 562; 687, pp. 137–55.
9 82, p. 195; 515, p. 223.
10 671, ff. 23–4.
11 206; 287; 576, pp. 64, 81, 116; 716. The first Dutch edition of Dürer (206) is dated 1622.
12 45; 262, vol. v, pp. 287–8; 446, p. 51.
13 *PSZ* V 2943 21 Oct. 1715, 3156 8 Feb. 1718, VI 3677 16 Nov. 1720, 4204 30 Apr. 1723, VII 4259 28 June 1723, XLV (*Kniga tarifov*), pp. 72–4; 626, pp. 14–53; 783, p. 230. According to Zaozerskaia (783) the linen of the Dutch type sold at between 60 and 76 kopecks, and of the Silesian type at 25 kopecks per arshin.
14 508, pp. 162–7; 626, pp. 14–53.
15 164, p. 423; 410, Appendix 1, p. 4.
16 783, pp. 213–23, 415.
17 508, p. 167; 783, pp. 124, 128, 213–32, 415. The figures given in these two works, pp. 167 and 124, 128 respectively, do not tally.
18 783, pp. 213–32, 415.
19 783, pp. 223, 285.
20 *PSZ* VII 4452 31 Jan. 1724, XLV (*Kniga tarifov*), p. 76. 410, pp. 61–4, Appendix 1, pp. 3–7.
21 626, p. 52.
22 *PSZ* V 3428 1 Oct. 1719, with reference to the original ordinance of 8 Apr. 1719, omitted from *PSZ*.
23 *PSZ* XLV (*Kniga tarifov*), p. 120; 445, p. 51.
24 783, pp. 230, 239, 353 (prices of linen and canvas goods).
25 314, p. 143; 626, p. 28; 783, p. 242. For Russia's foreign trade surplus see also Commentaries on Chapters 4 and 9.
26 495, p. 185.
27 18, p. 72.
28 67, pp. 191, 206; 783, p. 122.
29 783, pp. 427–93.
30 *PSZ* VII 4378 3 Dec. 1723, cf. VI 3590 24 May 1720. 783, p. 474.
31 *PSZ* V 3140 15 Jan. 1718, 3306 13 Feb. 1719, 3313 26 Feb. 1719, 3336 19 March 1719, VI 3808 26 July 1721. 783, p. 225.
32 *PSZ* VII 4624 1724 (undated). See also Chapter 10 of the Regulation of the Board of Civic Administration (*Reglament Glávnogo Magistráta*), *PSZ* VI 3708 21 Jan. 1721.
33 *PSZ* V 2965 11 Dec. 1715, 2989 26 Jan. 1716, 3030 22 June 1716, VII 4378 3 Dec. 1723. 314, p. 143; 416, vol. i, pp. 62, 65; 755, p. 139.
34 P. 133.
35 416, vol. i, pp. 71, 77.
36 *PB* III no. 623 7 Feb. 1704, p. 13, no. 765 8–9 Feb. 1705, pp. 229, 244, no. 798 30 March 1705, p. 792, IX, 1, no. 2992, 19 Jan. 1709, pp. 30–1, IX, 2, p. 593. 416, vol. i, p. 76; 417, p. 85; 612, p. 191; 668; 783, pp. 84–91.
37 544, pp. 284–97.

38 612, p. 85.
39 32; 656, pp. 59–72, 75.

Chapter 6. Of Brigandage

1 See 212; 333; 569 and also Chapter 7 below.
2 *Ulozhénie*, Chapter 21, articles 9, 10, 12–14, 16–18; *PRP* VII, pp. 457–8, 475, 478; *PSZ* I 105 20 Oct. 1653, 126 25 May 1654, 163 16 Aug. 1655, 165 4 Sep. 1656, 255 8 Aug. 1659, 334 11 May 1663, 383 24 Jan. 1666, 441 22 Jan. 1669, II 772 10 Sep. 1679, 970 28 Nov. 1682. For the remainder of the century see II 1265 17 Oct. 1687, 1413 3 Sep. 1691, III 1454 16 Nov. 1692, 1678 24 Feb. 1699.
3 Archiwum Czartoryskich, Cracow, MS 206, f. 1085; *PRP* VII, pp. 476–7; *PSZ* IV 2310 30 Nov. 1710. 646, vol. xv, p. 87.
4 *PRP* VII pp. 446, 476–7; *PSZ* IV 2310 30 Nov. 1710. 118, pp. 94–5, 150; 612, pp. 112, 132, 180, 281; 276, p. 535; 504, pp. 112–18; 569, pp. 202–10.
5 See Commentary on Chapter 2.
6 *PSZ* I 163 16 Aug. 1655, IV 1924 19 Jan. 1703, 1957 14 Jan. 1704, 2310 30 Nov. 1710, 2271 5 June 1710, 2373 14 June 1711, V 2823 3 June 1714, 3334 19 March 1719, 3445 30 Oct. 1719, 3477 24 Dec. 1719. 532, p. 268.
7 *ZA* no. 15, 18 Dec. 1713, p. 39 ('Town' here must be interpreted as 'place'); 504, p. 119.
8 *PSZ* IV 2271 5 June 1710, V 3445 30 Oct. 1719. 332; 590.
9 *PSZ* II 985 1 Jan. 1683, VII 4533 26 June 1724. For the poll-tax and the *zémskii komissár* see Introduction, pp. 102, 105–6.
10 *PRP* VIII, pp. 307, 311–14, 600; *PSZ* V 3477 24 Dec. 1719. 694, pp. 198–203, 209–16.
11 *Ulozhénie*, Chapter 21, articles 9, 10, 16; 266, pp. 78, 80; 777, pp. 72–3.
12 *PSZ* V 3203 25 May 1718, VI 3883 19 Jan. 1722, 4047 9 July 1722.
13 612, p. 72.

Chapter 7. Of the Peasantry

1 See 383, pp. 182–4, 190, 245–50; 444, p. 104; 477, p. 421.
2 See also 383, pp. 209–10; 646, vol. xvi, p. 492.
3 *AI* V no. 48 21 October 1679, pp. 72–5. Likewise *PSZ* V 3466 11 Dec. 1719 (Regulation for the *Kámer-kollégiia* or Board of Revenue), article 8.
4 383, pp. 92–6, 298, 302; 719, p. 231.
5 692, pp. 300, 309; 747, pp. 95, 102.
6 *PSZ* V 2884 12 Feb. 1715; 314, p. 166; 692, p. 302; 702, p. 122; 747, p. 114.
7 665, p. 327. See also 692, p. 277.
8 314, p. 159; 18, p. 191.
9 See Chapter 3, pp. 220–21, and Chapter 7, pp. 317, 321.
10 *SIE*, vol. 5, under *Inventárnye právila*.
11 383, p. 233; 444, p. 106, note 2.
12 625, pp. 5, 372–80.

13 *PSZ* V 3294 Jan. 1719, article 31.

14 Its substance contrasts strangely with the remark which the tsar is said to have made in the same year: 'There is no depopulation' (355, p. 422).

15 *PSZ* V 3466 11 Dec. 1719, article 8.

16 130, p. 57; 420; 512, vol. i, p. 214. *Georgica curiosa* was published in 1682 and again in 1687.

17 *PSZ* VI 3708 16 Jan. 1721 (Regulation for the *Glávnyi Magistrát* or Board of Civic Administration), Chapter 21.

18 759, pp. 2–3.

19 See 321; 369.

20 *ZA* no. 188 24 Jan. 1724, p. 140. 504, p. 137; 723, vol. iii, p. 512; 744, pp. 61, 68.

21 *PSZ* IV 1845 30 March 1701, VI 3466 11 Dec. 1719, article 13, 3668 26 Oct. 1720, article 9, 3941 6 Apr. 1722. 710, p. 140.

22 *PSZ* VI 4060 19 July 1722, VII 4379 3 Dec. 1723, 4995 30 Dec. 1726 (abolition of the office of *val'dméister*). Deciduous trees do not grow in the taiga which covers the region down to the south of Lake Ládoga and that of the northern Dviná. In the wooded steppe belt, on the rivers Don, Vorónezh, Bitiúg and their tributaries, a survey carried out in 1731 showed the presence of 'sufficient quantities' (for ship-building) of oak and pine forests (*PSZ* VIII 5612 28 Aug. 1730). 491 (map of natural vegetation zones on front end-paper); 713.

23 *PSZ* VI 4070 7 Aug. 1722, VII 4490 3 Apr. 1724.

24 269, p. 117.

Chapter 8. Of the Land

1 *PSZ* V 2789 23 March 1714. Cf. 557, pp. 162–3 and see Introduction, pp. 61–3.

2 *PSZ* V 3466 11 Dec. 1719.

3 685, pp. 105, 140.

4 See 210.

5 *PSZ* III 1074 Apr. 1684, articles 28, 29.

6 245, pp. 19, 138–40, 184–90, 217–18, 220, 227, 305; 460, pp. 487–501.

7 710, p. 111.

8 Cf. note 1 for this Chapter. 100,000 roubles from each of the eleven *gubérnii* would have brought in 1,100,000 roubles.

9 314, p. 390. On land measuring see also 209; 261, pp. 1–83; 477, p. 417; 584; 620; 738, vol. ii, pp. 362–402.

Chapter 9. Of the Tsar's Interest

1 See Introduction, pp. 16, 32.

2 See Introduction, pp. 31–2.

3 *PSZ* I 107 25 Oct. 1653, II 876 11 July 1681, 879 18 July 1681, III 1642 3 Aug. 1698, 1697 12 Sep. 1699, IV 2024 1 Feb. 1705, 2059 12 June 1705, 2084 1705 (undated), 2165 29 Oct. 1707, 2467 16 June 1712, 2610 9 Dec. 1712, XV 11184 11 Jan. 1761 with reference to 1723 (undated); *SGGD* IV no. 55, 6 May 2667; *Ulozhénie*, Chapter 18, articles 21, 23. 56, pt. i, pp. 1–22; 194; 231, pp. 118–37; 344, pp. 211, 239–40; 442, pp. 489–92, 669, 675; 550, pp. 12–56, 206–13; 632; 698, pp. 134–67.

4 *PSZ* IV 21 Jan. 1704, 1972 1 March 1704, 2033 15 Feb. 1705, V 2773 20 Feb. 1714, VII 4583 6 Nov. 1724. 344, p. 376; 442, pp. 156–9, 484, n. 6, 669–70; 486, pp. 123, 125.

5 373, pp. 588–90, 594.

6 *PSZ* II 879 18 July 1681, III 1697 12 Sep. 1699.

7 *PSZ* IV 2059 12 June 1705, 2165 29 Oct. 1707.

8 *DPV* IV, pp. 50, 292; *PSZ* II 879 18 July 1681, article 37, IV 2204 20 Aug. 1708, V 2990 28 Jan. 1716. 698, p. 165.

9 *PSZ* VI 3966 13 Apr. 1722, 4005 11 May 1722, 4097 24 Sep. 1722, VII 4312 27 Sep. 1723, 4388 9 Dec. 1723, 4620 21 Dec. 1724, VIII 5333 12 Sep. 1728.

10 *PSZ* VIII 5794 28 June 1731.

11 *PSZ* XIII 9734 6 Apr. 1750. 4 (1951 edition), p. 387.

12 *DAI* V no. 1, 1666, article 10, p. 6; *DP* V, 1, no. 360, p. 221; *PSZ* I 454 27 June 1669 (loans from *prikázy* forbidden), VII 4378 3 Dec. 1723. 122, pp. 14–16, 18, 21, 16, 18; 253; 256, pp. 268, 271; 762, vol. ii, p. 335. See also Commentary on Chapter 3 with reference to credit.

13 *DP* I no. 588 20 Aug. 1711, pp. 428–48; *PSZ* III 1700 6 Oct. 1699, IV 2401 16 July 1711. 270, p. 362.

14 *PSZ* V 3428 1 Oct. 1719 (with reference to 8 April 1719), VI 3672 10 Nov. 1720, 3959 11 Apr. 1722, VII 4452 31 Jan. 1724, 4246 14 June 1723, VII 4468 11 Feb. 1724. 367, p. 157.

15 *PSZ* XLV (*Kniga tarifov*), Appendix B, pp. 4, 50, 84 and p. 120. 364, pp. 193, 213.

16 *DP* II, 1 no. 21 9 Nov., p. 12, II 2 no. 763 12 Sep. 1712, p. 224, no. 869 4 Nov. 1712, p. 324; III, 1 no. 212 30 March 1713, pp. 175–6; *DPV* IV, p. 53; *PB* XI, 1 no. 4290 2 March 1711, p. 102 and p. 410; *PSZ* III 1519 5 Oct. 1695, IV 1776 11 March 1700, 1855 18 May 1701, 2349 13 Apr. 1711, 2357 2 May 1711, 2371 12 June 1711, 2383 21 June 1711, 2393 3 July 1711, 2416 16 Aug. 1711, 2444 26 Oct. 1711, 2601 4 Nov. 1712, 2762 24 Apr. 1713, V 3164 14 Feb. 1718. 317, pp. 90, 92; 442, pp. 149, 152, 360–2, 387, 520; 595, pp. 74–5; 703, pp. 65, 66, 68.

17 *DP* II, 1 no. 21, 9 Nov. 1712, p. 12; *PSZ* VI 3748 28 Feb. 1721, article 5. 129, pp. 94, 155–6; 442, pp. 520–1; 703, pp. 67–8; 540, vol. i, p. 518; 767, p. 200.

18 See Commentary on Chapter 4.

19 Archiwum Czartoryskich, Cracow, MS 206 f. 1095 (currency control on the frontier with Poland); *PSZ* V 2793 6 Apr. 1714, 3441 27 Oct. 1719, VI 3748 28 Feb. 1721, article 5. 80, p. 81; 118, pp. 328, 331, 353, 382, 461–5; 228, p. 110; 442, pp. 474, 494; 445, p. 50; 464, p. 481; 513, pp. 96, 106.

20 *PSZ* VII 4258 28 June 1723. 405, pp. 11–23, 16, 27–8, 31–6, 41, 52; 442, p. 521.

21 19; 89, pp. 9, 44–5; 129, pp. 3–71; 442, pp. 148–52; 703, p. 65.

22 80, p. 92; 149, pt i, pp. 117, 127; 599 under *Rubel*; 648, pp. 226, 275, 285, 300.

23 515, p. 250.

24 See Chapter 4.

25 *PSZ* I 107 23 Oct. 1653, IV 2009 1 Jan. 1705, 2123 Nov. 1706, 2350 11 Apr. 1711, 2366 31 May 1711; *Sb.RIO*, vol. 11, pp. 178–9, 394. 422, pp. 162–3, 364, 389–90; 477, pp. 106–11; 721, pp. 294, 296, 314.
26 See Introduction, p. 66.
27 Sergéi, Nikolái and Aleksándr, sons of Grigórii Dmítrievich Stróganov (1656–1715), barons from 1722 (*SIE*, vol. 13, under Stróganov, G. D.); 721, pp. 133–38, 141, 170.
28 *PSZ* VI 4007 11 May 1722, VII 4410 13 Jan. 1724. 226, pp. 103, 208, 213.
29 *PSZ* VII 5085 29 July 1727, VIII 5827 10 Aug. 1731.
30 371, pp. 201–05, 209; 658, pp. 70–71, 101, 434.
31 515, p. 167.
32 *PSZ* IV 2001 27 Dec. 1704, 2045 4 Apr. 1705, V 3071 3 March 1717, VIII 5164 26 Sep. 1727; *Sb.RIO* vol. 11, pp. 45, 328. 67, p. 205; 208, pp. 867–9; 235; 442, pp. 164, n. 2, 524; 542; 612, p. 337.
33 Cf. Chapters 3 and 7.
34 See Introduction, pp. 19–20, 26, 61–2, 79.
35 See Introduction, p. 61. The relevant ordinances were printed in March and April 1714. See 512, nos. 253 and 256, pp. 322–3.
36 *Sb.RIO*, vol. 40, p. 429. 464, p. 355.
37 226, pp. 127–270; 765, p. 604.
38 82, p. 57; 515, p. 248; 709, p. 39.

Pososhkóv: *The Book of Poverty and Wealth*

Chapter 1. Of the Clergy

1 It was the tsar's ordinance that enjoined attendance in church on holy days and commanded the clergy to keep registers of parishioners who did or did not attend confession (*PSZ* VI 4052 16 July 1722).
2 Household churches, signs of wealth and high social standing, were prohibited by Peter I in 1718 (*PSZ* 3171 19 Feb. 1718) and again by the Ecclesiastical Regulation of 1721 (451, p. 50). L. K. Narýshkin (1664–1705) was a maternal uncle of Peter I.
3 The three parts of the trivium.
4 An archimandrite may be either the head of a monastery (or a group of monasteries) or an ecclesiastical official ranking below a bishop and considered suitable for promotion to the episcopacy, even if a layman.
5 The Church Slavonic alphabet used in all ecclesiastical books and its simplified version (*grazhdánskii shrift*), officially introduced by Peter I in 1710 (*PB* X no. 3581, 29 Jan. 1710, pp. 27, 476–7; 512, vol. ii, pp. 642–5).
6 A collection of homilies – 'Pearls' – by St John Chrysostom, translated into Church Slavonic in the thirteenth and fourteenth centuries. The third printed edition appeared in Moscow in 1698.
7 *Chét'i minéi*: extracts from lives of the saints together with special prayers, arranged in their calendar sequence, for private reading and devotions.

8 *Mésiachnye* (or *sluzhébnye*) *minéi*: all that is required for the celebration of the offices of the saints throughout the year; divided into twelve monthly volumes.

9 Apollinarianism denied the complete manhood of Christ; the Eutychian and Severian heresies were forms of Monophysitism.

10 I Cor. 11.19.

11 The *Octoechos* contains the variable parts of the services, together with indications of the musical settings, except for periods before and after Easter when the *Triodion* and the *Pentecostarion* replace the *Octoechos*. The cycle covers eight weeks, one in each tone.

12 See Introduction, p. 8.

13 Probably an allusion to Num. 26 (especially v. 62) and 35. Cf. also II Chron. 31. 1–10; Deut. 14. 27–9, Deut. 18.

14 See note 16 on Ezekiel below.

15 Lev. 19.10.

16 The words, attributed by Pososhkóv to Ezekiel, are not an exact quotation but echo the general tenor of Chapter 17, especially vv. 11–21.

17 *Iarënok*: a parallel form to the earlier and commoner *erenga* or *iarenga* (a foreign word of uncertain origin), kersey, a Hanseatic export to Russia from at least the seventeenth century. Kersey (*karazéia*) was made in Russia from about 1714. See 509, p. 47; 298, vol. i, p. 772; and also Introduction, p. 115. For Russian ecclesiastical costume see 398, plates headed *Divers habillements des prêtres de Russie*.

18 The footwear of the peasantry, a kind of envelope for the foot of plaited bast, cord, etc. (but never of leather).

Chapter 2. *Of Military Affairs*

1 See also Commentary on Chapter 3.

2 One of the two regiments of life guards established by Peter I, the other being the Semënovskii. Both names are derived from villages near Moscow.

3 See *Textual Emendations*, p. 431 below.

4 Pososhkóv has but a hazy idea of naval warfare. Very little if any shooting was done from small boats but galleys were the mainstay of the Russian navy. For their honourable record in the war against Sweden see 127, pp. 28–38, 94–6. For the authorship of 127 see D. B. Smith, 'The authorship of *The Russian Fleet under Peter the Great*', *The Mariner's Mirror*, 20, 1934, 373–6. See further 40, pp. 158–61; 41, pp. 90–7.

5 In October 1695. See 478, vol. ii, pp. 618–19. In 1716 Swart or Schwartz fended off a raiding party of Kuban Tatars 'forty leagues beyond Kazan'. See 762, vol. i, pp. 124–5.

5 *Nártik*, probably the same as *nart*, both from the verb *nártit'sia* 'to act in a bold manner, (of horses) to rear, to prance'. See 198, under *nart*.

7 The establishment of the army as fixed in 1720 provided for thirty-three dragoon regiments comprising 43,824 men. See 314, p. 349.

8 Resting in a 'bucket' attached to the right stirrup.

Chapter 3. Of Justice and the Law

1 Prov. 10.2
2 See Textual Emendations, p. 431.
3 Unidentified.
4 See 441, pp. 101, 111–12.
5 See Introduction, pp. 7, 71–2.
6 '(*Gosudárevo*) *slóvo i délo*, – the form of words used to draw the attention of the authorities to evil intentions supposedly harboured against the sovereign.
7 *Kniaz'* Fëdor Iúr'evich Romodánovskii (d. 1717) was the head of the *Preobrazhénskii prikáz* which, being responsible for the maintenance of the political security of the state, handled all proceedings arising from 'the invocation of the name of the sovereign'. See 200; 255, pp. 14, 21, 26–7; 430; 341; 602, pp. 1–124.
8 28 June.
9 Cf. Commentary on Chapter 6, pp. 290–1.
10 At that time *oberlandríkhter* or chairman of the provincial court at Nóvgorod. See 18, p. 158, n. 96.
11 See Introduction, p. 12; 178.
12 See Introduction, pp. 7–9 and Commentary on Chapter 9.
13 Heb. 10.31.
14 A misleading statement. Under the ordinance on juridical procedure issued in 1697 (*PSZ* III 1572 21 Feb. 1697) the punishment for bearing false witness was death. For the same crime the Articles of War of 1715 (Chapter 18, article 32) prescribe beating with the knout (with the possible addition of ecclesiastical penance) or death (*PSZ* V 3006 30 March 1716). Cf. *PSZ* VI 3485 13 Jan. 1720, Chapter 18, article 132 (Naval Articles of War, also applied to the civil population). See *PRP* VIII, pp. 289–90, 293, 310, 317, 452–3, 522, 573.
15 The corner of a cottage where the icons were hung and, as the most honourable, where guests were received.
16 Susanna (OT Apocrypha).
17 Under the *Ulozhénie*, Chapter 1, article 1, the punishment for blasphemy was death by burning. The Articles of War (Chapter 1, articles 3–6, *PSZ* V 3006 30 March 1716) prescribed for blasphemy against God piercing the tongue with a red-hot iron, followed by beheading, for blasphemy against the Mother of God and the saints excision of the tongue or death. See *PRP* VIII, p. 371.
18 Matt. 12.31–2.
19 A section of Pososhkóv's *Manifest Mirror* (pt 1, pp. 32–56) attacks blasphemers; presumably here again he has the Old Believers in mind.
20 See Textual Emendations, p. 431.
21 The punishment for dishonouring a judge, inflicted on behalf of the tsar, was beating with the knout or with rods. In addition, the judge or magistrate was commanded to sue the culprit for damages in compensation for injured honour (*Ulozhénie*, Chapter 10, articles 105–10; *PRP* VI pp. 147–8). Cf. 186.
22 No such ordinance has been traced so far. In March 1721 debtors to the state who had been banished with hard labour were allowed to count 12 roubles a year towards the discharge of their debts. In November 1721, under a general amnesty, debts to the state, unpaid by reason of destitution, were remitted for the period 1700–18 but deliberate default on the part of those who could afford to pay was to be investigated (*PSZ* VI 3751 7 March 1721, 3842 4 Nov. 1721).

23 See Textual Emendations, p. 431.

24 Either the *kānūnnāme* of Sulaymān I or the *kānūnnāme-yi djedīd-i sultānī*. In Islam the Holy Law, the *Shari'a*, based on the Koran and the teaching of Muhammad, in theory regulates the whole of public and private life. In fact, extra provisions were necessary in common law, penal law and in administration – in particular the administration of the vast Ottoman Empire. The Sultans formulated *kānūns* in *kānūnnāmes* (books of secular laws) from early times. See *Encyclopaedia of Islam*, vol. 4, second edition, Leiden, 1978, under *Kānūnnāme*. We are indebted for this information to the late Dr Susan Skilliter. See also 592, pp. 22, 44, 79 and, for Turkomania, 214.

25 A likelier meaning of *liúdi boiárskie* than 'slaves'.

26 See Commentary on Chapter 7.

27 Cf. Introduction, p. 73.

28 See Introduction, p. 67.

29 Viz. receive over fifty strokes of the knout. 694, pp. 231, 234, 243.

30 For the increased cost of writing paper see p. 259.

31 See 694, p. 235.

32 Probably an allusion to Ps. 69.25. Cf. Isaiah 34.13.

33 See Textual Emendations, p. 431.

34 See Textual Emendations, p. 431.

35 Viz. Swedes and perhaps other foreigners recently recruited into the administration. In 1718 the tsar called upon Swedish prisoners of war to enter his civil service (*PSZ* V 3259 28 Dec. 1718).

36 See Introduction, p. 29.

37 No record has been found of the form *shesterlo*.

38 *Dvoriáne* in the upper echelons of court rank were first designated thus not later than 1712. See 501, p. 239.

39 Originally men of service entitled to receive their pay not in the provinces but in Moscow from the *chétverti*, the five *prikázy* concerned *inter alia* with the collection of taxes from certain regions. Obsolete as an administrative term, it is here used pejoratively. See N. E. Nosov, 'Boiarskaia kniga 1556 g (Iz istorii proiskhozhdeniia chetvertchikov)', in I. I. Smirnov, ed., *Voprosy èkonomiki i klassovykh otnoshenii v russkom gosudarstve XII–XVII vekov*, M, 1960, pp. 191–227 (pp. 222–3, 225, 227); 477, p. 373.

40 During the period 1714–24 Peter I sent a total of 328 tall Russian soldiers to King Frederick William I of Prussia who eagerly collected such human specimens. See 554 and cf. *PSZ* VI 4014 21 May 1722.

41 See Textual Emendations, p. 431.

42 *Stárosta*. His duties may be said to correspond to those of the manorial reeve, the bondman responsible for organizing the work of the peasants on the demesne land. The factor or bailiff (*prikázchik*) was normally a foreman responsible for the management of the whole estate or manor.

43 On the lower reaches of the Volga and the Don and in the eastern Ukraine. See Introduction, pp. 100–01.

44 *Bobýl'* – an agricultural labourer not entitled to a share in the communal land of the village.

45 *Vlastelínskie*. The term presumably includes the (formerly) patriarchal as well as episcopal lands.

46 See Textual Emendations, p. 431.

47 Literally 'Electors'. The specific sense of the term may have been unknown to Pososhkóv.

48 The fine prescribed by the *Ulozhénie* for costs incurred in this way was in fact 2 *grívny* per day. The *Ulozhénie* did not penalize genuine plaintiffs. See *Ulozhénie*, Chapter 16, article 26 and cf. Chapter 10, articles 18, 154; 197, pp. 420–3.

49 See Textual Emendations, p. 431.

50 Cracking eggs held in the hand against one another to see which would survive longest (especially at Easter). The Church disapproved of this sport not so much because of its pagan associations as because the competitors laid bets on the champion egg. See *Akty iuridicheskie*, SPg, 1838, no. 334, seventeenth century, p. 357; 33, pt iii, p. 181; 462, pp. 334, 340, 344.

51 For distilling see Commentary on Chapter 9.

52 The length of prison sentences (preceding banishment) for convicted criminals was between two and four years. See *Ulozhénie*, Chapter 21, articles 9, 10, 16.

53 107, pp. 19–26. Iamburg is now named Kingisepp (Leningrad *óblast'*).

Chapter 4. Of the Merchants

1 Matt. 6.24.

2 Matt. 6.21; Luke 12.34.

3 II Tim. 2.4. The Slavonic version is somewhat clearer: 'No soldier who engages in trading will be satisfactory to his commander.'

4 I.e. Stefán (Iavórskii), metropolitan of Riazán' and Múrom, in some respects the successor of the Patriarch of Moscow. See Introduction, p. 45.

5 See Chapter 9, p. 356.

6 The three grades are designated *sótskii*, *piatidesiátskii* and *desiátskii*, implying notional authority over one hundred, fifty and ten persons (or households).

7 Cf. the proverbial expression '*plókho ne kladí, v grékh ne vvodí*'.

8 Cheating on weights and measures was punishable under the Articles of War of 1715 (*PSZ* V 3006 30 March 1716, Chapter 12, article 200) by threefold restitution, a fine and flogging.

9 Cf. the sharp practices of Russian merchants recorded in 1823 by Lyall, 421, p. 291.

10 See Introduction, p. 44.

11 Cf. Chapter 9, pp. 374–8.

12 *Efímok*, derived colloquially from the first half of *Joachimstaler*, as 'dollar' is from the second.

13 For the manufacture of glass in Russia during this period see 107, pp. 19–26.

14 *Vókhra*: yellow ochre was to be found in Russia (especially near Kalúga) but the best kinds were imported; *cherlén'*: a reddish-brown pigment easily obtainable in Russia and therefore cheap. But there was also *prázelen' grétskaia* (perhaps 'Verona earth'), imported from south Europe; *pulmet* (and other spellings) properly *poliment* (It. *pulimento*): a compound used in icon painting and gilding generally as an undercoat where a glossy finish was needed. The vernacular name – *Olónetskaia glína* – shows that it was found in north Russia. It often contained *yar'* (verdigris, copper acetate, cf. Chapter 5, p. 285) or *cherlén'*. See 611, pp. 93–129.

15 *Tsaredvórtsy*. See Chapter 3, note 39.

16 See Textual Emendations, p. 431.

17 See Chapter 5, note 2.
18 *Gósti.* See Introduction, pp. 31–2, 42, and 83, 84.
19 See Textual Emendations, p. 431.
20 See Textual Emendations, p. 431.
21 See Textual Emendations, p. 431.
22 Luke 10.41–2.
23 *Karázinnye vódki* are mentioned in the *Slovar' Akademii Rossiiskoi*, vol. iii, SPg, 1792, without precise definition. *Karázin* (from the Turkic *karaz, kiraz*, 'cherry') would appear to be kirschwasser, a distillation of bitter cherries.
24 See Chapter 9, p. 374.
25 For tobacco see also Ch. 9 at end.
26 See Introduction, p. 40.

Chapter 5. Of the Craftsmen

1 Jer. 48.19.
2 Bombazines (*bumazéi*), calicoes (*mitkáli*) and cambrics (*kamórdki*) are properly wholly or partly of cotton; velvets are of silk and cotton but the word *trípy* may also include velours, which contain some linen but are used more for upholstery than for clothing, and velveteen which is mainly of cotton.
3 In 1711 Sir Randolph Knipe, a 'Russia merchant', wrote of hemp being sold at Archangel 'at extravagant high prices' (PRO, SP 104 22, 5 Dec. 1711). In 1712 the Russians were reported to have doubled the price of hemp at Archangel (PRO, CO 388 15, M 180, April 1712). In 1715 hemp was being offered at 9 roubles and in 1716 at 7 roubles 50 kopecks per *bérkovets*. Both prices were considered too high in London (Hampshire Record Office, Heathcote Papers, bundle 1, Russia, 26 Jan. 1716).
4 *Obrók*: a fixed annual payment for leased state land or property.
5 Woad (*krútik*) was made from the native indigo plant (*Isatis tinctoria*). Indigo (*lávra*): perhaps here the dye extracted from species of *Indigofera* (*kub*), otherwise called *kúbovaia kráska* and imported from India. Cinnabar (*kínovar'*): mercury sulphide, to be found in the Ukraine. Azure (*golubéts*): usually a mixture giving blue tones but sometimes an expensive cobalt pigment (*azzurro di smalto*?) imported since the later seventeenth century. Crimson (*bakán*): the word covers yellow and red pigments (arsenic sulphides). The 'ordinary' or native mineral was quite cheap; the imported 'Venetian' crimson presumably means *derevtsó*, a pigment extracted from various trees, especially Brazil wood (*varzíia*) and sandalwood. Verdigris (*iar'* or *iar'-mediánka*) or copper acetate could be made from copper and sour milk. 'Venetian' *iar'*, one of the copper-based blues used by Italian painters, was, like 'Venetian' *bakán*, an expensive import. The green tone of *iar'* was often improved by the addition of *shizhgil'*. Vegetable yellow: *shízhgil'* here, better *shíshgil'* or *shíshgel'*, sometimes *shízhgol'* or *shíshgol'*, from the Dutch *Schijtgeel*: a yellow or yellow-green pigment extracted from species of buckthorn, especially *Rhamnus cathartica*. The term is also used for a greenish-yellow dye extracted from birch leaves. See 298, vol. iii, pp. 667–8, 674, 715, 718, 763, 765, 798–9; 611, pp. 93–129.
6 Weidash (*smalchúga* or *smol'chúg*): from the German *Waidasch*, a crude form of potash.

7 A stockaded settlement on Kóla Peninsula, on Kóla gulf, founded in the thirteenth century by Nóvgorod.

8 Mineral pitch or asphaltum also known as maltha.

9 See note 14 in Chapter 4 regarding pigments, etc.

10 Prince Borís Alekséevich Golítsyn (1654–1714), between 1683 and 1713 head of the *Prikáz Kazánskogo dvortsá* concerned with the administration of the territories on the Volga to the south of Kazan.

Chapter 6. *Of Brigandage*

1 Ἐυστίγνιος, in Russian usually Evstígnii, popularly Evstignéi.

2 To the west of that river.

3 See Textual Emendations, p. 431.

4 Cf. Chapter 3 with reference to punishment for perjury. Branding on the face was usually done on the cheek and/or forehead; on the arm between elbow and wrist. See *PRP* VIII p. 312; 602, p. 9; 694, pp. 210–16.

5 I.e. those under the authority of each *sótskii* (warden over a hundred).

6 *Stároshchen'e*, the district under the authority of a *stárosta* (headman).

7 See Textual Emendations, p. 431.

8 *Pokróv*: the veil of the Blessed Virgin (Μαφόριον) was held to protect Byzantium from foreign attack. The feast of the Intercession celebrated on 1 October commemorates such a miraculous event.

Chapter 7. *Of the Peasantry*

1 Cf. Chapter 8, pp. 332–3 with reference to the optimum area of land per holding.

2 See Textual Emendations, p. 431.

3 See Textual Emendations, p. 431.

4 Cf. p. 268 in Chapter 4 with reference to the same towns, *ponizóvye gorodá*, on the lower course of the Volga and thence stretching towards the Don.

5 A Finno-Ugrian people living to the west of the middle Volga. For provision for their protection from oppression by Russians see *Ulozhénie*, Chapter 16, articles 41–5.

6 A Turkic people living in the angle of the Volga south-west of Kazan. Cheremís: a Finnic people living to the north of the middle Volga, north-west of Kazan, now called Mári.

7 See Textual Emendations, p. 431.

8 1 September.

9 *Sniatók* (dial. *snetók*), the sparling or freshwater smelt, common in the great lakes of North Russia. See 394, pp. 42–4.

10 *Obrók*: a fixed annual payment for the use of state land or property.

11 Cf. the double frontispiece of 598 (Schröder), 1718 edition bearing the captions *'Tonderi vult'*, *'Non deglubi'*. The inscription beneath reads:

Wann eines klugen Fürsten Heerden
Auf diesem Fuss genutzet werden
So können sie recht glücklich leben,
Und dem Regenten Wolle geben.
Doch wer sogleich das Fell abzieht
Bringt sich künftigen Profit.

Cf. also Introduction, pp. 11–12, 54.

12 In central Russia rye was usually sown in the autumn (*ózim'*), oats, barley, peas, flax and hemp were sown in the spring (*iarováia*), wheat in both seasons. The spring sowings were at about twice the rate of the autumn ones. The yield of hay was roughly reckoned at ten shocks (*kopná*, sing.) from one *desiatína*. The *chétvert'*, as well as being a measure of capacity, was also a measure of surface, one such *chétvert'* being sown with one *chétvert'* of grain. in the seventeenth century one *desiatína* of two *chétverti* (1.12 ha) was usually sown with two *chétverti* of rye or four of spring corn or oats. The weight of a *chétvert'* of rye has been put at five, seven, eight and even nine poods (82, 115, 131 and 147 kg). The 'official' *chétvert'* was equivalent to six poods of 98 kg. 18, p. 107; 167, pp. 31–2, 37, 126; 261, p. 342; 444, p. 66; 477, p. 42, n. 4; 620, pp. 18, 52–60, 62–3, 68–9; 720, pp. 321–5.

13 I.e. families and landholdings.

14 *Polovník*: a tenant or share-cropper.

Chapter 8. Of the Land

1 The three areas are 2, 1 and ¼ acre (0.810, 0.405 and 0.101 ha) approximately.

2 *Pustáia zemliá* or *pústosh'*: any land, cultivated or uncultivated, remote from dwellings. Thus the difference between 'occupied' and 'unoccupied' land is often similar to that between 'infield' and 'outfield'.

3 See Textual Emendations, p. 432.

4 See note 12 in Chapter 7.

5 The standard phrase defining a three-field system (unenclosed), one field being autumn-sown, one spring-sown and one fallow.

6 In pagan times solemn oaths were sworn in this fashion, whence the adverb *óderen'* (still used in some northern dialects): absolutely, irrevocably. See 505, pp. 427–34.

7 See Textual Emendations, p. 432.

8 See Introduction, p. 79.

9 See Textual Emendations, p. 432.

10 See Textual Emendations, p. 432.

11 There were several varieties of sazhen in use, from the everyday *makhováia sazhén'* (reach of the outstretched arms) of 2½ arshin (180 cm) to the *kosáia sazhén'* of 4 arshin (288 cm). The *kazënnaia sazhén'* (official), used especially for land, was of 3 arshin (216 cm). The 'official' *desiatína* was of 80 × 30 sazhen but Pososhkóv here adopts the earlier *kosáia desiatína* of 80 × 40 sazhen. There was also a *krúglaia desiatína* (square) of 60 × 60 sazhen.

12 See Introduction, pp. 102, 105–6.

13 See Introduction, pp. 47–8. From 1719 there were 11 *gubérnii* (*PSZ* V 3380 29 May 1719); 314, p. 326.

14 Because of the danger of the kilns' catching fire.

15 This equivalent of 6 *desiatíny* is apparently less than average for the second half of the seventeenth century which is given as between 7 and 9.3 *desiatíny*. Pososhkóv uses the *desiatína* of 80 × 40 sazhens in preference to that of 80 × 30. Cf. note 12 in Chapter 7 and see note 11.

16 See note 12 in Chapter 7.

17 See Textual Emendations, p. 432.

Chapter 9. Of the Tsar's Interest

1 *Interés* here has a double meaning, general and specific: (*a*) concern, (*b*) source of revenue.

2 Lake Ládoga lies beyond the habitat of the common oak but oak timber for the construction of the Baltic fleet was loaded on the Volga and carried by water to Lake Ládoga and thence to St Petersburg. See 157, p. 114 and 127, pp. 110–11. The reference here is to the time 'since the Tsar resolved on the Caspian expedition', i.e. 1722. As Pososhkóv mentions 1717 it would seem that the transportation of oak timber via Lake Ládoga began earlier than 1722.

3 *Traporékhii* (and derivatives): unrecorded word of uncertain etymology. *Driáblyi* is used as a synonym below. For shipbuilding see W. Sutherland, *Britain's Glory . . .*, London, 1717.

4 See Textual Emendations. p. 432.

5 Forbes?, a die engraver, still active in 1708. See 614, p. 131.

6 See Introduction, pp. 16, 46–7.

7 See Textual Emendations, p. 432.

8 Kurbátov, A. A. (d. 1721). From 1712 vice-governor of Archangel. At the turn of the century one of the superintendents of the Armoury (*Oruzhéinaia Paláta*) which was also responsible for the management of the Mint.

9 See Introduction, p. 32.

10 *Iávochyne dén'gi*: show-money, as it were. See 477, p. 427.

11 See Introduction, p. 106.

12 See Commentary on this chapter, p. 338.

13 See ibid., p. 348.

14 See *Ulozhénie*, Chapter 9, articles 6, 13 and *PRP* VI, p. 75.

15 See Textual Emendations, p. 432.

16 *Buzúk*: the same as *samosádka* below.

17 *Inozémskikh*, i.e. within the Russian Empire but having a non-Russian population.

18 *Samosádka*: naturally precipitated salt, e.g. from Lake Elton in the south-eastern steppes where summer evaporation is high.

19 Korchmín, V. D. (d. 1721). Major-general, military engineer, quartermaster-general during the Persian campaign of 1722. Connection with region of Olónets untraced.

20 See Textual Emendations, p. 432.

21 See Introduction, p. 107.

22 An anachronism. See Introduction, p. 47.

23 See Commentary on Chapter 3, p. 431–2.

24 About 68 proof (British standard).

25 *Vedró*. See Table of Weights and Measures, p. 433.

26 See Textual Emendations, p. 432.

27 This would bring a profit of 500 per cent on wholesale and of 620 per cent on retail trading.

28 See Chapter 3 at end.

29 *Próba*: there is not enough evidence to determine the system which Pososhkóv is using.

30 It seems clear that the corrupt passage here represents Latin terms which Pososhkóv knew by ear only and which have been further garbled in copying. For these terms see *Universal-Lexicon aller Wissenschaften und Künste*, Halle-Leipzig, 1733–54, vol. 19 under *Mastix*.

31 Natural honey (or mead) is (depending on the source) more or less white; when concentrated by heating (*varënye medý* above) it passes through yellow to a reddish colour. The concentrate is known as *krásnye medý*. But the term is apparently also used of mead flavoured with red fruit juices, cf. Chapter 4 above. The sing. *mëd* usually implies honey, the pl. *medý* mead but this is not an absolute distinction. See also 307, pp. 376–7.

32 See Introduction, p. 102.

33 Under the *Ulozhénie* (Chapter 5, article 1) forgers were put to death by having molten metal poured down their throats. The Articles of War of 1715 (*PSZ* V 3006 30 March 1716, Chapter 22, article 199) give a closer definition of counterfeiting and likewise prescribe the death penalty including, in extreme cases, burning. It would appear, however, that forgers were still being punished in accordance with the *Ulozhénie* because in 1723 the tsar commanded that criminals who did not die quickly from a dose of molten metal were to be beheaded (*PSZ* VI 4157 5 Feb. 1723).

34 See Introduction, p. 66.

35 *Saltan(')*: an Ottoman gold coin of approximately the same value as the ducat, known in the West as a sequin (Venetian *zecchino*).

36 *Továr*. The argument appears to require this sense but no confirmation has been found elsewhere. Above Pososhkóv uses the synonym *materiál*, translated as 'the content of metal'.

37 See previous note.

38 The tsar often went to take the waters at Olónets near Lake Ládoga. See 492, vol. iii, p. 92.

39 At the rate of 370 roubles per pood the profit on 2,000 poods would be 2,100,000 roubles. The difference between this figure and Pososhkóv's 1,840,000 could be attributed to costs.

40 To be provided for the protection of customers.

Bibliography

The works of Pososhkóv

1 *Ashche kto voskhoshchet* (1704?) (Should anyone wish . . .): a fragment also known as *Donoshenie ob ispravlenii vsekh neisprav* (A report on the correction of all shortcomings), first published in 1910 and reprinted in the 1951 edition of item 4, pp. 275–7.

2 *Donoshenie o novonachinaiushchikhsia den'gakh* (1718): a report on the newly introduced coinage. Lost.

3 *Donoshenie Petru I* (1724?): Pososhkóv's draft report to Peter I on *The Book of Poverty and Wealth*. Two versions: the longer one was first published in 1861 and reprinted in the 1937 edition of item 4, pp. 93–5; the shorter version was first published in 1904 and reprinted in the 1951 edition of item 4, pp. 314–15.

4 *Kniga o skudosti i bogatstve* (1724) (*The Book of Poverty and Wealth*), first published by M. Pogodin (M, 1842). A plain text with the addition of the memorandum on military affairs and the first letter to Stefan Iavorskii, with a foreword by A. A. Kizevetter, appeared in Moscow in 1911. A scholarly edition was first published by B. B. Kafengauz (M, 1937). A revised edition entitled '*Kniga o skudosti i bogatstve* i drugie sochineniia' appeared in 1951.

5 *O ratnom povedenii* (1701): a memorandum on military affairs. Two versions: the longer, first published in 1793, and the shorter, first published in 1888. Both versions reprinted in the 1951 edition of item 4, pp. 247–72 and 325–32.

6 *Pis'mo o denezhnom dele*: a memorandum on coinage submitted before 1701. Lost.

7 'Tri pis'ma mitropolitu Stefanu Iavorskomu (1704–1710)' (Three letters to the metropolitan Stefan Iavorskii), first published in full by V. I. Sreznevskii, *IORIaS*, 1899, no. 4, 1411–57.

8 *Zaveshchanie otecheskoe, k synu svoemu* (1719) (*A Father's Testament, for his son*, referred to as *A Paternal Testament*), first published in an incomplete version in 1873 and next by E. M. Prilezhaev, SPg, 1893.

9 *Zerkalo*, sirech' iz"iavlenie ochevidnoe i izvestnoe na suemudriia raskolnicha (1708) (The Mirror or manifest and public exposition of the sophistry of the schismatics), first published in an abridged version in 1863, published in full as *Zerkalo ochevidnoe* (*The Manifest Mirror*) by A. Tsarevskii, 2 pts, Kazan, 1898, 1905.

Some works on Pososhkóv

10 Babkin, A. M., 'Leksika *Knigi o skudosti i bogatstve* Pososhkova', *Uchenye Zapiski Leningradskogo Gosudarstvennogo Pedagogicheskogo Instituta*, 59, 1948, 51–88

11 Babkin, A. M., 'Frazeologiia Pososhkova (po materialam *Knigi o skudosti i bogatstve*)', ibid., 69, 1958, 77–96
12 Beauvois, Daniel, 'La question paysanne sous Pierre le Grand vue par Pososhkov', *Revue du Nord*, 52, 1970, 217–27
13 Brikner, A. G., *Ivan Pososhkov*, pt 1, *Pososhkov kak èkonomist*, SPg, 1867, also published in *ZhMNP*, pts 181, 183, 184 (1875, 1876)
14 ———, 'Mneniia Pososhkova o voiske', *Russkii Vestnik*, March 1879, 5–35
15 ———, 'Mneniia Pososhkova o sudoproizvodstve i zakonodatel'stve', ibid., June 1879, 491–529
16 Brückner, A. G., *Iwan Possoschkow. Ideen und Zustände in Russland zur Zeit Peters des Grossen*, Leipzig, 1878
17 Chambre, Henri, 'Pososhkov et le mercantilisme', *CMRS*, 4, 1963, 335–65
18 Kafengauz, B. B., *I. T. Pososhkov. Zhizn' i deiatel'nost'*, second edition, M, 1951. Includes texts of twenty-six documents relating to Pososhkóv
19 Klochkov, M. V., 'Zametka o Pososhkove', *Russkaia Starina*, 154, April–June 1913, 425–8
20 Lewitter, L. R., 'Pososhkov and "The Spirit of Capitalism"', *SEER*, 51, 1973, 524–53
21 ———, 'Women, Sainthood and Marriage in Muscovy', *Journal of Russian Studies*, 37, 1979, 3–11
22 O'Brien, Bickford, 'Ivan Pososhkov, Russian Critic of Mercantilist Principles', *American Slavic and East European Review*, 14, 1955, 503–11.
23 Pavlov-Sil'vanskii, N. P., 'I. T. Pososhkov', in his *Ocherki russkoi istorii XVIII–XIX vv.*, SPg, 1910, pp. 42–72
24 ———, 'Novye izvestiia o Pososhkove', ibid., pp. 73–99
25 ———, 'Pososhkov, I. T.', *RBS*, vol. 14
26 Schneider, Rita, *Die Sprache Pososkovs* (Phonetik und Morphologie), Münster, 1973

General Bibliography

27 Åberg, Alf, 'The Swedish Army, from Lützen to Narva', in Michael Roberts, ed., *Sweden's Age of Greatness*, London, 1973
28 Abramowski, Günter, *Das Geschichtsbild Max Webers*, Stuttgart, 1966
29 Adrianova, V., *Materialy dlia istorii tsen na knigi v drevnei Rusi: XVII–XVIII vv.*, SPg, 1912
30 Aleksandrov, V., 'K voprosu o proiskhozhdenii sosloviia gosudarstvennykh krest'ian', *VI*, 1950, 10, 85–95
31 Alekseev, G., Kopanev, A. I., 'Razvitie pomestnoi sistemy v XVI v.', in Pavlenko, ed., *Dvorianstvo . . .*, pp. 57–69
32 Alexander, J. T., 'Medical Development in Petrine Russia', *CASS*, 8, 1974, 198–221
33 Almazov, A. I., *Tainaia ispoved' v Pravoslavnoi Vostochnoi tserkvi*, 3 pts, Odessa, 1894–5
34 Almquist, Daniel, 'Feifs finansiella reformer och Wilhelm von Schröders *Fürstliche Schatz- und Rent-Cammer*', *Karolinska Förbundets Årsbok*, 1922, 233–53
35 Amburger, Erik, *Die Anwerbung ausländischer Fachkräfte für die Wirtschaft Russlands vom 15. bis zum 19. Jahrhundert*, Wiesbaden, 1968

36 Amburger, Erik, *Die Familie Marselis*. Studien zur russischen Wirtschaftsgeschichte, Giessen, 1957

37 —————, *Geschichte der Behördenorganisation Russlands von Peter dem Grossen bis 1917*, Leiden, 1966

38 —————, *Ingermanland*. Eine junge Provinz Russlands im Wirkungsbereich der Residenz- und Weltstadt St. Petersburg-Leningrad, 2 vols, Cologne-Vienna, 1980

39 —————, 'Zur Geschichte des Grosshandels in Russland: die *gosti*', *Vierteljahrschrift für Sozial- und Wirtschaftsgeschichte*, 46, 1959, 248–61

40 Anderson, R. C., *Naval Wars in the Baltic during the Sailing-Ship Epoch, 1522–1850*, London, 1910

41 —————, *Oared Fighting Ships*, London, 1952

42 Andreev, A. I., 'Osnovanie Akademii Nauk v Peterburge', in Andreev, ed., *Petr Velikii*, pp. 284–333

43 —————, ed., *Petr Velikii, Sbornik statei, M-L, 1947*

44 Andreevskii, I. E., *O namestnikakh, voevodakh i gubernatorakh*, SPg, 1864

45 Andreyev, N. E., 'Nikon and Avvakum on Icon-Painting', *Revue des études slaves*, 38, 1961, 37–44

46 Anisimov, E. V., 'Izmeneniia v sotsial'noi strukture russkogo obshchestva v kontse XVII – nachale XVIII veka', *ISSSR*, 1979, no. 5, 34–51

47 —————, *Podatnaia reforma Petra I*, L, 1982

48 Anners, Erik, *Den karolinska militärstraffrätten och Peter den Stores krigsartiklar*, *Acta Academiae Regiae Scientiarium Upsaliensis*, 9, Uppsala, 1961

49 [anon.] 'Delo, 1714–1718 godov, ob otpravlenii . . . kniazia Aleksandra Bekovicha Cherkaskogo na Kaspiiskoe more i v Khivu'; 'Vypiska iz stolpov ob otpravlenii na Kaspiiskoe more . . . kniaza Cherkaskogo 1714–1717', in Bychkov, ed., *Materialy . . '.*, pp. 196–309, 402–506 and notes, pp. 4–9

50 [—————.] *(The) Interest of Great Britain in Supplying Herself with Iron Impartially Consider'd*, (1725?), reprinted in *Journal of the Iron and Steel Institute*, 1885, no. 2, 753–78

51 [—————.] 'Materialy dlia svodnogo Ulozheniia 1701 goda', *Arkhiv istoricheskikh i prakticheskikh svedenii otnosiashchikhsia do Rossii* (edited by N. Kalachev), vol. 5, 1863, 45–54

52 [—————.] *Opisanie arkhiva Aleksandro-Nevskoi Lavry za vremia tsarstvovaniia imperatora Petra Velikogo*, 2 vols, SPg, 1903, 1911

53 [—————.] 'Podmetnoe pis'mo gosudariu Petru Pervomu', *ChOIDR*, 1860, pt 2, Smes', 27–30

54 [—————.] *Reasons for the Present Conduct of Sweden in Relation to the Trade in the Baltic*: set forth in a letter from a gentleman at Dantzick to his friend at Amsterdam. Translated from the French, London, 1715

55 [—————.] *Sbornik vypisok iz arkhivnykh bumag o Petre Velikom*, 2 vols, M, 1872

56 [—————.] *Svedeniia o piteinykh sborakh v Rossii*. Sostavleny v Gosudarstvennoi kantseliarii po Otdeleniiu gosudarstvennoi ekonomii, 4 pts, SPg, 1860

57 [—————.] 'Vruchenie . . . tsarevne Sofii Alekseevne privilegii na Akademiiu 21 ianvaria 1685 goda', *Drevniaia Rossiiskaia Vivliofika*, second edition, M, 1788, vol. 7, pp. 390–420

58 Anpilogov, G. N., 'Fiskalitet pri Petre Velikom', *Vestnik Moskovskogo Universiteta*, Istoriko-filologicheskaia seriia, 1956, no. 2, 63–80

59 —————, 'Gubernskie komissary pri Petre I, 1711–1718 gg.', *Doklady i*

soobshcheniia Istoricheskogo fakul'teta Moskovskogo Universiteta, 1948, no. 2, 33–8

60 Anpilogov, G. N., 'Senat pri Petre I', *Istoricheskii Zhurnal*, 1941, no. 1, 40–9

61 Aristotle, *Politics*, with an English translation by H. Rackham, London, 1967

62 Arkhangel'skii, A. S., *Tvoreniia ottsov tserkvi v drevnerusskoi pis'mennosti*, vol. iv, Kazan, 1890

63 Arkuditsa, V. E., 'Fontannykh del mastera', *VI*, 1973, 6, 207–9

64 Artsikhovskii, V. A., Sakharov, A. M., and others, eds, *Ocherki russkoi kul'tury XVII veka*, 2 vols, M, 1979

65 Avrich, R., *Russian Rebels, 1600–1800*, London, 1973

66 Avtokratov, V. N., 'Voennyi prikaz. (K istorii komplektovaniia i formirovaniia voisk v Rossii v nachale XVIII v.)', in Beskrovnyi, Kafengauz and others, eds, *Poltava*, pp. 228–45

67 Baburin, D. S., *Ocherki po istorii Manufaktur-kollegii*, M, 1931

68 Badalich, I., 'Iurii Krizhanich, predshestvennik I. T. Pososhkova', *Trudy Otdela Drevnerusskoi Literatury* (Institut Russkoi Literatury A. N. SSSR), 19, 1963, 390–403

69 Bagalei, D. I., *Ocherki iz istorii kolonizatsii stepnoi okrainy Moskovskogo gosudarstva*, M, 1887

70 Bagger, H., *Peter den Stores reformer. En forskningsoversigt*, Copenhagen, 1979

71 Bakhrushin, S. V., 'Remeslennye ucheniki v XVII veke', in vol. ii of his *Nauchnye trudy*, M, 1954, pp. 101–17

72 ————, and others, eds, *Istoriia Moskvy*, vol. i, M, 1952

73 Baklanov, N. B., Mavrodin, V. V., and Smirnov, I. I., *Tul'skie i Kashirskie zavody v XVII v.*, *Izvestiia Gosudarstvennoi Akademii Istorii Material'noi Kul'tury*, no. 98, M-L, 1934

74 Baklanova, I. A., 'Tetradi startsa Avraamiia', *IA*, 1951, 131–55

75 Baklanova, N. A., 'Russkii chitatel' XVII veka', in Derzhavina, ed., *Drevnerusskaia literatura . . .*, 1967, pp. 156–93

76 Baklanova, N. A., Chekan, I. V., and Zaozerskaia, E. I., *Ocherki po istorii torgovli i promyshlennosti v XVII i nachale XVIII stoletiia*, M, 1928

77 Baldwin, J. M., *The Medieval Theories of the Just Price*, Philadelphia, Pa, 1959

78 Bang, Nina Ellinger, and Korst, Knud, eds, *Tables de la navigation et du transport des marchandises passant par le Sund 1661–1783 et par le Grand-Belt 1701–1748*, deuxième partie, deuxième demi-tome, 1721–60, Copenhagen-Leipzig, 1945

79 Baranovich, A. I., and others, eds, *Ocherki istorii SSSR. Rossiia vo vtoroi chetverti XVIII v.*, M, 1957

80 Barbon, Nicholas, *A Discourse Concerning Coining the new money lighter . . .*, London, 1696

81 Barbour, Violet, *Capitalism in Amsterdam in the Seventeenth Century*, Baltimore, Md, 1950

82 Barker, Ernest, translator and ed., *Social and Political Thought in Byzantium*, Oxford, 1961

83 Baron, S. H., 'The fate of the *gosti* in the reign of Peter the Great', *CMRS*, 14, 1973, 488–512

84 ————, 'Who were the *gosti*?', *California Slavic Studies*, 7, 1974, 1–40

85 Barsov, E. V., ed., *Prichitaniia Severnogo kraia*, vol. ii, M, 1882

86 Barsov, T. V., 'O svetskikh fiskalakh i dukhovnykh inkvizitorakh', *ZhMNP*, February 1878, 307–400

87 Barsukov, A. P., *Spiski gorodovykh voevod i drugikh lits voevodskogo upravleniia Moskovskogo gosudarstva XVII stoletiia*, SPg, 1902

88 Bater, J. H., and French, R. A., eds, *Studies in Russian Historical Geography*, 2 vols, London-New York, 1983

89 Bazilevich, K. V., *Denezhnaia reforma Alekseia Mikhailovicha i vosstanie v Moskve v 1662 g.*, M, 1936

90 —————, 'Elementy merkantilizma v ėkonomicheskoi politike Alekseia Mikhailovicha', *Uchenye Zapiski Moskovskogo Gosudarstvennogo Universiteta*, 41 (Istoriia, no. 1), 1940, 3–34

91 —————, 'Novotorgovyi ustav 1667 goda', *IANSSSR*, 1932, Otdelenie obshchestvennykh nauk, no. 7, 589–622

92 Becher, Johann Joachim, *Politische Discours von den eigentlichen Ursachen dess Auff- und Abnehmen der Städt Länder und Republicken. In Spezie, wie ein Land Volckreich und Nahrhafft zu machen und eine rechte Societatem civilem zu bringen . . .* First edition (confiscated) Frankfurt, 1668; second edition ibid., 1673; reprinted 1688, 1721, 1754, 1759

93 Belokurov, S. A., *Iurii Krizhanich v Rossii* (po novym dokumentam), 3 pts, M, 1901–9

94 —————, ed., 'Podmetnye pis'ma Golosova, Pososhkova i drugikh (1700–05 gg.)', *ChOIDR*, 1888, pt 2, 1–80

95 Benson, Sumner, 'The Role of Western Political Thought in Petrine Russia', *CASS*, 8, 1974, 257–73

96 Berendts, E., *Baron A. Khr. von Liuberas i ego zapiska ob ustroistve kollegii v Rossii*, SPg, 1891

97 Berg, L. S., *Ocherki po istorii russkikh geograficheskikh otkrytii*, M-L, 1946

98 Berkh, V., *Tsarstvovanie Fedora Alekseevicha*, 2 pts, SPg, 1834–5

99 —————, ed., 'Zhizneopisanie general-leitenanta Vilima Ivanovicha Gennina', *Gornyi Zhurnal*, 1, 1826, no. 3, 51–129

100 Beskrovnyi, L. G., 'Proizvodstvo vooruzheniia i boepripasov na russkikh zavodakh v pervoi polovine XVIII v.', *IZ*, 36, 1951, 101–41

101 —————, *Russkaia armiia i flot v XVIII v.*, M, 1958

102 —————, ed., *Na rubezhe dvukh vekov; iz istorii preobrazovanii petrovskogo vremeni*, M, 1978

103 —————, and others, eds, *K voprosu o pervonachal'nom nakoplenii v Rossii* (XVII –XVIII vv.), M, 1958

104 Beskrovnyi, L. G., Kafengauz, B. B., and others, eds, *Poltava. K 250-letiiu Poltavskogo srazheniia. Sbornik statei*, M, 1959

105 Bespiatykh, Iu. N., 'Sochinenie L. Iu. Ernmal'ma [Lars Johan Ehrenmalm] *Sostoianie Rossii pri Petre I (1714)*', *ISSSR*, 1984, no. 5, 141–50

106 Bessel, Christian Georg, *Schmiede des politischen Glücks, darinnen viele nützliche Lehren enthalten*, Frankfurt and Hamburg, 1673

107 Bezborodov, M. A., *Ocherki po istorii russkogo steklodeliia*, Minsk, 1952

108 Birch, Thomas, *A Collection of the State Papers of John Thurloe, Esq.*, vol. ii, London, 1742

109 Bittner, Konrad, 'Beiträge zur Geschichte des Lebens und Wirkens Johann Friedrich (Andrei Ivanovich) Ostermanns', *JfGO*, 5, 1957, 106–24

110 Blagovidov, F. V., *Ober-prokurory Sviateishego Sinoda v XVIII i pervoi polovine XIX stoletiia*, second edition, Kazan, 1900

111 Blanc, Simone, 'La pratique de l'administration russe dans la première moitié du XVIIIe siècle', *Revue d'histoire moderne et contemporaine*, 10, 1963, 45–64

112 Bobrova, E. I., compiler, *Biblioteka Petra I*, ukazatel'-spravochnik, L, 1978
113 Bogoiavlenskii, S. K., 'Khovanshchina', *IZ*, 10, 1941, 180–221
114 ——————, 'Prikaznye d'iaki XVIII v.', *IZ*, 1, 1937, 220–39
115 ——————, *Prikaznye sud'i*, M-L, 1946
116 ——————,'Raspravnaia palata pri boiarskoi dume', in V. O. Kliuchevskii, dedicatee, *Sbornik statei . . .*, pp. 409–26
117 ——————, 'Vooruzhenie russkikh voisk v XVI – XVIII vv.', *IZ*, 4, 1938, 259–83
118 Bogoslovskii, M. M., *Oblastnaia reforma Petra Velikogo*. Provintsiia 1719–1727 gg., M, 1902
119 ——————, *Petr I, Materialy dlia biografii*, edited by V. I. Lebedev, 5 vols, L, 1940–8
120 ——————, *Zemskoe samoupravlenie na russkom Severe v XVII v.*, 2 vols, M, 1909
121 Bonnesen, S., *Peter den Store*, Stockholm, 1925
122 Borovoi, S. Ia., *Kredit i banki Rossii* (seredina XVII v.-1861 g.), M, 1958
123 ——————, 'Voprosy kreditovaniia torgovli i promyshlennosti v ėkonomicheskoi politike Rossii XVIII v.', *IZ*, 33, 1950, 92–122
124 Brandenburg, N. E., *Materialy dlia istorii artilleriiskogo upravleniia v Rossii*. 'Prikaz artillerii' (1701–1720 g.), SPg, 1876
125 Braudel, Fernand, and others, eds, *La Russie et l'Europe. XVIe–XVIIIe siècles*, Paris-Moscow, 1970
126 Brauleke, Heinz-Joachim, *Leben und Werk des Kameralisten Philipp Wilhelm von Hörnigk*, Frankfurt-Berne-Las Vegas, 1978
127 Bridge, C. A. G., ed., *History of the Russian Fleet during the Reign of Peter the Great*, by a contemporary Englishman [i.e. John Deane] (1724), London, 1899
128 Brikner, A. G., 'Khr.-Fr. Veber', *ZhMNP*, January 1881, 45–78, February 1881, 179–221
   Brikner see also Brückner
129 Brückner, Alexander, *Finanzgeschichtliche Studien*. Kupfergeldstudien, Kupfergeldkrisen, Dorpat, 1867
130 Brunner, Otto, *Adeliges Landleben und europäischer Geist*. Leben und Werk Wolf Helmhards von Hohberg, 1612–88, Salzburg, 1949
131 Bryner, E., *Der geistliche Stand in Russland*. Sozialgeschichtliche Untersuchungen, Göttingen, 1982
132 Buck, Hans-Robert, 'Die wirtschaftliche Voraussetzungen des klassischen Machtaufstieges unter Peter I', *Saeculum*, 19, 1968, 224–49
133 Buganov, V. I., *Krest'ianskie voiny v Rossii XVII–XVIII vv.*, M, 1976
134 ——————, *Moskovskie vosstaniia kontsa XVII veka*, M, 1969
135 ——————, *Moskovskoe vosstanie 1662 g.*, M, 1964
136 ——————, *Moskovskoe vosstanie 1682 g.*, M, 1969
137 Buganov, V. I., ed., Kazakevich, A. N., compiler, *Vosstanie moskovskikh strel'tsov 1698 g*. Sbornik dokumentov, M, 1980
138 Buganov, V. I., ed., Savich, N. G., compiler, *Vosstanie 1682 g. v Moskve*. Sbornik dokumentov, M, 1970
139 Bulmerincq, A. von, ed., *Aktenstücke und Urkunden zur Geschichte der Stadt Riga, 1710–40*, vol. i, Riga, 1902
140 Bushev, P. P., *Posol'stvo Artemiia Volynskogo v Iran v 1715–1718 gg.*, M, 1978
141 Bushkovitch, P., *The Merchants of Moscow, 1580–1650*, Cambridge, 1980
142 Bychkov, A. F., ed.,*Materialy Voenno-uchenogo arkhiva Glavnogo shtaba*, vol. 1, SPg, 1871

143 Bychkov, A. F., ed., *Pis'ma Petra Pervogo*, khraniashchiesia v Imperatorskoi Publichnoi Biblioteke, SPg, 1872

144 Bykova, T. A., and Gurevich, M. M., compilers, *Opisanie izdanii, napechatannykh pri Petre I*, 3 vols, M, 1955–8, L, 1972

145 Cederberg, A., *Heinrich Fick, Acta et Commentationes Universitatis Tartuensis (Dorpatensis), B, Humaniora*, 17, 1930

146 Chancellor, Richard, 'The newe Nauigation and discoverie of the Kingdome of Moscovia, 1533 . . .' Translated out of the former Latine into English, in Hakluyt, *The Principall Voiages* . . . vol. ii, pp. 280–92

147 Chappe d'Auteroche, Jean, *Voyage en Sibérie fait en 1761*, 4 vols, Amsterdam, 1769–70

148 [Charles XII] *Kongl. Maj:ts Rang-Ordning*, Uppsala, 1714

149 Chaudoir, S. de, *Aperçu sur les monnaies russes et sur les monnaies étrangères qui ont eu cours en Russie*, 3 pts, SPg, 1836–7

150 Chechulin, N. D., *Ocherki po istorii russkikh finansov v tsarstvovanie Ekateriny II*, SPg, 1906

151 Cherepnin, L. V., 'Akademik M. M. Bogoslovskii [1867–1929], *IZ*, 93, 1974, 223–71

152 ——————, *Zemskie sobory russkogo gosudarstva v XVI–XVII vv.*, M, 1978

153 Cherkas, M., 'Demidov, Nikita Demidych', RBS, vol. 7

154 Chernov, A. V., 'Astrakhanskoe vosstanie 1705–1706 gg.', *IZ*, 64, 1959, 186–216

155 ——————, *Vooruzhennye sily russkogo gosudarstva v XV–XVII vv.* S obrazovaniia tsentralizovannogo gosudarstva do reformy pri Petre I, M, 1954

156 Chicherin, B. N., *Oblastnye uchrezhdeniia v Rossii v XVII veke*, M, 1856

157 Chikov, P. S., ed., *Atlas arealov i resursov lekarstvennykh rastenii SSSR*, M, 1976

158 Chistiakova, E. V., 'Novotorgovyi ustav 1667 goda', *AE* for 1957, 1958, 102–26

159 ——————, 'Sotsial'no-ėkonomicheskie vzgliady A. L. Ordyna-Nashchokina', *Trudy Voronezhskogo Gosudarstvennogo Universiteta*, 20, 1950, 1–57

160 Chistovich, I. A., *Feofan Prokopovich i ego vremia*, *Sb. ORIaS*, 8, 1868

161 Christensen, S.Aa., *Ruslands historie i det 17. åhrhundrede.* En forskning- og kildeoversigt, Copenhagen, 1979

162 Chulkov, M. D., *Istoricheskoe opisanie rossiiskoi kommertsii pri vsekh portakh i granitsakh . . .*, 7 vols, M, 1781–8

163 Cieślak, E., and Rumiński, J., eds, *Les Rapports des résidents français à Gdańsk au XVIIIe siècle*, 2 vols, Gdańsk, 1964

164 Coleman, D. C., 'An Innovation and its Diffusion: the "New Draperies"', *Economic History Review*, series 2, 22, 1969, 417–29

165 ——————, ed., *Revisions in Mercantilism*, London, 1969

166 Collins, Samuel, *The Present State of Russia*, London, 1671

167 Confino, Michael, *Systèmes agraires et progrès agricole.* L'assolement triennial en Russie aux XVIIIe – XIXe siècles, Paris-The Hague, 1969

168 Consett, Thomas, *The Present State and Regulations of the Church of Russia*, 2 vols, London, 1729

169 Cordt, B., ed., 'Ein Brief Ph. Joh. von Strahlenberg's', *Verhandlungen der bei der Kaiserlichen Universität Dorpat bestehenden Gelehrten Estnischen Gesellschaft*, 13, 1888, 409–21

170 Cracraft, J., *The Church Reform of Peter the Great*, London, 1971

171 Crummey, R. O., *Aristocrats and Servitors.* The Boyar Elite in Russia, 1613–1689, Princeton, NJ, 1983

172 ——————, *The Old Believers and the World of Antichrist*: the Vyg Community and the Russian State, 1694–1855, Madison, Wis., 1970

173 Crummey R. O, 'Peter and the Boyar Aristocracy, 1689–1700', *CASS*, 8, 1974, 274–87

174 Czerska, Danuta, *Sobornoje Ułożenije 1649 roku*. Zagadnienia społeczno-ustrojowe. Wrocław, 1970

175 Danielson, Jan, *Just Juels rejse til Moskva 1709–1711*, Copenhagen, 1975

176 Danilov, M. V., 'Zapiski', *Russkii Arkhiv*, 1883, no. 2, 1–67

177 Deborin, A. M., and others, eds, *Kul'tura Ispanii*, M, 1940

178 De Madariaga, Isabel, 'Portrait of an Eighteenth-Century Russian Statesman: Prince D. M. Golitsyn', *SEER*, 62, 1984, 36–60

179 Demidova, N. F., 'Biurokratizatsiia gosudarstvennogo apparata absoliutizma v XVII–XVIII vv.', in Druzhinin, ed., *Absoliutizm . . .*, pp. 206–31

180 ————, 'Gosudarstvennyi apparat Rossii v XVII veke', *IZ*, 108, 1982, 109–54

181 ————, 'Prikaznye liudi XVII v. (Sotsial'nyi sostav i istochniki formirovaniia)' *IZ*, 90, 1972, 332–54

182 ————, 'Prikazy', *SIE*, vol. 11

183 ————, 'S. B. Veselovskii, *D'iaki i pod'iachie XV–XVII vv.*', *VI*, 1978, no. 7, 166–8

184 Demin, A. S., '*Zhezl pravleniia* i aforistika Simeona Polotskogo', in Robinson, ed., *Simeon Polotskii*, pp. 60–92

185 Derzhavina, O. A., ed., *Drevnerusskaia literatura i ee sviazi s novym vremenem*, M, 1967

186 Dewey, H. W., 'Old Muscovite Concepts of Injured Honour (*Beschestie*)', *SR*, 27, 1968, 594–603

187 Dewey, H. W., and Kleimola, Ann M., 'Coercion by Righter (*Pravezh*) in Old Russian Administration', *CASS*, 9, 1975, 156–7

188 ————————————————, translators and eds, *Russian Private Law, XIV–XVII Centuries*, Ann Arbor, Mich., 1973

189 Deyon, Pierre, *Le Mercantilisme*, Paris, 1959

190 Diderot, Denis, *Mémoires pour Catherine II*, edited by Paul Vernière, Paris, 1966

191 Ditiatin, I. I., 'Nashe gorodskoe samoupravlenie', in his *Stat'i . .*, pp. 232–71

192 ————, 'Russkii doreformennyi gorod', in his *Stat'i . . .*, pp. 1–32

193 ————, *Stat'i po istorii russkogo prava*, SPg, 1895

194 ————, 'Tsarskii kabak moskovskogo gosudarstva', in his *Stat'i . . .*, pp. 472–96

195 ————, *Ustroistvo i upravlenie gorodov v Rossii*. Goroda v Rossii v XVIII stoletii, SPg, 1874

196 Dittrich, Ehrhard, *Die deutschen und österreichischen Kameralisten*, Darmstadt, 1974

197 Dmitriev, F. M., *Istoriia sudebnykh instantsii (Sochineniia*, vol. i.), M, 1899

198 Dobrovol'skii, V. N., *Smolenskii oblastnoi slovar'*, Smolensk, 1914

199 Doerries, H., 'Dunkle Existenzen und dunkle Machenschaften im Schatten Peters des Grossen', *JfGO*, 4, 1939, 111–35

200 Domov, V. I. 'V Preobrazhenskikh zastenkakh', *VI*, 1966, no. 5, 216–18

201 Dovnar-Zapol'skii, M., 'Organizatsii moskovskikh remeslennikov v XVII v.', *ZhMNP*, September 1910, pt 2, 131–64

202 Druzhinin, N. M., ed., *Absoliutizm v Rossii*, Sbornik k semidesiatiletiiu . . . B. B. Kafengauza, M, 1964

203 ————, and others, eds, *Goroda feodal'noi Rossii*. Sbornik statei pamiati N. V. Ustiugova, M, 1966

204 Druzhinin, V. G., *Raskol na Donu v kontse XVII veka*, SPg, 1889

205 Duchesne, E., ed., *Le Stoglav ou les cent chapitres*. Recueil des décisions de l'assemblée ecclésiastique de Moscou, 1551, Paris, 1920

206 Dürer, Albrecht, *Vier Bücher von menschlicher Proportion*, Nuremberg, 1528

207 Durov, V. A., 'Ocherk nachal'nogo perioda deiatel'nosti Kadashevskogo monetnogo dvora', in Beskrovnyi, ed., *Na rubezhe . . .*, pp. 40–65

208 Dzhervis, M. V., 'Russkaia tabachnaia fabrika v XVIII i XIX vekakh', *IANSSSR*, 1932, Otdelenie obshchestvennykh nauk, 867–89

209 Eaton, H. L., 'Cadasters and Censuses of Muscovy', *SR*, 26, 1967, 54–69

210 Eeckaute, D., 'La mensuration générale des terres en Russie dans la deuxième moitié du XVIIIe siècle', *CMRS*, 3, 1964, 320–8

211 ————, 'Le commerce russe au milieu du XVIIe siècle d'après la correspondance du chargé d'affaires suédois Rodès', *Revue historique*, 233, 1965, 323–38

212 ————, 'Les brigands en Russie du XVIIe au XIXe siècle: mythe et réalité, *Revue d'histoire moderne et contemporaine*, 12, 1965, 161–202

213 Eekman, T., ed., *Juraj Križanić (1618–1683)*. A symposium, The Hague-Paris, 1976

214 Egorov, D., 'Ideia "turetskoi reformatsii" v XVI v.', *Russkaia Mysl'*, 1907, no. 2, 7–14

215 Ekegård, Einar, *Studier i svensk handelspolitik under den tidigare frihetstiden*, Uppsala, 1924

216 Eleonskii, F., ed., 'Zapiski igumena Oresta', *Arkheograficheskii Sbornik dokumentov otnosiashchikhsia k istorii Severozapadnoi Rusi*, Vil'na, 1867, Appendix, pp. i–ci

217 Epifanov, P. P., 'K voprosu o voennoi reforme Petra Velikogo', *VI*, 1945, 1, 34–58

218 ————, 'Voinskii Ustav Petra Velikogo', in Andreev, ed., *Petr Velikii*, pp. 167–213

219 Epstein, F. T., *Die Hof- und Zentralverwaltung im Moskauer Staat und die Bedeutung von G. K. Kotošikhins zeitgenössischem Werk 'Über Russland' für die russische Verwaltungsgeschichte*, edited by G. Specovius, Hamburg, 1978

220 Erdmann, Yella, *Der livländische Staatsmann Johann Reinhold von Patkul*, Berlin, 1970

221 Esipov, G. V., *Raskol'nich'i dela XVIII stoletiia* izvlechennye iz del Preobrazhenskogo prikaza i Tainoi rozysknykh del kantseliarii, 2 vols, SPg, 1861–3

222 Esmein, Adhémar, *A History of Continental Criminal Procedure*, London, 1914

223 Evreinov, V. A., *Grazhdanskoe chinoproizvodstvo v Rossii*, SPg, 1887

224 Falkus, M. E., *The Industrialization of Russia, 1700–1914*, London, 1972

225 Faust ab Aschaffenburg, Maximilian, *Consilia pro aerario civili ecclesiastico et militari, publico atque privato, sive iurium, artium ac remediorum omnium, universali orbis terrarum*, dadurch die oberkeitliche Rentcammern und Nahrungs-Cassen der Unterthanen vom Anfang hero, bis zum Ende der Welt, in allen Königreichen, Fürstenthumben und Herrschaften zu Kriegs- und Friedens-Zeiten angestellt, vermehrt, und erhalten worden . . ., Frankfurt-am-Main, 1641

226 Fedorov, V. S., ed., *200-letie Kabineta ego Imperatorskogo Velichestva, 1704–1904*, SPg, 1911

227 Feigina, S. A., *Alandskii kongress*. Vneshniaia politika Rossii v kontse Severnoi voiny, M, 1959

228 Fekhner, M. V., *Torgovlia russkogo gosudarstva so stranami Vostoka v XVI veke*, M, 1956

229 Filippov, A. N., Platonov, S. F., Chechulin, N. D., and others, eds, *Istoriia Pravitel'stvuiushchego senata za dvesti let, 1711–1911 gg.*, 5 vols, SPg, 1911

230 Firsov, N. N., *Russkie torgovye i promyshlennye kompanii v pervoi polovine XVIII v.*, Kazan, 1896

231 ————, 'Russkoe zakonodatel'stvo o khlebnom vine v XVIII stoletii', *Uchenye Zapiski Imperatorskogo Kazanskogo Universiteta*, 93, no. 3, 1892

232 Fleischhacker, Hedwig, '1730: Das Nachspiel der petrinischen Reform', *JfGO*, 6, 1941, 201–73

233 Fletcher, Giles, *Of the Russe Commonwealth*, with an Introduction by R. Pipes (facsimile of the first edition, London, 1591), Cambridge, Mass., 1966

234 Florovskii, A. V., 'Latinskie shkoly v Rossii v epokhu Petra I', *XVIII vek*, 5, 1962, 316–35

235 Frederiksen, O. J., 'Virginia Tobacco in Russia under Peter the Great', *SEER*, 21, 1942–3, 40–56

236 Freeze, G. L., *The Russian Levites*. Parish Clergy in the Eighteenth Century, Cambridge, Mass. and London, 1977

237 French, R. A., 'Canals in pre-revolutionary Russia', in Bater and French, eds, *Studies* . . . vol. ii, pp. 51–60

238 Fuhrmann, J. T., *The Origins of Capitalism in Russia*. Industry and Progress in the Sixteenth and Seventeenth Centuries, Chicago, 1972

239 Fursenko, V., 'Iaguzhinskii, P. I.', RBS, vol. 25

240 Gaisinovich, A. I., 'Tsekhi v Rossii v XVIII veke', *IANSSSR*, Otdelenie obshchestvennykh nauk, 1931, 522–68

241 Garrard, J. G., ed., *The Eighteenth Century in Russia*, Oxford, 1973

242 Geiman, V. G., 'Manufakturnaia promyshlennost' Peterburga petrovskogo vremeni', in Andreev, ed., *Petr Velikii*, pp. 248–83

243 Geraklitov, A. A., *Istoriia Saratovskogo kraia v XVI–XVIII vv.*, Saratov, 1923

244 Ger'e, V., ed., *Sbornik pisem i memorialov Leibnitsa otnosiashchikhsia k Rossii i k Petru Velikomu*, SPg, 1873

245 German, I. E., *Istoriia mezhevago zakonodatel'stva ot* Ulozheniia *do general'nogo mezhevaniia* (1649–1765), M, 1893

246 Glagoleva, A. P. *Olonetskie zavody v pervoi chetverti XVIII v.*, M, 1957

247 Goehrke, Carsten, *Die Wüstungen in der Moskauer Rus'*. Studien zur Siedlungs-, Bevölkerungs- und Sozialgeschichte, Wiesbaden, 1968

248 Goerdt, W., 'Pravda, Wahrheit (Istina) und Gerechtigkeit (Spravedlivost')', *Archiv für Begriffsgeschichte*, 12, 1968, 58–85

249 Gol'denberg, L. A., *Fedor Ivanovich Soimonov (1692–1780)*, M, 1966

250 Golikova, N. B., *Astrakhanskoe vosstanie 1705–1706 gg.*, M, 1975

251 ————, 'Iz istorii klassovykh protivorechii v russkoi armii (1700–09 gg.)', in Beskrovnyi, Kafengauz and others, eds, *Poltava*, pp. 269–85

252 ————, 'K voprosu o sostave russkogo kupechestva vo vtoroi polovine XVII – pervoi chetverti XVIII v.', in Ianin, V. I., ed., *Russkii Gorod*, vol. 3, M, 1980, pp. 37–65

253 ————, 'Kredit i ego rol'' v deiatel'nosti russkogo kupechestva v nachale XVIII v.', ibid., vol. 2, 1979, pp. 161–97

254 ————, 'Organy politicheskogo syska i ikh razvitie v XVII–XVIII vv.', in Druzhinin, ed., *Absoliutizm* . . ., pp. 255–8

255 ————, *Politicheskie protsessy pri Petre I*. Po materialam Preobrazhenskogo prikaza, M, 1957

256 ————, 'Rostovshchichestvo v Rossii nachala XVIII v.', in Skazkin and others, eds, *Problemy* . . ., pp. 242–90

257 Golubev, A. A., 'Raspravnaia palata pri Senate', in Opisanie MAMIu, vol. 5, 1888, section 3, pp. 103–43

258 Gorchakov, M. I., *Monastyrskii prikaz (1649–1725 gg.)*. Opyt istoriko-iuridicheskogo issledovaniia, SPg, 1868

259 Gorchakov, M. I., 'Monastyrskii prikaz', ES, vol. 38

260 ————, *O zemel'nykh vladeniiakh vserossiiskikh mitropolitov, patriarkhov i Sv. Sinoda (988–1738 gg.)*, SPg, 1871

Gordon *see* Obolensky

261 Got'e, Iu.V., *Zamoskovnyi krai v XVII veke*, second edition, M, 1937

262 Grabar', I. E., and others, eds., *Istoriia russkogo iskusstva*, vol. v, M, 1960

263 Gradov, B. A., Kloss, B. M., Koretskii, V. I., 'K istorii Arkhangel'skoi biblioteki D. M. Golitsyna', *AE* for 1978, 1979, 238–53

264 Gradovskii, A. D., 'Epizod iz istorii tserkovnogo upravleniia (po povodu knigi M. Gorchakova *Monastyrskii prikaz*', in his *Sobranie sochinenii*, vol. i, pp. 383–419

265 ————, *Sobranie sochinenii v 9-ti tomakh*, SPg, 1899–1908

266 Grand, Roger, 'La prison et la notion d'emprisonnement dans l'ancien droit', *Revue historique de droit français et étranger*, series 4, 19, 1940, 58–87

267 Grebeniuk, V. P., and Derzhavina, O. A., eds, *Panegiricheskaia literatura petrovskogo vremeni*, M, 1979

268 Griaznov, A., *Iaroslavskaia Bol'shaia Manufaktura za vremia s 1722 po 1856 g.*, M, 1910

269 Gromov, G. G., 'Russkaia material'naia kul'tura XVII veka', *VI*, 1975, no. 4, pp. 106–24

270 Grove, G. L., *Des Königlich Dänischen Envoyé G. Grund's Bericht über Russland in den Jahren 1705–1710, Izvestiia Imperatorskoi Akademii Nauk*, Istoriko-filologicheskoe otdelenie, 4, no. 9, 1900

271 ————, ed., *En rejsa til Rusland under tsar Peter*. Dagboks optegnelser of vice-admiral Just Juel, dansk gesandt i Rusland, 1709–1711, Copenhagen, 1893

272 Haintz, Otto, 'Peter der Grosse, Friedrich der Grosse und Voltaire. Zur Entstehungsgeschichte von Voltaires *Histoire de l'Empire Russe sous Pierre le Grand*', Akademie der Wissenschaften und der Literatur, *Abhandlungen der geistes- und sozialwissenschaftlichen Klasse*, 5, Wiesbaden, 1961, 511–56

273 Hakluyt, Richard, *The Principall Voiages and Discoveries of the English Nation*, London, 1589 (facsimile edition, 2 vols, Cambridge, 1965)

274 Halem, G. A. von, *Leben Peters des Grossen*, 3 vols, Münster and Leipzig, 1803–4

275 Hans, N., 'Henry Farquharson, Pioneer of Russian Education, 1698–1734', *Aberdeen University Review*, 36, 1959–60, 26–9

276 ————, 'The Moscow School of Mathematics and Navigation (1701)', *SEER*, 39, 1951, 532–6

277 Hart, Simon, 'Amsterdam Shipping and Trade to Northern Russia', *Economisch en Sociaal-Historisch Jaarboek*, 38, 1975, 5–30

278 ————, 'De handelsbetrekkingen van Amsterdam met Archangel en Lapland (Kola) in de 17e eeuw', *Nederlands Archievenblad*, 73, 1969, 66–80

279 Hassinger, Herbert, *Johann Joachim Becher, 1635–1682.* Ein Beitrag zur Geschichte des Merkantilismus, *Veröffentlichungen der Kommission für Neuere Geschichte Oesterreichs*, 38, Vienna, 1951

280 Hatton, R. M., *Charles XII of Sweden*, London, 1968

281 Heckscher, E. F., *Mercantilism*, revised edition, by E. F. Söderlund, 2 vols, London, 1955

282 Hellie, R., *Slavery in Russia, 1450–1725*, Chicago-London, 1982

283 ————, 'The Petrine Army: Continuity, Change, Impact', *CASS*, 8, 1974, 237–53

284 Hellie, R., 'The Stratification of Muscovite Society – the Townsman', *Russian History*, 5, 1978, pp. 119–75
285 Hennin, V. de, *Opisanie ural'skikh i sibirskikh zavodov, 1735*, M, 1937
286 Herrmann, Ernst, ed., *Russland unter Peter dem Grossen*, nach den handschriftlichen Berichten Johann Gotthilf Vockerodt's und Otto Pleyer's, Leipzig, 1872
287 Hetherington, Paul, translator, *The 'Painter's Manual' of Dionysius of Fourna*, London, 1974
288 Hicks, John, *A Theory of Economic History*, Oxford, 1969
289 Hildebrand, K. G., 'Foreign Markets for Swedish Iron in the Eighteenth Century', *Scandinavian Economic History Review*, 6, 1958, 3–52
290 Hill, C. E., *The Danish Sound Dues and the Command of the Baltic*, Durham, NC, 1926
291 Hitier, Joseph, *La Doctrine de l'absolutisme*, Paris, 1903
292 Hittle, J. M., *The Service City*. State and Townsmen in Russia, 1600–1800, Cambridge, Mass., 1979
293 Horbatsch, Olexa, *Die vier Ausgaben der Kirchenslavischen Grammatik von Meletij Smotryc'kyj*, Wiesbaden, 1964
294 Hughes, B. P., *Firepower*, London, 1974
295 Humpert, Magdalene, *Bibliographie der Kameralwissenschaften*, Cologne, 1973
296 Iablochkov, M., *Istoriia dvorianskogo sosloviia v Rossii*, SPg, 1876
297 Iaguzhinskii, P. I., 'Zapiska o sostoianii Rossii', *ChOIDR*, 1860, no. 4, 269–73
298 Iakovlev, A. I., ed., *Tamozhennye knigi Moskovskogo gosudarstva XVII veka*, 3 vols, M, 1950–1
299 ───────, *Zasechnaia cherta Moskovskogo gosudarstva v XVII veke, Zapiski Otdeleniia Russkoi i Slavianskoi Arkheologii Imperatorskogo Russkogo Arkheologicheskogo Obshchestva*, 13, 1916
300 Iakushkin, V. E., *Ocherki istorii russkoi pozemel'noi politiki v XVIII i XIX vv.*, M, 1890
301 Ianovskii, A. E., 'Kamer-kollegiia', ES, vol. 14
302 Indova, E. I., *Dvortsovoe khoziaistvo v Rossii*. Pervaia polovina XVIII veka, M, 1964
303 Iukht, A. I., 'Russkaia promyshlennost' i snabzhenie armii obmundirovaniem i ammunitsiei', in Beskrovnyi, Kafengauz and others, eds, *Poltava*, pp. 210–27
304 ───────, 'V. N. Tatishchev v Moskve. (K istorii denezhnogo obrashcheniia v Rossii v 20 – 30-kh godakh XVIII v.)', *IZ*, 101, 1978, 217–342
305 Ivanov, Petr Ivanovich, *Sistematicheskoe obozrenie pochetnykh prav i obiazannostei v Rossii sushchestvovavshikh*, s istoricheskim izlozheniem vsego do nikh otnosiashchegosia, M, 1836
306 Ivina, L. I., '*Ulozhenie 1649 g. i ego izdaniia*', *Vspomagatel'nye Istoricheskie Distsipliny*, 14, 1983, 152–74
307 Jenkinson, Anthony, *Early Voyages and Travels to Russia and Persia*. By Anthony Jenkinson and other Englishmen, edited by E. D. Morgan and C. H. Coote, 2 vols, London, 1886
308 Joannou, P.-P., ed., *Discipline générale antique*, Pontificia Commissione per la redazione del Codice del Diritto Canonico, fasc. 9, Rome, 1962
309 Johnson, Samuel, *Dictionary of the English Language*, 2 vols, London, 1755
310 Johnson, William A., *Christopher Polhem*, the Father of Swedish Technology, Hartford, Conn., 1963 (first published in 1911)
Juel see Shcherbachev
311 Kabuzan, V. M., *Narodonaselenie Rossii v XVIII–pervoi polovine XIX v.* (Po materialam revizii), M, 1963

312 Kafengauz, B. B., 'Geografiia vnutrennei torgovli i ėkonomicheskaia spetsializatsiia raionov Rossii v 20-kh godakh XVIII v., *Voprosy Geografii*, 20, 1950, 162–202

313 ———, *Istoriia khoziaistva Demidovykh v XVIII–XIX vv.*, M, 1923

314 Kafengauz, B. B., and Pavlenko, N. I., eds, *Ocherki istorii SSSR. Period feodalizma. Rossiia v pervoi chetverti XVIII v.* Preobrazovaniia Petra I, M, 1954

315 Kahan, Arcadius, 'Entrepreneurship in the Early Development of Iron Manufacturing in Russia', *Economic Development and Cultural Change*, 10, 1962, 395–422

316 ———, 'Observations on Petrine Foreign Trade', *CASS*, 8, 1974, 222–36

317 Kaim, Reinhold, *Russische Numismatik*, Brunswick, 1968

318 Kaiser, Friedhelm, 'Der europäische Anteil an der russischen Rechtsterminologie der petrinischen Zeit', *Forschungen zur Osteuropäischen Geschichte*, 10, 1965, 75–333

319 Kalinychev, F. I., 'Russkoe voisko vo vtoroi polovine XVII v.', *Doklady i soobshcheniia Instituta Istorii AN SSSR*, 2, 1954, 74–86

320 Kameneva, T. N., and Guseva, A. A., eds, *Ukrainskie knigi kirillovskoi pechati XVI–XVIII vv.*, M, 1976

321 Kappeler, A., *Russlands erste Nationalitäten: das Zarenreich und die Völker der Mittleren Wolga vom 16. bis zum 19. Jahrhundert*, Cologne-Vienna, 1982

322 Kapterev, N. F., 'M. Smentsovskii, *Brat'ia Likhudy*', *ZIAN*, Istoriko-filologicheskoe otdelenie, 6, no. 7, 1904, 85–115

323 ———, *Patriarkh Nikon i ego protivniki v dele ispravleniia tserkovnykh obriadov.* Vremia patriarshestva Iosifa, second edition, Sergiev Posad, 1913

324 ———, *Patriarkh Nikon i tsar' Aleksei Mikhailovich*, 2 vols, Sergiev Posad, 1909–12

325 ———, *Svetskie arkhiereiskie chinovniki v drevnei Rusi*, M, 1874

326 Karamzin, N. M., *Istoriia gosudarstva Rossiiskago*, vol. xii, SPg, 1829

327 Karnovich, E. P., *Zamechatel'nye bogatstva chastnykh lits v Rossii*, SPg, 1874

328 Kartashev, A. V., *Ocherki po istorii russkoi tserkvi*, 2 vols, Paris, 1959

329 Kartsov, V. G., 'Razintsy i raskol'niki', *VI*, 1977, no. 3, 121–31

330 Kasinec, E., 'A Bibliographical Essay on the Documentation of Russian Orthodoxy during the Imperial Era', in Nichols and Stavrou, eds, *Russian Orthodoxy . . .*, pp. 205–28

331 Kaufman-Rochard, Jacqueline, *Origines d'une bourgeoisie russe.* XVIe et XVIIe siècles, Paris, 1969

332 Kazantsev, B. N., 'Zakonodatel'stvo russkogo tsarizma po regulirovaniiu krest'ianskogo otkhoda v XVII–XIX vv.', *VI*, 1970, no. 6, 20–31

333 Keep, J. L. H., 'Bandits and the Law in Muscovy', *SEER*, 35, 1956, 201–22

334 ———, 'The Decline of the Zemskii Sobor', *SEER*, 36, 1958, 100–22

335 ———, 'Mutiny in Moscow 1682: A Contemporary Account', *Canadian Slavonic Papers*, 23, 1981, 410–42

336 Kellenbenz, H., 'Der russische Transithandel mit dem Orient im 17. und zu Beginn des 18. Jahrhunderts', *JfGO*, 1964, 481–98

337 ———, 'Marchands en Russie au XVIIe et XVIIIe siècles', *CMRS*, 11, 1970, 576–620; 12, 1971, 76–109

338 Kilburger, J.Ph., 'Kurzer Unterricht von dem Russischen Handel . . . 1674 . . .', *Magazin für die neue Historie und Geographie*, edited by A. F. Buesching, pt 3, 1769, 246–386 (Supplement in *Severnyi Arkhiv*, January 1823, pp. 169–87)

339 Kirby, D. G., 'The Balance of the North and Baltic Trade: George Mackenzie's Relation, August 1715', *SEER*, 54, 1976, 428–50

340 Kirillov, I. K., *Tsvetushchee sostoianie vserossiiskogo gosudarstva*, 2 vols, M, 1831, edited by B. A. Rybakov, L. A. Gol'denberg and S. M. Troitskii, M, 1977
341 Kirillov, V. I., 'Tainaia kantseliaria XVIII st.', *VI*, 1967, no. 12, 205–9
342 Kizevetter, A. A., 'Ekaterina I', *Entsiklopedicheskii Slovar' Russkogo bibliograficheskogo instituta Granat*, vol. 12, M [1927?]
343 ————, *Mestnoe samoupravlenie v Rossii*. IX–XIX st., M, 1909
344 ————, *Posadskaia obshchina v Rossii*. XVIII st., M, 1903
345 [Klenck, von] *Fürstliche Machtkunst oder unerschöpfliche Grube*, wodurch ein Fürst sich mächtig, und seine Unterthanen reich machen kan, published by Heinrich Boden, Halle 1702; Weissenfels 1703; reprinted 1737, 1740, 1748, 1753 (cf. Introduction, note 90)
346 Kliuchevskii, V. O., *Boiarskaia duma drevnei Rusi*, fifth edition, SPg, 1919
347 ————, 'Dobrye liudi drevnei Rusi' first published in 1892, in his *Tserkov' i Rossiia* . . ., reprinted in 354, pp. 61–87
348 ————, Istoriia soslovii v Rossii, in his *Sochineniia*, vol. vi, pp. 276–466
349 ————, *Kurs russkoi istorii*, 5 vols, M-Petrograd, 1923
350 ————, 'Podushnaia podat' i otmena kholopstva v Rossii', in his *Sochineniia*, vol. vii, pp. 318–402
351 ————, 'Russkii rubl' XVI–XVIII vv.', in his *Sochineniia*, vol. vii, pp. 170–236
352 ————, *Sochineniia v vos'mi tomakh* edited by N. N. Tikhomirov, M, 1956–9
353 ————, dedicatee, *Sbornik statei posviashchennykh V. O. Kliuchevskomy ego uchenikami*, M, 1909
354 ————, *Tri lektsii*, Paris, 1966
355 Klochkov, M. V., *Naselenie Rossii pri Petre Velikom po perepisiam togo vremeni. Tom pervyi. Perepis' dvorov i naseleniia (1678–1721)*, *ZIFF*, vol. 101, SPg, 1911
356 Klueting, H., and Klueting, E., eds, *Graf Ostermann, Urkunden und Regesten. Ostermaniana aus Hannover und Wolfenbüttel*, Amsterdam, 1974
357 Knoppers, J. V. Th., *Dutch Trade with Russia from the Time of Peter I to Alexander I. A Quantitative Study in Eighteenth-Century Shipping*, 3 vols, Montreal, 1976
358 Kolesnikov, P. A., ed., *Severnaia Rus'* (XVIII stoletie), Vologda, 1973
359 Kolosov, E. E., 'Razvitie artilleriiskogo vooruzheniia v Rossii vo vtoroi polovine XVII v.', *IZ*, 71, 1962, 259–69
360 Konarski, Stanisław, *O skutecznym rad sposobie*, 4 pts, Warsaw, 1923 (facsimile of the first edition, Warsaw, 1760–3)
361 Korchmarik, F. B., *Dukhovi vplivi Kieva na Moskovshchinu v dobu getmans'koi Ukraini*, New York, 1964
    Kordt see Cordt
362 Koser, R., and Droysen, H., eds, *Briefwechsel Friedrichs des Grossen mit Voltaire*, vol. i, Briefwechsel des Kronprinzen Friedrich, 1736–40, Leipzig, 1908
363 Kotoshikhin, Grigorii, *O Rossii v tsarstvovanie Alekseia Mikhailovicha*, edited by A. E. Pennington, Oxford, 1980
364 Kozintseva, R. I., 'Ot tamozhennogo tarifa 1724 g. k tarifu 1731 g.', in Mavrodin, ed., *Voprosy genezisa* . . ., pp. 182–216
365 ————, 'Uchastie kazny vo vneshnei torgovle Rossii v pervoi chetverti XVIII v.', *IZ*, 91, 1973, 267–337
366 ————, 'Vneshnetorgovyi oborot Arkhangel'skoi iarmarki i ee rol' v razvitii vserossiiskogo rynka', in Valk, ed., *Issledovaniia* . . ., pp. 116–63
367 ————, 'Vyrabotka pervogo russkogo tamozhennogo tarifa i ego redaktsii', *Problemy Istochnikovedeniia*, 10, 1962, 154–94

368 Kozlov, O. F., 'Delo Nikona', *VI*, 1976, no. 1, 102–14
369 Kozlov, V. I., and others, eds, *Mordva*. Istoriko-etnograficheskie ocherki, Saransk, 1981
370 Koz'min, B. P., 'A. P. Shchapov – istorik-demokrat', in *Ocherki istorii istoricheskoi nauki v SSSR*, vol. ii, edited by M. V. Nechkina and others, pp. 66–80, M, 1960
371 Krebel, Rudolph, *Der Scorbut in geschichtlich-literarischer, prophylaktischer und therapeutischer Beziehung*, Leipzig, 1862
372 Krestovskii, I. V., Petrova, E. N., and Belekhov, N. N., *Leningrad. Monumental'naia skul'ptura XVIII–XIX vekov*, M-L, 1951
373 Krizhanich, Iurii, *Politika*, text translated by A. L. Gol'dberg and edited by V. V. Zelenin, general editor M. N. Tikhomirov, M, 1965
374 —————, *Russian Statecraft*. The Political Economy of Iurii Krizhanich, edited and translated by J. M. Letiche and B. Dmytryshyn, Oxford, 1984
375 Krylova, T. K., 'K istorii torgovoi politiki Petra I v iugo-zapadnoi Evrope', *Uchenye Zapiski Leningradskogo Gosudarstvennogo Pedagogicheskogo Instituta im. A. Gertsena*, 19, 1939, 135–44
376 —————, 'Otnosheniia Rossii i Ispanii v pervoi chetverti XVIII veka', in Deborin, ed., *Kul'tura Ispanii*, pp. 327–52
377 —————, 'Rossiia i Venetsiia na rubezhe XVII i XVIII vv.', *Uchenye Zapiski Leningradskogo Gosudarstvennogo Pedagogicheskogo Instituta im. A. Gertsena*, 19, 1939, 43–82
378 Kurat, A. N., 'Der Prutfeldzug und der Prutfrieden von 1711', *JfGO*, 10, 1962, 13–66
379 Kurts, B. G., *Sochinenie Kil'burgera o russkoi torgovle v tsarstvovanie Alekseia Mikhailovicha*, Kiev, 1915
380 Lakier, A., *O votchinakh i pomest'iakh*, SPg, 1848
381 Lamare, Nicolas de, *Traité de la police*, Une description historique et topographique de Paris, 4 vols, Paris, 1705–38
382 Lantzeff, George V., and Pierce, R. A., *Eastward to Empire*: Exploration and Conquest on the Russian Open Frontier to 1750, Montreal, 1973
383 Lappo-Danilevskii, A. S., *Organizatsiia priamogo oblozheniia v Moskovskom gosudarstve s vremen smuty do epokhi preobrazovanii*, ZIFF, vol. 23, 1980
384 —————, *Russkie promyshlennye i torgovye kompanii v pervoi polovine XVIII stoletiia*, SPg, 1889
385 —————, 'Vysluzhennye votchiny v Moskovskom gosudarstve XVI–XVII vv.', *Istoricheskoe Obozrenie*, 3, 1891, 109–33
386 Latkin, V. N., *Uchebnik istorii russkogo prava*, SPg, 1909
387 —————, *Zakonodatel'nye kommissii v Rossii v XVIII stoletii*, SPg, 1887
388 Lauerma, Matti, *L'Artillerie de campagne française pendant les guerres de la révolution*, Helsinki, 1956
389 Lavrova, T. F., 'Torgovye sviazi g. Arkhangel'ska s zapadnoevropeiskimi stranami v pervoi chetverti XVIII v.', *Uchenye Zapiski Arkhangel'skogo Gosudarstvennogo Pedagogicheskogo Instituta*, 16, 1964, 209–28
390 Lebedev, D. M., *Geografiia v Rossii petrovskogo vremeni*, M, 1950
391 Lebedev, V. I., 'Bashkirskoe vosstanie 1705–1711 gg.', *IZ*, 1, 1937, 81–102
392 —————, *Bulavinskoe vosstanie*, M, 1934
393 —————, *Krest'ianskaia voina pod predvoditel'stvom Stepana Razina 1667–1671 gg.*, M, 1955

394 Leder, Irmgard, *Russische Fischnamen*, Wiesbaden, 1968
395 Leitsch, W., 'Stadtbevölkerung im Moskauer Staat', *Forschungen zur Osteuropäischen Geschichte*, 18, 1973, 221–48
396 Leonid, arkhimandrit, 'Petrovskie i drugie bumagi', *ChOIDR*, 1874, pt 2, Smes', 12–19
397 Leontief, W., 'Peter der Grosse: seine Wirtschaftspolitik und sein angeblicher Merkantilismus', *JfGO*, 2, 1937, 234–71
398 Le Prince, J. B., *Oeuvre . . . sur les moeurs, les coutumes et les habillements de différents peuples*, Paris, 1764
399 Lettenbauer, Wilhelm, *Moskau das Dritte Rom*. Zur Geschichte einer politischen Theorie, Munich, 1961
400 Lewitter, L. R., 'Russia, Poland and the Baltic, 1697–1721', *Historical Journal*, 11, 1968, 3–34
401 ————, 'The Russo-Polish Treaty of 1686 and its Antecedents', *Polish Review*, 9, 1964, no 3, 1–29, no. 4, 21–37
402 ————, *'The Spiritual Regulation of Peter the Great*, translated and edited by Alexander V. Muller', *SEER*, 52, 1974, 288–92
403 Lileev, M. I., *Iz istorii russkogo raskola na Vetke i v Starodube v XVII–XVIII vv.*, Izvestiia Filologicheskogo Instituta kn. Bezborodko, vols 12–14, Nezhin, 1895
404 Lindeberg, A. K., ed., *Istoricheskii ocherk 2-go Kadetskogo korpusa 1712–1912 gg. v dvukh tomakh*, vol. i, SPg, 1912
405 Lindeberg, Gösta, *Svensk ekonomisk politik under den Görtzka perioden*, Lund, 1941
406 Liubomirov, P., 'Staroobriadchestvo', *Entsiklopedicheskii Slovar' Russkogo bibliograficheskogo instituta Granat*, vol. 41–iv, M [1927?]
407 Liubomirov, P. G., *Ocherki po istorii metallurgicheskoi i metalloobrabatyvaiushchei promyshlennosti v Rossii*, L, 1937
408 ————, *Ocherki po istorii russkoi promyshlennosti*. XVII, XVIII i nachalo XIX veka, M, 1947
409 ————, 'Rol' kazennogo, dvorianskogo i kupecheskogo kapitala v stroitel'stve krupnoi promyshlennosti Rossii v XVII–XVIII vv.', *IZ*, 16, 1945, 65–9
410 Lodyzhenskii, K., *Istoriia russkogo tamozhennogo tarifa*, SPg, 1886
411 Longworth, P., *Alexis, Tsar of all the Russias*, London, 1984
412 ————, *The Cossacks*, London 1969
413 Louis XIV, *Oeuvres*, vol. i, Paris, 1806
414 Lubimenko, Inna, *Les Relations commerciales et politiques de l'Angleterre avec la Russie avant Pierre le Grand*, Paris, 1933
415 ————, 'The Struggle of the Dutch with the English for the Russian Market in the Seventeenth Century', *Transactions of the Royal Historical Society*, 7, 1924, 27–41
416 Luk'ianov, P. M., *Istoriia khimicheskikh promyslov i khimicheskoi promyshlennosti Rossii do kontsa XIX veka*, 6 vols, M–L, 1948–65
417 ————, 'Rol' Petra Velikogo v organizatsii khimicheskogo proizvodstva v Rossii', *VI*, 1947, no. 6, 79–85
418 Lupinin, N. B., *Religious Revolt in the Seventeenth Century*: the Schism in the Russian Church, Princeton, NJ, 1983
419 Luppov, S. P., *Istoriia stroitel'stva Peterburga v pervoi chetverti 18 v.*, M–L, 1957
420 L'vov, A., 'Popytka Petra I k rasprostraneniiu sredi russkogo naroda nauchnykh sel'skokhoziaistvennykh znanii', *ChOIDR*, 1892, pt 3, section 3, 1–11

421 Lyall, Robert, *The Character of the Russians and a Detailed History of Moscow*, London, 1823

422 Lystsov, V. P., *Persidskii pokhod Petra I, 1722–1723*, M, 1951

423 Magnitskii, Leontii, *Arifmetika, sirech nauka chislitelnaia* . . ., M, 1703

424 Maikov, L. N., ed., *Rasskazy Nartova o Petre Velikom, Sb.ORIaS*, 52, 1891, no. 8

425 Man'kov, A. G., 'K istorii vyrabotki zakonodatel'stva o krest'ianakh na rubezhe XVII –XVIII vv.', *AE* for 1958, 1960, 350–86

426 —————, 'Krepostnoe pravo i dvorianstvo v proekte Ulozheniia 1720–25 gg.', in Pavlenko and others, eds., *Dvorianstvo* . . ., pp. 150–80

427 —————, 'Proekt Ulozheniia rossiiskogo gosudarstva 1720–25 godov', in Peshtich, Shapiro and others, eds, *Problemy istorii* . . ., pp. 157–67

428 —————, Razvitie krepostnogo prava v Rossii vo vtoroi polovine XVII v., M, 1962

429 —————, *Ulozhenie 1649 goda*. Kodeks feodal'nogo prava Rossii, L, 1980

430 Mar'in, V. I., '"Slovo i delo gosudarevo"', *VI*, 1966, no. 3, 215–18

431 Markevich, A. I., *Istoriia mestnichestva v Moskovskom gosudarstve v XV–XVII vv.*, Odessa, 1888

432 Maslovskii, D., *Stroevaia i polevaia sluzhba russkikh voisk vremeni imperatora Petra Velikogo i imperatritsy Elizavety*, M, 1883

433 Mavrodin, V. V., ed., *Voprosy genezisa kapitalizma v Rossii*, L, 1960

434 Meehan-Waters, Brenda, *Autocracy and Aristocracy*. The Russian Service Elite of 1730, New Brunswick, NJ, 1982

435 —————, 'The Russian Aristocracy and the Reforms of Peter the Great', *CASS*, 8, 1974, 288–302

436 Meinecke, Friedrich, *Die Idee der Staatsraison in der neueren Geschichte*, second edition, Berlin, 1925

437 Merk, W., 'Das Gedanke des gemeinen Besten in der deutschen Staats- und Rechtsentwicklung', in Merk, ed., *Festschrift für Alfred Schultze*, pp. 451–520

438 —————, ed., *Festschrift für Alfred Schultze*, Weimar, 1934

439 Meshalin, I. V., ed., *Tekstil'naia promyshlennost' Moskovskoi gubernii v XVIII i nachale XIX v.* (Materialy po istorii krest'ianskoi promyshlennosti, vol. ii), M, 1950

440 Migne, J. P., ed., *Patrologiae cursus completus*. Patrologiae graecae tomus 48, 63, Paris, 1862

441 Mikhailov, M. M., *Russkoe grazhdanskoe sudoproizvodstvo* . . . ot Ulozheniia 1649 goda do izdaniia Svoda Zakonov, SPg, 1856

442 Miliukov, P. N., *Gosudarstvennoe khoziaistvo Rossii v pervoi chetverti XVIII stoletiia i reforma Petra Velikogo*, second edition, SPg, 1905

443 —————, 'Kommerts-kollegiia', *ES*, vol. 30

444 —————, *Spornye voprosy finansovoi istorii Moskovskogo gosudarstva*, SPg, 1892

445 Mironov, B. N., 'Revoliutsiia tsen v Rossii v XVII v.', *VI*, 1971, no. 11, 49–71

446 Moleva, N. M., 'Tsekhovaia organizatsiia khudozhnikov v Moskve XVII–XVIII vv.', *VI*, 1969, no. 11, 43–54

447 Mordukhovich, L. M., 'Juraj Križanić, W. Petty and Ivan Pososhkov', in Eekman, ed., *Juraj Križanić* . . ., pp. 223–44

448 Moroshkin, F. L., *Ob 'Ulozhenii' v posleduiushchem ego razvitii*, M, 1836

449 Mousnier, Roland, *Les Hiérarchies sociales de 1450 à nos jours*, Paris, 1969

450 Muller, A. V., 'The Inquisitorial Network of Peter the Great', in Nichols and Stavrou, eds, *Russian Orthodoxy* . . ., pp. 142–53

451 Muller, A. V., translator and ed., *The Spiritual Regulation of Peter the Great*, Seattle, W. and London, 1972
452 Mun, Thomas, *England's Treasure by Forraign Trade or The Ballance of our Forraign Trade is the Rule of our Treasure*, London, 1664
453 Murav'ev, N. V., *Prokurorskii nadzor v ego ustroistve i deiatel'nosti*, vol. i, M, 1889
454 Murav'eva, L. L., 'Voenno-istoricheskii plakat XVIII veka o persidskom pokhode Petra I', *AE* for 1961, 1962
455 Murzanova, M., 'Na moskovsko-novgorodskoi parusnoi fabrike', *Arkhiv Istorii Truda v Rossii* (edited by Iu. M. Gessen), 2, 1921, 1–7
456 Narochnitskii, A. L., and others, eds, *Istoricheskaia geografiia Rossii XII – nachalo XX v.* Sbornik k 70–letiiu L. G. Beskrovnogo, M, 1975
457 Nazarov, V. D., 'Cheti', *SIE*, vol. 15
458 Nechaiev, V. V., 'Raskol'nicheskaia kontora (1725–1763)', Opisanie MAMIu, vol. 7, pt 2, 1890, pp. 1–176
459 Nevolin, K. A., *Istoriia rossiiskikh grazhdanskikh zakonov*, pt 2 (*Polnoe sobranie sochinenii*, vol. iv), SPg, 1857
460 ————, 'Ob uspekhakh gosudarstvennogo mezhevaniia v Rossii do imperatritsy Ekateriny II', in his *Polnoe sobranie sochinenii*, vol. vi, pp. 431–517
461 ————, *Polnoe sobranie sochinenii*, 6 vols, SPg, 1857–9
462 Newall, Venetia, *An Egg at Easter*, London 1971
463 Nichols, R. L., and Stavrou, T. G., eds, *Russian Orthodoxy under the Old Régime*, Minneapolis, Minn., 1978
464 Nikiforov, L. A., *Vneshniaia politika Rossii v poslednie gody Severnoi voiny. Nishtadskii mir*, M, 1959
465 Nikitin, A. V., 'Oboronitel'nye sooruzheniia zasechnoi cherty XVI – XVII vv.', *Materialy i Issledovaniia po Arkheologii SSSR*, 44, 1955, pp. 116–213
466 Nikol'skii, K., *Anafemstvovanie (otluchenie ot tserkvi) . . .*, SPg, 1879
467 Nikonov, S. P., *Poruchitel'stvo v ego istoricheskom razvitii po russkomu pravu*, SPg, 1895
468 Nolte, H.-H., 'Die Reaktion auf die spätpetrinische Altgläubigenbedrückung', *Kirche im Osten*, 19, 1976, 11–28
469 ————, *Religiöse Toleranz in Russland 1600–1725*, Göttingen, 1969
470 ————, 'Sozialgeschichtliche Zusammenhänge der russischen Kirchenspaltung. Materialien zu einer vergleichenden Erklärung', *JfGO*, 41, 1975, 323–43
471 Nordmann, Claude J., *La Crise du Nord au début du XVIIIe siècle*, Paris, 1962
472 Novosel'skii, A. A., 'Pobegi krest'ian i kholopov i ikh syski v Moskovskom gosudarstve vo vtoroi polovine XVII v.' *Trudy Instituta Istorii* RANION, 1, 1926, 327–56
473 ————, 'Rasprostranenie krepostnicheskogo zemlevladeniia v iuzhnykh uezdakh Moskovskogo gosudarstva v XVII v.', *IZ*, 4, 1938, 21–40
474 ————, 'Rospis' krest'ianskikh dvorov nakhodiashchikhsia vo vladenii vysshego dukhovenstva, monastyrei i dumnykh liudei, po perepisnym knigam 1678 g.', *IA*, 4, 1949, 88–149
475 Novosel'skii, A. A., ed., Buganov, V. I., compiler, *Vosstanie 1662 g. v Moskve. Sbornik dokumentov*, M, 1964
476 Novosel'skii, A. A., Lebedev, V. I., and others, eds, Shvetsova, A. E., compiler, *Krest'ianskaia voina pod predvoditel'stvom Stepana Razina. Sbornik dokumentov*, 4 vols in 5, M, 1954–76

477 Novosel'skii, A. A., and Ustiugov, N. V., eds, *Ocherki istorii SSSR. Period feodalizma. XVII v.*, M, 1955

478 Obolensky, M. A., and Posselt, M. C., eds, *Tagebuch des Generals Patrick Gordon . . . 1665–1699*, 2 vols, M-SPg, 1849–52

479 O'Brien, C. Bickford, *Russia under Two Tsars, 1682–1689*. The Regency of Sophia Alekseevna, Berkeley, Calif., 1952

480 Ogorodnikov, S. F., *Ocherk istorii goroda Arkhangel'ska v torgovo-promyshlennom otnoshenii*, SPg, 1890

481 Okenfuss, M. J., 'The Jesuit Origins of Petrine Education', in Garrard, ed., *The Eighteenth . . .*, pp. 106–30

482 ——————, 'Russian Students in Europe in the Age of Peter', in Garrard, ed., *The Eighteenth . . .*, pp. 131–45

483 ——————, 'Technical Training in Russia under Peter the Great', *History of Education Quarterly*, 13, 1973, 325–46

484 Orfield, L. B., *The Growth of Scandinavian Law*, Philadelphia, Pa, 1953

485 Oshanina, O. N., 'K istorii zaseleniia srednego Povolzh'ia v XVII v.' in Ustiugov and others, eds, *Russkoe gosudarstvo . . .*, pp. 50–74

486 Osokin, E., *Vnutrennie tamozhennye poshliny v Rossii*, Kazan, 1850

487 Ostrogorskii, G., 'Das Projekt einer Rangtabelle aus der Zeit des Zaren Fedor Alekseevich', *Jahrbücher für Kultur und Geschichte der Slaven*, 9, 1933, 88–138

488 Palmer, William, *The Patriarch and the Tsar*, 6 vols, London, 1871–6

489 Pankov, D. V., ed., *Razvitie taktiki russkoi armii. XVIII v. – nachalo XX v.*, M, 1957

490 Pankratova, M. A., *Formirovanie proletariata v Rossii* (XVII–XVIII vv.), M, 1963

491 Parker, W. H., *An Historical Geography of Russia*, London, 1968

492 Paton, Henry, ed., *Report on the Manuscripts of Lord Polwarth*, 3 vols, London, 1916–31

493 Pavlenko, N. I., *Aleksandr Danilovich Menshikov*, M, 1981

494 ——————, 'Kazennaia metallurgicheskaia promyshlennost' Rossii v 20-40-kh gg. XVIII v. i sbyt', *IANSSSR*, Seriia istorii i filosofii, 8, no. 4, 1951, 323–37

495 ——————, 'Materialy o razvitii Ural'skoi promyshlennosti v 20-40-kh gg. XVIII v.', *IA*, 9, 1953, 156–282

496 ——————, *Razvitie metallurgicheskoi promyshlennosti Rossii v pervoi chetverti XVIII veka*, M, 1953

497 ——————, 'Torgovo-promyshlennaia politika pravitel'stva Rossii v pervoi chetverti XVIII veka', *ISSR*, 1978, no. 3, 49–69

498 ——————, ed., *Rossiia v period reform Petra I*, M, 1973

499 ——————, and others, eds, *Dvorianstvo i krepostnoi stroi Rossii XVI–XVIII vv.* Sbornik pamiati A. A. Novosel'skogo, M, 1975

500 Pavlov-Sil'vanskii, N. P., *Feodalizm v drevnei Rusi*, second edition, M-Petrograd, 1923

501 ——————, *Gosudarevy sluzhilye liudi. Liudi kabal'nye i dokladnye*, second edition (*Sochineniia*, vol. i), SPg, 1909

502 ——————, 'Mneniia verkhovnikov o reformakh Petra Velikogo', in his *Ocherki . . .*, pp. 373–401

503 ——————, *Ocherki russkoi istorii XVIII–XIX vv.*, SPg, 1910

504 ——————, *Proekty reform v zapiskakh sovremennikov Petra Velikogo*, ZIFF, vol. 42, 1897

505 ——————, 'Simvolizm v drevnem russkom prave', in his *Sochineniia*, vol. iii, pp. 423–66

506 ——————, *Sochineniia*, 3 vols, SPg, 1909–10

507 Pavlov-Sil'vanskii, N. P., 'Sud nad reformoi Petra Velikogo v Verkhovnom tainom sovete', in *O minuvshem*, Istoricheskii sbornik, SPg, 1909, pp. 1–10

508 Pazhitnov, K. A., *Ocherki istorii promyshlennosti dorevoliutsionnoi Rossii. Khlop-chatobumazhnaia*, l'no-pen'kovaia i shelkovaia promyshlennost', M, 1958

509 ———, *Ocherki istorii tekstil'noi promyshlennosti dorevoliutsionnoi Rossii. Sherstianaia promyshlennost'*, M, 1955

510 ———, *Problema remeslennykh tsekhov v zakonodatel'stve russkogo absoliutizma*, M, 1952

511 ———, 'Remeslennoe ustroistvo v Moskovskoi Rusi i reforma Petra I', *IZ*, 8, 1940, 163–73

512 Pekarskii, P. P., *Nauka i literatura pri Petre Velikom*, vol. i, Vvedenie v istoriiu prosveshcheniia v Rossii XVIII stol., vol. ii, Opisanie slaviano-russkikh knig i tipografii 1698–1725 gg., SPg, 1862

513 ———, ed., 'Ukaz Ekateriny I ob uluchshenii vnutrennikh del gosudarstva 9 ianvaria 1727 goda i mery priniatye Verkhovnym tainym sovetom po vyslushanii togo ukaza', *Sb.ORIaS*, 9, 1872, 84–109

514 Perry, John [late Captain of the Signet-Fireship], *A Regulation for Seamen . . . To which is added a narrative of his case relating to his loss of the said ship*, London, 1695

515 ———, *The State of Russia under the present Czar*, London 1716

516 Peshtich, S. L., Shapiro, A. L., and others, eds, *Problemy istorii feodal'noi Rossii*. Sbornik statei k 60-letiiu prof. V. V. Mavrodina, L, 1971

517 [Peter I] *Dukhovnyi Reglament Petra Pervogo*, Kiev, 1823 (reprinted)

518 Peterson, Claes, *Peter the Great's Administrative and Judicial Reforms*: Swedish Antecedents and the Process of Reception, Stockholm, 1979

519 Petrikeev, D. I., *Krupnoe krepostnoe khoziaistvo XVII v.*; po materialam votchiny boiarina B. I. Morozova, L, 1967

520 Petrov, A., 'Romodanovskii, Fedor Iur'evich', RBS, vol. 17

521 ———, 'Romodanovskii, Ivan Fedorovich', RBS, vol. 17

522 Petrov, P. N., *Istoriia Sankt-Peterburga . . . 1703–1782*, SPg, 1885

523 Petrovskii, S. A., *O Senate v tsarstvovanie Petra Velikogo*, M, 1875

524 Petschauer, P., 'The Philosopher and the Reformer. Leibniz and the College System', *CASS*, 13, 1979, 473–87

525 Pintner, W. McK., and Rowney, D. K., eds, *Russian Officialdom*. The Bureaucratization of Russian Society from the Seventeenth to the Twentieth Century, Chapel Hill, NC, 1980

526 Pirogov, A. E., ed., *Russkaia voennaia sila*, second edition, revised by A. N. Petrov, 2 vols, M, 1872

527 Plandovskii, V., *Narodnaia perepis'*, SPg, 1898

528 Platonov, S. F., 'Boiarskaia duma – predshestvennitsa Senata', in his *Sochineniia*, vol. i, pp. 444–94

529 ———, *Sochineniia*, 2 vols, SPg, 1912–13

530 ———, ed., *Patriarshaia ili Nikonovskaia letopis'*, M, 1965 (a reprint of *Polnoe sobranie russkikh letopisei*, vol. xiii, pt 1, SPg, 1904)

531 Plavsić, B., 'Seventeenth-century Chanceries and their Staffs', in Pintner and Rowney, eds, *Russian Officialdom*, pp. 19–49

532 Pobedonostsev, K. P., ed., 'Istoriko-iuridicheskie akty . . . XVII–XVIII v.', *ChOIDR*, 1886, pt 4, section 2, 191–295

533 Pod"iapol'skaia, E. P., *Vosstanie Bulavina*, M, 1962

534 Pokrovskii, M. N., ed., *Trudy Arkheograficheskoi Kommissii Akademii Nauk SSSR, Krepostnaia manufaktura v Rossii*, pt i: Tul'skie i Kashirskie zheleznye zavody, L, 1930

535 Polotskii, Simeon, *Izbrannye sochineniia*, edited by I. P. Eremin, L, 1953

536 Pönicke, Herbert, 'Johann Ernst Glück. Ein Widerstandskämpfer im Zeitalter der Frühaufklärung im Nordosten Europas', *Kirche im Osten*, 13, 1970, 104–32

537 Popov, N. A., ed., *Akty Moskovskogo gosudarstva*, vol. i, SPg, 1890

538 Porfir'ev, E. K., 'Taktika russkoi armii v pervoi chetverti XVIII v.', in Pankov, ed., *Razvitie . . .*, pp. 31–58

539 Portal, Roger, 'Razvitie novoi promyshlennosti v Rossii v XVII v.', *IZ*, 49, 1956, 360–5

540 Posthumus, N. W., *Inquiry into the History of Prices in Holland*, 2 vols, Leiden, 1946–64

541 Predtechenskii, A. V., ed., *Peterburg petrovskogo vremeni. Ocherki*, L, 1948

542 Price, J. M., 'The Tobacco Adventure in Russia', *Transactions of the American Philosophical Society*, vol. 51, 1961, pp. 1–120

543 Price, W. H., *The English Patents of Monopoly*, Cambridge, Mass., 1906

544 Probst, A. E., 'Iz istorii organizatsii v Rossii dobychi i pererabotki nefti', *IANSSSR*, Otdel ėkonomiki i prava, no. 4, 1950, 284–97

545 Prokopovich, Feofan, *Pravda voli monarshei vo opredelenii naslednika derzhavy svoei*, M-SPg, 1722

546 ————————, *Slovo na pogrebenie Petra Velikogo, Imperatora i Samoderzhtsa Vserossiiskogo, Ottsa Otechestva*, SPg-M, 1725 (English translation in Consett, *The Present State . . .*, vol. ii, pp. 274–87)

547 ————————, *Sochineniia*, edited by I. P. Eremin, L, 1956

548 Prokopovich, M. N., ed., 'O soderzhanii v nyneshnee mirnoe vremia armii i kakim obrazom krest'iän v luchshee sostoianie privest',' *ChOIDR*, 1897, pt 2, section 4, 29–52

549 Pronshtein, A. P., *Zemlia Donskaia v XVII veke*, Rostov-on-Don, 1961

550 Pryzhov, I. G., *Istoriia kabakov v Rossii*, M-SPg, 1868

551 ————————, N., *Nishchie na sviatoi Rusi*. Materialy dlia istorii obshchestvennogo i narodnogo byta v Rossii, M, 1862

552 Puparev, A., 'O bogadel'niakh v Kazani v XVIII stoletii', *Kazanskie Gubernskie Vedomosti*, no. 1, 1838, Chast' neoffitsial'naia, 3–5

553 Pushkarev, L. N., 'Kul'turnye sviazi Ukrainy i Rossii posle ikh vossoedineniia (vtoraia polovina XVII v.)' *ISSSR*, 1979, no. 3, 85–95

554 Putsillo, M., 'Russkie velikany v prusskoi sluzhbe 1711–46', *Sbornik Moskovskogo glavnogo arkhiva Ministerstva inostrannykh del*, vol. 1, Moscow, 1880, pp. 147–76

555 Puzyrevskii, A. K., *Razvitie postoiannykh reguliarnykh armii i sostoianie voennogo iskusstva v vek Liudovika XIV i Petra Velikogo*, SPg, 1889

556 Rabinovich, M. D., 'Formirovanie reguliarnoi russkoi armii nakanune Severnoi voiny', in Shunkov, ed., *Voprosy voennoi istorii . . .*, pp. 221–32

557 ————————, 'Sotsial'noe proiskhozhdenie i imushchestvennoe polozhenie ofitserov reguliarnoi russkoi armii v kontse Severnoi voiny', in Pavlenko, ed., *Rossiia . . .*, pp. 133–71

558 Raeff, Marc, 'The Well-Ordered Police State and the Development of Modernity in Seventeenth and Eighteenth-Century Europe: An Attempt at a Comparative Approach', *American Historical Review*, 80, 1975, 1221–43

559 ————————, *The Well-Ordered Police State*: Social and Institutional Change through Law in the Germanies and Russia, 1600–1800, New Haven, Conn., 1983

560 Rauch, Georg von, 'Protestantisch-ostkirchliche Begegnung im Baltischen Grenzraum zur Schwedenzeit', *Archiv für Reformationsgeschichte*, 43, 1952, 187–212

561 Repin, N. N., 'Kommercheskoe sudostroenie v Rossii v kontse XVII – pervoi polovine XVIII v.', *VI*, 1978, no. 1, 41–54

562 Ricca Salerno, Giuseppe, *Storia delle dottrine finanziarie in Italia*, second edition, Padua, 1960

563 Robinson, A. N., 'K probleme "bogatstva" i "bednosti" v russkoi literature v ee sviazi s novym vremenem', in Derzhavina, ed., *Drevnerusskaia literatura . . .*, pp. 124–155

564 —————————, ed., *Simeon Polotskii i ego knigoizdatel'skaia deiatel'nost'*, M, 1982

565 Rogers, H. C. B., *Weapons of the British Soldier*, London, 1960

566 Rogov, A. I., 'Narodnye massy i religioznye dvizheniia v Rossii vtoroi poloviny XVII veka', *VI*, 1973, no. 4, 32–43

567 —————————, 'Novye dannye o sostave uchenikov Slaviano-greko-latinskoi Akademii', *ISSSR*, 1959, no. 3, 140–7

568 Romanovich-Slavatinskii, A. V., *Dvorianstvo v Rossii ot nachala XVIII v. do otmeny krepostnogo prava*, SPg, 1870

569 Ronskii, O. M., 'Povstancheskie stanitsy v verkhnem Povolzh'e v nachale XVIII veka', *VI*, 1976, no. 11, 209–13

570 Roover, R. de, 'The Concept of the Just Price; Theory and Economic Policy', *Journal of Economic History*, 18, 1958, 419–34

571 Rosén, Jerker, *Den svenska utrikes politikens historia*, vol. ii, 1 (1697–1721), Stockholm, 1952

572 Rostovtsev, M. I., *The Social and Economic History of the Hellenistic World*, 3 vols, Oxford, 1941

573 —————————, *The Social and Economic History of the Roman Empire*, second edition, revised by P. M. Fraser, 2 vols, Oxford, 1952

574 Rousseau, Jean-Jacques, 'Discours sur l'économie politique', in *Oeuvres complètes*, published under the direction of B. Gagnebin and M. Raymond, vol. iii, Paris, 1964, pp. 241–78

575 Rousset de Missy, Jean, ed., *Recueil historique d'actes, négociations, mémoires et traités*, 21 vols, The Hague, etc., 1729–55

576 Rovinskii, D. A. *Obozrenie ikonopisaniia v Rossii do kontsa XVII veka*, SPg, 1903

577 Rozhdestvenskii, S. V., *Ocherki po istorii sistem narodnogo obrazovaniia v Rossii v XVII–XVIII vekakh*, vol. i, ZIFF, 104, 1912

578 —————————, 'O zemskom sobore 1642 goda', in *Sbornik statei po slavianovedeniiu, sostavlennykh i izdannykh uchenikami V. I. Lamanskogo*, SPg, 1883, pp. 95–103

579 —————————, *Sluzhiloe zemlevladenie v Moskovskom gosudarstve XVI veka*, ZIFF, 43, 1897

580 Rozhkov, V. I., 'Gornozavodskii promysel v Olonetskom krae', *Gornyi Zhurnal*, 1888, no. 2, 291–318

581 Rumiantseva, V. S., 'Rtishchevskaia shkola', *VI*, 1983, no. 5, 179–83

582 —————————, 'Russkaia shkola XVII veka', *VI*, 1978, no. 6, 214–19

583 Ryan, W. F., 'Peter the Great's English Yacht. Admiral Lord Carmarthen and the Russian Tobacco Monopoly', *The Mariner's Mirror*, 69, 1983, 65–87

584 —————————, 'Rathborne's *Surveyor*: the first Russian translation from English?', *Oxford Slavonic Papers*, 11, 1964, 1–7

585 Saint-Simon, Louis de Rouvray, duc de, *Mémoires*, edited by A. de Boislisle, 41 vols, Paris, 1879–1928

586 Sakharov, A. M., 'Neizvestnyi ukaz Petra I', *VI*, 1962, no. 12, 201–3

587 —————————, 'Ob évoliutsii feodal'noi sobstvennosti na zemliu v Rossiiskom gosudarstve XVI veka', *ISSSR*, 1978, no. 4, 19–41

588 —————————, 'Russkaia dukhovnaia kul'tura XVII veka', *VI*, 1975, no. 7, 94–114

589 Sakharov, I. P., ed., *Zapiski russkikh liudei*. Sobytiia vremen Petra Velikogo, SPg, 1841

590 Sakovich, S. I., 'Pamiati kormezhnye, naemnye i zhilye krest'ian-otkhodnikov kontsa XVII veka', *AE* for 1962, 1963, 166–73

591 —————————, 'Sotsial'nyi sostav moskovskikh tsekhovykh remeslennikov 1720-kh godov', *IZ*, 42, 1953, 238–61

592 Schacht, Joseph, *Esquisse d'une histoire du droit musulman*, Paris, 1953

593 Schauman, G. C. A., *Studier i frihetstidens nationalekonomisk skrifter*, Helsinki, 1910

594 Scheltema, Jacobus, *Peter de Groote, Keizer van Rusland in Holland en te Zaandam in 1697 en 1717*, 2 vols, second edition, Utrecht, 1842

595 Schloezer, A. L. von, *Geld- und Bergwerks-Geschichte des Russischen Kaiserthums* vom J. 1700 bis 1789, Göttingen, 1791

596 Schmoller, G., 'Die russische Kompagnie in Berlin 1724–1738', *Zeitschrift für Preussische Geschichte und Landeskunde*, 20, 1883, 1–116

597 —————————— and others, eds, *Acta Borussica, Behördenorganisation*, vols. i, iii, Berlin, 1901

598 Schröder, Wilhelm von, *Fürstliche Schatz- und Rent-Cammer*, first edition, Leipzig, 1685; reprinted 1704, 1713, 1718, 1721, 1737, 1744, 1752

599 Schrötter, Friedrich Freiherr von, *Wörterbuch der Münzkunde*, Berlin-Leipzig, 1930

600 Semenov, A., *Izuchenie istoricheskikh svedenii o rossiiskoi vneshnei torgovle i promyshlennosti s poloviny XVII-go stoletiia po 1858 god*, 3 vols, SPg, 1859

601 Semevskii, M. I., ed., *Arkhiv kniazia B. A. Kurakina*, vol. i, SPg, 1890

602 —————————, *Slovo i delo!*, third edition, SPg, 1885

603 Serbina, K. N., 'K voprosu ob uchenichestve v remesle russkogo goroda XVII veka', *IZ*, 18, 1946, 148–68

604 Shapiro, A. L., 'Krest'ianskaia torgovlia i krest'ianskie podriady v petrovskoe vremia', *IZ*, 27, 1948, 202–39

605 Sharkova, I. S., *Rossiia i Italia*. Torgovye otnosheniia XV – pervoi chetverti XVIII v., L, 1981

606 Shaw, D. J. B., 'Frontiers of Muscovy, 1550–1700', in Bater and French, eds, *Studies . . .*, vol. i, pp. 118–42

607 Shchapov, A. P., 'Russkii raskol staroobriadchestva' (first published in 1859), in his *Sochineniia*, vol. i, SPg, 1906, pp. 173–450

608 —————————, *Sochineniia v trekh tomakh*, SPg-Irkutsk, 1906–37

609 —————————, 'Zemstvo i raskol, 2', in his *Sochineniia*, vol. i, SPg, 1906, pp. 505–79

610 Shchapov, Ia. N., 'Mezhdunarodnyi seminar "Ot Rima k tret'emu Rimu"', *VI*, 1982, no. 3, 150–1

611 Shchavinskii, V. A., *Ocherki po istorii tekhniki zhivopisi i tekhnologii krasok v drevnei Rusi*, L, 1935

612 Shcherbachev, Iu. N., ed., *Zapiski Iusta Iulia*, datskogo poslannika pri Petre Velikom (1709–11), M, 1900

613 Shcherbatov, M. M., ed., *Zhurnal ili podennaia zapiska . . . imperatora Petra Velikogo s 1698 goda . . . po zakliuchenie Neishtatskogo mira*, SPg, 1770–2, 2 vols in 3

614 Shchukina, E. S., 'Rezchiki monetnykh shtempelei vtoroi poloviny XVII veka', in Sivers, ed., *Numizmaticheskii sbornik*, pp. 128–31

615 Shidlovskii, A. F., ed., *Petr Velikii na Severe. Sbornik statei i ukazov . . .*, Arkhangel'sk, 1909

616 Shilov, A. A., ed., *Sbornik statei, posviashchennykh A. S. Lappo-Danilevskomu*, Petrograd, 1916

617 Shimko, I. I., *Patriarshii Kazennyi prikaz, ego vneshniaia istoriia, ustroistvo i deiatel'nost'*, Moscow, 1894

618 Shliapkin, I. A., *Sv. Dimitrii Rostovskii i ego vremia*, SPg, 1891

619 Shmidt, S. O., 'Mestnichestvo i absoliutizm (postanovka voprosa)', in Druzhinin, ed., *Absoliutizm . . .*, pp. 168–205

620 Shost'in, N. A., *Ocherki istorii russkoi metrologii*, M, 1975

621 Shunkov, V. I., ed., *Voprosy voennoi istorii Rossii. XVIII i pervaia polovina XIX vekov*, M, 1969

622 Silberner, Edmond, *La guerre dans la pensée économique du XVIe au XVIIe siècle*, Paris, 1939

623 Sinaiskii, A., *Otnoshenie russkoi tserkovnoi vlasti k raskolu . . . 1721–1725*, SPg, 1895

624 Sivers, A. A., ed., *Numizmaticheskii sbornik*, M, 1955

625 Sivkov, K. V., ed., *Materialy po istorii krest'ianskogo i pomeshchich'ego khoziaistva pervoi chetverti XVIII v.*, M, 1951

626 ——————, general ed., Meshalin, I. V., compiler, *Materialy po istorii krest'ianskoi promyshlennosti*, vol. ii, Tekstil'naia promyshlennost' Moskovskoi gubernii v XVIII i nachale XIX v., M-L, 1950

627 Skazkin, S. D., and others, eds, *Problemy genezisa kapitalizma*, M, 1970

628 Small, Albion W., *The Cameralists. The Pioneers of German Social Policy* (first published Chicago, 1909), New York, 1967

629 Smentsovskii, M., *Brat'ia Likhudy*, SPg, 1899

630 ——————, 'Likhudy', RBS, vol. 10

631 Smirnov, I. I., Man'kov, A. G., Pod"iapol'skaia, E. P., Mavrodin, V. V., *Krest'ianskie voiny v Rossii XVII–XVIII vv.*, M-L, 1966

632 Smirnov, M. I., *Nizhegorodskie kazennye kabaki i kruzhechnye dvory XVII stoletiia*, Nizhnii Novgorod, 1913

633 Smirnov, N. A., ed., *Tserkov' v istorii Rossii (IX v. – 1917 g.)*, M, 1967

634 Smirnov, P. P., *Posadskie liudi i ikh klassovaia bor'ba do serediny XVII veka*, 2 vols, M, 1947–8

635 Smirnov, P. S., *Ioakim, patriarkh Moskovskii*, M, 1881

636 ——————, *Istoriia russkogo raskola staroobriadstva*, second edition, SPg, 1895

637 Smirnov, S. K., *Istoriia Moskovskoi Slaviano-greko-latinskoi Akademii*, M, 1855

638 Smirnov, V. D., *Krymskoe khanstvo pod verkhovenstvom Ottomanskoi Porty*, SPg, 1887

639 Smith, Adam, *Lectures on Justice, Police, Revenue, and Arms*, edited by E. Cannan, Oxford, 1896

640 Smith, R. E. F., and Christian, David, *Bread and Salt. A Social and Economic History of Food and Drink in Russia*, Cambridge, 1984

641 Smolitsch, Igor, *Geschichte der russischen Kirche*, vol. i, Leiden, 1964

642 Smotryc'kyj, Meletij, *Hrammatiki Slovenskija Pravilnoe Syntagma* (Jevje, 1619), edited by Olexa Horbatsch, Frankfurt-am-Main, 1974

643 Sobolevskii, A. I., *Obrazovannost' Moskovskoi Rusi v XVI–XVII vekakh*, SPg, 1892

644 Sofronenko, K. A., ed., *Sobornoe Ulozhenie tsaria Alekseia Mikhailovicha 1649 goda*, M, 1957 (= PRP vol. VI)

645 Solov'ev, N. I., *Istoricheskie ocherki ustroistva i dovol'stviia russkikh reguliarnykh voisk v pervoi polovine XVIII stoletiia*, vol. i, SPg, 1900

646 Solov'ev, S. M., *Istoriia Rossii s drevneishikh vremen*, edited by L. V. Cherepnin, vols xv, xvi, xvii, M, 1962

647 Sopikov, V. S., *Opyt russkoi bibliografii*, edited by V. N. Rogozhin, 5 pts, SPg 1904–6

648 Spasskii, I. G. 'Denezhnoe obrashchenie v Moskovskom gosudarstve s 1533 g. po 1617 g.', in *Materialy i Issledovaniia po Arkheologii SSSR*, no. 44, 1955, pp. 219–90

649 ————, *Russkaia monetnaia sistema*, third edition, L, 1962

650 Spassky, I. G., *The Russian Monetary System*, translated by Z. I. Gorishina, Amsterdam, 1967

651 Spieler, Silke, 'Heinrich von Fick, ein holsteinischer Mitarbeiter Peters des Grossen. Notizen zu einer Biographie', in Uwe Liszkowski, ed., *Russland und Deutschland*, Stuttgart, 1974, pp. 83–94

652 Spiridonova, E. V., *Ėkonomicheskaia politika i ėkonomicheskie vzgliady Petra I*, M, 1952

653 Srbik, Heinrich Ritter von, 'Wilhelm von Schröder', *Sitzungsberichte der Kaiserlichen Akademie der Wissenschaften in Wien*, Philosophisch-historische Klasse, 164, no. 1, 1910

654 Staehr, Georg, 'Die russische Kopfsteuer und ihre Reform', *Russische Revue*, 17, 1881, 1–55, 255–70

655 Stefanovich, D., *O Stoglave. Ego proiskhozhdenie i sostav*, SPg, 1909

656 Steinfeldt, V., *Das russische Medizinalwesen unter Peter dem Grossen*. Inaugural-Dissertation. Rheinische Friedrich-Wilhelms Universität, Bonn, 1968 (reproduced from typescript).

657 Steshenko, I. A., Sofronenko, K. A., *Gosudarstvennyi stroi Rossii v pervoi chetverti XVIII v.*, M, 1973 (reproduced from typescript)

658 Stewart, C. P., and Guthrie, D., eds, [James] *Lind's Treaty on Scurvy* [1753], Edinburgh, 1953

659 *Stoglav*, izdanie D. E. Kozhanchikova, SPg, 1863

660 Storozhev, V. N., 'Datochnye liudi', ES, vol. 10

661 ————, 'Ukaznaia kniga Pomestnogo prikaza', in Opisanie MAMIu, vol. 6, section 3, M, 1899

662 ————, 'Votchina', ES, vol. 7, 1892

663 Stoskova, N. N., *Pervye metallurgicheskie zavody Rossii*, M, 1962

664 Strahlenberg, P. J. von, *Das nord- und östliche Theil von Europa und Asia in so weit solches das gantze russische Reich mit Sibirien und der grossen Tatarey in sich begreiffet*, Stockholm, 1730

665 Strumilin, S. G., *Ocherki ėkonomicheskoi istorii Rossii*, M, 1960

666 Struve, P. B., *Collected Works* in fifteen volumes, Ann Arbor, Mich., 1970

667 ————, 'Tsena ukaznaia i tsena vol'naia' (first published in 1913), in his *Collected Works*, vol. x, item 451, pp. 101–314

668 Stuckenberg, J., 'Schwefelvorkommen in Russland', *Archiv für die wissenschaftliche Kunde von Russland*, 14, 1853, 382–407

669 Stupperich, R., 'Zur neuen Nikon-Forschung', *ZfOG*, 5, 1935, 173–84

670 Subbotin, N. I., ed., *Akty otnosiashchiesia k istorii Solovetskogo miatezha* (vol. iii of *Materialy dlia istorii raskola za pervoe vremia ego sushchestvovaniia*), M, 1878

671 ⸻, ed., *Deianiia moskovskikh soborov 1666 i 1667 godov*, M, 1893

672 Sukhomlinov, M. I., ed., *Materialy dlia istorii Imperatorskoi Akademii Nauk*, vol. iv, SPg, 1887

673 Svensson, Sven, 'En nederlänsk köpmansfamilj i Danmark och Ryssland vid 1600-tales mitt', *Historisk Tidskrift*, 78, 1958, 403–29

674 Symons, L., and White, C., *Russian Transport*, London, 1975

675 Syromiatnikov, B. I., *'Reguliarnoe khoziaistvo' Petra Pervogo i ego ideologiia*, M, 1943

676 Syrtsov, I. Ia., *Vozmushchenie solovetskikh monakhov staroobriadtsev v XVII veke*, Kostroma, 1888

677 Szeftel, M., 'The History of Suretyship in Old Russian Law', *Recueil de la Société Jean Bodin* pour l'Histoire Comparative des Institutions, vol. 29, Brussels, 1971, pp. 841–86

678 ⸻, 'The Legal Condition of the Foreign Merchants in Muscovy', *Recueil de la Société Jean Bodin* pour l'Histoire Comparative des Institutions, vol. 33, Brussels, 1972, pp. 336–58

679 Tal'berg, D. G., *Russkoe ugolovnoe sudoproizvodstvo*, vol. i, Kiev, 1889

680 Tal'man, E. M., 'Remeslennoe uchenichestvo Moskvy v XVII v.', *IZ*, 27, 1948, 67–95

681 Tarlovskaia, V. R., 'Torgovye krest'iane Povolzh'ia v kontse XVII–nachale XVIII veka', *ISSSR*, 1983, no 2, 149–58

682 Tatarskii, Ierofei, *Simeon Polotskii*, M, 1886

683 Tatishchev, V. N., *Dukhovnaia moemu synu*, SPg, 1896 [written 1733]

684 ⸻, *Istoriia rossiiskaia v semi tomakh*, edited by I. A. Andreev and others, vols i, vii, L, 1942

685 ⸻, *Sudebnik Gosudaria Tsaria . . . Ioanna Vasil'evicha* i nekotorye sego gosudaria i ego preemnikov ukazy, second edition, M, 1786

686 Tel'pukhovskii, V. S., *Severnaia voina 1700–1721*, M, 1946

687 Thon, Nikolaus, *Ikone und Liturgie*, Trier, 1979

688 Tikhomirov, M. N., *Klassovaia bor'ba v Rossii XVII v.*, edited by V. I. Shunkov and others, M, 1969

689 ⸻, 'Novgorodskoe vosstanie 1650 g.', in his *Klassovaia bor'ba . . .*, pp. 139–69

690 ⸻, 'Pskovskoe vosstanie 1650 g.', in his *Klassovaia bor'ba . . .*, pp. 23–138

691 Tikhomirov, M. N., and Epifanov, P. P., eds, *Sobornoe Ulozhenie 1649 goda*, M, 1961

692 Tikhonov, Iu. A., *Pomeshchich'i krest'iane. Feodal'naia renta v XVI–nachale XVIII v.*, M, 1974

693 Timofeev, A. G., *Istoriia S-Peterburgskoi birzhi*, SPg, 1903

694 ⸻, *Istoriia telesnykh nakazanii v russkom prave*, second edition, SPg, 1904

695 Titlinov, B. V., 'Feodosii (Ianovskii)', *RBS*, vol. 25

696 Tkacheva, N. K., 'Odnodvortsy XVIII veka v otechestvennoi istoriografii', in *Istoriia i istoriki, 1975*, M, 1978, 281–99

697 Tokarev, N. Ia., 'Blizhniaia kantseliariia pri Petre Velikom i ee dela', Opisanie MAMIu, vol. 5, 1888, section 2, pp. 43–102

698 Tolstoi, D., *Istoriia finansovykh uchrezhdenii Rossii so vremeni osnovaniia gosudarstva do konchiny imperatritsy Ekateriny II*, SPg, 1848

699 Tomsinskii, S. G., *Ural v russkoi publitsistike pervykh desiatiletii XVIII v.*, Perm', 1959

700 Tomsinskii, S. G., ed., *Bulavinskoe vosstanie (1707–1708 gg.)*, M, 1935
701 Torke, Hans-Joachim, *Die staatsbedingte Gesellschaft im Moskauer Reich*; Zar und Zemlja in der altrussichen Herrschaftsverfassung, 1613–89, Leyden, 1974
702 Troitskii, S. M., *Finansovaia politika russkogo absoliutizma v XVIII veke*, M, 1966
703 —————————, 'Iz istorii russkogo rublia,' *VI*, 1961, no. 1, 59–75
704 —————————, 'Iz istorii sozdaniia Tabeli o rangakh', *ISSSR*, 1974, no. 1, 98–111
705 —————————, 'Ob ispol'zovanii opyta Shvetsii pri provedenii administrativnykh reform v Rossii v pervoi chetverti XVIII veka', *VI*, 1977, no. 2, 67–75
706 —————————, *Russkii absoliutizm i dvorianstvo v XVIII v.* Formirovanie biurokratii, M, 1974
707 —————————, 'Zapiska I. I. Bibikova o torguiushchikh krest'ianakh', *AE* for 1961, 1962, 387–92
708 —————————, 'Le "système" de John Law et ses continuateurs russes', in Braudel and others, eds, *La Russie . . .*, pp. 39–68
709 Tschiževskij, D., *Das heilige Russland* (Russische Geistesgeschichte, i), Hamburg, 1959
710 Tsvetkov, M. A., *Izmenenie lesistosti evropeiskoi Rossii s kontsa XVII stoletiia po 1914 god*, M, 1957
711 Tugan-Baranovskii, M. I., *Russkaia fabrika v proshlom i nastoiashchem*, vol. i, SPg, 1898
712 Tumins, Valerie A., and Vernadsky, George, *Patriarch Nikon on Church and State*, Berlin-New York-Amsterdam, 1982
713 Turchanovich, L. F., 'Lesa evropeiskoi chasti SSSR v proshlom', *Zemledelie*, 3 (43), 1950, 80–106
714 Ulianitskii, V. A., *Russkie konsul'stva za granitseiu v XVIII veke*, 2 vols in 1, M, 1899
715 Unbegaun, B. O., 'Russian Grammars before Lomonosov', *Oxford Slavonic Papers*, 8, 1958, 96–116
716 Uspenskii, A. I., ed., *Podlinnik ikonopisnyi*, M, 1903
717 Ustiugov, N. V., 'Bashkiry', in Novosel'skii, ed., *Ocherki*, pp. 795–814
718 —————————, 'Instruktsiia votchinnomu prikazchiku pervoi chetverti XVIII v.', *IA*, 4, 1949, 150–83
719 —————————, 'K voprosu o raskladke povinnostei po dvorovomu chislu v kontse XVII v.', in Volgin, ed., *Akademiku B. D. Grekovu . . .*, pp. 221–31
720 —————————, 'Ocherk drevnerusskoi metrologii', *IZ*, 19, 1946, 294–348
721 —————————, *Solevarennaia promyshlennost' Soli Kamskoi v XVII veke*, M, 1957
722 ————————— and others, eds, *Russkoe gosudarstvo v XVII veke*. Novye iavleniia v sotsial'no-ekonomicheskoi, politicheskoi i kul'turnoi zhizni. Sbornik statei, M, 1961
723 Ustrialov, N. G., *Istoriia tsarstvovaniia Petra Velikogo*, vols. i–iv, vi, SPg, 1856–63
724 Val'denberg, V., 'Pososhkov i Krizhanich v ikh obshchestvenno-politicheskikh vozzreniakh', *Slavia*, 5, 1926–7, 754–62
725 Valk, S. N., ed., *Issledovaniia po istorii feodal'no-krepostnicheskoi Rossii*, M-L, 1964
726 Van Zuiden, D. S., 'Bijdrage tot de kennis van de Hollands-Russische relaties in de 16e–18e eeuw', *Economisch-Historisch Jaarboek*, 1911, 1–51

727 Vasilenko, N., 'Monastyrskie votchiny i dokhody', ES, vol. 38
728 —————————, 'Raskol', ES, vol. 51
729 Vazhinskii, V. M., 'Ia. E. Vodarskii, *Naselenie Rossii v kontse XVII–nachale XVIII veka*, M, 1977', *ISSSR*, 1980, no. 1, 216–19
730 Veretennikov, V. I., *Istoriia Tainoi kantseliarii petrovskogo vremeni*, Khar'kov, 1911
731 —————————, *Ocherki istorii general-prokuratury v Rossii do ekaterininskogo vremeni*, Khar'kov, 1915
732 Veriuzhskii, V., *Afanasii, arkhiepiskop Kholmogorskii*, SPg, 1908
733 Verkhovskoi, P. V., *Uchrezhdenie Dukhovnoi kollegii i Dukhovnyi Reglament*, 2 vols, Rostov-on-Don, 1916
734 Vernadsky, G., 'L'Industrie russe et Pierre le Grand,' *Le Monde Slave*, 1934, 283–99
735 Veselago, F. F., *Kratkaia istoriia russkogo flota*, 2 vols in 1, SPg, 1893–5
736 —————————, *Ocherk istorii morskogo kadetskogo korpusa*, SPg, 1852
737 Veselovskii, S. B., 'Prikaznyi stroi upravleniia Moskovskogo gosudarstva', in M. V. Dovnar-Zapol'skii, ed., *Russkaia istoriia v ocherkakh i stat'iakh*, vol. iii, Kiev, 1912, pp. 164–98
738 —————————, *Soshnoe pis'mo*. Issledovanie po istorii kadastra i pososhnogo oblozheniia Moskovskogo gosudarstva, 2 vols, M, 1915–16
739 Viatkin, M. P., ed., *Moskovskii Sukonnyi Dvor. Krepostnaia manufaktura v Rossii*, pt v, L, 1934
740 —————————, ed., *Ocherki istorii Leningrada*, vol. i, 1703–1861, L, 1955
741 Viazemskii, B. L., *Verkhovnyi tainyi sovet*, SPg, 1909
742 Viktorskii, S. K., *Istoriia smertnoi kazni v Rossii*, M, 1912
743 Viskovatov, A. V., *Istoricheskoe opisanie odezhdy i vooruzheniia rossiiskikh voisk*, 7 vols, SPg, 1841–8
744 Vladimirskii-Budanov, M. F., *Gosudarstvo i narodnoe obrazovanie v Rossii XVIII veka*, vol. i, Iaroslavl', 1874
745 —————————, *Obzor istorii russkogo prava*, second edition, SPg, 1888
746 Vlasov, I. I., 'Polotnianoi fabriki direktor Ivan Tames', offprint from *Trudy Ivanovo-Voznesenskogo Nauchnogo Obshchestva Kraevedenia*, no. 5, Ivanovo-Voznesensk, 1928
    Vockerodt see Herrmann
747 Vodarskii, Ia. E., *Naselenie Rossii v kontse XVII–nachale XVIII veka*, M, 1977
748 —————————, *Naselenie Rossii za 400 let* (XVI – nachalo XX vv.), M, 1973
749 —————————, 'Praviashchaia gruppa svetskikh feodalov v Rossii v XVII v.', in Pavlenko and others, eds., *Dvorianstvo . . .*, pp. 70–107
750 —————————, 'Proekt Reglamenta Glavnogo Magistrata i ego redaktsiia (1720 g.)', *Problemy Istochnikovedeniia*, 10, 1962, 195–207
751 —————————, 'Sluzhiloe dvorianstvo v Rossii v kontse XVII–nachale XVIII v.', in Shunkov, ed., *Voprosy . . .*, pp. 223–37
752 —————————, 'Tserkovnye organizatsii i ikh krepostnye krest'iane vo vtoroi polovine XVII–nachale XVIII v.', in Narochnitskii and others, eds, *Istoricheskaia geografiia . . .*, pp. 70–96
753 Vodarskii, Ia. E., and Pavlenko, V. V., 'Svodnye dannye o kolichestve podatnykh dvorov Evropeiskoi Rossii po perepisi 1678 g.', *Sovetskie Arkhivy*, 1971, no. 6, 65–88
754 Volgin, V. I., ed., *Akademiku B. D. Grekovu ko dniu semidesiatiletiia*, Sbornik statei, M, 1952
755 Volkov, M. Ia., 'Kupecheskie kozhevennye predpriatiia pervoi chetverti XVIII v.', *ISSSR*, 1966, no. 1, 138–51

756 Volkov, M. Ia., 'Monakh Avraamii i ego poslanie Petru I', in Pavlenko and others, eds., *Rossiia* . . ., pp. 311–36

757 —————, *Ocherki istorii promyslov Rossii.* Vtoraia polovina XVII-pervaia polovina XVIII v. Vinokurennoe proizvodstvo, M, 1979

758 —————, 'Ob otmene mestnichestva v Rossii', *ISSSR*, 1977, no. 2, 53–67

759 [Volynskii, A. P.] *Instruktsiia dvoretskomu Ivanu Nemchinovu o upravlenii domu i dereven' i Regula ob loshadiakh, Pamiatniki Drevnei Pis'mennosti i Iskusstva*, fasc. 24, SPg, 1881

760 Volynskoi, N. P., *Postepennoe razvitie russkoi reguliarnoi konnitsy v èpokhu Velikogo Petra*, vol. i, in 4 pts, SPg, 1912

761 Volz, G. B., ed., *Die politischen Testamente Friedrichs des Grossen*, Berlin, 1920

762 [Weber, F. C.] *Das veränderte Russland*, Neu-verbesserte Auflage, vol. i, Frankfurt and Leipzig, 1738, vol. ii, Hanover, 1738, vol. iii, ibid., 1740

763 Weber, Max, 'Agrarverhältnisse im Altertum' (first published in 1909), in his *Gesammelte Aufsätze zur Sozial- und Wirtschaftsgeschichte*, edited by Marianne Weber, Tübingen, 1924, pp. 1–288

764 —————, 'Vorbemerkungen zu den Gesamten Aufsätzen zur Religions-soziologie', in his *Gesammelte Aufsätze zur Religionssoziologie*, third edition, Tübingen, 1934, vol. i, pp. 1–16

765 —————, *Wirtschaft und Gesellschaft*, fourth edition prepared by J. Winckelmann, Tübingen, 1956

766 —————, *Wirtschaftsgeschichte.* Abriss der universalen Sozial- und Wirt-schaftsgeschichte, edited by S. Hellmann and M. Paly, Munich-Leipzig, 1923

767 Whitworth, Charles (Baron Whitworth), *An Account of Russia as it was in the year 1710*, Strawberry Hill, 1758

768 Williams-Ellis, Amabel, ed., *The White Sea Canal*, being an Account of the Con-struction of the new Canal between the White Sea and the Baltic Sea, written by I. Auerbach, etc., London, 1935

769 Wójcik, Z., 'From the Peace of Oliva to the truce of Bakhchisarai. International Relations in Europe, 1660–1681', *Acta Poloniae Historica*, 34, 1976, 255–80

770 Wolzendorff, Kurt, *Der Polizeigedanke des modernen Staats*, Breslau, 1918

771 Wortman, R., 'Peter the Great and Court Procedure', *CASS*, 7, 1974, 303–10

772 Yaney, G. L., *The Systematization of Russian Government.* Social Evolution in the Domestic Administration, Urbana, Ill., 1973

773 Zabelin, I. E., *Domashnii byt russkikh tsarits v XVI i XVII st.*, second edition, M, 1872

774 —————, *Opyty izucheniia russkikh drevnostei i istorii*, pt i, M, 1872

775 —————, 'Pervoe vodvorenie v Moskve grekolatinskoi i obshchei evropeiskoi nauki', *ChIODR*, 1886, no. 4, 1–24

776 Zagorovskii, V. P., *Belgorodskaia cherta*, Voronezh, 1969

777 Zagoskin, N. P., *Ocherk istorii smertnoi kazni v Rossii*, Kazan, 1892

778 Zalutskii, V., 'Prikhodskaia blagotvoritel'nost' v drevnei Rusi', *Pribavlenie k Irkutskim Eparkhial'nym Vedomostiam*, no. 29, 19 July 1875, 392–7

779 Zaozerskaia, E. I., 'Begstvo i otkhod krest'ian v pervoi polovine XVIII v.', in Beskrovnyi, ed. *K voprosu* . . ., pp. 144–88

780 —————*Manufaktura pri Petre I*, M–L, 1947

781 —————, 'Moskovskii posad pri Petre I', *VI*, 1947, no. 9, 18–35

782 —————, 'Pripisnye i krepostnye krest'iane v pervoi chetverti XVIII v.', *IZ*, 12, 1943, 128–43

783 Zaozerskaia, E. I., *Razvitie legkoi promyshlennosti v Moskve v pervoi chetverti XVIII v.*, M, 1955

784 —————————, ed., 'Vedomost' 1727 g. o sostoianii promyshlennykh predpriatii nakhodiashchikhsia v vedenii Kommerts-kollegii i Manufaktur-kontory', in A. A. Novosel'skii and others, eds, *Materialy po istorii SSSR*, vol. 5, M, 1957, pp. 205–82

785 Zaozerskii, A. I., *Tsarskaia votchina XVII v.* Iz istorii khoziaistvennoi i prikaznoi politiki tsaria Alekseia Mikhailovicha, second edition, M, 1937

786 Zernova, A. S., *Knigi kirillovskoi pechati izdannye v Moskve v XVI i XVII vekakh*, M, 1958

787 Zertsalov, A. N., and Belokurov, S. A., eds, 'O nemetskikh shkolakh v Moskve, 1701–1715, Dokumenty', *ChOIDR*, 1907, no. 1, pp. i–xcl, 1–244

788 Zheliabuzhskii, I. A., 'Zapiski', in Sakharov, ed., *Zapiski . . .*, pp. 1–103

789 Zhuravskii, D. I., 'Statisticheskoe obozrenie raskhodov na voennye potrebnosti s 1711 po 1825 g.', *Voennyi Sbornik*, 3, 1859, 3–27

790 Zlotnikov, M. F., 'Pod'iachie Ivanovskoi ploshchadi', in Shilov, ed., *Sbornik statei . . .*, pp. 82–130

791 Znamenskii, P. V., *Dukhovnye shkoly v Rossii do reformy 1808 goda*, Kazan, 1881

792 —————————, 'Otzyv o sochinenii N. F. Kaptereva *Patriarkh Nikon i Tsar' Aleksei Mikhailovich*', *ZIAN*, Istoriko-filologicheskoe otdelenie, 12, no. 6, 1915, 13–42

793 [Znamenskii, P. V.] 'Sposoby soderzhaniia dukhovenstva v XVII i XVIII stoletiiakh', *Pravoslavnyi Sobesednik*, 1865, no. 1, 145–88

794 —————————, *Uchebnoe rukovodstvo po istorii russkoi tserkvi*, second edition, SPg, 1904

795 Zolotarev, B. V., 'K voprosu o nachale artilleriiskogo i voenno-inzhenernogo obrazovaniia v Rossii', in Peshtich, Shapiro and others, eds, *Problemy istorii . . .*, pp. 195–206

796 Žužek, Ivan, *Kormčaja kniga*, Rome, 1964

Textual Emendations

See Translators' Note. The more substantial emendations are listed below.

The figures in the Text column refer to the pages in the text edited by Kafengauz (1951); t = line from top of page, b = line from bottom of page.

Chapter	Text	For	Read
2, n.3	46, 16t	приправленной	приправленную
3, n.2	55, 10b	в каковые	ни в каковые
n.5	56, 11b	707	717
n. 20	71, 9b	положа	положить
n. 23	79, 6b	отнюд имать не надлежит	*add* записей
n. 33	90, 13b	уставит	уставить
n. 34	92, 1t	богатым	свободным
n. 41	99, 7t	покинуть	покинут
n. 46	103, 7t	повешено	повелено + a missing infinitive
n. 49	106, 8t	ухватя бы его, привел	ухватя его, привел бы
4, n. 16	129, 3t	на верьхних кафтанех... кой купуются	верхние кафтаны... кое купуется
n. 19	129, 11b	покупает	покупаются
n. 20	129, 10b	белые и медные	белые или медные
n. 21	132, 6t	не строили	не носил
6, n. 3	152, 7t	и у приказных	и приказных
n. 7	162, 5t	о всеконечном... изпожение	о всеконечном... истреблении
7, n. 2	171, 2t	пограбленной пожиток	за пограбленный пожиток
n. 3	171, 6b	без грамотнаго	безграмотного
n. 7	173, 15b	семен леснова	семен лесных

The 1842 edition divides семен леснаго, березоваго but, although the hazel is also called лесной орех , the adjective makes better sense when applied to семен.

8, n. 3	185, 15t	уголовщине быть	уголовщине не быть
n. 7	186, 9b	не будет	ни будет
n. 9	190, 15b	ябедовать и нахаловать	ябедоват и нахаловат

Neither the verbs nor the adjectives are usual but the sense is virtually the same in either reading.

n. 10	191, 8–9t	по та	то та
n. 17	199, 10t	с огородные земли и с подгородные	огородные земли и подгородные
9, n. 4	203, 9t	ничим же	ничим не
n. 7	207, 13t	устоит	устроить
n. 15	212, 6t	коя	кой
n. 20	222, 6–5b	промыслы суть... въступатись в не надлежит	прибыль [питейная] есть... вступаться в нее не надлежит
n. 26	226, 13b	принимать будет	принимать будут

Russian Weights, Measures and Coins

The following tables give the approximate equivalents of the units in general use in the seventeenth and eighteenth centuries as employed by Pososhkóv.

Length	*Metric*	*British*
1 vershók	4.45 cm	1 ¾ in
16 v. = 1 arshin	71.1 cm	28 in
3 a. = 1 sazhen[1]	2.13 m	7 ft
500 s. = 1 verst	1 km	⅔ mile

Area		
1 chetverík	0.07 ha	⅙ acre
4 ch. = 1 osmína	0.27 ha	⅔ acre
2 o. = 1 chétvert'	0.55 ha	1⅓ acres
2 ch. = 1 desiatína		
reckoned as 80 × 30 sazhen	1.1 ha	2⅔ acres
80 × 40 sazhen		
(sorokováia)	1.5 ha	3⅗ acres

Volume (liquid)		
1 chárka	0.123 1	⅕ pint
10 ch. = 1 shtof	1.23 1	1 quart
10 sh. = 1 vedró (pl. vëdra)	12.3 1	2 ¾ gallons

The krúzhka was also used as an intermediate measure, often = 1 shtof but was usually somewhat larger.

Volume (dry)		
1 chetverík	26.25 1	¾ bushel
4 ch. = 1 osmína	105 1	3 b.
2 o. = 1 chétvert'	210 1	6 b.

Weight

1 zolotník	4.27 g	66 grains
96 z. = 1 funt	410 g	14½ oz
40 f. = 1 pood	16.4 kg	36 lb
10 p. = 1 bérkovets[2]	164 kg	360 lb

The funt was increasingly made equivalent to the Western pound (16 oz) and the pood correspondingly to 40 lb.

1 The sazhen of 3 arshin (kazënnaia sázhén') became the legal standard in 1649, especially for land measurement; it was then 218 cm (7' 2"). Peter I reduced it to 7 (English or Dutch) feet in the interests of shipbuilding. Sazhens of 4 arshin (kosáia) and 2½ arshin (makhováia) were also in everyday use.
2 Originally the 'cargo pound' (Schiffspfund) of 400 lb as used in the Baltic trade centred on Björkö (Birka) near Stockholm in the ninth and tenth centuries.

The relation of units of volume (dry) to area was:

1 basic measure of grain (usually rye) sowed 2 desiatíny;
hence: 1 chétvert' (= quarter) sowed ½ d. (0.55 ha)
　　　1 osmína (= eighth)　sowed ¼ d. (0.27 ha)

Coins

⅛ kopeck = 1 polupolúshka
¼ kopeck = 1 polúshka
½ kopeck = 1 den'gá
3 kopecks = 1 altýn
10 kopecks = 1 grívennik
25 kopecks = 1 polupoltína
50 kopecks = 1 poltína
100 kopecks = 1 rouble

Index of Proper Names

435

Subject index